Blackstone's Statutes on

Criminal Law

Blackstone's Statutes on

Criminal Law

2008–2009

18th edition

edited by

P. R. Glazebrook

Emeritus Fellow of Jesus College, Cambridge

OXFORD
UNIVERSITY PRESS

OXFORD
UNIVERSITY PRESS

Great Clarendon Street, Oxford OX2 6DP

Oxford University Press is a department of the University of Oxford.
It furthers the University's objective of excellence in research, scholarship,
and education by publishing worldwide in

Oxford New York

Auckland Cape Town Dar es Salaam Hong Kong Karachi
Kuala Lumpur Madrid Melbourne Mexico City Nairobi
New Delhi Shanghai Taipei Toronto

With offices in

Argentina Austria Brazil Chile Czech Republic France Greece
Guatemala Hungary Italy Japan Poland Portugal Singapore
South Korea Switzerland Thailand Turkey Ukraine Vietnam

Published in the United States
by Oxford University Press Inc., New York

First published by Blackstone Press

First edition 1989	Fifth edition 1995	Twelfth edition 2002
Second edition 1991	Sixth edition 1996	Thirteenth edition 2003
Reprinted 1992	Seventh edition 1997	Fourteenth edition 2004
Third edition 1993	Eight edition 1998	Fifteenth edition 2005
Reprinted 1993	Ninth edition 1999	Sixteenth edition 2006
Fourth edition 1994	Tenth edition 2000	Seventeenth edition 2007
Reprinted 1994	Eleventh edition 2001	Eighteenth edition 2008

British Library Cataloguing in Publication Data

Data available

Library of Congress Cataloging in Publication Data

Data available

Typeset by Newgen Imaging Systems (P) Ltd, Chennai, India
Printed in Italy
on acid-free paper by
L.E.G.O. S.p.A

ISBN 978–0–19–923822–4

10 9 8 7 6 5 4 3 2 1

Editor's preface

England is one of only a handful of jurisdictions among the developed countries of the world which is still without a Criminal Code. Most of the underdeveloped countries are, in this respect at least, better provided for. For close on forty years the Law Commission's declared aim has been to make good this lack of a single, comprehensive enactment specifying both the conduct which is prohibited under threat of imprisonment and other severe penalties, and the conditions which must be satisfied before a person who has engaged in such conduct may be convicted and punished. But though there has been much labouring, little has been achieved. A Draft Criminal Code Bill, and accompanying Report, published in1989 (Law Com. No. 177) was in many respects a disappointing document and attracted severe criticism. It was not based on any clearly identified or consistent principles, and suffered from many of the defects proverbially attributed to buildings designed by a committee (in this case several committees) rather than an architect.

The Commission has since published a series of Consultation Papers and Reports, under the general title 'Legislating the Criminal Code', some but not all containing bills in the style of the 1989 Draft. These draft bills deal with areas of the law where the need for reform has been thought to be particularly urgent, and they show that the Commission has been having second—or third—thoughts. Only time will tell whether such very limited bills (Appendix 2 prints four of them) represent, as the Commission hopes, the first stages in implementing the Code project, or the fatal first steps towards its abandonment. At present the Commission appears to be running around in ever diminishing circles, while the Home Office, reckless of the shape and intelligibility of the law, has treated its recommendations with ill-disguised disdain and continued to add new offences and heavier penalties to the statute book in a manner reminiscent of the late eighteenth century, while enthusiastically developing an ersatz criminal law by means of the offence of disobeying an antisocial behaviour order (Crime and Disorder Act 1998, section 1). And the drafting becomes ever more prolix and convoluted. The prize for the most worthless statute of last year (within the scope of this collection) goes to the Corporate Manslaughter and Corporate Homicide Act 2007. It redeems, after a decade's delay, an emotional but ill-considered pledge in New Labour's 1997 election manifesto, but otherwise achieves nothing and may well lead to some very protracted and costly trials.

Students and teachers of criminal law (not to mention police officers, magistrates, jurors, lawyers and judges) have therefore to confront a great jumble of statutory provisions, exhibiting many different drafting styles, which are replete with detail, but short on principle. There are believed to be close on 8,000 different criminal offences on the statute-book—some 700 of them added in the last ten years. This present selection, which is intended to be no more than a convenient means of reference to the main statutory framework of the substantive criminal law, is inevitably a personal and, to a degree, an arbitrary one. But it is hoped that it is extensive and varied enough to meet the needs both of those students following criminal law courses of a traditional sort, which involve a detailed study of the principal offences of personal violence and fraud (who will learn much about their inadequacies by studying the less familiar legislation designed to supplement them) and of those whose courses place more emphasis on the use of the criminal law to regulate less obvious, yet often equally harmful, forms of objectionable behaviour. Considerations of space and cost have, however, demanded the excision of most of the procedural, evidentiary, and administrative provisions of these statutes, as also of almost all penalty provisions where these are separate from the offence-creating ones. Whether an offence is (when an adult is charged) triable solely on indictment, or either way, or only summarily has, however, been indicated by the addition of the letters [I], [E] and [S] respectively.

In general the statutory provisions selected are printed in the form in which they were law on 1 June 2008 (amending legislation being incorporated silently).

P. R. Glazebrook

Contents

Alphabetical contents

Chronological contents

Classification of offence

The mode of trial for an offence, when the person charged is an adult, has been indicated by the addition of a letter at the end of the provision creating it—

[I]: triable only on indictment (i.e., only in the Crown Court)

[E]: triable either way (i.e., in either Crown or Magistrates' Court)

[S]: triable only summarily (i.e., only in the Magistrates' Court)

This classification, it should be noted, is different from that of the Schedule to section 5, Interpretation Act 1978 (page 1, below), which does not distinguish offences triable only on indictment from those triable either way.

Part I

General Rules

(a) Interpretation

Interpretation Act 1978

5 Definitions

In any Act, unless the contrary intention appears, words and expressions listed in Schedule 1 to this Act are to be construed according to that Schedule.

SCHEDULE 1

'Person' includes a body of persons corporate or unincorporate.

In relation to England and Wales—

(a) 'indictable offence' means an offence which, if committed by an adult, is triable on indictment, whether it is exclusively so triable or triable either way;

(b) 'summary offence' means an offence which, if committed by an adult, is triable only summarily;

(c) 'offence triable either way' means an offence (other than an offence triable on indictment only by virtue of Part V of the Criminal Justice Act 1988) which, if committed by an adult, is triable either on indictment or summarily;

and the terms 'indictable', 'summary' and 'triable either way', in their application to offences, are to be construed accordingly.

In the above definitions references to the way or ways in which an offence is triable are to be construed without regard to the effect, if any, of section 22 of the Magistrates' Courts Act 1980 on the mode of trial in a particular case.

6 Gender and number

In any Act, unless the contrary intention appears,—

(a) words importing the masculine gender include the feminine;

(b) words importing the feminine gender include the masculine;

(c) words in the singular include the plural and words in the plural include the singular.

15 Repeal of repeal

Where an Act repeals a repealing enactment, the repeal does not revive any enactment previously repealed unless words are added reviving it.

16 General savings

(1) Without prejudice to section 15, where an Act repeals an enactment, the repeal does not, unless the contrary intention appears,—

(a) revive anything not in force or existing at the time at which the repeal takes effect;
(b) affect the previous operation of the enactment repealed or anything duly done or suffered under that enactment;
(c) affect any right, privilege, obligation or liability acquired, accrued, or incurred under that enactment;
(d) affect any penalty, forfeiture or punishment incurred in respect of any offence committed against that enactment;
(e) affect any investigation, legal proceeding or remedy in respect of any such right, privilege, obligation, liability, penalty, forfeiture or punishment;

and any such investigation, legal proceeding or remedy may be instituted, continued or enforced, and any such penalty, forefeiture or punishment may be imposed, as if the repealing Act had not been passed.

(2) This section applies to the expiry of a temporary enactment as if it were repealed by an Act.

18 Duplicated offences

Where an act or omission constitutes an offence under two or more Acts, or both under an Act and at common law, the offender shall, unless the contrary intention appears, be liable to be prosecuted and punished under either or any of those Acts or at common law, but shall not be liable to be punished more than once for the same offence.

Gender Recognition Act 2004

9 General

(1) Where a full gender recognition certificate is issued to a person, the person's gender becomes for all purposes the acquired gender (so that, if the acquired gender is the male gender, the person's sex becomes that of a man and, if it is the female gender, the person's sex becomes that of a woman).

(2) Subsection (1) does not affect things done, or events occurring, before the certificate is issued; but it does operate for the interpretation of enactments passed, and instruments and other documents made, before the certificate is issued (as well as those passed or made afterwards).

(3) Subsection (1) is subject to provision made by this Act or any other enactment or any subordinate legislation.

20 Gender-specific offences

(1) Where (apart from this subsection) a relevant gender-specific offence could be committed or attempted only if the gender of a person to whom a full gender recognition certificate has been issued were not the acquired gender, the fact that the person's gender has become the acquired gender does not prevent the offence being committed or attempted.

(2) An offence is a 'relevant gender-specific offence' if—
(a) either or both of the conditions in subsection (3) are satisfied, and
(b) the commission of the offence involves the accused engaging in sexual activity.

(3) The conditions are—
(a) that the offence may be committed only by a person of a particular gender, and
(b) that the offence may be committed only on, or in relation to, a person of a particular gender,

and the references to a particular gender include a gender identified by reference to the gender of the other person involved.

Human Rights Act 1998

1 The Convention Rights

(1) In this Act 'the Convention rights' means the rights and fundamental freedoms set out in—

(a) Articles 2 to 12 and 14 of the Convention,

(b) Articles 1 to 3 of the First Protocol, and

(c) Articles 1 and 2 of the Sixth Protocol,

as read with Articles 16 to 18 of the Convention.

(2) Those Articles are to have effect for the purposes of this Act subject to any designated derogation or reservation (as to which see sections 14 and 15).

(3) The Articles are set out in Schedule 1.

3 Interpretation of legislation

(1) So far as it is possible to do so, primary legislation and subordinate legislation must be read and given effect in a way which is compatible with the Convention rights.

(2) This section—

(a) applies to primary legislation and subordinate legislation whenever enacted;

(b) does not affect the validity, continuing operation or enforcement of any incompatible primary legislation; and

(c) does not affect the validity, continuing operation or enforcement of any incompatible subordinate legislation if (disregarding any possibility of revocation) primary legislation prevents removal of the incompatibility.

4 Declaration of incompatibility

(1) Subsection (2) applies in any proceedings in which a court determines whether a provision of primary legislation is compatible with a Convention right.

(2) If the court is satisfied that the provision is incompatible with a Convention right, it may make a declaration of that incompatibility.

(3) Subsection (4) applies in any proceedings in which a court determines whether a provision of subordinate legislation, made in the exercise of a power conferred by primary legislation, is compatible with a Convention right.

(4) If the court is satisfied—

(a) that the provision is incompatible with a Convention right, and

(b) that (disregarding any possibility of revocation) the primary legislation concerned prevents removal of the incompatibility,

it may make a declaration of that incompatibility.

(5) In this section 'court' means—

(a) the House of Lords;

(b) the Judicial Committee of the Privy Council;

(c) the Courts-Martial Appeal Court;

(d) in Scotland, the High Court of Justiciary sitting otherwise than as a trial court or the Court of Session;

(e) in England and Wales or Northern Ireland, the High Court or the Court of Appeal.

(6) A declaration under this section ('a declaration of incompatibility')—

(a) does not affect the validity, continuing operation or enforcement of the provision in respect of which it is given; and

(b) is not binding on the parties to the proceedings in which it is made.

SCHEDULE 1 THE ARTICLES

PART I THE CONVENTION

Rights and freedoms

Article 2 Right to life

1. Everyone's right to life shall be protected by law. No one shall be deprived of his life intentionally save in the execution of a sentence of a court following his conviction of a crime for which this penalty is provided by law.

2. Deprivation of life shall not be regarded as inflicted in contravention of this Article when it results from the use of force which is no more than absolutely necessary:

(a) in defence of any person from unlawful violence;
(b) in order to effect a lawful arrest or to prevent the escape of a person lawfully detained;
(c) in action lawfully taken for the purpose of quelling a riot or insurrection.

Article 3 Prohibition of torture

No one shall be subjected to torture or to inhuman or degrading treatment or punishment.

Article 4 Prohibition of slavery and forced labour

1. No one shall be held in slavery or servitude.
2. No one shall be required to perform forced or compulsory labour.
3. For the purpose of this Article the term "forced or compulsory labour" shall not include:
   (a) any work required to be done in the ordinary course of detention imposed according to the provisions of Article 5 of this Convention or during conditional release from such detention;
   (b) any service of a military character or, in case of conscientious objectors in countries where they are recognised, service exacted instead of compulsory military service;
   (c) any service exacted in case of an emergency or calamity threatening the life or well-being of the community;
   (d) any work or service which forms part of normal civic obligations.

Article 5 Right to liberty and security

1. Everyone has the right to liberty and security of person. No one shall be deprived of his liberty save in the following cases and in accordance with a procedure prescribed by law:

(a) the lawful detention of a person after conviction by a competent court;
(b) the lawful arrest or detention of a person for non-compliance with the lawful order of a court or in order to secure the fulfilment of any obligation prescribed by law;
(c) the lawful arrest or detention of a person effected for the purpose of bringing him before the competent legal authority on reasonable suspicion of having committed an offence or when it is reasonably considered necessary to prevent his committing an offence or fleeing after having done so;
(d) the detention of a minor by lawful order for the purpose of educational supervision or his lawful detention for the purpose of bringing him before the competent legal authority;
(e) the lawful detention of persons for the prevention of the spreading of infectious diseases, of persons of unsound mind, alcoholics or drug addicts or vagrants;
(f) the lawful arrest or detention of a person to prevent his effecting an unauthorised entry into the country or of a person against whom action is being taken with a view to deportation or extradition.

2. Everyone who is arrested shall be informed promptly, in a language which he understands, of the reasons for his arrest and of any charge against him.

Article 6 Right to a fair trial

2. Everyone charged with a criminal offence shall be presumed innocent until proved guilty according to law.

Article 7 No punishment without law

1. No one shall be held guilty of any criminal offence on account of any act or omission which did not constitute a criminal offence under national or international law at the time when it was committed. Nor shall a heavier penalty be imposed than the one that was applicable at the time the criminal offence was committed.

2. This Article shall not prejudice the trial and punishment of any person for any act or omission which, at the time when it was committed, was criminal according to the general principles of law recognised by civilised nations.

Article 8 Right to respect for private and family life

1. Everyone has the right to respect for his private and family life, his home and his correspondence.

2. There shall be no interference by a public authority with the exercise of this right except such as is in accordance with the law and is necessary in a democratic society in the interests of national security, public safety or the economic well being of the country, for the prevention of disorder or crime, for the protection of health or morals, or for the protection of the rights and freedoms of others.

Article 9 Freedom of thought, conscience and religion

1. Everyone has the right to freedom of thought, conscience and religion; this right includes freedom to change his religion or belief and freedom, either alone or in community with others and in public or private, to manifest his religion or belief, in worship, teaching, practice and observance.

2. Freedom to manifest one's religion or beliefs shall he subject only to such limitations as are prescribed by law and are necessary in a democratic society in the interests of public safety, for the protection of public order, health or morals, or for the protection of the rights and freedoms of others.

Article 10 Freedom of expression

1. Everyone has the right to freedom of expression. This right shall include freedom to hold opinions and to receive and impart information and ideas without interference by public authority and regardless of frontiers. This Article shall not prevent States from requiring the licensing of broadcasting television or cinema enterprises.

2. The exercise of these freedoms, since it carries with it duties and responsibilities, may be subject to such formalities, conditions, restrictions or penalties as are prescribed by law and are necessary in a democratic society, in the interests of national security, territorial integrity or public safety, for the prevention of disorder or crime, for the protection of health or morals, for the protection of the reputation or rights of others, for preventing the disclosure of information received in confidence, or for maintaining the authority and impartiality of the judiciary.

Article 11 Freedom of assembly and association

1. Everyone has the right to freedom of peaceful assembly and to freedom of association with others, including the right to form and to join trade unions for the protection of his interests.

2. No restrictions shall be placed on the exercise of these rights other than such as are prescribed by law and are necessary in a democratic society in the interests of national security or public safety, for the prevention of disorder or crime, for the protection of health or morals or for the protection of the rights and freedoms of others. This Article shall not prevent the imposition of lawful restrictions on the exercise of these rights by members of the armed forces, of the police or of the administration of the State.

Article 14 Prohibition of discrimination

The enjoyment of the rights and freedoms set forth in this Convention shall be secured without discrimination on any ground such as sex, race, colour, language, religion, political or other opinion, national or social origin, association with a national minority, property, birth or other status.

Article 16 Restrictions on political activity of aliens

Nothing in Articles 10, 11 and 14 shall be regarded as preventing the High Contracting Parties from imposing restrictions on the political activity of aliens.

Article 17 Prohibition of abuse of rights

Nothing in this Convention may be interpreted as implying for any State, group or person any right to engage in any activity or perform any act aimed at the destruction of any of the rights and freedoms set forth herein or at their limitation to a greater extent than is provided for in the Convention.

Article 18 Limitation on use of restrictions on rights

The restrictions permitted under this Convention to the said rights and freedoms shall not be applied for any purpose other than those for which they have been prescribed.

PART II THE FIRST PROTOCOL

Article 1 Protection of property

Every natural or legal person is entitled to the peaceful enjoyment of his possessions. No one shall be deprived of his possessions except in the public interest and subject to the conditions provided for by law and by the general principles of international law.

The preceding provisions shall not, however, in any way impair the right of a State to enforce such laws as it deems necessary to control the use of property in accordance with the general interest or to secure the payment of taxes or other contributions or penalties.

PART III THE SIXTH PROTOCOL

Article 1 Abolition of the death penalty

The death penalty shall be abolished. No one shall be condemned to such penalty or executed.

(b) Liability

Criminal Law Act 1967

1 Abolition of distinction between felony and misdemeanour

(1) All distinctions between felony and misdemeanour are hereby abolished.

(2) Subject to the provisions of this Act, on all matters on which a distinction has previously been made between felony and misdemeanour, including mode of trial, the law and practice in relation to all offences cognisable under the law of England and Wales (including piracy) shall be the law and practice applicable at the commencement of this Act in relation to misdemeanour.

6 Trial of offences

(1) Where a person is arraigned on an indictment—

(a) he shall in all cases be entitled to make a plea of not guilty in addition to any demurrer or special plea;

(b) he may plead not guilty of the offence specifically charged in the indictment but guilty of another offence of which he might be found guilty on that indictment;

(c) if he stands mute of malice or will not answer directly to the indictment, the court may order a plea of not guilty to be entered on his behalf, and he shall then be treated as having pleaded not guilty.

(2) On an indictment for murder a person found not guilty of murder may be found guilty—

(a) of manslaughter, or of causing grievous bodily harm with intent to do so; or

(b) of any offence of which he may be found guilty under an enactment specifically so providing, or under section 4(2) of this Act; or

(c) of any attempt to commit murder, or an attempt to commit any other offence of which he might be found guilty;

but may not be found guilty of any offence not included above.

(3) Where, on a person's trial on indictment for any offence except treason or murder, the jury find him not guilty of the offence specifically charged in the indictment, but the allegations in the indictment amount to or include (expressly or by implication) an allegation of another offence falling within the jurisdiction of the court of trial, the jury may find him guilty of that other offence or of an offence of which he could be found guilty on an indictment specifically charging that other offence.

(4) For purposes of subsection (3) above any allegation of an offence shall be taken as including an allegation of attempting to commit that offence; and where a person is charged on an indictment

with attempting to commit an offence or with any assault or other act preliminary to an offence, but not with the completed offence, then (subject to the discretion of the court to discharge the jury with a view to the preferment of an indictment for the completed offence) he may be convicted of the offence charged notwithstanding that he is shown to be guilty of the completed offence.

(5) Where a person arraigned on an indictment pleads not guilty of an offence charged in the indictment but guilty of some other offence of which he might be found guilty on that charge, and he is convicted on that plea of guilty without trial for the offence of which he has pleaded not guilty, then (whether or not the two offences are separately charged in distinct counts) his conviction of the one offence shall be an acquittal of the other.

Road Traffic Offenders Act 1988

24 Alternative verdicts

(A1) Where—

(a) a person charged with manslaughter in connection with the driving of a mechanically propelled vehicle by him is found not guilty of that offence, but

(b) the allegations in the indictment amount to or include an allegation of any of the relevant offences,

he may be convicted of that offence.

(A2) For the purposes of subsection (A1) above the following are the relevant offences—

(a) an offence under section 1 of the Road Traffic Act 1988 (causing death by dangerous driving),

(b) an offence under section 2 of that Act (dangerous driving),

(c) an offence under section 3A of that Act (causing death by careless driving when under influence of drink or drugs), and

(d) an offence under section 35 of the Offences Against the Person Act 1861 (furious driving).

Children and Young Persons Act 1933

50 Age of criminal responsibility

It shall be conclusively presumed that no child under the age of ten years can be guilty of any offence.

Theft Act 1968

30 Husband and wife

(2) Subject to subsection (4) below, a person shall have the same right to bring proceedings against that person's wife or husband for any offence (whether under this Act or otherwise) as if they were not married, and a person bringing any such proceedings shall be competent to give evidence for the prosecution at every stage of the proceedings.

(4) Proceedings shall not be instituted against a person for any offence of stealing or doing unlawful damage to property which at the time of the offence belongs to that person's wife or husband, or for any attempt, incitement or conspiracy to commit such an offence, unless the proceedings are instituted by or with the consent of the Director of Public Prosecutions:

Provided that—

(a) this subsection shall not apply to proceedings against a person for an offence—

(i) if that person is charged with committing the offence jointly with the wife or husband; or

(ii) if by virtue of any judicial decree or order (wherever made) that person and the wife or husband are at the time of the offence under no obligation to cohabit.

Criminal Justice Act 1967

8 Proof of criminal intent

A court or jury, in determining whether a person has committed an offence,—

(a) shall not be bound in law to infer that he intended or foresaw a result of his actions by reason only of its being a natural and probable consequence of those actions; but

(b) shall decide whether he did intend or foresee that result by reference to all the evidence, drawing such inferences from the evidence as appear proper in the circumstances.

Accessories and Abettors Act 1861

8 Abettors

Whosoever shall aid, abet, counsel, or procure the commission of any indictable offence, whether the same be an offence at common law or by virtue of any Act passed or to be passed, shall be liable to be tried, indicted, and punished as a principal offender.

Magistrates' Courts Act 1980

44 Aiders and abettors

(1) A person who aids, abets, counsels or procures the commission by another person of a summary offence shall be guilty of the like offence and may be tried (whether or not he is charged as a principal) either by a court having jurisdiction to try that other person or by a court having by virtue of his own offence jurisdiction to try him.

(2) Any offence consisting in aiding, abetting, counselling or procuring the commission of an offence triable either way (other than an offence listed in Schedule 1 to this Act) shall by virtue of this subsection be triable either way.

Criminal Justice Act 1948

31 Jurisdiction and procedure in respect of certain indictable offences committed in foreign countries

(1) Any British subject employed under His Majesty's Government in the United Kingdom in the service of the Crown who commits in a foreign country, when acting or purporting to act in the course of his employment, any offence which, if committed in England, would be punishable on indictment, shall be guilty of an offence . . . and subject to the same punishment, as if the offence had been committed in England.

Merchant Shipping Act 1995

282 Offences committed by British seamen

(1) Any act in relation to property or person done in or at any place (ashore or afloat) outside the United Kingdom by any master or seaman who at the time is employed in a United Kingdom ship,

which, if done in any part of the United Kingdom, would be an offence under the law of any part of the United Kingdom, shall—

(a) be an offence under that law, and

(b) be treated for the purposes of jurisdiction and trial, as if it had been done within the jurisdiction of the Admiralty of England.

(2) Subsection (1) above also applies in relation to a person who had been so employed within the period of three months expiring with the time when the act was done.

(3) Subsections (1) and (2) above apply to omissions as they apply to acts.

Territorial Waters Jurisdiction Act 1878

2 Amendment of law as to jurisdiction of the Admiral

An offence committed by a person, whether he is or is not a subject of Her Majesty, on the open sea within the territorial waters of Her Majesty's dominions, is an offence within the jurisdiction of the Admiral, although it may have been committed on board or by means of a foreign ship, and the person who committed such offence may be arrested, tried, and punished accordingly.

Suppression of Terrorism Act 1978

4 Jurisdiction in respect of offences committed outside United Kingdom

(1) If a person, whether a citizen of the United Kingdom and Colonies or not, does in a convention country any act which, if he had done it in a part of the United Kingdom, would have made him guilty in that part of the United Kingdom of—

(a) an offence mentioned in paragraph 1, 2, 4, 5, 10, 11, 11B, 12, 13, 14 or 15 of Schedule 1 to this Act; or

(b) an offence of attempting to commit any offence so mentioned, he shall, in that part of the United Kingdom, be guilty of the offence or offences aforesaid of which the act would have made him guilty if he had done it there.

(3) If a person who is a national of a convention country but not a citizen of the United Kingdom and Colonies does outside the United Kingdom and that convention country any act which makes him in that convention country guilty of an offence and which, if he had been a citizen of the United Kingdom and Colonies, would have made him in any part of the United Kingdom guilty of an offence mentioned in paragraph 1, 2 or 13 of Schedule 1 to this Act, he shall, in any part of the United Kingdom, be guilty of the offence or offences aforesaid of which the act would have made him guilty if he had been such a citizen.

(7) For the purposes of this section any act done—

(a) on board a ship registered in a convention country, being an act which, if the ship had been registered in the United Kingdom, would have constituted an offence within the jurisdiction of the Admiralty; or

(b) on board an aircraft registered in a convention country while the aircraft is in flight elsewhere than in or over that country; or

(c) on board a hovercraft registered in a convention country while the hovercraft is in journey elsewhere than in or over that country,

shall be treated as done in that convention country; and subsection (4) of section 92 of the Civil Aviation Act 1982 (definition of 'in flight' or, as applied to hovercraft, 'in journey') shall apply for the purposes of this subsection as it applies for the purposes of that section.

8 Provisions as to interpretation and orders

(1) In this Act—

'act' includes omission;

'convention country' means a country for the time being designated in an order made by the Secretary of State as a party to the European Convention on the Suppression of Terrorism signed at Strasbourg on the 27th January 1977;

'country' includes any territory;

'enactment' includes an enactment of the Parliament of Northern Ireland, a Measure of the Northern Ireland Assembly, and an Order in Council under the Northern Ireland (Temporary Provisions) Act 1972 or the Northern Ireland Act 1974.

SCHEDULE 1

Common law offences

1. Murder.
2. Manslaughter or culpable homicide.
4. Kidnapping, abduction or plagium.
5. False imprisonment.

Abduction

10. An offence under any of the following provisions of the Offences against the Person Act 1861—

(a) section 55 (abduction of unmarried girl under 16)

(b) section 56 (child-stealing or receiving stolen child).

11. An offence under section 20 of the Sexual Offences Act 1956 (abduction of unmarried girl under 16).

Explosives

12. An offence under any of the following provisions of the Offences against the Person Act 1861—

(a) section 28 (causing bodily injury by gunpowder);

(b) section 29 (causing gunpowder to explode etc. with intent to do grievous bodily harm);

(c) section 30 (placing gunpowder near a building etc. with intent to cause bodily injury).

13. An offence under any of the following provisions of the Explosive Substances Act 1883—

(a) section 2 (causing explosion likely to endanger life or property);

(b) section 3 (doing any act with intent to cause such an explosion, conspiring to cause such an explosion, or making or possessing explosive with intent to endanger life or property).

13A. An offence under any provision of the Nuclear Material (Offences) Act 1983.

Firearms

14. The following offences under the Firearms Act 1968—

(a) an offence under section 16 (possession of firearm with intent to injure);

(b) an offence under subsection (1) of section 17 (use of firearm or imitation firearm to resist arrest) involving the use or attempted use of a firearm within the meaning of that section.

Terrorism Act 2000

59 Inciting terrorism overseas

[See page 302]

62 Terrorist bombing: jurisdiction

(1) If—

(a) a person does anything outside the United Kingdom as an act of terrorism or for the purposes of terrorism, and
(b) his action would have constituted the commission of one of the offences listed in subsection (2) if it had been done in the United Kingdom,

he shall be guilty of the offence.

(2) The offences referred to in subsection (1)(b) are—
(a) an offence under section 2, 3 or 5 of the Explosive Substances Act 1883 (causing explosions, &c.),
(b) an offence under section 1 of the Biological Weapons Act 1974 (biological weapons), and
(c) an offence under section 2 of the Chemical Weapons Act 1996 (chemical weapons).

Civil Aviation Act 1982

92 Application of criminal law to aircraft

(1) Any act or omission taking place on board a British-controlled aircraft or (subject to subsection (1A) below) a foreign aircraft while in flight elsewhere than in or over the United Kingdom which, if taking place in, or in a part of, the United Kingdom, would constitute an offence under the law in force in, or in that part of, the United Kingdom shall constitute that offence; but this subsection shall not apply to any act or omission which is expressly or impliedly authorised by or under that law when taking place outside the United Kingdom.

(1A) Subsection (1) above shall only apply to an act or omission which takes place on board a foreign aircraft where—
(a) the next landing of the aircraft is in the United Kingdom, and
(b) in the case of an aircraft registered in a country other than the United Kingdom, the act or omission would, if taking place there, also constitute an offence under the law in force in that country.

(1B) Any act or omission punishable under the law in force in any country is an offence under that law for the purposes of subsection (1A) above, however it is described in that law.

(4) For the purposes of this section the period during which an aircraft is in flight shall be deemed to include any period from the moment when power is applied for the purpose of the aircraft taking off on a flight until the moment when the landing run (if any) at the termination of that flight ends; and any reference in this section to an aircraft in flight shall include a reference to an aircraft during any period when it is on the surface of the sea or land but not within the territorial limits of any country.

(5) In this section, except where the context otherwise requires—

'aircraft' means any aircraft, whether or not a British-controlled aircraft, other than—
(a) a military aircraft; or
(b) subject to section 101(1)(b) below, an aircraft which, not being a military aircraft, belongs to or is exclusively employed in the service of Her Majesty in right of the United Kingdom;

'British-controlled aircraft' means an aircraft—
(a) which is for the time being registered in the United Kingdom; or
(b) which is not for the time being registered in any country but in the case of which either the operator of the aircraft or each person entitled as owner to any legal or beneficial interest in it satisfies the following requirements, namely—
(i) that he is a person qualified to be the owner of a legal or beneficial interest in an aircraft registered in the United Kingdom; and
(ii) that he resides or has his principal place of business in the United Kingdom; or
(c) which, being for the time being registered in some other country, is for the time being chartered by demise to a person who, or to persons each of whom, satisfies the requirements aforesaid; . . .

'foreign aircraft' means any aircraft other than a British-controlled aircraft.

Offences Against the Person Act 1861

9 Murder or manslaughter abroad
[See page 35]

Criminal Law Act 1977

1A Conspiracy to commit offences outside the United Kingdom
[See page 352]

Criminal Attempts Act 1981

1A Extended jurisdiction in relation to certain attempts
[See page 346]

Aviation Security Act 1982

1 Hijacking
[See page 119]

2 Destroying, damaging or endangering safety of aircraft
[See page 119]

3 Other Acts endangering or likely to endanger safety of aircraft
[See page 120]

4 Offences in relation to certain dangerous articles
[See page 120]

Taking of Hostages Act 1982

1 Hostage-taking
[See page 295]

Official Secrets Act 1989

15 Acts done abroad
[See page 325]

Criminal Justice Act 1988

134 Torture
[See page 42]

Aviation and Maritime Security Act 1990

9 Hijacking of ships
[See page 123]

10 Seizing or exercising control of fixed platforms
[See page 124]

11 Destroying ships or fixed platforms or endangering their safety
[See page 124]

12 Other acts endangering or likely to endanger safe navigation
[See page 125]

13 Offences involving threats
[See page 125]

Computer Misuse Act 1990

4 Territorial scope of offences under this Act
[See page 171]

War Crimes Act 1991

1 Jurisdiction over certain war crimes
[See page 35]

International Criminal Court Act 2001

51 Genocide, crimes against humanity and war crimes

(1) It is an offence against the law of England and Wales for a person to commit genocide, a crime against humanity or a war crime. [I]

(2) This section applies to acts committed—

(a) in England or Wales, or

(b) outside the United Kingdom by a United Kingdom national, a United Kingdom resident or a person subject to UK service jurisdiction.

52 Conduct ancillary to genocide, etc. committed outside jurisdiction

(1) It is an offence against the law of England and Wales for a person to engage in conduct ancillary to an act to which this section applies. [I]

(2) This section applies to an act that if committed in England or Wales would constitute—

(a) an offence under section 51 (genocide, crime against humanity or war crime), or

(b) an offence under this section,

but which, being committed (or intended to be committed) outside England and Wales, does not constitute such an offence.

(3) The reference in subsection (1) to conduct ancillary to such an act is to conduct that would constitute an ancillary offence in relation to that act if the act were committed in England or Wales.

(4) This section applies where the conduct in question consists of or includes an act committed—

(a) in England or Wales, or
(b) outside the United Kingdom by a United Kingdom national, a United Kingdom resident or a person subject to UK service jurisdiction.

55 Meaning of 'ancillary offence'

(1) References in this Part to an ancillary offence under the law of England and Wales are to—
(a) aiding, abetting, counselling or procuring the commission of an offence,
(b) inciting a person to commit an offence,
(c) attempting or conspiring to commit an offence, or
(d) assisting an offender or concealing the commission of an offence.

(2) In subsection (1)(a) the reference to aiding, abetting, counselling or procuring is to conduct that in relation to an indictable offence would be punishable under section 8 of the Accessories and Abettors Act 1861.

(3) In subsection (1)(b) the reference to incitement is to conduct amounting to an offence of incitement at common law.

(4) In subsection (1)(c)—
(a) the reference to an attempt is to conduct amounting to an offence under section 1 of the Criminal Attempts Act 1981; and
(b) the reference to conspiracy is to conduct amounting to an offence of conspiracy under section 1 of the Criminal Law Act 1977.

(5) In subsection (1)(d)—
(a) the reference to assisting an offender is to conduct that in relation to a relevant offence would amount to an offence under section 4(1) of the Criminal Law Act 1967; and
(b) the reference to concealing an offence is to conduct that in relation to a relevant offence would amount to an offence under section 5(1) of that Act.

65 Responsibility of commanders and other superiors

(1) This section applies in relation to—
(a) offences under this Part, and
(b) offences ancillary to such offences.

(2) A military commander, or a person effectively acting as a military commander, is responsible for offences committed by forces under his effective command and control, or (as the case may be) his effective authority and control, as a result of his failure to exercise control properly over such forces where—
(a) he either knew, or owing to the circumstances at the time, should have known that the forces were committing or about to commit such offences, and
(b) he failed to take all necessary and reasonable measures within his power to prevent or repress their commission or to submit the matter to the competent authorities for investigation and prosecution.

(3) With respect to superior and subordinate relationships not described in subsection (2), a superior is responsible for offences committed by subordinates under his effective authority and control, as a result of his failure to exercise control properly over such subordinates where—
(a) he either knew, or consciously disregarded information which clearly indicated, that the subordinates were committing or about to commit such offences,
(b) the offences concerned activities that were within his effective responsibility and control, and
(c) he failed to take all necessary and reasonable measures within his power to prevent or repress their commission or to submit the matter to the competent authorities for investigation and prosecution.

(4) A person responsible under this section for an offence is regarded as aiding, abetting, counselling or procuring the commission of the offence.

(5) In interpreting and applying the provisions of this section (which corresponds to article 28) the court shall take into account any relevant judgment or decision of the ICC.

Account may also be taken of any other relevant international jurisprudence.

(6) Nothing in this section shall be read as restricting or excluding—

(a) any liability of the commander or superior apart from this section, or

(b) the liability of persons other than the commander or superior.

67 Meaning of 'UK national', 'UK resident' and 'person subject to UK service jurisdiction

(1) In this Part a 'United Kingdom national' means an individual who is—

(a) a British citizen, a British Dependent Territories citizen, a British National (Overseas) or a British Overseas Citizen,

(b) a person who under the British Nationality Act 1981 (c. 61) is a British subject, or

(c) a British protected person within the meaning of that Act.

(2) In this Part a 'United Kingdom resident' means a person who is resident in the United Kingdom.

(3) In this Part a 'person subject to UK service jurisdiction' means—

(a) a person subject to military law, air force law or the Naval Discipline Act 1957;

(b) any such person as is mentioned in section 208A or 209(1) or (2) of the Army Act 1955 or the Air Force Act 1955 (application of Act to passengers in HM ships and aircraft and to certain civilians); or

(c) any such person as is mentioned in section 117 or 118 of the Naval Discipline Act 1957 (application of Act to passengers in HM ships and to certain civilians).

Criminal Justice Act 1993

PART I JURISDICTION

1 Offences to which this Part applies

(1) This Part applies to two groups of offences—

(a) any offence mentioned in subsection (2) (a 'Group A offence'); and

(b) any offence mentioned in subsection (3) (a 'Group B offence').

(2) The Group A offences are—

(a) an offence under any of the following provisions of the Theft Act 1968—
section 1 (theft);
section 17 (false accounting);
section 19 (false statements by company directors etc.);
section 21 (blackmail);
section 22 (handling stolen goods);
section 24A (retaining credits from dishonest sources, etc.);

(bb) an offence under any of the following provisions of the Fraud Act 2006—

(i) section 1 (fraud);

(ii) section 6 (possession etc. of articles for use in frauds);

(iii) section 7 (making or supplying articles for use in frauds);

(iv) section 9 (participating in fraudulent business carried on by sole trader etc.);

(v) section 11 (obtaining services dishonestly).

(c) an offence under any of the following provisions of the Forgery and Counterfeiting Act 1981—
section 1 (forgery);
section 2 (copying a false instrument);
section 3 (using a false instrument);
section 4 (using a copy of a false instrument);
section 5 (offences which relate to money orders, share certificates, passports, etc.);

(ca) an offence under section 25 of the Identity Cards Act 2006;
(d) the common law offence of cheating in relation to the public revenue.

(3) The Group B offences are—
(a) conspiracy to commit a Group A offence;
(b) conspiracy to defraud;
(c) attempting to commit a Group A offence;
(d) incitement to commit a Group A offence.

2 Jurisdiction in respect of Group A offences

(1) For the purposes of this Part, 'relevant event', in relation to any Group A offence, means (subject to subsection (1A)) any act or omission or other event (including any result of one or more acts or omissions) proof of which is required for conviction of the offence.

(1A) In relation to an offence under section 1 of the Fraud Act 2006 (fraud), 'relevant event' includes—
(a) if the fraud involved an intention to make a gain and the gain occurred, that occurrence;
(b) if the fraud involved an intention to cause a loss or to expose another to a risk of loss and the loss occurred, that occurrence.

(2) For the purpose of determining whether an event is a relevant event, any question as to where it occurred is to be disregarded.

(3) A person may be guilty of a Group A offence if any of the events which are relevant events in relation to the offence occurred in England and Wales.

3 Questions immaterial to jurisdiction in the case of certain offences

(1) A person may be guilty of a Group A or Group B offence whether or not—
(a) he was a British citizen at any material time;
(b) he was in England and Wales at any such time.

(2) On a charge of conspiracy to commit a Group A offence, or on a charge of conspiracy to defraud in England and Wales, the defendant may be guilty of the offence whether or not—
(a) he became a party to the conspiracy in England and Wales;
(b) any act or omission or other event in relation to the conspiracy occurred in England and Wales.

(3) On a charge of attempting to commit a Group A offence, the defendant may be guilty of the offence whether or not—
(a) the attempt was made in England and Wales;
(b) it had an effect in England and Wales.

(4) Subsection (1)(a) does not apply where jurisdiction is given to try the offence in question by an enactment which makes provision by reference to the nationality of the person charged.

(5) Subsection (2) does not apply in relation to any charge under the Criminal Law Act 1977 brought by virtue of section 1A of that Act.

(6) Subsection (3) does not apply in relation to any charge under the Criminal Attempts Act 1981 brought by virtue of section 1A of that Act.

4 Rules for determining certain jurisdictional questions relating to the location of events

In relation to a Group A or Group B offence—
(a) there is an obtaining of property in England and Wales if the property is either despatched from or received at a place in England and Wales; and
(b) there is a communication in England and Wales of any information, instruction, request, demand or other matter if it is sent by any means—
(i) from a place in England and Wales to a place elsewhere; or
(ii) from a place elsewhere to a place in England and Wales.

5 Extended jurisdiction over conspiracies to defraud and incitement

(3) A person may be guilty of conspiracy to defraud if—

(a) a party to the agreement constituting the conspiracy, or a party's agent, did anything in England and Wales in relation to the agreement before its formation, or
(b) a party to it became a party in England and Wales (by joining it either in person or through an agent), or
(c) a party to it, or a party's agent, did or omitted anything in England and Wales in pursuance of it,

and the conspiracy would be triable in England and Wales but for the fraud which the parties to it had in view not being intended to take place in England and Wales.

(4) A person may be guilty of incitement to commit a Group A offence if—
(a) the incitement takes place in England and Wales; and
(b) a charge in respect of incitement would be triable in England and Wales but for what the person charged had in view not being an offence triable in England and Wales.

(5) Subsections (3) and (4) are subject to section 6.

6 Relevance of external law

(1) A person is guilty of an offence triable by virtue of section 5(3), only if the pursuit of the agreed course of conduct would at some stage involve—
(a) an act or omission by one or more of the parties, or
(b) the happening of some other event, constituting an offence under the law in force where the act, omission or other event was intended to take place.

(2) A person is guilty of an offence triable by virtue of section 1A of the Criminal Attempts Act 1981, or by virtue of section 5(4), only if what he had in view would involve the commission of an offence under the law in force where the whole or any part of it was intended to take place.

(3) Conduct punishable under the law in force in any place is an offence under that law for the purposes of this section, however it is described in that law.

(4) Subject to subsection (6), a condition specified in subsection (1) or (2) shall be taken to be satisfied unless, not later than rules of court may provide, the defence serve on the prosecution a notice—
(a) stating that, on the facts as alleged with respect to the relevant conduct, the condition is not in their opinion satisfied;
(b) showing their grounds for that opinion; and
(c) requiring the prosecution to show that it is satisfied.

(5) In subsection (4) 'the relevant conduct' means—
(a) where the condition in subsection (1) is in question, the agreed course of conduct; and
(b) where the condition in subsection (2) is in question, what the defendant had in view.

(6) The court, if it thinks fit, may permit the defence to require the prosecution to show that the condition is satisfied without the prior service of a notice under subsection (4).

(7) In the Crown Court, the question whether the condition is satisfied shall be decided by the judge alone.

Female Genital Mutilation Act 2003

3 Offence of assisting a non-UK person to mutilate overseas a girl's genitalia

[See page 44]

4 Extension of sections 1 to 3 to extra-territorial acts

[See page 44]

Sexual Offences Act 2003

72 Offences outside the United Kingdom

[See page 76]

Serious Crime Act 2007

52 Jurisdiction over offences of assisting or encouraging an offence
[See page 350]

(c) Defences

Criminal Law Act 1967

3 Use of force in making arrest, etc.

(1) A person may use such force as is reasonable in the circumstances in the prevention of crime, or in effecting or assisting in the lawful arrest of offenders or suspected offenders or of persons unlawfully at large.

(2) Subsection (1) above shall replace the rules of the common law on the question when force used for a purpose mentioned in the subsection is justified by that purpose.

Criminal Justice and Immigration Act 2008

76 Reasonable force for purposes of self-defence etc.

(1) This section applies where in proceedings for an offence—

- (a) an issue arises as to whether a person charged with the offence ("D") is entitled to rely on a defence within subsection (2), and
- (b) the question arises whether the degree of force used by D against a person ("V") was reasonable in the circumstances.

(2) The defences are—

- (a) the common law defence of self-defence; and
- (b) the defences provided by section 3(1) of the Criminal Law Act 1967 (use of force in prevention of crime or making arrest).

(3) The question whether the degree of force used by D was reasonable in the circumstances is to be decided by reference to the circumstances as D believed them to be, and subsections (4) to (8) also apply in connection with deciding that question.

(4) If D claims to have held a particular belief as regards the existence of any circumstances—

- (a) the reasonableness or otherwise of that belief is relevant to the question whether D genuinely held it; but
- (b) if it is determined that D did genuinely hold it, D is entitled to rely on it for the purposes of subsection (3), whether or not—
  - (i) it was mistaken, or
  - (ii) (if it was mistaken) the mistake was a reasonable one to have made.

(5) But subsection (4)(b) does not enable D to rely on any mistaken belief attributable to intoxication that was voluntarily induced.

(6) The degree of force used by D is not to be regarded as having been reasonable in the circumstances as D believed them to be if it was disproportionate in those circumstances.

(7) In deciding the question mentioned in subsection (3) the following considerations are to be taken into account (so far as relevant in the circumstances of the case)—

- (a) that a person acting for a legitimate purpose may not be able to weigh to a nicety the exact measure of any necessary action; and

(b) that evidence of a person's having only done what the person honestly and instinctively thought was necessary for a legitimate purpose constitutes strong evidence that only reasonable action was taken by that person for that purpose.

(8) Subsection (7) is not to be read as preventing other matters from being taken into account where they are relevant to deciding the question mentioned in subsection (3).

(9) This section is intended to clarify the operation of the existing defences mentioned in subsection (2).

(10) In this section—

(a) "legitimate purpose" means—

(i) the purpose of self-defence under the common law, or

(ii) the prevention of crime or effecting or assisting in the lawful arrest of persons mentioned in the provisions referred to in subsection (2)(b);

(b) references to self-defence include acting in defence of another person; and

(c) references to the degree of force used are to the type and amount of force used.

Police and Criminal Evidence Act 1984

24 Arrest without warrant: constables

(1) A constable may arrest without a warrant—

(a) anyone who is about to commit an offence;

(b) anyone who is in the act of committing an offence;

(c) anyone whom he has reasonable grounds for suspecting to be about to commit an offence;

(d) anyone whom he has reasonable grounds for suspecting to be committing an offence.

(2) If a constable has reasonable grounds for suspecting that an offence has been committed, he may arrest without a warrant anyone whom he has reasonable grounds to suspect of being guilty of it.

(3) If an offence has been committed, a constable may arrest without a warrant—

(a) anyone who is guilty of the offence;

(b) anyone whom he has reasonable grounds for suspecting to be guilty of it.

(4) But the power of summary arrest conferred by subsection (1), (2) or (3) is exercisable only if the constable has reasonable grounds for believing that for any of the reasons mentioned in subsection (5) it is necessary to arrest the person in question.

(5) The reasons are—

(a) to enable the name of the person in question to be ascertained (in the case where the constable does not know, and cannot readily ascertain, the person's name, or has reasonable grounds for doubting whether a name given by the person as his name is his real name);

(b) correspondingly as regards the person's address;

(c) to prevent the person in question—

(i) causing physical injury to himself or any other person;

(ii) suffering physical injury;

(iii) causing loss of or damage to property;

(iv) committing an offence against public decency (subject to subsection (6)); or

(v) causing an unlawful obstruction of the highway;

(d) to protect a child or other vulnerable person from the person in question;

(e) to allow the prompt and effective investigation of the offence or of the conduct of the person in question;

(f) to prevent any prosecution for the offence from being hindered by the disappearance of the person in question.

(6) Subsection (5)(c)(iv) applies only where members of the public going about their normal business cannot reasonably be expected to avoid the person in question.

24A Arrest without warrant: other persons

(1) A person other than a constable may arrest without a warrant—

(a) anyone who is in the act of committing an indictable offence;

(b) anyone whom he has reasonable grounds for suspecting to be committing an indictable offence.

(2) Where an indictable offence has been committed, a person other than a constable may arrest without a warrant—

(a) anyone who is guilty of the offence;

(b) anyone whom he has reasonable grounds for suspecting to be guilty of it.

(3) But the power of summary arrest conferred by subsection (1) or (2) is exercisable only if—

(a) the person making the arrest has reasonable grounds for believing that for any of the reasons mentioned in subsection (4) it is necessary to arrest the person in question; and

(b) it appears to the person making the arrest that it is not reasonably practicable for a constable to make it instead.

(4) The reasons are to prevent the person in question—

(a) causing physical injury to himself or any other person;

(b) suffering physical injury;

(c) causing loss of or damage to property; or

(d) making off before a constable can assume responsibility for him.

(5) This section does not apply in relation to an offence under Part 3 or 3A of the Public Order Act 1986.

117 Power of constable to use reasonable force

Where any provision of this Act—

(a) confers a power on a constable; and

(b) does not provide that the power may only be exercised with the consent of some person, other than a police officer, the officer may use reasonable force, if necessary, in the exercise of the power.

Fire and Rescue Services Act 2004

44 Powers of fire-fighters etc in an emergency etc.

(1) An employee of a fire and rescue authority who is authorised in writing by the authority for the purposes of this section may do anything he reasonably believes to be necessary—

(a) if he reasonably believes a fire to have broken out or to be about to break out, for the purpose of extinguishing or preventing the fire or protecting life or property;

(b) if he reasonably believes a road traffic accident to have occurred, for the purpose of rescuing people or protecting them from serious harm;

(c) if he reasonably believes an emergency of another kind to have occurred, for the purpose of discharging any function conferred on the fire and rescue authority in relation to the emergency;

(d) for the purpose of preventing or limiting damage to property resulting from action taken as mentioned in paragraph (a), (b) or (c).

(2) In particular, an employee of a fire and rescue authority who is authorised as mentioned in subsection (1) may under that subsection—

(a) enter premises or a place, by force if necessary, without the consent of the owner or occupier of the premises or place;

(b) move or break into a vehicle without the consent of its owner;

(c) close a highway;

(d) stop and regulate traffic;
(e) restrict the access of persons to premises or a place.

Children Act 2004

58 Reasonable punishment

(1) In relation to any offence specified in subsection (2), battery of a child cannot be justified on the ground that it constituted reasonable punishment.

(2) The offences referred to in subsection (1) are—

(a) an offence under section 18 or 20 of the Offences against the Person Act 1861 (wounding and causing grievous bodily harm);
(b) an offence under section 47 of that Act (assault occasioning actual bodily harm);
(c) an offence under section 1 of the Children and Young Persons Act 1933 (cruelty to persons under 16).

(4) For the purposes of subsection (3) 'actual bodily harm' has the same meaning as it has for the purposes of section 47 of the Offences against the Person Act 1861.

Education Act 1996

550A Power of members of staff to restrain pupils

[See page 64]

550B Detention outside school hours lawful despite absence of parental consent

[See page 65]

Criminal Justice Act 1925

47 Abolition of presumption of coercion of married woman by husband

Any presumption of law that an offence committed by a wife in the presence of her husband is committed under the coercion of the husband is hereby abolished, but on a charge against a wife for any offence other than treason or murder it shall be a good defence to prove that the offence was committed in the presence of, and under the coercion of, the husband.

Crime and Disorder Act 1998

34 Abolition of rebuttable presumption that a child is doli incapax

The rebuttable presumption of criminal law that a child aged 10 or over is incapable of committing an offence is hereby abolished.

Statutory Instruments Act 1946

3 Supplementary provisions as to publication

(1) Regulations made for the purposes of this Act shall make provision for the publication by His Majesty's Stationery Office of lists showing the date upon which every statutory instrument printed

and sold by or under the authority of the King's printer of Acts of Parliament was first issued by or under the authority of that office; and in any legal proceedings a copy of any list so published purporting to bear the imprint of the King's printer shall be received in evidence as a true copy, and an entry therein shall be conclusive evidence of the date on which any statutory instrument was first issued by or under the authority of His Majesty's Stationery Office.

(2) In any proceedings against any person for an offence consisting of a contravention of any such statutory instrument, it shall be a defence to prove that the instrument had not been issued by or under the authority of His Majesty's Stationery Office at the date of the alleged contravention unless it is proved that at that date reasonable steps had been taken for the purpose of bringing the purport of the instrument to the notice of the public, or of persons likely to be affected by it, or of the person charged.

Magistrates' Courts Act 1980

101 Onus of proving exceptions, etc.

Where the defendant to an information or complaint relies for his defence on any exception, exemption, proviso, excuse or qualification, whether or not it accompanies the description of the offence or matter of complaint in the enactment creating the offence or on which the complaint is founded, the burden of proving the exception, exemption, proviso, excuse or qualification shall be on him; and this notwithstanding that the information or complaint contains an allegation negativing the exception, exemption, proviso, excuse or qualification.

Trial of Lunatics Act 1883

2 Special verdict where accused found guilty, but insane at date of act or omission charged, and orders thereupon

(1) Where in any indictment or information any act or omission is charged against any person as an offence, and it is given in evidence on the trial of such person for that offence that he was insane, so as not to be responsible, according to law, for his actions at the time when the act was done or omission made, then, if it appears to the jury before whom such person is tried that he did the act or made the omission charged, but was insane as aforesaid at the time when he did or made the same, the jury shall return a special verdict that the accused is not guilty by reason of insanity.

Criminal Procedure (Insanity and Unfitness to Plead) Act 1991

1 Acquittals on grounds of insanity

(1) A jury shall not return a special verdict under section 2 of the Trial of Lunatics Act 1883 (acquittal on ground of insanity) except on the written or oral evidence of two or more registered medical practitioners at least one of whom is duly approved.

6 Interpretation etc.

(1) In this Act—

'duly approved', in relation to a registered medical practitioner, means approved for the purposes of section 12 of the 1983 Act by the Secretary of State as having special experience in the diagnosis or treatment of mental disorder.

(d) Appeals

Criminal Appeal Act 1968

2 Grounds for allowing and dismissing appeals

(1) Subject to the provisions of this Act, the Court of Appeal—

(a) shall allow an appeal against conviction if they think that the conviction is unsafe; and

(b) shall dismiss such an appeal in any other case.

3 Power to substitute conviction of alternative offence

(1) This section applies on an appeal against conviction, where the appellant has been convicted of an offence and the jury could on the indictment have found him guilty of some other offence, and on the finding of the jury it appears to the Court of Appeal that the jury must have been satisfied of facts which proved him guilty of the other offence.

(2) The Court may, instead of allowing or dismissing the appeal, substitute for the verdict found by the jury a verdict of guilty of the other offence, and pass such sentence in substitution for the sentence passed at the trial as may be authorised by law for the other offence, not being a sentence of greater severity.

12 Appeal against verdict of not guilty by reason of insanity

A person in whose case there is returned a verdict of not guilty by reason of insanity may appeal to the Court of Appeal against the verdict—

(a) with the leave of the Court of Appeal; or

(b) if the judge of the court of trial grants a certificate that the case is fit for appeal.

Magistrates' Courts Act 1980

108 Right of appeal to the Crown Court

(1) A person convicted by a magistrates' court may appeal to the Crown Court—

(a) if he pleaded guilty, against his sentence;

(b) if he did not, against the conviction or sentence.

(1A) Section 14 of the Power of Criminal Courts (Sentencing) Act 2000 (under which a conviction of an offence for which an order for conditional or absolute discharge is made is deemed not to be a conviction except for certain purposes) shall not prevent an appeal under this Act, whether against conviction or otherwise.

111 Statement of case by magistrates' court

(1) Any person who was a party to any proceeding before a magistrates' court or is aggrieved by the conviction, order, determination or other proceeding of the court may question the proceeding on the ground that it is wrong in law or is in excess of jurisdiction by applying to the justices composing the court to state a case for the opinion of the High Court on the question of law or jurisdiction involved; but a person shall not make an application under this section in respect of a decision against which he has a right of appeal to the High Court or which by virtue of any enactment passed after 31st December 1879 is final.

(2) On the making of an application under this section in respect of a decision any right of the applicant to appeal against the decision to the Crown Court shall cease.

(3) If the justices are of opinion that an application under this section is frivolous, they may refuse to state a case, and, if the applicant so requires, shall give him a certificate stating that the application has been refused; but the justices shall not refuse to state a case if the application is made by or under the direction of the Attorney General.

(4) Where justices refuse to state a case, the High Court may, on the application of the person who applied for the case to be stated, make an order of mandamus requiring the justices to state a case.

Part II

Homicide and Foeticide

Homicide Act 1957

1 Abolition of 'constructive malice'

(1) Where a person kills another in the course or furtherance of some other offence, the killing shall not amount to murder unless done with the same malice aforethought (express or implied) as is required for a killing to amount to murder when not done in the course or furtherance of another offence.

(2) For the purposes of the foregoing subsection, a killing done in the course or for the purpose of resisting an officer of justice, or of resisting or avoiding or preventing a lawful arrest, or of effecting or assisting an escape or rescue from legal custody, shall be treated as a killing in the course or furtherance of an offence.

2 Persons suffering from diminished responsibility

(1) Where a person kills or is a party to the killing of another, he shall not be convicted of murder if he was suffering from such abnormality of mind (whether arising from a condition of arrested or retarded development of mind or any inherent causes or induced by disease or injury) as substantially impaired his mental responsibility for his acts and omissions in doing or being a party to the killing.

(2) On a charge of murder, it shall be for the defence to prove that the person charged is by virtue of this section not liable to be convicted of murder.

(3) A person who but for this section would be liable, whether as a principal or as accessory, to be convicted of murder shall be liable instead to be convicted of manslaughter.

(4) The fact that one party to a killing is by virtue of this section not liable to be convicted of murder shall not affect the question whether the killing amounted to murder in the case of any other party to it.

3 Provocation

Where on a charge of murder there is evidence on which the jury can find that the person charged was provoked (whether by things done or by things said or by both together) to lose his self-control, the question whether the provocation was enough to make a reasonable man do as he did shall be left to be determined by the jury; and in determining that question the jury shall take into account everything both done and said according to the effect which, in their opinion, it would have on a reasonable man.

4 Suicide pacts

(1) It shall be manslaughter, and shall not be murder, for a person acting in pursuance of a suicide pact between him and another to kill the other or be a party to the other... being killed by a third person.

(2) Where it is shown that a person charged with the murder of another killed the other or was a party to his . . . being killed, it shall be for the defence to prove that the person charged was acting in pursuance of a suicide pact between him and the other.

(3) For the purposes of this section 'suicide pact' means a common agreement between two or more persons having for its object the death of all of them, whether or not each is to take his own life, but nothing done by a person who enters into a suicide pact shall be treated as done by him in pursuance of the pact unless it is done while he has the settled intention of dying in pursuance of the pact.

Criminal Procedure (Insanity) Act 1964

6 Evidence by prosecution of insanity or diminished responsibility

Where on a trial for murder the accused contends—

(a) that at the time of the alleged offence he was insane so as not to be responsible according to law for his actions; or

(b) that at that time he was suffering from such abnormality of mind as is specified in subsection (1) of section 2 of the Homicide Act 1957 (diminished responsibility),

the court shall allow the prosecution to adduce or elicit evidence tending to prove the other of those contentions, and may give directions as to the stage of the proceedings at which the prosecution may adduce such evidence.

Infanticide Act 1938

1 Offence of infanticide

(1) Where a woman by any wilful act or omission causes the death of her child being a child under the age of twelve months, but at the time of the act or omission the balance of her mind was disturbed by reason of her not having fully recovered from the effect of giving birth to the child or by reason of the effect of lactation consequent upon the birth of the child, then, notwithstanding that the circumstances were such that but for this Act the offence would have amounted to murder, she shall be guilty of felony, to wit of infanticide, and may for such offence be dealt with and punished as if she had been guilty of the offence of manslaughter of the child. [I]

(2) Where upon the trial of a woman for the murder of her child, being a child under the age of twelve months, the jury are of opinion that she by any wilful act or omission caused its death, but that at the time of the act or omission the balance of her mind was disturbed by reason of her not having fully recovered from the effect of giving birth to the child or by reason of the effect of lactation consequent upon the birth of the child, then the jury may, notwithstanding that the circumstances were such that but for the provisions of this Act they might have returned a verdict of murder, return in lieu thereof a verdict of infanticide.

(3) Nothing in this Act shall affect the power of the jury upon an indictment for the murder of a child to return a verdict of manslaughter, or a verdict of guilty but insane . . .

Domestic Violence, Crime and Victims Act 2004

5 Causing or allowing the death of a child or vulnerable adult

(1) A person ('D') is guilty of an offence if—

(a) a child or vulnerable adult ('V') dies as a result of the unlawful act of a person who—

(i) was a member of the same household as V, and

(ii) had frequent contact with him,

(b) D was such a person at the time of that act,

(c) at that time there was a significant risk of serious physical harm being caused to V by the unlawful act of such a person, and

(d) either D was the person whose act caused V's death or—

(i) D was, or ought to have been, aware of the risk mentioned in paragraph (c),

(ii) D failed to take such steps as he could reasonably have been expected to take to protect V from the risk, and

(iii) the act occurred in circumstances of the kind that D foresaw or ought to have foreseen.

(2) The prosecution does not have to prove whether it is the first alternative in subsection (1)(d) or the second (sub-paragraphs (i) to (iii)) that applies.

(3) If D was not the mother or father of V—

(a) D may not be charged with an offence under this section if he was under the age of 16 at the time of the act that caused V's death;

(b) for the purposes of subsection (1)(d)(ii) D could not have been expected to take any such step as is referred to there before attaining that age.

(4) For the purposes of this section—

(a) a person is to be regarded as a 'member' of a particular household, even if he does not live in that household, if he visits it so often and for such periods of time that it is reasonable to regard him as a member of it;

(b) where V lived in different households at different times, 'the same household as V' refers to the household in which V was living at the time of the act that caused V's death.

(5) For the purposes of this section an 'unlawful' act is one that—

(a) constitutes an offence, or

(b) would constitute an offence but for being the act of—

(i) a person under the age of ten, or

(ii) a person entitled to rely on a defence of insanity.

Paragraph (b) does not apply to an act of D.

(6) In this section—

'act' includes a course of conduct and also includes omission;

'child' means a person under the age of 16;

'serious' harm means harm that amounts to grievous bodily harm for the purposes of the Offences against the Person Act 1861 (c. 100);

'vulnerable adult' means a person aged 16 or over whose ability to protect himself from violence, abuse or neglect is significantly impaired through physical or mental disability or illness, through old age or otherwise. [I]

6 Evidence and procedure: England and Wales

(1) Subsections (2) to (4) apply where a person ('the defendant') is charged in the same proceedings with an offence of murder or manslaughter and with an offence under section 5 in respect of the same death ('the section 5 offence').

(2) Where by virtue of section 35(3) of the Criminal Justice and Public Order Act 1994 a court or jury is permitted, in relation to the section 5 offence, to draw such inferences as appear proper from the defendant's failure to give evidence or refusal to answer a question, the court or jury may also draw such inferences in determining whether he is guilty—

(a) of murder or manslaughter, or

(b) of any other offence of which he could lawfully be convicted on the charge of murder or manslaughter,

even if there would otherwise be no case for him to answer in relation to that offence.

(3) The charge of murder or manslaughter is not to be dismissed under paragraph 2 of Schedule 3 to the Crime and Disorder Act 1998 (unless the section 5 offence is dismissed).

(4) At the defendant's trial the question whether there is a case for the defendant to answer on the charge of murder or manslaughter is not to be considered before the close of all the evidence (or, if at some earlier time he ceases to be charged with the section 5 offence, before that earlier time).

Corporate Manslaughter and Corporate Homicide Act 2007

1 The offence

(1) An organisation to which this section applies is guilty of an offence if the way in which its activities are managed or organised—

(a) causes a person's death, and

(b) amounts to a gross breach of a relevant duty of care owed by the organisation to the deceased. [I]

(2) The organisations to which this section applies are—

(a) a corporation;

(b) a department or other body listed in Schedule 1 [not printed];

(c) a police force;

(d) a partnership, or a trade union or employers' association, that is an employer.

(3) An organisation is guilty of an offence under this section only if the way in which its activities are managed or organised by its senior management is a substantial element in the breach referred to in subsection (1).

(4) For the purposes of this Act—

(a) 'relevant duty of care' has the meaning given by section 2, read with sections 3 to 7;

(b) a breach of a duty of care by an organisation is a 'gross' breach if the conduct alleged to amount to a breach of that duty falls far below what can reasonably be expected of the organisation in the circumstances;

(c) 'senior management', in relation to an organisation, means the persons who play significant roles in—

(i) the making of decisions about how the whole or a substantial part of its activities are to be managed or organised, or

(ii) the actual managing or organising of the whole or a substantial part of those activities.

2 Meaning of 'relevant duty of care'

(1) A 'relevant duty of care', in relation to an organisation, means any of the following duties owed by it under the law of negligence—

(a) a duty owed to its employees or to other persons working for the organisation or performing services for it;

(b) a duty owed as occupier of premises;

(c) a duty owed in connection with—

(i) the supply by the organisation of goods or services (whether for consideration or not),

(ii) the carrying on by the organisation of any construction or maintenance operations,

(iii) the carrying on by the organisation of any other activity on a commercial basis, or

(iv) the use or keeping by the organisation of any plant, vehicle or other thing;

(d) a duty owed to a person who, by reason of being a person within subsection (2), is someone for whose safety the organisation is responsible.

(2) A person is within this subsection if—

(a) he is detained at a custodial institution or in a custody area at a court or police station;

(b) he is detained at a removal centre or short-term holding facility;

(c) he is being transported in a vehicle, or being held in any premises, in pursuance of prison escort arrangements or immigration escort arrangements;

(d) he is living in secure accommodation in which he has been placed;

(e) he is a detained patient.

(3) Subsection (1) is subject to sections 3 to 7.

(4) A reference in subsection (1) to a duty owed under the law of negligence includes a reference to a duty that would be owed under the law of negligence but for any statutory provision under which liability is imposed in place of liability under that law.

(5) For the purposes of this Act, whether a particular organisation owes a duty of care to a particular individual is a question of law. The judge must make any findings of fact necessary to decide that question.

(6) For the purposes of this Act there is to be disregarded—

(a) any rule of the common law that has the effect of preventing a duty of care from being owed by one person to another by reason of the fact that they are jointly engaged in unlawful conduct;

(b) any such rule that has the effect of preventing a duty of care from being owed to a person by reason of his acceptance of a risk of harm.

(7) In this section—

'construction or maintenance operations' means operations of any of the following descriptions—

(a) construction, installation, alteration, extension, improvement, repair, maintenance, decoration, cleaning, demolition or dismantling of—

(i) any building or structure,

(ii) anything else that forms, or is to form, part of the land, or

(iii) any plant, vehicle or other thing;

(b) operations that form an integral part of, or are preparatory to, or are for rendering complete, any operations within paragraph (a);

'custodial institution' means a prison, a young offender institution, a secure training centre, a young offenders institution, a young offenders centre, a juvenile justice centre or a remand centre;

'detained patient' means—

(a) a person who is detained in any premises under—

(i) Part 2 or 3 of the Mental Health Act 1983 ('the 1983 Act'),

(b) a person who (otherwise than by reason of being detained as mentioned in paragraph (a)) is deemed to be in legal custody by—

(i) section 137 of the 1983 Act,

'immigration escort arrangements' means arrangements made under section 156 of the Immigration and Asylum Act 1999; 'the law of negligence' includes—

(a) in relation to England and Wales, the Occupiers' Liability Act 1957, the Defective Premises Act 1972 and the Occupiers' Liability Act 1984;

'prison escort arrangements' means arrangements made under section 80 of the Criminal Justice Act 1991 or under section 102 or 118 of the Criminal Justice and Public Order Act 1994;

'removal centre' and 'short-term holding facility' have the meaning given by section 147 of the Immigration and Asylum Act 1999;

'secure accommodation' means accommodation, not consisting of or forming part of a custodial institution, provided for the purpose of restricting the liberty of persons under the age of 18.

3 Public policy decisions, exclusively public functions and statutory inspections

(1) Any duty of care owed by a public authority in respect of a decision as to matters of public policy (including in particular the allocation of public resources or the weighing of competing public interests) is not a 'relevant duty of care'.

(2) Any duty of care owed in respect of things done in the exercise of an exclusively public function is not a 'relevant duty of care' unless it falls within section 2(1)(a), (b) or (d).

(3) Any duty of care owed by a public authority in respect of inspections carried out in the exercise of a statutory function is not a 'relevant duty of care' unless it falls within section 2(1)(a) or (b).

(4) In this section—

'exclusively public function' means a function that falls within the prerogative of the Crown or is, by its nature, exercisable only with authority conferred—

(a) by the exercise of that prerogative, or

(b) by or under a statutory provision;

'statutory function' means a function conferred by or under a statutory provision

4 Military activities

(1) Any duty of care owed by the Ministry of Defence in respect of—

(a) operations within subsection (2),

(b) activities carried on in preparation for, or directly in support of, such operations, or

(c) training of a hazardous nature, or training carried out in a hazardous way, which it is considered needs to be carried out, or carried out in that way, in order to improve or maintain the effectiveness of the armed forces with respect to such operations, is not a 'relevant duty of care'.

(2) The operations within this subsection are operations, including peacekeeping operations and operations for dealing with terrorism, civil unrest or serious public disorder, in the course of which members of the armed forces come under attack or face the threat of attack or violent resistance.

(3) Any duty of care owed by the Ministry of Defence in respect of activities carried on by members of the special forces is not a 'relevant duty of care'.

(4) In this section 'the special forces' means those units of the armed forces the maintenance of whose capabilities is the responsibility of the Director of Special Forces or which are for the time being subject to the operational command of that Director

5 Policing and law enforcement

(1) Any duty of care owed by a public authority in respect of—

(a) operations within subsection (2),

(b) activities carried on in preparation for, or directly in support of, such operations, or

(c) training of a hazardous nature, or training carried out in a hazardous way, which it is considered needs to be carried out, or carried out in that way, in order to improve or maintain the effectiveness of officers or employees of the public authority with respect to such operations, is not a 'relevant duty of care'.

(2) Operations are within this subsection if—

(a) they are operations for dealing with terrorism, civil unrest or serious disorder,

(b) they involve the carrying on of policing or law-enforcement activities, and

(c) officers or employees of the public authority in question come under attack, or face the threat of attack or violent resistance, in the course of the operations.

(3) Any duty of care owed by a public authority in respect of other policing or law-enforcement activities is not a 'relevant duty of care' unless it falls within section 2(1)(a), (b) or (d).

(4) In this section 'policing or law-enforcement activities' includes—

(a) activities carried on in the exercise of functions that are—

(i) functions of police forces, or

(ii) functions of the same or a similar nature exercisable by public authorities other than police forces;

(b) activities carried on in the exercise of functions of constables employed by a public authority;

(c) activities carried on in the exercise of functions exercisable under Chapter 4 of Part 2 of the Serious Organised Crime and Police Act 2005 (protection of witnesses and other persons);

(d) activities carried on to enforce any provision contained in or made under the Immigration Acts.

6 Emergencies

(1) Any duty of care owed by an organisation within subsection (2) in respect of the way in which it responds to emergency circumstances is not a 'relevant duty of care' unless it falls within section 2(1)(a) or (b).

(2) The organisations within this subsection are—

(a) a fire and rescue authority in England and Wales;

(d) any other organisation providing a service of responding to emergency circumstances either—

(i) in pursuance of arrangements made with an organisation within paragraph (a), or
(ii) (if not in pursuance of such arrangements) otherwise than on a commercial basis;

(e) a relevant NHS body;

(f) an organisation providing ambulance services in pursuance of arrangements—
(i) made by, or at the request of, a relevant NHS body, or
(ii) made with the Secretary of State or with the Welsh Ministers;

(g) an organisation providing services for the transport of organs, blood, equipment or personnel in pursuance of arrangements of the kind mentioned in paragraph (f);

(h) an organisation providing a rescue service;

(i) the armed forces.

(3) For the purposes of subsection (1), the way in which an organisation responds to emergency circumstances does not include the way in which—
(a) medical treatment is carried out, or
(b) decisions within subsection (4) are made.

(4) The decisions within this subsection are decisions as to the carrying out of medical treatment, other than decisions as to the order in which persons are to be given such treatment.

(5) Any duty of care owed in respect of the carrying out, or attempted carrying out, of a rescue operation at sea in emergency circumstances is not a 'relevant duty of care' unless it falls within section 2(1)(a) or (b).

(6) Any duty of care owed in respect of action taken—
(a) in order to comply with a direction under Schedule 3A to the Merchant Shipping Act 1995 (safety directions), or
(b) by virtue of paragraph 4 of that Schedule (action in lieu of direction), is not a 'relevant duty of care' unless it falls within section 2(1)(a) or (b).

(7) In this section—

'emergency circumstances' means circumstances that are present or imminent and—
(a) are causing, or are likely to cause, serious harm or a worsening of such harm, or
(b) are likely to cause the death of a person;

'medical treatment' includes any treatment or procedure of a medical or similar nature;

'relevant NHS body' means—
(a) a Strategic Health Authority, Primary Care Trust, NHS trust, Special Health Authority or NHS foundation trust in England;
(b) a Local Health Board, NHS trust or Special Health Authority in Wales;

'serious harm' means—
(a) serious injury to or the serious illness (including mental illness) of a person;
(b) serious harm to the environment (including the life and health of plants and animals);
(c) serious harm to any building or other property.

(8) A reference in this section to emergency circumstances includes a reference to circumstances that are believed to be emergency circumstances

7 Child-protection and probation functions

(1) A duty of care to which this section applies is not a 'relevant duty of care' unless it falls within section 2(1)(a), (b) or (d).

(2) This section applies to any duty of care that a local authority or other public authority owes in respect of the exercise by it of functions conferred by or under—
(a) Parts 4 and 5 of the Children Act 1989,

(3) This section also applies to any duty of care that a local probation board or other public authority owes in respect of the exercise by it of functions conferred by or under—
(a) Chapter 1 of Part 1 of the Criminal Justice and Court Services Act 2000.

8 Factors for jury

(1) This section applies where—
(a) it is established that an organisation owed a relevant duty of care to a person, and

(b) it falls to the jury to decide whether there was a gross breach of that duty.

(2) The jury must consider whether the evidence shows that the organisation failed to comply with any health and safety legislation that relates to the alleged breach, and if so—

(a) how serious that failure was;

(b) how much of a risk of death it posed.

(3) The jury may also—

(a) consider the extent to which the evidence shows that there were attitudes, policies, systems or accepted practices within the organisation that were likely to have encouraged any such failure as is mentioned in subsection (2), or to have produced tolerance of it;

(b) have regard to any health and safety guidance that relates to the alleged breach.

(4) This section does not prevent the jury from having regard to any other matters they consider relevant.

(5) In this section 'health and safety guidance' means any code, guidance, manual or similar publication that is concerned with health and safety matters and is made or issued (under a statutory provision or otherwise) by an authority responsible for the enforcement of any health and safety legislation.

11 Application to Crown bodies

(1) An organisation that is a servant or agent of the Crown is not immune from prosecution under this Act for that reason.

(2) For the purposes of this Act—

(a) a department or other body listed in Schedule 1, or

(b) a corporation that is a servant or agent of the Crown, is to be treated as owing whatever duties of care it would owe if it were a corporation that was not a servant or agent of the Crown.

(3) For the purposes of section 2—

(a) a person who is—

(i) employed by or under the Crown for the purposes of a department or other body listed in Schedule 1, or

(ii) employed by a person whose staff constitute a body listed in that Schedule, is to be treated as employed by that department or body;

(b) any premises occupied for the purposes of—

(i) a department or other body listed in Schedule 1, or

(ii) a person whose staff constitute a body listed in that Schedule, are to be treated as occupied by that department or body.

(4) For the purposes of sections 2 to 7 anything done purportedly by a department or other body listed in Schedule 1, although in law by the Crown or by the holder of a particular office, is to be treated as done by the department or other body itself.

12 Application to armed forces

(1) In this Act 'the armed forces' means any of the naval, military or air forces of the Crown raised under the law of the United Kingdom.

(2) For the purposes of section 2 a person who is a member of the armed forces is to be treated as employed by the Ministry of Defence.

(3) A reference in this Act to members of the armed forces includes a reference to—

(a) members of the reserve forces (within the meaning given by section 1(2) of the Reserve Forces Act 1996) when in service or undertaking training or duties;

(b) persons serving on Her Majesty's vessels (within the meaning given by section 132(1) of the Naval Discipline Act 1957).

13 Application to police forces

(1) In this Act 'police force' means—

(a) a police force within the meaning of—

(i) the Police Act 1996, or

(d) the British Transport Police Force;
(e) the Civil Nuclear Constabulary;
(f) the Ministry of Defence Police.

(2) For the purposes of this Act a police force is to be treated as owing whatever duties of care it would owe if it were a body corporate.

(3) For the purposes of section 2—

(a) a member of a police force is to be treated as employed by that force;
(b) a special constable appointed for a police area in England and Wales is to be treated as employed by the police force maintained by the police authority for that area;
(c) a special constable appointed for a police force mentioned in paragraph (d) or (f) of subsection (1) is to be treated as employed by that force;
(d) a police cadet undergoing training with a view to becoming a member of a police force mentioned in paragraph (a) or (d) of subsection (1) is to be treated as employed by that force;
(g) a member of a police force seconded to the Serious Organised Crime Agency or the National Policing Improvement Agency to serve as a member of its staff is to be treated as employed by that Agency.

(4) A reference in subsection (3) to a member of a police force is to be read, in the case of a force mentioned in paragraph (a)(ii) of subsection (1), as a reference to a constable of that force.

(5) For the purposes of section 2 any premises occupied for the purposes of a police force are to be treated as occupied by that force.

(6) For the purposes of sections 2 to 7 anything that would be regarded as done by a police force if the force were a body corporate is to be so regarded.

(7) Where—

(a) by virtue of subsection (3) a person is treated for the purposes of section 2 as employed by a police force, and
(b) by virtue of any other statutory provision (whenever made) he is, or is treated as, employed by another organisation, the person is to be treated for those purposes as employed by both the force and the other organisation.

14 Application to partnerships

(1) For the purposes of this Act a partnership is to be treated as owing whatever duties of care it would owe if it were a body corporate.

(4) This section does not apply to a partnership that is a legal person under the law by which it is governed.

18 No individual liability

(1) An individual cannot be guilty of aiding, abetting, counselling or procuring the commission of an offence of corporate manslaughter.

(1A) An individual cannot be guilty of an offence under Part 2 of the Serious Crime Act 2007 (encouraging or assisting crime) by reference to an offence of corporate manslaughter.

19 Convictions under this Act and under health and safety legislation

(1) Where in the same proceedings there is—

(a) a charge of corporate manslaughter or corporate homicide arising out of a particular set of circumstances, and
(b) a charge against the same defendant of a health and safety offence arising out of some or all of those circumstances, the jury may, if the interests of justice so require, be invited to return a verdict on each charge.

(2) An organisation that has been convicted of corporate manslaughter or corporate homicide arising out of a particular set of circumstances may, if the interests of justice so require, be charged with a health and safety offence arising out of some or all of those circumstances.

(3) In this section 'health and safety offence' means an offence under any health and safety legislation.

20 Abolition of liability of corporations for manslaughter at common law

The common law offence of manslaughter by gross negligence is abolished in its application to corporations, and in any application it has to other organisations to which section 1 applies.

25 Interpretation

In this Act—

'armed forces' has the meaning given by section 12(1);

'corporation' does not include a corporation sole but includes any body corporate wherever incorporated;

'employee' means an individual who works under a contract of employment or apprenticeship (whether express or implied and, if express, whether oral or in writing), and related expressions are to be construed accordingly; see also sections 11(3)(a), 12(2) and 13(3) (which apply for the purposes of section 2);

'employers' association' has the meaning given by section 122 of the Trade Union and Labour Relations (Consolidation) Act 1992;

'enforcement authority' means an authority responsible for the enforcement of any health and safety legislation;

'health and safety legislation' means any statutory provision dealing with health and safety matters, including in particular provision contained in the Health and Safety at Work etc. Act 1974;

'member', in relation to the armed forces, is to be read in accordance with section 12(3);

'partnership' means—

(a) a partnership within the Partnership Act 1890, or

(b) a limited partnership registered under the Limited Partnerships Act 1907,

or a firm or entity of a similar character formed under the law of a country or territory outside the United Kingdom;

'police force' has the meaning given by section 13(1);

'premises' includes land, buildings and moveable structures;

'public authority' has the same meaning as in section 6 of the Human Rights Act 1998 (disregarding subsections (3)(a) and (4) of that section);

'publicity order' means an order under section 10(1);

'remedial order' means an order under section 9(1);

'statutory provision', except in section 15, means provision contained in, or in an instrument made under, any Act;

'trade union' has the meaning given by section 1 of the Trade Union and Labour Relations (Consolidation) Act 1992;

28 Extent and territorial application

(3) Section 1 applies if the harm resulting in death is sustained in the United Kingdom or—

(a) within the seaward limits of the territorial sea adjacent to the United Kingdom;

(b) on a ship registered under Part 2 of the Merchant Shipping Act 1995;

(c) on a British-controlled aircraft as defined in section 92 of the Civil Aviation Act 1982;

(d) on a British-controlled hovercraft within the meaning of that section as applied in relation to hovercraft by virtue of provision made under the Hovercraft Act 1968;

(e) in any place to which an Order in Council under section 10(1) of the Petroleum Act 1998 applies (criminal jurisdiction in relation to offshore activities).

(4) For the purposes of subsection (3)(b) to (d) harm sustained on a ship, aircraft or hovercraft includes harm sustained by a person who—

(a) is then no longer on board the ship, aircraft or hovercraft in consequence of the wrecking of it or of some other mishap affecting it or occurring on it, and

(b) sustains the harm in consequence of that event.

Law Reform (Year and a Day Rule) Act 1996

1 Abolition of 'year and a day rule'
The rule known as the 'year and a day rule' (that is, the rule that, for the purposes of offences involving death and of suicide, an act or omission is conclusively presumed not to have caused a person's death if more than a year and a day elapsed before he died) is abolished for all purposes.

2 Restriction on institution of proceedings for a fatal offence
(1) Proceedings to which this section applies may only be instituted by or with the consent of the Attorney General.
(2) This section applies to proceedings against a person for a fatal offence if—
(a) the injury alleged to have caused the death was sustained more than three years before the death occurred, or
(b) the person has previously been convicted of an offence committed in circumstances alleged to be connected with the death.
(3) In subsection (2) 'fatal offence' means—
(a) murder, manslaughter, infanticide or any other offence of which one of the elements is causing a person's death,
(b) the offence of aiding, abetting, counselling or procuring a person's suicide.

3 Commencement etc.
(2) Section 1 does not affect the continued application of the rule referred to in that section to a case where the act or omission (or the last of the acts or omissions) which caused the death occurred before the day on which this Act is passed.

Offences Against the Person Act 1861

9 Murder or manslaughter abroad
Where any murder or manslaughter shall be committed on land out of the United Kingdom, whether within the Queen's dominions or without, and whether the person killed were a subject of Her Majesty or not, every offence committed by any subject of Her Majesty in respect of any such case, whether the same shall amount to the offence of murder or of manslaughter, . . . may be dealt with, inquired of, tried, determined, and punished . . . in England or Ireland . . .

10 Provision for the trial of murder and manslaughter where the death or cause of death only happens in England or Ireland
Where any person being criminally stricken, poisoned, or otherwise hurt upon the sea, or at any place out of England or Ireland, shall die of such stroke, poisoning, or hurt in England or Ireland, or, being criminally stricken, poisoned or otherwise hurt in any place in England or Ireland, shall die of such stroke, poisoning, or hurt upon the sea, or at any place out of England or Ireland, every offence committed in respect of any such case, whether the same shall amount to the offence of murder or of manslaughter, . . . may be dealt with, inquired of, tried, determined, and punished . . . in England or Ireland . . .

War Crimes Act 1991

1 Jurisdiction over certain war crimes
(1) Subject to the provisions of this section, proceedings for murder, manslaughter or culpable homicide may be brought against a person in the United Kingdom irrespective of his nationality at the time of the alleged offence if that offence—

(a) was committed during the period beginning with 1st September 1939 and ending with 5th June 1945 in a place which at the time was part of Germany or under German occupation; and

(b) constituted a violation of the laws and customs of war.

(2) No proceedings shall by virtue of this section be brought against any person unless he was on 8th March 1990, or has subsequently become, a British citizen or resident in the United Kingdom, the Isle of Man or any of the Channel Islands.

Criminal Law Act 1967

6(2) [Trial of offences]

[See page 6]

Suicide Act 1961

1 Suicide to cease to be a crime

The rule of law whereby it is a crime for a person to commit suicide is hereby abrogated.

2 Criminal liability for complicity in another's suicide

(1) A person who aids, abets, counsels or procures the suicide of another, or an attempt by another to commit suicide shall be liable on conviction on indictment to imprisonment for a term not exceeding fourteen years. [I]

(2) If on the trial of an indictment for murder or manslaughter it is proved that the accused aided, abetted, counselled or procured the suicide of the person in question, the jury may find him guilty of that offence.

Mental Capacity Act 2005

62 Scope of the Act

For the avoidance of doubt, it is hereby declared that nothing in this Act is to be taken to affect the law relating to murder or manslaughter or the operation of section 2 of the Suicide Act 1961 (assisting suicide).

Road Traffic Act 1988

1 Causing death by dangerous driving

[See page 97]

2B Causing death by careless or inconsiderative driving

[See page 97]

3A Causing death by careless driving when under influence of drink or drugs

[See page 98]

3ZB Causing death by driving: unlicensed, disqualified or uninsured drivers

[See page 98]

Theft Act 1968

12A(4) Aggravated vehicle-taking causing death
[See page 177]

Offences Against the Person Act 1861

60 Concealing the birth of a child
If any woman shall be delivered of a child, every person who shall, by any secret disposition of the dead body of the said child, whether such child died before, at, or after its birth, endeavour to conceal the birth thereof, shall be guilty of a misdemeanour, and being convicted thereof shall be liable, at the discretion of the court, to be imprisoned for any term not exceeding two years. [E]

Infant Life (Preservation) Act 1929

1 Punishment for child destruction
(1) Subject as hereinafter in this subsection provided, any person who, with intent to destroy the life of a child capable of being born alive, by any wilful act causes a child to die before it has an existence independent of its mother, shall be guilty of felony, to wit, of child destruction, and shall be liable on conviction thereof on indictment to penal servitude for life:

Provided that no person shall be found guilty of an offence under this section unless it is proved that the act which caused the death of the child was not done in good faith for the purpose only of preserving the life of the mother. [I]

(2) For the purposes of this Act, evidence that a woman had at any material time been pregnant for a period of twenty-eight weeks or more shall be a prima facie proof that she was at that time pregnant of a child capable of being born alive.

2 Prosecution of offences
(2) Where upon the trial of any person for the murder or manslaughter of any child, or for infanticide, or for an offence under section fifty-eight of the Offences against the Person Act, 1861 (which relates to administering drugs or using instruments to procure abortion), the jury are of opinion that the person charged is not guilty of murder, manslaughter or infanticide, or of an offence under the said section fifty-eight, as the case may be, but that he is shown by the evidence to be guilty of the felony of child destruction, the jury may find him guilty of that felony, and thereupon the person convicted shall be liable to be punished as if he had been convicted upon an indictment for child destruction.

(3) Where upon the trial of any person for the felony of child destruction the jury are of opinion that the person charged is not guilty of any felony, but that he is shown by the evidence to be guilty of an offence under the said section fifty-eight of the Offences against the Person Act, 1861, the jury may find him guilty of that offence, and thereupon the person convicted shall be liable to be punished as if he had been convicted upon an indictment under that section.

Offences Against the Person Act 1861

58 Administering drugs or using instruments to procure abortion
Every woman, being with child, who, with intent to procure her own miscarriage, shall unlawfully administer to herself any poison or other noxious thing, or shall unlawfully use any instrument or

other means whatsoever with the like intent, and whosoever, with intent to procure the miscarriage of any woman, whether she be or be not with child, shall unlawfully administer to her or cause to be taken by her any poison or other noxious thing, or shall unlawfully use any instrument or other means whatsoever with the like intent, shall be guilty of felony, and being convicted thereof shall be liable . . . to be kept in penal servitude for life . . . [I]

59 Procuring drugs, etc., to cause abortion

Whosoever shall unlawfully supply or procure any poison or other noxious thing, or any instrument or thing whatsoever, knowing that the same is intended to be unlawfully used or employed with intent to procure the miscarriage of any woman, whether she be or be not with child, shall be guilty of a misdemeanour, and being convicted thereof shall be liable . . . to be kept in penal servitude . . . [I]

Abortion Act 1967

1 Medical termination of pregnancy

(1) Subject to the provisions of this section, a person shall not be guilty of any offence under the law relating to abortion when a pregnancy is terminated by a registered medical practitioner if two medical practitioners are of the opinion, formed in good faith—

(a) that the pregnancy has not exceeded its twenty-fourth week and that the continuance of the pregnancy would involve risk, greater than if the pregnancy were terminated, of injury to the physical or mental health of the pregnant woman or any existing children of her family; or

(b) that the termination is necessary to prevent grave permanent injury to the physical or mental health of the pregnant woman; or

(c) that the continuance of the pregnancy would involve risk to the life of the pregnant woman, greater than if the pregnancy were terminated; or

(d) that there is a substantial risk that if the child were born it would suffer from such physical or mental abnormalities as to be seriously handicapped.

(2) In determining whether the continuance of a pregnancy would involve such risk of injury to health as is mentioned in paragraph (a) or (b) of subsection (1) of this section, account may be taken of the pregnant woman's actual or reasonably foreseeable environment.

(3) Except as provided by subsection (4) of this section, any treatment for the termination of pregnancy must be carried out in a hospital vested in the Secretary of State for the purpose of his functions under the National Health Service Act 1977 or the National Health Service (Scotland) Act 1978 or in a hospital vested in a National Health Service trust, or in a place for the time being approved for the purposes of this section by the Secretary of State.

(4) Subsection (3) of this section, and so much of subsection (1) as relates to the opinion of two registered medical practitioners, shall not apply to the termination of a pregnancy by a registered practitioner in a case where he is of the opinion, formed in good faith, that the termination is immediately necessary to save the life or to prevent grave permanent injury to the physical or mental health of the pregnant woman.

2 Notification

(1) The Minister of Health in respect of England and Wales, and the Secretary of State in respect of Scotland, shall by statutory instrument make regulations to provide—

(a) for requiring any such opinion as is referred to in section 1 of this Act to be certified by the practitioners or practitioner concerned in such form and at such time as may be prescribed by the regulations, and for requiring the preservation and disposal of certificates made for the purposes of the regulations;

(b) for requiring any registered medical practitioner who terminates a pregnancy to give notice of the termination and such other information relating to the termination as may be so prescribed;

(c) for prohibiting the disclosure, except to such persons or for such purposes as may be so prescribed, of notices given or information furnished pursuant to the regulations.

(3) Any person who wilfully contravenes or wilfully fails to comply with the requirements of regulations under subsection (1) of this section shall be liable on summary conviction to a fine not exceeding level 5 on the standard scale. [S]

4 Conscientious objection to participation in treatment

(1) Subject to subsection (2) of this section, no person shall be under any duty, whether by contract or by any statutory or other legal requirement, to participate in any treatment authorised by this Act to which he has a conscientious objection:

Provided that in any legal proceedings the burden of proof of conscientious objection shall rest on the person claiming to rely on it.

(2) Nothing in subsection (1) of this section shall affect any duty to participate in treatment which is necessary to save the life or to prevent grave permanent injury to the physical or mental health of a pregnant woman.

5 Supplementary provisions

(1) No offence under the Infant Life (Preservation) Act 1929 shall be committed by a registered medical practitioner who terminates a pregnancy in accordance with the provisions of this Act.

(2) For the purposes of the law relating to abortion, anything done with intent to procure a woman's miscarriage (or, in the case of a woman carrying more than one foetus, her miscarriage of any foetus) is unlawfully done unless authorised by section 1 of this Act and, in the case of a woman carrying more than one foetus, anything done with intent to procure her miscarriage of any foetus is authorised by that section if—

(a) the ground for termination of the pregnancy specified in subsection (1)(d) of that section applies in relation to any foetus and the thing is done for the purpose of procuring the miscarriage of that foetus, or

(b) any of the other grounds for termination of the pregnancy specified in that section applies.

6 Interpretation

In this Act, the following expressions have meanings hereby assigned to them:—

'the law relating to abortion' means sections 58 and 59 of the Offences against the Person Act 1861, and any rule of law relating to the procurement of abortion.

Nurses, Midwives and Health Visitors Act 1997

16 Attendance by unqualified persons at childbirth

(1) A person other than a registered midwife or a registered medical practitioner shall not attend a woman in childbirth. [S]

(2) Subsection (1) does not apply—

(a) where the attention is given in a case of sudden or urgent necessity; or

(b) in the case of a person who, while undergoing training with a view to becoming a medical practitioner or to becoming a midwife, attends a woman in childbirth as part of a course of practical instruction in midwifery recognised by the General Medical Council or one of the National Boards.

Part III

Personal Injury, Molestation and Harassment

(a) Personal Injury

Offences Against the Person Act 1861

4 Soliciting to commit murder

[See page 357]

16 Threats to kill

[See page 45]

17 Impeding a person endeavouring to save himself or another from shipwreck

[See page 45]

18 Wounding, or causing grievous bodily harm with intent to do grievous bodily harm, or to resist apprehension

Whosoever shall unlawfully and maliciously by any means whatsoever wound or cause any grievous bodily harm to any person . . . with intent . . . to do some . . . grievous bodily harm to any person, or with intent to resist or prevent the lawful apprehension or detainer of any person, shall be guilty of an offence, and being convicted thereof shall be liable, . . . to imprisonment for life . . . [I]

20 Wounding or inflicting grievous bodily harm

Whosoever shall unlawfully and maliciously wound or inflict any grievous bodily harm upon any other person, either with or without any weapon or instrument, shall be guilty of an offence, and being convicted thereof shall be liable . . . to imprisonment for a term not exceeding five years. [E]

21 Attempting to choke, etc., in order to commit or assist in the committing of any indictable offence

Whosoever shall, by any means whatsoever, attempt to choke, suffocate, or strangle any other person, or shall by any means calculated to choke, suffocate, or strangle, attempt to render any other person insensible, unconscious, or incapable of resistance, with intent in any of such cases thereby to enable himself or any other person to commit, or with intent in any of such cases thereby to assist any other person in committing any indictable offence, shall be guilty of an offence, and being convicted thereof shall be liable . . . to imprisonment for life . . . [I]

22 Using chloroform, etc., to commit or assist in the committing of any indictable offence

Whosoever shall unlawfully apply or administer to or cause to be taken by, or attempt to apply or administer to or attempt to cause to be administered to or taken by, any person, any chloroform, laudanum, or other stupefying or overpowering drug, matter, or thing, with intent in any of such cases thereby to enable himself or any other person to commit, or with intent in any of such cases thereby to assist any other person in committing any indictable offence, shall be guilty of an offence, and being convicted thereof shall be liable . . . to imprisonment for life . . . [I]

23 Maliciously administering poison, etc., so as to endanger life or inflict grievous bodily harm

Whosoever shall unlawfully and maliciously administer to or cause to be administered to or taken by any other person any poison or other destructive or noxious thing, so as thereby to endanger the life of such person, or so as thereby to inflict upon such person any grievous bodily harm, shall be guilty of an offence, and being convicted thereof shall be liable . . . to imprisonment for any term not exceeding ten years . . . [I]

24 Maliciously administering poison, etc., with intent to injure, aggrieve, or annoy any other person

[See page 45]

26 Not providing apprentices or servants with food, etc., or doing bodily harm, whereby life is endangered, or health permanently injured

Whosoever, being legally liable, either as a master or mistress, to provide for any apprentice or servant necessary food, clothing, or lodging, shall wilfully and without lawful excuse refuse or neglect to provide the same, or shall unlawfully and maliciously do or cause to be done any bodily harm to any such apprentice or servant, so that the life of such apprentice or servant shall be endangered, or the health of such apprentice or servant shall be likely to be permanently injured, shall be guilty of an offence, and being convicted thereof shall be liable . . . to imprisonment for a term not exceeding five years. [E]

28 Causing bodily injury by gunpowder

Whosoever shall unlawfully and maliciously, by the explosion of gunpowder or other explosive substance, burn, maim, disfigure, disable, or do any grievous bodily harm to any person, shall be guilty of an offence, and being convicted thereof shall be liable, at the discretion of the court, to imprisonment for life. [I]

29 Causing gunpowder to explode, or sending to any person an explosive substance, or throwing corrosive fluid on a person, with intent to do grievous bodily harm

Whosoever shall unlawfully and maliciously cause any gunpowder or other explosive substance to explode, or send or deliver to or cause to be taken or received by any person any explosive substance or any other dangerous or noxious thing, or put or lay at any place, or cast or throw at or upon or otherwise apply to any person, any corrosive fluid or any destructive or explosive substance, with intent in any of the cases aforesaid to burn, maim, disfigure, or disable any person, or to do some grievous bodily harm to any person, shall, whether any bodily injury be effected or not, be guilty of an offence, and being convicted thereof shall be liable, at the discretion of the court, to imprisonment for life. [I]

30 Placing gunpowder near a building, etc., with intent to do bodily injury to any person

Whosoever shall unlawfully and maliciously place or throw in, into, upon, against, or near any building, ship, or vessel any gunpowder or other explosive substance, with intent to do any bodily injury to any person, shall, whether or not any explosion take place, and whether or not any bodily injury be effected, be guilty of an offence, and being convicted thereof shall be liable, at the discretion of the court, to imprisonment for any term not exceeding fourteen years. [I]

31 Setting or allowing to remain spring guns, etc., with intent to inflict grievous bodily harm

[See page 136]

32 Placing wood, etc., on railway, taking up rails, showing or hiding signals, etc., with intent to endanger passengers

[See page 118]

33 Casting stone, etc., upon a railway carriage, with intent to endanger the safety of any person therein, or in any part of the same train
[See page 118]

34 Doing or omitting anything so as to endanger passengers by railway
[See page 118]

35 Drivers of carriages injuring persons by furious driving
Whosoever, having the charge of any carriage or vehicle, shall by wanton or furious driving or racing, or other wilful misconduct, or by wilful neglect, do or cause to be done any bodily harm to any person whatsoever, shall be guilty of an offence, and being convicted thereof shall be liable, at the discretion of the court, to be imprisoned for any term not exceeding two years. [I]

38 Assault with intent to resist arrest
[See page 45]

47 Assault occasioning bodily harm
Whosoever shall be convicted upon an indictment of any assault occasioning actual bodily harm shall be liable . . . to be imprisoned for any term not exceeding five years. [E]

64 Making or having anything with intent to commit an offence in this Act
Whosoever shall knowingly have in his possession, or make or manufacture, any gunpowder, explosive substance, or any dangerous or noxious thing, or any machine, engine, instrument, or thing, with intent by means thereof to commit, or for the purpose of enabling any other person to commit, any of the offences in this Act mentioned shall be guilty of a misdemeanour, and being convicted thereof shall be liable, at the discretion of the court, to be imprisoned for any term not exceeding two years . . . [I]

Crime and Disorder Act 1998

29 Racially or religiously aggravated assaults
[See page 293]

Conspiracy and Protection of Property Act 1875

6 Penalty for neglect by master to provide food, clothing, etc., for servant or apprentice
Where a master, being legally liable to provide for his servant or apprentice necessary food, clothing, medical aid, or lodging, wilfully and without lawful excuse refuses or neglects to provide the same, whereby the health of the servant or apprentice is or is likely to be seriously or permanently injured, he shall on summary conviction be liable either to pay a penalty not exceeding level 2 on the standard scale or to be imprisoned for a term not exceeding six months. [S]

Criminal Justice Act 1988

134 Torture

(1) A public official or person acting in an official capacity, whatever his nationality, commits the offence of torture if in the United Kingdom or elsewhere he intentionally inflicts severe pain or suffering on another in the performance or purported performance of his official duties. [I]

(2) A person not falling within subsection (1) above commits the offence of torture, whatever his nationality, if—

(a) in the United Kingdom or elsewhere he intentionally inflicts severe pain or suffering on another at the instigation or with the consent or acquiescence—

(i) of a public official; or

(ii) of a person acting in an official capacity; and

(b) the official or other person is performing or purporting to perform his official duties when he instigates the commission of the offence or consents to or acquiesces in it. [I]

(3) It is immaterial whether the pain or suffering is physical or mental and whether it is caused by an act or an omission.

(4) It shall be a defence for a person charged with an offence under this section in respect of any conduct of his to prove that he had lawful authority, justification or excuse for that conduct.

(5) For the purposes of this section 'lawful authority, justification or excuse' means—

(a) in relation to pain or suffering inflicted in the United Kingdom, lawful authority, justification or excuse under the law of the part of the United Kingdom where it was inflicted;

(b) in relation to pain or suffering inflicted outside the United Kingdom—

(i) if it was inflicted by a United Kingdom official acting under the law of the United Kingdom or by a person acting in an official capacity under that law, lawful authority, justification or excuse under that law;

(ii) if it was inflicted by a United Kingdom official acting under the law of any part of the United Kingdom or by a person acting in an official capacity under such law, lawful authority, justification or excuse under the law of the part of the United Kingdom under whose law he was acting; and

(iii) in any other case, lawful authority, justification or excuse under the law of the place where it was inflicted.

Dangerous Dogs Act 1991

3 Keeping dogs under proper control

[See page 149]

Female Genital Mutilation Act 2003

1 Offence of female genital mutilation

(1) a person is guilty of an offence if he excises, infibulates or otherwise mutilates the whole or any part of a girl's labia majora, labia minora or clitoris. [E]

(2) But no offence is committed by an approved person who performs—

(a) a surgical operation on a girl which is necessary for her physical or mental health, or

(b) a surgical operation on a girl who is in any stage of labour, or has just given birth, for purposes connected with the labour or birth.

(3) The following are approved persons—

(a) in relation to an operation falling within subsection (2)(a), a registered medical practitioner,

(b) in relation to an operation falling within subsection (2)(b), a registered medical practitioner, a registered midwife or a person undergoing a course of training with a view to becoming such a practitioner or midwife.

(4) There is also no offence committed by a person who—

(a) performs a surgical operation falling within subsection (2)(a) or (b) outside the United Kingdom, and

(b) in relation to such an operation exercises functions corresponding to those of an approved person.

(5) For the purpose of determining whether an operation is necessary for the mental health of a girl it is immaterial whether she or any other person believes that the operation is required as a matter of custom or ritual.

2 Offence of assisting a girl to mutilate her own genitalia

A person is guilty of an offence if he aids, abets, counsels or procures a girl to excise, infibulate or otherwise mutilate the whole or any part of her own labia majora, labia minora or clitoris. [E]

3 Offence of assisting a non-UK person to mutilate overseas a girl's genitalia

(1) A person is guilty of an offence if he aids, abets, counsels or procures a person who is not a United Kingdom national or permanent United Kingdom resident to do a relevant act of female genital mutilation outside the United Kingdom. [E]

(2) An act is a relevant act of female genital mutilation if—

(a) it is done in relation to a United Kingdom national or permanent United Kingdom resident, and

(b) it would, if done by such a person, constitute an offence under section 1.

(3) But no offence is committed if the relevant act of female genital mutilation—

(a) is a surgical operation falling within section 1(2)(a) or (b), and

(b) is performed by a person who, in relation to such an operation, is an approved person or exercises functions corresponding to those of an approved person.

4 Extension of sections 1 to 3 to extra-territorial acts

(1) Sections 1 to 3 extend to any act done outside the United Kingdom by a United Kingdom national or permanent United Kingdom resident.

(2) If an offence under this Act is committed outside the United Kingdom—

(a) proceedings may be taken, and

(b) the offence may for incidental purposes be treated as having been committed,

in any place in England and Wales or Northern Ireland.

6 Definitions

(1) Girl includes woman.

(2) A United Kingdom national is an individual who is—

(a) a British citizen, a British overseas territories citizen, a British National (Overseas) or a British Overseas citizen,

(b) a person who under the British Nationality Act 1981 is a British subject, or

(c) a British protected person within the meaning of that Act.

(3) A permanent United Kingdom resident is an individual who is settled in the United Kingdom (within the meaning of the Immigration Act 1971).

(4) This section has effect for the purposes of this Act.

(b) Molestation and Harassment

Criminal Justice Act 1988

39 Common assault and battery to be summary offences

Common assault and battery shall be summary offences and a person guilty of either of them shall be liable to a fine not exceeding level 5 on the standard scale, to imprisonment for a term not exceeding six months, or to both. [S]

Offences Against the Person Act 1861

16 Threats to kill

A person who without lawful excuse makes to another a threat, intending that that other would fear it would be carried out, to kill that other or a third person, shall be guilty of an offence and liable on conviction on indictment to imprisonment for a term not exceeding ten years. [E]

17 Impeding a person endeavouring to save himself or another from shipwreck

Whosoever shall unlawfully and maliciously prevent or impede any person, being on board of or having quitted any ship or vessel which shall be in distress, or wrecked, stranded, or cast on shore, in his endeavour to save his life, or shall unlawfully and maliciously prevent or impede any person in his endeavour to save the life of any such person as in this section first aforesaid, shall be guilty of an offence, and being convicted thereof shall be liable . . . to imprisonment for life. [I]

24 Maliciously administering poison, etc., with intent to injure, aggrieve, or annoy any other person

Whosoever shall unlawfully and maliciously administer to or cause to be administered to or taken by any other person any poison or other destructive or noxious thing, with intent to injure, aggrieve, or annoy such person, shall be guilty of an offence, and being . . . convicted thereof shall be liable to imprisonment for a term not exceeding five years. [I]

38 Assault with intent to resist arrest

Whosoever . . . shall assault any person with intent to resist or prevent the lawful apprehension or detainer of himself or of any other person for any offence, shall be guilty of an offence, and being convicted thereof shall be liable, at the discretion of the court, to be imprisoned for any term not exceeding two years. [E]

Police Act 1996

89 Assaults on constables

[See page 331]

Sexual Offences Act 2003

1 Rape

(1) a person (A) commits an offence if—

(a) he intentionally penetrates the vagina, anus or mouth of another person (B) with his penis,

(b) B does not consent to the penetration, and

(c) A does not reasonably believe that B consents. [I]

(2) Whether a belief is reasonable is to be determined having regard to all the circumstances, including any steps A has taken to ascertain whether B consents.

(3) Sections 75 and 76 apply to an offence under this section.

2 Assault by penetration

(1) A person (A) commits an offence if—

(a) he intentionally penetrates the vagina or anus of another person (B) with a part of his body or anything else,

(b) the penetration is sexual,

(c) B does not consent to the penetration, and

(d) A does not reasonably believe that B consents. [I]

(2) Whether a belief is reasonable is to be determined having regard to all the circumstances, including any steps A has taken to ascertain whether B consents.

(3) Sections 75 and 76 apply to an offence under this section.

3 Sexual assault

(1) a person (A) commits an offence if—

(a) he intentionally touches another person (B),

(b) the touching is sexual,

(c) B does not consent to the touching, and

(d) A does not reasonably believe that B consents.

(2) Whether a belief is reasonable is to be determined having regard to all the circumstances, including any steps A has taken to ascertain whether B consents.

(3) Sections 75 and 76 apply to an offence under this section. [E]

4 Causing a person to engage in sexual activity without consent

(1) A person (A) commits an offence if—

(a) he intentionally causes another person (B) to engage in an activity,

(b) the activity is sexual,

(c) B does not consent to engaging in the activity, and

(d) A does not reasonably believe that B consents.

(2) Whether a belief is reasonable is to be determined having regard to all the circumstances, including any steps A has taken to ascertain whether B consents.

(3) Sections 75 and 76 apply to an offence under this section.

(4) A person guilty of an offence under this section, if the activity caused involved—

(a) penetration of B's anus or vagina,

(b) penetration of B's mouth with a person's penis,

(c) penetration of a person's anus or vagina with a part of B's body or by B with anything else, or

(d) penetration of a person's mouth with B's penis,

is liable, on conviction on indictment, to imprisonment for life. [E] and [I]

61 Administering a substance with intent

(1) A person commits an offence if he intentionally administers a substance to, or causes a substance to be taken by, another person (B)—

(a) knowing that B does not consent, and

(b) with the intention of stupefying or overpowering B, so as to enable any person to engage in a sexual activity that involves B. [E]

62 Committing an offence with intent to commit a sexual offence

(1) A person commits an offence under this section if he commits any offence with the intention of committing a relevant sexual offence.

(2) In this section, 'relevant sexual offence' means any offence under [sections 1–73 of this Act] (including an offence of aiding, abetting, counselling or procuring such an offence). [I] and [E]

(3) A person guilty of an offence under this section is liable on conviction on indictment, where the offence is committed by kidnapping or false imprisonment, to imprisonment for life.

63 Trespass with intent to commit a sexual offence

[See page 230]

66 Exposure

(1) A person (A) commits an offence if—

(a) he intentionally exposes his genitals, and

(b) he knows or intends that someone will see them and be caused alarm or distress. [E]

67 Voyeurism

[See page 239]

74 'Consent'

For the purposes of this [Act] a person consents if he agrees by choice, and has the freedom and capacity to make that choice.

75 Evidential presumptions about consent

(1) If in proceedings for an offence to which this section applies it is proved—

(a) that the defendant did the relevant act,

(b) that any of the circumstances specified in subsection (2) existed, and

(c) that the defendant knew that those circumstances existed,

the complainant is to be taken not to have consented to the relevant act unless sufficient evidence is adduced to raise an issue as to whether he consented, and the defendant is to be taken not to have reasonably believed that the complainant consented unless sufficient evidence is adduced to raise an issue as to whether he reasonably believed it.

(2) The circumstances are that—

(a) any person was, at the time of the relevant act or immediately before it began, using violence against the complainant or causing the complainant to fear that immediate violence would be used against him;

(b) any person was, at the time of the relevant act or immediately before it began, causing the complainant to fear that violence was being used, or that immediate violence would be used, against another person;

(c) the complainant was, and the defendant was not, unlawfully detained at the time of the relevant act;

(d) the complainant was asleep or otherwise unconscious at the time of the relevant act;

(e) because of the complainant's physical disability, the complainant would not have been able at the time of the relevant act to communicate to the defendant whether the complainant consented;

(f) any person had administered to or caused to be taken by the complainant, without the complainant's consent, a substance which, having regard to when it was administered or taken, was capable of causing or enabling the complainant to be stupified or overpowered at the time of the relevant act.

(3) In subsection (2)(a) and (b), the reference to the time immediately before the relevant act began is, in the case of an act which is one of a continuous series of sexual activities, a reference to the time immediately before the first sexual activity began.

76 Conclusive presumptions about consent

(1) If in proceedings for an offence to which this section applies it is proved that the defendant did the relevant act and that any of the circumstances specified in subsection (2) existed, it is to be conclusively presumed—

(a) that the complainant did not consent to the relevant act, and

(b) that the defendant did not believe that the complainant consented to the relevant act.

(2) The circumstances are that—

(a) the defendant intentionally deceived the complainant as to the nature or purpose of the relevant act;

(b) the defendant intentionally induced the complainant to consent to the relevant act by impersonating a person known personally to the complainant.

77 Sections 75 and 76: relevant acts

In relation to an offence to which sections 76 and *77* apply, references in those sections to the relevant act and to the complainant are to be read as follows—

Offence	Relevant Act
An offence under section 1 (rape).	The defendant intentionally penetrating, with his penis, the vagina, anus or mouth of another person ('the complainant').
An offence under section 2 (assault by penetration).	The defendant intentionally penetrating, with a part of his body or anything else, the vagina or anus of another person ('the complainant'), where the penetration is sexual.
An offence under section 3 (sexual assault).	The defendant intentionally touching another person ('the complainant'), where the touching is sexual.
An offence under section 4 (causing a person to engage in sexual activity without consent).	The defendant intentionally causing another person ('the complainant') to engage in an activity, where the activity is sexual.

78 'Sexual'

For the purposes of this [Act] (except section 71) penetration, touching or any other activity is sexual if a reasonable person would consider that—

(a) whatever the circumstances or any person's purpose in relation to it, it is because of its nature sexual, or

(b) because of its nature it may be sexual and because of the circumstances or the purpose of any person in relation to it (or both) it is sexual.

79 General interpretation

(1) The following apply for the purposes of this [Act].

(2) Penetration is a continuing act from entry to withdrawal.

(3) References to a part of the body include references to a part surgically constructed (in particular, through gender reassignment surgery).

(4) 'Image' means a moving or still image and includes an image produced by any means and, where the context permits, a three-dimensional image.

(5) References to an image of a person include references to an image of an imaginary person.

(6) 'Mental disorder' has the meaning given by section 1 of the Mental Health Act 1983.

(7) References to observation (however expressed) are to observation whether direct or by looking at an image.

(8) Touching includes touching—

(a) with any part of the body,

(b) with anything else,

(c) through anything,

and in particular includes touching amounting to penetration.

(9) 'Vagina' includes vulva.

(10) In relation to an animal, references to the vagina or anus include references to any similar part.

Sexual Offences Act 1993

1 Abolition of presumption of sexual incapacity

The presumption of criminal law that a boy under the age of fourteen is incapable of sexual intercourse is hereby abolished.

Public Order Act 1986

PART I

1 Riot
[See page 288]

2 Violent disorder
[See page 288]

3 Affray
(1) A person is guilty of affray if he uses or threatens unlawful violence towards another and his conduct is such as would cause a person of reasonable firmness present at the scene to fear for his personal safety. [E]

(2) Where 2 or more persons use or threaten the unlawful violence, it is the conduct of them taken together that must be considered for the purposes of subsection (1).

(3) For the purposes of this section a threat cannot be made by the use of words alone.

(4) No person of reasonable firmness need actually be, or be likely to be, present at the scene.

(5) Affray may be committed in private as well as in public places.

4 Fear or provocation of violence
(1) A person is guilty of an offence if he—

(a) uses towards another person threatening, abusive or insulting words or behaviour; or

(b) distributes or displays to another person any writing, sign or other visible representation which is threatening, abusive or insulting,

with intent to cause that person to believe that immediate unlawful violence will be used against him or another by any person, or to provoke the immediate use of unlawful violence by that person or another, or whereby that person is likely to believe that such violence will be used or it is likely that such violence will be provoked. [S]

(2) An offence under this section may be committed in a public or a private place, except that no offence is committed where the words or behaviour are used, or the writing, sign or other visible representation is distributed or displayed, by a person inside a dwelling and the other person is also inside that or another dwelling.

4A Intentional harassment, alarm or distress
(1) A person is guilty of an offence if, with intent to cause a person harassment, alarm or distress, he—

(a) uses threatening, abusive or insulting words or behaviour, or disorderly behaviour, or

(b) displays any writing, sign or other visible representation which is threatening, abusive or insulting,

thereby causing that or another person harassment, alarm or distress. [S]

(2) An offence under this section may be committed in a public or a private place, except that no offence is committed where the words or behaviour are used, or the writing, sign or other visible representation is displayed, by a person inside a dwelling and the person who is harassed, alarmed or distressed is also inside that or another dwelling.

(3) It is a defence for the accused to prove—

(a) that he was inside a dwelling and had no reason to believe that the words or behaviour used, or the writing, sign or other visible representation displayed would be heard or seen by a person outside that or any other dwelling, or

(b) that his conduct was reasonable.

5 Harassment, alarm or distress

(1) A person is guilty of an offence if he—

(a) uses threatening, abusive or insulting words or behaviour, or disorderly behaviour, or

(b) displays any writing, sign or other visible representation which is threatening, abusive or insulting,

within the hearing or sight of a person likely to be caused harassment, alarm or distress thereby. [S]

(2) An offence under this section may be committed in a public or a private place, except that no offence is committed where the words or behaviour are used, or the writing, sign or other visible representation is displayed, by a person inside a dwelling and the other person is also inside that or another dwelling.

(3) It is a defence for the accused to prove—

(a) that he had no reason to believe that there was any person within hearing or sight who was likely to be caused harassment, alarm or distress, or

(b) that he was inside a dwelling and had no reason to believe that the words or behaviour used, or the writing, sign or other visible representation displayed, would be heard or seen by a person outside that or any other dwelling, or

(c) that his conduct was reasonable.

6 Mental element: miscellaneous

(1) A person is guilty of riot only if he intends to use violence or is aware that his conduct may be violent.

(2) A person is guilty of violent disorder or affray only if he intends to use or threaten violence or is aware that his conduct may be violent or threaten violence.

(3) A person is guilty of an offence under section 4 only if he intends his words or behaviour, or the writing, sign or other visible representation, to be threatening, abusive or insulting, or is aware that it may be threatening, abusive or insulting.

(4) A person is guilty of an offence under section 5 only if he intends his words or behaviour, or the writing, sign or other visible representation, to be threatening, abusive or insulting, or is aware that it may be threatening, abusive or insulting or (as the case may be) he intends his behaviour to be or is aware that it may be disorderly.

(5) For the purposes of this section a person whose awareness is impaired by intoxication shall be taken to be aware of that of which he would be aware if not intoxicated, unless he shows either that his intoxication was not self-induced or that it was caused solely by the taking or administration of a substance in the course of medical treatment.

(6) In subsection (5) 'intoxication' means any intoxication, whether caused by drink, drugs or other means, or by a combination of means.

(7) Subsections (1) and (2) do not affect the determination for the purposes of riot or violent disorder of the number of persons who use or threaten violence.

8 Interpretation

In this Part—

'dwelling' means any structure or part of a structure occupied as a person's home or as other living accommodation (whether the occupation is separate or shared with others) but does not include any part not so occupied, and for this purpose 'structure' includes a tent, caravan, vehicle, vessel or other temporary or movable structure;

'violence' means any violent conduct, so that—

(a) except in the context of affray, it includes violent conduct towards property as well as violent conduct towards persons, and

(b) it is not restricted to conduct causing or intended to cause injury or damage but includes any other violent conduct (for example, throwing at or towards a person a missile of a kind capable of causing injury which does not hit or falls short).

Firearms Act 1968

16A Possession of firearm with intent to cause fear of violence
[See page 141]

Theft Act 1968

21 Blackmail
[See page 178]

Criminal Damage Act 1971

2 Threats to destroy or damage property
[See page 168]

Criminal Justice and Public Order Act 1994

51 Intimidation, etc., of witnesses, jurors and others
[See page 336]

Family Law Act 1996

42A Offence of breaching non-molestation order

(1) A person who without reasonable excuse does anything that he is prohibited from doing by a non-molestation order is guilty of an offence.

(2) In the case of a non-molestation order made by virtue of section 45(1), a person can be guilty of an offence under this section only in respect of conduct engaged in at a time when he was aware of the existence of the order.

(3) Where a person is convicted of an offence under this section in respect of any conduct, that conduct is not punishable as a contempt of court.

(4) A person cannot be convicted of an offence under this section in respect of any conduct which has been punished as a contempt of court. [E]

Protection from Harassment Act 1997

1 Prohibition of harassment

(1) A person must not pursue a course of conduct—

(a) which amounts to harrassment of another, and

(b) which he knows or ought to know amounts to harassment of the other.

(2) For the purposes of this section, the person whose course of conduct is in question ought to know that it amounts to or involves harassment of another if a reasonable person in possession of

the same information would think the course of conduct amounted to or involved harassment of the other.

(3) Subsection (1) or (1A) does not apply to a course of conduct if the person who pursued it shows—

(a) that it was pursued for the purpose of preventing or detecting crime,
(b) that it was pursued under any enactment or rule of law or to comply with any condition or requirement imposed by any person under any enactment, or
(c) that in the particular circumstances the pursuit of the course of conduct was reasonable.

2 Offence of harassment

(1) A person who pursues a course of conduct in breach of section 1 is guilty of an offence. [S]

4 Putting people in fear of violence

(1) A person whose course of conduct causes another to fear, on at least two occasions, that violence will be used against him is guilty of an offence if he knows or ought to know that his course of conduct will cause the other so to fear on each of those occasions. [E]

(2) For the purposes of this section, the person whose course of conduct is in question ought to know that it will cause another to fear that violence will be used against him on any occasion if a reasonable person in possession of the same information would think the course of conduct would cause the other so to fear on that occasion.

(3) It is a defence for a person charged with an offence under this section to show that—

(a) his course of conduct was pursued for the purpose of preventing or detecting crime,
(b) his course of conduct was pursued under any enactment or rule of law or to comply with any condition or requirement imposed by any person under any enactment, or
(c) the pursuit of his course of conduct was reasonable for the protection of himself or another or for the protection of his or another's property.

(5) If on the trial on indictment of a person charged with an offence under this section the jury find him not guilty of the offence charged, they may find him guilty of an offence under section 2.

(6) The Crown Court has the same powers and duties in relation to a person who is by virtue of subsection (5) convicted before it of an offence under section 2 as a magistrates' court would have on convicting him of the offence.

5 Restraining orders

(1) A court sentencing or otherwise dealing with a person ('the defendant') convicted of an offence under section 2 or 4 may (as well as sentencing him or dealing with him in any other way) make an order under this section.

(2) The order may, for the purpose of protecting the victim or victims of the offence, or any other person mentioned in the order, from conduct which—

(a) amounts to harassment, or
(b) will cause a fear of violence,

prohibit the defendant from doing anything described in the order.

(3) The order may have effect for a specified period or until further order.

(4) The prosecutor, the defendant or any other person mentioned in the order may apply to the court which made the order for it to be varied or discharged by a further order.

(5) If without reasonable excuse the defendant does anything which he is prohibited from doing by an order under this section, he is guilty of an offence. [E]

7 Interpretation of this group of sections

(1) This section applies for the interpretation of sections 1 to 5.

(2) References to harassing a person include alarming the person or causing the person distress.

(3) A 'course of conduct' must involve conduct on at least two occasions.

(3A) A person's conduct on any occasion shall be taken, if aided, abetted, counselled or procured by another—

(a) to be conduct on that occasion of the other (as well as conduct of the person whose conduct it is); and

(b) to be conduct in relation to which the other's knowledge and purpose, and what he ought to have known, are the same as they were in relation to what was contemplated or reasonably foreseeable at the time of the aiding, abetting, counselling or procuring.

(4) 'Conduct' includes speech.

12 National security, etc.

(1) If the Secretary of State certifies that in his opinion anything done by a specified person on a specified occasion related to—

(a) national security,

(b) the economic well-being of the United Kingdom, or

(c) the prevention or detection of serious crime,

and was done on behalf of the Crown, the certificate is conclusive evidence that this Act does not apply to any conduct of that person on that occasion.

(2) In subsection (1), 'specified' means specified in the certificate in question.

Crime and Disorder Act 1998

1 Anti-social behaviour orders

(1) An application for an order under this section may be made by a relevant authority if it appears to the authority that the following conditions are fulfilled with respect to any person aged 10 or over, namely—

(a) that the person has acted, since the commencement date, in an anti-social manner, that is to say, in a manner that caused or was likely to cause harassment, alarm or distress to one or more persons not of the same household as himself; and

(b) that such an order is necessary to protect relevant persons from further anti-social acts by him.

(1A) In this section and sections 1B and 1E 'relevant authority' means—

(a) the council for a local government area;

(b) the chief officer of police of any police force maintained for a police area;

(c) the chief constable of the British Transport Police Force; or

(d) any person registered under section 1 of the Housing Act 1996 as a social landlord who provides or manages any houses or hostel in a local government area.

(1B) In this section 'relevant persons' means—

(a) in relation to a relevant authority falling within paragraph (a) of subsection (1A), persons within the local government area of that council;

(b) in relation to a relevant authority falling within paragraph (b) of that subsection, persons within the police area;

(c) in relation to a relevant authority falling within paragraph (c) of that subsection—

(i) persons who are on or likely to be on policed premises in a local government area; or

(ii) persons who are in the vicinity of or likely to be in the vicinity of such premises;

(d) in relation to a relevant authority falling within paragraph (d) of that subsection—

(i) persons who are residing in or who are otherwise on or likely to be on premises provided or managed by that authority; or

(ii) persons who are in the vicinity of or likely to be in the vicinity of such premises.

(4) If, on such an application, it is proved that the conditions mentioned in subsection (1) above are fulfilled, the magistrates' court may make an order under this section (an 'anti-social behaviour order') which prohibits the defendant from doing anything described in the order.

(5) For the purpose of determining whether the condition mentioned in subsection (1)(a) above is fulfilled, the court shall disregard any act of the defendant which he shows was reasonable in the circumstances.

(6) The prohibitions that may be imposed by an anti-social behaviour order are those necessary for the purpose of protecting persons (whether relevant persons or persons elsewhere in England and Wales) from further anti-social acts by the defendant.

(7) An anti-social behaviour order shall have effect for a period (not less than two years) specified in the order or until further order.

(10) If without reasonable excuse a person does anything which he is prohibited from doing by an anti-social behaviour order, he is guilty of an offence . . . [E]

32 Racially or religiously aggravated harassment, etc.
[See page 293]

Criminal Justice and Police Act 2001

39 Intimidation of witnesses
[See page 337]

40 Harming witnesses etc.
[See page 338]

42 Police directions stopping the harassment etc. of a person in his home

(1) Subject to the following provisions of this section, a constable who is at the scene may give a direction under this section to any person if—

- (a) that person is present outside or in the vicinity of any premises that are used by any individual ('the resident') as his dwelling;
- (b) that constable believes, on reasonable grounds, that that person is present there for the purpose (by his presence or otherwise) of representing to the resident or another individual (whether or not one who uses the premises as his dwelling), or of persuading the resident or such another individual—
  - (i) that he should not do something that he is entitled or required to do; or
  - (ii) that he should do something that he is not under any obligation to do; and
- (c) that constable also believes, on reasonable grounds, that the presence of that person (either alone or together with that of any other persons who are also present)—
  - (i) amounts to, or is likely to result in, the harassment of the resident; or
  - (ii) is likely to cause alarm or distress to the resident.

(2) A direction under this section is a direction requiring the person to whom it is given to do all such things as the constable giving it may specify as the things he considers necessary to prevent one or both of the following—

- (a) the harassment of the resident; or
- (b) the causing of any alarm or distress to the resident.

(3) A direction under this section may be given orally; and where a constable is entitled to give a direction under this section to each of several persons outside, or in the vicinity of, any premises, he may give that direction to those persons by notifying them of his requirements either individually or all together.

(4) The requirements that may be imposed by a direction under this section include—

- (a) a requirement to leave the vicinity of the premises in question, and
- (b) a requirement to leave that vicinity and not to return to it within such period as the constable may specify, not being longer than 3 months;

and (in either case) the requirement to leave the vicinity may be to do so immediately or after a specified period of time.

(7) Any person who knowingly contravenes a direction given to him under this section shall be guilty of an offence . . . [S]

(9) In this section 'dwelling' has the same meaning as in Part I of the Public Order Act 1986.

42A Offence of harassment etc. of a person in his home

(1) A person commits an offence if—

(a) that person is present outside or in the vicinity of any premises that are used by any individual ('the resident') as his dwelling;

(b) that person is present there for the purpose (by his presence or otherwise) of representing to the resident or another individual (whether or not one who uses the premises as his dwelling), or of persuading the resident or such another individual—

(i) that he should not do something that he is entitled or required to do; or

(ii) that he should do something that he is not under any obligation to do;

(c) that person—

(i) intends his presence to amount to the harassment of, or to cause alarm or distress to, the resident; or

(ii) knows or ought to know that his presence is likely to result in the harassment of, or to cause alarm or distress to, the resident; and

(d) the presence of that person—

(i) amounts to the harassment of, or causes alarm or distress to, any person falling within subsection (2); or

(ii) is likely to result in the harassment of, or to cause alarm or distress to, any such person. [S]

(2) A person falls within this subsection if he is—

(a) the resident,

(b) a person in the resident's dwelling, or

(c) a person in another dwelling in the vicinity of the resident's dwelling.

(3) The references in subsection (1)(c) and (d) to a person's presence are references to his presence either alone or together with that of any other persons who are also present.

(4) For the purposes of this section a person (A) ought to know that his presence is likely to result in the harassment of, or to cause alarm or distress to, a resident if a reasonable person in possession of the same information would think that A's presence was likely to have that effect.

(7) In this section 'dwelling' has the same meaning as in Part 1 of the Public Order Act 1986.

Trade Union and Labour Relations (Consolidation) Act 1992

241 Intimidation or annoyance by violence or otherwise

(1) a person commits an offence who, with a view to compelling another person to abstain from doing or to do any act which that person has a legal right to do or abstain from doing, wrongfully and without legal authority—

(a) uses violence to or intimidates that person or his wife or children, or injures his property,

(b) persistently follows that person about from place to place,

(c) hides any tools, clothes or other property owned or used by that person, or deprives him of or hinders him in the use thereof,

(d) watches or besets the house or other place where that person resides, works, carries on business or happens to be, or the approach to any such house or place, or

(e) follows that person with two or more other persons in a disorderly manner in or through any street or road. [E]

Serious Organised Crime and Police Act 2005

145 Interference with contractual relationships so as to harm animal research organisation

(1) A person (A) commits an offence if, with the intention of harming an animal research organisation, he—

(a) does a relevant act, or

(b) threatens that he or somebody else will do a relevant act,

in circumstances in which that act or threat is intended or likely to cause a second person (B) to take any of the steps in subsection (2). [E]

(2) The steps are—

(a) not to perform any contractual obligation owed by B to a third person (C) (whether or not such non-performance amounts to a breach of contract);

(b) to terminate any contract B has with C;

(c) not to enter into a contract with C.

(3) For the purposes of this section, a 'relevant act' is—

(a) an act amounting to a criminal offence, or

(b) a tortious act causing B to suffer loss or damage of any description;

but paragraph (b) does not include an act which is actionable on the ground only that it induces another person to break a contract with B.

(4) For the purposes of this section, 'contract' includes any other arrangement (and 'contractual' is to be read accordingly).

(5) For the purposes of this section, to 'harm' an animal research organisation means—

(a) to cause the organisation to suffer loss or damage of any description, or

(b) to prevent or hinder the carrying out by the organisation of any of its activities.

(6) This section does not apply to any act done wholly or mainly in contemplation or furtherance of a trade dispute.

(7) In subsection (6) 'trade dispute' has the same meaning as in Part 4 of the Trade Union and Labour Relations (Consolidation) Act 1992 (c. 52), except that section 218 of that Act shall be read as if—

(a) it made provision corresponding to section 244(4) of that Act, and

(b) in subsection (5), the definition of 'worker' included any person falling within paragraph (b) of the definition of 'worker' in section 244(5).

146 Intimidation of persons connected with animal research organisation

(1) A person (A) commits an offence if, with the intention of causing a second person (B) to abstain from doing something which B is entitled to do (or to do something which B is entitled to abstain from doing)—

(a) A threatens B that A or somebody else will do a relevant act, and

(b) A does so wholly or mainly because B is a person falling within subsection (2). [E]

(2) A person falls within this subsection if he is—

(a) an employee or officer of an animal research organisation;

(b) a student at an educational establishment that is an animal research organisation;

(c) a lessor or licensor of any premises occupied by an animal research organisation;

(d) a person with a financial interest in, or who provides financial assistance to, an animal research organisation;

(e) a customer or supplier of an animal research organisation;

(f) a person who is contemplating becoming someone within paragraph (c), (d) or (e);

(g) a person who is, or is contemplating becoming, a customer or supplier of someone within paragraph (c), (d), (e) or (f);

(h) an employee or officer of someone within paragraph (c), (d), (e), (f) or (g);
(i) a person with a financial interest in, or who provides financial assistance to, someone within paragraph (c), (d), (e), (f) or (g);
(j) a spouse, civil partner, friend or relative of, or a person who is known personally to, someone within any of paragraphs (a) to (i);
(k) a person who is, or is contemplating becoming, a customer or supplier of someone within paragraph (a), (b), (h), (i) or (j); or
(l) an employer of someone within paragraph (j).

(3) For the purposes of this section, an 'officer' of an animal research organisation or a person includes—
(a) where the organisation or person is a body corporate, a director, manager or secretary;
(b) where the organisation or person is a charity, a charity trustee (within the meaning of the Charities Act 1993 (c. 10));
(c) where the organisation or person is a partnership, a partner.

(4) For the purposes of this section—
(a) a person is a customer or supplier of another person if he purchases goods, services or facilities from, or (as the case may be) supplies goods, services or facilities to, that other; and
(b) 'supplier' includes a person who supplies services in pursuance of any enactment that requires or authorises such services to be provided.

(5) For the purposes of this section, a 'relevant act' is—
(a) an act amounting to a criminal offence, or
(b) a tortious act causing B or another person to suffer loss or damage of any description.

(6) The Secretary of State may by order amend this section so as to include within subsection (2) any description of persons framed by reference to their connection with—
(a) an animal research organisation, or
(b) any description of persons for the time being mentioned in that subsection.

(7) This section does not apply to any act done wholly or mainly in contemplation or furtherance of a trade dispute.

(8) In subsection (7) 'trade dispute' has the meaning given by section 145(7).

148 Animal research organisations

(1) For the purposes of sections 145 and 146 'animal research organisation' means any person or organisation falling within subsection (2) or (3).

(2) A person or organisation falls within this subsection if he or it is the owner, lessee or licensee of premises constituting or including—
(a) a place specified in a licence granted under section 4 or 5 of the 1986 Act,
(b) a scientific procedure establishment designated under section 6 of that Act, or
(c) a breeding or supplying establishment designated under section 7 of that Act.

(3) A person or organisation falls within this subsection if he or it employs, or engages under a contract for services, any of the following in his capacity as such—
(a) the holder of a personal licence granted under section 4 of the 1986 Act,
(b) the holder of a project licence granted under section 5 of that Act,
(c) a person specified under section 6(5) of that Act, or
(d) a person specified under section 7(5) of that Act.

(4) The Secretary of State may by order amend this section so as to include a reference to any description of persons whom he considers to be involved in, or to have a direct connection with persons who are involved in, the application of regulated procedures.

(5) In this section—
'the 1986 Act' means the Animals (Scientific Procedures) Act 1986 (c. 14);
'organisation' includes any institution, trust, undertaking or association of persons;
'premises' includes any place within the meaning of the 1986 Act;
'regulated procedures' has the meaning given by section 2 of the 1986 Act.

149 Extension of sections 145 to 147

(1) The Secretary of State may by order provide for sections 145, 146 and 147 to apply in relation to persons or organisations of a description specified in the order as they apply in relation to animal research organisations.

(2) The Secretary of State may, however, only make an order under this section if satisfied that a series of acts has taken place and—

(a) that those acts were directed at persons or organisations of the description specified in the order or at persons having a connection with them, and

(b) that, if those persons or organisations had been animal research organisations, those acts would have constituted offences under section 145 or 146.

(3) In this section 'organisation' and 'animal research organisation' have the meanings given by section 148.

Malicious Communications Act 1988

1 Offence of sending letters etc. with intent to cause distress or anxiety

(1) Any person who sends to another person—

(a) a letter, electronic communication of any description which conveys—

(i) a message which is indecent or grossly offensive;

(ii) a threat; or

(iii) information which is false and known or believed to be false by the sender; or

(b) any article or electronic communication which is, in whole or part, of an indecent or grossly offensive nature,

is guilty of an offence if his purpose, or one of his purposes, in sending it is that it should, so far as falling within paragraph (a) or (b) above, cause distress or anxiety to the recipient or to any other person to whom he intends that it or its contents or nature should be communicated. [S]

(2) A person is not guilty of an offence by virtue of subsection (1)(a)(ii) above if he shows—

(a) that the threat was used to reinforce a demand made by him on reasonable grounds; and

(b) that he believed, and had reasonable grounds for believing, that the use of the threat was a proper means of reinforcing the demand.

(2A) In this section 'electronic communication' includes—

(a) any oral or other communication by means of a telecommunication system (within the meaning of the Telecommunications Act 1984); and

(b) any communication (however sent) that is in electronic form.

(3) In this section references to sending include references to delivering or transmitting and to causing to be sent, delivered or transmitted and 'sender' shall be construed accordingly.

Communications Act 2003

127 Improper use of public electronic communications network

(1) A person is guilty of an offence if he—

(a) sends by means of a public electronic communications network a message or other matter that is grossly offensive or of an indecent, obscene or menacing character; or

(b) causes any such message or matter to be so sent. [S]

(2) A person is guilty of an offence if, for the purpose of causing annoyance, inconvenience or needless anxiety to another, he—

(a) sends by means of a public electronic communications network, a message that he knows to be false,

(b) causes such a message to be sent; or

(c) persistently makes use of a public electronic communications network. [S]

(4) Subsections (1) and (2) do not apply to anything done in the course of providing a programme service (within the meaning of the Broadcasting Act 1990).

Administration of Justice Act 1970

40 Punishment for unlawful harassment of debtors

(1) A person commits an offence if, with the object of coercing another person to pay money claimed from the other as a debt due under a contract, he—

(a) harasses the other with demands for payment which, in respect of their frequency or the manner or occasion of making any such demand, or of any threat or publicity by which any demand is accompanied, are calculated to subject him or members of his family or household to alarm, distress or humiliation;

(b) falsely represents, in relation to the money claimed, that criminal proceedings lie for failure to pay it;

(c) falsely represents himself to be authorised in some official capacity to claim or enforce payment; or

(d) utters a document falsely represented by him to have some official character or purporting to have some official character which he knows it has not. [S]

(2) A person may be guilty of an offence by virtue of subsection 1 (a) above if he concerts with others in the taking of such action as is described in that paragraph, notwithstanding that his own course of conduct does not by itself amount to harassment.

(3) Subsection 1 (a) above does not apply to anything done by a person which is reasonable (and otherwise permissible in law) for the purpose—

(a) of securing the discharge of an obligation due, or believed by him to be due, to himself or to persons for whom he acts, or protecting himself or them from future loss; or

(b) of the enforcement of any liability by legal process.

Protection from Eviction Act 1977

1 Unlawful eviction and harassment of occupier

(1) In this section 'residential occupier', in relation to any premises, means a person occupying the premises as a residence, whether under a contract or by virtue of any enactment or rule of law giving him the right to remain in occupation or restricting the right of any person to recover possession of the premises.

(2) If any person unlawfully deprives the residential occupier of any premises of his occupation of the premises or any part thereof, or attempts to do so, he shall be guilty of an offence unless he proves that he believed, and had reasonable cause to believe, that the residential occupier had ceased to reside in the premises. [E]

(3) If any person with intent to cause the residential occupier of any premises—

(a) to give up the occupation of the premises or any part thereof; or

(b) to refrain from exercising any right or pursuing any remedy in respect of the premises or part thereof;

does acts likely to interfere with the peace or comfort of the residential occupier or members of his household, or persistently withdraws or withholds services reasonably required for the occupation of the premises as a residence, he shall be guilty of an offence. [E]

(3A) Subject to subsection (3B) below, the landlord of a residential occupier or an agent of the landlord shall be guilty of an offence if—

(a) he does acts likely to interfere with the peace or comfort of the residential occupier or members of his household, or

(b) he persistently withdraws or withholds services reasonably required for the occupation of the premises in question as a residence,

and (in either case) he knows, or has reasonable cause to believe, that that conduct is likely to cause the residential occupier to give up the occupation of the whole or part of the premises or to refrain from exercising any right or pursuing any remedy in respect of the whole or part of the premises. [E]

(3B) A person shall not be guilty of an offence under subsection (3A) above if he proves that he had reasonable grounds for doing the acts or withdrawing or withholding the services in question.

(3C) In subsection (3A) above 'landlord', in relation to a residential occupier of any premises, means the person who, but for—

(a) the residential occupier's right to remain in occupation of the premises, or

(b) a restriction on the person's right to recover possession of the premises,

would be entitled to occupation of the premises and any superior landlord under whom that person derives title.

Criminal Law Act 1977

51 Bomb hoaxes

(1) A person who—

(a) places any article in any place whatever; or

(b) dispatches any article by post, rail or any other means whatever of sending things from one place to another,

with the intention (in either case) of inducing in some other person a belief that it is likely to explode or ignite and thereby cause personal injury or damage to property is guilty of an offence.

In this subsection 'article' includes substance. [E]

(2) A person who communicates any information which he knows or believes to be false to another person with the intention of inducing in him or any other person a false belief that a bomb or other thing liable to explode or ignite is present in any place or location whatever is guilty of an offence. [E]

(3) For a person to be guilty of an offence under subsection (1) or (2) above it is not necessary for him to have any particular person in mind as the person in whom he intends to induce the belief mentioned in that subsection.

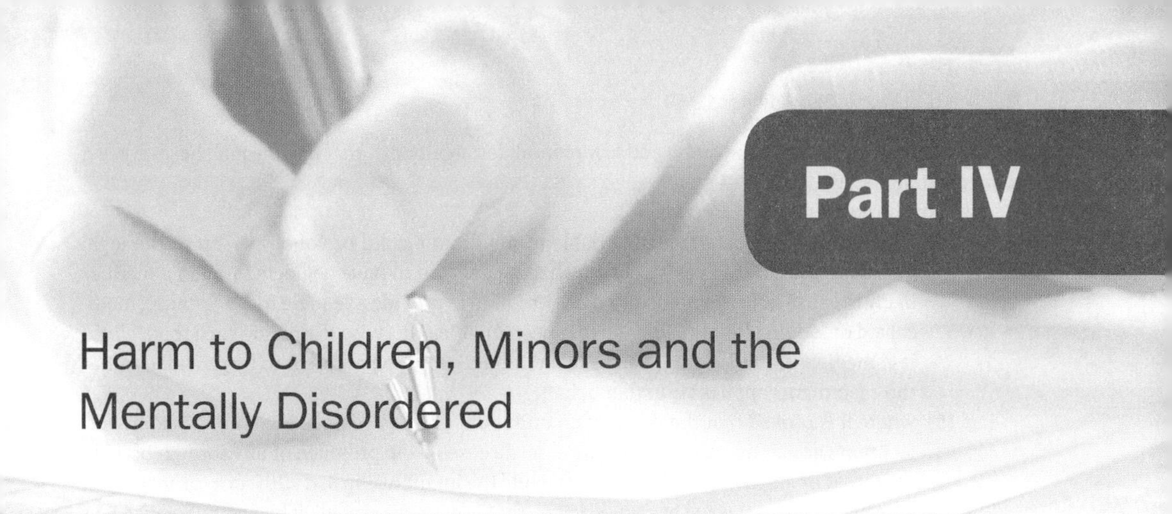

Part IV

Harm to Children, Minors and the Mentally Disordered

(a) Children and Minors

Offences Against the Person Act 1861

27 Exposing child, whereby life is endangered, or health permanently injured
Whosoever shall unlawfully abandon or expose any child, being under the age of two years, whereby the life of such child shall be endangered, or the health of such child shall have been or shall be likely to be permanently injured, shall be guilty of an offence, and being convicted thereof shall be liable to imprisonment for a term not exceeding five years. [E]

Licensing Act 1902

2 Penalty for being drunk while in charge of child

(1) If any person is found drunk in any highway or other public place, whether a building or not, or on any licensed premises, while having the charge of a child apparently under the age of seven years, he may be apprehended, and shall, if the child is under that age, be liable on summary conviction, to a fine not exceeding level 2 on the standard scale or to imprisonment for any period not exceeding one month. [S]

(2) If the child appears to the court to be under the age of seven the child shall, for the purposes of this section, be deemed to be under that age unless the contrary is proved.

8 Interpretation of 'public place'
For the purposes of section twelve of the Licensing Act, 1872, and of sections one and two of this Act, the expression 'public place' shall include any place to which the public have access, whether on payment or otherwise.

Children and Young Persons Act 1933

1 Cruelty to persons under sixteen

(1) If any person who has attained the age of sixteen years and has responsibility for any child or young person under that age, wilfully assaults, ill-treats, neglects, abandons, or exposes him, or causes or procures him to be assaulted, ill-treated, neglected, abandoned, or exposed, in a manner likely to cause him unnecessary suffering or injury to health (including injury to or loss of sight, or

hearing, or limb, or organ of the body, and any mental derangement), that person shall be guilty of a misdemeanour . . . [E]

(2) For the purposes of this section—

(a) a parent or other person legally liable to maintain a child or young person or the legal guardian of a child or young person shall be deemed to have neglected him in a manner likely to cause injury to his health if he has failed to provide adequate food, clothing, medical aid or lodging for him, or if, having been unable otherwise to provide such food, clothing, medical aid or lodging, he has failed to take steps to procure it to be provided under the enactments applicable in that behalf;

(b) where it is proved that the death of an infant under three years of age was caused by suffocation (not being suffocation caused by disease or the presence of any foreign body in the throat or air passages of the infant) while the infant was in bed with some other person who has attained the age of sixteen years, that other person shall, if he was, when he went to bed, under the influence of drink, be deemed to have neglected the infant in a manner likely to cause injury to its health.

(3) A person may be convicted of an offence under this section—

(a) notwithstanding that actual suffering or injury to health, or the likelihood of actual suffering or injury to health, was obviated by the action of another person;

(b) notwithstanding the death of the child or young person in question.

3 Allowing persons under sixteen to be in brothels

(1) If any person having responsibility for a child or young person who has attained the age of four years and is under the age of sixteen years, allows that child or young person to reside in or to frequent a brothel, he shall be liable on summary conviction, to a fine not exceeding level 2 on the standard scale, or alternatively . . . or in addition thereto, to imprisonment for any term not exceeding six months. [S]

5 Giving intoxicating liquor to children under five

If any person gives, or causes to be given, to any child under the age of five years any intoxicating liquor, except upon the order of a duly qualified medical practitioner, or in case of sickness, apprehended sickness, or other urgent cause, he shall, on summary conviction, be liable to a fine not exceeding level 1 on the standard scale. [S]

7 Sale of tobacco, etc., to persons under sixteen

(1) Any person who sells to a person under the age of sixteen years any tobacco or cigarette papers, whether for his own use or not, shall be liable on summary conviction to a fine not exceeding level 4 on the standard scale. [S]

(1A) It shall be a defence for a person charged with an offence under subsection (1) above to prove that he took all reasonable precautions and exercised all due diligence to avoid the commission of the offence.

(5) For the purposes of this section the expression 'tobacco' includes cigarettes, any product containing tobacco and intended for oral or nasal use and smoking mixtures intended as a substitute for tobacco, and the expression 'cigarette' includes cut tobacco rolled up in papers, tobacco leaf, or other material in such form as to be capable of immediate use for smoking.

11 Exposing children under twelve to risk of burning

If any person who has attained the age of sixteen years, having responsibility for any child under the age of twelve years, allows the child to be in any room containing an open fire grate or any heating appliance liable to cause injury to a person by contact therewith not sufficiently protected to guard against the risk of his being burnt or scalded without taking reasonable precautions against that risk, and by reason thereof the child is killed or suffers serious injury, he shall on summary conviction be liable to a fine not exceeding level 1 on the standard scale:

Provided that neither this section, nor any proceedings taken thereunder shall affect any liability of any such person to be proceeded against by indictment for any indictable offence. [S]

17 Interpretation of Part I

(1) For the purposes of this Part of this Act, the following shall be presumed to have responsibility for a child or young person—

(a) Any person who—

(i) has parental responsibility for him (within the meaning of the Children Act 1989); or

(ii) is otherwise legally liable to maintain him; and

(b) any person who has care of him.

(2) A person who is presumed to be responsible for a child or young person by virtue of subsection (1)(a) shall not be taken to have ceased to be responsible for him by reason only that he does not have care of him.

18 Restrictions on employment of children

(1) Subject to the provisions of this section and of any byelaws made thereunder no child shall be employed—

(a) so long as he is under the age of fourteen years; or

(b) to do any work other than light work before the close of school hours on any day on which he is required to attend school; or

(c) before seven o'clock in the morning or after seven o'clock in the evening on any day; or

(d) for more than two hours on any day on which he is required to attend school; or

(e) for more than two hours on any Sunday; or

(f) to lift, carry or move anything so heavy as to be likely to cause injury to him. [S]

23 Prohibition against persons under sixteen taking part in performances endangering life or limb

No person under the age of sixteen, and no child aged sixteen years shall take part in any performance to which section 37 of the Children and Young Persons Act 1963 applies and in which his life or limbs are endangered and every person who causes or procures such a person or child, or being his parent or guardian allows him, to take part in such a performance, shall be liable on summary conviction to a fine not exceeding level 3 on the standard scale:

Provided that no proceedings shall be taken under this subsection except by or with the authority of a chief officer of police. [S]

24 Restrictions on training for performances of a dangerous nature

(1) No child under the age of twelve years shall be trained to take part in performances of a dangerous nature, and no child who has attained that age shall be trained to take part in such performances except under and in accordance with the terms of a licence granted and in force under this section; and every person who causes or procures a person, or being his parent or guardian allows him, to be trained to take part in performances of a dangerous nature in contravention of this section, shall be liable on summary conviction to a fine not exceeding level 3 on the standard scale. [S]

(2) A local authority may grant a licence for a child who has attained the age of twelve years but is under the age of sixteen years to be trained to take part in performances of a dangerous nature.

Education Act 1996

548 No right to give corporal punishment

(1) Corporal punishment given by, or on the authority of, a member of staff to a child—

(a) for whom education is provided at any school, or

(b) for whom education is provided, otherwise than at school, under any arrangements made by a local education authority, or

(c) for whom specified nursery education is provided otherwise than at school, cannot be justified in any proceedings on the ground that it was given in pursuance of a right exercisable by the member of staff by virtue of his position as such.

(2) Subsection (1) applies to corporal punishment so given to a child at any time, whether at the school or other place at which education is provided for the child, or elsewhere.

(3) The following provisions have effect for the purposes of this section.

(4) Any reference to giving corporal punishment to a child is to doing anything for the purpose of punishing that child (whether or not there are other reasons for doing it) which, apart from any justification, would constitute battery.

(5) However, corporal punishment shall not be taken to be given to a child by virtue of anything done for reasons that include averting—

(a) an immediate danger of personal injury to, or
(b) an immediate danger to the property of,

any person (including the child himself).

(6) 'Member of staff', in relation to the child concerned, means—

(a) any person who works as a teacher at the school or other place at which education is provided for the child, or
(b) any other person who (whether in connection with the provision of education for the child or otherwise)—
  (i) works at that school or place, or—
  (ii) otherwise provides his services there (whether or not for payment), and has lawful control or charge of the child.

(7) 'Child' (except in subsection (8)) means a person under the age of 18.

(8) 'Specified nursery education' means full-time or part-time education suitable for children who have not attained compulsory school age which is provided—

(a) by a local education authority; or
(b) by any other person—
  (i) who is (or is to be) in receipt of financial assistance given by such an authority and whose provision of nursery education is taken into account by the authority in formulating proposals for the purposes of section 120(2)(a) of the School Standards and Framework Act 1998, or
  (ii) who is (or is to be) in receipt of grants under section 1 of the Nursery Education and Grant-Maintained Schools Act 1996; or
(c) (otherwise than as mentioned in paragraph (a) or (b)) in any educational institution which would fall within section 4(1) above (definition of 'school') but for the fact that it provides part-time, rather than full-time, primary education.

550A Power of members of staff to restrain pupils

(1) A member of the staff of a school may use, in relation to any pupil at the school, such force as is reasonable in the circumstances for the purpose of preventing the pupil from doing (or continuing to do) any of the following, namely—

(a) committing any offence,
(b) causing personal injury to, or damage to the property of, any person (including the pupil himself), or
(c) engaging in any behaviour prejudicial to the maintenance of good order and discipline at the school or among any of its pupils, whether that behaviour occurs during a teaching session or otherwise.

(2) Subsection (1) applies where a member of the staff of a school is—

(a) on the premises of the school, or
(b) elsewhere at a time when, as a member of its staff, he has lawful control or charge of the pupil concerned;

but it does not authorise anything to be done in relation to a pupil which constitutes the giving of corporal punishment within the meaning of section 548.

(3) Subsection (1) shall not be taken to prevent any person from relying on any defence available to him otherwise than by virtue of this section.

(4) In this section—

'member of the staff', in relation to a school, means any teacher who works at the school and any other person who, with the authority of the head teacher, has lawful control or charge of pupils at the school;

'offence' includes anything that would be an offence but for the operation of any presumption that a person under a particular age is incapable of committing an offence.

550B Detention outside school hours lawful despite absence of parental consent

(1) Where a pupil to whom this section applies is required on disciplinary grounds to spend a period of time in detention at his school after the end of any school session, his detention shall not be rendered unlawful by virtue of the absence of his parent's consent to it if the conditions set out in subsection (3) are satisfied.

(2) This section applies to any pupil who has not attained the age of 18 and is attending—

(a) a school maintained by a local education authority; or

(c) a city technology college, city college for the technology of the arts, or city academy.

(3) The conditions referred to in subsection (1) are as follows—

(a) the head teacher of the school must have previously determined, and have—

(i) made generally known within the school, and

(ii) taken steps to bring to the attention of the parent of every person who is for the time being a registered pupil there,

that the detention of pupils after the end of a school session is one of the measures that may be taken with a view to regulating the conduct of pupils;

(b) the detention must be imposed by the head teacher or by another teacher at the school specifically or generally authorised by him for the purpose;

(c) the detention must be reasonable in all the circumstances; and

(d) the pupil's parent must have been given at least 24 hours' notice in writing that the detention was due to take place.

(4) In determining for the purposes of subsection (3)(c) whether a pupil's detention is reasonable, the following matters in particular shall be taken into account—

(a) whether the detention constitutes a proportionate punishment in the circumstances of the case; and

(b) any special circumstances relevant to its imposition on the pupil which are known to the person imposing it (or of which he ought reasonably to be aware) including in particular—

(i) the pupil's age,

(ii) any special educational needs he may have,

(iii) any religious requirements affecting him, and

(iv) here arrangements have to be made for him to travel from the school to his home, whether suitable alternative arrangements can reasonably be made by his parent.

Children Act 2004

58 Reasonable punishment

[see page 21]

Sexual Offences Act 2003

5 Rape of a child under 13

(1) A person commits an offence if—

(a) he intentionally penetrates the vagina, anus or mouth of another person with his penis, and

(b) the other person is under 13. [I]

6 Assault of a child under 13 by penetration

(1) A person commits an offence if—

(a) he intentionally penetrates the vagina or anus of another person with a part of his body or anything else,

(b) the penetration is sexual, and

(c) the other person is under 13. [I]

7 Sexual assault of a child under 13

(1) A person commits an offence if—

(a) he intentionally touches another person,

(b) the touching is sexual, and

(c) the other person is under 13. [E]

8 Causing or inciting a child under 13 to engage in sexual activity

(1) A person commits an offence if—

(a) he intentionally causes or incites another person (B) to engage in an activity,

(b) the activity is sexual, and

(c) B is under 13. [E]

(2) A person guilty of an offence under this section, if the activity caused or incited involved—

(a) penetration of B's anus or vagina,

(b) penetration of B's mouth with a person's penis,

(c) penetration of a person's anus or vagina with a part of B's body or by B with anything else, or

(d) penetration of a person's mouth with B's penis,

is liable, on conviction on indictment, to imprisonment for life.

9 Sexual activity with a child

(1) A person aged 18 or over (A) commits an offence if—

(a) he intentionally touches another person (B),

(b) the touching is sexual, and

(c) either—

(i) B is under 16 and A does not reasonably believe that B is 16 or over, or

(ii) B is under 13. [E]

(2) A person guilty of an offence under this section, if the touching involved—

(a) penetration of B's anus or vagina with a part of A's body or anything else,

(b) penetration of B's mouth with A's penis,

(c) penetration of A's anus or vagina with a part of B's body, or

(d) penetration of A's mouth with B's penis,

is liable, on conviction on indictment, to imprisonment for a term not exceeding 14 years.

10 Causing or inciting a child to engage in sexual activity

Sexual Offences Act 2003

(1) A person aged 18 or over (A) commits an offence if—

(a) he intentionally causes or incites another person (B) to engage in an activity,

(b) the activity is sexual, and

(c) either—

(i) B is under 16 and A does not reasonably believe that B is 16 or over, or
(ii) B is under 13. [E]

(2) A person guilty of an offence under this section, if the activity caused or incited involved—
(a) penetration of B's anus or vagina,
(b) penetration of B's mouth with a person's penis,
(c) penetration of a person's anus or vagina with a part of B's body or by B with anything else, or
(d) penetration of a person's mouth with B's penis,

is liable, on conviction on indictment, to imprisonment for a term not exceeding 14 years.

11 Engaging in sexual activity in the presence of a child

(1) A person aged 18 or over (A) commits an offence if—
(a) he intentionally engages in an activity,
(b) the activity is sexual,
(c) for the purpose of obtaining sexual gratification, he engages in it—
(i) when another person (B) is present or is in a place from which A can be observed, and,
(ii) knowing or believing that B is aware, or intending that B should be aware,

that he is engaging in it, and
(d) either—
(i) B is under 16 and A does not reasonably believe that B is 16 or over, or
(ii) B is under 13. [E]

12 Causing a child to watch a sexual act

(1) A person aged 18 or over (A) commits an offence if—
(a) for the purpose of obtaining sexual gratification, he intentionally causes another person (B) to watch a third person engaging in an activity, or to look at an image of any person engaging in an activity,
(b) the activity is sexual, and
(c) either—
(i) B is under 16 and A does not reasonably believe that B is 16 or over, or
(ii) B is under 13. [E]

13 Child sex offences committed by children or young persons

(1) A person under 18 commits an offence if he does anything which would be an offence under any of sections 9 to 12 if he were aged 18. [E]

14 Arranging or facilitating commission of a child sex offence

(1) A person commits an offence if—
(a) he intentionally arranges or facilitates something that he intends to do, intends another person to do, or believes that another person will do, in any part of the world, and
(b) doing it will involve the commission of an offence under any of sections 9 to 13.

(2) A person does not commit an offence under this section if—
(a) he arranges or facilitates something that he believes another person will do, but that he does not intend to do or intend another person to do, and
(b) any offence within subsection (1)(b) would be an offence against a child for whose protection he acts.

(3) For the purposes of subsection (2), a person acts for the protection of a child if he acts for the purpose of—
(a) protecting the child from sexually transmitted infection,
(b) protecting the physical safety of the child,
(c) preventing the child from becoming pregnant, and
(d) promoting the child's emotional well-being by the giving of advice,

and not for the purpose of obtaining sexual gratification or for the purpose of causing or encouraging the activity constituting the offence within subsection (1)(b) or the child's participation in it. [E]

15 Meeting a child following sexual grooming, etc.

(1) A person aged 18 or over (A) commits an offence if—

(a) A has met or communicated with another person (B) on at least two occasions and subsequently—

(i) A intentionally meets B,

(ii) A travels with the intention of meeting B in any part of the world or arranges to meet B in any part of the world, or

(iii) B travels with the intention of meeting A in any part of the world,

(b) A intends to do anything to or in respect of B, during or after the meeting mentioned in paragraph (a)(i) to (iii) and in any part of the world, which if done will involve the commission by A of a relevant offence.

(c) B is under 16, and

(d) A does not reasonably believe that B is 16 or over.

(2) In subsection (1)—

(a) the reference to A having met or communicated with B is a reference to A having met B in any part of the world or having communicated with B by any means from, to or in any part of the world;

(b) 'relevant offence' means—

(i) an offence under this Act,

(ii) an offence within any of paragraphs 61 to 92 of Schedule 3, or

(iii) anything done outside England and Wales and Northern Ireland which is not an offence within sub-paragraph (i) or (ii) but would be an offence within sub-paragraph (i) if done in England and Wales. [E]

16 Abuse of position of trust: sexual activity with a child

(1) A person aged 18 or over (A) commits an offence if—

(a) he intentionally touches another person (B),

(b) the touching is sexual,

(c) A is in a position of trust in relation to B, and

(d) where subsection (2) applies, A knows or could reasonably be expected to know of the circumstances by virtue of which he is in a position of trust in relation to B, and

(e) either—

(i) B is under 18 and A does not reasonably believe that B is 18 or over, or

(ii) B is under 13.

(2) This subsection applies where A—

(a) is in a position of trust in relation to B by virtue of circumstances within section 21 (2), (3), (4) or (5), and

(b) is not in such a position of trust by virtue of other circumstances.

(3) Where in proceedings for an offence under this section it is proved that the other person was under 18, the defendant is to be taken not to have reasonably believed that that person was 18 or over unless sufficient evidence is adduced to raise an issue as to whether he reasonably believed it.

(4) Where in proceedings for an offence under this section—

(a) it is proved that the defendant was in a position of trust in relation to the other person by virtue of circumstances within section 21(2), (3), (4) or (5), and

(b) it is not proved that he was in such a position of trust by virtue of other circumstances,

it is to be taken that the defendant knew or could reasonably have been expected to know of the circumstances by virtue of which he was in such a position of trust unless sufficient evidence is adduced to raise an issue as to whether he knew or could reasonably have been expected to know of those circumstances. [E]

17 Abuse of position of trust: causing or inciting a child to engage in sexual activity

(1) A person aged 18 or over (A) commits an offence if—

(a) he intentionally causes or incites another person (B) to engage in an activity,
(b) the activity is sexual,
(c) A is in a position of trust in relation to B,
(d) where subsection (2) applies, A knows or could reasonably be expected to know of the circumstances by virtue of which he is in a position of trust in relation to B, and
(e) either—
(i) B is under 18 and A does not reasonably believe that B is 18 or over, or
(ii) B is under 13.

(2) This subsection applies where A—
(a) is in a position of trust in relation to B by virtue of circumstances within section 21 (2), (3), (4) or (5), and
(b) is not in such a position of trust by virtue of other circumstances.

(3) Where in proceedings for an offence under this section it is proved that the other person was under 18, the defendant is to be taken not to have reasonably believed that that person was 18 or over unless sufficient evidence is adduced to raise an issue as to whether he reasonably believed it.

(4) Where in proceedings for an offence under this section—
(a) it is proved that the defendant was in a position of trust in relation to the other person by virtue of circumstances within section 21(2), (3), (4) or (5), and
(b) it is not proved that he was in such a position of trust by virtue of other circumstances,

it is to be taken that the defendant knew or could reasonably have been expected to know of the circumstances by virtue of which he was in such a position of trust unless sufficient evidence is adduced to raise an issue as to whether he knew or could reasonably have been expected to know of those circumstances. [E]

18 Abuse of position of trust: sexual activity in the presence of a child

(1) A person aged 18 or over (A) commits an offence if—
(a) he intentionally engages in an activity,
(b) the activity is sexual,
(c) for the purpose of obtaining sexual gratification, he engages in it (i) when another person (B) is present, or is in a place from which A can be observed, and (ii), knowing or believing that B is aware, or intending that B should be aware, that he is engaging in it,
(d) A is in a position of trust in relation to B,
(e) where subsection (2) applies, A knows or could reasonably be expected to know of the circumstances by virtue of which he is in a position of trust in relation to B, and
(f) either—
(i) B is under 18 and A does not reasonably believe that B is 18 or over, or
(ii) B is under 13.

(2) This subsection applies where A—
(a) is in a position of trust in relation to B by virtue of circumstances within section 21 (2), (3), (4) or (5), and
(b) is not in such a position of trust by virtue of other circumstances.

(3) Where in proceedings for an offence under this section it is proved that the other person was under 18, the defendant is to be taken not to have reasonably believed that that person was 18 or over unless sufficient evidence is adduced to raise an issue as to whether he reasonably believed it.

(4) Where in proceedings for an offence under this section—
(a) it is proved that the defendant was in a position of trust in relation to the other person by virtue of circumstances within section 21(2), (3), (4) or (5), and
(b) it is not proved that he was in such a position of trust by virtue of other circumstances,

it is to be taken that the defendant knew or could reasonably have been expected to know of the circumstances by virtue of which he was in such a position of trust unless sufficient evidence is adduced to raise an issue as to whether he knew or could reasonably have been expected to know of those circumstances. [E]

19 Abuse of position of trust: causing a child to watch a sexual act

(1) A person aged 18 or over (A) commits an offence if—

(a) for the purpose of obtaining sexual gratification, he intentionally causes another person (B) to watch a third person engaging in an activity, or to look at an image of any person engaging in an activity,

(b) the activity is sexual,

(c) A is in a position of trust in relation to B,

(d) where subsection (2) applies, A knows or could reasonably be expected to know of the circumstances by virtue of which he is in a position of trust in relation to B, and

(e) either—

(i) B is under 18 and A does not reasonably believe that B is 18 or over, or

(ii) B is under 13.

(2) This subsection applies where A—

(a) is in a position of trust in relation to B by virtue of circumstances within section 21(2), (3), (4) or (5), and

(b) is not in such a position of trust by virtue of other circumstances.

(3) Where in proceedings for an offence under this section it is proved that the other person was under 18, the defendant is to be taken not to have reasonably believed that that person was 18 or over unless sufficient evidence is adduced to raise an issue as to whether he reasonably believed it.

(4) Where in proceedings for an offence under this section—

(a) it is proved that the defendant was in a position of trust in relation to the other person by virtue of circumstances within section 21(2), (3), (4) or (5), and

(b) it is not proved that he was in such a position of trust by virtue of other circumstances, it is to be taken that the defendant knew or could reasonably have been expected to know of the circumstances by virtue of which he was in such a position of trust unless sufficient evidence is adduced to raise an issue as to whether he knew or could reasonably have been expected to know of those circumstances. [E]

20 Abuse of position of trust: acts done in Scotland

Anything which, if done in England and Wales, . . . would constitute an offence under any of sections 16 to 19 also constitutes that offence if done in Scotland.

21 Positions of trust

(1) For the purposes of sections 16 to 19, a person (A) is in a position of trust in relation to another person (B) if—

(a) any following subsections applies, or

(b) any condition specified in an order made by the Secretary of State is met.

(2) This subsection applies if A looks after persons under 18 who are detained in an institution by virtue of a court order or under an enactment, and B is so detained in that institution.

(3) This subsection applies if A looks after persons under 18 who are resident in a home or other place in which—

(a) accommodation and maintenance are provided by an authority under section 23(2) of the Children Act 1989, . . . or

(b) accommodation is provided by a voluntary organisation under section 59(1) of that Act . . .

and B is resident, and is so provided with accommodation and maintenance or accommodation, in that place.

(4) This subsection applies if A looks after persons under 18 who are accommodated and cared for in one of the following institutions—

(a) a hospital,

(b) an independent clinic,

(c) a care home, residential care home or private hospital,

(d) a community home, voluntary home or children's home,
(e) a home provided under section 82(5) of the Children Act 1989, or
(f) a residential family centre,

and B is accommodated and cared for in that institution.

(5) This subsection applies if A looks after persons under 18 who are receiving education at an educational institution and B is receiving, and A is not receiving, education at that institution.

(7) This subsection applies if A is engaged in the provision of services under, or pursuant to anything done under—

(a) sections 8 to 10 of the Employment and Training Act 1973, or
(b) section 114 of the Learning and Skills Act 2000,

and, in that capacity, looks after B on an individual basis.

(8) This subsection applies if A regularly has unsupervised contact with B (whether face to face or by any other means)—

(a) in the exercise of functions of a local authority under section 20 or 21 of the Children Act 1989,...

(9) This subsection applies if A, as a person who is to report to the court under section 7 of the Children Act 1989... on matters relating to the welfare of B, regularly has unsupervised contact with B (whether face to face or by any other means).

(10) This subsection applies if A is a personal adviser appointed for B under—

(a) section 23B(2) of, or paragraph 19C of Schedule 2 to, the Children Act 1989... and, in that capacity, looks after B on an individual basis.

(11) This subsection applies if—

(a) B is subject to a care order, a supervision order or an education supervision order, and
(b) in the exercise of functions conferred by virtue of the order on an authorised person or the authority designated by the order, A looks after B on an individual basis.

(12) This subsection applies if A—

(a) is an officer of the Service appointed for B under section 41(1) of the Children Act 1989,
(b) is appointed a children's guardian of B under rule 6 or rule 18 of the Adoption Rules 1984 (S.I. 1984/265), or
(c) is appointed to be the guardian ad litem of B under rule 9.5 of the Family Proceedings Rules 1991 (S.I. 1991/1247)...

and, in that capacity, regularly has unsupervised contact with B (whether face to face or by any other means).

(13) This subsection applies if—

(a) B is subject to requirements imposed by or under an enactment on his release from detention for a criminal offence, or is subject to requirements imposed by a court order made in criminal proceedings, and
(b) A looks after B on an individual basis in pursuance of the requirements.

22 Positions of trust: interpretation

(1) The following provisions apply for the purposes of section 21.

(2) Subject to subsection (3), a person looks after persons under 18 if he is regularly involved in caring for, training, supervising or being in sole charge of such persons.

(3) A person (A) looks after another person (B) on an individual basis if—

(a) A is regularly involved in caring for, training or supervising B, and
(b) in the course of his involvement, A regularly has unsupervised contact with B alone (whether face to face or by any other means).

(4) A person receives education at an educational institution if—

(a) he is registered or otherwise enrolled as a pupil or student at the institution, or
(b) he receives education at the institution under arrangements with another educational institution at which he is so registered or otherwise enrolled.

(5) In section 21—

'authority'—

(a) in relation to England and Wales, means a local authority;

...

'care home' means an establishment which is a care home for the purposes of the Care Standards Act 2000;

'children's home' has—

(a) in relation to England and Wales, the meaning given by section 1 of the Care Standards Act 2000,

...

'community home' has the meaning given by section 53 of the Children Act 1989 (c. 41);

'hospital'—

(a) in relation to England and Wales, means a hospital within the meaning given by section 128(1) of the National Health Service Act 1977, or any other establishment which is a hospital within the meaning given by section 2(3) of the Care Standards Act 2000;

...

'independent clinic' has—

(a) in relation to England and Wales, the meaning given by section 2 of the Care Standards Act 2000;

...

'voluntary home' has—

(a) in relation to England and Wales, the meaning given by section 60(3) of the Children Act 1989.

23 Sections 16 to 19: marriage exception

(1) Conduct by a person (A) which would otherwise be an offence under any of sections 16 to 19 against another person (B) is not an offence under that section if at the time—

(a) B is 16 or over, and

(b) A and B are lawfully married.

(2) In proceedings for such an offence it is for the defendant to prove that A and B were lawfully married at the time.

24 Sections 16 to 19: sexual relationships which pre-date position of trust

(1) Conduct by a person (A) which would otherwise be an offence under any of sections 16 to 19 against another person (B) is not an offence under that section if, immediately before the position of trust arose, a sexual relationship existed between A and B.

(2) Subsection (1) does not apply if at that time sexual intercourse between A and B would have been unlawful.

(3) In proceedings for an offence under any of sections 16 to 19 it is for the defendant to prove that such a relationship existed at that time.

25 Sexual activity with a child family member

(1) A person (A) commits an offence if—

(a) he intentionally touches another person (B),

(b) the touching is sexual,

(c) the relation of A to B is within section 27,

(d) A knows or could reasonably be expected to know that his relation to B is of a description falling within that section, and

(e) either—

(i) B is under 18 and A does not reasonably believe that B is 18 or over, or

(ii) B is under 13.

(2) Where in proceedings for an offence under this section it is proved that the other person was under 18, the defendant is to be taken not to have reasonably believed that that person was 18 or over unless sufficient evidence is adduced to raise an issue as to whether he reasonably believed it.

(3) Where in proceedings for an offence under this section it is proved that the relation of the defendant to the other person was of a description falling within section 27, it is to be taken that the defendant knew or could reasonably have been expected to know that his relation to the other person was of that description unless sufficient evidence is adduced to raise an issue as to whether he knew or could reasonably have been expected to know that it was. [E]

(4) A person guilty of an offence under this section, if aged 18 or over at the time of the offence, is liable—

(a) where subsection (6) applies, on conviction on indictment to imprisonment for a term not exceeding 14 years;

(b) in any other case—

(i) on summary conviction, to imprisonment for a term not exceeding 6 months or a fine not exceeding the statutory maximum or both;

(ii) on conviction on indictment, to imprisonment for a term not exceeding 14 years.

(5) Unless subsection (4) applies, a person guilty of an offence under this section is liable—

(a) on summary conviction, to imprisonment for a term not exceeding 6 months or a fine not exceeding the statutory maximum or both;

(b) on conviction on indictment, to imprisonment for a term not exceeding 5 years.

(6) This subsection applies where the touching involved—

(a) penetration of B's anus or vagina with a part of A's body or anything else,

(b) penetration of B's mouth with A's penis,

(c) penetration of A's anus or vagina with a part of B's body, or

(d) penetration of A's mouth with B's penis.

26 Inciting a child family member to engage in sexual activity

(1) A person (A) commits an offence if—

(a) he intentionally incites another person (B) to touch, or allow himself to be touched by, A,

(b) the touching is sexual,

(c) the relation of A to B is within section 27,

(d) A knows or could reasonably be expected to know that his relation to B is of a description falling within that section, and

(e) either—

(i) B is under 18 and A does not reasonably believe that B is 18 or over, or

(ii) B is under 13.

(2) Where in proceedings for an offence under this section it is proved that the other person was under 18, the defendant is to be taken not to have reasonably believed that that person was 18 or over unless sufficient evidence is adduced to raise an issue as to whether he reasonably believed it.

(3) Where in proceedings for an offence under this section it is proved that the relation of the defendant to the other person was of a description falling within section 27, it is to be taken that the defendant knew or could reasonably have been expected to know that his relation to the other person was of that description unless sufficient evidence is adduced to raise an issue as to whether he knew or could reasonably have been expected to know that it was. [E]

(4) A person guilty of an offence under this section, if he was aged 18 or over at the time of the offence, is liable—

(a) where subsection (6) applies, on conviction on indictment to imprisonment for a term not exceeding 14 years;

(b) in any other case—

(i) on summary conviction, to imprisonment for a term not exceeding 6 months or a fine not exceeding the statutory maximum or both;

(ii) on conviction on indictment, to imprisonment for a term not exceeding 14 years.

(5) Unless subsection (4) applies, a person guilty of an offence under this section is liable—

(a) on summary conviction, to imprisonment for a term not exceeding 6 months or a fine not exceeding the statutory maximum or both;

(b) on conviction on indictment, to imprisonment for a term not exceeding 5 years.

(6) This subsection applies where the touching to which the incitement related involved—
(a) penetration of B's anus or vagina with a part of A's body or anything else,
(b) penetration of B's mouth with A's penis,
(c) penetration of A's anus or vagina with a part of B's body, or
(d) penetration of A's mouth with B's penis.

27 Family relationships

(1) The relation of one person (A) to another (B) is within this section if—
(a) it is within any of subsections (2) to (4), or
(b) it would be within one of those subsections but for section 39 of the Adoption Act 1976 or section 67 of the Adoption and Children Act 2002 (status conferred by adoption).
(2) The relation of A to B is within this subsection if—
(a) one of them is the other's parent, grandparent, brother, sister, half-brother, half-sister, aunt or uncle, or
(b) A is or has been B's foster parent.
(3) The relation of A to B is within this subsection if A and B live or have lived in the same household, or A is or has been regularly involved in caring for, training, supervising or being in sole charge of B, and—
(a) one of them is or has been the partner of the other's step-parent,
(b) A and B are cousins, or
(c) one of them is or has been the other's stepbrother or stepsister, or
(d) the parent or present or former foster parent of one of them is or has been the other's foster parent.
(4) The relation of A to B is within this subsection if—
(a) A and B live in the same household, and
(b) A is regularly involved in caring for, training, supervising or being in sole charge of B.
(5) For the purposes of this section—
(a) 'aunt' means the sister or half-sister of a person's parent, and 'uncle' has a corresponding meaning;
(b) 'cousin' means the child of an aunt or uncle;
(c) a person is a child's foster parent if—
(i) he is a person with whom the child has been placed under sections 23 (2) (a) or 59(1)(a) of the Children Act 1989 (fostering for local authority or voluntary organisation), or
(ii) he fosters the child privately, within the meaning given by section 66(1) (b) of that Act;
(d) a person is another's partner (whether they are of different sexes or the same sex) if they live together as partners in an enduring family relationship;
(e) 'stepbrother' and 'stepsister' include the child of a parent's partner.

28 Sections 25 and 26: marriage exception

(1) Conduct by a person (A) which would otherwise be an offence under section 25 or 26 against another person (B) is not an offence under that section if at the time—
(a) B is 16 or over, and
(b) A and B are lawfully married.
(2) In proceedings for such an offence it is for the defendant to prove that A and B were lawfully married at the time.

29 Sections 25 and 26: sexual relationships which pre-date family relationships

(1) Conduct by a person (A) which would otherwise be an offence under section 25 or 26 against another person (B) is not an offence under that section if—
(a) the relation of A to B is not within subsection (2) of section 27,
(b) it would not be within that subsection if section 39 of the Adoption Act 1976 or section 67 of the Adoption and Children Act 2002 did not apply, and
(c) immediately before the relation of A to B first became such as to fall within section 27, a sexual relationship existed between A and B.

(2) Subsection (1) does not apply if at the time referred to in subsection (1)(c) sexual intercourse between A and B would have been unlawful.

(3) In proceedings for an offence under section 25 or 26 it is for the defendant to prove the matters mentioned in subsection (1)(a) to (c).

47 Paying for sexual services of a child

(1) A person (A) commits an offence if—

(a) he intentionally obtains for himself the sexual services of another person (B),

(b) before obtaining those services, he has made or promised payment for those services to B or a third person, or knows that another person has made or promised such a payment, and

(c) either—

(i) B is under 18, and A does not reasonably believe that B is 18 or over, or

(ii) B is under 13.

(2) In this section, 'payment' means any financial advantage, including the discharge of an obligation to pay or the provision of goods or services (including sexual services) gratuitously or at a discount. [E]

(3) A person guilty of an offence under this section against a person under 13, where subsection (6) applies, is liable on conviction on indictment to imprisonment for life.

(6) This subsection applies where the offence involved—

(a) penetration of B's anus or vagina with a part of A's body or anything else,

(b) penetration of B's mouth with A's penis,

(c) penetration of A's anus or vagina with a part of B's body or by B with anything else, or

(d) penetration of A's mouth with B's penis.

48 Causing or inciting child prostitution or pornography

(1) A person (A) commits an offence if—

(a) he intentionally causes or incites another person (B) to become a prostitute, or to be involved in pornography, in any part of the world, and

(b) either—

(i) B is under 18, and A does not reasonably believe that B is 18 or over, or

(ii) B is under 13. [E]

49 Controlling a child prostitute or a child involved in pornography

(1) A person (A) commits an offence if—

(a) he intentionally controls any of the activities of another person (B) relating to B's prostitution or involvement in pornography in any part of the world, and

(b) either—

(i) B is under 18, and A does not reasonably believe that B is 18 or over, or

(ii) B is under 13. [E]

50 Arranging or facilitating child prostitution or pornography

(1) A person (A) commits an offence if—

(a) he intentionally arranges or facilitates the prostitution or involvement in pornography in any part of the world of another person (B), and

(b) either—

(i) B is under 18, and A does not reasonably believe that B is 18 or over, or

(ii) B is under 13. [E]

51 Sections 48 to 50: interpretation

(1) For the purposes of sections 48 to 50, a person is involved in pornography if an indecent image of that person is recorded; and similar expressions, and 'pornography', are to be interpreted accordingly.

(2) In those sections 'prostitute' means a person (A) who, on at least one occasion and whether or not compelled to do so, offers or provides sexual services to another person in return for payment or a promise of payment to A or a third person; and 'prostitution' is to be interpreted accordingly.

(3) In subsection (2), 'payment' means any financial advantage, including the discharge of an obligation to pay or the provision of goods or services (including sexual services) gratuitously or at a discount.

72 Offences outside the United Kingdom

(1) If—

(a) a United Kingdom national does an act in a country outside the United Kingdom, and

(b) the act, if done in England and Wales or Northern Ireland, would constitute a sexual offence to which this section applies,

the United Kingdom national is guilty in that part of the United Kingdom of that sexual offence.

(2) If—

(a) a United Kingdom resident does an act in a country outside the United Kingdom,

(b) the act constitutes an offence under the law in force in that country, and

(c) the act, if done in England and Wales or Northern Ireland, would constitute a sexual offence to which this section applies,

the United Kingdom resident is guilty in that part of the United Kingdom of that sexual offence.

(3) If—

(a) a person does an act in a country outside the United Kingdom at a time when the person was not a United Kingdom national or a United Kingdom resident,

(b) the act constituted an offence under the law in force in that country,

(c) the act, if done in England and Wales or Northern Ireland, would have constituted a sexual offence to which this section applies, and

(d) the person meets the residence or nationality condition at the relevant time,

proceedings may be brought against the person in that part of the United Kingdom for that sexual offence as if the person had done the act there.

(4) The person meets the residence or nationality condition at the relevant time if the person is a United Kingdom national or a United Kingdom resident at the time when the proceedings are brought.

(5) An act punishable under the law in force in any country constitutes an offence under that law for the purposes of subsections (2) and (3) however it is described in that law.

(6) The condition in subsection (2)(b) or (3)(b) is to be taken to be met unless, not later than rules of court may provide, the defendant serves on the prosecution a notice—

(a) stating that, on the facts as alleged with respect to the act in question, the condition is not in the defendant's opinion met,

(b) showing the grounds for that opinion, and

(c) requiring the prosecution to prove that it is met.

(7) But the court, if it thinks fit, may permit the defendant to require the prosecution to prove that the condition is met without service of a notice under subsection (6).

(8) In the Crown Court the question whether the condition is met is to be decided by the judge alone.

(9) In this section—

"country" includes territory;

"United Kingdom national" means an individual who is—

(a) a British citizen, a British overseas territories citizen, a British National (Overseas) or a British Overseas citizen;

(b) a person who under the British Nationality Act 1981 is a British subject; or

(c) a British protected person within the meaning of that Act;

"United Kingdom resident" means an individual who is resident in the United Kingdom.

(10) Schedule 2 lists the sexual offences to which this section applies.

SCHEDULE 2

1. In relation to England and Wales, the following are sexual offences to which section 72 applies—

(a) an offence under any of sections 5 to 19, 25 and 26, and 47 to 50;

(b) an offence under any of sections 1 to 4, 30–41, and 61 where the victim of the offence was under 18 at the time of the offence;

(c) an offence under section 62 or 63 where the intended offence was an offence against a person under 18;

(d) an offence under—

(i) section 1 of the Protection of Children Act 1978 (indecent photographs of children), or

(ii) section 160 of the Criminal Justice Act 1988 (possession of indecent photograph of child)

73 Exceptions to aiding, abetting and counselling

(1) A person is not guilty of aiding, abetting or counselling the commission against a child of an offence to which this section applies if he acts for the purpose of—

(a) protecting the child from sexually transmitted infection,

(b) protecting the physical safety of the child,

(c) preventing the child from becoming pregnant, or

(d) promoting the child's emotional well-being by the giving of advice,

and not for the purpose of causing or encouraging either the activity constituting the offence or the child's participation in it.

(2) This section applies to—

(a) an offence under any of sections 5 to 7 (offences against children under 13);

(b) an offence under section 9 (sexual activity with a child);

(c) an offence under section 13 which would be an offence under section 9 if the offender were aged 18;

(d) an offence under any of sections 16, 25, 30, 34 and 38 (sexual activity) against a person under 16.

(3) This section does not affect any other enactment or any rule of law restricting the circumstances in which a person is guilty of aiding, abetting or counselling an offence under this [Act.]

78 'Sexual'

[see page 48]

79 General interpretation

[see page 48]

Protection of Children Act 1978

1 Indecent photographs of children

(1) Subject to sections 1A and 1B, it is an offence for a person—

(a) to take, or permit to be taken, or to make any indecent photograph or pseudo-photograph of a child; or

(b) to distribute or show such indecent photographs or pseudo-photographs; or

(c) to have in his possession such indecent photographs, or pseudo-photographs with a view to their being distributed or shown by himself or others; or

(d) to publish or cause to be published any advertisement likely to be understood as conveying that the advertiser distributes or shows such indecent photographs or pseudo-photographs, or intends to do so. [E]

(2) For purposes of this Act, a person is to be regarded as distributing an indecent photograph or pseudo-photograph if he parts with possession of it to, or exposes or offers it for acquisition by, another person.

(4) Where a person is charged with an offence under subsection (1)(b) or (c), it shall be a defence for him to prove—

(a) that he had a legitimate reason for distributing or showing the photographs or pseudo-photographs or (as the case may be) having them in his possession; or

(b) that he had not himself seen the photographs or pseudo-photographs and did not know, nor had any cause to suspect, them to be indecent.

1A Marriage and other relationships

(1) This section applies where, in proceedings for an offence under section 1(1)(a) of taking or making an indecent photograph of a child, or for an offence under section 1(1)(b) or (c) relating to an indecent photograph of a child, the defendant proves that the photograph was of the child aged 16 or over, and that at the time of the offence charged the child and he—

(a) were married, or

(b) lived together as partners in an enduring family relationship.

(2) Subsections (5) and (6) also apply where, in proceedings for an offence under section 1 (1)(b) or (c) relating to an indecent photograph of a child, the defendant proves that the photograph was of the child aged 16 or over, and that at the time when he obtained it the child and he—

(a) were married, or

(b) lived together as partners in an enduring family relationship.

(3) This section applies whether the photograph showed the child alone or with the defendant, but not if it showed any other person.

(4) In the case of an offence under section 1(1) (a), if sufficient evidence is adduced to raise an issue as to whether the child consented to the photograph being taken or made, or as to whether the defendant reasonably believed that the child so consented, the defendant is not guilty of the offence unless it is proved that the child did not so consent and that the defendant did not reasonably believe that the child so consented.

(5) In the case of an offence under section 1(1) (b), the defendant is not guilty of the offence unless it is proved that the showing or distributing was to a person other than the child.

(6) In the case of an offence under section 1(1) (c), if sufficient evidence is adduced to raise an issue both—

(a) as to whether the child consented to the photograph being in the defendant's possession, or as to whether the defendant reasonably believed that the child so consented, and

(b) as to whether the defendant had the photograph in his possession with a view to its being distributed or shown to anyone other than the child,

the defendant is not guilty of the offence unless it is proved either that the child did not so consent and that the defendant did not reasonably believe that the child so consented, or that the defendant had the photograph in his possession with a view to its being distributed or shown to a person other than the child.

1B Exception for criminal proceedings, investigations, etc.

(1) In proceedings for an offence under section 1(1)(a) of making an indecent photograph or pseudo-photograph of a child, the defendant is not guilty of the offence if he proves that—

(a) it was necessary for him to make the photograph or pseudo-photograph for the purposes of the prevention, detection or investigation of crime, or for the purposes of criminal proceedings, in any part of that world,

(b) at the time of the offence charged he was a member of the Security Service or the Secret Intelligence Service, and it was necessary for him to make the photograph or pseudo-photograph for the exercise of any of the functions of that Service, or

(c) at the time of the offence charged he was a member of GCHQ, and it was necessary for him to make the photograph or pseudo-photograph for the exercise of any of the functions of GCHQ.

(2) In this section 'GCHQ' has the same meaning as in the Intelligence Services Act 1994.

2 Evidence

(3) In proceedings under this Act [relating to indecent photographs of children] a person is to be taken as having been a child at any material time if it appears from the evidence as a whole that he was then under the age of 16.

7 Interpretation

(1) The following subsections apply for the interpretation of this Act.

(2) References to an indecent photograph include an indecent film, a copy of an indecent photograph or film, and an indecent photograph comprised in a film.

(3) Photographs (including those comprised in a film) shall, if they show children and are indecent, be treated for all purposes of this Act as indecent photographs of children, and so as respects pseudo-photographs.

(4) References to a photograph include—

(a) the negative as well as the positive version; and

(b) data stored on a computer disc or by other electronic means which is capable of conversion into a photograph.

(4A) References to a photograph also include—

(a) a tracing or other image, whether made by electronic or other means (of whatever nature) —

(i) which is not itself a photograph or pseudo-photograph, but

(ii) which is derived from the whole or part of a photograph or pseudo-photograph (or a combination of either or both); and

(b) data stored on a computer disc or by other electronic means which is capable of conversion into an image within paragraph (a);

and subsection (8) applies in relation to such an image as it applies in relation to a pseudo-photograph.

(5) 'Film' includes any form of video-recording.

(6) 'Child', subject to subsection (8), means a person under the age of 16.

(7) 'Pseudo-photograph' means an image, whether made by computer-graphics or otherwise howsoever, which appears to be a photograph.

(8) If the impression conveyed by a pseudo-photograph is that the person shown is a child, the pseudo-photograph shall be treated for all purposes of this Act as showing a child and so shall a pseudo-photograph where the predominant impression conveyed is that the person shown is a child notwithstanding that some of the physical characteristics shown are those of an adult.

(9) References to an indecent pseudo-photograph include—

(a) a copy of an indecent pseudo-photograph; and

(b) data stored on a computer disc or by other electronic means which is capable of conversion into an indecent pseudo-photograph.

Criminal Justice Act 1988

160 Possession of indecent photograph of child

(1) Subject to subsection (1A), it is an offence for a person to have any indecent photograph or psuedo-photograph of a child (meaning in this section a person under the age of 18) in his possession. [I]

(2) Where a person is charged with an offence under subsection (1) above, it shall be a defence for him to prove—

(a) that he had a legitimate reason for having the photograph or pseudo-photograph in his possession; or

(b) that he had not himself seen the photograph or pseudo-photograph and did not know, nor had any cause to suspect, it to be indecent; or

(c) that the photograph or pseudo-photograph was sent to him without any prior request made by him or on his behalf and that he did not keep it for an unreasonable time.

(4) Sections 1(3), 2(3), 3 and 7 of the Protection of Children Act 1978 shall have effect as if any reference in them to that Act included a reference to this section.

160A Marriage and other relationships

(1) This section applies where, in proceedings for an offence under section 160 relating to an indecent photograph of a child, the defendant proves that the photograph was of the child aged 16 or over, and that at the time of the offence charged the child and he—

(a) were married, or

(b) lived together as partners in an enduring family relationship.

(2) This section also applies where, in proceedings for an offence under section 160 relating to an indecent photograph of a child, the defendant proves that the photograph was of the child aged 16 or over, and that at the time when he obtained it the child and he—

(a) were married, or

(b) lived together as partners in an enduring family relationship.

(3) This section applies whether the photograph showed the child alone or with the defendant, but not if it showed any other person.

(4) If sufficient evidence is adduced to raise an issue as to whether the child consented to the photograph being in the defendant's possession, or as to whether the defendant reasonably believed that the child so consented, the defendant is not guilty of the offence unless it is proved that the child did not so consent and that the defendant did not reasonably believe that the child so consented.

Education Act 1996

444 Failure to secure regular attendance at school of registered pupil

(1) If a child of compulsory school age who is a registered pupil at a school fails to attend regularly at the school, his parent is guilty of an offence. [S]
Children and Young Persons (Harmful Publications) Act 1955

(1A) If in the circumstances mentioned in subsection (1) the parent knows that his child is failing to attend regularly at the school and fails without reasonable justification to cause him to do so, he is guilty of an offence. [S]

(2) Subsections (3) to (6) below apply in proceedings for an offence under this section in respect of a child who is not a boarder at the school at which he is a registered pupil.

(3) The child shall not be taken to have failed to attend regularly at the school by reason of his absence from the school—

(a) with leave,

(b) at any time when he was prevented from attending by reason of sickness or any unavoidable cause, or

(c) on any day exclusively set apart for religious observance by the religious body to which his parent belongs.

(4) The child shall not be taken to have failed to attend regularly at the school if the parent proves—

(a) that the school at which the child is a registered pupil is not within walking distance of the child's home, and

(b) that no suitable arrangements have been made by the local education authority or the funding authority for any of the following—
(i) his transport to and from the school,
(ii) boarding accommodation for him at or near the school, and
(iii) enabling him to become a registered pupil at a school nearer to his home.

(5) In subsection (4) above, 'walking distance' means—
(a) in relation to a child who is under the age of eight years, two miles, and
(b) in relation to a child who has attained the age of eight years, three miles,
in each case measured by the nearest available route.

(6) If it is proved that the child has no fixed abode, subsection (4) above shall not apply, but the parent shall be acquitted if he proves—
(a) that he is engaged in a trade or business of such a nature as to require him to travel from place to place,
(b) that the child has attended at a school as a registered pupil as regularly as the nature of that trade or business permits, and
(c) if the child has attained the age of six years, that he has made at least two hundred attendances during the period of twelve months ending with the date on which the proceedings were instituted.

(7) In proceedings for an offence under this section in respect of a child who is a boarder at the school at which he is a registered pupil, the child shall be taken to have failed to attend regularly at the school if he is absent from it without leave during any part of the school term at a time when he was not prevented from being present by reason of sickness or any unavoidable cause.

(8B) If, on the trial of an offence under subsection (1A), the court finds the defendant not guilty of that offence but is satisfied that he is guilty of an offence under subsection (1), the court may find him guilty of that offence.

(9) In this section 'leave', in relation to a school, means leave granted by any person authorised to do so by the governing body or proprietor of the school.

Hypnotism Act 1952

3 Prohibition on hypnotising persons under eighteen

A person who gives an exhibition, demonstration or performance of hypnotism on a person who has not attained the age of eighteen years at or in connection with an entertainment to which the public are admitted, whether on payment or otherwise, shall, unless he had reasonable cause to believe that that person had attained that age, be liable on summary conviction to a fine not exceeding level 3 on the standard scale. [S]

Children and Young Persons (Harmful Publications) Act 1955

1 Works to which this Act applies

This Act applies to any book, magazine or other like work which is of a kind likely to fall into the hands of children or young persons and consists wholly or mainly of stories told in pictures (with or without the addition of written matter), being stories portraying—
(a) the commission of crimes; or
(b) acts of violence or cruelty; or
(c) incidents of a repulsive or horrible nature;
in such a way that the work as a whole would tend to corrupt a child or young person into whose hands it might fall.

2 Penalty for printing, publishing, selling, etc., works to which this Act applies

(1) A person who prints, publishes, sells or lets on hire a work to which this Act applies, or has any such work in his possession for the purpose of selling it or letting it on hire, shall be guilty of an offence and liable, on summary conviction, to imprisonment for a term not exceeding four months or to a fine not exceeding level 3 on the standard scale or to both:

Provided that, in any proceedings taken under this subsection against a person in respect of selling or letting on hire a work or of having it in his possession for the purpose of selling it or letting it on hire, it shall be a defence for him to prove that he had not examined the contents of the work and had no reasonable cause to suspect that it was one to which this Act applies. [S]

(2) A prosecution for an offence under this section shall not, in England or Wales, be instituted except by, or with the consent of, the Attorney-General.

4 Prohibition of importation of works to which this Act applies and articles for printing them

The importation of—

(a) any work to which this Act applies; and

(b) any plate prepared for the purpose of printing copies of any such work and any photographic film prepared for that purpose;

is hereby prohibited.

Tattooing of Minors Act 1969

1 Prohibition of tattooing of minors

It shall be an offence to tattoo a person under the age of eighteen except when the tattoo is performed for medical reasons by a duly qualified medical practitioner or by a person working under his direction, but it shall be a defence for a person charged to show that at the time the tattoo was performed he had reasonable cause to believe that the person tattooed was of or over the age of eighteen and did in fact so believe. [S]

3 Definition

For the purposes of this Act 'tattoo' shall mean the insertion into the skin of any colouring material designed to leave a permanent mark.

Child Abduction Act 1984

1 Offence of abduction of child by parent, etc.

(1) Subject to subsections (5) and (8) below, a person connected with a child under the age of sixteen commits an offence if he takes or sends the child out of the United Kingdom without the appropriate consent. [E]

(2) A person is connected with a child for the purposes of this section if—

(a) he is a parent of the child; or

(b) in the case of a child whose parents were not married to each other at the time of his birth, there are reasonable grounds for believing that he is the father of the child; or

(c) he is a guardian of the child; or

(d) he is a person in whose favour a residence order is in force with respect to the child; or

(e) he has custody of the child.

(3) In this section 'the appropriate consent' in relation to a child, means—

(a) the consent of each of the following—

(i) the child's mother;

(ii) the child's father, if he has parental responsibility for him;
(iii) any guardian of the child;
(iv) any person in whose favour a residence order is in force with respect to the child;
(v) any person who has custody of the child; or

(b) the leave of the court granted under or by virtue of any provision of Part II of the Children Act 1989; or

(c) if any person has custody of the child, the leave of the court which awarded custody to him.

(4) A person does not commit an offence under this section by taking or sending a child out of the United Kingdom without obtaining the appropriate consent if—

(a) he is a person in whose favour there is a residence order in force with respect to the child, and

(b) he takes or sends him out of the United Kingdom for a period of less than one month.

(4A) Subsection (4) above does not apply if the person taking or sending the child out of the United Kingdom does so in breach of an order under Part II of the Children Act 1989.

(5) A person does not commit an offence under this section by doing anything without the consent of another person whose consent is required under the foregoing provisions if—

(a) he does it in the belief that the other person—
(i) has consented; or
(ii) would consent if he was aware of all the relevant circumstances; or

(b) he has taken all reasonable steps to communicate with the other person but has been unable to communicate with him; or

(c) the other person has unreasonably refused to consent.

(5A) Subsection (5)(c) above does not apply if—

(a) the person who refused to consent is a person—
(i) in whose favour there is a residence order in force with respect to the child; or
(ii) who has custody of the child; or

(b) the person taking or sending the child out of the United Kingdom is, by so acting, in breach of an order made by a court in the United Kingdom.

(6) Where, in proceedings for an offence under this section, there is sufficient evidence to raise an issue as to the application of subsection (5) above, it shall be for the prosecution to prove that the subsection does not apply.

(7) For the purposes of this section—

(a) 'guardian of a child', 'residence order' and 'parental responsibility' have the same meaning as in the Children Act 1989; and

(b) a person shall be treated as having custody of a child if there is in force an order of a court in the United Kingdom awarding him (whether solely or jointly with another person) custody, legal custody or care and control of the child.

(8) This section shall have effect subject to the provisions of the Schedule to this Act in relation to a child who is in the care of a local authority detained in a place of safety, remanded to a local authority accommodation or the subject of proceedings or an order relating to adoption.

2 Offence of abduction of child by other persons

(1) Subject to subsection (3) below, a person, other than one mentioned in subsection (2) below, commits an offence if, without lawful authority or reasonable excuse, he takes or detains a child under the age of sixteen—

(a) so as to remove him from the lawful control of any person having lawful control of the child; or

(b) so as to keep him out of the lawful control of any person entitled to lawful control of the child. [E]

(2) The persons are—

(a) where the father and mother of the child in question were married to each other at the time of his birth, the child's father and mother;

(b) where the father and mother of the child in question were not married to each other at the time of his birth, the child's mother; and

(c) any other person mentioned in section 1(2)(c) to (e) above.

(3) In proceedings against any person for an offence under this section, it shall be a defence for that person to prove—

(a) where the father and mother of the child in question were not married to each other at the time of his birth—

(i) that he is the child's father; or

(ii) that, at the time of the alleged offence, he believed, on reasonable grounds, that he was the child's father; or

(b) that, at the time of the alleged offence, he believed that the child had attained the age of sixteen.

3 Construction of references to taking, sending and detaining

For the purposes of this Part of this Act—

(a) a person shall be regarded as taking a child if he causes or induces the child to accompany him or any other person or causes the child to be taken;

(b) a person shall be regarded as sending a child if he causes the child to be sent;

(c) a person shall be regarded as detaining a child if he causes the child to be detained or induces the child to remain with him or any other person; and

(d) references to a child's parents and to a child whose parents were (or were not) married to each other at the time of his birth shall be construed in accordance with section 1 of the Family Law Reform Act 1987 (which extends their meaning).

Intoxicating Substances (Supply) Act 1985

1 Offence of supplying intoxicating substance to or for person under 18

[see page 282]

Horses (Protective Headgear for Young Riders) Act 1990

1 Causing or permitting child under 14 to ride on road without protective headgear

(1) Except as provided by regulations, it is an offence for any person to whom this subsection applies to cause or permit a child under the age of 14 years to ride a horse on a road unless the child is wearing protective headgear, of such description as may be specified in regulations, in such manner as may be so specified. [S]

(2) Subsection (1) above applies to the following persons—

(a) any person who—

(i) for the purposes of Part I of the Children and Young Persons Act 1933, has responsibility for the child;

(b) any owner of the horse;

(c) any person other than its owner who has custody of or is in possession of the horse immediately before the child rides it; and

(d) where the child is employed, his employer and any other person to whose orders the child is subject in the course of his employment.

3 Interpretation

(1) In this Act—

'horse' includes pony, mule, donkey or other equine animal;

'regulations' means regulations under section 2 of this Act; and

'road' does not include a footpath or bridleway but, subject to that, has—

(a) in England and Wales the meaning given by section 192(1) of the Road Traffic Act 1988...

(2) For the purposes of the definition of 'road' in subsection (1) above—

(a) 'footpath' means a way—

(i) over which the public have a right of way or, in Scotland, of passage on foot only; and

(ii) which is not associated with a carriageway; and

(b) 'bridleway' means a way over which the public have the following, but no other, rights of way: a right of way on foot and a right of way on horseback or leading a horse, with or without a right to drive animals of any description along the way.

Children and Young Persons (Protection from Tobacco) Act 1991

3 Sale of unpackaged cigarettes

(1) It shall be an offence for any person carrying on a retail business to sell cigarettes to any person other than in pre-packed quantities of 10 or more cigarettes in their original package. [S]

(3) In this section, 'original package' means the package in which the cigarettes were supplied for the purpose of retail sale by the manufacturer or importer; and 'package' means any box, carton or other container.

4 Display of warning statements in retail premises and on vending machines

(1) A notice displaying the following statement—

'It is illegal to sell tobacco products to anyone under the age of 16'

shall be exhibited at every premises at which tobacco is sold by retail, and shall be so exhibited in a prominent position where the statement is readily visible to persons at the point of sale of the tobacco; and where—

(a) any person carries on a business involving the sale of tobacco by retail at any premises, and

(b) no notice is exhibited at those premises in accordance with this subsection, that person shall be guilty of an offence. [S]

(2) A notice displaying the following statement—

'This machine is only for the use of people aged 16 or over'

shall be exhibited on every automatic machine for the sale of tobacco which is kept available for use as such at any premises, and shall be so exhibited in such a way that the statement is readily visible to persons using the machine and where—

(a) any person is the owner of any such machine which is so kept or the owner of the premises at which any such machine is so kept, and

(b) no notice is exhibited on the machine in accordance with this subsection, that person shall be guilty of an offence. [S]

(3) The dimensions of the notice to be exhibited in accordance with subsection (1) or (2) above, and the size of the statement to be displayed on it, shall be such as may be prescribed by regulations made by the Secretary of State; and any such regulations may make different provision for different cases.

(5) It shall be a defence for a person charged with any such offence to prove that he took all reasonable precautions and exercised all due diligence to avoid the commission of the offence.

(6) Where any such offence is committed by a body corporate and is proved to have been committed with the consent or connivance of, or to be attributable to any neglect on the part of, any

director, manager, secretary or other similar officer of the body corporate, or any person who was purporting to act in any such capacity, he as well as the body corporate shall be guilty of that offence and shall be liable to be proceeded against and punished accordingly. In relation to a body corporate whose affairs are managed by its members, 'director' means a member of the body corporate.

(8) In this section—

'premises' includes any place and any vehicle, vessel, aircraft, hovercraft, stall or moveable structure; and

'tobacco' (except where it appears in the statement required by subsection (1)) has the same meaning as in section 7 of the Children and Young Persons Act 1933.

Licensing Act 2003

146–153 Sale and supply of alcohol to persons under 18

[see pages 268–272]

(b) The Mentally Disordered

Mental Health Act 1983

PART IV

56 Patients to whom Part IV applies

(1) Section 57 and, so far as relevant to that section, sections 59 to 62 below apply to any patient.

(2) Subject to that and to subsection (5) below, this Part of this Act applies to a patient only if he falls within subsection (3) or (4) below.

(3) A patient falls within this subsection if he is liable to be detained under this Act but not if—

(a) he is so liable by virtue of an emergency application and the second medical recommendation referred to in section 4(4)(a) above has not been given and received;

(b) he is so liable by virtue of section 5(2) or (4) or 35 above or section 135 or 136 below or by virtue of a direction for his detention in a place of safety under section 37(4) or 45A(5) above; or

(c) he has been conditionally discharged under section 42(2) above or section 73 or 74 below and he is not recalled to hospital.

(4) A patient falls within this subsection if—

(a) he is a community patient; and

(b) he is recalled to hospital under section 17E above.

(5) Section 58A and, so far as relevant to that section, sections 59 to 62 below also apply to any patient who—

(a) does not fall within subsection (3) above;

(b) is not a community patient; and

(c) has not attained the age of 18 years.

57 Treatment requiring consent and a second opinion

(1) This section applies to the following forms of medical treatment for mental disorder—

(a) any surgical operation for destroying brain tissue or for destroying the functioning of brain tissue; and

(b) such other forms of treatment as may be specified for the purposes of this section by regulations made by the Secretary of State.

(2) Subject to section 62 below, a patient shall not be given any form of treatment to which this section applies unless he has consented to it and—

(a) a registered medical practitioner appointed for the purposes of this Part of this Act by the Secretary of State (not being the responsible clinician (if there is one) or, the person in charge of the treatment in question) and two other persons appointed for the purposes of this paragraph by the Secretary of State (not being registered medical practitioners) have certified in writing that the patient is capable of understanding the nature, purpose and likely effects of the treatment in question and has consented to it; and

(b) the registered medical practitioner referred to in paragraph (a) above has certified in writing that it is appropriate for the treatment to be given.

(3) Before giving a certificate under subsection (2)(b) above the registered medical practitioner concerned shall consult two other persons who have been professionally concerned with the patient's medical treatment, but, of those persons—

(a) one shall be a nurse and the other shall be neither a nurse nor a registered medical practitioner; and

(b) neither shall be the responsible clinician (if there is one) or the person in charge of the treatment in question.

58 Treatment requiring consent or a second opinion

(1) This section applies to the following forms of medical treatment for mental disorder—

(a) such forms of treatment as may be specified for the purposes of this section by regulations made by the Secretary of State;

(b) the administration of medicine to a patient by any means (not being a form of treatment specified under paragraph (a) above or section 57 above or section 58A(1)(b)) below at any time during a period for which he is liable to be detained as a patient to whom this Part of this Act applies if three months or more have elapsed since the first occasion in that period when medicine was administered to him by any means for his mental disorder.

(3) Subject to section 62 below, a patient shall not be given any form of treatment to which this section applies unless—

(a) he has consented to that treatment and either the approved clinician in charge of it or a registered medical practitioner appointed for the purposes of this Part of this Act by the Secretary of State has certified in writing that the patient is capable of understanding its nature, purpose and likely effects and has consented to it; or

(b) a registered medical practitioner appointed as aforesaid (not being the responsible clinician or the approved clinician in charge of the treatment in question) has certified in writing that the patient is not capable of understanding the nature, purpose and likely effects of that treatment or being so capable has not consented to it but that it is appropriate for the treatment to be given.

(4) Before giving a certificate under subsection (3)(b) above the registered medical practitioner concerned shall consult two other persons who have been professionally concerned with the patient's medical treatment, but, of those persons—

(a) one shall be a nurse and the other shall be neither a nurse nor a registered medical practitioner; and

(b) neither shall be the responsible clinician or the approved clinician in charge of the treatment in question.

58A Electro-convulsive therapy, etc.

(1) This section applies to the following forms of medical treatment for mental disorder—

(a) electro-convulsive therapy; and

(b) such other forms of treatment as may be specified for the purposes of this section by regulations made by the appropriate national authority.

(2) Subject to section 62 below, a patient shall be not be given any form of treatment to which this section applies unless he falls within subsection (3), (4) or (5) below.

(3) A patient falls within this subsection if—

(a) he has attained the age of 18 years;

(b) he has consented to the treatment in question; and

(c) either the approved clinician in charge of it or a registered medical practitioner appointed as mentioned in section 58(3) above has certified in writing that the patient is capable of understanding the nature, purpose and likely effects of the treatment and has consented to it.

(4) A patient falls within this subsection if—

(a) he has not attained the age of 18 years; but

(b) he has consented to the treatment in question; and

(c) a registered medical practitioner appointed as aforesaid (not being the approved clinician in charge of the treatment) has certified in writing—

(i) that the patient is capable of understanding the nature, purpose and likely effects of the treatment and has consented to it; and

(ii) that it is appropriate for the treatment to be given.

(5) A patient falls within this subsection if a registered medical practitioner appointed as aforesaid (not being the responsible clinician (if there is one) or the approved clinician in charge of the treatment in question) has certified in writing—

(a) that the patient is not capable of understanding the nature, purpose and likely effects of the treatment; but

(b) that it is appropriate for the treatment to be given; and

(c) that giving him the treatment would not conflict with—

(i) an advance decision which the registered medical practitioner concerned is satisfied is valid and applicable; or

(ii) a decision made by a donee or deputy or by the Court of Protection.

(6) Before giving a certificate under subsection (5) above the registered medical practitioner concerned shall consult two other persons who have been professionally concerned with the patient's medical treatment but, of those persons—

(a) one shall be a nurse and the other shall be neither a nurse nor a registered medical practitioner; and

(b) neither shall be the responsible clinician (if there is one) or the approved clinician in charge of the treatment in question.

(7) This section shall not by itself confer sufficient authority for a patient who falls within section 56(5) above to be given a form of treatment to which this section applies if he is not capable of understanding the nature, purpose and likely effects of the treatment (and cannot therefore consent to it).

(9) In this section—

(a) a reference to an advance decision is to an advance decision (within the meaning of the Mental Capacity Act 2005) made by the patient;

(b) 'valid and applicable', in relation to such a decision, means valid and applicable to the treatment in question in accordance with section 25 of that Act;

(c) a reference to a donee is to a donee of a lasting power of attorney (within the meaning of section 9 of that Act) created by the patient, where the donee is acting within the scope of his authority and in accordance with that Act; and

(d) a reference to a deputy is to a deputy appointed for the patient by the Court of Protection under section 16 of that Act, where the deputy is acting within the scope of his authority and in accordance with that Act.

59 Plans of treatment

Any consent or certificate under section 57, 58 or 58A above may relate to a plan of treatment under which the patient is to be given (whether within a specified period or otherwise) one or more of the forms of treatment to which that section applies.

60 Withdrawal of consent

(1) Where the consent of a patient to any treatment has been given for the purposes of section 57, 58 or 58A above, the patient may, subject to section 62 below, at any time before the completion of the treatment withdraw his consent, and those sections shall then apply as if the remainder of the treatment were a separate form of treatment.

(1A) Subsection (1B) below applies where—

(a) the consent of a patient to any treatment has been given for the purposes of section 57, 58 or 58A above; but

(b) before the completion of the treatment, the patient ceases to be capable of understanding its nature, purpose and likely effects.

(1B) The patient shall, subject to section 62 below, be treated as having withdrawn his consent, and those sections shall then apply as if the remainder of the treatment were a separate form of treatment.

(1C) Subsection (1D) below applies where—

(a) a certificate has been given under section 58 or 58A above that a patient is not capable of understanding the nature, purpose and likely effects of the treatment to which the certificate applies; but

(b) before the completion of the treatment, the patient becomes capable of understanding its nature, purpose and likely effects.

(1D) The certificate shall, subject to section 62 below, cease to apply to the treatment and those sections shall then apply as if the remainder of the treatment were a separate form of treatment.

(2) Without prejudice to the application of subsections (1)to (1D) above to any treatment given under the plan of treatment to which a patient has consented, a patient who has consented to such a plan may, subject to section 62 below, at any time withdraw his consent to further treatment, or to further treatment of any description, under the plan.

62 Urgent treatment

(1) Sections 57 and 58 above shall not apply to any treatment—

(a) which is immediately necessary to save the patient's life; or

(b) which (not being irreversible) is immediately necessary to prevent a serious deterioration of his condition; or

(c) which (not being irreversible or hazardous) is immediately necessary to alleviate serious suffering by the patient; or

(d) which (not being irreversible or hazardous) is immediately necessary and represents the minimum interference necessary to prevent the patient from behaving violently or being a danger to himself or to others.

(1A) Section 58A above, in so far as it relates to electro-convulsive therapy by virtue of subsection (1)(a) of that section, shall not apply to any treatment which falls within paragraph (a) or (b) of subsection (1) above.

(1B) Section 58A above, in so far as it relates to a form of treatment specified by virtue of subsection (1)(b) of that section, shall not apply to any treatment which falls within such of paragraphs (a) to (d) of subsection (1) above as may be specified in regulations under that section.

(1C) For the purposes of subsection (1B) above, the regulations—

(a) may make different provision for different cases (and may, in particular, make different provision for different forms of treatment);

(b) may make provision which applies subject to specified exceptions; and

(c) may include transitional, consequential, incidental or supplemental provision.

(2) Sections 60 and 61(3) above shall not preclude the continuation of any treatment or of treatment under any plan pending compliance with section 57, 58 or 58A above if the approved clinician in charge of the treatment considers that the discontinuance of the treatment or of treatment under the plan would cause serious suffering to the patient.

(3) For the purposes of this section treatment is irreversible if it has unfavourable irreversible physical or psychological consequences and hazardous if it entails significant physical hazard.

63 Treatment not requiring consent

The consent of a patient shall not be required for any medical treatment given to him for the mental disorder from which he is suffering, not being a form of treatment to which section 57, 58 or 58A applies, if the treatment is given by or under the direction of the approved clinician in charge of the treatment.

PART IX

127 Ill-treatment of patients

(1) It shall be an offence for any person who is an officer on the staff of or otherwise employed in, or who is one of the managers of, a hospital, independent hospital or mental nursing home—

(a) to ill-treat or wilfully to neglect a patient for the time being receiving treatment for mental disorder as an in-patient in that hospital or home; or

(b) to ill-treat or wilfully to neglect, on the premises of which the hospital or home forms part, a patient for the time being receiving such treatment there as an out-patient. [E]

(2) It shall be an offence for any individual to ill-treat or wilfully to neglect a mentally disordered patient who is for the time being subject to his guardianship under this Act or otherwise in his custody or care (whether by virtue of a legal or moral obligation or otherwise). [E]

(2A) It shall be an offence for any individual to ill-treat or wilfully to neglect a mentally disordered patient who is for the time being subject to after-care under supervision. [E]

Mental Capacity Act 2005

2 People who lack capacity

(1) For the purposes of this Act, a person lacks capacity in relation to a matter if at the material time he is unable to make a decision for himself in relation to the matter because of an impairment of, or a disturbance in the functioning of, the mind or brain.

(2) It does not matter whether the impairment or disturbance is permanent or temporary.

(3) A lack of capacity cannot be established merely by reference to—

(a) a person's age or appearance, or

(b) a condition of his, or an aspect of his behaviour, which might lead others to make unjustified assumptions about his capacity.

(4) In proceedings under this Act or any other enactment, any question whether a person lacks capacity within the meaning of this Act must be decided on the balance of probabilities.

(5) No power which a person ('D') may exercise under this Act—

(a) in relation to a person who lacks capacity, or

(b) where D reasonably thinks that a person lacks capacity,

is exercisable in relation to a person under 16.

(6) Subsection (5) is subject to section 18(3).

3 Inability to make decisions

(1) For the purposes of section 2, a person is unable to make a decision for himself if he is unable—

(a) to understand the information relevant to the decision,

(b) to retain that information,

(c) to use or weigh that information as part of the process of making the decision, or

(d) to communicate his decision (whether by talking, using sign language or any other means).

(2) A person is not to be regarded as unable to understand the information relevant to a decision if he is able to understand an explanation of it given to him in a way that is appropriate to his circumstances (using simple language, visual aids or any other means).

(3) The fact that a person is able to retain the information relevant to a decision for a short period only does not prevent him from being regarded as able to make the decision.

(4) The information relevant to a decision includes information about the reasonably foreseeable consequences of—

(a) deciding one way or another, or
(b) failing to make the decision.

44 Ill-treatment or neglect

(1) Subsection (2) applies if a person ('D')—

(a) has the care of a person ('P') who lacks, or whom D reasonably believes to lack, capacity,
(b) is the donee of a lasting power of attorney, or an enduring power of attorney (within the meaning of Schedule 4), created by P, or
(c) is a deputy appointed by the court for P.

(2) D is guilty of an offence if he ill-treats or wilfully neglects P. [E]

Sexual Offences Act 2003

30 Sexual activity with a person with a mental disorder impeding choice

(1) A person (A) commits an offence if—

(a) he intentionally touches another person (B),
(b) the touching is sexual,
(c) B is unable to refuse because of or for a reason related to a mental disorder, and
(d) A knows or could reasonably be expected to know that B has a mental disorder and that because of it or for a reason related to it B is likely to be unable to refuse.

(2) B is unable to refuse if—

(a) he lacks the capacity to choose whether to agree to the touching (whether because he lacks sufficient understanding of the nature or reasonably foreseeable consequences of what is being done, or for any other reason), or
(b) he is unable to communicate such a choice to A. [E]

(3) A person guilty of an offence under this section, if the touching involved—

(a) penetration of B's anus or vagina with a part of A's body or anything else,
(b) penetration of B's mouth with A's penis,
(c) penetration of A's anus or vagina with a part of B's body, or
(d) penetration of A's mouth with B's penis,

is liable, on conviction on indictment, to imprisonment for life.

31 Causing or inciting a person with a mental disorder impeding choice to engage in sexual activity

(1) A person (A) commits an offence if—

(a) he intentionally causes or incites another person (B) to engage in an activity,
(b) the activity is sexual,
(c) B is unable to refuse because of or for a reason related to a mental disorder, and
(d) A knows or could reasonably be expected to know that B has a mental disorder and that because of or for a reason related to it B is likely to be unable to refuse.

(2) B is unable to refuse if—

(a) he lacks the capacity to choose whether to agree to engaging in the activity caused or incited (whether because he lacks sufficient understanding of the nature or reasonably foreseeable consequences of the activity, or for any other reason), or
(b) he is unable to communicate such a choice to A. [E]

(3) A person guilty of an offence under this section, if the activity caused or incited involved—

(a) penetration of B's anus or vagina,

(b) penetration of B's mouth with a person's penis,
(c) penetration of a person's anus or vagina with a part of B's body or by B with anything else, or
(d) penetration of a person's mouth with B's penis,

is liable, on conviction on indictment, to imprisonment for life.

32 Engaging in sexual activity in the presence of a person with a mental disorder impeding choice

(1) A person (A) commits an offence if—
(a) he intentionally engages in an activity,
(b) the activity is sexual,
(c) for the purpose of obtaining sexual gratification, he engages in it—
(i) when another person (B) is present or is in a place from which A can be observed, and
(ii) knowing or believing that B is aware, or intending that B should be aware, that he is engaging in it,
(d) B is unable to refuse because of a mental disorder, and
(e) A knows or could reasonably be expected to know that B has a mental disorder and that because of it B is likely to be unable to refuse.
(2) B is unable to refuse if—
(a) he lacks the capacity to choose whether to agree to being present (whether because he lacks sufficient understanding of the nature of the activity, or for any other reason),
(b) Sexual Offences Act 2003 he is unable to communicate such a choice to A. [E]

33 Causing a person with a mental disorder impeding choice to watch a sexual act

(1) A person (A) commits an offence if—
(a) for the purpose of obtaining sexual gratification, he intentionally causes another person (B) to watch a third person engaging in an activity, or to look at an image of any person engaging in an activity,
(b) the activity is sexual,
(c) B is unable to refuse because of or for a reason related to a mental disorder, and
(d) A knows or could reasonably be expected to know that B has a mental disorder and that because of it or for a reason related to it B is likely to be unable to refuse.
(2) B is unable to refuse if—
(a) he lacks the capacity to choose whether to agree to watching or looking (whether because he lacks sufficient understanding of the nature of the activity, or for any other reason), or
(b) he is unable to communicate such a choice to A. [E]

34 Inducement, threat or deception to procure sexual activity with a person with a mental disorder

(1) A person (A) commits an offence if—
(a) with the agreement of another person (B) he intentionally touches that person,
(b) the touching is sexual,
(c) A obtains B's agreement by means of an inducement offered or given, a threat made or a deception practised by A for that purpose,
(d) B has a mental disorder, and
(e) A knows or could reasonably be expected to know that B has a mental disorder. [E]
(2) A person guilty of an offence under this section, if the touching involved—
(a) penetration of B's anus or vagina with a part of A's body or anything else,
(b) penetration of B's mouth with A's penis,
(c) penetration of A's anus or vagina with a part of B's body, or
(d) penetration of A's mouth with B's penis,

is liable, on conviction on indictment, to imprisonment for life.

35 Causing a person with a mental disorder to engage in sexual activity by inducement, threat or deception

(1) A person (A) commits an offence if—

(a) by means of an inducement offered or given, a threat made or a deception practised by him for this purpose, he intentionally causes a person (B) to engage in an activity,

(b) the activity is sexual,

(c) B has a mental disorder, and

(d) A knows or could reasonably be expected to know that B has a mental disorder. [E]

(2) A person guilty of an offence under this section, if the activity caused involved—

(a) penetration of B's anus or vagina,

(b) penetration of B's mouth with a person's penis,

(c) penetration of a person's anus or vagina with a part of B's body or by B with anything else, or

(d) penetration of a person's mouth with B's penis, is liable, on conviction on indictment, to imprisonment for life.

36 Engaging in sexual activity in the presence, procured by inducement, threat or deception, of a person with a mental disorder

(1) A person (A) commits an offence if—

(a) he intentionally engages in an activity,

(b) the activity is sexual,

(c) for the purpose of obtaining sexual gratification, he engages in it—

(i) when another person (B) is present or is in a place from which A can be observed, and

(ii) knowing or believing that B is aware, or intending that B should be aware, that he is engaging in it,

(d) B agrees to be present or in the place refered to in paragraph (c) (i) because of an inducement offered or given, a threat made or a deception practised by A for the purpose of obtaining that agreement,

(e) B has a mental disorder, and

(f) A knows or could reasonably be expected to know that B has a mental disorder. [E]

37 Causing a person with a mental disorder to watch a sexual act by inducement, threat or deception

(1) A person (A) commits an offence if—

(a) for the purpose of obtaining sexual gratification, he intentionally causes another person (B) to watch a third person engaging in an activity, or to look at an image of any person engaging in an activity,

(b) the activity is sexual,

(c) B agrees to watch or look because of an inducement offered or given, a threat made or a deception practised by A for the purpose of obtaining that agreement,

(d) B has a mental disorder, and

(e) A knows or could reasonably be expected to know that B has a mental disorder. [E]

38 Care workers: sexual activity with a person with a mental disorder

(1) A person (A) commits an offence if—

(a) he intentionally touches another person (B),

(b) the touching is sexual,

(c) B has a mental disorder,

(d) A knows or could reasonably be expected to know that B has a mental disorder, and

(e) A is involved in B's care in a way that falls within section 42.

(2) Where in proceedings for an offence under this section it is proved that the other person had a mental disorder, it is to be taken that the defendant knew or could reasonably have been expected

to know that that person had a mental disorder unless sufficient evidence is adduced to raise an issue as to whether he knew or could reasonably have been expected to know it. [E]

(3) A person guilty of an offence under this section, if the touching involved—

(a) penetration of B's anus or vagina with a part of A's body or anything else,

(b) penetration of B's mouth with A's penis,

(c) penetration of A's anus or vagina with a part of B's body, or

(d) penetration of A's mouth with B's penis,

is liable, on conviction on indictment, to imprisonment for a term not exceeding 14 years.

39 Care workers: causing or inciting sexual activity

(1) A person (A) commits an offence if—

(a) he intentionally causes or incites another person (B) to engage in an activity,

(b) the activity is sexual,

(c) B has a mental disorder,

(d) A knows or could reasonably be expected to know that B has a mental disorder, and

(e) A is involved in B's care in a way that falls within section 42.

(2) Where in proceedings for an offence under this section it is proved that the other person had a mental disorder, it is to be taken that the defendant knew or could reasonably have been expected to know that that person had a mental disorder unless sufficient evidence is adduced to raise an issue as to whether he knew or could reasonably have been expected to know it. [E]

(3) A person guilty of an offence under this section, if the activity caused or incited involved—

(a) penetration of B's anus or vagina,

(b) penetration of B's mouth with a person's penis,

(c) penetration of a person's anus or vagina with a part of B's body or by B with anything else, or

(d) penetration of a person's mouth with B's penis,

is liable, on conviction on indictment, to imprisonment for a term not exceeding 14 years.

40 Care workers: sexual activity in the presence of a person with a mental disorder

(1) A person (A) commits an offence if—

(a) he intentionally engages in an activity,

(b) the activity is sexual,

(c) for the purpose of obtaining sexual gratification, he engages in it—

(i) when another person (B) is present or is in a place from which A can be observed, and

(ii) knowing or believing that B is aware, or intending that B should be aware, that he is engaging in it,

(d) B has a mental disorder,

(e) A knows or could reasonably be expected to know that B has a mental disorder, and

(f) A is involved in B's care in a way that falls within section 42.

(2) Where in proceedings for an offence under this section it is proved that the other person had a mental disorder, it is to be taken that the defendant knew or could reasonably have been expected to know that that person had a mental disorder unless sufficient evidence is adduced to raise an issue as to whether he knew or could reasonably have been expected to know it. [E]

41 Care workers: causing a person with a mental disorder to watch a sexual act

(1) A person (A) commits an offence if—

(a) for the purpose of obtaining sexual gratification, he intentionally causes another person (B) to watch a third person engaging in an activity, or to look at an image of any person engaging in an activity,

(b) the activity is sexual,

(c) B has a mental disorder,

(d) A knows or could reasonably be expected to know that B has a mental disorder, and

(e) A is involved in B's care in a way that falls within section 42.

(2) Where in proceedings for an offence under this section it is proved that the other person had a mental disorder, it is to be taken that the defendant knew or could reasonably have been expected to know that that person had a mental disorder unless sufficient evidence is adduced to raise an issue as to whether he knew or could reasonably have been expected to know it. [E]

42 Care workers: interpretation

(1) For the purposes of sections 38 to 41, a person (A) is involved in the care of another person (B) in a way that falls within this section if any of subsections (2) to (4) applies.

(2) This subsection applies if—

(a) B is accommodated and cared for in a care home, community home, voluntary home or children's home, and

(b) A has functions to perform in the home in the course of employment which have brought him or are likely to bring him into regular face to face contact with B.

(3) This subsection applies if B is a patient for whom services are provided—

(a) by a National Health Service body or an independent medical agency, or

(b) in an independent clinic or an independent hospital,

and A has functions to perform for the body or agency or in the clinic or hospital in the course of employment which have brought him or are likely to bring him into regular face to face contact with B.

(4) This subsection applies if A—

(a) is, whether or not in the course of employment, a provider of care, assistance or services to B in connection with B's mental disorder, and

(b) as such, has had or is likely to have regular face to face contact with B.

(5) In this section—

'care home' means an establishment which is a care home for the purposes of the Care Standards Act 2000;

'children's home' has the meaning given by section 1 of that Act;

'community home' has the meaning given by section 53(1) of the Children Act 1989;

'employment' means any employment, whether paid or unpaid and whether under a contract of service or apprenticeship, under a contract for services, or otherwise than under a contract;

'independent clinic', 'independent hospital' and 'independent medical agency' have the meaning given by section 2 of the Care Standards Act 2000;

'National Health Service body' means—

(a) a Health Authority,

(b) a National Health Service trust,

(c) a Primary Care Trust, or

(d) a Special Health Authority;

'voluntary home' has the meaning given by section 60(3) of the Children Act 1989.

43 Sections 38 to 41: marriage exception

(1) Conduct by a person (A) which would otherwise be an offence under any of sections 38 to 41 against another person (B) is not an offence under that section if at the time—

(a) B is 16 or over, and

(b) A and B are lawfully married.

(2) In proceedings for such an offence it is for the defendant to prove that A and B were lawfully married at the time.

48 Sections 38 to 41: sexual relationships which pre-date care relationships

(1) Conduct by a person (A) which would otherwise be an offence under any of sections 38 to 41 against another person (B) is not an offence under that section if, immediately before A became

involved in B's care in a way that falls within section 42, a sexual relationship existed between A and B.

(2) Subsection (1) does not apply if at that time sexual intercourse between A and B would have been unlawful.

(3) In proceedings for an offence under any of sections 38 to 41 it is for the defendant to prove that such a relationship existed at that time.

62 Committing an offence with intent to commit a sexual offence

[see page 46]

63 Trespass with intent to commit a sexual offence

[see page 230]

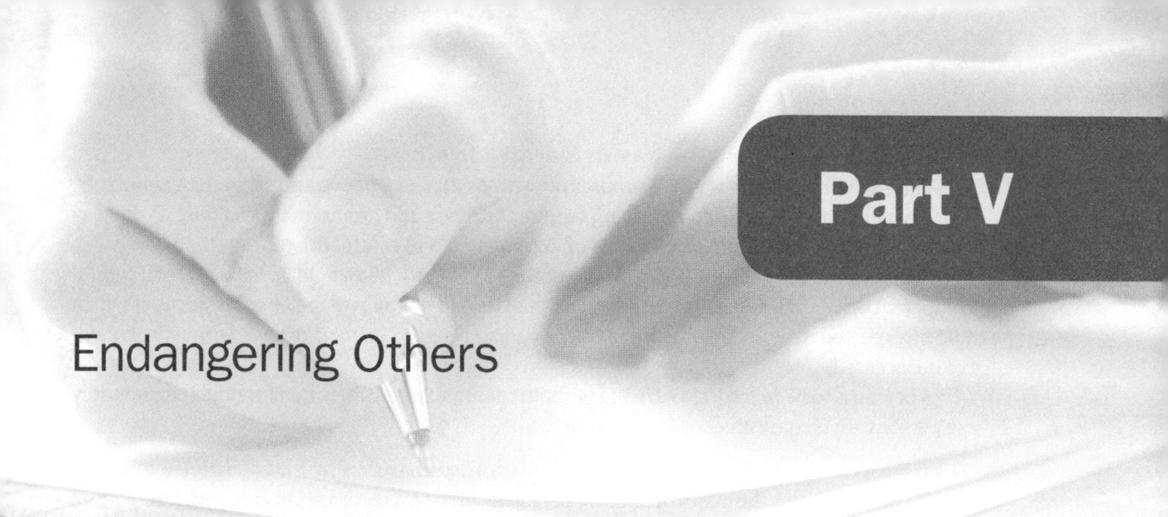

Part V

Endangering Others

(a) Traffic

Road Traffic Act 1988

1 Causing death by dangerous driving

A person who causes the death of another person by driving a mechanically propelled vehicle dangerously on a road or other public place is guilty of an offence. [I]

2 Dangerous driving

A person who drives a mechanically propelled vehicle dangerously on a road or other public place is guilty of an offence. [E]

2A Meaning of dangerous driving

(1) For the purposes of sections 1 and 2 above a person is to be regarded as driving dangerously if (and, subject to subsection (2) below, only if)—

(a) the way he drives falls far below what would be expected of a competent and careful driver, and

(b) it would be obvious to a competent and careful driver that driving in that way would be dangerous.

(2) A person is also to be regarded as driving dangerously for the purposes of sections 1 and 2 above if it would be obvious to a competent and careful driver that driving the vehicle in its current state would be dangerous.

(3) In subsections (1) and (2) above 'dangerous' refers to danger either of injury to any person or of serious damage to property; and in determining for the purposes of those subsections what would be expected of, or obvious to, a competent and careful driver in a particular case, regard shall be had not only to the circumstances of which he could be expected to be aware but also to any circumstances shown to have been within the knowledge of the accused.

(4) In determining for the purposes of subsection (2) above the state of a vehicle, regard may be had to anything attached to or carried on or in it and to the manner in which it is attached or carried.

2B Causing death by careless or inconsiderate driving

A person who causes the death of another person by driving a mechanically propelled vehicle on a road or other public place without due care and attention, or without reasonable consideration for other persons using the road or place, is guilty of an offence. [E]

3 Careless, and inconsiderate, driving

If a person drives a mechanically propelled vehicle on a road or other public place without due care and attention, or without reasonable consideration for other persons using the road or place, he is guilty of an offence. [S]

3ZA Meaning of careless, or inconsiderate, driving

(1) This section has effect for the purposes of sections 2B and 3 above and section 3A below.

(2) A person is to be regarded as driving without due care and attention if (and only if) the way he drives falls below what would be expected of a competent and careful driver.

(3) In determining for the purposes of subsection (2) above what would be expected of a careful and competent driver in a particular case, regard shall be had not only to the circumstances of which he could be expected to be aware but also to any circumstances shown to have been within the knowledge of the accused.

(4) A person is to be regarded as driving without reasonable consideration for other persons only if those persons are inconvenienced by his driving.

3A Causing death by careless driving when under influence of drink or drugs

(1) If a person causes the death of another person by driving a mechanically propelled vehicle on a road or other public place without due care and attention, or without reasonable consideration for other persons using the road or place, and—

(a) he is, at the time when he is driving, unfit to drive through drink or drugs, or

(b) he has consumed so much alcohol that the proportion of it in his breath, blood or urine at that time exceeds the prescribed limit, or

(c) he is, within 18 hours after that time, required to provide a specimen in pursuance of section 7 of this Act, but without reasonable excuse fails to provide it, or

(d) he is required by a constable to give his permission for a laboratory test of a specimen of blood taken from him under section 7A of this Act, but without reasonable excuse fails to do so

he is guilty of an offence. [I]

(2) For the purposes of this section a person shall be taken to be unfit to drive at any time when his ability to drive properly is impaired.

(3) Subsection (1)(b)(c) and (d) above shall not apply in relation to a person driving a mechanically propelled vehicle other than a motor vehicle.

3ZB Causing death by driving: unlicensed, disqualified or uninsured drivers

A person is guilty of an offence under this section if he causes the death of another person by driving a motor vehicle on a road and, at the time when he is driving, the circumstances are such that he is committing an offence under—

(a) section 87(1) of this Act (driving otherwise than in accordance with a licence),

(b) section 103(1)(b) of this Act (driving while disqualified), or

(c) section 143 of this Act (using motor vehicle while uninsured or unsecured against third party risks). [E]

4 Driving, or being in charge, when under influence of drink or drugs

(1) A person who, when driving or attempting to drive a mechanically propelled vehicle on a road or other public place, is unfit to drive through drink or drugs is guilty of an offence. [S]

(2) Without prejudice to subsection (1) above, a person who, when in charge of a mechanically propelled vehicle which is on a road or other public place, is unfit to drive through drink or drugs is guilty of an offence. [S]

(3) For the purposes of subsection (2) above, a person shall be deemed not to have been in charge of a mechanically propelled vehicle if he proves that at the material time the circumstances were such that there was no likelihood of his driving it so long as he remained unfit to drive through drink or drugs.

(4) The court may, in determining whether there was such a likelihood as is mentioned in subsection (3) above, disregard any injury to him and any damage to the vehicle.

(5) For the purposes of this section, a person shall be taken to be unfit to drive if his ability to drive properly is for the time being impaired.

5 Driving or being in charge of a motor vehicle with alcohol concentration above prescribed limit

(1) If a person—

(a) drives or attempts to drive a motor vehicle on a road or other public place, or

(b) is in charge of a motor vehicle on a road or other public place,

after consuming so much alcohol that the proportion of it in his breath, blood or urine exceeds the prescribed limit he is guilty of an offence. [S]

(2) It is a defence for a person charged with an offence under subsection (1)(b) above to prove that at the time he is alleged to have committed the offence the circumstances were such that there was no likelihood of his driving the vehicle whilst the proportion of alcohol in his breath, blood or urine remained likely to exceed the prescribed limit.

(3) The court may, in determining whether there was such a likelihood as is mentioned in subsection (2) above, disregard any injury to him and any damage to the vehicle.

6 Breath tests

(1) Where a constable in uniform has reasonable cause to suspect—

(a) that a person driving or attempting to drive or in charge of a motor vehicle on a road or other public place has alcohol in his body or has committed a traffic offence whilst the vehicle was in motion, or

(b) that a person has been driving or attempting to drive or been in charge of a motor vehicle on a road or other public place with alcohol in his body and that that person still has alcohol in his body, or

(c) that a person has been driving or attempting to drive or been in charge of a motor vehicle on a road or other public place and has committed a traffic offence whilst the vehicle was in motion,

he may, subject to section 9 of this Act, require him to provide a specimen of breath for a breath test.

(2) If an accident occurs owing to the presence of a motor vehicle on a road or other public place, a constable may, subject to section 9 of this Act, require any person who he has reasonable cause to believe was driving or attempting to drive or in charge of the vehicle at the time of the accident to provide a specimen of breath for a breath test.

(3) A person may be required under subsection (1) or subsection (2) above to provide a specimen either at or near the place where the requirement is made or, if the requirement is made under subsection (2) above and the constable making the requirement thinks fit, at a police station specified by the constable.

(4) A person who, without reasonable excuse, fails to provide a specimen of breath when required to do so in pursuance of this section is guilty of an offence. [S]

(8) In this section 'traffic offence' means an offence under—

(a) any provision of Part II of the Public Passenger Vehicles Act 1981,

(b) any provision of the Road Traffic Regulation Act 1984,

(c) any provision of the Road Traffic Offenders Act 1988 except Part III, or

(d) any provision of this Act except Part V.

7 Provision of specimens for analysis

(1) In the course of an investigation into whether a person has committed an offence under section 3A, 4 or 5 of this Act a constable may, subject to the following provisions of this section and section 9 of this Act, require him—

(a) to provide two specimens of breath for analysis by means of a device of a type approved by the Secretary of State, or

(b) to provide a specimen of blood or urine for a laboratory test.

(2) A requirement under this section to provide specimens of breath can only be made at a police station.

(3) A requirement under this section to provide a specimen of blood or urine can only be made at a police station or at a hospital; and it cannot be made at a police station unless—

(a) the constable making the requirement has reasonable cause to believe that for medical reasons a specimen of breath cannot be provided or should not be required, or

(b) at the time the requirement is made a device or a reliable device of the type mentioned in subsection (1)(a) above is not available at the police station or it is then for any other reason not practicable to use such a device there, or

(bb) a device of the type mentioned in subsection (1)(a) above has been used at the police station but the constable who required the specimens of breath has reasonable came to believe that the device has not produced a reliable indication of the proportion of alcohol in the breath of the person concerned, or

(c) the suspected offence is one under section 3A or 4 of this Act and the constable making the requirement has been advised by a medical practitioner that the condition of the person required to provide the specimen might be due to some drug;

but may then be made notwithstanding that the person required to provide the specimen has already provided or been required to provide two specimens of breath.

(4) If the provision of a specimen other than a specimen of breath may be required in pursuance of this section the question whether it is to be a specimen of blood or a specimen of urine shall be decided by the constable making the requirement, but if a medical practitioner is of the opinion that for medical reasons a specimen of blood cannot or should not be taken the specimen shall be a specimen of urine.

(5) A specimen of urine shall be provided within one hour of the requirement for its provision being made and after the provision of a previous specimen of urine.

(6) A person who, without reasonable excuse, fails to provide a specimen when required to do so in pursuance of this section is guilty of an offence. [S]

(7) A constable must, on requiring any person to provide a specimen in pursuance of this section, warn him that a failure to provide it may render him liable to prosecution.

8 Choice of specimens of breath

(1) Subject to subsection (2) below, of any two specimens of breath provided by any person in pursuance of section 7 of this Act that with the lower proportion of alcohol in the breath shall be used and the other shall be disregarded.

(2) If the specimen with the lower proportion of alcohol contains no more than 50 microgrammes of alcohol in 100 millilitres of breath, the person who provided it may claim that it should be replaced by such specimen as may be required under section 7(4) of this Act and, if he then provides such a specimen, neither specimen of breath shall be used.

9 Protection for hospital patients

(1) While a person is at a hospital as a patient he shall not be required to provide a specimen of breath for a breath test or to provide a specimen for a laboratory test unless the medical practitioner in immediate charge of his case has been notified of the proposal to make the requirement; and—

(a) if the requirement is then made, it shall be for the provision of a specimen at the hospital, but

(b) if the medical practitioner objects on the ground specified in subsection (2) below, the requirement shall not be made.

(1A) While a person is at a hospital as a patient, no specimen of blood shall be taken from him under section 7A of this Act and he shall not be required to give his permission for a laboratory test of a specimen taken under that section unless the medical practitioner in immediate charge of his case—

(a) has been notified of the proposal to take the specimen or to make the requirement; and

(b) has not objected on the ground specified in subsection (2).

(2) The ground on which the medical practitioner may object is—

(a) in a case falling within subsection (1), that the requirement or the provision of the specimen or (if one is required) the warning required by section *7(7)* of this Act would be prejudicial to the proper care and treatment of the patient; and

(b) in a case falling within subsection (1A), that the taking of the specimen, the requirement or the warning required by section 7A(5) of this Act would be so prejudicial.

11 Interpretation of sections 4 to 10

(1) The following provisions apply for the interpretation of sections 3A to 10 of this Act.

(2) In those sections—

'breath test' means a preliminary test for the purpose of obtaining, by means of a device of a type approved by the Secretary of State, an indication whether the proportion of alcohol in a person's breath or blood is likely to exceed the prescribed limit,

'drug' includes any intoxicant other than alcohol,

'fail' includes refuse,

'hospital' means an institution which provides medical or surgical treatment for in-patients or out-patients,

'the prescribed limit' means, as the case may require—

(a) 35 microgrammes of alcohol in 100 millilitres of breath,

(b) 80 milligrammes of alcohol in 100 millilitres of blood, or

(c) 107 milligrammes of alcohol in 100 millilitres of urine,

or such other proportion as may be prescribed by regulations made by the Secretary of State.

'registered health care professional' means a person (other than a medical practitioner) who is—

(a) a registered nurse; or

(b) a registered member of a health care profession which is designated for the purposes of this paragraph by an order made by the Secretary of State.

(2A) A health care profession is any profession mentioned in section 60(2) of the Health Act 1999 other than the profession of practising medicine and the profession of nursing.

(3) A person does not provide a specimen of breath for a breath test or for analysis unless the specimen—

(a) is sufficient to enable the test or the analysis to be carried out, and

(b) is provided in such a way as to enable the objective of the test or analysis to be satisfactorily achieved.

(4) A person provides a specimen of blood if and only if he consents to its being taken by a medical practitioner and it is so taken.

12 Motor racing on public ways

(1) A person who promotes or takes part in a race or trial of speed between motor vehicles on a public way is guilty of an offence. [S]

(2) In this section 'public way' means, in England and Wales, a highway...

13 Regulation of motoring events on public ways

(1) A person who promotes or takes part in a competition or trial (other than a race or trial of speed) involving the use of motor vehicles on a public way is guilty of an offence unless the competition or trial—

(a) is authorised, and

(b) is conducted in accordance with any conditions imposed,

by or under regulations under this section. [S]

(4) In this section 'public way' means, in England and Wales, a public highway...

13A Disapplication of sections 1 to 3 for authorised motoring events

(1) A person shall not be guilty of an offence under sections 1, 2 or 3 of this Act by virtue of driving a vehicle in a public place other than a road if he shows that he was driving in accordance with an authorisation for a motoring event given under regulations made by the Secretary of State.

14 Seat belts: adults

(1) The Secretary of State may make regulations requiring, subject to such exceptions as may be prescribed, persons who are driving or riding in motor vehicles on a road to wear seat belts of such description as may be prescribed.

(3) A person who drives or rides in a motor vehicle in contravention of regulations under this section is guilty of an offence; but, notwithstanding any enactment or rule of law, no person other

than the person actually committing the contravention is guilty of an offence by reason of the contravention. [S]

(6) Regulations under this section requiring the wearing of seat belts by persons riding in motor vehicles shall not apply to children under the age of fourteen years.

15 Restriction on carrying children not wearing seat belts in motor vehicles

(1) Except as provided by regulations, where a child under the age of fourteen years is in the front of a motor vehicle, a person must not without reasonable excuse drive the vehicle on a road unless the child is wearing a seat belt in conformity with regulations.

(2) It is an offence for a person to drive a motor vehicle in contravention of subsection (1) above. [S]

(3) Except as provided by regulations, where a child under the age of fourteen years is in the rear of a motor vehicle and any seat belt is fitted in the rear of that vehicle, a person must not without reasonable excuse drive the vehicle on a road unless the child is wearing a seat belt in conformity with regulations.

(3A) Except as provided by regulations, where—

- (a) a child who is under the age of 12 years and less than 150 centimetres in height is in the rear of a passenger car,
- (b) no seat belt is fitted in the rear of the passenger car, and
- (c) a seat in the front of the passenger car is provided with a seat belt but is not occupied by any person,

a person must not without reasonable excuse drive the passenger car on a road.

(4) It is an offence for a person to drive a motor vehicle in contravention of subsection (3) or (3A) above. [S]

(9) In this section—

'regulations' means regulations made by the Secretary of State under this section, and

'seat belt' includes any description of restraining device for a child and any reference to wearing a seat belt is to be construed accordingly.

16 Wearing of protective headgear

(1) The Secretary of State may make regulations requiring, subject to such exceptions as may be specified in the regulations, persons driving or riding (otherwise than in side-cars) on motor cycles of any class specified in the regulations to wear protective headgear of such description as may be so specified.

(2) A requirement imposed by regulations under this section shall not apply to any follower of the Sikh religion while he is wearing a turban.

(4) A person who drives or rides a motor cycle in contravention of regulations under this section is guilty of an offence; but notwithstanding any enactment or rule of law no person other than the person actually committing the contravention is guilty of an offence by reason of the contravention unless the person actually committing the contravention is a child under the age of sixteen years. [S]

18 Authorisation of head-worn appliances for use on motor cycles

(1) The Secretary of State may make regulations prescribing (by reference to shape, construction or any other quality) types of appliance of any description to which this section applies as authorised for use by persons driving or riding (otherwise than in sidecars) on motor cycles of any class specified in the regulations.

(3) If a person driving or riding on a motor cycle on a road uses an appliance of any description for which a type is prescribed under this section and that appliance—

- (a) is not of a type so prescribed, or
- (b) is otherwise used in contravention of regulations under this section, he is guilty of an offence. [S]

(4) If a person sells, or offers for sale, an appliance of any such description as authorised for use by persons on or in motor cycles, or motor cycles of any class, and that appliance is not of a type

prescribed under this section as authorised for such use, he is, subject to subsection (5) below, guilty of an offence. [S]

(5) A person shall not be convicted of an offence under this section in respect of the sale or offer for sale of an appliance if he proves that it was sold or, as the case may be, offered for sale for export from Great Britain.

(7) This section applies to appliances of any description designed or adapted for use—

(a) with any headgear, or

(b) by being attached to or placed upon the head, (as, for example, eye protectors or earphones).

(8) References in this section to selling or offering for sale include respectively references to letting on hire and offering to let on hire.

22 Leaving vehicles in dangerous positions

If a person in charge of a vehicle causes or permits the vehicle or a trailer drawn by it to remain at rest on a road in such a position or in such condition or in such circumstances as to involve a danger of injury to other persons using the road, he is guilty of an offence. [S]

22A Causing danger to road-users

(1) A person is guilty of an offence if he intentionally and without lawful authority or reasonable cause—

(a) causes anything to be on or over a road, or

(b) interferes with a motor vehicle, trailer or cycle, or

(c) interferes (directly or indirectly) with traffic equipment,

in such circumstances that it would be obvious to a reasonable person that to do so would be dangerous. [E]

(2) In subsection (1) above 'dangerous' refers to danger either of injury to any person while on or near a road, or of serious damage to property on or near a road; and in determining for the purposes of that subsection what would be obvious to a reasonable person in a particular case, regard shall be had not only to the circumstances of which he could be expected to be aware but also to any circumstances shown to have been within the knowledge of the accused.

(3) In subsection (1) above 'traffic equipment' means—

(a) anything lawfully placed on or near a road by a highway authority;

(b) a traffic sign lawfully placed on or near a road by a person other than a highway authority;

(c) any fence, barrier or light lawfully placed on or near a road—

(i) in pursuance of section 174 of the Highways Act 1980, or section 65 of the New Roads and Street Works Act 1991 (which provide for guarding, lighting and signing in streets where works are undertaken), or

(ii) by a constable or a person acting under the instructions (whether general or specific) of a chief officer of police.

(4) For the purposes of subsection (3) above anything placed on or near a road shall unless the contrary is proved be deemed to have been lawfully placed there.

(5) In this section 'road' does not include a footpath or bridleway.

23 Restriction of carriage of persons on motor cycles

(1) Not more than one person in addition to the driver may be carried on a motor cycle.

(2) No person in addition to the driver may be carried on a motor cycle otherwise than sitting astride the motor cycle and on a proper seat securely fixed to the motor cycle behind the driver's seat.

(3) If a person is carried on a motor cycle in contravention of this section, the driver of the motor cycle is guilty of an offence. [S]

24 Restriction of carriage of persons on bicycles

(1) Not more than one person may be carried on a road on a bicycle not propelled by mechanical power unless it is constructed or adapted for the carriage of more than one person.

(2) In this section—

(a) references to a person carried on a bicycle include references to a person riding the bicycle, and

(b) 'road' includes bridleway.

(3) If a person is carried on a bicycle in contravention of subsection (1) above, each of the persons carried is guilty of an offence. [S]

25 Tampering with motor vehicles

If, while a motor vehicle is on a road or on a parking place provided by a local authority, a person—

(a) gets on to the vehicle, or

(b) tampers with the brake or other part of its mechanism,

without lawful authority or reasonable cause he is guilty of an offence. [S]

26 Holding or getting on to vehicle in order to be towed or carried

(1) If, for the purpose of being carried, a person without lawful authority or reasonable cause takes or retains hold of, or gets on to, a motor vehicle or trailer while in motion on a road he is guilty of an offence.

(2) If, for the purpose of being drawn, a person takes or retains hold of a motor vehicle or trailer while in motion on a road he is guilty of an offence. [S]

27 Control of dogs on roads

(1) A person who causes or permits a dog to be on a designated road without the dog being held on a lead is guilty of an offence. [S]

(2) In this section 'designated road' means a length of road specified by an order in that behalf of the local authority in whose area the length of road is situated.

(4) An order under this section may provide that subsection (1) above shall apply subject to such limitations or exceptions as may be specified in the order, and (without prejudice to the generality of this subsection) subsection (1) above does not apply to dogs proved—

(a) to be kept for driving or tending sheep or cattle in the course of a trade or business, or

(b) to have been at the material time in use under proper control for sporting purposes.

28 Dangerous cycling

(1) A person who rides a cycle on a road dangerously is guilty of an offence. [S]

(2) For the purposes of subsection (1) above a person is to be regarded as riding dangerously if (and only if)—

(a) the way he rides falls far below what would be expected of a competent and careful cyclist, and

(b) it would be obvious to a competent and careful cyclist that riding in that way would be dangerous.

(3) In subsection (2) above 'dangerous' refers to danger either of injury to any person or of serious damage to property; and in determining for the purposes of that subsection what would be obvious to a competent and careful cyclist in a particular case, regard shall be had not only to the circumstances of which he could be expected to be aware but also to any circumstances shown to have been within the knowledge of the accused.

29 Careless, and inconsiderate, cycling

If a person rides a cycle on a road without due care and attention, or without reasonable consideration for other persons using the road, he is guilty of an offence. [S]

30 Cycling when under influence of drink or drugs

(1) A person who, when riding a cycle on a road or other public place, is unfit to ride through drink or drugs (that is to say, is under the influence of drink or a drug to such an extent as to be incapable of having proper control of the cycle) is guilty of an offence. [S]

31 Regulation of cycle racing on public ways

(1) A person who promotes or takes part in a race or trial of speed on a public way between cycles is guilty of an offence, unless the race or trial—

(a) is authorised, and
(b) is conducted in accordance with any conditions imposed, by or under regulations under this section. [S]

(6) In this section 'public way' means, in England and Wales, a highway . . .

34 Prohibition of driving motor vehicles elsewhere than on roads

(1) Subject to the provisions of this section, if without lawful authority a person drives a motor vehicle—

(a) on to or upon any common land, moorland or land of any other description, not being land forming part of a road, or
(b) on any road being a footpath, bridleway, or restricted byway, he is guilty of an offence. [S]

(3) It is not an offence under this section to drive a mechanically propelled vehicle on any land within fifteen yards of a road, being a road on which a motor vehicle may lawfully be driven, for the purpose only of parking the vehicle on that land.

(4) A person shall not be convicted of an offence under this section with respect to a vehicle if he proves to the satisfaction of the court that it was driven in contravention of this section for the purpose of saving life or extinguishing fire or meeting any other like emergency.

35 Drivers to comply with traffic directions

(1) Where a constable is for the time being engaged in the regulation of traffic in a road, a person driving or propelling a vehicle who neglects or refuses—

(a) to stop the vehicle, or
(b) to make it proceed in, or keep to, a particular line of traffic,

when directed to do so by the constable in the execution of his duty is guilty of an offence. [S]

(2) Where—

(a) a traffic survey of any description is being carried out on or in the vicinity of a road, and
(b) a constable gives to a person driving or propelling a vehicle a direction—
  (i) to stop the vehicle,
  (ii) to make it proceed in, or keep to, a particular line of traffic, or
  (iii) to proceed to a particular point on or near the road on which the vehicle is being driven or propelled,

being a direction given for the purposes of the survey (but not a direction requiring any person to provide any information for the purposes of a traffic survey),

the person is guilty of an offence if he neglects or refuses to comply with the direction.

36 Drivers to comply with traffic signs

(1) Where a traffic sign, being a sign—

(a) of the prescribed size, colour and type, or
(b) of another character authorised by the Secretary of State under the provisions in that behalf of the Road Traffic Regulation Act 1984,

has been lawfully placed on or near a road, a person driving or propelling a vehicle who fails to comply with the indication given by the sign is guilty of an offence. [S]

(2) A traffic sign shall not be treated for the purposes of this section as having been lawfully placed unless either—

(a) the indication given by the sign is an indication of a statutory prohibition, restriction or requirement, or
(b) it is expressly provided by or under any provision of the Traffic Acts that this section shall apply to the sign or to signs of a type of which the sign is one;

and, where the indication mentioned in paragraph (a) of this subsection is of the general nature only of the prohibition, restriction or requirement to which the sign relates, a person shall not be convicted of failure to comply with the indication unless he has failed to comply with the prohibition, restriction or requirement to which the sign relates.

(3) For the purposes of this section a traffic sign placed on or near a road shall be deemed—

(a) to be of the prescribed size, colour and type, or of another character authorised by the Secretary of State under the provisions in that behalf of the Road Traffic Regulation Act 1984, and

(b) (subject to subsection (2) above) to have been lawfully so placed,

unless the contrary is proved.

(4) Where a traffic survey of any description is being carried out on or in the vicinity of a road, this section applies to a traffic sign by which a direction is given—

(a) to stop a vehicle,

(b) to make it proceed in, or keep to, a particular line of traffic, or

(c) to proceed to a particular point on or near the road on which the vehicle is being driven or propelled,

being a direction given for the purposes of the survey (but not a direction requiring any person to provide any information for the purposes of the survey).

37 Directions to pedestrians

Where a constable in uniform is for the time being engaged in the regulation of vehicular traffic in a road, a person on foot who proceeds across or along the carriageway in contravention of a direction to stop given by the constable in the execution of his duty, either to persons on foot or to persons on foot and other traffic, is guilty of an offence. [S]

40A Using vehicles in dangerous condition

A person is guilty of an offence if he uses, or causes or permits another to use, a motor vehicle or trailer on a road when—

(a) the condition of the motor vehicle or trailer, or of its accessories or equipment, or

(b) the purpose for which it is used, or

(c) the number of passengers carried by it or the manner in which they are carried, or

(d) the weight, position or distribution of its load, or the manner in which it is secured, is such that the use of the motor vehicle or trailer involves a danger of injury to any person. [S]

41A Breach of requirement as to brakes, steering-gear or tyres

A person who—

(a) contravenes or fails to comply with a construction and use requirement as to brakes, steering-gear or tyres, or

(b) uses on a road a motor vehicle or trailer which does not comply with such a requirement, or causes or permits a motor vehicle or trailer to be so used,

is guilty of an offence. [S]

41B Breach of requirement as to weight: goods and passenger vehicles

(1) A person who—

(a) contravenes or fails to comply with a construction and use requirement as to any description of weight applicable to—

(i) a goods vehicle, or

(ii) a motor vehicle or trailer adapted to carry more than eight passengers, or

(b) uses on a road a vehicle which does not comply with such a requirement, or causes or permits a vehicle to be so used,

is guilty of an offence. [S]

(2) In any proceedings for an offence under this section in which there is alleged a contravention of or failure to comply with a construction and use requirement as to any description of weight applicable to a goods vehicle, it shall be a defence to prove either—

(a) that at the time when the vehicle was being used on the road—

(i) it was proceeding to a weighbridge which was the nearest available one to the place where the loading of the vehicle was completed for the purpose of being weighed, or

(ii) it was proceeding from a weighbridge after being weighed to the nearest point at which it was reasonably practicable to reduce the weight to the relevant limit, without causing an obstruction on any road, or

(b) in a case where the limit of that weight was not exceeded by more than 5 per cent—

(i) that that limit was not exceeded at the time when the loading of the vehicle was originally completed, and

(ii) that since that time no person has made any addition to the load.

42 Breach of other construction and use requirements

A person who—

(a) contravenes or fails to comply with any construction or use requirement other than one within section 41A(a) or 41B(1)(a) of this Act, or

(b) uses on a road a motor vehicle or trailer which does not comply with such a requirement, or causes or permits a motor vehicle or trailer to be so used,

is guilty of an offence. [S]

75 Vehicles not to be sold in unroadworthy condition or altered so as to be unroadworthy

(1) Subject to the provisions of this section no person shall supply a motor vehicle or trailer in an unroadworthy condition.

(2) In this section references to supply include—

(a) sell,

(b) offer to sell or supply, and

(c) expose for sale.

(3) For the purposes of subsection (1) above a motor vehicle or trailer is in an unroadworthy condition if—

(a) it is in such a condition that the use of it on a road in that condition would be unlawful by virtue of any provision made by regulations under section 41 of this Act as respects—

(i) brakes, steering-gear or tyres, or

(ii) the construction, weight or equipment of vehicles, or

(b) it is in such a condition that its use on a road would involve a danger of injury to any person.

(4) Subject to the provisions of this section no person shall alter a motor vehicle or trailer so as to render its condition such that the use of it on a road in that condition

(a) would be unlawful by virtue of any provision made as respects the construction, weight or equipment of vehicles by regulations under section 41, or

(b) would involve a danger of injury to any person.

(5) A person who supplies or alters a motor vehicle or trailer in contravention of this section, or causes or permits it to be so supplied or altered, is guilty of an offence. [S]

(6) A person shall not be convicted of an offence under this section in respect of the supply or alteration of a motor vehicle or trailer if he proves—

(a) that it was supplied or altered, as the case may be, for export from Great Britain, or

(b) that he had reasonable cause to believe that the vehicle or trailer would not be used on a road in Great Britain, or would not be so used until it had been put into a condition in which it might lawfully be so used.

(6A) Paragraph (b) of subsection (6) above shall not apply in relation to a person who, in the course of a trade or business—

(a) exposes a vehicle or trailer for sale, unless he also proves that he took all reasonable steps to ensure that any prospective purchaser would be aware that its use in its current condition on a road in Great Britain would be unlawful, or

(b) offers to sell a vehicle or trailer, unless he also proves that he took all reasonable steps to ensure that the person to whom the offer was made was aware of that fact.

76 Fitting and supply of defective or unsuitable vehicle parts

(1) If any person—

(a) fits a vehicle part to a vehicle, or

(b) causes or permits a vehicle part to be fitted to a vehicle,

in such circumstances that the use of the vehicle on a road would, by reason of that part being fitted to the vehicle involve a danger of injury to any person, or, constitute a contravention of or failure to comply with any of the construction and use requirements, he is guilty of an offence. [S]

(2) A person shall not be convicted of an offence under subsection (1) above if he proves—

(a) that the vehicle to which the part was fitted was to be exported from Great Britain, or

(b) that he had reasonable cause to believe that that vehicle—

(i) would not be used on a road in Great Britain, or

(ii) that it would not be so used until it had been put into a condition in which its use on a road would not constitute a contravention of or a failure to comply with any of the construction and use requirements, and would not involve a danger of injury to any person.

(3) If a person—

(a) supplies a vehicle part or causes or permits a vehicle part to be supplied, and

(b) has reasonable cause to believe that the part is to be fitted to a motor vehicle, or to a vehicle of a particular class, or to a particular vehicle,

he is guilty of an offence if that part could not be fitted to a motor vehicle, or, as the case may require, to a vehicle of that class or of a class to which the particular vehicle belongs, except in such circumstances that the use of the vehicle on a road would, by reason of that part being fitted to the vehicle, constitute a contravention of or failure to comply with any of the construction and use requirement or involve a danger of injury to any person. [S]

(4) In this section references to supply include—

(a) sell, and

(b) offer to sell or supply.

(5) A person shall not be convicted of an offence under subsection (3) above in respect of the supply of a vehicle part if he proves—

(a) that the part was supplied for export from Great Britain, or

(b) that he had reasonable cause to believe that—

(i) it would not be fitted to a vehicle used on a road in Great Britain, or

(ii) it would not be so fitted until it had been put into such a condition that it could be fitted otherwise than in such circumstances that the use of the vehicle on a road would, by reason of that part being fitted to the vehicle, constitute a contravention of or failure to comply with any of the construction and use requirements, or involve a danger of injury to any person.

87 Drivers of motor vehicles to have driving licences

(1) It is an offence for a person to drive on a road a motor vehicle of any class otherwise than in accordance with a licence authorising him to drive a motor vehicle of that class.

(2) It is an offence for a person to cause or permit another person to drive on a road a motor vehicle of any class otherwise than in accordance with a licence authorising that person to drive a motor vehicle of that class. [S]

103 Obtaining licence, or driving, while disqualified

(1) A person is guilty of an offence if, while disqualified for holding or obtaining a licence, he—

(a) obtains a licence, or

(b) drives a motor vehicle on a road. [S]

(2) A licence obtained by a person who is disqualified is of no effect (or, where the disqualification relates only to vehicles of a particular class, is of no effect in relation to vehicles of that class).

143 Users of motor vehicles to be insured or secured against third-party risks

(1) Subject to the provisions of Part [VI] of this Act—

(a) a person must not use a motor vehicle on a road or other public place unless there is in force in relation to the use of the vehicle by that person such a policy of insurance or such a security in respect of third party risks as complies with the requirements of this Part of this Act, and

(b) a person must not cause or permit any other person to use a motor vehicle on a road or other public place unless there is in force in relation to the use of the vehicle by that other person such a policy of insurance or such a security in respect of third party risks as complies with the requirements of this Part of this Act.

(2) If a person acts in contravention of subsection (1) above he is guilty of an offence. [S]

(3) A person charged with using a motor vehicle in contravention of this section shall not be convicted if he proves—

(a) that the vehicle did not belong to him and was not in his possession under a contract of hiring or of loan,

(b) that he was using the vehicle in the course of his employment, and

(c) that he neither knew nor had reason to believe that there was not in force in relation to the vehicle such a policy of insurance of security as is mentioned in subsection (1) above.

(4) Part [VI] of this Act does not apply to invalid carriages.

144A Offence of keeping vehicle which does not meet insurance requirements

(1) If a motor vehicle registered under the Vehicle Excise and Registration Act 1994 does not meet the insurance requirements, the person in whose name the vehicle is registered is guilty of an offence. [S]

(2) For the purposes of this section a vehicle meets the insurance requirements if—

(a) it is covered by such a policy of insurance or such a security in respect of third party risks as complies with the requirements of this Part of this Act, and

(b) either of the following conditions is satisfied.

(3) The first condition is that the policy or security, of the certificate of insurance or security which relates to it, identifies the vehicle by its registration mark as a vehicle which is covered by the policy or security.

(4) The second condition is that the vehicle is covered by the policy or security because—

(a) the policy or security covers any vehicle, or any vehicle of a particular description, the owner of which is a person named in the policy or security or in the certificate of insurance or security which relates to it, and

(b) the vehicle is owned by that person.

(5) For the purposes of this section a vehicle is covered by a policy of insurance or security if the policy of insurance or security is in force in relation to the use of the vehicle.

144B Exceptions to section 144A offence

(1) A person ('the registered keeper') in whose name a vehicle which does not meet the insurance requirements is registered at any particular time ('the relevant time') does not commit an offence under section 144A of this Act at that time if any of the following conditions are satisfied.

(2) The first condition is that at the relevant time the vehicle is owned as described—

(a) in subsection (1) of section 144 of this Act, or

(b) in paragraph (a), (b), (da), (db), (dc) or (g) of subsection (2) of that section,

(whether or not at the relevant time it is being driven as described in that provision).

(3) The second condition is that at the relevant time the vehicle is owned with the intention that it should be used as described in paragraph (c), (d), (e) or (f) of section 144(2) of this Act.

(4) The third condition is that the registered keeper—

(a) is not at the relevant time the person keeping the vehicle, and

(b) if previously he was the person keeping the vehicle, he has by the relevant time complied with any requirements under subsection (7)(a) below that he is required to have complied with by the relevant of any earlier time.

(5) The fourth condition is that—

(a) the registered keeper is at the relevant time the person keeping the vehicle,

(b) at the relevant time the vehicle is not used on a road or other public place, and

(c) the registered keeper has by the relevant time complied with any requirements under subsection (7)(a) below that he is required to have complied with by the relevant or any earlier time.

(6) The fifth condition is that—

(a) the vehicle has been stolen before the relevant time,

(b) the vehicle has not been recovered by the relevant time, and

(c) any requirements under subsection (7)(b) below that, in connection with the theft, are required to have been complied with by the relevant or any earlier time have been complied with by the relevant time.

(9) A person accused of an offence under section 144A of this Act is not entitled to the benefit of an exception conferred by or under this section unless evidence is adduced that is sufficient to raise an issue with respect to that exception; but where evidence is so adduced it is for the prosecution to prove beyond reasonable doubt that the exception does not apply.

168 Failure to give, or giving false, name and address in case of dangerous or careless or inconsiderate driving or cycling

Any of the following persons—

(a) the driver of a mechanically propelled vehicle who is alleged to have committed an offence under section 2 or 3 of this Act, or

(b) the rider of a cycle who is alleged to have committed an offence under section 28 or 29 of this Act,

who refuses, on being so required by any person having reasonable ground for so requiring, to give his name or address, or gives a false name or address, is guilty of an offence. [S]

169 Pedestrian contravening constable's direction to stop to give name and address

A constable may require a person committing an offence under section 37 of this Act to give his name and address, and if that person fails to do so he is guilty of an offence. [S]

170 Duty of driver to stop, report accident and give information or documents

(1) This section applies in a case where, owing to the presence of a mechanically propelled vehicle on a road, an accident occurs by which—

(a) personal injury is caused to a person other than the driver of that mechanically propelled vehicle, or

(b) damage is caused—

(i) to a vehicle other than that mechanically propelled vehicle or a trailer drawn by that mechanically propelled vehicle, or

(ii) to an animal other than an animal in or on that mechanically propelled vehicle or a trailer drawn by that mechanically propelled vehicle, or

(iii) to any other property constructed on, fixed to, growing in or otherwise forming part of the land on which the road in question is situated or land adjacent to such land.

(2) The driver of the mechanically propelled vehicle must stop and, if required to do so by any person having reasonable grounds for so requiring, give his name and address and also the name and address of the owner and the identification marks of the vehicle.

(3) If for any reason the driver of the mechanically propelled vehicle does not give his name and address under subsection (2) above, he must report the accident.

(4) A person who fails to comply with subsection (2) or (3) above is guilty of an offence. [S]

(5) If, in a case where this section applies by virtue of subsection (1)(a) above, the driver of a motor vehicle does not at the time of the accident produce such a certificate of insurance or security, or other evidence, as is mentioned in section 165(2)(a) of this Act—

(a) to a constable, or

(b) to some person who, having reasonable grounds for so doing, has required him to produce it,

the driver must report the accident and produce such a certificate or other evidence.

This subsection does not apply to the driver of an invalid carriage.

(6) To comply with a duty under this section to report an accident or to produce such a certificate of insurance or security, or other evidence, as is mentioned in section 165(2)(a) of this Act, the driver—

(a) must do so at a police station or to a constable, and

(b) must do so as soon as is reasonably practicable and, in any case, within twenty-four hours of the occurrence of the accident.

(7) A person who fails to comply with a duty under subsection (5) above is guilty of an offence, but he shall not be convicted by reason only of a failure to produce a certificate or other evidence if, within seven days after the occurrence of the accident, the certificate or other evidence is produced at a police station that was specified by him at the time when the accident was reported. [S]

(8) In this section 'animal' means horse, cattle, ass, mule, sheep, pig, goat or dog.

171 Duty of owner of motor vehicle to give information for verifying compliance with requirement of compulsory insurance or security

(1) For the purpose of determining whether a motor vehicle was or was not being driven in contravention of section 143 of this Act on any occasion when the driver was required under section 165(1) or 170 of this Act to produce such a certificate of insurance or security, or other evidence, as is mentioned in section 165(2)(a) of this Act, the owner of the vehicle must give such information as he may be required, by or on behalf of a chief officer of police, to give.

(2) A person who fails to comply with the requirement of subsection (1) above is guilty of an offence. [S]

(3) In this section 'owner', in relation to a vehicle which is the subject of a hiring agreement, includes each party to the agreement.

172 Duty to give information as to identity of driver, etc., in certain circumstances

(1) This section applies—

(a) to any offence under the preceding provisions of this Act except—

(i) an offence under Part V, or

(ii) an offence under section 13, 16, 51(2), 61(4), 67(9), 68(4), 96 or 120, and to an offence under section 178 of this Act,

(b) to any offence under sections 25, 26 or 27 of the Road Traffic Offenders Act 1988,

(c) to any offence against any other enactment relating to the use of vehicles on roads, except an offence under paragraph 8 of Schedule 1 to the Road Traffic (Driver Licensing and Information Systems) Act 1989, and

(d) to manslaughter... by the driver of a motor vehicle.

(2) Where the driver of a vehicle is alleged to be guilty of an offence to which this section applies—

(a) the person keeping the vehicle shall give such information as to the identity of the driver as he may be required to give by or on behalf of a chief officer of police, and

(b) any other person shall if required as stated above give any information which it is in his power to give and may lead to identification of the driver.

(3) Subject to the following provisions, a person who fails to comply with a requirement under subsection (2) above shall be guilty of an offence. [S]

(4) A person shall not be guilty of an offence by virtue of paragraph (a) of subsection (2) above if he shows that he did not know and could not with reasonable diligence have ascertained who the driver of the vehicle was.

(5) Where a body corporate is guilty of an offence under this section and the offence is proved to have been committed with the consent or connivance of, or to be attributable to neglect on the part of, a director, manager, secretary or other similar officer of the body corporate, or a person who was purporting to act in any such capacity, he, as well as the body corporate, is guilty of that offence and liable to be proceeded against and punished accordingly.

(6) Where the alleged offender is a body corporate, . . . or the proceedings are brought against him by virtue of subsection (5) above or subsection (11) below, subsection (4) above shall not apply unless, in addition to the matters there mentioned, the alleged offender shows that no record was kept of the persons who drove the vehicle and that the failure to keep a record was reasonable.

(7) A requirement under subsection (2) may be made by written notice served by post; and where it is so made—

(a) it shall have effect as a requirement to give the information within the period of 28 days beginning with the day on which the notice is served, and

(b) the person on whom the notice is served shall not be guilty of an offence under this section if he shows either that he gave the information as soon as reasonably practicable after the end of that period or that it has not been reasonably practicable for him to give it.

(8) Where the person on whom a notice under subsection (7) above is to be served is a body corporate, the notice is duly served if it is served on the secretary or clerk of that body.

(9) For the purposes of section 7 of the Interpretation Act 1978 as it applies for the purposes of this section the proper address of any person in relation to the service on him of a notice under subsection (7) above is—

(a) in the case of the secretary or clerk of a body corporate, that of the registered or principal office of that body or (if the body corporate is the registered keeper of the vehicle concerned) the registered address, and

(b) in any other case, his last known address at the time of service.

(10) In this section—

'registered address', in relation to the registered keeper of a vehicle, means the address recorded in the record kept under the Vehicles (Excise) and Registration Act 1994 with respect to that vehicle as being that person's address, and

'registered keeper', in relation to a vehicle, means the person in whose name the vehicle is registered under that Act;

and references to the driver of a vehicle include references to the rider of a cycle.

185 Meaning of 'motor vehicle' and other expressions relating to vehicles

(1) In this Act—

. . .

'invalid carriage' means a mechanically propelled vehicle the weight of which unladen does not exceed 254 kilograms and which is specially designed and constructed, and not merely adapted, for the use of a person suffering from some physical defect or disability and is used solely by such a person,

'motor car' means a mechanically propelled vehicle, not being a motor cycle or an invalid carriage, which is constructed itself to carry a load or passengers and the weight of which unladen—

(a) if it is constructed solely for the carriage of passengers and their effects, is adapted to carry not more than seven passengers exclusive of the driver and is fitted with tyres of such type as may be specified in regulations made by the Secretary of State, does not exceed 3050 kilograms,

(b) if it is constructed or adapted for use for the conveyance of goods or burden of any description, does not exceed 3050 kilograms, or 3500 kilograms if the vehicle carries a container or containers for holding for the purposes of its propulsion any fuel which is wholly gaseous at 17.5 degrees Celsius under a pressure of 1.013 bar or plant and materials for producing such fuel,

(c) does not exceed 2540 kilograms in a case not falling within sub-paragraph (a) or (b) above,

'motor cycle' means a mechanically propelled vehicle, not being an invalid carriage, with less than four wheels and the weight of which unladen does not exceed 410 kilograms,

. . .

'motor vehicle' means, subject to section 20 of the Chronically Sick and Disabled Persons Act 1970 (which makes special provision about invalid carriages, within the meaning of that Act), a mechanically propelled vehicle intended or adapted for use on roads, and

'trailer' means a vehicle drawn by a motor vehicle.

. . .

192 General interpretation of Act

(1) In this Act—

'bridleway' means a way over which the public have the following, but no other, rights of way: a right of way on foot and a right of way on horseback or leading a horse, with or without a right to drive animals of any description along the way,

'carriage of goods' includes the haulage of goods,

'cycle' means a bicycle, a tricycle, or a cycle having four or more wheels, not being in any case a motor vehicle,

'driver', where a separate person acts as a steersman of a motor vehicle, includes (except for the purposes of section 1 of this Act) that person as well as any other person engaged in the driving of the vehicle, and 'drive' is to be interpreted accordingly,

'footpath', in relation to England and Wales, means a way over which the public have a right of way on foot only,

'goods' includes goods or burden of any description,

'goods vehicle' means a motor vehicle constructed or adapted for use for the carriage of goods, or a trailer so constructed or adapted,

'highway authority', in England and Wales, means—

(a) in relation to a road for which he is the highway authority within the meaning of the Highway Act 1980, the Secretary of State, and

(b) in relation to any other road, the council of the county, metropolitan district or London borough or the Common Council of the City of London as the case may be.

. . .

'owner', in relation to a vehicle which is the subject of a hiring agreement or hire-purchase agreement, means the person in possession of the vehicle under that agreement,

'prescribed' means prescribed by regulations made by the Secretary of State,

'road', in relation to England and Wales, means any highway and any other road to which the public has access, and includes bridges over which a road passes,

'the Road Traffic Acts' means the Road Traffic Offenders Act 1988, the Road Traffic (Consequential Provisions) Act 1988 (so far as it reproduces the effect of provisions repealed by that Act) and this Act,

'statutory', in relation to any prohibition, restriction, requirement or provision, means contained in, or having effect under, any enactment (including any enactment contained in this Act),

'the Traffic Acts' means the Road Traffic Acts and the Road Traffic Regulation Act 1984,

'traffic sign' has the meaning given by section 64(1) of the Road Traffic Regulation Act 1984,

'tramcar' includes any carriage used on any road by virtue of an order under the Light Railways Act 1896, and

'trolley vehicle' means a mechanically propelled vehicle adapted for use on roads without rails under power transmitted to it from some external source whether or not there is in addition a source of power on board the vehicle.

. . .

(3) References in this Act to a class of vehicles are to be interpreted as references to a class defined or described by reference to any characteristics of the vehicles or to any other circumstances whatsoever, and accordingly an authorising the use of 'category' to indicate a class of vehicles, however defined or described.

Theft Act 1968

12A Aggravated vehicle-taking

[See page 177]

Highways Act 1980

137 Penalty for wilful obstruction

(1) If a person, without lawful authority or excuse, in any way wilfully obstructs the free passage along a highway he is guilty of an offence and liable to a fine not exceeding level 3 on the standard scale. [S]

161 Penalties for causing certain kinds of danger or annoyance

(1) If a person, without lawful authority or excuse, deposits any thing whatsoever on a highway in consequence of which a user of the highway is injured or endangered, that person is guilty of an offence and liable to a fine not exceeding level 3 on the standard scale. [S]

(2) If a person, without lawful authority or excuse,

(a) lights any fire on or over a highway which consists of or comprises a carriageway; or

(b) discharges any firearm or firework within 50 feet of the centre of such a highway, and in consequence a user of the highway is injured, interrupted or endangered, that person is guilty of an offence and liable to a fine not exceeding level 3 on the standard scale. [S]

(3) If a person plays at football or any other game on a highway to the annoyance of a user of the highway he is guilty of an offence and liable to a fine not exceeding level 1 on the standard scale. [S]

(4) If a person, without lawful authority or excuse, allows any filth, dirt, lime or other offensive matter or thing to run or flow on to a highway from any adjoining premises, he is guilty of an offence and liable to a fine not exceeding level 1 on the standard scale. [S]

162 Penalty for placing rope, etc., across highway

A person who for any purpose places any rope, wire or other apparatus across a highway in such a manner as to be likely to cause danger to persons using the highway is, unless he proves that he had taken all necessary means to give adequate warning of the danger, guilty of an offence and liable, to a fine not exceeding level 3 on the standard scale. [S]

Road Traffic Regulation Act 1984

81 General speed limit for restricted roads

(1) It shall not be lawful for a person to drive a motor vehicle on a restricted road at a speed exceeding 30 miles per hour. [S]

82 What roads are restricted roads

(1) Subject to the provisions of this section and of section 84(3) of this Act, a road is a restricted road for the purposes of section 81 of this Act if there is provided on it a system of street lighting furnished by means of lamps placed not more than 200 yards apart.

84 Speed limits on roads other than restricted roads

(1) An order made under this subsection as respects any road may prohibit—

(a) the driving of motor vehicles on that road at a speed exceeding that specified in the order,

(b) the driving of motor vehicles on that road at a speed exceeding that specified in the order during periods specified in the order, or

(c) the driving of motor vehicles on that road at a speed exceeding the speed for the time being indicated by traffic signs in accordance with the order.

(1A) An order made by virtue of subsection (1)(c) above may—

(a) make provision restricting the speeds that may be indicated by traffic signs or the periods during which the indication may be given, and

(b) provide for the indications to be given only in such circumstances as may be determined by or under the order;

but any such order must comply with regulations made under subsection (1B) below, except where the Secretary of State authorises otherwise in a particular case.

(3) While an order made by virtue of subsection (1)(a) above is in force as respects a road, that road shall not be a restricted road for the purposes of section 81 of this Act.

85 Traffic signs for indicating speed restrictions

(4) Where no such system of street or carriageway lighting as is mentioned in section 82(1) is provided on a road, but a limit of speed is to be observed on the road, a person shall not be convicted of driving a motor vehicle on the road at a speed exceeding the limit unless the limit is indicated by means of such traffic signs as are mentioned in subsection (1) or subsection (2) above.

(5) In any proceedings for a contravention of section 81 of this Act, where the proceedings relate to driving on a road provided with such a system of street or carriageway lighting, evidence of the absence of traffic signs displayed in pursuance of this section to indicate that the road is not a restricted road for the purposes of that section shall be evidence that the road is a restricted road for those purposes.

86 Speed limits for particular classes of vehicles

(1) It shall not be lawful for a person to drive a motor vehicle of any class on a road at a speed greater than the speed specified in Schedule 6 to this Act as the maximum speed in relation to a vehicle of that class. [S]

87 Exemptions from speed limits

(1) No statutory provision imposing a speed limit on motor vehicles shall apply to any vehicle on an occasion when—

(a) it is being used for fire and rescue authority purposes or for or in connection with the exercise of any function of a relevant authority as defined in section 6 of the Fire (Scotland) Act 2005, for ambulance purposes or for police or Serious Organised Crime Agency purposes,

(b) it is being used for other prescribed purposes in such circumstances as may be prescribed, or

(c) it is being used for training persons to drive vehicles for use for any of the purposes mentioned in paragraph (a) or (b) above,

if the observance of that provision would be likely to hinder the use of the vehicle for the purpose for which it is being used on that occasion.

(2) Subsection (1) above does not apply unless the vehicle is being driven by a person who—

(a) has satisfactorily completed a course of training in the driving of vehicles at high speed provided in accordance with regulations under this section, or

(b) is driving the vehicle as part of such a course.

89 Speeding offences generally

(1) A person who drives a motor vehicle on a road at a speed exceeding a limit imposed by or under any enactment to which this section applies shall be guilty of an offence. [S]

(4) If a person who employs other persons to drive motor vehicles on roads publishes or issues any time-table or schedule, or gives any directions, under which any journey, or any stage or part of any journey, is to be completed within some specified time, and it is not practicable in the circumstances of the case for that journey (or that stage or part of it) to be completed in the specified time without the commission of such an offence as is mentioned in subsection (1) above, the publication or issue of the time-table or schedule, or the giving of the directions may be produced as prima facie evidence that the employer procured or (as the case may be) incited the persons employed by him to drive the vehicles to commit such an offence.

Town Police Clauses Act 1847

28 Penalty on persons committing any of the offences herein named

Every person who in any street, to the obstruction, annoyance, or danger of the residents or passengers, commits any of the following offences, shall be liable to a penalty not exceeding [level 3 on the standard scale] for each offence, or, in the discretion of the justice before whom he is convicted, may be committed to prison, there to remain for a period not exceeding fourteen days; . . . ; (that is to say,)

Every person who exposes for show, hire, or sale (except in a market or market place or fair lawfully appointed for that purpose) any horse or other animal, or exhibits in a caravan or otherwise any show or public entertainment, or shoes, bleeds, or farries any horse or animal (except in cases of accident), or cleans, dresses, exercises, trains, or breaks, or turns loose any horse or animal, or makes or repairs any part of any cart or carriage (except in cases of accident where repair on the spot is necessary):

Every person who suffers to be at large any unmuzzled ferocious dog, or sets on or urges any dog or other animal to attack, worry, or put in fear any person or animal:

Every person who slaughters or dresses any cattle, or any part thereof, except in the case of any cattle over-driven which may have met with any accident, and which for the public safety or other reasonable cause ought to be killed on the spot:

Every person having the care of any waggon, cart, or carriage who rides on the shafts thereof, or who without having reins, and holding the same, rides upon such waggon, cart, or carriage or on any animal drawing the same, or who is at such a distance from such waggon, cart, or carriage, as not to have due control over every animal drawing the same, or who does not, in meeting any other carriage, keep his waggon, cart, or carriage to the left or near side or who in passing any other carriage does not keep his waggon, cart, or carriage on the right or off side of the road, (except in cases of actual necessity, or some sufficient reason for deviation,) or who, by obstructing the street, wilfully prevents any person or carriage from passing him, or any waggon, cart, or carriage under his care:

Every person who rides or drives furiously any horse or carriage, or drives furiously any cattle:

Every person who causes any public carriage, sledge, truck, or barrow, with or without horses, or any beast of burden, to stand longer than is necessary for loading or unloading goods, or for taking up or setting down passengers, (except hackney carriages, and horses and other beasts of draught or burthen, standing for hire in any place appointed for that purpose by the commissioners or other lawful authority,) and every person who, by means of any cart, carriage, sledge, truck, or barrow, or any animal, or other means wilfully interrupts any public crossing, or wilfully causes any obstruction in any public footpath or other public thoroughfare:

Every person who causes any tree or timber or iron beam to be drawn in or upon any carriage, without having sufficient means of safely guiding the same:

Every person who leads or rides any horse or other animal, or draws or drives any cart or carriage, sledge, truck, or barrow, upon any footway of any street, or fastens any horse or other animal so that it stands across or upon any footway:

Every person who places or leaves any furniture, goods, wares, or merchandize, or any cask, tub, basket, pail, or bucket, or places or uses any standing-place, stool, bench, stall, or show-board, on any footway, or who places any blind, shade, covering, awning, or other projection over or along any such footway, unless such blind, shade, covering, awning, or other projection is eight feet in height at least in every part thereof from the ground:

Every person who places, hangs up, or otherwise exposes to sale any goods, wares, merchandize, matter, or thing whatsoever, so that the same project into or over any footway, or beyond the line of any house, shop, or building at which the same are so exposed, so as to obstruct or incommode the passage of any person over or along such footway:

Every person who rolls or carries any cask, tub, hoop, or wheel, or any ladder, plank, pole, timber, or log of wood, upon any footway, except for the purpose of loading or unloading any cart or carriage, or of crossing the footway:

Every person who places any line, cord, or pole across any street, or hangs or places any clothes thereon:

Every person who wilfully and indecently exposes his person:

Every person who publicly offers for sale or distribution, or exhibits to public view any profane... book, paper, print, drawing, painting, or representation, or sings any profane or obscene song or ballad, or uses any profane or obscene language:

Every person who wantonly discharges any firearm, or throws or discharges any stone or other missile, or makes any bonfire, or throws or sets fire to any firework:

Every person who wilfully and wantonly disturbs any inhabitant, by pulling or ringing any door bell, or knocking at any door, or who wilfully and unlawfully extinguishes the light of any lamp:

Every person who flies any kite, or who makes or uses any slide upon ice or snow:

Every person who cleanses, hoops, fires, washes, or scalds any cask or tub, or hews, saws, bores, or cuts any timber or stone, or slacks, sifts, or screens any lime:

Every person who throws or lays down any stones, coals, slate, shells, lime, bricks, timber, iron, or other materials (except building materials so inclosed as to prevent mischief to passengers):

Every person who beats or shakes any carpet, rug, or mat (except door mats beaten or shaken before the hour of eight in the morning):

Every person who fixes or places any flower-pot or box, or other heavy article, in any upper window, without sufficiently guarding the same against being blown down:

Every person who throws from the roof or any part of any house or other building any slate, brick, wood, rubbish, or other thing, except snow thrown so as not to fall on any passenger:

Every occupier of any house or other building, or other person, who orders or permits any person in his service to stand on the sill of any window, in order to clean, paint, or perform any other operation upon the outside of such window, or upon any house or other building within the said limits, unless such window be in the sunk or basement storey:

Every person who leaves open any vault or cellar, or the entrance from any street to any cellar or room underground, without a sufficient fence or handrail, or leaves defective the door, window, or other covering of any vault or cellar, or who does not sufficiently fence any area, pit, or sewer left open, or who leaves such open area, pit, or sewer, without a sufficient light after sunset to warn and prevent persons from falling thereinto:

Every person who throws or lays any dirt, litter, or ashes, or night-soil, or any carrion, fish, offal, or rubbish, on any street, or causes any offensive matter to run from any manufactory, brewery, slaughter-house, butcher's shop, or dunghill, into any street: Provided always, that it shall not be deemed an offence to lay sand or other materials in any street in time of frost, to prevent accidents, or litter or other suitable materials to prevent the freezing of water in pipes, or in the case of sickness to prevent noise, if the party laying any such things causes them to be removed as soon as the occasion for them ceases:

Every person who keeps any pigstye to the front of any street, not being shut out from such street by a sufficient wall or fence, or who keeps any swine in or near any street, so as to be a common nuisance. [S]

Offences Against the Person Act 1861

32 Placing wood, etc., on railway, taking up rails, showing or hiding signals, etc., with intent to endanger passengers

Whosoever shall unlawfully and maliciously put or throw upon or across any railway any wood, stone, or other matter or thing, or shall unlawfully and maliciously take up, remove, or displace any rail, sleeper, or other matter or thing belonging to any railway, or shall unlawfully and maliciously turn, move or divert any points or other machinery belonging to any railway, or shall unlawfully and maliciously make or show, hide or remove, any signal or light upon or near to any railway, or shall unlawfully and maliciously do or cause to be done any other matter or thing, with intent, in any of the cases aforesaid, to endanger the safety of any person travelling or being upon such railway, shall be guilty of an offence, and being convicted thereof shall be liable, at the discretion of the court, to imprisonment for life. [I]

33 Casting stone, etc., upon a railway carriage, with intent to endanger the safety of any person therein, or in any part of the same train

Whosoever shall unlawfully and maliciously throw, or cause to fall or strike, at, against, into, or upon any engine, tender, carriage, or truck used upon any railway, any wood, stone, or other matter or thing, with intent to injure or endanger the safety of any person being in or upon such engine, tender, carriage, or truck, or in or upon any other any other engine, tender, carriage, or truck of any train of which such first-mentioned engine, tender, carriage, or truck shall form part, shall be guilty of an offence, and being convicted thereof shall be liable . . . to imprisonment for life. [I]

34 Doing or omitting anything so as to endanger passengers by railway

Whosoever, by any unlawful act, or by any wilful omission or neglect, shall endanger or cause to be endangered the safety of any person conveyed or being in or upon a railway, or shall aid or assist therein, shall be guilty of an offence, and being convicted thereof shall be liable, at the discretion of the court, to be imprisoned for any term not exceeding two years. [E]

Malicious Damage Act 1861

35 Placing wood, etc., on railway, taking up rails, etc., turning points, showing or hiding signals, etc., with intent to obstruct or overthrow any engine, etc.

Whosoever shall unlawfully and maliciously put, place, cast, or throw upon or across any railway any wood, stone, or other matter or thing, or shall unlawfully and maliciously take up, remove, or displace any rail, sleeper, or other matter or thing belonging to any railway, or shall unlawfully and maliciously turn, move, or divert any points or other machinery belonging to any railway, or shall unlawfully and maliciously make or show, hide or remove, any signal or light upon or near to any railway, or shall unlawfully and maliciously do or cause to be done any other matter or thing, with intent, in any of the cases aforesaid, to obstruct, upset, overthrow, injure, or destroy any engine, tender, carriage, or truck using such railway, shall be guilty of felony, and being convicted thereof shall be liable, at the discretion of the court, to be kept in penal servitude for life . . . or to be imprisoned . . . [I]

36 Obstructing engines or carriages on railways

Whosoever, by any unlawful act, or by any wilful omission or neglect, shall obstruct or cause to be obstructed any engine or carriage using any railway, or shall aid or assist therein, shall be guilty of a misdemeanour, and being convicted thereof shall be liable, at the discretion of the court, to be imprisoned for any term not exceeding two years. [E]

58 Malice against owner of property unnecessary

Every punishment and forfeiture by this Act imposed on any person maliciously committing any offence, whether the same be punishable upon indictment or upon summary conviction, shall equally apply and be enforced, whether the offence shall be committed from malice conceived against the owner of the property in respect of which it shall be committed, or otherwise.

Aviation Security Act 1982

1 Hijacking

(1) A person on board an aircraft in flight who unlawfully, by the use of force or by threats of any kind, seizes the aircraft or exercises control of it commits the offence of hijacking, whatever his nationality, whatever the State in which the aircraft is registered and whether the aircraft is in the United Kingdom or elsewhere, but subject to subsection (2) below. [I]

(2) If—

(a) the aircraft is used in military, customs or police service, or

(b) both the place of take-off and the place of landing are in the territory of the State in which the aircraft is registered,

subsection (1) above shall not apply unless—

(i) the person seizing or exercising control of the aircraft is a United Kingdom national; or

(ii) his act is committed in the United Kingdom; or

(iii) the aircraft is registered in the United Kingdom or is used in the military or customs service of the United Kingdom or in the service of any police force in the United Kingdom.

(5) For the purposes of this section the territorial waters of any State shall be treated as part of its territory.

2 Destroying, damaging or endangering safety of aircraft

(1) It shall, subject to subsection (4) below, be an offence for any person unlawfully and intentionally—

(a) to destroy an aircraft in service or so to damage such an aircraft as to render it incapable of flight or as to be likely to endanger its safety in flight; or

(b) to commit on board an aircraft in flight any act of violence which is likely to endanger the safety of the aircraft. [I]

(2) It shall also, subject to subsection (4) below, be an offence for any person unlawfully and intentionally to place, or cause to be placed, on an aircraft in service any device or substance which is likely to destroy the aircraft, or is likely so to damage it as to render it incapable of flight or as to be likely to endanger its safety in flight; but nothing in this subsection shall be construed as limiting the circumstances in which the commission of any act—

(a) may constitute an offence under subsection (1) above, or

(b) may constitute attempting or conspiring to commit, or aiding, abetting, counselling or procuring, or being art and part in, the commission of such an offence. [I]

(3) Except as provided by subsection (4) below, subsections (1) and (2) above shall apply whether any such act as is therein mentioned is committed in the United Kingdom or elsewhere, whatever the nationality of the person committing the act and whatever the State in which the aircraft is registered.

(4) Subsections (1) and (2) above shall not apply to any act committed in relation to an aircraft used in military, customs or police service unless—

(a) the act is committed in the United Kingdom, or

(b) where the act is committed outside the United Kingdom, the person committing it is a United Kingdom national.

(6) In this section 'unlawfully'—

(a) in relation to the commission of an act in the United Kingdom, means so as (apart from this Act) to constitute an offence under the law of the part of the United Kingdom in which the act is committed, and

(b) in relation to the commission of an act outside the United Kingdom, means so that the commission of the act would (apart from this Act) have been an offence under the law of England and Wales if it had been committed in England and Wales or of Scotland if it had been committed in Scotland.

(7) In this section 'act of violence' means—

(a) any act done in the United Kingdom which constitutes the offence of murder, attempted murder, manslaughter, culpable homicide or assault or an offence under section 18, 20, 21, 22, 23, 24, 28 or 29 of the Offences against the Person Act 1861 or under section 2 of the Explosive Substances Act 1883, and

(b) any act done outside the United Kingdom which, if done in the United Kingdom, would constitute such an offence as is mentioned in paragraph (a) above.

3 Other acts endangering or likely to endanger safety of aircraft

(1) It shall, subject to subsections (5) and (6) below, be an offence for any person unlawfully and intentionally to destroy or damage any property to which this subsection applies, or to interfere with the operation of any such property, where the destruction, damage or interference is likely to endanger the safety of aircraft in flight. [I]

(2) Subsection (1) above applies to any property used for the provision of air navigation facilities, including any land, building or ship so used, and including any apparatus or equipment so used, whether it is on board an aircraft or elsewhere.

(3) It shall also, subject to subsections (4) and (5) below, be an offence for any person intentionally to communicate any information which is false, misleading or deceptive in a material particular, where the communication of the information endangers the safety of an aircraft in flight or is likely to endanger the safety of aircraft in flight. [I]

(4) It shall be a defence for a person charged with an offence under subsection (3) above to prove—

(a) that he believed, and had reasonable grounds for believing, that the information was true; or

(b) that, when he communicated the information, he was lawfully employed to perform duties which consisted of or included the communication of information and that he communicated the information in good faith in the performance of those duties.

(5) Subsections (1) and (3) above shall not apply to the commission of any act unless either the act is committed in the United Kingdom, or, where it is committed outside the United Kingdom—

(a) the person committing it is a United Kingdom national; or

(b) the commission of the act endangers or is likely to endanger the safety in flight of a civil aircraft registered in the United Kingdom or chartered by demise to a lessee whose principal place of business, or (if he has no place of business) whose permanent residence, is in the United Kingdom; or

(c) the act is committed on board a civil aircraft which is so registered or so chartered; or

(d) the act is committed on board a civil aircraft which lands in the United Kingdom with the person who committed the act still on board.

(6) Subsection (1) above shall also not apply to any act committed outside the United Kingdom and so committed in relation to property which is situated outside the United Kingdom and is not used for the provision of air navigation facilities in connection with international air navigation, unless the person committing the act is a United Kingdom national.

(8) In this section 'civil aircraft' means any aircraft other than an aircraft used in military, customs or police service and 'unlawfully' has the same meaning as in section 2 of this Act.

4 Offences in relation to certain dangerous articles

(1) It shall be an offence for any person without lawful authority or reasonable excuse (the proof of which shall lie on him) to have with him—

(a) in any aircraft registered in the United Kingdom, whether at a time when the aircraft is in the United Kingdom or not, or

(b) in any other aircraft at a time when it is in, or in flight over, the United Kingdom, or
(c) in any part of an aerodrome in the United Kingdom, or
(d) in any air navigation installation in the United Kingdom which does not form part of an aerodrome,

any article to which this section applies. [E]

(2) This section applies to the following articles, that is to say—

(a) any firearm, or any article having the appearance of being a firearm, whether capable of being discharged or not;
(b) any explosive, any article manufactured or adapted (whether in the form of a bomb, grenade or otherwise) so as to have the appearance of being an explosive, whether it is capable of producing a practical effect by explosion or not, or any article marked or labelled so as to indicate that it is or contains an explosive; and
(c) any article (not falling within either of the preceding paragraphs) made or adapted for use for causing injury to or incapacitating a person or for destroying or damaging property, or intended by the person having it with him for such use, whether by him or by any other person.

(3) For the purposes of this section a person who is for the time being in an aircraft, or in part of an aerodrome, shall be treated as having with him in the aircraft, or in that part of the aerodrome, as the case may be, an article to which this section applies if—

(a) where he is in an aircraft, the article, or an article in which it is contained, is in the aircraft and has been caused (whether by him or by any other person) to be brought there as being, or as forming part of, his baggage on a flight in the aircraft or has been caused by him to be brought there as being, or as forming part of, any other property to be carried on such a flight, or
(b) where he is in part of an aerodrome (otherwise than in an aircraft), the article, or an article in which it is contained, is in that or any other part of the aerodrome and has been caused (whether by him or by any other person) to be brought into the aerodrome as being, or as forming part of, his baggage on a flight from that aerodrome or has been caused by him to be brought there as being, or as forming part of, any other property to be carried on such a flight on which he is also to be carried,

notwithstanding that the circumstances may be such that (apart from this subsection) he would not be regarded as having the article with him in the aircraft or in a part of the aerodrome, as the case may be.

(5) Nothing in subsection (3) above shall be construed as limiting the circumstances in which a person would, apart from that subsection, be regarded as having an article with him as mentioned in subsection (1) above.

38 Interpretation, etc.

(1) In this Act, except in so far as the context otherwise requires—

'aerodrome' means the aggregate of the land, buildings and works comprised in an aerodrome within the meaning of the Civil Aviation Act 1982 and (if and so far as not comprised in an aerodrome as defined in that Act) any land, building or works situated within the boundaries of an area designated, by an order made by the Secretary of State which is for the time being in force, as constituting the area of an aerodrome for the purposes of this Act;

'air navigation installation' means any building, works, apparatus or equipment used wholly or mainly for the purpose of assisting air traffic control or as an aid to air navigation, together with any land contiguous or adjacent to any such building, works, apparatus or equipment and used wholly or mainly for purposes connected therewith;

'aircraft registered or operating in the United Kingdom' means any aircraft which is either—

(a) an aircraft registered in the United Kingdom, or
(b) an aircraft not so registered which is for the time being allocated for use on flights which (otherwise than in exceptional circumstances) include landing at or taking off from one or more aerodromes in the United Kingdom;

'article' includes any substance, whether in solid or liquid form or in the form of a gas or vapour;

'constable' includes any person having the powers and privileges of a constable;

'explosive' means any article manufactured for the purpose of producing a practical effect by explosion, or intended for that purpose by a person having the article with him;

'firearm' includes an airgun or air pistol;

'manager', in relation to an aerodrome, means the person (whether . . . the Civil Aviation Authority, a local authority or any other person) by whom the aerodrome is managed;

'military service' includes naval and air force service;

'measures' (without prejudice to the generality of that expression) includes the construction, execution, alteration, demolition or removal of buildings or other works and also includes the institution or modification, and the supervision and enforcement, of any practice or procedure;

'operator' has the same meaning as in the Civil Aviation Act 1982;

'property' includes any land, buildings or works, any aircraft or vehicle and any baggage, cargo or other article of any description;

'United Kingdom national' means an individual who is—

(a) a British citizen, a British Dependent Territories citizen, a British National (Overseas) or a British Overseas citizen;

(b) a person who under the British Nationality Act 1981 is a British subject; or

(c) a British protected person (within the meaning of that Act).

(2) For the purposes of this Act—

(a) in the case of an air navigation installation provided by, or used wholly or mainly by, the Civil Aviation Authority, that Authority, and

(b) in the case of any other air navigation installation, the person by whom it is provided, or by whom it is wholly or mainly used,

shall be taken to be the authority responsible for that air navigation installation.

(3) For the purposes of this Act—

(a) the period during which an aircraft is in flight shall be deemed to include any period from the moment when all its external doors are closed following embarkation until the moment when any such door is opened for disembarkation, and, in the case of a forced landing, any period until the competent authorities take over responsibility for the aircraft and for persons and property on board; and

(b) an aircraft shall be taken to be in service during the whole of the period which begins with the pre-flight preparation of the aircraft for a flight and ends 24 hours after the aircraft lands having completed that flight, and also at any time (not falling within that period) while, in accordance with the preceding paragraph, the aircraft is in flight,

and anything done on board an aircraft while in flight over any part of the United Kingdom shall be treated as done in that part of the United Kingdom.

(4) For the purposes of this Act the territorial waters adjacent to any part of the United Kingdom shall be treated as included in that part of the United Kingdom.

Civil Aviation Act 1982

81 Dangerous flying

(1) Where an aircraft is flown in such a manner as to be the cause of unnecessary danger to any person or property on land or water, the pilot or the person in charge of the aircraft, and also the owner thereof, unless he proves to the satisfaction of the court that the aircraft was so flown without his actual fault or privity, shall be liable on summary conviction to a fine not exceeding [level 4 on the standard scale] or to imprisonment for a term not exceeding six months or to both. [S]

(2) In this section the expression 'owner' in relation to an aircraft includes any person by whom the aircraft is hired at the time of the offence.

Aviation and Maritime Security Act 1990

1 Endangering safety at aerodromes

(1) It is an offence for any person by means of any device, substance or weapon intentionally to commit at an aerodrome serving international civil aviation any act of violence which—

(a) causes or is likely to cause death or serious personal injury, and

(b) endangers or is likely to endanger the safe operation of the aerodrome or the safety of persons at the aerodrome. [I]

(2) It is also, subject to subsection (4) below, an offence for any person by means of any device, substance or weapon unlawfully and intentionally—

(a) to destroy or seriously to damage—

(i) property used for the provision of any facilities at an aerodrome serving international civil aviation (including any apparatus or equipment so used), or

(ii) any aircraft which is at such an aerodrome but is not in service, or

(b) to disrupt the services of such an aerodrome, in such a way as to endanger or be likely to endanger the safe operation of the aerodrome or the safety of persons at the aerodrome. [I]

(3) Except as provided by subsection (4) below, subsections (1) and (2) above apply whether any such act as is referred to in those subsections is committed in the United Kingdom or elsewhere and whatever the nationality of the person committing the act.

(4) Subsection (2)(a)(ii) above does not apply to any act committed in relation to an aircraft used in military, customs or police service unless—

(a) the act is committed in the United Kingdom, or

(b) where the act is committed outside the United Kingdom, the person committing it is a United Kingdom national.

(9) In this section—

'act of violence' means—

(a) any act done in the United Kingdom which constitutes the offence of murder, attempted murder, manslaughter, culpable homicide or assault or an offence under section 18, 20, 21, 22, 23, 24, 28 or 29 of the Offences against the Person Act 1861 or under section 2 of the Explosive Substances Act 1883, and

(b) any act done outside the United Kingdom which, if done in the United Kingdom, would constitute such an offence as is mentioned in paragraph (a) above;

'aerodrome' has the same meaning as in the Civil Aviation Act 1982;

'military service' and 'United Kingdom national' have the same meaning as in the Aviation Security Act 1982; and

'unlawfully'—

(a) in relation to the commission of an act in the United Kingdom, means so as (apart from this section) to constitute an offence under the law of the part of the United Kingdom in which the act is committed, and

(b) in relation to the commission of an act outside the United Kingdom, means so that the commission of the act would (apart from this section) have been an offence under the law of England and Wales if it had been committed in England and Wales...

9 Hijacking of ships

(1) A person who unlawfully, by the use of force or by threats of any kind, seizes a ship or exercises control of it, commits the offence of hijacking a ship, whatever his nationality and whether the ship is in the United Kingdom or elsewhere, but subject to subsection (2) below.

(2) Subsection (1) above does not apply in relation to a warship or any other ship used as a naval auxiliary or in customs or police service unless—

(a) the person seizing or exercising control of the ship is a United Kingdom national, or

(b) his act is committed in the United Kingdom, or

(c) the ship is used in the naval or customs service of the United Kingdom or in the service of any police force in the United Kingdom. [I]

10 Seizing or exercising control of fixed platforms

(1) A person who unlawfully, by the use of force or by threats of any kind, seizes a fixed platform or exercises control of it, commits an offence, whatever his nationality and whether the fixed platform is in the United Kingdom or elsewhere. [I]

11 Destroying ships or fixed platforms or endangering their safety

(1) Subject to subsection (5) below, a person commits an offence if he unlawfully and intentionally—

(a) destroys a ship or a fixed platform,

(b) damages a ship, its cargo or a fixed platform so as to endanger, or to be likely to endanger, the safe navigation of the ship, or as the case may be, the safety of the platform, or

(c) commits on board a ship or on a fixed platform an act of violence which is likely to endanger the safe navigation of the ship, or as the case may be, the safety of the platform. [I]

(2) Subject to subsection (5) below, a person commits an offence if he unlawfully and intentionally places, or causes to be placed, on a ship or fixed platform any device or substance which—

(a) in the case of a ship, is likely to destroy the ship or is likely so to damage it or its cargo as to endanger its safe navigation, or

(b) in the case of a fixed platform, is likely to destroy the fixed platform or so to damage it as to endanger its safety.

(3) Nothing in subsection (2) above is to be construed as limiting the circumstances in which the commission of any act—

(a) may constitute an offence under subsection (1) above, or

(b) may constitute attempting or conspiring to commit, or aiding, abetting, counselling, procuring or inciting, or being art and part in, the commission of such an offence.

(4) Except as provided by subsection (5) below, subsections (1) and (2) above apply whether any such act as is mentioned in those subsections is committed in the United Kingdom or elsewhere and whatever the nationality of the person committing the act.

(5) Subsections (1) and (2) above do not apply in relation to any act committed in relation to a warship or any other ship used as a naval auxiliary or in customs or police service unless—

(a) the person committing the act is a United Kingdom national, or

(b) his act is committed in the United Kingdom, or

(c) the ship is used in the naval or customs service of the United Kingdom or in the service of any police force in the United Kingdom.

(7) In this section—

'act of violence' means—

(a) any act done in the United Kingdom which constitutes the offence of murder, attempted murder, manslaughter, culpable homicide or assault or an offence under section 18, 20, 21, 22, 23, 24, 28 or 29 of the Offences against the Person Act 1861 or under section 2 of the Explosive Substances Act 1883, and

(b) any act done outside the United Kingdom which, if done in the United Kingdom, would constitute such an offence as is mentioned in paragraph (a) above, and

'unlawfully'—

(a) in relation to the commission of an act in the United Kingdom, means so as (apart from this Act) to constitute an offence under the law of the part of the United Kingdom in which the act is committed, and

(b) in relation to the commission of an act outside the United Kingdom means so that the commission of the act would (apart from this Act) have been an offence under the law of England and Wales if it had been committed in England and Wales . . .

12 Other acts endangering or likely to endanger safe navigation

(1) Subject to subsection (6) below, it is an offence for any person unlawfully and intentionally—

(a) to destroy or damage any property to which this subsection applies, or

(b) seriously to interfere with the operation of any such property,

where the destruction, damage or interference is likely to endanger the safe navigation of any ship. [I]

(2) Subsection (1) above applies to any property used for the provision of maritime navigation facilities, including any land, building or ship so used, and including any apparatus or equipment so used, whether it is on board a ship or elsewhere.

(3) Subject to subsection (6) below, it is also an offence for any person intentionally to communicate any information which he knows to be false in a material particular, where the communication of the information endangers the safe navigation of any ship.

(4) It is a defence for a person charged with an offence under subsection (3) above to prove that, when he communicated the information, he was lawfully employed to perform duties which consisted of or included the communication of information and that he communicated the information in good faith in performance of those duties.

(5) Except as provided by subsection (6) below, subsections (1) and (3) above apply whether any such act as is mentioned in those subsections is committed in the United Kingdom or elsewhere and whatever the nationality of the person committing the act.

(6) For the purposes of subsections (1) and (3) above any danger, or likelihood of danger, to the safe navigation of a warship or any other ship used as a naval auxiliary or in customs or police service is to be disregarded unless—

(a) the person committing the act is a United Kingdom national, or

(b) his act is committed in the United Kingdom, or

(c) the ship is used in the naval or customs service of the United Kingdom or in the service of any police force in the United Kingdom.

(8) In this section 'unlawfully' has the same meaning as in section 11 of this Act.

13 Offences involving threats

(1) A person commits an offence if—

(a) in order to compel any other person to do or abstain from doing any act, he threatens that he or some other person will do in relation to any ship or fixed platform an act which is an offence by virtue of section 11(1) of this Act, and

(b) the making of that threat is likely to endanger the safe navigation of the ship or, as the case may be, the safety of the fixed platform. [I]

(2) Subject to subsection (4) below, a person commits an offence if—

(a) in order to compel any other person to do or abstain from doing any act, he threatens that he or some other person will do an act which is an offence by virtue of section 12(1) of this Act, and

(b) the making of that threat is likely to endanger the safe navigation of any ship. [I]

(3) Except as provided by subsection (4) below, subsections (1) and (2) above apply whether any such act as is mentioned in those subsections is committed in the United Kingdom or elsewhere and whatever the nationality of the person committing the act.

(4) Section 12(6) of this Act applies for the purposes of subsection (2)(b) above as it applies for the purposes of section 12(1) and (3) of this Act.

17 Interpretation of Part II

(1) In this Part of this Act—

'fixed platform' means—

(a) any offshore installation, within the meaning of the Mineral Workings (Offshore Installations) Act 1971, which is not a ship, and

(b) any other artificial island, installation or structure which—

(i) permanently rests on, or is permanently attached to, the seabed,

(ii) is maintained for the purposes of the exploration or exploitation of resources or for other economic purposes, and

(iii) is not connected with dry land by a permanent structure providing access at all times and for all purposes;

'naval service' includes military and air force service;

'ship' means any vessel (including hovercraft, submersible craft and other floating craft) other than one which—

(a) permanently rests on, or is permanently attached to, the seabed, or

(b) has been withdrawn from navigation or laid up; and

'United Kingdom national' means an individual who is—

(a) a British citizen, a British Dependent Territories citizen, a British National (Overseas) or a British Overseas citizen,

(b) a person who under the British Nationality Act 1981 is a British subject, or

(c) a British protected person (within the meaning of that Act).

(2) For the purposes of this Part of this Act the territorial waters adjacent to any part of the United Kingdom shall be treated as included in that part of the United Kingdom.

Merchant Shipping Act 1995

58 Conduct endangering ships, structures or individuals

(1) This section applies—

(a) to the master of, or any seaman employed in, a United Kingdom ship; and

(b) to the master of, or any seaman employed in, a ship which—

(i) is registered under the law of any country outside the United Kingdom, and

(ii) is in a port in the United Kingdom or within the United Kingdom while proceeding to or from any such port.

(2) If a person to whom this section applies, while on board his ship or in its immediate vicinity—

(a) does any act which causes or is likely to cause—

(i) the loss or destruction of or serious damage to his ship or its machinery, navigational equipment or safety equipment, or

(ii) the loss or destruction of or serious damage to any other ship or any structure, or

(iii) the death of or serious injury to any person, or

(b) omits to do anything required—

(i) to preserve his ship or its machinery, navigational equipment or safety equipment from being lost, destroyed or seriously damaged, or

(ii) to preserve any person on board his ship from death or serious injury, or

(iii) to prevent his ship from causing the loss or destruction of or serious damage to any other ship or any structure, or the death of or serious injury to any person not on board his ship,

and either of the conditions specified in subsection (3) of this section is satisfied with respect to that act or omission, he shall (subject to subsections (6) and (7) of this section) be guilty of an offence. [E]

(3) Those conditions are—

(a) that the act or omission was deliberate or amounted to a breach or neglect of duty;

(b) that the master or seaman in question was under the influence of drink or a drug at the time of the act or omission.

(4) If a person to whom this section applies—

(a) discharges any of his duties, or performs any other function in relation to the operation of his ship or its machinery or equipment, in such a manner as to cause, or to be likely to cause, any such loss, destruction, death or injury as is mentioned in subsection (2)(a) above, or

(b) fails to discharge any of his duties, or to perform any such function, properly to such an extent as to cause, or to be likely to cause, any of those things,

he shall (subject to subsections (6) and (7) of this section) be guilty of an offence. [E]

(6) In proceedings for an offence under this section it shall be a defence to prove—

(a) in the case of an offence under subsection (2) above where the act or omission alleged against the defendant constituted a breach or neglect of duty, that the defendant took all reasonable steps to discharge that duty;

(b) in the case of an offence under subsection (2) above, that at the time of the act or omission alleged against the accused he was under the influence of a drug taken by him for medical purposes and either that he took it on medical advice and complied with any directions given as part of that advice, or that he had no reason to believe the drug might have the influence it had;

(c) in the case of an offence under subsection (4) above, that the defendant took all reasonable precautions and exercised all due diligence to avoid committing the offence; or

(d) in the case of an offence under either of those subsections—

(i) that he could have avoided committing the offence only by disobeying a lawful command, or

(ii) that in all the circumstances the loss, destruction, damage, death or injury in question, or (as the case may be) the likelihood of its being caused, either could not reasonably have been foreseen by the defendant or could not reasonably have been avoided by him.

(7) In the application of this section to any person falling within subsection (1)(b) above, subsections (2) and (4) shall have effect as if (a)(i) and (b)(i) paragraphs of subsection (2) were omitted...

(8) In this section—

'breach or neglect of duty', except in relation to a master, includes any disobedience to a lawful command;

'duty'—

(a) in relation to a master or seaman, means any duty falling to be discharged by him in his capacity as such; and

(b) in relation to a master, includes his duty with respect to the good management of his ship and his duty with respect to the safety of operation of his ship, its machinery and equipment; and

'structure' means any fixed or movable structure (of whatever description) other than a ship.

59 Concerted disobedience and neglect of duty

(1) If a seaman employed in a United Kingdom ship combines with other seamen employed in that ship—

(a) to disobey lawful commands which are required to be obeyed at a time while the ship is at sea;

(b) to neglect any duty which is required to be discharged at such a time; or

(c) to impede, at such a time, the progress of a voyage or the navigation of the ship,

he shall be liable—

(i) on summary conviction, to a fine not exceeding the statutory maximum;

(ii) on conviction on indictment, to imprisonment for a term not exceeding two years or a fine or both. [E]

(2) For the purposes of this section a ship shall be treated as being at sea at any time when it is not securely moored in a safe berth.

92 Duty of ship to assist the other in case of collision

(1) In every case of collision between two ships, it shall be the duty of the master of each ship, if and so far as he can do so without danger to his own ship, crew and passengers (if any)—

(a) to render to the other ship, its master, crew and passengers (if any) such assistance as may be practicable, and may be necessary to save them from any danger caused by the collision, and to stay by the other ship until he has ascertained that it has no need of further assistance; and

(b) to give to the master of the other ship the name of his own ship and also the names of the ports from which it comes and to which it is bound.

(2) The duties imposed on the master of a ship by subsection (1) above apply to the masters of United Kingdom ships and to the masters of foreign ships when in United Kingdom waters.

(3) The failure of the master of a ship to comply with the provisions of this section shall not raise any presumption of law that the collision was caused by his wrongful act, neglect, or default.

(4) If the master fails without reasonable excuse to comply with this section, he shall—

(a) in the case of a failure to comply with subsection (1)(a) above, be liable—

(i) on summary conviction, to a fine not exceeding £50,000 or imprisonment for a term not exceeding six months or both;

(ii) on conviction on indictment, to a fine or imprisonment for a term not exceeding two years or both; and

(b) in the case of a failure to comply with subsection (1)(b) above, be liable—

(i) on summary conviction, to a fine not exceeding the statutory maximum;

(ii) on conviction on indictment, to a fine;

and in either case if he is a certified officer, an inquiry into his conduct may be held, and his certificate cancelled or suspended. [E]

93 Duty to assist persons in distress

(1) The master of a ship, on receiving at sea a signal of distress from an aircraft or information from any source that an aircraft is in distress, shall proceed with all speed to the assistance of the persons in distress (informing them if possible that he is doing so) unless he is unable, or in the special circumstances of the case considers it unreasonable or unnecessary, to do so, or unless he is released from this duty under subsection (5) below.

(3) The duties imposed on the master of a ship by subsection (1) above apply to the masters of United Kingdom ships and to the masters of foreign ships when in United Kingdom waters.

(5) A master shall be released from the duty imposed by subsection (1) above, if he is informed by the persons in distress, or by the master of any ship that has reached the persons in distress, that assistance is no longer required. [E]

94 Meaning of 'dangerously unsafe ship'

(1) For the purposes of sections 95, 96, 97 and 98 a ship in port is 'dangerously unsafe' if, having regard to the nature of the service for which it is intended, the ship is, by reason of the matters mentioned in subsection (2) below, unfit to go to sea without serious danger to human life.

(1A) For the purposes of those sections a ship at sea is 'dangerously unsafe' if, having regard to the nature of the service for which it is being used or is intended, the ship is, by reason of the matters mentioned in subsection (2) below either—

(a) unfit to remain at sea without serious danger to human life, or

(b) unfit to go on a voyage without serious danger to human life.

(2) Those matters are—

(a) the condition, or the unsuitability for its purpose, of—

(i) the ship or its machinery or equipment, or

(ii) any part of the ship or its machinery or equipment;

(b) undermanning;

(c) overloading or unsafe or improper loading;

(d) any other matter relevant to the safety of the ship;

and are referred to in those sections, in relation to any ship, as 'the matters relevant to its safety'.

(3) Any reference in those sections to 'going to sea' shall, in a case where the service for which the ship is intended consists of going on voyages or excursions that do not involve going to sea, be construed as a reference to going on such a voyage or excursion.

98 Owner and master liable in respect of dangerously unsafe ship

(1) If a ship which—

(a) is in a port in the United Kingdom, or

(b) is a United Kingdom ship and is in any other port,

is dangerously unsafe, then, subject to subsections (4) and (5) below, the master and the owner of the ship shall each be guilty of an offence. [E]

(2) Where, at the time when a ship is dangerously unsafe, any responsibilities of the owner with respect to the matters relevant to its safety have been assumed (whether wholly or in part) by any person or persons other than the owner, and have been so assumed by that person or (as the case may be) by each of those persons either—

(a) directly, under the terms of a charter-party or management agreement made with the owner, or

(b) indirectly, under the terms of a series of charter-parties or management agreements,

the reference to the owner in subsection (1) above shall be construed as a reference to that other person or (as the case may be) to each of those other persons.

(4) It shall be a defence in proceedings for an offence under this section to prove that at the time of the alleged offence—

(a) arrangements had been made which were appropriate to ensure that before the ship went to sea it was made fit to do so without serious danger to human life by reason of the matters relevant to its safety which are specified in the charge (or, in Scotland, which are libelled in the complaint, petition or indictment); or

(b) it was reasonable for such arrangements not to have been made.

(5) It shall also be a defence in proceedings for an offence under this section to prove—

(a) that, under the terms of one or more charter-parties or management agreements entered into by the accused, the relevant responsibilities, namely—

(i) where the accused is the owner, his responsibilities with respect to the matters relevant to the ship's safety, or

(ii) where the accused is liable to proceedings under this section by virtue of subsection (2) above, so much of those responsibilities as had been assumed by him as mentioned in that subsection,

had at the time of the alleged offence been wholly assumed by some other person or persons party thereto; and

(b) that in all the circumstances of the case the accused had taken such steps as it was reasonable for him to take, and exercised such diligence as it was reasonable for him to exercise, to secure the proper discharge of the relevant responsibilities during the period during which they had been assumed by some other person or persons as mentioned in paragraph (a) above;

and, in determining whether the accused had done so, regard shall be had in particular to the matters mentioned in subsection (6) below.

(6) Those matters are—

(a) whether prior to the time of the alleged offence the accused was, or in all the circumstances ought reasonably to have been, aware of any deficiency in the discharge of the relevant responsibilities; and

(b) the extent to which the accused was or was not able, under the terms of any such charter-party or management agreement as is mentioned in subsection (5)(a) above—

(i) to terminate it, or

(ii) to intervene in the management of the ship,

in the event of any such deficiency, and whether it was reasonable for the accused to place himself in that position.

(8) In this section—

'management agreement', in relation to a ship, means any agreement (other than a charter-party or a contract of employment) under which the ship is managed, either wholly or in part, by a person other than the owner (whether on behalf of the owner or on behalf of some other person); and

'relevant responsibilities' shall be construed in accordance with subsection (5) above.

(9) References in this section to responsibilities being assumed by a person under the terms of a charter-party or management agreement are references to their being so assumed by him whether or not he has entered into a further charter-party or management agreement providing for them to be assumed by some other person.

100 Owner liable for unsafe operation of ship

(1) It shall be the duty of the owner of a ship to which this section applies to take all reasonable steps to secure that the ship is operated in a safe manner.

(2) This section applies to—

(a) any United Kingdom ship; and

(b) any ship which—

(i) is registered under the law of any country outside the United Kingdom, and

(ii) is within United Kingdom waters while proceeding to or from a port in the United Kingdom,

unless the ship would not be so proceeding but for weather conditions or any other unavoidable circumstances. [E]

(4) Where any such ship—

(a) is chartered by demise, or

(b) is managed, either wholly or in part, by a person other than the owner under the terms of a management agreement within the meaning of section 98,

any reference to the owner of the ship in subsection (1) or (3) above shall be construed as including a reference—

(i) to the charterer under the charter by demise, or

(ii) to any such manager as is referred to in paragraph (b) above, or

(iii) (if the ship is both chartered and managed as mentioned above) to both the charterer and any such manager,

and accordingly the reference in subsection (1) above to the taking of all reasonable steps shall, in relation to the owner, the charterer or any such manager, be construed as a reference to the taking of all such steps as it is reasonable for him to take in the circumstances of the case.

101 Offences in connection with passenger ships

(1) A person commits an offence if, in relation to a ship to which this section applies, he does any of the following things, that is to say—

(a) if, being drunk or disorderly, he has been on that account refused admission to the ship by the owner or any person in his employment, and, after having the amount of his fare (if he has paid it) returned or tendered to him, nevertheless persists in attempting to enter the ship;

(b) if, being drunk or disorderly on board the ship, he is requested by the owner or any person in his employment to leave the ship at any place in the United Kingdom at which he can conveniently do so, and, after having the amount of his fare (if he has paid it) returned or tendered to him, does not comply with the request;

(c) if, on board the ship, after warning by the master or other officer thereof, he molests or continues to molest any passenger;

(d) if, after having been refused admission to the ship by the owner or any person in his employment on account of the ship being full, and having had the amount of his fare (if he has paid it) returned or tendered to him, he nevertheless persists in attempting to enter the ship;

(e) if, having gone on board the ship at any place, and being requested, on account of the ship being full, by the owner or any person in his employment to leave the ship before it has left that place, and having had the amount of his fare (if he has paid it) returned or tendered to him, he does not comply with that request;

(f) if, on arriving in the ship at a point to which he has paid his fare, he knowingly and intentionally refuses or neglects to leave the ship; and

(g) if, on board the ship he fails, when requested by the master or other officer thereof, either to pay his fare or show such ticket or other receipt, if any, showing the payment of his fare, as is usually given to persons travelling by and paying their fare for the ship;

but his liability in respect of any such offence shall not prejudice the recovery of any fare payable by him. [S]

(2) A person commits an offence if, on board any ship to which this section applies he intentionally does or causes to be done anything in such a manner as to—

(a) obstruct or damage any part of the machinery or equipment of the ship, or

(b) obstruct, impede or molest the crew, or any of them, in the navigation or management of the ship, or otherwise in the execution of their duty on or about the ship. [S]

(3) The master or other officer of any ship to which this section applies, and all persons called by him to his assistance, may, without any warrant, detain any person who commits any offence against subsection (1) or (2) above and whose name and address are unknown to the master or officer, and deliver that person to a constable.

(5) If any person commits an offence against subsection (1) or (2) above and on the application of the master of the ship, or any other person in the employment of the owner thereof, refuses to give his name and address, or gives a false name or address, that person shall be liable, on summary conviction, to a fine not exceeding level 2 on the standard scale. [S]

(6) This section applies to a ship for which there is in force a Passenger Ship Safety Certificate or Passenger Certificate, as the case may be, issued under or recognised by safety regulations.

Wireless Telegraphy Act 2006

47 Misleading messages

(1) A person commits an offence if, by means of wireless telegraphy, he sends or attempts to send a message to which this section applies. [E]

(2) This section applies to a message which, to the person's knowledge—

(a) is false or misleading; and

(b) is likely to prejudice the efficiency of a safety of life service or to endanger the safety of a person or of a ship, aircraft or vehicle.

(3) This section applies in particular to a message which, to the person's knowledge, falsely suggests that a ship or aircraft—

(a) is in distress or in need of assistance; or

(b) is not in distress or not in need of assistance.

(b) Employment

Health and Safety at Work etc. Act 1974

2 General duties of employers to their employees

(1) It shall be the duty of every employer to ensure, so far as is reasonably practicable, the health, safety and welfare at work of all his employees.

(2) Without prejudice to the generality of an employer's duty under the preceding subsection, the matters to which that duty extends include in particular—

(a) the provision and maintenance of plant and systems of work that are, so far as is reasonably practicable, safe and without risks to health;

(b) arrangements for ensuring, so far as is reasonably practicable, safety and absence of risks to health in connection with the use, handling, storage and transport of articles and substances;

(c) the provision of such information, instruction, training and supervision as is necessary to ensure, so far as is reasonably practicable, the health and safety at work of his employees;

(d) so far as is reasonably practicable as regards any place of work under the employer's control, the maintenance of it in a condition that is safe and without risks to health and the provision and maintenance of means of access to and egress from it that are safe and without such risks;

(e) the provision and maintenance of a working environment for his employees that is, so far as is reasonably practicable, safe, without risks to health, and adequate as regards facilities and arrangements for their welfare at work.

(3) Except in such cases as may be prescribed, it shall be the duty of every employer to prepare and as often as may be appropriate revise a written statement of his general policy with respect to the health and safety at work of his employees and the organisation and arrangements for the time being in force for carrying out that policy, and to bring the statement and any revision of it to the notice of all of his employees.

3 General duties of employers and self-employed to persons other than their employees

(1) It shall be the duty of every employer to conduct his undertaking in such a way as to ensure, so far is reasonably practicable, that persons not in his employment who may be affected thereby are not thereby exposed to risks to their health or safety.

(3) In such cases as may be prescribed, it shall be the duty of every employer and every self-employed person, in the prescribed circumstances and in the prescribed manner, to give to persons (not being his employees) who may be affected by the way in which he conducts his undertaking the prescribed information about such aspects of the way in which he conducts his undertaking as might affect their health or safety.

4 General duties of persons concerned with premises to persons other than their employees

(1) This section has effect for imposing on persons duties in relation to those who—

(a) are not their employees; but

(b) use non-domestic premises made available to them as a place of work or as a place where they may use plant or substances provided for their use there,

and applies to premises so made available and other non-domestic premises used in connection with them.

(2) It shall be the duty of each person who has, to any extent, control of premises to which this section applies or of the means of access thereto or egress therefrom or of any plant or substance in such premises to take such measures as it is reasonable for a person in his position to take to ensure, so far as is reasonably practicable, that the premises, all means of access thereto or egress therefrom available for use by persons using the premises, and any plant or substance in the premises or, as the case may be, provided for use there, is or are safe and without risks to health.

(3) Where a person has, by virtue of any contract or tenancy, an obligation of any extent in relation to—

(a) the maintenance or repair of any premises to which this section applies or any means of access thereto or egress therefrom; or

(b) the safety of or the absence of risks to health arising from plant or substances in any such premises;

that person shall be treated, for the purposes of subsection (2) above, as being a person who has control of the matters to which his obligation extends.

(4) Any reference in this section to a person having control of any premises or matter is a reference to a person having control of the premises or matter in connection with the carrying on by him of a trade, business or other undertaking (whether for profit or not).

5 General duty of persons in control of certain premises in relation to harmful emissions into atmosphere

(1) Subject to subsection (5) below, it shall be the duty of the person having control of any premises of a class prescribed for the purposes of section 1(1)(d) to use the best practicable means for preventing the emission into the atmosphere from the premises of noxious or offensive substances and for rendering harmless and inoffensive such substances as may be so emitted.

(2) The reference in subsection (1) above to the means to be used for the purposes there mentioned includes a reference to the manner in which the plant provided for those purposes is used and to the supervision of any operation involving the emission of the substances to which that subsection applies.

(3) Any substance or a substance of any description prescribed for the purposes of subsection (1) above as noxious or offensive shall be a noxious or, as the case may be, an offensive substance for those purposes whether or not it would be so apart from this subsection.

(4) Any reference in this section to a person having control of any premises is a reference to a person having control of the premises in connection with the carrying on by him of a trade, business or other undertaking (whether for profit or not) and any duty imposed on any such person by this section shall extend only to matters within his control.

(5) The foregoing provisions of this section shall not apply in relation to any process which is a prescribed process as from the date which is the determination date for that process.

6 General duties of manufacturers etc., as regards articles and substances for use at work

(1) It shall be the duty of any person who designs, manufactures, imports or supplies any article for use at work or any article of fairground equipment—

- (a) to ensure, so far as is reasonably practicable, that the article is so designed and constructed that it will be safe and without risks to health at all times when it is being set, used, cleaned or maintained by a person at work;
- (b) to carry out or arrange for the carrying out of such testing and examination as may be necessary for the performance of the duty imposed on him by the preceding paragraph;
- (c) to take such steps as are necessary to secure that persons supplied by that person with the article are provided with adequate information about the use for which the article is designed or has been tested and about any conditions necessary to ensure that it will be safe and without risks to health at all such times as are mentioned in paragraph (a) above and when it is being dismantled or disposed of; and
- (d) to take such steps as are necessary to secure, so far as is reasonably practicable, that persons so supplied are provided with all such revisions of information provided to them by virtue of the preceding paragraph as are necessary by reason of its becoming known that anything gives rise to a serious risk to health and safety.

(1A) It shall be the duty of any person who designs, manufactures, imports or supplies any article of fairground equipment—

- (a) to ensure, so far as is reasonably practicable, that the article is so designed and constructed that it will be safe and without risks to health at all times when it is being used for or in connection with the entertainment of members of the public;
- (b) to carry out or arrange for the carrying out of such testing and examination as may be necessary for the performance of the duty imposed on him by the preceding paragraph;
- (c) to take such steps as are necessary to secure that persons supplied by that person with the article are provided with adequate information about the use for which the article is designed or has been tested and about any conditions necessary to ensure that it will be safe and without risks to health at all times when it is being used for or in connection with the entertainment of members of the public; and

(d) to take such steps as are necessary to secure, so far as is reasonably practicable, that persons so supplied are provided with all such revisions of information provided to them by virtue of the preceding paragraph as are necessary by reason of its becoming known that anything gives rise to a serious risk to health or safety.

(2) It shall be the duty of any person who undertakes the design or manufacture of any article for use at work or of any article of fairground equipment to carry out or arrange for the carrying out of any necessary research with a view to the discovery and, so far as is reasonably practicable, the elimination or minimisation of any risks to health or safety to which the design or article may give rise.

(3) It shall be the duty of any person who erects or installs any article for use at work in any premises where that article is to be used by persons at work or who erects or installs any article of fairground equipment to ensure, so far as is reasonably practicable, that nothing about the way in which the article is erected or installed makes it unsafe or a risk to health at any such time as is mentioned in paragraph (a) of subsection (1) or, as the case may be, in paragraph (a) of subsection (1) or (1A).

(4) It shall be the duty of any person who manufactures, imports or supplies any substance—

(a) to ensure, so far as is reasonably practicable, that the substance will be safe and without risks to health at all times when it is being used, handled, processed, stored or transported by a person at work or in premises to which section 4 above applies;

(b) to carry out or arrange for the carrying out of such testing and examination as may be necessary for the performance of the duty imposed on him by the preceding paragraph;

(c) to take such steps as are necessary to secure that persons supplied by that person with the substance are provided with adequate information about any risks to health or safety to which the inherent properties of the substance may give rise, about the results of any relevant tests which have been carried out on or in connection with the substance and about any conditions necessary to ensure that the substance will be safe and without risks to health at all such times as are mentioned in paragraph (a) above and when the substance is being disposed of; and

(d) to take such steps as are necessary to secure, so far as is reasonably practicable, that persons so supplied are provided with all such revisions of information provided to them by virtue of the preceding paragraph as are necessary by reason of its becoming known that anything gives rise to a serious risk to health or safety.

(5) It shall be the duty of any person who undertakes the manufacture of any substance to carry out or arrange for the carrying out of any necessary research with a view to the discovery and, so far as is reasonable practicable, the elimination or minimisation of any risks to health or safety to which the substance may give rise at all such times as are mentioned in paragraph (a) of subsection (4) above.

(6) Nothing in the preceding provisions of this section shall be taken to require a person to repeat any testing, examination or research which has been carried out otherwise than by him or at his instance, in so far as it is reasonable for him to rely on the results thereof for the purposes of those provisions.

(7) Any duty imposed on any person by any of the preceding provisions of this section shall extend only to things done in the course of a trade, business or other undertaking carried on by him (whether for profit or not) and to matters within his control.

(8) Where a person designs, manufactures, imports or supplies an article for use at work or an article of fairground equipment and does so for or to another on the basis of a written undertaking by that other to take specified steps sufficient to ensure, so far as is reasonably practicable, that the article will be safe and without risks to health at all such times as are mentioned in paragraph (a) of subsection (1) or, as the case may be, in paragraph (a) of subsection (1) or (1A) above, the undertaking shall have the effect of relieving the first-mentioned person from the duty imposed by virtue of that paragraph to such extent as is reasonable having regard to the terms of the undertaking.

(8A) Nothing in subsection (7) or (8) above shall relieve any person who imports any article or substance from any duty in respect of anything which—

(a) in the case of an article designed outside the United Kingdom, was done by and in the course of any trade, profession or other undertaking carried on by, or was within the control of, the person who designed the article; or

(b) in the case of an article or substance manufactured outside the United Kingdom, was done by and in the course of any trade, profession or other undertaking carried on by, or was within the control of, the person who manufactured the article or substance.

(9) Where a person ('the ostensible supplier') supplies any article or substance to another ('the customer') under a hire-purchase agreement, conditional sale agreement or credit-sale agreement, and the ostensible supplier—

(a) carries on the business of financing the acquisition of goods by others by means of such agreements; and

(b) in the course of that business acquired his interest in the article or substance supplied to the customer as a means of financing its acquisition by the customer from a third person ('the effective supplier'),

the effective supplier and not the ostensible supplier shall be treated for the purposes of this section as supplying the article or substance to the customer, and any duty imposed by the preceding provisions of this section on suppliers shall accordingly fall on the effective supplier and not on the ostensible supplier.

(10) For the purposes of this section an absence of safety or a risk to the health shall be disregarded in so far as the case in or in relation to which it would arise is shown to be one the occurrence of which could not reasonably be foreseen; and in determining whether any duty imposed by virtue of paragraph (a) of subsection (1), (1A) or (4) above has been performed regard shall be had to any relevant information or advice which has been provided to any person by the person by whom the article has been designed, manufactured, imported or supplied or, as the case may be, by the person by whom the substance has been manufactured, imported or supplied.

7 General duties of employees at work

It shall be the duty of every employee while at work—

(a) to take reasonable care for the health and safety of himself and of other persons who may be affected by his acts or omissions at work; and

(b) as regards any duty or requirement imposed on his employer or any other person by or under any of the relevant statutory provisions, to co-operate with him so far as is necessary to enable that duty or requirement to be performed or complied with.

8 Duty not to interfere with or misuse things provided pursuant to certain provisions

No person shall intentionally or recklessly interfere with or misuse anything provided in the interests of health, safety or welfare in pursuance of any of the relevant statutory provisions.

33 Offences

(1) It is an offence for a person—

(a) to fail to discharge a duty to which he is subject by virtue of section 2 to 7;

(b) to contravene section 8 or 9;

(c) to contravene any health and safety regulations or agricultural health and safety regulations or any requirement or prohibition imposed under any such regulations (including any requirement or prohibition to which he is subject by virtue of the terms of or any condition or restriction attached to any licence, approval, exemption or other authority issued, given or granted under the regulations);

(k) to make a statement which he knows to be false or recklessly to make a statement which is false where the statement is made—

(i) in purported compliance with a requirement to furnish any information imposed by or under any of the relevant statutory provisions; or

(ii) for the purpose of obtaining the issue of a document under any of the relevant statutory provisions to himself or another person;

(l) intentionally to make a false entry in any register, book, notice or other document required by or under any of the relevant statutory provisions to be kept, served or given or, with intent to deceive, to make use of any such entry which he knows to be false;

(m) with intent to deceive, to forge or use a document issued or authorised to be issued under any of the relevant statutory provisions or required for any purpose there under or to make or have in his possession a document so closely resembling any such document as to be calculated to deceive;

(n) falsely to pretend to be an inspector. [E]

36 Offences due to fault of other person

(1) Where the commission by any person of an offence under any of the relevant statutory provisions is due to the act or default of some other person, that other person shall be guilty of the offence, and a person may be charged with and convicted of the offence by virtue of this subsection whether or not proceedings are taken against the first-mentioned person. [E]

(2) Where there would be or have been the commission of an offence under section 33 by the Crown but for the circumstance that that section does not bind the Crown, and that fact is due to the act or default of a person other than the Crown, that person shall be guilty of the offence which, but for that circumstance, the Crown would be committing or would have committed, and may be charged with and convicted of that offence accordingly. [E]

40 Onus of proving limits of what is practicable etc.

In any proceedings for an offence under any of the relevant statutory provisions consisting of a failure to comply with a duty or requirement to do something so far as is practicable or so far as is reasonably practicable, or to use the best means to do something, it shall be for the accused to prove (as the case may be) that it was not practicable or not reasonably practicable to do more than was in fact done to satisfy the duty or requirement, or that there was no better practicable means than was in fact used to satisfy the duty or requirement.

Corporate Manslaughter and Corporate Homicide Act 2007

19 Convictions under this Act and under health and safety legislation

[See page 33]

(c) Explosives and Firearms

Offences Against the Person Act 1861

31 Setting or allowing to remain spring guns, etc., with intent to inflict grievous bodily harm

Whosoever shall set or place, or cause to be set or placed, any spring gun, man trap, or other engine calculated to destroy human life or inflict grievous bodily harm, with the intent that the same or whereby the same may destroy or inflict grievous bodily harm upon a trespasser or other person coming in contact therewith, shall be guilty of an offence, and being convicted thereof shall be liable . . . to imprisonment for a term not exceeding five years; and whosoever shall knowingly and wilfully permit any such spring gun, man trap, or other engine which may have been set or placed in any place then being in or afterwards coming into his possession or occupation by some other person to continue so set or placed, shall be deemed to have set and placed such gun, trap, or engine with such intent as aforesaid: Provided, that nothing in this section contained shall extend to make it illegal to set or place any gun or trap such as may have been or may be usually set or placed with the intent of destroying vermin: Provided also, that nothing in this section shall be deemed to make it unlawful to set or place, or cause to be set or placed, or to be continued set or placed, from sunset to sunrise, any spring gun, man trap, or other engine which shall be set or placed, or caused or continued to be set or placed, in a dwelling-house, for the protection thereof. [I]

Explosive Substances Act 1883

2 Causing explosion likely to endanger life or property

[See page 294]

Firearms Act 1968

1 Requirement of firearm certificate

(1) Subject to any exemption under this Act, it is an offence for a person—

(a) to have in his possession, or to purchase or acquire, a firearm to which this section applies without holding a firearm certificate in force at the time, or otherwise than as authorised by such a certificate;

(b) to have in his possession, or to purchase or acquire, any ammunition to which this section applies without holding a firearm certificate in force at the time, or otherwise than as authorised by such a certificate, or in quantities in excess of those so authorised. [E]

(2) It is an offence for a person to fail to comply with a condition subject to which a firearm certificate is held by him. [S]

(3) This section applies to every firearm except—

(a) a shot gun within the meaning of this Act, that is to say a smooth-bore gun (not being an air gun) which—

(i) has a barrel not less than 24 inches in length and does not have any barrel with a bore exceeding 2 inches in diameter;

(ii) either has no magazine or has a non-detachable magazine incapable of holding more than two cartridges; and

(iii) is not a revolver gun; and

(b) an air weapon (that is to say, an air rifle, air gun or air pistol which does not fall within section 5(1) and which is not of a type declared by rules made by the Secretary of State under section 53 of this Act to be specially dangerous).

(3A) A gun which has been adapted to have such a magazine as is mentioned in subsection (3)(a)(ii) above shall not be regarded as falling within that provision unless the magazine bears a mark approved by the Secretary of State for denoting that fact and that mark has been made, and the adaptation has been certified in writing as having been carried out in a manner approved by him, either by one of the two companies mentioned in section 58(1) of this Act or by such other person as may be approved by him for that purpose.

(4) This section applies to any ammunition for a firearm, except the following articles, namely:—

(a) cartridges containing five or more shot, none of which exceeds 0.36 inch in diameter;

(b) ammunition for an air gun, air rifle or air pistol; and

(c) blank cartridges not more than one inch in diameter measured immediately in front of the rim or cannelure of the base of the cartridge.

2 Requirement of certificate for possession of shot guns

(1) Subject to any exemption under this Act, it is an offence for a person to have in his possession, or to purchase or acquire, a shot gun without holding a certificate under this Act authorising him to possess shot guns. [E]

(2) It is an offence for a person to fail to comply with a condition subject to which a shot gun certificate is held by him. [S]

3 Business and other transactions with firearms and ammunition

(1) A person commits an offence if, by way of trade or business, he—

(a) manufactures, sells, transfers, repairs, tests or proves any firearm or ammunition to which section 1 of this Act applies, or a shot gun; or

(b) exposes for sale or transfer, or has in his possession for sale, transfer, repair, test or proof any such firearm or ammunition, or a shot gun, or

(c) sells or transfers an air weapon, exposes such a weapon for sale or transfer or has such a weapon in his possession for sale or transfer or has such a weapon in his possession for sale or transfer,

without being registered under this Act as a firearms dealer. [E]

(2) It is an offence for a person to sell or transfer to any other person in the United Kingdom, other than a registered firearms dealer, any firearm or ammunition to which section 1 of this Act applies, or a shot gun, unless that other produces a firearm certificate authorising him to purchase or acquire it or as the case may be, his shot gun certificate, or shows that he is by virtue of this Act entitled to purchase or acquire it without holding a certificate. [E]

(3) It is an offence for a person to undertake the repair, tests or proof of a firearm or ammunition to which section 1 of this Act applies, or of a shot gun, for any other person in the United Kingdom other than a registered firearms dealer as such, unless that other produces or causes to be produced a firearm certificate authorising him to have possession of the firearm or ammunition or, as the case may be, his shot gun certificate, or shows that he is by virtue of this Act entitled to have possession of it without holding a certificate. [E]

(4) Subsections (1) and (3) above have effect subject to any exemption under subsequent provisions of this Part of this Act.

(5) A person commits an offence if, with a view to purchasing or acquiring, or procuring the repair, test or proof of, any firearm or ammunition to which section 1 of this Act applies, or a shot gun, he produces a false certificate or a certificate in which any false entry has been made, or personates a person to whom a certificate has been granted, or knowingly or recklessly makes a statement false in any material particular. [E]

(6) It is an offence for a pawnbroker to take in pawn any firearm or ammunition to which section 1 of this Act applies, or a shot gun. [S]

4 Conversion of weapons

(1) Subject to this section, it is an offence to shorten the barrel of a shot gun to a length less than 24 inches. [E]

(2) It is not an offence under subsection (1) above for a registered firearms dealer to shorten the barrel of a shot gun for the sole purpose of replacing a defective part of the barrel so as to produce a barrel not less than 24 inches in length.

(3) It is an offence for a person other than a registered firearms dealer to convert into a firearm anything which, though having the appearance of being a firearm, is so constructed as to be incapable of discharging any missile through its barrel. [E]

(4) A person who commits an offence under section 1 of this Act by having in his possession, or purchasing or acquiring, a shotgun which has been shortened contrary to subsection (1) above or a firearm which has been converted contrary to subsection (3) above (whether by a registered firearms dealer or not), without holding a firearm certificate authorising him to have it in his possession, or to purchase or acquire it, shall be treated for the purposes of provisions of this Act relating to the punishment of offences as committing that offence in an aggravated form.

5 Weapons subject to general prohibition

(1) A person commits an offence if, without the authority of the Defence Council, he has in his possession, or purchases or acquires, or manufactures, sells or transfers—

(a) any firearm which is so designed or adapted that two or more missiles can be successively discharged without repeated pressure on the trigger;

(ab) any self-loading or pump-action rifled gun other than one which is chambered for .22 rim-fire cartridges;

(aba) any firearm which either has a barrel less than 30 centimetres in length or is less than 60 centimetres in length overall, other than an air weapon, a muzzleloading gun or a firearm designed as signalling apparatus;

(ac) any self-loading or pump-action smooth-bore gun which is not an air weapon or chambered for .22 rim-fire cartridges and either has a barrel less than 24 inches in length or (excluding any detachable folding, retractable or other movable butt-stock) is less than 40 inches in length overall;

(ad) any smooth-bore revolver gun other than one which is chambered for 9mm rim-fire cartridges or a muzzle-loading gun;

(ae) any rocket launcher, or any mortar, for projecting a stabilised missile, other than a launcher or mortar designed for line-throwing or pyrotechnic purposes or as signalling apparatus;

(b) any weapon of whatever description designed or adapted for the discharge of any noxious liquid, gas or other thing; and

(c) any cartridge with a bullet designed to explode on or immediately before impact, any ammunition containing or designed or adapted to contain any such noxious thing as is mentioned in paragraph (b) above and, if capable of being used with a firearm of any description, any grenade, bomb (or other like missile), or rocket or shell designed to explode as aforesaid. [I]

(1A) Subject to section 5A of this Act, a person commits an offence if, without the authority of the Secretary of State, he has in his possession, or purchases or acquires, or sells or transfers—

(a) any firearm which is disguised as another object [I];

(b) any rocket or ammunition not falling within paragraph (c) of subsection (1) of this section which consists in or incorporates a missile designed to explode on or immediately before impact and is for military use;

(c) any launcher or other projecting apparatus not falling within paragraph (ae) of that subsection which is designed to be used with any rocket or ammunition falling within paragraph (b) above or with ammunition which would fall within that paragraph but for its being ammunition falling within paragraph (c) of this subsection;

(d) any ammunition for military use which consists in or incorporates a missile designed so that a substance contained in the missile will ignite on or immediately before impact;

(e) any ammunition for military use which consists in or incorporates a missile designed, on account of its having a jacket and hard-core, to penetrate armour plating, armour screening or body armour;

(f) any ammunition which incorporates a missile designed or adapted to expand on impact;

(g) anything which is designed to be projected as a missile from any weapon and is designed to be, or has been, incorporated in—

(i) any ammunition falling within any of the preceding paragraphs; or

(ii) any ammunition which would fall within any of those paragraphs but for its being specified in subsection (1) of this section. [E]

(2) The weapons and ammunition specified in subsections (1) and (1A) of this section (including, in the case of ammunition, any missiles falling within subsection (1A)(g) of this section) are referred to in this Act as 'prohibited weapons' and 'prohibited ammunition' respectively.

(3) An authority given to a person by the Defence Council under this section shall be in writing and be subject to conditions specified therein.

(5) It is an offence for a person to whom an authority is given under this section to fail to comply with any condition of the authority. [S]

(7) For the purposes of this section and section 5A of this Act—

(a) any rocket or ammunition which is designed to be capable of being used with a military weapon shall be taken to be for military use;

(b) references to a missile designed so that a substance contained in the missile will ignite on or immediately before impact include references to any missile containing a substance that ignites on exposure to air; and

(c) references to a missile's expanding on impact include references to its deforming in any predictable manner on or immediately after impact.

(8) For the purposes of subsection (1)(aba) and (ac) above, any detachable, folding, retractable or other movable butt-stock shall be disregarded in measuring the length of any firearm.

(9) Any reference in this section to a muzzle-loading gun is a reference to a gun which is designed to be loaded at the muzzle end of the barrel or chamber with a loose charge and a separate ball (or other missile).

5A Exemptions from requirement of authority under section 5

(1) Subject to subsection (2) below, the authority of the Secretary of State shall not be required by virtue of subsection (1A) of section 5 of this Act for any person to have in his possession, or to purchase, acquire, sell or transfer, any prohibited weapon or ammunition if he is authorised by a certificate under this Act to possess, purchase or acquire that weapon or ammunition subject to a condition that he does so only for the purpose of its being kept or exhibited as part of a collection.

(2) No sale or transfer may be made under subsection (1) above except to a person who—

(a) produces the authority of the Secretary of State under section 5 of this Act for his purchase or acquisition; or

(b) shows that he is, under this section or a licence under the Schedule to the Firearms (Amendment) Act 1988 (museums etc.), entitled to make the purchase or acquisition without the authority of the Secretary of State.

(3) The authority of the Secretary of State shall not be required by virtue of subsection (1A) of section 5 of this Act for any person to have in his possession, or to purchase or acquire, any prohibited weapon or ammunition if his possession, purchase or acquisition is exclusively in connection with the carrying on of activities in respect of which—

(a) that person; or

(b) the person on whose behalf he has possession, or makes the purchase or acquisition, is recognised, for the purposes of the law of another member State relating to firearms, as a collector of firearms or a body concerned in the cultural or historical aspects of weapons.

(4) The authority of the Secretary of State shall not be required by virtue of subsection (1A) of section 5 of this Act for any person to have in his possession, or to purchase or acquire or to sell or transfer, any expanding ammunition or the missile for any such ammunition if—

(a) he is authorised by a firearm certificate or visitor's firearm permit to possess, or purchase or acquire, any expanding ammunition; and

(b) the certificate or permit is subject to a condition restricting the use of any expanding ammunition to use in connection with any one or more of the following, namely—

(i) the lawful shooting of deer;

(ii) the shooting of vermin or, in the course of carrying on activities in connection with the management of any estate other wildlife;

(iii) the humane killing of animals;

(iv) the shooting of animals for the protection of other animals or humans.

(5) The authority of the Secretary of State shall not be required by virtue of subsection (1A) of section 5 of this Act for any person to have in his possession any expanding ammunition or the missile for any such ammunition if—

(a) he is entitled, under section 10 of this Act, to have a slaughtering instrument and the ammunition for it in his possession; and

(b) the ammunition or missile in question is designed to be capable of being used with a slaughtering instrument.

(6) The authority of the Secretary of State shall not be required by virtue of subsection (1A) of section 5 of this Act for the sale or transfer of any expanding ammunition or the missile for any such ammunition to any person who produces a certificate by virtue of which he is authorised under subsection (4) above to purchase or acquire it without the authority of the Secretary of State.

(7) The authority of the Secretary of State shall not be required by virtue of subsection (1A) of section 5 of this Act for a person carrying on the business of a firearms dealer, or any servant of his, to have in his possession, or to purchase, acquire, sell or transfer, any expanding ammunition or the missile for any such ammunition in the ordinary course of that business.

(8) In this section—

(a) references to expanding ammunition are references to any ammunition which is designed to be used with a pistol and incorporates a missile which is designed to expand on impact; and

(b) references to the missile for any such ammunition are references to anything which, in relation to any such ammunition, falls within section 5(1A)(g) of this Act.

7 Police permit

(1) A person who has obtained from the chief officer of police for the area in which he resides a permit for the purpose in the prescribed form may, without holding a certificate under this Act, have in his possession a firearm and ammunition in accordance with the terms of the permit.

(2) It is an offence for a person knowingly or recklessly to make any statement which he knows to be false in any material particular for the purpose of procuring, whether for himself or for another person, the grant of a permit under this section. [S]

16 Possession of firearm with intent to injure

It is an offence for a person to have in his possession any firearm or ammunition with intent by means thereof to endanger life . . . or to enable another person by means thereof to endanger life . . . whether any injury has been caused or not. [I]

16A Possession of firearm with intent to cause fear of violence

It is an offence for a person to have in his possession any firearm or imitation firearm with intent—

(a) by means thereof to cause, or

(b) to enable another person by means thereof to cause,

any person to believe that unlawful violence will be used against him or another person. [I]

17 Use of firearm to resist arrest

(1) It is an offence for a person to make or attempt to make any use whatsoever of a firearm or imitation firearm with intent to resist or prevent the lawful arrest or detention of himself or another person. [I]

(2) If a person, at the time of his committing or being arrested for an offence specified in Schedule 1 to this Act, has in his possession a firearm or imitation firearm, he shall be guilty of an offence under this subsection unless he shows that he had it in his possession for a lawful object. [I]

(4) For purposes of this section, the definition of 'firearm' in section 57(1) of this Act shall apply without paragraphs (b) and (c) of that subsection, and 'imitation firearm' shall be construed accordingly.

18 Carrying firearm with criminal intent

(1) It is an offence for a person to have with him a firearm or imitation firearm with intent to commit an indictable offence, or to resist arrest or prevent the arrest of another, in either case while he has the firearm or imitation firearm with him. [I]

(2) In proceedings for an offence under this section proof that the accused had a firearm or imitation firearm with him and intended to commit an offence, or to resist or prevent arrest, is evidence that he intended to have it with him while doing so.

19 Carrying firearm in a public place

A person commits an offence if, without lawful authority or reasonable excuse (the proof whereof lies on him) he has with him in a public place a loaded shot gun, or a loaded air weapon, or any other firearm (whether loaded or not) together with ammunition suitable for use in that firearm. [E]

20 Trespassing with firearm

(1) A person commits an offence if, while he has a firearm or imitation firearm with him, he enters or is in any building or part of a building as a trespasser and without reasonable excuse (the proof whereof lies on him). [E]

(2) A person commits an offence if, while he has a firearm or imitation firearm with him, he enters or is on any land as a trespasser and without reasonable excuse (the proof whereof lies on him). [S]

(3) In subsection (2) of this section the expression 'land' includes land covered with water.

21A Firing an air weapon beyond premises

(1) A person commits an offence if—

(a) he has with him an air weapon on any premises; and

(b) he uses it for firing a missile beyond those premises.

(2) In proceedings against a person for an offence under this section it shall be a defence for him to show that the only premises into or across which the missile was fired were premises the occupier of which had consented to the firing of the missile (whether specifically or by way of a general consent). [S]

22 Acquisition and possession of firearms by minors

(1) It is an offence—

(a) for a person under the age of eighteen to purchase or hire an air weapon or ammunition for an air weapon;

(b) for a person under the age of seventeen to purchase or hire a firearm or ammunition of any other description. [S]

(1A) When a person under the age of eighteen is entitled, as the holder of a certificate under this Act, to have a firearm in his possession, it is an offence for that person to use that firearm for a purpose not authorised by the European weapons directive. [E]

(2) It is an offence for a person under the age of fourteen to have in his possession any firearm or ammunition to which section 1 of this Act or section 15 of the Firearms Amendment Act 1988 applies, except in circumstances where under section 11 (1), (3) or (4) of this Act he is entitled to have possession of it without holding a firearm certificate. [S]

(3) It is an offence for a person under the age of fifteen to have with him an assembled shot gun except while under the supervision of a person of or over the age of twenty-one, or while the shot gun is so covered with a securely fastened gun cover that it cannot be fired. [S]

(4) Subject to section 23 below, it is an offence for a person under the age of eighteen to have with him an air weapon or ammunition for an air weapon. [S]

(5) Subject to section 23 below, it is an offence for a person under the age of seventeen to have an air weapon with him in a public place, except an air gun or air rifle which is so covered with a securely fastened gun cover that it cannot be fired. [S]

23 Exceptions from s. 22(4) and (5)

(1) It is not an offence under section 22 (4) of this Act for a person to have with him an air weapon or ammunition while he is under the supervision of a person of or over the age of twenty-one; but where a person has with him an air weapon on any premises in circumstances where he would be prohibited from having it with him but for this subsection, it is an offence for the person under whose supervision he is to allow him so to use it for firing any missile beyond those premises.

(1A) In proceedings against a person for an offence under subsection (1) it shall be a defence for him to show that the only premises into or across which the missile was fired were premises the occupier of which had consented to the firing of the missile (whether specifically or by way of a general consent);

(2) It is not an offence under section 22(4) or (5) of this Act for a person to have with him an air weapon or ammunition at a time when—

(a) being a member of a rifle club or miniature rifle club for the time being approved by the Secretary of State for the purposes of this section or section 15 of the Firearms (Amendment) Act 1988, he is engaged as such a member in or in connection with target shooting; or

(b) he is using the weapon or ammunition at a shooting gallery where the only firearms used are either air weapons or miniature rifles not exceeding 0.23 inch calibre.

24 Supplying firearms to minors

(1) It is an offence—

(a) to sell or let on hire an air weapon or ammunition for an air weapon to a person under the age of eighteen;

(b) to sell or let on hire a firearm or ammunition of any other description to a person under the age of seventeen. [S]

(2) It is an offence—

(a) to make a gift of or lend any firearm or ammunition to which section 1 of this Act applies to a person under the age of fourteen; or

(b) to part with the possession of any such firearm or ammunition to a person under that age, except in circumstances where that person is entitled under section 11 (1), (3) or (4) of this Act or section 15 of the Firearms (Amendment) Act 1988 to have possession thereof without holding a firearm certificate. [S]

(3) It is an offence to make a gift of a shot gun or ammunition for a shot gun to a person under the age of fifteen. [S]

(4) It is an offence—

(a) to make a gift of an air weapon or ammunition for an air weapon to a person under the age of eighteen; or

(b) to part with the possession of an air weapon or ammunition for an air weapon to a person under that age except where by virtue of section 23 of this Act the person is not prohibited from having it with him. [S]

(5) In proceedings for an offence under any provision of this section it is a defence to prove that the person charged with the offence believed the other person to be of or over the age mentioned in that provision and had reasonable ground for the belief.

24A Supplying imitation firearms to minors

(1) It is an offence for a person under the age of eighteen to purchase an imitation firearm. [S]

(2) It is an offence to sell an imitation firearm to a person under the age of eighteen. [S]

(3) In proceedings for an offence under subsection (2) it is a defence to show that the person charged with the offence—

(a) believed the other person to be aged eighteen or over; and

(b) had reasonable ground for that belief.

(4) For the purposes of this section a person shall be taken to have shown the matters specified in subsection (3) if—

(a) sufficient evidence of those matters is adduced to raise an issue with respect to them; and

(b) the contrary is not proved beyond a reasonable doubt.

25 Supplying firearm to person drunk or insane

It is an offence for a person to sell or transfer any firearm or ammunition to, or to repair, prove or test any firearm or ammunition for, another person whom he knows or has reasonable cause for believing to be drunk or of unsound mind. [S]

57 Interpretation

(1) In this Act, the expression 'firearm' means a lethal barrelled weapon of any description from which any shot, bullet or other missile can be discharged and includes—

(a) any prohibited weapon, whether it is such a lethal weapon as aforesaid or not; and
(b) any component part of such a lethal or prohibited weapon; and
(c) any accessory to any such weapon designed or adapted to diminish the noise or flash caused by firing the weapon;

and so much of section 1 of this Act as excludes any description of firearm from the category of firearms to which that section applies shall be construed as also excluding component parts of, and accessories to, firearms of that description.

(2) In this Act, the expression 'ammunition' means ammunition for any firearm and includes grenades, bombs and other like missiles, whether capable of use with a firearm or not, and also includes prohibited ammunition.

(2A) In this Act 'self-loading' and 'pump-action' in relation to any weapon mean respectively that it is designed or adapted (otherwise that as mentioned in section 5(1)(a)) so that it is automatically re-loaded or that it is so designed or adapted that it is re-loaded by the manual operation of the fore-end or forestock of the weapon.

(2B) In this Act 'revolver', in relation to a smooth-bore gun, means a gun containing a series of chambers which revolve when the gun is fired.

(4) In this Act—

'acquire' means hire, accept as a gift or borrow and 'acquisition' shall be construed accordingly;

'air weapon' has the meaning assigned to it by section 1 (3)(b) of this Act;

'area' means a police area;

'another member State' means a member State other than the United Kingdom, and 'other member State' shall be construed accordingly;

'Article 7 authority' means a document issued by virtue of section 32A(1)(b) or (2) of this Act;

'British Transport Police Force' means the constables appointed under section 53 of the British Transport commission Act 1949;

'certificate' (except in a context relating to the registration of firearms dealers) and 'certificate under this Act' means a firearm certificate or a shot gun certificate and—

(a) 'firearm certificate' means a certificate granted by a chief officer of police under this Act in respect of any firearm or ammunition to which section 1 of this Act applies; and
(b) 'shot gun certificate' means a certificate granted by a chief officer of police under this Act and authorising a person to possess shot guns;

'civilian officer' means—

(a) a person employed by a police authority or the Corporation of the City of London who is under the direction and control of a chief officer of police;

'European firearms pass' means a document to which the holder of a certificate under this Act is entitled by virtue of section 32A(1)(a) of this Act;

'European weapons directive' means the directive of the Council of the European Communities No. 91/477/EEC (directive on the control of the acquisition and possession of weapons);

'firearms dealer' means a person who, by way of trade or business,

(a) manufactures, sells, transfers, repairs, tests or proves firearms or ammunition to which section 1 of this Act applies or shot guns; or
(b) sells or transfers air weapons.

'imitation firearm' means any thing which has the appearance of being a firearm (other than such a weapon as is mentioned in section 5 (1)(b) of this Act) whether or not it is capable of discharging any shot, bullet or other missile;

'premises' includes any land;

'prescribed' means prescribed by rules made by the Secretary of State under section 53 of this Act;

'prohibited weapon' and 'prohibited ammunition' have the meanings assigned to them by section 5(2) of this Act;

'public place' includes any highway and any other premises or place to which at the material time the public have or are permitted to have access, whether on payment or otherwise;

'registered', in relation to a firearms dealer, means registered either—

(a) in Great Britain, under section 33 of this Act, or

(b) in Northern Ireland, under section 8 of the Firearms Act 1920 or any enactment of the Parliament of Northern Ireland amending or substituted for that section;

and references to 'the register', 'registration' and a 'certificate of registration' shall be construed accordingly, except in section 40;

'rifle' includes carbine;

'shot gun' has the meaning assigned to it by section 1 (3)(a) of this Act and, in sections 3 (1) and 45 (2) of this Act and in the definition of 'firearms dealer', includes any component part of a shot gun and any accessory to a shot gun designed or adapted to diminish the noise or flash caused by firing the gun;

'slaughtering instrument' means a firearm which is specially designed or adapted for the instantaneous slaughter of animals or for the instantaneous stunning of animals with a view to slaughtering them; and

'transfer' includes let on hire, give, lend and part with possession, and 'transferee' and 'transferor' shall be construed accordingly.

(4A) For the purposes of any reference in this Act to the use of any firearm or ammunition for a purpose not authorised by the European weapons directive, the directive shall be taken to authorise the use of a firearm or ammunition as or with a slaughtering instrument and the use of a firearm and ammunition—

(a) for sporting purposes;

(b) for the shooting of vermin, or, in the course of carrying on activities in connection with the management of any estate, of other wildlife; and

(c) for competition purposes and target shooting outside competitions.

(5) The definitions in subsections (1) to (3) above apply to the provisions of this Act except where the context otherwise requires.

(6) For the purposes of this Act—

(a) the length of the barrel of a firearm shall be measured from the muzzle to the point at which the charge is exploded on firing; and

(b) a shot gun or an air weapon shall be deemed to be loaded if there is ammunition in the chamber or barrel or in any magazine or other device which is in such a position that the ammunition can be fed into the chamber or barrel by the manual or automatic operation of some part of the gun or weapon.

58 Particular savings

(2) Nothing in this Act relating to firearms shall apply to an antique firearm which is sold, transferred, purchased, acquired or possessed as a curiosity or ornament.

(3) The provisions of this Act relating to ammunition shall be in addition to and not in derogation of any enactment relating to the keeping and sale of explosives.

SCHEDULE 1 OFFENCES TO WHICH SECTION 17(2) APPLIES

1. Offences under section 1 of the Criminal Damage Act 1971

2. Offences under any of the following provisions of the Offences against the Person Act 1861—

section 20 to 22 (inflicting bodily injury; garrotting; criminal use of stupefying drugs);

section 30 (laying explosive to building etc.);

section 32 (endangering railway passengers by tampering with track);

section 38 (assault with intent to commit felony or resist arrest);

section 47 (criminal assaults);

2A. Offences under Part 1 of the Child Abduction Act 1984 (abduction of children).

4. Theft, robbery, burglary, blackmail and any offence under section 12(1) (taking of motor vehicle or other conveyance without owner's consent) of the Theft Act 1968.

5. Offences under section 89(1) of the Police Act 1996 (assaulting constable in execution of his duty).

5A. An offence under section 90(1) of the Criminal Justice Act 1991 (assaulting prisoner custody officer).

5B. An offence under section 13(1) of the Criminal Justice and Public Order Act 1994 (assaulting secure training centre custody officer).

6. Offences under any of the following provisions of the Sexual Offences Act 1956— section 1 (rape);

sections 17, 18 and 20 (abduction of women).

8. Aiding or abetting the commission of any offence specified in paragraphs 1 to 6 of this Schedule.

9. Attempting to commit any offence so specified.

Firearms (Amendment) Act 1988

5 Restriction on sale of ammunition for smooth-bore guns

(1) This section applies to ammunition to which section 1 of the Firearms Act 1968 does not apply and which is capable of being used in a shot gun or in a smooth-bore gun to which that section applies.

(2) It is an offence for a person to sell any such ammunition to another person in the United Kingdom who is neither a registered firearms dealer nor a person who sells such ammunition by way of trade or business unless that other person—

(a) produces a certificate authorising him to possess a gun of a kind mentioned in subsection (1) above; or

(b) shows that he is by virtue of that Act or this Act entitled to have possession of such a gun without holding a certificate; or

(c) produces a certificate authorising another person to possess such a gun, together with that person's written authority to purchase the ammunition on his behalf. [S]

6 Shortening of barrels

(1) Subject to subsection (2) below, it is an offence to shorten to a length less than 24 inches the barrel of any smooth-bore gun to which section 1 of the Firearms Act 1968 applies other than one which has a barrel with a bore exceeding 2 inches in diameter . . . [E]

(2) It is not an offence under this section for a registered firearms dealer to shorten the barrel of a gun for the sole purpose of replacing a defective part of the barrel so as to produce a barrel not less than 24 inches in length.

14 Auctioneers, carriers and warehousemen

(1) It is an offence for an auctioneer, carrier or warehouseman—

(a) to fail to take reasonable precautions for the safe custody of any firearm or ammunition which, by virtue of section 9(1) of the Firearms Act 1968 he or any servant of his has in his posession without holding a certificate; or

(b) to fail to report forthwith to the police the loss or theft of any such firearm or ammunition. [S]

Firearms (Amendment) Act 1997

2 Slaughtering instruments

The authority of the Secretary of State is not required by virtue of subsection (1)(aba) of section 5 of the 1968 Act—

(a) for a person to have in his possession, or to purchase or acquire, or to sell or transfer, a slaughtering instrument if he is authorised by a firearm certificate to have the instrument in his possession, or to purchase or acquire it;
(b) for a person to have a slaughtering instrument in his possession if he is entitled, under section 10 of the 1968 Act, to have it in his possession without a firearm certificate.

3 Firearms used for humane killing of animals

The authority of the Secretary of State is not required by virtue of subsection (1)(aba) of section 5 of the 1968 Act for a person to have in his possession, or to purchase or acquire, or to sell or transfer, a firearm if he is authorised by a firearm certificate to have the firearm in his possession, or to purchase or acquire it, subject to a condition that it is only for use in connection with the humane killing of animals.

4 Shot pistols used for shooting vermin

(1) The authority of the Secretary of State is not required by virtue of subsection (1)(aba) of section 5 of the 1968 Act for a person to have in his possession, or to purchase or acquire, or to sell or transfer, a shot pistol if he is authorised by a firearm certificate to have the shot pistol in his possession, or to purchase or acquire it, subject to a condition that it is only for use in connection with the shooting of vermin.

(2) For the purposes of this section, 'shot pistol' means a smooth-bored gun which is chambered for .410 cartridges or 9mm rim-fire cartridges.

5 Races at athletic meetings

The authority of the Secretary of State is not required by virtue of subsection (1)(aba) of section 5 of the 1968 Act—

(a) for a person to have a firearm in his possession at an athletic meeting for the purpose of starting races at that meeting; or
(b) for a person to have in his possession, or to purchase or acquire, or to sell or transfer, a firearm if he is authorised by a firearm certificate to have the firearm in his possession, or to purchase or acquire it, subject to a condition that it is only for use in connection with starting races at athletic meetings.

6 Trophies of war

The authority of the Secretary of State is not required by virtue of subsection (1)(aba) of section 5 of the 1968 Act for a person to have in his possession a firearm which was acquired as a trophy of war before 1st January 1946 if he is authorised by a firearm certificate to have it in his possession.

7 Firearms of historic interest

(1) The authority of the Secretary of State is not required by virtue of subsection (1)(aba) of section 5 of the 1968 Act for a person to have in his possession, or to purchase or acquire, or to sell or transfer, a firearm which—

(a) was manufactured before 1st January 1919; and
(b) is of a description specified under subsection (2) below,

if he is authorised by a firearm certificate to have the firearm in his possession, or to purchase or acquire it, subject to a condition that he does so only for the purpose of its being kept or exhibited as part of a collection.

(2) The Secretary of State may by order made by statutory instrument specify a description of firearm for the purposes of subsection (1) above if it appears to him that—

(a) firearms of that description were manufactured before 1st January 1919, and
(b) ammunition for firearms of that type is not readily available.

(3) The authority of the Secretary of State is not required by virtue of subsection (1)(aba) of section 5 of the 1968 Act for a person to have in his possession, or to purchase or acquire, or to sell or transfer, a firearm which—

(a) is of particular rarity, aesthetic quality or technical interest, or
(b) is of historical importance,

if he is authorised by a firearm certificate to have the firearm in his possession subject to a condition requiring it to be kept and used only at a place designated for the purposes of this subsection by the Secretary of State.

(4) This section has effect without prejudice to section 58(2) of the 1968 Act (antique firearms).

8 Weapons and ammunition used for treating animals

The authority of the Secretary of State is not required by virtue of subsection (1)(aba), (b) or (c) of section 5 of the 1968 Act for a person to have in his possession, or to purchase or acquire, or to sell or transfer, any firearm, weapon or ammunition designed or adapted for the purpose of tranquillising or otherwise treating any animal, if he is authorised by a firearm certificate to possess, or to purchase or acquire, the firearm, weapon or ammunition subject to a condition restricting its use to use in connection with the treatment of animals.

48 Firearms powered by compressed carbon dioxide

Any reference to an air rifle, air pistol or air gun—

(a) in the Firearms Acts 1968 to 1997; or

(b) in the Firearms (Dangerous Air Weapons) Rules 1969 or the Firearms (Dangerous Air Weapons)(Scotland) Rules 1969,

shall include a reference to a rifle, pistol or gun powered by compressed carbon dioxide.

(d) Dogs

Dangerous Dogs Act 1991

1 Dogs bred for fighting

(1) This section applies to—

(a) any dog of the type known as the pit bull terrier;

(b) any dog of the type known as the Japanese tosa; and

(c) any dog of any type designated for the purposes of this section by an order of the Secretary of State, being a type appearing to him to be bred for fighting or to have the characteristics of a type bred for that purpose.

(2) No person shall—

(a) breed, or breed from, a dog to which this section applies;

(b) sell or exchange such a dog or offer, advertise or expose such a dog for sale or exchange;

(c) make or offer to make a gift of such a dog or advertise or expose such a dog as a gift;

(d) allow such a dog of which he is the owner or of which he is for the time being in charge to be in a public place without being muzzled and kept on a lead; or

(e) abandon such a dog of which he is the owner or, being the owner or for the time being in charge of such a dog, allow it to stray.

(7) Any person who contravenes this section is guilty of an offence and liable on summary conviction to imprisonment for a term not exceeding six months or a fine not exceeding level 5 on the standard scale or both except that a person who publishes an advertisement in contravention of subsection (2)(b) or (c)—

(a) shall not on being convicted be liable to imprisonment if he shows that he published the advertisement to the order of someone else and did not himself devise it; and

(b) shall not be convicted if, in addition, he shows that he did not know and had no reasonable cause to suspect that it related to a dog to which this section applies. [S]

3 Keeping dogs under proper control

(1) If a dog is dangerously out of control in a public place—

(a) the owner; and

(b) if different, the person for the time being in charge of the dog, is guilty of an offence [S], or, if the dog while so out of control injures any person, an aggravated offence [E], under this subsection.

(2) In proceedings for an offence under subsection (1) above against a person who is the owner of a dog but was not at the material time in charge of it, it shall be a defence for the accused to prove that the dog was at the material time in the charge of a person whom he reasonably believed to be a fit and proper person to be in charge of it.

(3) If the owner or, if different, the person for the time being in charge of a dog allows it to enter a place which is not a public place but where it is not permitted to be and while it is there—

(a) it injures any person; or

(b) there are grounds for reasonable apprehension that it will do so, he is guilty of an offence, or, if the dog injures any person, an aggravated offence, under this subsection.

6 Dogs owned by young persons

Where a dog is owned by a person who is less than sixteen years old any reference to its owner in section 1(2)(d) or (e) or 3 above shall include a reference to the head of the household, if any, of which that person is a member…

7 Muzzling and leads

(1) In this Act—

(a) references to a dog being muzzled are to its being securely fitted with a muzzle sufficient to prevent it biting any person; and

(b) references to its being kept on a lead are to its being securely held on a lead by a person who is not less than sixteen years old.

10 Interpretation

(2) In this Act—

'advertisement' includes any means of bringing a matter to the attention of the public and 'advertise' shall be construed accordingly;

'public place' means any street, road or other place (whether or not enclosed) to which the public have or are permitted to have access whether for payment or otherwise and includes the common parts of a building containing two or more separate dwellings.

(3) For the purposes of this Act a dog shall be regarded as dangerously out of control on any occasion on which there are grounds for reasonable apprehension that it will injure any person whether or not it actually does so, but references to a dog injuring a person or there being grounds for reasonable apprehension that it will do so do not include references to any case in which the dog is being used for a lawful purpose by a constable or a person in the service of the Crown.

(e) Supply of Goods and Services

Food Safety Act 1990

1 Meaning of 'food' and other basic expressions

(1) In this Act 'food' includes—

(a) drink;

(b) articles and substances of no nutritional value which are used for human consumption;

(c) chewing gum and other products of a like nature and use; and

(d) articles and substances used as ingredients in the preparation of food or anything falling within this subsection.

(2) In this Act 'food' does not include—

(a) live animals or birds, or live fish which are not used for human consumption while they are alive;

(b) fodder or feeding stuffs for animals, birds or fish;

(c) controlled drugs within the meaning of the Misuse of Drugs Act 1971; or

(d) subject to such exceptions as may be specified in an order made by the Secretary of State—

(i) medicinal products within the meaning of the Medicines Act 1968 in respect of which product licences within the meaning of that Act are for the time being in force; or

(ii) other articles or substances in respect of which such licences are for the time being in force in pursuance of orders under section 104 or 105 of that Act (application of Act to other articles and substances).

(3) In this Act, unless the context otherwise requires—

'business' includes the undertaking of a canteen, club, school, hospital or institution, whether carried on for profit or not, and any undertaking or activity carried on by a public or local authority;

'commercial operation', in relation to any food or contact material, means any of the following, namely—

(a) selling, possessing for sale and offering, exposing or advertising for sale;

(b) consigning, delivering or serving by way of sale;

(c) preparing for sale or presenting, labelling or wrapping for the purpose of sale;

(d) storing or transporting for the purpose of sale;

(e) importing and exporting;

and, in relation to any food source, means deriving food from it for the purpose of sale or for purposes connected with sale;

'contact material' means any article or substance which is intended to come into contact with food;

'food business' means any business in the course of which commercial operations with respect to food or food sources are carried out;

'food premises' means any premises used for the purposes of a food business; 'food source' means any growing crop or live animal, bird or fish from which food is intended to be derived (whether by harvesting, slaughtering, milking, collecting eggs or otherwise);

'premises' includes any place, any vehicle, stall or moveable structure and, for such purposes as may be specified in an order made by the Secretary of State, any ship or aircraft of a description so specified.

(4) The reference in subsection (3) above to preparing for sale shall be construed, in relation to any contact material, as a reference to manufacturing or producing for the purpose of sale.

2 Extended meaning of 'sale', etc.

(1) For the purposes of this Act—

(a) the supply of food, otherwise than on sale, in the course of a business; and

(b) any other thing which is done with respect to food and is specified in an order made by the Secretary of State,

shall be deemed to be a sale of the food, and references to purchasers and purchasing shall be construed accordingly.

(2) This Act shall apply—

(a) in relation to any food which is offered as a prize or reward or given away in connection with any entertainment to which the public are admitted, whether on payment of money or not, as if the food were, or had been, exposed for sale by each person concerned in the organisation of the entertainment;

(b) in relation to any food which, for the purpose of advertisement or in furtherance of any trade or business, is offered as a prize or reward or given away, as if the food were, or had been, exposed for sale by the person offering or giving away the food; and

(c) in relation to any food which is exposed or deposited in any premises for the purpose of being so offered or given away as mentioned in paragraph (a) or (b) above, as if the food were, or had been, exposed for sale by the occupier of the premises;

and in this subsection 'entertainment' includes any social gathering, amusement, exhibition, performance, game, sport or trial of skill.

3 Presumptions that food intended for human consumption

(1) The following provisions shall apply for the purposes of this Act.

(2) Any food commonly used for human consumption shall, if sold or offered, exposed or kept for sale, be presumed, until the contrary is proved, to have been sold or, as the case may be, to have been or to be intended for sale for human consumption.

(3) The following, namely—

(a) any food commonly used for human consumption which is found on premises used for the preparation, storage, or sale of that food; and

(b) any article or substance commonly used in the manufacture of food for human consumption which is found on premises used for the preparation, storage or sale of that food,

shall be presumed, until the contrary is proved, to be intended for sale, or for manufacturing food for sale, for human consumption.

(4) Any article or substance capable of being used in the composition or preparation of any food commonly used for human consumption which is found on premises on which that food is prepared shall, until the contrary is proved, be presumed to be intended for such use.

7 Rendering food injurious to health

(1) Any person who renders any food injurious to health by means of any of the following operations, namely—

(a) adding any article or substance to the food;

(b) using any article or substance as an ingredient in the preparation of the food;

(c) abstracting any constituent from the food; and

(d) subjecting the food to any other process or treatment,

with intent that it shall be sold for human consumption, shall be guilty of an offence. [E]

(2) In determining for the purposes of this section and section 8(2) below whether any food is injurious to health, regard shall be had—

(a) not only to the probable effect of that food on the health of a person consuming it; but

(b) also to the probable cumulative effect of food of substantially the same composition on the health of a person consuming it in ordinary quantities.

(3) In this Part 'injury', in relation to health, includes any impairment, whether permanent or temporary, and 'injurious to health' shall be construed accordingly.

8 Selling food not complying with food safety requirements

(1) Any person who—

(a) sells for human consumption, or offers, exposes or advertises for sale for such consumption, or has in his possession for the purpose of such sale or of preparation for such sale; or

(b) deposits with, or consigns to, any other person for the purpose of such sale or of preparation for such sale,

any food which fails to comply with food safety requirements shall be guilty of an offence. [E]

(2) For the purposes of this Part food fails to comply with food safety requirements if—

(a) it has been rendered injurious to health by means of any of the operations mentioned in section 7(1) above;

(b) it is unfit for human consumption; or

(c) it is so contaminated (whether by extraneous matter or otherwise) that it would not be reasonable to expect it to be used for human consumption in that state;

and references to such requirements or to food complying with such requirements shall be construed accordingly.

(3) Where any food which fails to comply with food safety requirements is part of a batch, lot or consignment of food of the same class or description, it shall be presumed for the purposes of this section and section 9 below, until the contrary is proved, that all of the food in that batch, lot or consignment fails to comply with those requirements.

(4) For the purposes of this Part, any part of, or product derived wholly or partly from, an animal—

(a) which has been slaughtered in a knacker's yard, or of which the carcase has been brought into a knacker's yard;. . .

shall be deemed to be unfit for human consumption.

14 Selling food not of the nature or substance or quality demanded

(1) Any person who sells to the purchaser's prejudice any food which is not of the nature or substance or quality demanded by the purchaser shall be guilty of an offence. [E]

(2) In subsection (1) above the reference to sale shall be construed as a reference to sale for human consumption; and in proceedings under that subsection it shall not be a defence that the purchaser was not prejudiced because he bought for analysis or examination.

15 Falsely describing or presenting food

(1) Any person who gives with any food sold by him, or displays with any food offered or exposed by him for sale or in his possession for the purpose of sale, a label, whether or not attached to or printed on the wrapper or container, which—

(a) falsely described the food; or

(b) is likely to mislead as to the nature or substance or quality of the food, shall be guilty of an offence. [E]

(2) Any person who publishes, or is a party to the publication of, an advertisement (not being such a label given or displayed by him as mentioned in subsection (1) above) which—

(a) falsely describes any food; or

(b) is likely to mislead as to the nature or substance or quality of any food, shall be guilty of an offence. [E]

(3) Any person who sells, or offers or exposes for sale, or has in his possession for the purpose of sale, any food the presentation of which is likely to mislead as to the nature or substance or quality of the food shall be guilty of an offence. [E]

(4) In proceedings for an offence under subsection (1) or (2) above, the fact that a label or advertisement in respect of which the offence is alleged to have been committed contained an accurate statement of the composition of the food shall not preclude the court from finding that the offence was committed.

(5) In this section references to sale shall be construed as references to sale for human consumption.

20 Offences due to fault of another person

Where the commission by any person of an offence under any of the preceding provisions of this Part is due to an act or default of some other person, that other person shall be guilty of the offence; and a person may be charged with and convicted of the offence by virtue of this section whether or not proceedings are taken against the first-mentioned person.

21 Defence of due diligence

(1) In any proceedings for an offence under any of the preceding provisions of this Part (in this section referred to as 'the relevant provision'), it shall, subject to subsection (5) below, be a defence for the person charged to prove that he took all reasonable precautions and exercised all due diligence to avoid the commission of the offence by himself or by a person under his control. (2) Without

prejudice to the generality of subsection (1) above, a person charged with an offence under section 8, 14 or 15 above who neither—

(a) prepared the food in respect of which the offence is alleged to have been committed; nor

(b) imported it into Great Britain,

shall be taken to have established the defence provided by that subsection if he satisfies the requirements of subsection (3) or (4) below.

(3) A person satisfies the requirements of this subsection if he proves—

(a) that the commission of the offence was due to an act or default of another person who was not under his control, or to reliance on information supplied by such a person;

(b) that he carried out all such checks of the food in question as were reasonable in all the circumstances, or that it was reasonable in all the circumstances for him to rely on checks carried out by the person who supplied the food to him; and

(c) that he did not know and had no reason to suspect at the time of the commission of the alleged offence that his act or omission would amount to an offence under the relevant provision.

(4) A person satisfies the requirements of this subsection if he proves—

(a) that the commission of the offence was due to an act or default of another person who was not under his control, or to reliance on information supplied by such a person;

(b) that the sale or intended sale of which the alleged offence consisted was not a sale or intended sale under his name or mark; and

(c) that he did not know, and could not reasonably have been expected to know, at the time of the commission of the alleged offence that his act or omission would amount to an offence under the relevant provision.

(5) If in any case the defence provided by subsection (1) above involves the allegation that the commission of the offence was due to an act or default of another person, or to reliance on information supplied by another person, the person charged shall not, without leave of the court, be entitled to rely on that defence unless—

(a) at least seven clear days before the hearing; and

(b) where he has previously appeared before a court in connection with the alleged offence, within one month of his first such appearance,

he has served on the prosecutor a notice in writing giving such information identifying or assisting in the identification of that other person as was then in his possession.

(6) In subsection (5) above any reference to appearing before a court shall be construed as including a reference to being brought before a court.

22 Defence of publication in the course of business

In proceedings for an offence under any of the preceding provisions of this Part consisting of the advertisement for sale of any food, it shall be a defence for the person charged to prove—

(a) that he is a person whose business it is to publish or arrange for the publication of advertisements; and

(b) that he received the advertisement in the ordinary course of business and did not know and had no reason to suspect that its publication would amount to an offence under that provision.

33 Obstruction, etc., of officers

(1) Any person who—

(a) intentionally obstructs any person acting in the execution of this Act; or

(b) without reasonable cause, fails to give to any person acting in the execution of this Act any assistance or information which that person may reasonably require of him for the performance of his functions under this Act,

shall be guilty of an offence. [S]

(2) Any person who, in purported compliance with any such requirement as is mentioned in subsection (1)(b) above—

(a) furnishes information which he knows to be false or misleading in a material particular; or

(b) recklessly furnishes information which is false or misleading in a material particular, shall be guilty of an offence. [E]

(3) Nothing in subsection (1)(b) above shall be construed as requiring any person to answer any question or give information if to do so might incriminate him.

36 Offences by bodies corporate

(1) Where an offence under this Act which has been committed by a body corporate is proved to have been committed with the consent or connivance of, or to be attributable to any neglect on the part of—

(a) any director, manager, secretary or other similar officer of the body corporate; or

(b) any person who was purporting to act in any such capacity,

he as well as the body corporate shall be deemed to be guilty of that offence and shall be liable to be proceeded against and punished accordingly.

(2) In subsection (1) above 'director', in relation to any body corporate established by or under any enactment for the purpose of carrying on under national ownership any industry or part of an industry or undertaking, being a body corporate whose affairs are managed by its members, means a member of that body corporate.

Consumer Protection Act 1987

10 The general safety requirement

(1) A person shall be guilty of an offence if he—

(a) supplies any consumer goods which fail to comply with the general safety requirement;

(b) offers or agrees to supply any such goods; or

(c) exposes or possesses any such goods for supply. [S]

(2) For the purposes of this section consumer goods fail to comply with the general safety requirement if they are not reasonably safe having regard to all the circumstances, including—

(a) the manner in which, and purposes for which, the goods are being or would be marketed, the get-up of the goods, the use of any mark in relation to the goods and any instructions or warnings which are given or would be given with respect to the keeping, use or consumption of the goods;

(b) any standards of safety published by any person either for goods of a description which applies to the goods in question or for matters relating to goods of that description; and

(c) the existence of any means by which it would have been reasonable (taking into account the cost, likelihood and extent of any improvement) for the goods to have been made safer.

(3) For the purposes of this section consumer goods shall not be regarded as failing to comply with the general safety requirement in respect of—

(a) anything which is shown to be attributable to compliance with any requirement imposed by or under any enactment or with any Community obligation;

(b) any failure to do more in relation to any matter than is required by—

(i) any safety regulations imposing requirements with respect to that matter;

(iii) any provision of any enactment or subordinate legislation imposing such requirements with respect to that matter as are designated for the purposes of this subsection by any such regulations.

(4) In any proceedings against any person for an offence under this section in respect of any goods it shall be a defence for that person to show—

(a) that he reasonably believed that the goods would not be used or consumed in the United Kingdom; or

(b) that the following conditions are satisfied, that is to say—

(i) that he supplied the goods, offered or agreed to supply them, or as the case may be, exposed or possessed them for supply in the course of carrying on a retail business; and
(ii) that, at the time he supplied the goods or offered or agreed to supply them or exposed or possessed them for supply, he neither knew nor had reasonable grounds for believing that the goods failed to comply with the general safety requirement; or

(c) that the terms on which he supplied the goods or agreed or offered to supply them or, in the case of goods which he exposed or possessed for supply, the terms on which he intended to supply them—
(i) indicated that the goods were not supplied or to be supplied as new goods; and
(ii) provided for, or contemplated, the acquisition of an interest in the goods by the person supplied or to be supplied.

(5) For the purposes of subsection (4)(b) above goods are supplied in the course of carrying on a retail business if—
(a) whether or not they are themselves acquired for a person's private use or consumption, they are supplied in the course of carrying on a business of making a supply of consumer goods available to persons who generally acquire them for private use or consumption; and
(b) the descriptions of goods the supply of which is made available in the course of that business do not, to a significant extent, include manufactured or imported goods which have not previously been supplied in the United Kingdom.

(6) A person guilty of an offence under this section shall be liable on summary conviction to imprisonment for a term not exceeding six months or to a fine not exceeding level 5 on the standard scale or to both.

(7) In this section 'consumer goods' means any goods which are ordinarily intended for private use or consumption, not being—
(a) growing crops or things comprised in land by virtue of being attached to it;
(b) water, food, feeding stuff or fertiliser;
(c) gas which is, is to be or has been supplied by a person authorised to supply it by or under section 7A of the Gas Act 1986; (licensing of gas suppliers and gas shippers) or paragraph 5 of Schedule 2A to that Act (supply to very large customers an exception to prohibition on unlicensed activities);
(d) aircraft (other than hang-gliders) or motor vehicles;
(e) controlled drugs or licensed medicinal products;
(f) tobacco.

11 Safety regulations

(1) The Secretary of State may by regulations under this section ('safety regulations') make such provision as he considers appropriate for the purposes of section 10(3) above and for the purpose of securing—
(a) that goods to which this section applies are safe;
(b) that goods to which this section applies which are unsafe, or would be unsafe in the hands of persons of a particular description, are not made available to persons generally or, as the case may be, to persons of that description; and
(c) that appropriate information is, and inappropriate information is not, provided in relation to goods to which this section applies.

12 Offences against the safety regulations

(1) Where safety regulations prohibit a person from supplying or offering or agreeing to supply any goods or from exposing or possessing any goods for supply, that person shall be guilty of an offence if he contravenes the prohibition. [S]

(2) Where safety regulations require a person who makes or processes any goods in the course of carrying on a business—
(a) to carry out a particular test or use a particular procedure in connection with the making or processing of the goods with a view to ascertaining whether the goods satisfy any requirements of such regulations; or

(b) to deal or not to deal in a particular way with a quantity of the goods of which the whole or part does not satisfy such a test or does not satisfy standards connected with such a procedure,

that person shall be guilty of an offence if he does not comply with the requirement. [S]

(3) If a person contravenes a provision of safety regulations which prohibits or requires the provision, by means of a mark or otherwise, of information of a particular kind in relation to goods, he shall be guilty of an offence. [S]

(4) Where safety regulations require any person to give information to another for the purpose of enabling that other to exercise any function, that person shall be guilty of an offence if—

(a) he fails without reasonable cause to comply with the requirement; or

(b) in giving the information which is required of him—

(i) he makes any statement which he knows is false in a material particular; or

(ii) he recklessly makes any statement which is false in a material particular. [S]

39 Defence of due diligence

(1) Subject to the following provisions of this section, in proceedings against any person for an offence to which this section applies it shall be a defence for that person to show that he took all reasonable steps and exercised all due diligence to avoid committing the offence.

(2) Where in any proceedings against any person for such an offence the defence provided by subsection (1) above involves an allegation that the commission of the offence was due—

(a) to the act or default of another; or

(b) to reliance on information given by another,

that person shall not, without the leave of the court, be entitled to rely on the defence unless, not less than seven clear days before the hearing of the proceedings, he has served a notice under subsection (3) below on the person bringing the proceedings.

(3) A notice under this subsection shall give such information identifying or assisting in the identification of the person who committed the act or default or gave the information as is in the possession of the person serving the notice at the time he serves it.

(4) It is hereby declared that a person shall not be entitled to rely on the defence provided by subsection (1) above by reason of his reliance on information supplied by another, unless he shows that it was reasonable in all the circumstances for him to have relied on the information, having regard in particular—

(a) to the steps which he took, and those which might reasonably have been taken, for the purpose of verifying the information; and

(b) to whether he had any reason to disbelieve the information.

(5) This section shall apply to an offence under section 10, 12(1), (2) or (3), 13(4), 14(6) or 20(1) above.

40 Liability of persons other than the principal offender

(1) Where the commission by any person of an offence to which section 39 above applies is due to an act or default committed by some other person in the course of any business of his, the other person shall be guilty of the offence and may be proceeded against and punished by virtue of this subsection whether or not proceedings are taken against the first-mentioned person. [S]

(2) Where a body corporate is guilty of an offence under this Act (including where it is so guilty by virtue of subsection (1) above) in respect of any act or default which is shown to have been committed with the consent or connivance of, or to be attributable to any neglect on the part of, any director, manager, secretary or other similar officer of the body corporate or any person who was purporting to act in any such capacity he, as well as the body corporate, shall be guilty of that offence and shall be liable to be proceeded against and punished accordingly. [S]

(3) Where the affairs of a body corporate are managed by its members, subsection (2) above shall apply in relation to the acts and defaults of a member in connection with his functions of management as if he were a director of the body corporate.

(f) Miscellaneous

Offences Against the Person Act 1861

23 Maliciously administering poison, so as to endanger life
[See page 41]

Criminal Damage Act 1971

1(2) Endangering life by destroying or damaging property
[See page 168]

Postal Services Act 2000

85 Prohibition on sending certain articles by post

(1) A person commits an offence if he sends by post a postal packet which encloses any creature, article or thing of any kind which is likely to injure other postal packets in course of their transmission by post or any person engaged in the business of a postal operator. [E]

(2) Subsection (1) does not apply to postal packets which enclose anything permitted (whether generally or specifically) by the postal operator concerned.

Health Act 2006

7 Offence of smoking in smoke-free place

(1) In this section, a 'smoke-free place' means any of the following—

- (a) premises, so far as they are smoke-free under or by virtue of sections 2 and 3 (including premises which by virtue of regulations under section 3(5) are smoke-free except in relation to performers),
- (b) a place, so far as it is smoke-free by virtue of section 4,
- (c) a vehicle, so far as it is smoke-free by virtue of section 5. (2) A person who smokes in a smoke-free place commits an offence. [S]

(3) But a person who smokes in premises which are not smoke-free in relation to performers by virtue of regulations under section 3(5) does not commit an offence if he is such a performer.

(4) It is a defence for a person charged with an offence under subsection (2) to show that he did not know, and could not reasonably have been expected to know, that it was a smoke-free place.

(5) If a person charged with an offence under this section relies on a defence in subsection (4), and evidence is adduced which is sufficient to raise an issue with respect to that defence, the court must assume that the defence is satisfied unless the prosecution proves beyond reasonable doubt that it is not.

8 Offence of failing to prevent smoking in smoke-free place

(1) It is the duty of any person who controls or is concerned in the management of smoke-free premises to cause a person smoking there to stop smoking.

(2) The reference in subsection (1) to a person smoking does not include a performer in relation to whom the premises are not smoke-free by virtue of regulations under section 3(5).

(3) Regulations made by the appropriate national authority may provide for a duty corresponding to that mentioned in subsection (1) in relation to—

(a) places which are smoke-free by virtue of section 4,

(b) vehicles which are smoke-free by virtue of section 5.

The duty is to be imposed on persons, or on persons of a description, specified in the regulations.

(4) A person who fails to comply with the duty in subsection (1), or any corresponding duty in regulations under subsection (3), commits an offence. [S]

(5) It is a defence for a person charged with an offence under subsection (4) to show—

(a) that he took reasonable steps to cause the person in question to stop smoking, or

(b) that he did not know, and could not reasonably have been expected to know, that the person in question was smoking, or

(c) that on other grounds it was reasonable for him not to comply with the duty.

(6) If a person charged with an offence under this section relies on a defence in subsection (5), and evidence is adduced which is sufficient to raise an issue with respect to that defence, the court must assume that the defence is satisfied unless the prosecution proves beyond reasonable doubt that it is not.

(8) The references in this section, however expressed, to premises, places or vehicles which are smoke-free, are to those premises, places or vehicles so far as they are smoke-free under or by virtue of this Chapter (and references to smoke-free premises include premises which by virtue of regulations under section 3(5) are smoke-free except in relation to performers).

76 Offences by bodies corporate etc.

(1) If an offence committed by a body corporate is proved—

(a) to have been committed with the consent or connivance of an officer, or

(b) to be attributable to any neglect on his part,

the officer as well as the body corporate is guilty of the offence and liable to be proceeded against and punished accordingly.

(2) In subsection (1) 'officer', in relation to the body corporate, means a director, manager, secretary or other similar officer of the body, or a person purporting to act in any such capacity.

(3) If the affairs of a body corporate are managed by its members, subsection (1) applies in relation to the acts and defaults of a member in connection with his functions of management as if he were a director of the body corporate.

(4) If an offence committed by a partnership is proved—

(a) to have been committed with the consent or connivance of a partner, or

(b) to be attributable to any neglect on his part,

the partner as well as the partnership is guilty of the offence and liable to be proceeded against and punished accordingly.

(5) In subsection (4) 'partner' includes a person purporting to act as a partner.

(6) If an offence committed by an unincorporated association (other than a partnership) is proved—

(a) to have been committed with the consent or connivance of an officer of the association or a member of its governing body, or

(b) to be attributable to any neglect on the part of such an officer or member,

the officer or member as well as the association is guilty of the offence and liable to be proceeded against and punished accordingly.

(7) In this section and section *77* 'offence' means an offence under any provision of this Act.

Part VI

Harm to Animals and the Environment

Animal Welfare Act 2006

1 Animals to which the Act applies

(1) In this Act, except subsections (4) and (5), 'animal' means a vertebrate other than man.

(2) Nothing in this Act applies to an animal while it is in its foetal or embryonic form.

(3) The appropriate national authority may by regulations for all or any of the purposes of this Act—

(a) extend the definition of 'animal' so as to include invertebrates of any description;

(b) make provision in lieu of subsection (2) as respects any invertebrates included in the definition of 'animal';

(c) amend subsection (2) to extend the application of this Act to an animal from such earlier stage of its development as may be specified in the regulations.

(4) The power under subsection (3)(a) or (c) may only be exercised if the appropriate national authority is satisfied, on the basis of scientific evidence, that animals of the kind concerned are capable of experiencing pain or suffering.

(5) In this section, 'vertebrate' means any animal of the Sub-phylum Vertebrata of the Phylum Chordata and 'invertebrate' means any animal not of that Sub-phylum.

2 'Protected animal'

An animal is a 'protected animal' for the purposes of this Act if—

(a) it is of a kind which is commonly domesticated in the British Islands,

(b) it is under the control of man whether on a permanent or temporary basis, or

(c) it is not living in a wild state.

3 Responsibility for animals

(1) In this Act, references to a person responsible for an animal are to a person responsible for an animal whether on a permanent or temporary basis.

(2) In this Act, references to being responsible for an animal include being in charge of it.

(3) For the purposes of this Act, a person who owns an animal shall always be regarded as being a person who is responsible for it.

(4) For the purposes of this Act, a person shall be treated as responsible for any animal for which a person under the age of 16 years of whom he has actual care and control is responsible.

4 Unnecessary suffering

(1) A person commits an offence if—

(a) an act of his, or a failure of his to act, causes an animal to suffer,

(b) he knew, or ought reasonably to have known, that the act, or failure to act, would have that effect or be likely to do so,

(c) the animal is a protected animal, and

(d) the suffering is unnecessary. [E]

(2) A person commits an offence if—
(a) he is responsible for an animal,
(b) an act, or failure to act, of another person causes the animal to suffer,
(c) he permitted that to happen or failed to take such steps (whether by way of supervising the other person or otherwise) as were reasonable in all the circumstances to prevent that happening, and
(d) the suffering is unnecessary. [E]

(3) The considerations to which it is relevant to have regard when determining for the purposes of this section whether suffering is unnecessary include—
(a) whether the suffering could reasonably have been avoided or reduced;
(b) whether the conduct which caused the suffering was in compliance with any relevant enactment or any relevant provisions of a licence or code of practice issued under an enactment;
(c) whether the conduct which caused the suffering was for a legitimate purpose, such as—
(i) the purpose of benefiting the animal, or
(ii) the purpose of protecting a person, property or another animal;
(d) whether the suffering was proportionate to the purpose of the conduct concerned;
(e) whether the conduct concerned was in all the circumstances that of a reasonably competent and humane person.

(4) Nothing in this section applies to the destruction of an animal in an appropriate and humane manner.

5 Mutilation

(1) A person commits an offence if—
(a) he carries out a prohibited procedure on a protected animal;
(b) he causes such a procedure to be carried out on such an animal. [S]

(2) A person commits an offence if—
(a) he is responsible for an animal,
(b) another person carries out a prohibited procedure on the animal, and
(c) he permitted that to happen or failed to take such steps (whether by way of supervising the other person or otherwise) as were reasonable in all the circumstances to prevent that happening. [S]

(3) References in this section to the carrying out of a prohibited procedure on an animal are to the carrying out of a procedure which involves interference with the sensitive tissues or bone structure of the animal, otherwise than for the purpose of its medical treatment.

(4) Subsections (1) and (2) do not apply in such circumstances as the appropriate national authority may specify by regulations.

(5) Before making regulations under subsection (4), the appropriate national authority shall consult such persons appearing to the authority to represent any interests concerned as the authority considers appropriate.

(6) Nothing in this section applies to the removal of the whole or any part of a dog's tail.

6 Docking of dogs' tails

(1) A person commits an offence if—
(a) he removes the whole or any part of a dog's tail, otherwise than for the purpose of its medical treatment;
(b) he causes the whole or any part of a dog's tail to be removed by another person, otherwise than for the purpose of its medical treatment. [S]

(2) A person commits an offence if—
(a) he is responsible for a dog,
(b) another person removes the whole or any part of the dog's tail, otherwise than for the purpose of its medical treatment, and

(c) he permitted that to happen or failed to take such steps (whether by way of supervising the other person or otherwise) as were reasonable in all the circumstances to prevent that happening. [S]

(3) Subsections (1) and (2) do not apply if the dog is a certified working dog that is not more than 5 days old.

(4) For the purposes of subsection (3), a dog is a certified working dog if a veterinary surgeon has certified, in accordance with regulations made by the appropriate national authority, that the first and second conditions mentioned below are met.

(5) The first condition referred to in subsection (4) is that there has been produced to the veterinary surgeon such evidence as the appropriate national authority may by regulations require for the purpose of showing that the dog is likely to be used for work in connection with—

(a) law enforcement,
(b) activities of Her Majesty's armed forces,
(c) emergency rescue,
(d) lawful pest control, or
(e) the lawful shooting of animals.

(6) The second condition referred to in subsection (4) is that the dog is of a type specified for the purposes of this subsection by regulations made by the appropriate national authority.

(7) It is a defence for a person accused of an offence under subsection (1) or (2) to show that he reasonably believed that the dog was one in relation to which subsection (3) applies.

(8) A person commits an offence if—

(a) he owns a subsection (3) dog, and
(b) fails to take reasonable steps to secure that, before the dog is 3 months old, it is identified as a subsection (3) dog in accordance with regulations made by the appropriate national authority.

(9) A person commits an offence if—

(a) he shows a dog at an event to which members of the public are admitted on payment of a fee,
(b) the dog's tail has been wholly or partly removed (in England and Wales or elsewhere), and
(c) removal took place on or after the commencement day.

(10) Where a dog is shown only for the purpose of demonstrating its working ability, subsection (9) does not apply if the dog is a subsection (3) dog.

(11) It is a defence for a person accused of an offence under subsection (9) to show that he reasonably believed—

(a) that the event was not one to which members of the public were admitted on payment of an entrance fee,
(b) that the removal took place before the commencement day, or
(c) that the dog was one in relation to which subsection (10) applies.

(12) A person commits an offence if he knowingly gives false information to a veterinary surgeon in connection with the giving of a certificate for the purposes of this section.

(16) In this section—

'commencement day' means the day on which this section comes into force;

'subsection (3) dog' means a dog whose tail has, on or after the commencement day, been wholly or partly removed without contravening subsection (1), because of the application of subsection (3).

7 Administration of poisons etc.

(1) A person commits an offence if, without lawful authority or reasonable excuse, he—

(a) administers any poisonous or injurious drug or substance to a protected animal, knowing it to be poisonous or injurious, or
(b) causes any poisonous or injurious drug or substance to be taken by a protected animal, knowing it to be poisonous or injurious. [S]

(2) A person commits an offence if—
(a) he is responsible for an animal,
(b) without lawful authority or reasonable excuse, another person administers a poisonous or injurious drug or substance to the animal or causes the animal to take such a drug or substance, and
(c) he permitted that to happen or, knowing the drug or substance to be poisonous or injurious,he failed to take such steps (whether by way of supervising the other person or otherwise) as were reasonable in all the circumstances to prevent that happening. [S]

(3) In this section, references to a poisonous or injurious drug or substance include a drug or substance which, by virtue of the quantity or manner in which it is administered or taken, has the effect of a poisonous or injurious drug or substance.

8 Fighting etc.

(1) A person commits an offence if he—
(a) causes an animal fight to take place, or attempts to do so;
(b) knowingly receives money for admission to an animal fight;
(c) knowingly publicises a proposed animal fight;
(d) provides information about an animal fight to another with the intention of enabling or encouraging attendance at the fight;
(e) makes or accepts a bet on the outcome of an animal fight or on the likelihood of anything occurring or not occurring in the course of an animal fight;
(f) takes part in an animal fight;
(g) has in his possession anything designed or adapted for use in connection with an animal fight with the intention of its being so used;
(h) keeps or trains an animal for use for in connection with an animal fight;
(i) keeps any premises for use for an animal fight. [S]

(2) A person commits an offence if, without lawful authority or reasonable excuse, he is present at an animal fight. [S]

(3) A person commits an offence if, without lawful authority or reasonable excuse, he—
(a) knowingly supplies a video recording of an animal fight,
(b) knowingly publishes a video recording of an animal fight,
(c) knowingly shows a video recording of an animal fight to another, or
(d) possesses a video recording of an animal fight, knowing it to be such a recording, with the intention of supplying it. [S]

(4) Subsection (3) does not apply if the video recording is of an animal fight that took place—
(a) outside Great Britain, or
(b) before the commencement date.

(5) Subsection (3) does not apply—
(a) in the case of paragraph (a), to the supply of a video recording for inclusion in a programme service;
(b) in the case of paragraph (b) or (c), to the publication or showing of a video recording by means of its inclusion in a programme service;
(c) in the case of paragraph (d), by virtue of intention to supply for inclusion in a programme service.

(7) In this section—

'animal fight' means an occasion on which a protected animal is placed with an animal, or with a human, for the purpose of fighting, wrestling or baiting;

'commencement date' means the date on which subsection (3) comes into force; 'information society services' has the meaning given in Article 2(a) of Directive 2000/31/EC of the European Parliament and of the Council of 8 June 2000 on certain legal aspects of information society services, in particular electronic commerce in the Internal Market (Directive on electronic commerce);

'programme service' has the same meaning as in the Communications Act 2003 (c. 21);

'video recording' means a recording, in any form, from which a moving image may by any means be reproduced and includes data stored on a computer disc or by other electronic means which is capable of conversion into a moving image.

(8) In this section—

(a) references to supplying or publishing a video recording are to supplying or publishing a video recording in any manner, including, in relation to a video recording in the form of data stored electronically, by means of transmitting such data;

(b) references to showing a video recording are to showing a moving image reproduced from a video recording by any means.

9 Duty of person responsible for animal to ensure welfare

(1) A person commits an offence if he does not take such steps as are reasonable in all the circumstances to ensure that the needs of an animal for which he is responsible are met to the extent required by good practice.

(2) For the purposes of this Act, an animal's needs shall be taken to include—

(a) its need for a suitable environment,

(b) its need for a suitable diet,

(c) its need to be able to exhibit normal behaviour patterns,

(d) any need it has to be housed with, or apart from, other animals, and

(e) its need to be protected from pain, suffering, injury and disease.

(3) The circumstances to which it is relevant to have regard when applying subsection (1) include, in particular—

(a) any lawful purpose for which the animal is kept, and

(b) any lawful activity undertaken in relation to the animal.

(4) Nothing in this section applies to the destruction of an animal in an appropriate and humane manner.

11 Transfer of animals by way of sale or prize to persons under 16

(1) A person commits an offence if he sells an animal to a person whom he has reasonable cause to believe to be under the age of 16 years.

(2) For the purposes of subsection (1), selling an animal includes transferring, or agreeing to transfer, ownership of the animal in consideration of entry by the transferee into another transaction.

(3) Subject to subsections (4) to (6), a person commits an offence if—

(a) he enters into an arrangement with a person whom he has reasonable cause to believe to be under the age of 16 years, and

(b) the arrangement is one under which that person has the chance to win an animal as a prize.

(4) A person does not commit an offence under subsection (3) if—

(a) he enters into the arrangement in the presence of the person with whom the arrangement is made, and

(b) he has reasonable cause to believe that the person with whom the arrangement is made is accompanied by a person who is not under the age of 16 years.

(5) A person does not commit an offence under subsection (3) if—

(a) he enters into the arrangement otherwise than in the presence of the person with whom the arrangement is made, and

(b) he has reasonable cause to believe that a person who has actual care and control of the person with whom the arrangement is made has consented to the arrangement.

(6) A person does not commit an offence under subsection (3) if he enters into the arrangement in a family context.

57 Offences by bodies corporate

(1) Where an offence under this Act is committed by a body corporate and is proved to have been committed with the consent or connivance of or to be attributable to any neglect on the part of—

(a) any director, manager, secretary or other similar officer of the body corporate, or

(b) any person who was purporting to act in any such capacity,

he (as well as the body corporate) commits the offence and shall be liable to be proceeded against and punished accordingly.

(2) Where the affairs of a body corporate are managed by its members, subsection (1) applies in relation to the acts and defaults of a member in connection with his functions of management as if he were a director of the body corporate.

58 Scientific research

(1) Nothing in this Act applies to anything lawfully done under the Animals (Scientific Procedures) Act 1986.

(2) No power of entry, inspection or search conferred by or under this Act, except for any such power conferred by section 28, may be exercised in relation to a place which is—

(a) designated under section 6 of the Animals (Scientific Procedures) Act 1986 as a scientific procedure establishment, or

(b) designated under section 7 of that Act as a breeding establishment or as a supplying establishment.

(3) Section 9 does not apply in relation to an animal which—

(a) is being kept, at a place designated under section 6 of the Animals (Scientific Procedures) Act 1986 as a scientific procedure establishment, for use in regulated procedures,

(b) is being kept, at a place designated under section 7 of that Act as a breeding establishment, for use for breeding animals for use in regulated procedures,

(c) is being kept at such a place, having been bred there for use in regulated procedures, or

(d) is being kept, at a place designated under section 7 of that Act as a supplying establishment, for the purpose of being supplied for use elsewhere in regulated procedures.

(4) In subsection (3), 'regulated procedure' has the same meaning as in the Animals (Scientific Procedures) Act 1986.

59 Fishing

Nothing in this Act applies in relation to anything which occurs in the normal course of fishing.

Wild Mammals (Protection) Act 1996

1 Offences

If, save as permitted by this Act, any person mutilates, kicks, beats, nails or otherwise impales, stabs, burns, stones, crushes, drowns, drags or asphyxiates any wild mammal with intent to inflict unnecessary suffering he shall be guilty of an offence. [S]

2 Exceptions from offences under the Act

(1) A person shall not be guilty of an offence under this Act by reason of—

(a) the attempted killing of any such wild mammal as an act of mercy if he shows that the mammal had been so seriously disabled otherwise than by his unlawful act that there was no reasonable chance of its recovering;

(b) the killing in a reasonably swift and humane manner of any such wild mammal if he shows that the wild mammal had been injured or taken in the course of either lawful shooting, hunting, coursing or lawful pest control activity;

(c) doing anything which is authorised by or under any enactment;

(d) any act made unlawful by section 1 if the act was done by means of any snare, trap, dog, or bird lawfully used for the purpose of killing or taking any wild mammal; or

(e) the lawful use of any poisonous or noxious substance on any wild mammal.

3 Interpretation

In this Act 'wild mammal' means any mammal which is not a domestic or captive animal within the meaning of the Protection of Animals Act 1911 or the Protection of Animals (Scotland) Act 1912.

Fur Farming (Prohibition) Act 2000

1 Offences relating to fur farming

[See page 286]

Hunting Act 2004

1 Hunting wild mammals with dogs

[See page 284]

5 Hare coursing

[See page 284]

Environmental Protection Act 1990

87 Offence of leaving litter

(1) If any person throws down, drops or otherwise deposits in, into or from any place to which this section applies, and leaves, any thing whatsoever in such circumstances as to cause, or contribute to, or tend to lead to, the defacement by litter of any place to which this section applies, he shall, subject to subsection (2) below, be guilty of an offence. [S]

(2) No offence is committed under this section where the depositing and leaving of the thing was—

(a) authorised by law, or

(b) done with the consent of the owner, occupier or other person or authority having control of the place in or into which that thing was deposited.

(3) This section applies to any public open place and, in so far as the place is not a public open place, also to the following places—

(a) any relevant highway or relevant road and any trunk road which is a special road;

(b) any place on relevant land of a principal litter authority;

(c) any place on relevant Crown land;

(d) any place on relevant land of any designated statutory undertaker;

(e) any place on relevant land of any designated educational institution;

(f) any place on relevant land within a litter control area of a local authority.

(4) In this section 'public open place' means a place in the open air to which the public are entitled or permitted to have access without payment; and any covered place open to the air on at least one side and available for public use shall be treated as a public open place.

Water Resources Act 1991

85 Offences of polluting controlled waters

(1) A person contravenes this section if he causes or knowingly permits any poisonous, noxious or polluting matter or any solid waste matter to enter any controlled waters.

(3) A person contravenes this section if he causes or knowingly permits any trade effluent or sewage effluent to be discharged—

(a) into any controlled waters; or

(b) from land in England and Wales, through a pipe, into the sea outside the seaward limits of controlled waters.

(5) A person contravenes this section if he causes or knowingly permits any matter whatever to enter any inland freshwaters so as to tend (either directly or in combination with other matter which he or another person causes or permits to enter those waters) to impede the proper flow of the waters in a manner leading, or likely to lead, to a substantial aggravation of—

(a) pollution due to other causes; or

(b) the consequences of such pollution.

(6) Subject to the following provisions of this Chapter, a person who contravenes this section or the conditions of any consent given under this Chapter for the purposes of this section shall be guilty of an offence. [E]

89 Other defences to principal offences

(1) A person shall not be guilty of an offence under section 85 above in respect of the entry of any matter into any waters or any discharge if—

(a) the entry is caused or permitted, or the discharge is made, in an emergency in order to avoid danger to life or health;

(b) that person takes all such steps as are reasonably practicable in the circumstances for minimising the extent of the entry or discharge and of its polluting effects; and

(c) particulars of the entry or discharge are furnished to the Authority as soon as reasonably practicable after the entry occurs.

(2) A person shall not be guilty of an offence under section 85 above by reason of his causing or permitting any discharge of trade or sewage effluent from a vessel.

(3) A person shall not be guilty of an offence under section 85 above by reason only of his permitting water from an abandoned mine to enter controlled waters.

(4) A person shall not, otherwise than in respect of the entry of any poisonous, noxious or polluting matter into any controlled waters, be guilty of an offence under section 85 above by reason of his depositing the solid refuse of a mine or quarry on any land so that it falls or is carried into inland freshwaters if—

(a) he deposits the refuse on the land with the consent of the Authority;

(b) no other site for the deposit is reasonably practicable; and

(c) he takes all reasonably practicable steps to prevent the refuse from entering those inland freshwaters.

Merchant Shipping Act 1995

Chapter II

131 Discharge of oil from ships into certain United Kingdom waters

(1) If any oil or mixture containing oil is discharged as mentioned in the following paragraphs into United Kingdom national waters which are navigable by sea-going ships, then, subject to the following provisions of this Chapter, the following shall be guilty of an offence, that is to say—

(a) if the discharge is from a ship, the owner or master of the ship, unless he proves that the discharge took place and was caused as mentioned in paragraph (b) below;

(b) if the discharge is from a ship but takes place in the course of a transfer of oil to or from another ship or a place on land and is caused by the act or omission of any person in charge of any apparatus in that other ship or that place, the owner or master of that other ship or, as the case may be, the occupier of that place. [E]

(2) Subsection (1) above does not apply to any discharge which—

(a) is made into the sea; and

(b) is of a kind or is made in circumstances for the time being prescribed by regulations made by the Secretary of State.

(4) In this section 'sea' includes any estuary or arm of the sea.

(5) In this section 'place on land' includes anything resting on the bed or shore of the sea, or of any other waters included in United Kingdom national waters, and also includes anything afloat (other than a ship) if it is anchored or attached to the bed or shore of the sea or any such waters.

(6) In this section 'occupier', in relation to any such thing as is mentioned in subsection (5) above, if it has no occupier, means the owner thereof.

132 Defences of owner or master charged with offence under section 131

(1) Where a person is charged with an offence under section 131 as the owner or master of a ship, it shall be a defence to prove that the oil or mixture was discharged for the purpose of—

(a) securing the safety of any ship;

(b) preventing damage to any ship or cargo, or

(c) saving life,

unless the court is satisfied that the discharge of the oil or mixture was not necessary for that purpose or was not a reasonable step to take in the circumstances.

(2) Where a person is charged with an offence under section 131 as the owner or master of a ship, it shall also be a defence to prove—

(a) that the oil or mixture escaped in consequence of damage to the ship, and that as soon as practicable after the damage occurred all reasonable steps were taken for preventing, or (if it could not be prevented) for stopping or reducing, the escape of the oil or mixture; or

(b) that the oil or mixture escaped by reason of leakage, that neither the leakage nor any delay in discovering it was due to any want of reasonable care, and that as soon as practicable after the escape was discovered all reasonable steps were taken for stopping or reducing it.

133 Defences of occupier charged with offence under section 131

Where a person is charged, in respect of the escape of any oil or mixture containing oil, with an offence under section 131 as the occupier of a place on land, it shall be a defence to prove that neither the escape nor any delay in discovering it was due to any want of reasonable care and that as soon as practicable after it was discovered all reasonable steps were taken for stopping or reducing it.

Anti-social Behaviour Act 2003

54 Sale of aerosol paint to children

(1) A person commits an offence if he sells an aerosol paint container to a person under the age of sixteen.

(2) In subsection (1) 'aerosol paint container' means a device which—

(a) contains paint stored under pressure, and

(b) is designed to permit the release of the paint as a spray.

(4) It is a defence for a person charged with an offence under this section in respect of a sale to prove that—

(a) he took all reasonable steps to determine the purchaser's age, and

(b) he reasonably believed that the purchaser was not under the age of sixteen.

(5) It is a defence for a person charged with an offence under this section in respect of a sale effected by another person to prove that he (the defendant) took all reasonable steps to avoid the commission of an offence under this section. [S]

Part VII

Property Damage

Criminal Damage Act 1971

1 Destroying or damaging property

(1) A person who without lawful excuse destroys or damages any property belonging to another intending to destroy or damage any such property or being reckless as to whether any such property would be destroyed or damaged shall be guilty of an offence. [E]

(2) A person who without lawful excuse destroys or damages any property, whether belonging to himself or another—

(a) intending to destroy or damage any property or being reckless as to whether any property would be destroyed or damaged; and

(b) intending by the destruction or damage to endanger the life of another or being reckless as to whether the life of another would be thereby endangered;

shall be guilty of an offence. [I]

(3) An offence committed under this section by destroying or damaging property by fire shall be charged as arson.

2 Threats to destroy or damage property

A person who without lawful excuse makes to another a threat, intending that that other would fear it would be carried out,—

(a) to destroy or damage any property belonging to that other or a third person; or

(b) to destroy or damage his own property in a way which he knows is likely to endanger the life of that other or a third person;

shall be guilty of an offence. [E]

3 Possessing anything with intent to destroy or damage property

A person who has anything in his custody or under his control intending without lawful excuse to use it or cause or permit another to use it—

(a) to destroy or damage any property belonging to some other person; or

(b) to destroy or damage his own or the user's property in a way which he knows is likely to endanger the life of some other person;

shall be guilty of an offence. [E]

4 Punishment of offences

(1) A person guilty of arson under section 1 above or of an offence under section 1(2) above (whether arson or not)shall on conviction on indictment be liable to imprisonment for life.

(2) A person guilty of any other offence under this Act shall on conviction on indictment be liable to imprisonment for a term not exceeding ten years.

5 'Without lawful excuse'

(1) This section applies to any offence under section 1(1) above and any offence under section 2 or 3 above other than one involving a threat by the person charged to destroy or damage property

in a way which he knows is likely to endanger the life of another or involving an intent by the person charged to use or cause or permit the use of something in his custody or under his control so to destroy or damage property.

(2) A person charged with an offence to which this section applies shall whether or not he would be treated for the purposes of this Act as having a lawful excuse apart from this subsection, be treated for those purposes as having a lawful excuse—

- (a) if at the time of the act or acts alleged to constitute the offence he believed that the person or persons whom he believed to be entitled to consent to the destruction of or damage to the property in question had so consented, or would have so consented to it if he or they had known of the destruction or damage and its circumstances; or
- (b) if he destroyed or damaged or threatened to destroy or damage the property in question or, in the case of a charge of an offence under section 3 above, intended to use or cause or permit the use of something to destroy or damage it, in order to protect property belonging to himself or another or a right or interest in property which was or which he believed to be vested in himself or another, and at the time of the act or acts alleged to constitute the offence he believed—
  - (i) that the property, right or interest was in immediate need of protection; and
  - (ii) that the means of protection adopted or proposed to be adopted were or would be reasonable having regard to all the circumstances.

(3) For the purposes of this section it is immaterial whether a belief is justified or not if it is honestly held.

(4) For the purposes of subsection (2) above a right or interest in property includes any right or privilege in or over land, whether created by grant, licence or otherwise.

(5) This section shall not be construed as casting doubt on any defence recognised by law as a defence to criminal charges.

10 Interpretation

(1) In this Act 'property' means property of a tangible nature, whether real or personal, including money and—

- (a) including wild creatures which have been tamed or are ordinarily kept in captivity, and any other wild creatures or their carcasses if, but only if, they have been reduced into possession which has not been lost or abandoned or are in the course of being reduced into possession; but
- (b) not including mushrooms growing wild on any land or flowers, fruit or foliage of a plant growing wild on any land.

For the purposes of this subsection 'mushroom' includes any fungus and 'plant' includes any shrub or tree.

(2) Property shall be treated for the purposes of this Act as belonging to any person—

- (a) having the custody or control of it;
- (b) having in it any proprietary right or interest (not being an equitable interest arising only from an agreement to transfer or grant an interest); or
- (c) having a charge on it.

(3) Where property is subject to a trust, the persons to whom it belongs shall be so treated as including any person having a right to enforce the trust.

(4) Property of a corporation sole shall be so treated as belonging to the corporation not-withstanding a vacancy in the corporation.

Theft Act 1968

30 Husband and wife

[See page 7]

Crime and Disorder Act 1998

30 Racially or religiously aggravated criminal damage

[See page 293]

Postal Services Act 2000

86 Additional protection for universal postal service

(1) A person commits an offence if, without due authority, he affixes any advertisement, document, board or thing in or on any universal postal service post office, universal postal service letter box or other property belonging to, or used by, a universal service provider in connection with the provision of a universal postal service. [S]

(2) A person commits an offence if, without due authority, he paints or in any way disfigures any such office, box or property. [S]

(4) In this Act—

'universal postal service letter box' means any box or receptacle provided by a universal service provider for the purpose of receiving postal packets, or any class of postal packets, for onwards transmission in connection with the provision of a universal postal service, and

'universal postal service post office' includes any house, building, room, vehicle or place used for the provision of any postal services in connection with the provision of a universal postal service or a part of such a service.

Computer Misuse Act 1990

1 Unauthorised access to computer material

(1) A person is guilty of an offence if—

(a) he causes a computer to perform any function with intent to secure access to any program or data held in any computer or to enable any such access to be secured;

(b) the access he intends to secure or to enable to be secured is unauthorised; and

(c) he knows at the time when he causes the computer to perform the function that that is the case. [E]

2 Unauthorised access with intent to commit or facilitate commission of further offences

(1) A person is guilty of an offence under this section if he commits an offence under section 1 above ('the unauthorised access offence') with intent—

(a) to commit an offence to which this section applies; or

(b) to facilitate the commission of such an offence (whether by himself or by any other person);

and the offence he intends to commit or facilitate is referred to below in this section as the further offence. [E]

(2) This section applies to offences—

(a) for which the sentence is fixed by law; or

(b) for which a person of twenty-one years of age or over (not previously convicted) may be sentenced to imprisonment for a term of five years (or, in England and Wales, might be so sentenced but for the restrictions imposed by section 33 of the Magistrates' Courts Act 1980).

(3) It is immaterial for the purposes of this section whether the further offence is to be committed on the same occasion as the unauthorised access offence or on any future occasion.

(4) A person may be guilty of an offence under this section even though the facts are such that the commission of the further offence is impossible.

3 Unauthorised acts with intent to impair, or with recklessness as to impairing, operation of computer, etc.

(1) A person is guilty of an offence if—

(a) he does any unauthorised act in relation to a computer;

(b) at the time when he does the act he knows that it is unauthorised; and

(c) either subsection (2) or subsection (3) below applies. [E]

(2) This subsection applies if the person intends by doing the act—

(a) to impair the operation of any computer;

(b) to prevent or hinder access to any program or data held in any computer; or

(c) to impair the operation of any such program or the reliability of any such data.

(3) This subsection applies if the person is reckless as to whether the act will do any of the things mentioned in paragraphs (a) to (c) of subsection (2) above.

(4) The intention referred to in subsection (2) above, or the recklessness referred to in subsection (3) above, need not relate to—

(a) any particular computer;

(b) any particular program or data; or

(c) a program or data of any particular kind.

(5) In this section—

(a) a reference to doing an act includes a reference to causing an act to be done;

(b) 'act' includes a series of acts;

(c) a reference to impairing, preventing or hindering something includes a reference to doing so temporarily.

3A Making, supplying or obtaining articles for use in offence under section 1 or 3

(1) A person is guilty of an offence if he makes, adapts, supplies or offers to supply any article intending it to be used to commit, or to assist in the commission of, an offence under section 1 or 3. [E]

(2) A person is guilty of an offence if he supplies or offers to supply any article believing that it is likely to be used to commit, or to assist in the commission of, an offence under section 1 or 3. [E]

(3) A person is guilty of an offence if he obtains any article with a view to its being supplied for use to commit, or to assist in the commission of, an offence under section 1 or 3. [E]

(4) In this section 'article' includes any program or data held in electronic form.

4 Territorial scope of offences under this Act

(1) Except as provided below in this section, it is immaterial for the purposes of any offence under section 1 or 3 above—

(a) whether any act or other event proof of which is required for conviction of the offence occurred in the home country concerned; or

(b) whether the accused was in the home country concerned at the time of any such act or event.

(2) Subject to subsection (3) below, in the case of such an offence at least one significant link with domestic jurisdiction must exist in the circumstances of the case for the offence to be committed.

(3) There is no need for any such link to exist for the commission of an offence under section 1 above to be established in proof of an allegation to that effect in proceedings for an offence under section 2 above.

(4) Subject to section 8 below, where—

(a) any such link does infact exist in the case of an offence under section 1 above; and

(b) commission of that offence is alleged in proceedings for an offence under section 2 above;

section 2 above shall apply as if anything the accused intended to do or facilitate in any place outside the home country concerned which would be an offence to which section 2 applies if it took place in the home country concerned were the offence in question.

(6) References in this Act to the home country concerned are references—

(a) in application of this Act to England and Wales, to England and Wales;
(b) in the application of this Act to Scotland, to Scotland; and
(c) in the application of this Act to Northern Ireland, to Northern Ireland.

5 Significant links with domestic jurisdiction

(1) The following provisions of this section apply for the interpretation of section 4 above.

(2) In relation to an offence under section 1, either of the following is a significant link with domestic jurisdiction—

(a) that the accused was in the home country concerned at the time when he did the act which caused the computer to perform the function; or
(b) that any computer containing any program or data to which the accused secured or intended to secure unauthorised access by doing that act was in the home country concerned at that time.

(3) In relation to an offence under section 3, either of the following is a significant link with domestic jurisdiction—

(a) that the accused was in the home country concerned at the time when he did the act which caused the unauthorised modification; or
(b) that the unauthorised modification took place in the home country concerned.

6 Territorial scope of inchoate offences related to offences under this Act

(1) On a charge of conspiracy to commit an offence under this Act the following questions are immaterial to the accused's guilt—

(a) the question where any person became a party to the conspiracy; and
(b) the question whether any act, omission or other event occured in the home country concerned.

(2) On a charge of attempting to commit an offence under section 3 above the following questions are immaterial to the accused's guilt—

(a) the question where the attempt was made; and
(b) the question whether it had an effect in the home country concerned.

8 Relevance of external law

(1) A person is guilty of an offence triable by virtue of section 4(4) above only if what he intended to do or facilitate would involve the commission of an offence under the law in force where the whole or any part of it was intended to take place.

(3) A person is guilty of an offence triable by virtue of section 1(1A) of the Criminal Attempts Act 1981 only if what he had in view would involve the commission of an offence under the law in force where the whole or any part of it was intended to take place.

(4) Conduct punishable under the law in force in any place is an offence under that law for the purposes of this section, however it is described in that law.

(5) Subject to subsection (7) below, a condition specified in subsections (1) or (3) above shall be taken to be satisfied unless not later than rules of court may provide the defence serve on the prosecution a notice—

(a) stating that, on the facts as alleged with respect to the relevant conduct, the condition is not in their opinion satisfied;
(b) showing their grounds for that opinion; and
(c) requiring the prosecution to show that it is satisfied.

(6) In subsection (5) above 'the relevant conduct' means—

(a) where the condition in subsection (1) above is in question, what the accused intended to do or facilitate; and
(c) where the condition in subsection (3) above is in question, what the accused had in view.

(7) The court, if it thinks fit, may permit the defence to require the prosecution to show that the condition is satisfied without the prior service of a notice under subsection (5) above.

(9) In the Crown Court the question whether the condition is satisfied shall be decided by the judge alone.

9 British citizenship immaterial

(1) In any proceedings brought in England and Wales in respect of any offence to which this section applies it is immaterial to guilt whether or not the accused was a British citizen at the time of any act, omission or other event proof of which is required for conviction of the offence.

(2) This section applies to the following offences—

(a) any offence under this Act;

(c) any attempt to commit an offence under section 3 above.

17 Interpretation

(1) The following provisions of this section apply for the interpretation of this Act.

(2) A person secures access to any program or data held in a computer if by causing a computer to perform any function he—

(a) alters or erases the program or data;

(b) copies or moves it to any storage medium other than that in which it is held or to a different location in the storage medium in which it is held;

(c) uses it; or

(d) has it output from the computer in which it is held (whether by having it displayed or in any other manner);

and references to access to a program or data (and to an intent to secure such access) shall be read accordingly.

(3) For the purposes of subsection (2)(c) above a person uses a program if the function he causes the computer to perform—

(a) causes the program to be executed; or

(b) is itself a function of the program.

(4) For the purposes of subsection (2)(d) above—

(a) a program is output if the instructions of which it consists are output; and

(b) the form in which any such instructions or any other data is output (and in particular whether or not it represents a form in which, in the case of instructions, they are capable of being executed or, in the case of data, it is capable of being processed by a computer) is immaterial.

(5) Access of any kind by any person to any program or data held in a computer is unauthorised if—

(a) he is not himself entitled to control access of the kind in question to the program or data; and

(b) he does not have consent to access by him of the kind in question to the program or data from any person who is so entitled.

(6) References to any program or data held in a computer include references to any program or data held in any removable storage medium which is for the time being in the computer; and a computer is to be regarded as containing any program or data held in any such medium.

(7) A modification of the contents of any computer takes place if, by the operation of any function of the computer concerned or any other computer—

(a) any program or data held in the computer concerned is altered or erased; or

(b) any program or data is added to its contents; and any act which contributes towards causing such a modification shall be regarded as causing it.

(8) Such a modification is unauthorised if—

(a) the person whose act causes it is not himself entitled to determine whether the modification should be made; and

(b) he does not have consent to the modification from any person who is so entitled.

(9) References to the home country concerned shall be read in accordance with section 4(6) above.

(10) References to a program include references to part of a program.

Part VIII

Theft, Fraud and Commercial Malpractice

(a) Theft and Fraud

Theft Act 1968

1 Basic definition of theft

(1) A person is guilty of theft if he dishonestly appropriates property belonging to another with the intention of permanently depriving the other of it; and 'theft' and 'steal' shall be construed accordingly. [E]

(2) It is immaterial whether the appropriation is made with a view to gain, or is made for the thief's own benefit.

(3) The five following sections of this Act shall have effect as regards the interpretation and operation of this section (and, except as otherwise provided by this Act, shall apply only for purposes of this section).

2 'Dishonestly'

(1) A person's appropriation of property belonging to another is not to be regarded as dishonest—

- (a) if he appropriates the property in the belief that he has in law the right to deprive the other of it, on behalf of himself or of a third person; or
- (b) if he appropriates the property in the belief that he would have the other's consent if the other knew of the appropriation and the circumstances of it; or
- (c) (except where the property came to him as trustee or personal representative) if he appropriates the property in the belief that the person to whom the property belongs cannot be discovered by taking reasonable steps.

(2) A person's appropriation of property belonging to another may be dishonest notwithstanding that he is willing to pay for the property.

3 'Appropriates'

(1) Any assumption by a person of the rights of an owner amounts to an appropriation, and this includes, where he has come by the property (innocently or not) without stealing it, any later assumption of a right to it by keeping or dealing with it as owner.

(2) Where property or a right or interest in property is or purports to be transferred for value to a person acting in good faith, no later assumption by him of rights which he believed himself to be acquiring shall, by reason of any defect in the transferor's title, amount to theft of the property.

4 'Property'

(1) 'Property' includes money and all other property, real or personal, including things in action and other intangible property.

(2) A person cannot steal land, or things forming part of land and severed from it by him or by his directions, except in the following cases, that is to say—

(a) when he is a trustee or personal representative, or is authorised by power of attorney, or as liquidator of a company, or otherwise, to sell or dispose of land belonging to another, and he appropriates the land or anything forming part of it by dealing with it in breach of the confidence reposed in him; or

(b) when he is not in possession of the land and appropriates anything forming part of the land by severing it or causing it to be severed, or after it has been severed; or

(c) when, being in possession of the land under a tenancy, he appropriates the whole or part of any fixture or structure let to be used with the land.

For purposes of this subsection 'land' does not include incorporeal hereditaments; 'tenancy' means a tenancy for years or less period and includes an agreement for such a tenancy, but a person who after the end of a tenancy remains in possession as statutory tenant or otherwise is to be treated as having possession under the tenancy, and 'let' shall be construed accordingly.

(3) A person who picks mushrooms growing wild on any land, or who picks flowers, fruit or foliage from a plant growing wild on any land, does not (although not in possession of the land) steal what he picks, unless he does it for reward or for sale or other commercial purpose. For purposes of this subsection 'mushroom' includes any fungus, and 'plant' includes any shrub or tree.

(4) Wild creatures, tamed or untamed, shall be regarded as property; but a person cannot steal a wild creature not tamed nor ordinarily kept in captivity, or the carcase of any such creature, unless either it has been reduced into possession by or on behalf of another person and possession of it has not since been lost or abandoned, or another person is in course of reducing it into possession.

5 'Belonging to another'

(1) Property shall be regarded as belonging to any person having possession or control of it, or having in it any proprietary right or interest (not being an equitable interest arising only from an agreement to transfer or grant an interest).

(2) Where property is subject to a trust, the persons to whom it belongs shall be regarded as including any person having a right to enforce the trust, and an intention to defeat the trust shall be regarded accordingly as an intention to deprive of the property any person having that right.

(3) Where a person receives property from or on account of another, and is under an obligation to the other to retain and deal with that property or its proceeds in a particular way, the property or proceeds shall be regarded (as against him) as belonging to the other.

(4) Where a person gets property by another's mistake, and is under an obligation to make restoration (in whole or in part) of the property or its proceeds or of the value thereof, then to the extent of that obligation the property or proceeds shall be regarded (as against him) as belonging to the person entitled to restoration, and an intention not to make restoration shall be regarded accordingly as an intention to deprive that person of the property or proceeds.

(5) Property of a corporation sole shall be regarded as belonging to the corporation notwithstanding a vacancy in the corporation.

6 'With the intention of permanently depriving the other of it'

(1) A person appropriating property belonging to another without meaning the other permanently to lose the thing itself is nevertheless to be regarded as having the intention of permanently depriving the other of it if his intention is to treat the thing as his own to dispose of regardless of the other's rights; and a borrowing or lending of it may amount to so treating it if, but only if, the borrowing or lending is for a period and in circumstances making it equivalent to an outright taking or disposal.

(2) Without prejudice to the generality of subsection (1) above, where a person, having possession or control (lawfully or not) of property belonging to another, parts with the property under a condition as to its return which he may not be able to perform, this (if done for purposes of his own and without the other's authority) amounts to treating the property as his own to dispose of regardless of the other's rights.

7 Theft

A person guilty of theft shall on conviction on indictment be liable to imprisonment for a term not exceeding seven years. [E]

8 Robbery

(1) A person is guilty of robbery if he steals, and immediately before or at the time of doing so, and in order to do so, he uses force on any person or puts or seeks to put any person in fear of being then and there subjected to force.

(2) A person guilty of robbery, or of an assault with intent to rob, shall on conviction on indictment be liable to imprisonment for life. [I]

9 Burglary

[See page 221]

10 Aggravated burglary

[See page 221]

11 Removal of articles from places open to the public

(1) Subject to subsections (2) and (3) below, where the public have access to a building in order to view the building or part of it, or a collection or part of a collection housed in it, any person who without lawful authority removes from the building or its grounds the whole or part of any article displayed or kept for display to the public in the building or that part of it or in its grounds shall be guilty of an offence.

For this purpose 'collection' includes a collection got together for a temporary purpose, but references in this section to a collection do not apply to a collection made or exhibited for the purpose of effecting sales or other commercial dealings. [E]

(2) It is immaterial for purposes of subsection (1) above, that the public's access to a building is limited to a particular period or particular occasion; but where anything removed from a building or its grounds is there otherwise than as forming part of, or being on loan for exhibition with, a collection intended for permanent exhibition to the public, the person removing it does not thereby commit an offence under this section unless he removes it on a day when the public have access to the building as mentioned in subsection (1) above.

(3) A person does not commit an offence under this section if he believes that he has lawful authority for the removal of the thing in question or that he would have it if the person entitled to give it knew of the removal and the circumstances of it.

12 Taking motor vehicle or other conveyance without authority

(1) Subject to subsections (5) and (6) below, a person shall be guilty of an offence if, without having the consent of the owner or other lawful authority, he takes any conveyance for his own or another's use or, knowing that any conveyance has been taken without such authority, drives it or allows himself to be carried in or on it. [S]

(4) If on the trial of an indictment for theft the jury are not satisfied that the accused committed theft, but it is proved that the accused committed an offence under subsection (1) above, the jury may find him guilty of the offence under subsection (1), and if he is found guilty of it, he shall be liable as he would have been liable under subsection (2) above on summary conviction.

(5) Subsection (1) above shall not apply in relation to pedal cycles; but, subject to subsection (6) below, a person who, without having the consent of the owner or other lawful authority, takes a pedal cycle for his own or another's use, or rides a pedal cycle knowing it to have been taken without such authority, shall on summary conviction be liable to a fine not exceeding level 3 on the standard scale.

(6) A person does not commit an offence under this section by anything done in the belief that he has lawful authority to do it or that he would have the owner's consent if the owner knew of his doing it and the circumstances of it.

(7) For purposes of this section—

(a) 'conveyance' means any conveyance constructed or adapted for the carriage of a person or persons whether by land, water, or air, except that it does not include a conveyance constructed or adapted for use only under the control of a person not carried in or on it, and 'drive' shall be construed accordingly; and

(b) 'owner', in relation to conveyance which is the subject of a hiring agreement or hire-purchase agreement, means the person in possession of the conveyance under that agreement.

12A Aggravated vehicle-taking

(1) Subject to subsection (3) below, a person is guilty of aggravated taking of a vehicle if—

(a) he commits an offence under section 12(1) above (in this section referred to as a 'basic offence') in relation to a mechanically propelled vehicle; and

(b) it is proved that, at any time after the vehicle was unlawfully taken (whether by him or another) and before it was recovered, the vehicle was driven, or injury or damage was caused, in one or more of the circumstances set out in paragraphs (a) to (d) of subsection (2) below. [I]

(2) The circumstances referred to in subsection (1)(b) above are—

(a) that the vehicle was driven dangerously on a road or other public place;

(b) that, owing to the driving of the vehicle, an accident occurred by which injury was caused to any person;

(c) that, owing to the driving of the vehicle, an accident occurred by which damage was caused to any property, other than the vehicle;

(d) that damage was caused to the vehicle.

(3) A person is not guilty of an offence under this section if he proves that, as regards any such proven driving, injury or damage as is referred to in subsection (1)(b) above, either—

(a) the driving, accident or damage referred to in subsection (2) above occurred before he committed the basic offence; or

(b) he was neither in nor on nor in the immediate vicinity of the vehicle when that driving, accident or damage occurred.

(4) A person guilty of an offence under this section shall be liable on conviction on indictment to imprisonment for a term not exceeding two years or, if it is proved that, in circumstances falling within subsection (2)(b) above, the accident caused the death of the person concerned, fourteen years.

(5) If a person who is charged with an offence under this section is found not guilty of that offence but it is proved that he committed a basic offence, he may be convicted of the basic offence.

(7) For the purposes of this section a vehicle is driven dangerously if—

(a) it is driven in a way which falls far below what would be expected of a competent and careful driver; and

(b) it would be obvious to a competent and careful driver that driving the vehicle in that way would be dangerous.

(8) For the purposes of this section a vehicle is recovered when it is restored to its owner or to other lawful possession or custody; and in this subsection 'owner' has the same meaning as in section 12 above.

13 Abstracting of electricity

A person who dishonestly uses without due authority, or dishonestly causes to be wasted or diverted, any electricity shall on conviction on indictment be liable to imprisonment for a term not exceeding five years. [E]

17 False accounting

(1) Where a person dishonestly, with a view to gain for himself or another or with intent to cause loss to another,—

(a) destroys, defaces, conceals or falsifies any account or any record or document made or required for any accounting purpose; or

(b) in furnishing information for any purpose produces or makes use of any account, or any such record or document as aforesaid, which to his knowledge is or may be misleading, false or deceptive in a material particular;

he shall, on conviction on indictment, be liable to imprisonment for a term not exceeding seven years. [E]

(2) For purposes of this section a person who makes or concurs in making in an account or other document an entry which is or may be misleading, false or deceptive in a material particular, or who omits or concurs in omitting a material particular from an account or other document, is to be treated as falsifying the account or document.

18 Liability of company officers for certain offences by company

(1) Where an offence committed by a body corporate under section 17 of this Act is proved to have been committed with the consent or connivance of any director, manager, secretary or other similar officer of the body corporate or any person who was purporting to act in any such capacity, he as well as the body corporate shall be guilty of that offence, and shall be liable to be proceeded against and punished accordingly.

(2) Where the affairs of a body corporate are managed by its members, this section shall apply in relation to the acts and defaults of a member in connection with his functions of management as if he were a director of the body corporate.

19 False statements by company directors, etc.

(1) Where an officer of a body corporate or unincorporated association (or person purporting to act as such), with intent to deceive members or creditors of the body corporate or association about its affairs, publishes or concurs in publishing a written statement or account which to his knowledge is or may be misleading, false or deceptive in a material particular, he shall on conviction on indictment be liable to imprisonment for a term not exceeding seven years. [E]

(2) For the purposes of this section a person who has entered into a security for the benefit of a body corporate or association is to be treated as a creditor of it.

(3) Where the affairs of a body corporate or association are managed by its members, this section shall apply to any statement which a member publishes or concurs in publishing in connection with his functions or management as if he were an officer of the body corporate or association.

20 Suppression, etc., of documents

(1) A person who dishonestly, with a view to gain for himself or another or with intent to cause loss to another, destroys, defaces or conceals any valuable security, any will or other testamentary document or any original document of or belonging to, or filed or deposited in, any court of justice or any government department shall on conviction on indictment be liable to imprisonment for a term not exceeding seven years. [E]

21 Blackmail

(1) A person is guilty of blackmail if, with a view to gain for himself or another or with intent to cause loss to another, he makes any unwarranted demand with menaces; and for this purpose a demand with menaces is unwarranted unless the person making it does so in the belief—

(a) that he has reasonable grounds for making the demand; and

(b) that the use of the menaces is a proper means of reinforcing the demand. [I]

(2) The nature of the act or omission demanded is immaterial, and it is also immaterial whether the menaces relate to action to be taken by the person making the demand.

22 Handling stolen goods

(1) A person handles stolen goods if (otherwise than in the course of the stealing) knowing or believing them to be stolen goods he dishonestly receives the goods, or dishonestly undertakes or assists in their retention, removal, disposal or realisation by or for the benefit of another person, or if he arranges to do so. [E]

23 Advertising rewards for return of goods stolen or lost

Where any public advertisement of a reward for the return of any goods which have been stolen or lost uses any words to the effect that no questions will be asked, or that the person producing the goods will be safe from apprehension or inquiry, or that any money paid for the purchase of the goods or advances by way of a loan on them will be repaid, the person advertising the reward and any person who prints or publishes the advertisement shall on summary conviction be liable to a fine not exceeding level 3 on the standard scale. [S]

24 Scope of offences relating to stolen goods

(1) The provisions of this Act relating to goods which have been stolen shall apply whether the stealing occurred in England or Wales or elsewhere, and whether it occurred before or after the commencement of this Act, provided that the stealing (if not an offence under this Act) amounted to an offence where and at the time when the goods were stolen; and references to stolen goods shall be construed accordingly.

(2) For purposes of those provisions references to stolen goods shall include, in addition to the goods originally stolen and parts of them (whether in their original state or not),—

- (a) any other goods which directly or indirectly represent or have at any time represented the stolen goods in the hands of the thief as being the proceeds of any disposal or realisation of the whole or part of the goods stolen or of goods so representing the stolen goods; and
- (b) any other goods which directly or indirectly represent or have at any time represented the stolen goods in the hands of a handler of the stolen goods or any part of them as being the proceeds of any disposal or realisation of the whole or part of the stolen goods handled by him or of goods so representing them.

(3) But no goods shall be regarded as having continued to be stolen goods after they have been restored to the person from whom they were stolen or to other lawful possession or custody, or after that person and any other person claiming through him have otherwise ceased as regards those goods to have any right to restitution in respect of the theft.

(4) For purposes of the provisions of this Act relating to goods which have been stolen (including subsections (1) to (3) above) goods obtained in England or Wales or elsewhere either by blackmail or, subject to subsection (5) below, by fraud (within the meaning of the Fraud Act 2006), shall be regarded as stolen; and 'steal', 'theft' and 'thief' shall be construed accordingly.

(5) Subsection (1) above applies in relation to goods obtained by fraud as if—

- (a) the reference to the commencement of this Act were a reference to the commencement of the Fraud Act 2006, and
- (b) the reference to an offence under this Act were a reference to an offence under section 1 of that Act.

24A Dishonestly retaining a wrongful credit

(1) A person is guilty of an offence if—

- (a) a wrongful credit has been made to an account kept by him or in respect of which he has any right or interest;
- (b) he knows or believes that the credit is wrongful; and
- (c) he dishonestly fails to take such steps as are reasonable in the circumstances to secure that the credit is cancelled. [E]

(2) References to a credit are to a credit of an amount of money.

(2A) A credit to an account is wrongful to the extent that it derives from—

- (a) theft;
- (b) blackmail;
- (c) fraud (contrary to section 1 of the Fraud Act 2006); or
- (d) stolen goods.

(5) In determining whether a credit to an account is wrongful, it is immaterial (in particular) whether the account is overdrawn before or after the credit is made.

(7) Subsection (8) below applies for purposes of provisions of this Act relating to stolen goods (including subsection (2A) above).

(8) References to stolen goods include money which is dishonestly withdrawn from an account to which a wrongful credit has been made, but only to the extent that the money derives from the credit.

(9) 'Account' means an account kept with—

(a) a bank;

(b) a person carrying on a business which falls within subsection (10) below; or

(c) an issuer of electronic money (as defined for the purposes of Part 2 of the Financial Services and Markets Act 2000).

(10) A business falls within this subsection if—

(a) in the course of the business money received by way of deposit is lent to others; or

(b) any other activity of the business is financed, wholly or to any material extent, out of the capital of or the interest on money received by way of deposit.

(11) References in subsection (10) above to a deposit must be read with—

(a) section 22 of the Financial Services and Markets Act 2000;

(b) any relevant order under that section; and

(c) Schedule 2 to that Act;

but any restriction on the meaning of deposit which arises from the identity of the person making it is to be disregarded.

(12) For the purposes of subsection (10) above—

(a) all the activities which a person carries on by way of business shall be regarded as a single business carried on by him; and

(b) 'money' includes money expressed in a currency other than sterling.

25 Going equipped for stealing, etc.

(1) A person shall be guilty of an offence if, when not at his place of abode, he has with him any article for use in the course of or in connection with any burglary or theft. [E]

(3) Where a person is charged with an offence under this section, proof that he had with him any article made or adapted for use in committing a burglary or theft shall be evidence that he had it with him for such use.

(5) For purposes of this section an offence under section 12 (1) of this Act of taking a conveyance shall be treated as theft.

27 Evidence and procedure on charge of theft or handling stolen goods

(3) Where a person is being proceeded against for handling stolen goods (but not for any offence other than handling stolen goods), then at any stage of the proceedings, if evidence has been given of his having or arranging to have in his possession the goods the subject of the charge, or of his undertaking or assisting in, or arranging to undertake or assist in, their retention, removal, disposal or realisation, the following evidence shall be admissible for the purpose of proving that he knew or believed the goods to be stolen goods:—

(a) evidence that he has had in his possession, or has undertaken or assisted in the retention, removal, disposal or realisation of, stolen goods from any theft taking place not earlier than twelve months before the offence charged; and

(b) (provided that seven days' notice in writing has been given to him of the intention to prove the conviction) evidence that he has within the five years preceding the date of the offence charged been convicted of theft or of handling stolen goods.

30 Husband and wife

[See page 7]

32 Effect on existing law and construction of references to offences

(1) The following offences are hereby abolished for all purposes not relating to offences committed before the commencement of this Act, that is to say—

(a) any offence at common law of larceny, robbery, burglary, receiving stolen property, obtaining property by threats, extortion by colour of office or franchise, false accounting by public officers, concealment of treasure trove and, except as regards offences relating to the public revenue, cheating; . . .

34 Interpretation

(1) Sections 4(1) and 5 (1) of this Act shall apply generally for purposes of this Act as they apply for purposes of section 1.

(2) For purposes of this Act—

(a) 'gain' and 'loss' are to be construed as extending only to gain or loss in money or other property, but as extending to any such gain or loss whether temporary or permanent; and—

(i) 'gain' includes a gain by keeping what one has, as well as a gain by getting what one has not; and

(ii) 'loss' includes a loss by not getting what one might get, as well as a loss by parting with what one has;

(b) 'goods' except in so far as the context otherwise requires, includes money and every other description of property except land, and includes things severed from the land by stealing.

SCHEDULE 1 OFFENCES OF TAKING, ETC. FISH

2 Taking or destroying fish

(1) Subject to sub-paragraph (2) below, a person who unlawfully takes or destroys, or attempts to take or destroy, any fish in water which is private property or in which there is any private right of fishery shall on summary conviction be liable to a fine not exceeding fifty pounds or, for an offence committed after a previous conviction of an offence under this sub-paragraph, to imprisonment for a term not exceeding three months or to a fine not exceeding one hundred pounds or to both. [S]

(2) Sub-paragraph (1) above shall not apply to taking or destroying fish by angling in the daytime (that is to say, in the period beginning one hour before sunrise and ending one hour after sunset); but a person who by angling in the daytime unlawfully takes or destroys, or attempts to take or destroy, any fish in water which is private property or in which there is any private right of fishery shall on summary conviction be liable to a fine not exceeding level 1 on the standard scale.

Salmon Act 1986

32 Handling salmon in suspicious circumstances

(1) Subject to subsections (3) and (4) below, a person shall be guilty of an offence if, at a time when he believes or it would be reasonable for him to suspect that a relevant offence has at any time been committed in relation to any salmon, he receives the salmon, or undertakes or assists in its retention, removal or disposal by or for the benefit of another person, or if he arranges to do so. [E]

(2) For the purposes of this section an offence is a relevant offence in relation to a salmon if—

(a) it is committed by taking, killing or landing that salmon, either in England and Wales or in Scotland; or

(b) that salmon is taken, killed or landed, either in England and Wales or in Scotland, in the course of the commission of the offence.

(3) It shall be immaterial for the purposes of subsection (1) above that a person's belief or the grounds for suspicion relate neither specifically to a particular offence that has been committed nor

exclusively to a relevant offence or to relevant offences; but it shall be a defence in proceedings for an offence under this section to show that no relevant offence had in fact been committed in relation to the salmon in question.

(4) A person shall not be guilty of an offence under this section in respect of conduct which constitutes a relevant offence in relation to any salmon or in respect of anything done in good faith for the purposes connected with the prevention or detection of crime or the investigation or treatment of disease.

(7) In this section 'offence', in relation to the taking, killing or landing of a salmon either in England and Wales or in Scotland, means an offence under the law applicable to the place where the salmon is taken, killed or landed.

Night Poaching Act 1828

1 Persons taking or destroying game or rabbits by night

[See page 225]

Deer Act 1991

1 Poaching of deer

[See page 227]

Theft Act 1978

3 Making off without payment

(1) Subject to subsection (3) below, a person who, knowing that payment on the spot for any goods supplied or service done is required or expected from him, dishonestly makes off without having paid as required or expected and with intent to avoid payment of the amount due shall be guilty of an offence. [E]

(2) For purposes of this section 'payment on the spot' includes payment at the time of collecting goods on which work has been done or in respect of which service has been provided.

(3) Subsection (1) above shall not apply where the supply of the goods or the doing of the service is contrary to law, or where the service done is such that payment is not legally enforceable.

5 Supplementary

(2) Sections 30(1) (husband and wife), 31(1) (effect on civil proceedings) and 34 (interpretation) of the Theft Act 1968, so far as they are applicable in relation to this Act, shall apply as they apply in relation to that Act.

Road Traffic Regulation Act 1984

47 Interfering with parking meters

(3) A person who, with intent to defraud, interferes with a parking meter, or operates or attempts to operate a parking meter by the insertion of objects other than current coins or bank notes of the appropriate denomination, or the appropriate credit or debit cards, shall be guilty of an offence. [S]

Gas Act 1995

SCHEDULE 2

10 Injury to gas fittings and interference with meters

(1) If any person intentionally or by culpable negligence—

(a) injures or allows to be injured any gas fitting belonging to a public gas transporter or gas supplier or any service pipe by which any premises are connected to such transporter's mains;

(b) alters the index to any meter used for measuring the quantity of gas supplied by such a transporter or supplier; or

(c) prevents any such meter from duly registering the quantity of gas conveyed or supplied,

he shall be guilty of an offence and liable on summary conviction to a fine not exceeding level 3 on the standard scale. [S]

(2) In the case of any offence under sub-paragraph (1) above, the transporter or supplier may disconnect the premises or cut off the supply of gas to the person so offending.

(3) Where any person is prosecuted for an offence under sub-paragraph (1)(b) or (c) above, the possession by him of artificial means for causing an alteration of the index of the meter or, as the case may be, the prevention of the meter from duly registering shall, if the meter was in his custody or under his control, be prima facie evidence that the alteration or prevention was intentionally caused by him.

11 Restoration of supply without consent

(1) Where a consumer's premises has been disconnected by a public gas transporter or a supply of gas to a consumer's premises has been cut off by a gas supplier otherwise than in the exercise of certain powers, no person shall, without the relevant consent, reconnect the premises or restore the supply.

(2) If any person acts in contravention of sub-paragraph (1) above, (a) he shall be guilty of an offence and liable on summary conviction to a fine not exceeding level 3 on the standard scale and (b) the transporter or supplier may again disconnect the premises or, as the case may be, cut off the supply. [S]

Communications Act 2003

125 Dishonestly obtaining electronic communications services

(1) A person who—

(a) dishonestly obtains an electronic communications service, and

(b) does so with intent to avoid payment of a charge applicable to the provision of that service, is

guilty of an offence. [E]

(2) It is not an offence under this section to obtain a service mentioned in section 297(1) of the Copyright, Designs and Patents Act 1988 (dishonestly obtaining a broadcasting service provided from a place in the UK).

126 Possession or supply of apparatus etc. for contravening s. 125

(1) A person is guilty of an offence if, with an intention falling within subsection (3), he has in his possession or under his control anything that may be used—

(a) for obtaining an electronic communications service; or

(b) in connection with obtaining such a service. [E]

(2) A person is guilty of an offence if—

(a) he supplies or offers to supply anything which may be used as mentioned in subsection (1); and

(b) he knows or believes that the intentions in relation to that thing of the person to whom it is supplied or offered fall within subsection (3). [E]

(3) A person's intentions fall within this subsection if he intends—

(a) to use the thing to obtain an electronic communications service dishonestly;

(b) to use the thing for a purpose connected with the dishonest obtaining of such a service;

(c) dishonestly to allow the thing to be used to obtain such a service; or

(d) to allow the thing to be used for a purpose connected with the dishonest obtaining of such a service.

(4) An intention does not fall within subsection (3) if it relates exclusively to the obtaining of a service mentioned in section 297(1) of the Copyright, Designs and Patents Act 1988.

(6) In this section, references, in the case of a thing used for recording data, to the use of that thing include references to the use of data recorded by it.

Treasure Act 1996

8 Duty of finder of treasure to notify coroner

(1) A person who finds an object which he believes or has reasonable grounds for believing is treasure must notify the coroner for the district in which the object was found before the end of the notice period.

(2) The notice period is fourteen days beginning with—

(a) the day after the find; or

(b) if later, the day on which the finder first believes or has reason to believe the object is treasure.

(3) Any person who fails to comply with subsection (1) is guilty of an offence . . . [S]

(4) In proceedings for an offence under this section, it is a defence for the defendant to show that he had, and has continued to have, a reasonable excuse for failing to notify the coroner.

Dealing in Cultural Objects (Offences) Act 2003

1 Offence of dealing in tainted cultural objects

[See page 382]

Postal Services Act 2000

83 Interfering with the mail: postal operators

(1) A person who is engaged in the business of a postal operator commits an offence if, contrary to his duty and without reasonable excuse, he—

(a) intentionally delays or opens a postal packet in the course of its transmission by post, or

(b) intentionally opens a mail-bag. [E]

(2) Subsection (1) does not apply to the delaying or opening of a postal packet or the opening of a mail-bag under the authority of—

(a) this Act or any other enactment (including, in particular, in pursuance of a warrant issued under any other enactment), or

(b) any directly applicable Community provision.

(3) Subsection (1) does not apply to the delaying or opening of a postal packet in accordance with any terms and conditions applicable to its transmission by post.

(4) Subsection (1) does not apply to the delaying of a postal packet as a result of industrial action in contemplation or furtherance of a trade dispute.

(5) In subsection (4) 'trade dispute' has the meaning given by section 244 of the Trade Union and Labour Relations (Consolidation) Act 1992; and the reference to industrial action shall be construed in accordance with that Act.

84 Interfering with the mail: general

(1) A person commits an offence if, without reasonable excuse, he—

(a) intentionally delays or opens a postal packet in the course of its transmission by post, or

(b) intentionally opens a mail-bag. [S]

(2) Subsections (2) to (5) of section 83 apply to subsection (1) above as they apply to subsection (1) of that section.

(3) A person commits an offence if, intending to act to a person's detriment and without reasonable excuse, he opens a postal packet which he knows or reasonably suspects has been incorrectly delivered to him. [S]

(4) Subsections (2) and (3) of section 83 (so far as they relate to the opening of postal packets) apply to subsection (3) above as they apply to subsection (1) of that section.

Forgery and Counterfeiting Act 1981

PART I FORGERY AND KINDRED OFFENCES

1 The offence of forgery

A person is guilty of forgery if he makes a false instrument, with the intention that he or another shall use it to induce somebody to accept it as genuine, and by reason of so accepting it to do or not to do some act to his own or any other person's prejudice. [E]

2 The offence of copying a false instrument

It is an offence for a person to make a copy of an instrument which is, and which he knows or believes to be, a false instrument, with the intention that he or another shall use it to induce somebody to accept it as a copy of a genuine instrument, and by reason of so accepting it to do or not to do some act to his own or any other person's prejudice. [E]

3 The offence of using a false instrument

It is an offence for a person to use an instrument which is, and which he knows or believes to be, false, with the intention of inducing somebody to accept it as genuine, and by reason of so accepting it to do or not to do some act to his own or any other person's prejudice. [E]

4 The offence of using a copy of a false instrument

It is an offence for a person to use a copy of an instrument which is, and which he knows or believes to be, a false instrument, with the intention of inducing somebody to accept it as a copy of a genuine instrument, and by reason of so accepting it to do or not to do some act to his own or any other person's prejudice. [E]

5 Offences relating to money orders, share certificates, passports, etc.

(1) It is an offence for a person to have in his custody or under his control an instrument to which this section applies which is, and which he knows or believes to be, false, with the intention that he or another shall use it to induce somebody to accept it as genuine, and by reason of so accepting it to do or not to do some act to his own or any other person's prejudice. [E]

(2) It is an offence for a person to have in his custody or under his control, without lawful authority or excuse, an instrument to which this section applies which is, and which he knows or believes to be, false. [E]

(3) It is an offence for a person to make or to have in his custody or under his control a machine or implement, or paper or any other material, which to his knowledge is or has been specially designed or adapted for the making of an instrument to which this section applies, with the intention that he or another shall make an instrument to which this section applies which is false and that he or another shall use the instrument to induce somebody to accept it as genuine, and by reason of so accepting it to do or not to do some act to his own or any other person's prejudice. [E]

(4) It is an offence for a person to make or to have in his custody or under his control any such machine, implement, paper or material, without lawful authority or excuse. [E]

(5) The instruments to which this section applies are—

- (a) money orders;
- (b) postal orders;
- (c) United Kingdom postage stamps;
- (d) Inland Revenue stamps;
- (e) share certificates;
- (f) passports and documents which can be used instead of passports;
- (fa) Immigration documents;
- (g) cheques and other bills of exchange;
- (h) travellers' cheques;
- (ha) bankers' drafts;
- (hb) promissory notes;
- (i) cheque cards;
- (j) credit cards;
- (ja) debit cards;
- (k) Certified copies relating to an entry in a register of births, adoptions, marriages, civil partnerships, or deaths and issued by the Registrar General, the Registrar General for Northern Ireland, a registration officer or person lawfully authorised to issue Certified copies relating to such entries; and
- (l) certificates relating to entries in such registers.

(6) In subsection (5) (e) above 'share certificate' means an instrument entitling or evidencing the title of a person to a share or interest—

- (a) in any public stock, annuity, fund or debt of any government or state, including a state which forms part of another state; or
- (b) in any stock, fund or debt of a body (whether corporate or unincorporated) established in the United Kingdom or elsewhere.

(7) An instrument is also an instrument to which this section applies if it is a monetary instrument specified for the purposes of this section by the Secretary of State.

8 Meaning of 'instrument'

(1) Subject to subsection (2) below, in this Part of this Act 'instrument' means—

- (a) any document, whether of a formal or informal character;
- (b) any stamp issued or sold by a postal operator;
- (c) any Inland Revenue stamp; and
- (d) any disc, tape, sound track or other device on or in which information is recorded or stored by mechanical, electronic or other means.

(2) A currency note within the meaning of Part II of this Act is not an instrument for the purposes of this Part of this Act.

(3) A mark denoting payment of postage which the postal operator authorises to be used instead of an adhesive stamp is to be treated for the purposes of this Part of this Act as if it were a stamp issued by the postal operator concerned.

9 Meaning of 'false' and 'making'

(1) An instrument is false for the purposes of this Part of this Act—

(a) if it purports to have been made in the form in which it is made by a person who did not in fact make it in that form; or

(b) if it purports to have been made in the form in which it is made on the authority of a person who did not in fact authorise its making in that form; or

(c) if it purports to have been made in the terms in which it is made by a person who did not in fact make it in those terms; or

(d) if it purports to have been made in the terms in which it is made on the authority of a person who did not in fact authorise its making in those terms; or

(e) if it purports to have been altered in any respect by a person who did not in fact alter it in that respect; or

(f) if it purports to have been altered in any respect on the authority of a person who did not in fact authorise the alteration in that respect; or

(g) if it purports to have been made or altered on a date on which, or at a place at which, or otherwise in circumstances in which, it was not in fact made or altered; or

(h) if it purports to have been made or altered by an existing person but he did not in fact exist.

(2) A person is to be treated for the purposes of this Part of this Act as making a false instrument if he alters an instrument so as to make it false in any respect (whether or not it is false in some other respect apart from that alteration).

10 Meaning of 'prejudice' and 'induce'

(1) Subject to subsections (2) and (4) below, for the purposes of this Part of this Act an act or omission intended to be induced is to a person's prejudice if, and only if, it is one which if it occurs—

(a) will result—

(i) in his temporary or permanent loss of property; or

(ii) in his being deprived of an opportunity to earn remuneration or greater remuneration; or

(iii) in his being deprived of an opportunity to gain a financial advantage otherwise than by way of remuneration; or

(b) will result in somebody being given an opportunity—

(i) to earn remuneration or greater remuneration from him; or

(ii) to gain a financial advantage from him otherwise than by way of remuneration; or

(c) will be the result of his having accepted a false instrument as genuine, or a copy of a false instrument as a copy of a genuine one, in connection with his performance of any duty.

(2) An act which a person has an enforceable duty to do and an omission to do an act which a person is not entitled to do shall be disregarded for the purposes of this Part of this Act.

(3) In this Part of this Act references to inducing somebody to accept a false instrument as genuine, or a copy of a false instrument as a copy of a genuine one, include references to inducing a machine to respond to the instrument or copy as if it were a genuine instrument or, as the case may be, a copy of a genuine one.

(4) Where subsection (3) above applies, the act or omission intended to be induced by the machine responding to the instrument or copy shall be treated as an act or omission to a person's prejudice.

(5) In this section 'loss' includes not getting what one might get as well as parting with what one has.

PART II COUNTERFEITING AND KINDRED OFFENCES

14 Offences of counterfeiting notes and coins

(1) It is an offence for a person to make a counterfeit of a currency note or of a protected coin, intending that he or another shall pass or tender it as genuine. [E]

(2) It is an offence for a person to make a counterfeit of a currency note or of a protected coin without lawful authority or excuse. [E]

15 Offences of passing, etc., counterfeit notes and coins

(1) It is an offence for a person—

(a) to pass or tender as genuine any thing which is, and which he knows or believes to be, a counterfeit of a currency note or of a protected coin; or

(b) to deliver to another any thing which is, and which he knows or believes to be, such a counterfeit, intending that the person to whom it is delivered or another shall pass or tender it as genuine. [E]

(2) It is an offence for a person to deliver to another, without lawful authority or excuse, any thing which is, and which he knows or believes to be, a counterfeit of a currency note or of a protected coin. [E]

16 Offences involving the custody or control of counterfeit notes and coins

(1) It is an offence for a person to have in his custody or under his control any thing which is, and which he knows or believes to be, a counterfeit of a currency note or of a protected coin, intending either to pass or tender it as genuine or to deliver it to another with the intention that he or another shall pass or tender it as genuine. [E]

(2) It is an offence for a person to have in his custody or under his control, without lawful authority or excuse, anything which is, and which he knows or believes to be, a counterfeit of a currency note or of a protected coin. [E]

(3) It is immaterial for the purposes of subsections (1) and (2) above that a coin or note is not in a fit state to be passed or tendered or that the making or counterfeiting of a coin or note has not been finished or perfected.

17 Offences involving the making or custody or control of counterfeiting materials and implements

(1) It is an offence for a person to make, or to have in his custody or under his control, anything which he intends to use, or to permit any other person to use, for the purpose of making a counterfeit of a currency note or of a protected coin with the intention that it be passed or tendered as genuine. [E]

(2) It is an offence for a person without lawful authority or excuse—

(a) to make; or

(b) to have in his custody or under his control, anything which, to his knowledge, is or has been specially designed or adapted for the making of a counterfeit of a currency note. [E]

(3) Subject to subsection (4) below, it is an offence for a person to make, or to have in his custody or under his control, any implement which, to his knowledge, is capable of imparting to anything a resemblance—

(a) to the whole or part of either side of a protected coin; or

(b) to the whole or part of the reverse of the image on either side of a protected coin. [E]

(4) It shall be a defence for a person charged with an offence under subsection (3) above to show—

(a) that he made the implement or, as the case may be, had it in his custody or under his control, with the written consent of the Treasury; or

(b) that he had lawful authority otherwise than by virtue of paragraph (4) above, or a lawful excuse, for making it or having it in his custody or under his control.

18 The offence of reproducing British currency notes

(1) It is an offence for any person, unless the relevant authority has previously consented in writing, to reproduce on any substance whatsoever, and whether or not on the correct scale, any British currency note or any part of a British currency note. [E]

(2) In this section—

'British currency note' means any note which—

(a) has been lawfully issued in England and Wales, Scotland or Northern Ireland; and

(b) is or has been customarily used as money in the country where it was issued; and
(c) is payable on demand; and

'the relevant authority', in relation to a British currency note of any particular description, means the authority empowered by law to issue notes of that description.

19 Offences in making, etc., imitation British coins

(1) It is an offence for a person—

(a) to make an imitation British coin in connection with a scheme intended to promote the sale of any product or the making of contracts for the supply of any service; or
(b) to sell or distribute imitation British coins in connection with any such scheme, or to have imitation British coins in his custody or under his control with a view to such sale or distribution,

unless the Treasury have previously consented in writing to the sale or distribution of such imitation British coins in connection with that scheme. [E]

(2) In this section—

'British coin' means any coin which is legal tender in any part of the United Kingdom; and

'imitation British coin' means any thing which resembles a British coin in shape, size and the substance of which it is made.

20 Prohibition of importation of counterfeit notes and coins

The importation, landing or unloading of a counterfeit of a currency note or of a protected coin without the consent of the Treasury is hereby prohibited.

21 Prohibition of exportation of counterfeit notes and coins

(1) The exportation of a counterfeit of a currency note or of a protected coin without the consent of the Treasury is hereby prohibited.

27 Meaning of 'currency note' and 'protected coin'

(1) In this Part of this Act—

'currency note' means—

(a) any note which—
  (i) has been lawfully issued in England and Wales, Scotland, Northern Ireland, any of the Channel Islands, the Isle of Man or the Republic of Ireland; and
  (ii) is or has been customarily used as money in the country where it was issued; and
  (iii) is payable on demand; or
(b) any note which—
  (i) has been lawfully issued in some country other than those mentioned in paragraph (a) (i) above; and
  (ii) is customarily used as money in that country; and

'protected coin' means any coin which—

(a) is customarily used as money in any country; or
(b) is specified in an order made by the Treasury for the purposes of this Part of this Act.

28 Meaning of 'counterfeit'

(1) For the purposes of this Part of this Act a thing is a counterfeit of a currency note or of a protected coin—

(a) if it is not a currency note or a protected coin but resembles a currency note or protected coin (whether on one side only or on both) to such an extent that it is reasonably capable of passing for a currency note or protected coin of that description; or
(b) if it is a currency note or protected coin which has been so altered that it is reasonably capable of passing for a currency note or protected coin of some other description.

(2) For the purposes of this Part of this Act—

(a) a thing consisting of one side only of a currency note, with or without the addition of other material, is a counterfeit of such a note;

(b) a thing consisting—
    (i) of parts of two or more currency notes; or
    (ii) of parts of a currency note, or of parts of two or more currency notes, with the addition of other material,

is capable of being a counterfeit of a currency note.

(3) References in this Part of this Act to passing or tendering a counterfeit of a currency note or a protected coin are not to be construed as confined to passing or tendering it as legal tender.

Copyright, Designs and Patents Act 1988

107 Criminal liability for making or dealing with infringing articles, etc.

(1) A person commits an offence who, without the licence of the copyright owner—

(a) makes for sale or hire, [E] or
(b) imports into the United Kingdom otherwise than for his private and domestic use, [E] or
(c) possesses in the course of a business with a view to committing any act infringing the copyright [S], or
(d) in the course of a business—
    (i) sells or lets for hire, or
    (ii) offers or exposes for sale or hire, or
    (iii) exhibits in public, or
    (iv) distributes, [E] or
(e) distributes otherwise than in the course of a business to such an extent as to affect prejudicially the owner of the copyright, [E]

an article which is, and which he knows or has reason to believe is, an infringing copy of a copyright work.

(2) A person commits an offence who—

(a) makes an article specifically designed or adapted for making copies of a particular copyright work, or
(b) has such an article in his possession, knowing or having reason to believe that it is to be used to make infringing copies for sale or hire or for use in the course of a business. [S]

(3) Where copyright is infringed (otherwise than by reception of a broadcast or cable programme)—

(a) by the public performance of a literary, dramatic or musical work, or
(b) by the playing or showing in public of a sound recording or film, any person who caused the work to be so performed, played or shown is guilty of an offence if he knew or had reason to believe that copyright would be infringed. [S]

Trade Marks Act 1994

92 Unauthorised use of trade mark, etc., in relation to goods

(1) A person commits an offence who with a view to gain for himself or another, or with intent to cause loss to another, and without the consent of the proprietor—

(a) applies to goods or their packaging a sign identical to or likely to be mistaken for, a registered trade mark, or
(b) sells or lets for hire, offers or exposes for sale or hire or distributes goods which bear, or the packaging of which bears, such a sign, or
(c) has in his possession, custody or control in the course of a business any such goods with a view to the doing of anything, by himself or another, which would be an offence under paragraph (b). [E]

(2) A person commits an offence who with a view to gain for himself or another, or with intent to cause loss to another, and without the consent of the proprietor—

(a) applies a sign identical to, or likely to be mistaken for, a registered trade mark to material intended to be used—

(i) for labelling or packaging goods

(ii) as a business paper in relation to goods, or

(iii) for advertising goods, or

(b) uses in the course of a business material bearing such a sign for labelling or packaging goods, as a business paper in relation to goods, or for advertising goods, or

(c) has in his possession, custody or control in the course of a business any such material with a view to the doing of anything, by himself or another, which would be an offence under paragraph (b). [E]

(3) A person commits an offence who with a view to gain for himself or another, or with intent to cause loss to another, and without the consent of the proprietor—

(a) makes an article specifically designed or adapted for making copies of a sign identical to, or likely to be mistaken for, a registered trade mark, or

(b) has such an article in his possession, custody or control in the course of a business,

knowing or having reason to believe that it has been, or is to be, used to produce goods, or material for labelling or packaging goods, as a business paper in relation to goods, or for advertising goods. [E]

(4) A person does not commit an offence under this section unless—

(a) the goods are goods in respect of which the trade mark is registered, or

(b) the trade mark has a reputation in the United Kingdom and the use of the sign takes or would take unfair advantage of, or is or would be detrimental to, the distinctive character or the repute of the trade mark.

(5) It is a defence for a person charged with an offence under this section to show that he believed on reasonable grounds that the use of the sign in the manner in which it was used, or was to be used, was not an infringement of the registered trade mark.

Fraud Act 2006

1 Fraud

(1) A person is guilty of fraud if he is in breach of any of the sections listed in subsection (2) (which provide for different ways of committing the offence). [E]

(2) The sections are—

(a) section 2 (fraud by false representation),

(b) section 3 (fraud by failing to disclose information), and

(c) section 4 (fraud by abuse of position).

2 Fraud by false representation

(1) A person is in breach of this section if he—

(a) dishonestly makes a false representation, and

(b) intends, by making the representation—

(i) to make a gain for himself or another, or

(ii) to cause loss to another or to expose another to a risk of loss.

(2) A representation is false if—

(a) it is untrue or misleading, and

(b) the person making it knows that it is, or might be, untrue or misleading.

(3) 'Representation' means any representation as to fact or law, including a representation as to the state of mind of—

(a) the person making the representation, or

(b) any other person.

(4) A representation may be express or implied.

(5) For the purposes of this section a representation may be regarded as made if it (or anything implying it) is submitted in any form to any system or device designed to receive, convey or respond to communications (with or without human intervention).

3 Fraud by failing to disclose information

A person is in breach of this section if he—

(a) dishonestly fails to disclose to another person information which he is under a legal duty to disclose, and

(b) intends, by failing to disclose the information—

(i) to make a gain for himself or another, or

(ii) to cause loss to another or to expose another to a risk of loss.

4 Fraud by abuse of position

(1) A person is in breach of this section if he—

(a) occupies a position in which he is expected to safeguard, or not to act against, the financial interests of another person,

(b) dishonestly abuses that position, and

(c) intends, by means of the abuse of that position—

(i) to make a gain for himself or another, or

(ii) to cause loss to another or to expose another to a risk of loss.

(2) A person may be regarded as having abused his position even though his conduct consisted of an omission rather than an act.

5 'Gain' and 'loss'

(1) The references to gain and loss in sections 2 to 4 are to be read in accordance with this section.

(2) 'Gain' and 'loss'—

(a) extend only to gain or loss in money or other property;

(b) include any such gain or loss whether temporary or permanent;

and 'property' means any property whether real or personal (including things in action and other intangible property).

(3) 'Gain' includes a gain by keeping what one has, as well as a gain by getting what one does not have.

(4) 'Loss' includes a loss by not getting what one might get, as well as a loss by parting with what one has.

6 Possession etc. of articles for use in frauds

(1) A person is guilty of an offence if he has in his possession or under his control any article for use in the course of or in connection with any fraud. [E]

7 Making or supplying articles for use in frauds

(1) A person is guilty of an offence if he makes, adapts, supplies or offers to supply any article—

(a) knowing that it is designed or adapted for use in the course of or in connection with fraud, or

(b) intending it to be used to commit, or assist in the commission of, fraud. [E]

8 'Article'

(1) For the purposes of—

(a) sections 6 and 7, and

(b) the provisions listed in subsection (2), so far as they relate to articles for use in the course of or in connection with fraud,

'article' includes any program or data held in electronic form.

(2) The provisions are—

(a) section 1(7)(b) of the Police and Criminal Evidence Act 1984,

(b) section 2(8)(b) of the Armed Forces Act 2001.

9 Participating in fraudulent business carried on by sole trader etc.

(1) A person is guilty of an offence if he is knowingly a party to the carrying on of a business to which this section applies. [E]

(2) This section applies to a business which is carried on—
(a) by a person who is outside the reach of section 993 of the Companies Act 2006... and
(b) with intent to defraud creditors of any person or for any other fraudulent purpose.
(3) The following are within the reach of section 993 of the 2006 Act—
(a) a company (within the meaning of that Act);
(b) a person to whom that section applies (with or without adaptations or modifications) as if the person were a company;
(c) a person exempted from the application of that section.
(5) 'Fraudulent purpose' has the same meaning as in section 993 of the 2006 Act.

11 Obtaining services dishonestly

(1) A person is guilty of an offence under this section if he obtains services for himself or another—
(a) by a dishonest act, and
(b) in breach of subsection (2). [E]
(2) A person obtains services in breach of this subsection if—
(a) they are made available on the basis that payment has been, is being or will be made for or in respect of them,
(b) he obtains them without any payment having been made for or in respect of them or without payment having been made in full, and
(c) when he obtains them, he knows—
(i) that they are being made available on the basis described in paragraph (a), or
(ii) that they might be,
but intends that payment will not be made, or will not be made in full.

12 Liability of company officers for offences by company

(1) Subsection (2) applies if an offence under this Act is committed by a body corporate.
(2) If the offence is proved to have been committed with the consent or connivance of—
(a) a director, manager, secretary or other similar officer of the body corporate, or
(b) a person who was purporting to act in any such capacity,
he (as well as the body corporate) is guilty of the offence and liable to be proceeded against and punished accordingly.

(3) If the affairs of a body corporate are managed by its members, subsection (2) applies in relation to the acts and defaults of a member in connection with his functions of management as if he were a director of the body corporate.

Finance Act 2000

144 Offence of fraudulent evasion of income tax

(1) A person commits an offence if he is knowingly concerned in the fraudulent evasion of income tax by him or any other person. [E]

Gambling Act 2005

3 Gambling

In this Act 'gambling' means—
(a) gaming (within the meaning of section 6),
(b) betting (within the meaning of section 9), and
(c) participating in a lottery (within the meaning of section 14 and subject to section 15).

6 Gaming & game of chance

(1) In this Act 'gaming' means playing a game of chance for a prize.

(2) In this Act 'game of chance'—

(a) includes—

(i) a game that involves both an element of chance and an element of skill,

(ii) a game that involves an element of chance that can be eliminated by superlative skill, and

(iii) a game that is presented as involving an element of chance, but

(b) does not include a sport.

(3) For the purposes of this Act a person plays a game of chance if he participates in a game of chance—

(a) whether or not there are other participants in the game, and

(b) whether or not a computer generates images or data taken to represent the actions of other participants in the game.

(4) For the purposes of this Act a person plays a game of chance for a prize—

(a) if he plays a game of chance and thereby acquires a chance of winning a prize, and

(b) whether or not he risks losing anything at the game.

(5) In this Act 'prize' in relation to gaming (except in the context of a gaming machine)—

(a) means money or money's worth, and

(b) includes both a prize provided by a person organising gaming and winnings of money staked.

(6) The Secretary of State may by regulations provide that a specified activity, or an activity carried on in specified circumstances, is or is not to be treated for the purposes of this Act as—

(a) a game;

(b) a game of chance;

(c) a sport.

9 Betting: general

(1) In this Act 'betting' means making or accepting a bet on—

(a) the outcome of a race, competition or other event or process,

(b) the likelihood of anything occurring or not occurring, or

(c) whether anything is or is not true.

(2) A transaction that relates to the outcome of a race, competition or other event or process may be a bet within the meaning of subsection (1) despite the facts that—

(a) the race, competition, event or process has already occurred or been completed, and

(b) one party to the transaction knows the outcome.

(3) A transaction that relates to the likelihood of anything occurring or not occurring may be a bet within the meaning of subsection (1) despite the facts that—

(a) the thing has already occurred or failed to occur, and

(b) one party to the transaction knows that the thing has already occurred or failed to occur.

14 Lottery

(1) For the purposes of this Act an arrangement is a lottery, irrespective of how it is described, if it satisfies one of the descriptions of lottery in subsections (2) and (3).

(2) An arrangement is a simple lottery if—

(a) persons are required to pay in order to participate in the arrangement,

(b) in the course of the arrangement one or more prizes are allocated to one or more members of a class, and

(c) the prizes are allocated by a process which relies wholly on chance.

(3) An arrangement is a complex lottery if—

(a) persons are required to pay in order to participate in the arrangement,

(b) in the course of the arrangement one or more prizes are allocated to one or more members of a class,
(c) the prizes are allocated by a series of processes, and
(d) the first of those processes relies wholly on chance.

(4) In this Act 'prize' in relation to lotteries includes any money, articles or services—
(a) whether or not described as a prize, and
(b) whether or not consisting wholly or partly of money paid, or articles or services provided, by the members of the class among whom the prize is allocated.

(5) A process which requires persons to exercise skill or judgment or to display knowledge shall be treated for the purposes of this section as relying wholly on chance if—
(a) the requirement cannot reasonably be expected to prevent a significant proportion of persons who participate in the arrangement of which the process forms part from receiving a prize, and
(b) the requirement cannot reasonably be expected to prevent a significant proportion of persons who wish to participate in that arrangement from doing so.

15 National Lottery

(2) Participating in a lottery which forms part of the National Lottery is gambling for the purposes of—
(a) section 42.

42 Cheating

(1) A person commits an offence if he—
(a) cheats at gambling, or
(b) does anything for the purpose of enabling or assisting another person to cheat at gambling. [E]

(2) For the purposes of subsection (1) it is immaterial whether a person who cheats—
(a) improves his chances of winning anything, or
(b) wins anything.

(3) Without prejudice to the generality of subsection (1) cheating at gambling may, in particular, consist of actual or attempted deception or interference in connection with—
(a) the process by which gambling is conducted, or
(b) a real or virtual game, race or other event or process to which gambling relates.

Companies Act 2006

993 Punishment for fraudulent trading

(1) If any business of a company is carried on with intent to defraud creditors of the company or creditors of any other person, or for any fraudulent purpose, every person who was knowingly a party to the carrying on of the business in that manner commits an offence. [E]

(2) This applies whether or not the company has been, or is in the course of being, wound up. [E]

Insolvency Act 1986

CHAPTER VI BANKRUPTCY OFFENCES

350 Scheme of this Chapter

(1) Subject to section 360(3) below, this Chapter applies where the court has made a bankruptcy order on a bankruptcy petition.

(2) This Chapter applies whether or not the bankruptcy order is annulled, but proceedings for an offence under this Chapter shall not be instituted after the annulment.

(3) Without prejudice to his liability in respect of a subsequent bankruptcy, the bankrupt is not guilty of an offence under this Chapter in respect of anything done after his discharge; but nothing in this Group of Parts prevents the institution of proceedings against a discharged bankrupt for an offence committed before his discharge.

(4) It is not a defence in proceedings for an offence under this Chapter that anything relied on, in whole or in part, as constituting that offence was done outside England and Wales.

...

351 Definitions

In the following provisions of this Chapter—

(a) references to property comprised in the bankrupt's estate or to property possession of which is required to be delivered up to the official receiver or the trustee of the bankrupt's estate include any property which would be such property if a notice in respect of it were given under section 307 (after-acquired property) or 308 (personal property and effects of bankrupt having more than replacement value) or section 308A (vesting in trustee of certain tenancies);

(b) 'the initial period' means the period between the presentation of the bankruptcy petition and the commencement of the bankruptcy; and

(c) a reference to a number of months or years before petition is to that period ending with the presentation of the bankruptcy petition.

352 Defence of innocent intention

Where in the case of an offence under any provision of this Chapter it is stated that this section applies, a person is not guilty of the offence if he proves that, at the time of the conduct constituting the offence, he had no intent to defraud or to conceal the state of his affairs.

353 Non-disclosure

(1) The bankrupt is guilty of an offence if—

(a) he does not to the best of his knowledge and belief disclose all the property comprised in his estate to the official receiver or the trustee, or

(b) he does not inform the official receiver or the trustee of any disposal of any property which but for the disposal would be so comprised, stating how, when, to whom and for what consideration the property was disposed of. [E]

(2) Subsection (1)(b) does not apply to any disposal in the ordinary course of a business carried on by the bankrupt or to any payment of the ordinary expenses of the bankrupt or his family.

(3) Section 352 applies to this offence.

354 Concealment of property

(1) The bankrupt is guilty of an offence if—

(a) he does not deliver up possession to the official receiver or trustee, or as the official receiver or trustee may direct, of such part of the property comprised in his estate as is in his possession or under his control and possession of which he is required by law so to deliver up,

(b) ... he conceals any property the value of which is not less than the prescribed amount and possession of which he is required to deliver up to the official receiver or trustee, or

(c) in the 12 months before petition, or in the initial period, he did anything which would have been an offence under paragraph (b) above if the bankruptcy order had been made immediately before he did it.

Section 352 applies to this offence. [E]

(2) The bankrupt is guilty of an offence if he removes, or in the initial period removed, any property the value of which was not less than the prescribed amount and possession of which he has or would have been required to deliver up to the official receiver or the trustee.

Section 352 applies to this offence. [E]

(3) The bankrupt is guilty of an offence if he without reasonable excuse fails, on being required to do so by the official receiver or the court—

(a) to account for the loss of any substantial part of his property incurred in the 12 months before petition or in the initial period, or

(b) to give a satisfactory explanation of the manner in which such a loss was incurred. [E]

355 Concealment of books and papers; falsification

(1) The bankrupt is guilty of an offence if he does not deliver up possession to the official receiver or the trustee, or as the official receiver or trustee may direct, of all books, papers and other records of which he has possession or control and which relate to his estate or his affairs.

Section 352 applies to this offence. [E]

(2) The bankrupt is guilty of an offence if—

(a) he prevents, or in the initial period prevented, the production of any books, papers or records relating to his estate or affairs;

(b) he conceals, destroys, mutilates or falsifies, or causes or permits the concealment, destruction, mutilation or falsification of, any books, papers or other records relating to his estate or affairs;

(c) he makes, or causes or permits the making of, any false entries in any book, document or record relating to his estate or affairs; or

(d) in the 12 months before petition, or in the initial period, he did anything which would have been an offence under paragraph (b) or (c) above if the bankruptcy order had been made before he did it.

Section 352 applies to this offence. [E]

(3) The bankrupt is guilty of an offence if—

(a) he disposes of, or alters or makes any omission in, or causes or permits the disposal, altering or making of any omission in, any book, document or record relating to his estate or affairs, or

(b) in the 12 months before petition, or in the initial period he did anything which would have been an offence under paragraph (a) if the bankruptcy order had been made before he did it.

Section 352 applies to this offence. [E]

356 False statements

(1) The bankrupt is guilty of an offence if he makes or has made any material omission in any statement made under any provision in this Group of Parts and relating to his affairs.

Section 352 applies to this offence. [E]

(2) The bankrupt is guilty of an offence if—

(a) knowing or believing that a false debt has been proved by any person under the bankruptcy, he fails to inform the trustee as soon as practicable; or

(b) he attempts to account for any part of his property by fictitious losses or expenses; or

(c) at any meeting of his creditors in the 12 months before petition or (whether or not at such a meeting) at any time in the initial period, he did anything which would have been an offence under paragraph (b) if the bankruptcy order had been made before he did it; or

(d) he is, or at any time has been, guilty of any false representation or other fraud for the purpose of obtaining the consent of his creditors, or any of them, to an agreement with reference to his affairs or to his bankruptcy. [E]

357 Fraudulent disposal of property

(1) The bankrupt is guilty of an offence if he makes or causes to be made, or has in the period of 5 years ending with the commencement of the bankruptcy made or caused to be made, any gift or transfer of, or any charge on, his property.

Section 352 applies to this offence. [E]

(2) The reference to making a transfer of or charge on any property includes causing or conniving at the levying of any execution against that property.

(3) The bankrupt is guilty of an offence if he conceals or removes, or has at any time before the commencement of the bankruptcy concealed or removed, any part of his property after, or within 2 months before, the date on which a judgment or order for the payment of money has been obtained against him, being a judgment or order which was not satisfied before the commencement of the bankruptcy.

Section 352 applies to this offence. [E]

358 Absconding

The bankrupt is guilty of an offence if—

(a) he leaves, or attempts or makes preparations to leave, England and Wales with any property the value of which is not less than the prescribed amount and possession of which he is required to deliver up to the official receiver or the trustee, or

(b) in the 6 months before petition, or in the initial period, he did anything which would have been an offence under paragraph (a) if the bankruptcy order had been made immediately before he did it.

Section 352 applies to this offence. [E]

359 Fraudulent dealing with property obtained on credit

(1) The bankrupt is guilty of an offence if, in the 12 months before petition, or in the initial period, he disposed of any property which he had obtained on credit and, at the time he disposed of it, had not paid for.

Section 352 applies to this offence. [E]

(2) A person is guilty of an offence if, in the 12 months before petition or in the initial period, he acquired or received property from the bankrupt knowing or believing—

(a) that the bankrupt owed money in respect of the property, and

(b) that the bankrupt did not intend, or was unlikely to be able, to pay the money he so owed. [E]

(3) A person is not guilty of an offence under subsection (1) or (2) if the disposal, acquisition or receipt of the property was in the ordinary course of a business carried on by the bankrupt at the time of the disposal, acquisition or receipt.

(4) In determining for the purposes of this section whether any property is disposed of, acquired or received in the ordinary course of a business carried on by the bankrupt, regard may be had, in particular, to the price paid for the property.

(5) In this section references to disposing of property include pawning or pledging it; and references to acquiring or receiving property shall be read accordingly.

360 Obtaining credit; engaging in business

(1) The bankrupt is guilty of an offence if—

(a) either alone or jointly with any other person, he obtains credit to the extent of the prescribed amount or more without giving the person from whom he obtains it the relevant information about his status; or

(b) he engages (whether directly or indirectly) in any business under a name other than that in which he was adjudged bankrupt without disclosing to all persons with whom he enters into any business transaction the name in which he was so adjudged. [E]

(2) The reference to the bankrupt obtaining credit includes the following cases—

(a) where goods are bailed to him under a hire-purchase agreement, or agreed to be sold to him under a conditional sale agreement, and

(b) where he is paid in advance (whether in money or otherwise) for the supply of goods or services.

(3) A person whose estate has been sequestrated in Scotland, or who has been adjudged bankrupt in Northern Ireland, is guilty of an offence if, before his discharge, he does anything in England and Wales which would be an offence under subsection (1) if he were an undischarged bankrupt and the sequestration of his estate or the adjudication in Northern Ireland were an adjudication under this Part. [E]

(4) For the purposes of subsection (1)(a), the relevant information about the status of the person in question is the information that he is an undischarged bankrupt or, as the case may be, that his estate has been sequestrated in Scotland and that he has not been discharged.

Criminal Justice Act 1993

Sections 1–6:

Jurisdiction in Relation to Offences of Theft and Fraud

[See pages 15–17]

(b) Commercial Malpractice

Prevention of Corruption Act 1906

1 Corrupt transactions by agents

(1) If any agent corruptly accepts or obtains, or agrees to accept or attempts to obtain, from any person, for himself or for any other person, any gift or consideration as an inducement or reward for doing or forbearing to do, or for having after the passing of this Act done or forborne to do, any act in relation to his principal's affairs or business, or for showing or forbearing to show favour or disfavour to any person in relation to his principal's affairs or business; or

If any person corruptly gives or agrees to give or offers any gift or consideration to any agent as an inducement or reward for doing or forbearing to do, or for having after the passing of this Act done or forborne to do, any act in relation to his principal's affairs or business, or for showing or forbearing to show favour or disfavour to any person in relation to his principal's affairs or business; or

If any person knowingly gives to any agent, or if any agent knowingly uses with intent to deceive his principal, any receipt, account, or other document in respect of which the principal is interested, and which contains any statement which is false or erroneous or defective in any material particular, and which to his knowledge is intended to mislead the principal; he shall be guilty of a misdemeanour, . . . [E]

(2) For the purposes of this Act the expression 'consideration' includes valuable consideration of any kind; the expression 'agent' includes any person employed by or acting for another; and the expression 'principal' includes an employer.

(3) A person serving under the Crown or under any corporation or any municipal, borough, county, or district council, or any board of guardians, is an agent within the meaning of this Act.

(4) For the purposes of this Act it is immaterial if—

(a) the principal's affairs or business have no connection with the United Kingdom and are conducted in a country or territory outside the United Kingdom;

(b) the agent's functions have no connection with the United Kingdom and are carried out in a country or territory outside the United Kingdom.

Prevention of Corruption Act 1916

2 Presumption of corruption in certain cases

[See page 314]

Auctions (Bidding Agreements) Act 1927

1 Certain bidding agreements to be illegal

(1) If any dealer agrees to give, or gives, or offers any gift or consideration to any other person as an inducement or reward for abstaining, or for having abstained, from bidding at a sale by auction either generally or for any particular lot, or if any person agrees to accept, or accepts, or attempts to obtain from any dealer any such gift or consideration as aforesaid, he shall be guilty of an offence under this Act, . . .

Provided that, where it is proved that a dealer has previously to an auction entered into an agreement in writing with one or more persons to purchase goods at the auction bona fide on a joint account and has before the goods were purchased at the auction deposited a copy of the agreement with the auctioneer, such an agreement shall not be treated as an agreement made in contravention of this section. [S]

(2) For the purposes of this section the expression 'dealer' means a person who in the normal course of his business attends sales by auction for the purpose of purchasing goods with a view to reselling them.

Mock Auctions Act 1961

1 Penalties for promoting or conducting mock auctions

(1) It shall be an offence to promote or conduct, or to assist in the conduct of, a mock auction at which one or more lots to which this Act applies are offered for sale. [E]

(3) Subject to the following provisions of this section, for the purposes of this Act a sale of goods by way of competitive bidding shall be taken to be a mock auction if, but only if, during the course of the sale—

- (a) any lot to which this Act applies is sold to a person bidding for it, and either it is sold to him at a price lower than the amount of his highest bid for that lot, or part of the price at which it is sold to him is repaid or credited to him or is stated to be so repaid or credited, or
- (b) the right to bid for any lot to which this Act applies is restricted, or is stated to be restricted, to persons who have bought or agreed to buy one or more articles, or
- (c) any articles are given away or offered as gifts.

(4) A sale of goods shall not be taken to be a mock auction by virtue of paragraph (a) of the last preceding subsection, if it is proved that the reduction in price, or the repayment or credit as the case may be—

- (a) was on account of a defect discovered after the highest bid in question had been made, being a defect of which the person conducting the sale was unaware when that bid was made, or
- (b) was on account of damage sustained after that bid was made.

3 Interpretation

(1) In this Act 'sale of goods by way of competitive bidding' means any sale of goods at which the persons present, or some of them, are invited to buy articles by way of competitive bidding, and 'competitive bidding' includes any mode of sale whereby prospective purchasers may be enabled to compete for the purchase of articles, whether by way of increasing bids or by the offer of articles to be bid for at successively decreasing prices or otherwise.

(2) In this Act 'lot to which this Act applies' means a lot consisting of or including one or more prescribed articles; and 'prescribed articles' means any plate, plated articles, linen, china, glass, books, pictures, prints, furniture, jewellery, articles of household or personal use or ornament or any musical or scientific instrument or apparatus.

(3) In this Act 'stated', in relation to a sale of goods by way of competitive bidding, means stated by or on behalf of the person conducting the sale, by an announcement made to the persons for the time being present at the sale.

(4) For the purposes of this Act any bid stated to have been made at a sale of goods by way of competitive bidding shall be conclusively presumed to have been made, and to have been a bid of the amount stated; and any reference in this Act to the sale of a lot to a person who has made a bid for it includes a reference to a purported sale thereof to a person stated to have bid for it, whether that person exists or not.

(5) For the purposes of this Act anything done in or about the place where a sale of goods by way of competitive bidding is held, if done in connection with the sale, shall be taken to be done during the course of the sale, whether it is done at the time when the articles are being sold or offered for sale by way of competitive bidding or before or after any such time.

Trade Descriptions Act 1968

1 Prohibition of false trade descriptions

(1) Any person who, in the course of a trade or business,—

(a) applies a false trade description to any goods; or

(b) supplies or offers to supply any goods to which a false trade description is applied; shall, subject to the provisions of this Act, be guilty of an offence. [E]

(2) Sections 2 to 6 of this Act shall have effect for the purposes of this section and for the interpretation of expressions used in this section, wherever they occur in this Act.

2 Trade description

(1) A trade description is an indication, direct or indirect, and by whatever means given, of any of the following matters with respect to any goods or parts of goods, that is to say—

(a) quantity, size or gauge;

(b) method of manufacture, production, processing or reconditioning;

(c) composition;

(d) fitness for purpose, strength, performance, behaviour or accuracy;

(e) any physical characteristics not included in the preceding paragraphs;

(f) testing by any person and results thereof;

(g) approval by any person or conformity with a type approved by any person;

(h) place or date of manufacture, production, processing or reconditioning;

(i) person by whom manufactured, produced, processed or reconditioned;

(j) other history, including previous ownership or use.

(2) The matters specified in subsection (1) of this section shall be taken—

(a) in relation to any animal, to include sex, breed or cross, fertility and soundness;

(b) in relation to any semen, to include the identity and characteristics of the animal from which it was taken and measure of dilution.

(3) In this section 'quantity' includes length, width, height, area, volume, capacity, weight and number.

3 False trade description

(1) A false trade description is a trade description which is false to a material degree.

(2) A trade description which though not false, is misleading, that is to say, likely to be taken for such an indication of any of the matters specified in section 2 of this Act as would be false to a material degree, shall be deemed to be a false trade description.

(3) Anything which, though not a trade description, is likely to be taken for an indication of any of those matters and, as such an indication, would be false to a material degree, shall be deemed to be a false trade description.

(4) A false indication, or anything likely to be taken as an indication which would be false, that any goods comply with a standard specified or recognised by any person or implied by the approval of any person shall be deemed to be a false trade description, if there is no such person or no standard so specified, recognised or implied.

4 Applying a trade description to goods

(1) A person applies a trade description to goods if he—

(a) affixes or annexes it to or in any manner marks it on or incorporates it with—

(i) the goods themselves, or

(ii) anything in, on or with which the goods are supplied; or

(b) places the goods in, on or with anything which the trade description has been affixed or annexed to, marked on or incorporated with, or places any such thing with the goods; or

(c) uses the trade description in any manner likely to be taken as referring to the goods.

(2) An oral statement may amount to the use of a trade description.

(3) Where goods are supplied in pursuance of a request in which a trade description is used and the circumstances are such as to make it reasonable to infer that the goods are supplied as goods corresponding to that trade description, the person supplying the goods shall be deemed to have applied that trade description to the goods.

5 Trade descriptions used in advertisements

(1) The following provisions of this section shall have effect where in an advertisement a trade description is used in relation to any class of goods.

(2) The trade description shall be taken as referring to all goods of the class, whether or not in existence at the time the advertisement is published—

(a) for the purpose of determining whether an offence has been committed under paragraph (a) of section 1(1) of this Act; and

(b) where goods of the class are supplied or offered to be supplied by a person publishing or displaying the advertisement, also for the purpose of determining whether an offence has been committed under paragraph (b) of the said section 1(1).

(3) In determining for the purposes of this section whether any goods are of a class to which a trade description used in an advertisement relates regard shall be had not only to the form and content of the advertisement but also to the time, place, manner and frequency of its publication and all other matters making it likely or unlikely that a person to whom the goods are supplied would think of the goods as belonging to the class in relation to which the trade description is used in the advertisement.

6 Offer to supply

A person exposing goods for supply or having goods in his possession for supply shall be deemed to offer to supply them.

13 False representations as to supply of goods or services

If any person, in the course of any trade or business, gives, by whatever means, any false indication, direct or indirect, that any goods or services supplied by him are of a kind supplied to any person he shall, subject to the provisions of this Act, be guilty of an offence. [S]

14 False or misleading statements as to services, etc.

(1) It shall be an offence for any person in the course of any trade or business—

(a) to make a statement which he knows to be false; or

(b) recklessly to make a statement which is false; as to any of the following matters, that is to say,—

(i) the provision in the course of any trade or business of any services, accommodation or facilities;

(ii) the nature of any services, accommodation or facilities provided in the course of any trade or business;

(iii) the time at which, manner in which or persons by whom any services, accommodation or facilities are so provided;

(iv) the examination, approval or evaluation by any person of any services, accommodation or facilities so provided; or

(v) the location or amenities of any accommodation so provided. [E]

(2) For the purposes of this section—

(a) anything (whether or not a statement as to any of the matters specified in the preceding subsection) likely to be taken for such a statement as to any of those matters as would be false shall be deemed to be a false statement as to that matter; and

(b) a statement made regardless of whether it is true or false shall be deemed to be made recklessly, whether or not the person making it had reasons for believing that it might be false.

(3) In relation to any services consisting of or including the application of any treatment or process or the carrying out of any repair, the matters specified in subsection (1) of this section shall be taken to include the effect of the treatment, process or repair.

(4) In this section 'false' means false to a material degree and 'services' does not include anything done under a contract of service.

23 Offences due to fault of other person

Where the commission by any person of an offence under this Act is due to the act or default of some other person that other person shall be guilty of the offence, and a person may be charged with and convicted of the offence by virtue of this section whether or not proceedings are taken against the first-mentioned person.

24 Defence of mistake, accident, etc.

(1) In any proceedings for an offence under this Act it shall, subject to subsection (2) of this section, be a defence for the person charged to prove—

(a) that the commission of the offence was due to a mistake or to reliance on information supplied to him or to the act or default of another person, an accident or some other cause beyond his control; and

(b) that he took all reasonable precautions and exercised all due diligence to avoid the commission of such an offence by himself or any person under his control.

(2) If in any case the defence provided by the last foregoing subsection involves the allegation that the commission of the offence was due to the act or default of another person or to reliance on information supplied by another person, the person charged shall not, without leave of the court, be entitled to rely on that defence unless, within a period ending seven clear days before the hearing, he has served on the prosecutor a notice in writing giving such information identifying or assisting in the identification of that other person as was then in his possession.

(3) In any proceedings for an offence under this Act of supplying or offering to supply goods to which a false trade description is applied it shall be a defence for the person charged to prove that he did not know, and could not with reasonable diligence have ascertained, that the goods did not conform to the description or that the description had been applied to the goods.

25 Innocent publication of advertisement

In proceedings for an offence under this Act committed by the publication of an advertisement it shall be a defence for the person charged to prove that he is a person whose business it is to publish or arrange for the publication of advertisements and that he received the advertisement for publication in the ordinary course of business and did not know and had no reason to suspect that its publication would amount to an offence under this Act.

Weights and Measures Act 1985

28 Short weight, etc.

(1) Subject to sections 33 to 37 below, any person who, in selling or purporting to sell any goods by weight or other measurement or by number, delivers or causes to be delivered to the buyer—

(a) a lesser quantity than that purported to be sold, or

(b) a lesser quantity than corresponds with the price charged, shall be guilty of an offence. [S]

(2) For the purposes of this section—

(a) the quantity of the goods in a package, or of a loaf of bread, to which the packaged goods regulations apply shall be deemed to be the nominal quantity (within the meaning of those regulations) of the package or the loaf of bread; and

(b) any statement, whether oral or in writing, as to the weight of any goods shall be taken, unless otherwise expressed, to be a statement as to the net weight of the goods.

29 Misrepresentation

(1) Subject to sections 33 to 37 below, any person who—

(a) on or in connection with the sale or purchase of any goods,

(b) in exposing or offering any goods for sale,

(c) in purporting to make known to the buyer the quantity of any goods sold, or

(d) in offering to purchase any goods,

makes any misrepresentation whether oral or otherwise as to the quantity of the goods, or does any other act calculated to mislead a person buying or selling the goods as to the quantity of the goods, shall be guilty of an offence. [S]

(2) Subsection (2) of section 28 above shall have effect for the purposes of this section as it has effect for the purposes of that section.

30 Quantity less than stated

(1) If, in the case of any goods pre-packed in or on a container marked with a statement in writing with respect to the quantity of the goods, the quantity of the goods is at any time found to be less than that stated, then, subject to sections 33 to 37 below—

(a) any person who has those goods in his possession for sale shall be guilty of an offence, and

(b) if it is shown that the deficiency cannot be accounted for by anything occurring after the goods had been sold by retail and delivered to, or to a person nominated in that behalf by, the buyer, any person by whom or on whose behalf those goods have been sold or agreed to be sold at any time while they were pre-packed in or on the container in question, shall be guilty of an offence. [S]

(2) If—

(a) in the case of a sale of or agreement to sell any goods which, not being pre-packed, are made up for sale or for delivery after sale in or on a container marked with a statement in writing with respect to the quantity of the goods, or

(b) in the case of any goods which, in connection with their sale or an agreement for their sale, have associated with them a document containing such a statement, the quantity of the goods is at any time found to be less than that stated, then, if it is shown that the deficiency cannot be accounted for by anything occurring after the goods had been delivered to, or to a person nominated in that behalf by, the buyer, and subject to sections 33 to 37 below and paragraph 10 of Schedule 4 to this Act, the person by whom, and any other person on whose behalf, the goods were sold or agreed to be sold shall be guilty of an offence.

(3) Subsections (1) and (2) above shall have effect notwithstanding that the quantity stated is expressed to be the quantity of the goods at a specified time falling before the time in question, or is expressed with some other qualification of whatever description, except where

(a) that quantity is so expressed in pursuance of an express requirement of this Part of this Act or any instrument made under this Part, or

(b) the goods, although falling within subsection (1) or subsection (2)(a) above—

(i) are not required by or under this Part of this Act to be pre-packed as mentioned in subsection (1) or, as the case may be, to be made up for sale or for delivery after sale in or on a container only if the container is marked as mentioned in subsection (2)(a), and

(ii) are not goods on a sale of which (whether any sale or a sale of any particular description) the quantity sold is required by or under any provision of this Part of this Act other than section 26, to be made known to the buyer at or before a particular time, or

(c) the goods, although falling within subsection (2)(b) above, are not required by or under this Part of this Act to have associated with them such a document as is mentioned in that provision.

(4) In any case to which, by virtue of paragraph (a), (b) or (c) of subsection (3) above, the provisions of subsection (1) or (2) above do not apply, if it is found at any time that the quantity of the goods in question is less than that stated and it is shown that the deficiency is greater than can be reasonably justified on the ground justifying the qualification in question, then, subject to sections 33 to 37 below—

(a) in the case of goods such as are mentioned in subsection (1) above, if it is further shown as mentioned in that subsection, then—

(i) where the container in question was marked in Great Britain, the person by whom, and any other person on whose behalf, the container was marked, or

(ii) where the container in question was marked outside Great Britain, the person by whom, and any other person on whose behalf, the goods were first sold in Great Britain,

shall be guilty of an offence; [S]

(b) in the case of goods such as are mentioned in subsection (2) above, the person by whom, and any other person on whose behalf, the goods were sold or agreed to be sold shall be guilty of an offence if, but only if, he would, but for paragraph (a), (b) or (c) of subsection (3) above have been guilty of an offence under subsection (2). [S]

(5) Subsection (2) of section 28 above shall have effect for the purposes of this section as it has effect for the purposes of that section.

31 Incorrect statements

(1) Without prejudice to section 30(2) to (4) above, if in the case of any goods required by or under this Part of this Act to have associated with them a document containing particular statements, that document is found to contain any such statement which is materially incorrect, any person who, knowing or having reasonable cause to suspect that statement to be materially incorrect, inserted it or caused it to be inserted in the document, or used the document for the purposes of this Part of this Act while that statement was contained in the document, shall be guilty of an offence. [S]

(2) Subsection (2) of section 28 above shall have effect for the purposes of this section as it has effect for the purposes of that section.

32 Offences due to default of third person

Where the commission by any person of an offence under this Part of this Act or an instrument made under this Part is due to the act or default of some other person, the other person shall be guilty of an offence and may be charged with and convicted of the offence whether or not proceedings are taken against the first-mentioned person. [S]

33 Warranty

(1) Subject to the following provisions of this section, in any proceedings for an offence under this Part of this Act or any instrument made under this Part, being an offence relating to the quantity or pre-packing of any goods, it shall be a defence for the person charged to prove—

(a) that he bought the goods from some other person—

(i) as being of the quantity which the person charged purported to sell or represented, or which was marked on any container or stated in any document to which the proceedings relate, or

(ii) as conforming with the statement marked on any container to which the proceedings relate, or with the requirements with respect to the pre-packing of goods of this Part of this Act or any instrument made under this Part,

as the case may require, and

(b) that he so bought the goods with a written warranty from that other person that they were of that quantity or, as the case may be, did so conform, and

(c) that at the time of the commission of the offence he did in fact believe the statement contained in the warranty to be accurate and had no reason to believe it to be inaccurate, and

(d) if the warranty was given by a person who at the time he gave it was resident outside Great Britain and any designated country, that the person charged had taken reasonable steps to check the accuracy of the statement contained in the warranty, and

(e) in the case of proceedings relating to the quantity of any goods, that he took all reasonable steps to ensure that, while in his possession, the quantity of the goods remained unchanged and, in the case of such or any other proceedings, that apart from any change in their quantity the goods were at the time of the commission of the offence in the same state as when he bought them.

(2) A warranty shall not be a defence in any such proceedings as are mentioned in subsection (1) above unless, not later than three days before the date of the hearing, the person charged has sent to the prosecutor a copy of the warranty with a notice stating that he intends to rely on it and specifying the name and address of the person from whom the warranty was received, and has also sent a like notice to that person.

(3) Where the person charged is the employee of a person who, if he had been charged, would have been entitled to plead a warranty as a defence under this section, subsection (1) above shall have effect—

(a) with the substitution, for any reference (however expressed) in paragraphs (a), (b), (d), and (e) to the person charged, of a reference to his employer, and

(b) with the substitution for paragraph (c) of the following—

'(c) that at the time of the commission of the offence his employer did in fact believe the statement contained in the warranty to be accurate and the person charged had no reason to believe it to be inaccurate'.

(4) The person by whom the warranty is alleged to have been given shall be entitled to appear at the hearing and to give evidence.

(5) If the person charged in any such proceedings as are mentioned in subsection (1) above wilfully attributes to any goods a warranty given in relation to any other goods, he shall be guilty of an offence.

(6) A person who, in respect of any goods sold by him in respect of which a warranty might be pleaded under this section, gives to the buyer a false warranty in writing shall be guilty of an offence unless he proves that when he gave the warranty he took all reasonable steps to ensure that the statements contained in it were, and would continue at all relevant times to be, accurate.

(7) Where in any such proceedings as are mentioned in subsection (1) above ('the original proceedings') the person charged relies successfully on a warranty given to him or to his employer, any proceedings under subsection (6) above in respect of the warranty may, at the option of the prosecutor, be taken either before a court having jurisdiction in the place where the original proceedings were taken or before a court having jurisdiction in the place where the warranty was given.

(8) For the purposes of this section, any statement with respect to any goods which is contained in any document required by or under this Part of this Act to be associated with the goods or in any invoice, and, in the case of goods made up in or on a container for sale or for delivery after sale, any statement with respect to those goods with which that container is marked, shall be taken to be a written warranty of the accuracy of that statement.

34 Reasonable precautions and due diligence

(1) In any proceedings for an offence under this Part of this Act or any instrument made under this Part, it shall be a defence for the person charged to prove that he took all reasonable precautions and exercised all due diligence to avoid the commission of the offence.

(2) If in any case the defence provided by subsection (1) above involves an allegation that the commission of the offence in question was due to the act or default of another person or due to reliance on information supplied by another person, the person charged shall not, without the leave of the court, be

entitled to rely on the defence unless, before the beginning of the period of seven days ending with the date when the hearing of the charge began, he served on the prosecutor a notice giving such information identifying or assisting in the identification of the other person as was then in his possession.

35 Subsequent deficiency

(1) This subsection applies to any proceedings for an offence under this Part of this Act, or any instrument made under this Part, by reason of the quantity—

(a) of any goods made up for sale or for delivery after sale (whether by way of pre-packing or otherwise) in or on a container marked with an indication of quantity,

(b) of any goods which, in connection with their sale or an agreement for their sale, have associated with them a document purporting to state the quantity of the goods, or

(c) of any goods required by or under this Part of this Act to be pre-packed, or to be otherwise made up in or on a container for sale or for delivery after sale, or to be made for sale, only in particular quantities,

being less than that marked on the container or stated in the document in question or than the relevant particular quantity, as the case may be.

(2) In any proceedings to which subsection (1) above applies, it shall be a defence for the person charged to prove that the deficiency arose—

(a) in a case falling within paragraph (a) of subsection (1) above, after the making up of the goods and the marking of the container,

(b) in a case falling within paragraph (b) of that subsection, after the preparation of the goods for delivery in pursuance of the sale or agreement and after the completion of the document,

(c) in a case falling within paragraph (c) of that subsection, after the making up or making, as the case may be, of the goods for sale,

and was attributable wholly to factors for which reasonable allowance was made in stating the quantity of the goods in the marking or document or in making up or making the goods for sale, as the case may be.

(3) In the case of a sale by retail of food, other than food pre-packed in a container which is, or is required by or under this Part of this Act to be, marked with an indication of quantity, in any proceedings for an offence under this Part of this Act or any instrument made under this Part, by reason of the quantity delivered to the buyer being less than that purported to be sold, it shall be a defence for the person charged to prove that the deficiency was due wholly to unavoidable evaporation or drainage since the sale and that due care and precaution were taken to minimise any such evaporation or drainage.

(4) If in any proceedings for an offence under this Part of this Act or any instrument made under this Part, being an offence in respect of any deficiency in the quantity of any goods sold, it is shown that between the sale and the discovery of the deficiency the goods were with the consent of the buyer subjected to treatment which could result in a reduction in the quantity of those goods for delivery to, or to any person nominated in that behalf by, the buyer, the person charged shall not be found guilty of that offence unless it is shown that the deficiency cannot be accounted for by the subjecting of the goods to that treatment.

36 Excess due to precautions

In any proceedings for an offence under this Part of this Act or any instrument made under this Part, being an offence in respect of any excess in the quantity of any goods, it shall be a defence for the person charged to prove that the excess was attributable to the taking of measures reasonably necessary in order to avoid the commission of an offence in respect of a deficiency in those or other goods.

37 Provisions as to testing

(1) If proceedings for an offence under this Part of this Act, or any instrument made under this Part, in respect of any deficiency or excess in the quantity—

(a) of any goods made up for sale (whether by way of pre-packing or otherwise) in or on a container marked with an indication of quantity, or

(b) of any goods which have been pre-packed or otherwise made up in or on a container for sale or for delivery after sale, or which have been made for sale, and which are required by or under this Part of this Act to be pre-packed, or to be otherwise so made up, or to be so made, as the case may be, only in particular quantities,

are brought with respect to any article, and it is proved that, at the time and place at which that article was tested, other articles of the same kind, being articles which, or articles containing goods which, had been sold by the person charged or were in that person's possession for sale or for delivery after sale, were available for testing, the person charged shall not be convicted of such an offence with respect to that article unless a reasonable number of those other articles was also tested.

(2) In any proceedings for such an offence as is mentioned in subsection (1) above, the court—

(a) if the proceedings are with respect to one or more of a number of articles tested on the same occasion, shall have regard to the average quantity in the articles tested,

(b) if the proceedings are with respect to a single article, shall disregard any inconsiderable deficiency or excess, and

(c) shall have regard generally to all the circumstances of the case.

(3) Subsections (1) and (2) above shall apply with the necessary modifications to proceedings for an offence in respect of the size, capacity or contents of a container as they apply to proceedings for an offence in respect of the excess or deficiency in the quantity of certain goods.

(4) Where by virtue of section 32 above a person is charged with an offence with which some other person might have been charged, the reference in subsection (1) above to articles or goods sold by or in the possession of the person charged shall be construed as a reference to articles or goods sold by or in the possession of that other person.

82 Offences by corporations

(1) Where an offence under, or under any instrument made under, this Act which has been committed by a body corporate is proved to have been committed with the consent or connivance of, or to be attributable to any neglect on the part of, any director, manager, secretary or other similar officer of the body corporate, or any person who was purporting to act in any such capacity, he as well as the body corporate shall be guilty of that offence and shall be liable to be proceeded against and punished accordingly. [S]

(2) In subsection (1) above 'director' in relation to any body corporate established by or under any enactment for the purpose of carrying on under national ownership any industry or part of an industry or undertaking, being a body corporate whose affairs are managed by its members, means a member of that body corporate.

Consumer Protection Act 1987

20 Offence of giving misleading indication of price

(1) Subject to the following provisions of this Part, a person shall be guilty of an offence if, in the course of any business of his, he gives (by any means whatever) to any consumers an indication which is misleading as to the price at which any goods, services, accommodation or facilities are available (whether generally or from particular persons). [S]

(2) Subject as aforesaid, a person shall be guilty of an offence if—

(a) in the course of any businss of his, he has given an indication to any consumers which, after it was given, has become misleading as mentioned in subsection (1) above; and

(b) some or all of those consumers might reasonably be expected to rely on the indication at a time after it has become misleading; and

(c) he fails to take all such steps as are reasonable to prevent those consumers from relying on the indication. [S]

(3) For the purposes of this section it shall be immaterial—

(a) whether the person who gives or gave the indication is or was acting on his own behalf or on behalf of another;
(b) whether or not that person is the person, or included among the persons, from whom the goods, services, accommodation or facilities are available; and
(c) whether the indication is or has become misleading in relation to all the consumers to whom it is or was given or only in relation to some of them.

(5A) A person is not guilty of an offence under subsection (1) or (2) above if, in giving the misleading indication which would otherwise constitute an offence under either of those subsections he is guilty of an offence under section 397 of the Financial Services and Markets Act 2000 (misleading statements and practices).

(6) In this Part—

'Consumer'—
(a) in relation to any goods, means any person who might wish to be supplied with the goods for his own private use or consumption;
(b) in relation to any services or facilities, means any person who might wish to be provided with the services or facilities otherwise than for the purposes of any business of his; and
(c) in relation to any accommodation, means any person who might wish to occupy the accommodation otherwise than for the purposes of any business of his;

'price', in relation to any goods, services, accommodation or facilities, means—
(a) the aggregate of the sums required to be paid by a consumer for or otherwise in respect of the supply of the goods or the provision of the services, accommodation or facilities; or
(b) except in section 21 below, any method which will be or has been applied for the purpose of determining that aggregate.

21 Meaning of 'misleading'

(1) For the purposes of section 20 above an indication given to any consumers is misleading as to a price if what is conveyed by the indication, or what those consumers might reasonably be expected to infer from the indication or any omission from it, includes any of the following, that is to say—
(a) that the price is less than in fact it is;
(b) that the applicability of the price does not depend on facts or circumstances on which its applicability does in fact depend;
(c) that the price covers matters in respect of which an additional charge is in fact made;
(d) that a person who in fact has no such expectation—
  (i) expects the price to be increased or reduced (whether or not at a particular time or by a particular amount); or
  (ii) expects the price, or the price as increased or reduced, to be maintained (whether or not for a particular period); or
(e) that the facts or circumstances by reference to which the consumers might reasonably be expected to judge the validity of any relevant comparison made or implied by the indication are not what in fact they are.

(2) For the purposes of section 20 above, an indication given to any consumers is misleading as to a method of determining a price if what is conveyed by the indication, or what those consumers might reasonably be expected to infer from the indication or any omission from it, includes any of the following, that is to say—
(a) that the method is not what in fact it is;
(b) that the applicability of the method does not depend on facts or circumstances on which its applicability does in fact depend;
(c) that the method takes into account matters in respect of which an additional charge will in fact be made;
(d) that a person who in fact has no such expectation—

(i) expects the method to be altered (whether or not at a particular time or in a particular respect); or

(ii) expects the method, or that method as altered, to remain unaltered (whether or not for a particular period); or

(e) that the facts or circumstances by reference to which the consumers might reasonably be expected to judge the validity of any relevant comparison made or implied by the indication are not what in fact they are.

(3) For the purposes of subsection (1)(e) and (2)(e) above a comparison is a relevant comparison in relation to a price or method of determining a price if it is made between that price or that method, or any price which has been or may be determined by that method, and—

(a) any price or value which is stated or implied to be, to have been or to be likely to be attributed or attributable to the goods, services, accommodation or facilities in question or to any other goods, services, accommodation, or facilities; or

(b) any method, or other method, which is stated or implied to be, to have been or to be likely to be applied or applicable for the determination of the price or value of the goods, services, accommodation or facilities in question or of the price or value of any other goods, services, accommodation or facilities.

22 Application to provision of services and facilities

(1) Subject to the following provisions of this section, references in this Part to services or facilities are references to any services or facilities whatever including, in particular—

(a) the provision of credit or of banking or insurance services and the provision of facilities incidental to the provision of such services;

(b) the purchase or sale of foreign currency;

(c) the supply of electricity;

(d) the provision of a place, other than on a highway, for the parking of a motor vehicle;

(e) the making of arrangements for a person to put or keep a caravan on any land other than arrangements by virtue of which that person may occupy the caravan as his only or main residence.

(2) References in this Part to services shall not include references to services provided to an employer under a contract of employment.

(4) In relation to a service consisting in the purchase or sale of foreign currency, references in this Part to the method by which the price of the service is determined shall include references to the rate of exchange.

(5) In this section—

'caravan' has the same meaning as in the Caravan Sites and Control of Development Act 1960;

'contract of employment' and 'employer' have the same meanings as in the Employment Rights Act 1996;

'credit' has the same meaning as in the Consumer Credit Act 1974.

23 Application to provision of accommodation, etc.

(1) Subject to subsection (2) below, references in this Part to accommodation or facilities being available shall not include references to accommodation or facilities being available to be provided by means of the creation or disposal of an interest in land except where—

(a) the person who is to create or dispose of the interest will do so in the course of any business of his; and

(b) the interest to be created or disposed of is a relevant inretest in a new dwelling and is to be created or disposed of for the purpose of enabling that dwelling to be occupied as a residence, or one of the residences, of the person acquiring the interest.

(2) Subsection (1) above shall not prevent the application of any provision of this Part in relation to—

(a) the supply of any goods as part of the same transaction as any creation or disposal of an interest in land; or

(b) the provision of any services or facilities for the purposes of, or in connection with, any transaction for the creation or disposal of such an interest.

(3) In this section—

'new dwelling' means any building or part of a building in Great Britain which—

(a) has been constructed or adapted to be occupied as a residence; and

(b) has not previously been so occupied or has been so occupied only with other premises or as more than one residence,

and includes any yard, garden, out-house or appurtenances which belong to that building or part or are to be enjoyed with it;

'relevant interest'—

(a) in relation to a new dwelling in England and Wales, means the freehold estate in the dwelling or a leasehold interest in the dwelling for a term of years absolute of more than twenty-one years, not being a term of which twenty-one years or less remains unexpired; . . .

24 Defences

(1) In any proceedings against a person for an offence under subsection (1) or (2) of section 20 above in respect of any indication it shall be a defence for the person to show that his acts or omissions were authorised for the purposes of this subsection by regulations made under section 26 below.

(2) In proceedings against a person for an offence under subsection (1) or (2) of section 20 above in respect of an indication published in a book, newspaper, magazine, or film or in a programme included in a programme service (within the meaning of the Broadcasting Act 1990) it shall be a defence for that person to show that the indication was not contained in an advertisement.

(3) In proceedings against a person for an offence under subsection (1) or (2) of section 20 above in respect of an indication published in an advertisement it shall be a defence for that person to show that—

(a) he is a person who carries on a business of publishing or arranging for the publication of advertisements;

(b) he received the advertisement for publication in the ordinary course of that business; and

(c) at the time of publication he did not know and had no grounds for suspecting that the publication would involve the commission of the offence.

(4) In any proceedings against a person for an offence under subsection (1) of section 20 above in respect of any indication, it shall be a defence for that person to show that—

(a) the indication did not relate to the availability from him of any goods, services, accommodation or facilities;

(b) a price had been recommended to every person from whom the goods, services, accommodation or facilities were indicated as being available;

(c) the indication related to that price and was misleading as to that price only by reason of a failure by any person to follow the recommendation; and

(d) it was reasonable for the person who gave the indication to assume that the recommendation was for the most part being followed.

(5) The provisions of this section are without prejudice to the provisions of section 39 below.

(6) In this section—

'advertisement' includes a catalogue, a circular and a price list.

39 Defence of due diligence

[See page 156]

40 Liability of persons other than the principal offender

[See page 156]

Criminal Justice Act 1993

PART V INSIDER DEALING

52 The offence of insider dealing

(1) An individual who has information as an insider is guilty of insider dealing if, in the circumstances mentioned in subsection (3), he deals in securities that are price-affected securities in relation to the information. [E]

(2) An individual who has information as an insider is also guilty of insider dealing if—

(a) he encourages another person to deal in securities that are (whether or not that other knows it) price-affected securities in relation to the information, knowing or having reasonable cause to believe that the dealing would take place in the circumstances mentioned in subsection (3); or

(b) he discloses the information, otherwise than in the proper performance of the functions of his employment, office or profession, to another person. [E]

(3) The circumstances referred to above are that the acquisition or disposal in question occurs on a regulated market, or that the person dealing relies on a professional intermediary or is himself acting as a professional intermediary.

(4) This section has effect subject to section 53.

53 Defences

(1) An individual is not guilty of insider dealing by virtue of dealing in securities if he shows—

(a) that he did not at the time expect the dealing to result in a profit attributable to the fact that the information in question was price-sensitive information in relation to the securities, or

(b) that at the time he believed on reasonable grounds that the information had been disclosed widely enough to ensure that none of those taking part in the dealing would be prejudiced by not having the information, or

(c) that he would have done what he did even if he had not had the information.

(2) An individual is not guilty of insider dealing by virtue of encouraging another person to deal in securities if he shows—

(a) that he did not at the time expect the dealing to result in a profit attributable to the fact that the information in question was price-sensitive information in relation to the securities, or

(b) that at the time he believed on reasonable grounds that the information had been or would be disclosed widely enough to ensure that none of those taking part in the dealing would be prejudiced by not having the information, or

(c) that he would have done what he did even if he had not had the information.

(3) An individual is not guilty of insider dealing by virtue of a disclosure of information if he shows—

(a) that he did not at the time expect any person, because of the disclosure, to deal in securities in the circumstances mentioned in subsection (3) of section 52; or

(b) that, although he had such an expectation at the time, he did not expect the dealing to result in a profit attributable to the fact that the information was price-sensitive information in relation to the securities.

(4) Schedule 1 (special defences) shall have effect.

(6) In this section references to a profit include references to the avoidance of a loss.

54 Securities to which Part V applies

(1) This Part applies to any security which—

(a) falls within any paragraph of Schedule 2; and

(b) satisfies any conditions applying to it under an order made by the Treasury for the purposes of this subsection;

and in the provisions of this Part (other than that Schedule) any reference to a security is a reference to a security to which this Part applies.

55 Meaning of 'dealing'

(1) For the purposes of this Part, a person deals in securities if—

(a) he acquires or disposes of the securities (whether as principal or agent); or

(b) he procures, directly or indirectly, an acquisition or disposal of the securities by any other person.

(2) For the purposes of this Part, 'acquire', in relation to a security, includes—

(a) agreeing to acquire the security; and

(b) entering into a contract which creates the security.

(3) For the purposes of this Part, 'dispose', in relation to a security, includes—

(a) agreeing to dispose of the security; and

(b) bringing to an end a contract which created the security.

(4) For the purposes of subsection (1), a person procures an acquisition or disposal of a security if the security is acquired or disposed of by a person who is—

(a) his agent,

(b) his nominee, or

(c) a person who is acting at his direction, in relation to the acquisition or disposal.

(5) Subsection (4) is not exhaustive as to the circumstances in which one person may be regarded as procuring an acquisition or disposal of securities by another.

56 Meaning of 'inside information'

(1) For the purposes of this section and section 57, 'inside information' means information which—

(a) relates to particular securities or to a particular issuer of securities or to particular issuers of securities and not to securities generally or to the issuers of securities generally;

(b) is specific or precise;

(c) has not been made public; and

(d) if it were made public would be likely to have a significant effect on the price of any securities.

(2) For the purposes of this Part, securities are 'price-affected securities' in relation to inside information, and inside information is 'price-sensitive information' in relation to securities, if and only if the information would, if made public, be likely to have a significant effect on the price of the securities.

(3) For the purpose of this section 'price' includes value.

57 'Insiders'

(1) For the purposes of this Part, a person has information as an insider if and only if—

(a) it is, and he knows that it is, inside information, and

(b) he has it, and knows that he has it, from an inside source.

(2) For the purposes of subsection (1), a person has information from an inside source if and only if—

(a) he has it through—

(i) being a director, employee or shareholder of an issuer of securities; or

(ii) having access to the information by virtue of his employment, office or profession; or

(b) the direct or indirect source of his information is a person within paragraph (a).

58 Information 'made public'

(1) For the purposes of section 56, 'made public', in relation to information, shall be construed in accordance with the following provisions of this section; but those provisions are not exhaustive as to the meaning of that expression.

(2) Information is made public if—

(a) it is published in accordance with the rules of a regulated market for the purpose of informing investors and their professional advisers;

(b) it is contained in records which by virtue of any enactment are open to inspection by the public;

(c) it can be readily acquired by those likely to deal in any securities—

(i) to which the information relates, or

(ii) of an issuer to which the information relates; or

(d) it is derived from information which has been made public.

(3) Information may be treated as made public even though—

(a) it can be acquired only by persons exercising diligence or expertise;

(b) it is communicated to a section of the public and not to the public at large;

(c) it can be acquired only by observation;

(d) it is communicated only on payment of a fee; or

(e) it is published only outside the United Kingdom.

59 'Professional intermediary'

(1) For the purposes of this Part, a 'professional intermediary' is a person—

(a) who carries on a business consisting of an activity mentioned in subsection (2) and who holds himself out to the public or any section of the public (including a section of the public constituted by persons such as himself) as willing to engage in any such business; or

(b) who is employed by a person falling within paragraph (a) to carry out any such activity.

(2) The activities referred to in subsection (1) are—

(a) acquiring or disposing of securities (whether as principal or agent); or

(b) acting as an intermediary between persons taking part in any dealing in securities.

(3) A person is not to be treated as carrying on a business consisting of an activity mentioned in subsection (2)—

(a) if the activity in question is merely incidental to some other activity not falling within subsection (2); or

(b) merely because he occasionally conducts one of those activities.

(4) For the purposes of section 52, a person dealing in securities relies on a professional intermediary if and only if a person who is acting as a professional intermediary carries out an activity mentioned in subsection (2) in relation to that dealing.

60 Other interpretation provisions

(1) For the purposes of this Part, 'regulated market' means any market, however operated, which, by an order made by the Treasury, is identified (whether by name or by reference to criteria prescribed by the order) as a regulated market for the purposes of this Part.

(2) For the purposes of this Part an 'issuer', in relation to any securities, means any company, public sector body or individual by which or by whom the securities have been or are to be issued.

(3) For the purposes of this Part—

(a) 'company' means any body (whether or not incorporated and wherever incorporated or constituted) which is not a public sector body; and

(b) 'public sector body' means—

(i) the government of the United Kingdom, of Northern Ireland or of any country or territory outside the United Kingdom;

(ii) a local authority in the United Kingdom or elsewhere;

(iii) any international organisation the members of which include the United Kingdom or another member state;

(iv) the Bank of England; or

(v) the central bank of any sovereign State.

(4) For the purposes of this Part, information shall be treated as relating to an issuer of securities which is a company not only where it is about the company but also where it may affect the company's business prospects.

62 Territorial scope of offence of insider dealing

(1) An individual is not guilty of an offence falling within subsection (1) of section 52 unless—

(a) he was within the United Kingdom at the time when he is alleged to have done any act constituting or forming part of the alleged dealing;

(b) the regulated market on which the dealing is alleged to have occurred is one which is declared by an order made by the Treasury to be a market which for the purposes of this Part is to be treated as regulated in the United Kingdom; or

(c) the professional intermediary was within the United Kingdom at the time when he is alleged to have done anything by means of which the offence is alleged to have been committed.

(2) An individual is not guilty of an offence falling within subsection (2) of section 52 unless—

(a) he was within the United Kingdom at the time when he is alleged to have disclosed the information or encouraged the dealing; or

(b) the alleged recipient of the information or encouragement was within the United Kingdom at the time when he is alleged to have received the information or encouragement.

63 Limits on section 52

(1) Section 52 does not apply to anything done by an individual acting on behalf of a public sector body in pursuit of monetary policies or policies with respect to exchange rates or the management of public debt or foreign exchange reserves.

SCHEDULE 1 SPECIAL DEFENCES

Market makers

1. (1) An individual is not guilty of insider dealing by virtue of dealing in securities or encouraging another person to deal if he shows that he acted in good faith in the course of—

(a) his business as a market maker, or

(b) his employment in the business of a market maker.

(2) A market maker is a person who—

(a) holds himself out at all normal times in compliance with the rules of a regulated market or an approved organisation as willing to acquire or dispose of securities; and

(b) is recognised as doing so under those rules.

(3) In this paragraph 'approved organisation' means an international securities self-regulating organisation approved under paragraph 25B of Schedule 1 to the Financial Services Act 1986.

Market information

2. (1) An individual is not guilty of insider dealing by virtue of dealing in securities or encouraging another person to deal if he shows that—

(a) the information which he had as an insider was market information; and

(b) is was reasonable for an individual in his position to have acted as he did despite having that information as an insider at the time.

(2) In determining whether it is reasonable for an individual to do any act despite having market information at the time, there shall, in particular, be taken into account—

(a) the content of the information;

(b) the circumstances in which he first had the information and in what capacity; and

(c) the capacity in which he now acts.

3. An individual is not guilty of insider dealing by virtue of dealing in securities or encouraging another person to deal if he shows—

(a) that he acted—

(i) in connection with an acquisition or disposal which was under consideration or the subject of negotiation, or in the course of a series of such acquisitions or disposals; and

(ii) with a view to facilitating the accomplishment of the acquisition or disposal or the series of acquisitions or disposals; and

(b) that the information which he had as an insider was market information arising directly out of his involvement in the acquisition or disposal or series of acquisitions or disposals.

4. For the purposes of paragraphs 2 and 3 market information is information consisting of one or more of the following facts—

(a) that securities of a particular kind have been or are to be acquired or disposed of, or that their acquisition or disposal is under consideration or the subject of negotiation;

(b) that securities of a particular kind have not been or are not to be acquired or disposed of;

(c) the number of securities acquired or disposed of or to be acquired or disposed of or whose acquisition or disposal is under consideration or the subject of negotiation;

(d) the price (or range of prices) at which securities have been or are to be acquired or disposed of or the price (or range of prices) at which securities whose acquisition or disposal is under consideration or the subject of negotiation may be acquired or disposed of;

(e) the identity of the persons involved or likely to be involved in any capacity in an acquisition or disposal.

Price stabilisation

5. (1) An individual is not guilty of insider dealing by virtue of dealing in securities or encouraging another person to deal if he shows that he acted in conformity with the price stabilisation rules, or with there valiant provisions of Commission Regulation (EC) No 2273/2003. . . .

(2) In this paragraph 'the price stabilisation rules' means rules which—

(a) are made under section 48 of the Financial Services Act 1986 (conduct of business rules); and

(b) make provision of a description mentioned in paragraph (i) of subsection (2) of that section (price stabilisation rules).

SCHEDULE 2 SECURITIES

Shares

1. Shares and stock in the share capital of a company ('shares').

Debt securities

2. Any instrument creating or acknowledging indebtedness which is issued by a company or public sector body, including, in particular, debentures, debenture stock, loan stock, bonds and certificates of deposit ('debt securities').

Warrants

3. Any right (whether conferred by warrant or otherwise) to subscribe for shares or debt securities ('warrants').

Depositary receipts

4. (1) The rights under any depositary receipt.

(2) For the purposes of sub-paragraph (1)a 'depositary receipt' means a certificate or other record (whether or not in the form of a document)—

(a) which is issued by or on behalf of a person who holds any relevant securities of a particular issuer; and

(b) which acknowledges that another person is entitled to rights in relation to the relevant securities or relevant securities of the same kind.

(3) In sub-paragraph (2) 'relevant securities' means shares, debt securities and warrants.

Options

5. Any option to acquire or dispose of any thing falling within any other paragraph of this Schedule.

Futures

6. (1) Rights under a contract for the acquisition or disposal at a future date of any relevant securities at a price agreed when the contract is made.

(2) In sub-paragraph (1)—

(a) the references to a future date and to a price agreed when the contract is made include references to a date and a price determined in accordance with terms of the contract; and

(b) 'relevant securities' means any security falling within any other paragraph of this Schedule.

Contracts, for differences

7. (1) Rights under a contract which does not provide for the delivery of securities but whose purpose or pretended purpose is to secure a profit or avoid a loss by reference to fluctuations in—

(a) a share index or other similar factor connected with relevant securities;

(b) the price of particular relevant securities; or

(c) the interest rate offered on money placed on deposit.

(2) In sub-paragraph (1) 'relevant securities' means any thing falling within any other paragraph of this Schedule.

Financial Services and Markets Act 2000

397 Misleading statements and practices

(1) This subsection applies to a person who—

(a) makes a statement, promise or forecast which he knows to be misleading, false or deceptive in a material particular.

(b) dishonestly conceals any material facts whether in connection with a statement, promise or forecast made by him or otherwise; or

(c) recklessly makes (dishonestly or otherwise) a statement, promise or forecast which is misleading, false or deceptive in a material particular.

(2) A person to whom subsection (1) applies is guilty of an offence if he makes the statement, promise or forecast or conceals the facts for the purpose of inducing, or is reckless as to whether it may induce, another person (whether or not the person to whom the statement, promise or forecast is made)—

(a) to enter or offer to enter into, or to refrain from entering or offering to enter into, a relevant agreement; or

(b) to exercise, or refrain from exercising, any rights conferred by a relevant investment. [E]

(3) Any person who does any act or engages in any course of conduct which creates a false or misleading impression as to the market in or the price or value of any relevant investments is guilty of an offence if he does so for the purpose of creating that impression and of thereby inducing another person to acquire, dispose of, subscribe for or underwrite those investments or to refrain from doing so or to exercise, or refrain from exercising, any rights conferred by those investments. [E]

(4) In proceedings for an offence under subsection (2) brought against a person to whom subsection (1) applies as a result of paragraph (a) of that subsection, it is a defence for him to show that the statement, promise or forecast was made in conformity with price stabilising rules or control of information rules.

(5) In proceedings brought against any person for an offence under subsection (3) it is a defence for him to show—

(a) that he reasonably believed that his act or conduct would not create an impression that was false or misleading as to the matters mentioned in that subsection:

(b) that he acted or engaged in the conduct—

(i) for the purpose of stabilising the price of investments; and
(ii) in conformity with price stabilising rules; or

(c) that he acted or engaged in the conduct in conformity with control of information rules.

(6) Subsections (1) and (2) do not apply unless—

(a) the statement, promise or forecast is made in or from, or the facts are concealed in or from, the United Kingdom or arrangements are made in or from the United Kingdom for the statement, promise or forecast to be made or the facts to be concealed:

(b) the person on whom the inducement is intended to or may have effect is in the United Kingdom; or

(c) the agreement is or would be entered into or the rights are or would be exercised in the United Kingdom.

(7) Subsection (3) does not apply unless—

(a) the act is done, or the course of conduct is engaged in, in the United Kingdom; or

(b) the false or misleading impression is created there.

(9) 'Relevant agreement' means an agreement—

(a) the entering into or performance of which by either party constitutes an activity of a specified kind or one which falls within a specified class of activity; and

(b) which relates to a relevant investment.

(10) 'Relevant investment' means an investment of a specified kind or one which falls within a prescribed class of investment.

(13) 'Investment' includes any asset, right or interest.

(14) 'Specified' means specified in an order made by the Treasury.

400 Offences by bodies corporate, etc.

(1) If an offence under this Act committed by a body corporate is shown—

(a) to have been committed with the consent or connivance of an officer, or

(b) to be attributable to any neglect on his part,

the officer as well as the body corporate is guilty of the offence and liable to be proceeded against and punished accordingly.

(2) If the affairs of a body corporate are managed by its members, subsection (1) applies in relation to the acts and defaults of a member in connection with his functions of management as if he were a director of the body.

(3) If an offence under this Act committed by a partnership is shown—

(a) to have been committed with the consent or connivance of a partner, or

(b) to be attributable to any neglect on his part,

the partner as well as the partnership is guilty of the offence and liable to be proceeded against and punished accordingly.

(4) In subsection (3) 'partner' includes a person purporting to act as a partner.

(5) 'Officer', in relation to a body corporate, means—

(a) a director, member of the committee of management, chief executive, manager, secretary or other similar officer of the body, or a person purporting to act in any such capacity; and

(b) an individual who is a controller of the body.

(6) If an offence under this Act committed by an unincorporated association (other than a partnership) is shown—

(a) to have been committed with the consent or connivance of an officer of the association or a member of its governing body, or

(b) to be attributable to any neglect on the part of such an officer or member, that officer or member as well as the association is guilty of the offence and liable to be proceeded against and punished accordingly.

Enterprise Act 2002

188 Cartel offence

(1) An individual is guilty of an offence if he dishonestly agrees with one or more other persons to make or implement, or to cause to be made or implemented, arrangements of the following kind relating to at least two undertakings (A and B). [E]

(2) The arrangements must be ones which, if operating as the parties to the agreement intend, would—

- (a) directly or indirectly fix a price for the supply by A in the United Kingdom (otherwise than to B) of a product or service,
- (b) limit or prevent supply by A in the United Kingdom of a product or service,
- (c) limit or prevent production by A in the United Kingdom of a product,
- (d) divide between A and B the supply in the United Kingdom of a product or service to a customer or customers,
- (e) divide between A and B customers for the supply in the United Kingdom of a product or service, or
- (f) be bid-rigging arrangements.

(3) Unless subsection (2)(d), (e) or (f) applies, the arrangements must also be ones which, if operating as the parties to the agreement intend, would—

- (a) directly or indirectly fix a price for the supply by B in the United Kingdom (otherwise than to A) of a product or service,
- (b) limit or prevent supply by B in the United Kingdom of a product or service, or
- (c) limit or prevent production by B in the United Kingdom of a product.

(4) In subsections (2)(a) to (d) and (3), references to supply or production are to supply or production in the appropriate circumstances (for which see section 189).

(5) 'Bid-rigging arrangements' are arrangements under which, in response to a request for bids for the supply of a product or service in the United Kingdom, or for the production of a product in the United Kingdom—

- (a) A but not B may make a bid, or
- (b) A and B may each make a bid but, in one case or both, only a bid arrived at in accordance with the arrangements.

(6) But arrangements are not bid-rigging arrangements if, under them, the person requesting bids would be informed of them at or before the time when a bid is made.

(7) 'Undertaking' has the same meaning as in Part 1 of the 1998 Act.

189 Cartel offence: supplementary

(1) For section 188(2)(a), the appropriate circumstances are that A's supply of the product or service would be at a level in the supply chain at which the product or service would at the same time be supplied by B in the United Kingdom.

(2) For section 188(2)(b), the appropriate circumstances are that A's supply of the product or service would be at a level in the supply chain—

- (a) at which the product or service would at the same time be supplied by B in the United Kingdom, or
- (b) at which supply by B in the United Kingdom of the product or service would be limited or prevented by the arrangements.

(3) For section 188(2)(c), the appropriate circumstances are that A's production of the product would be at a level in the production chain—

- (a) at which the product would at the same time be produced by B in the United Kingdom, or
- (b) at which production by B in the United Kingdom of the product would be limited or prevented by the arrangements.

(4) For section 188(2)(d), the appropriate circumstances are that A's supply of the product or service would be at the same level in the supply chain as B's.

(5) For section 188(3)(a), the appropriate circumstances are that B's supply of the product or service would be at a level in the supply chain at which the product or service would at the same time be supplied by A in the United Kingdom.

(6) For section 188(3)(b), the appropriate circumstances are that B's supply of the product or service would be at a level in the supply chain—

(a) at which the product or service would at the same time be supplied by A in the United Kingdom, or

(b) at which supply by A in the United Kingdom of the product or service would be limited or prevented by the arrangements.

(7) For section 188(3)(c), the appropriate circumstances are that B's production of the product would be at a level in the production chain—

(a) at which the product would at the same time be produced by A in the United Kingdom, or

(b) at which production by A in the United Kingdom of the product would be limited or prevented by the arrangements.

Part IX

Trespass and Invasion of Privacy

(a) Trespass

Theft Act 1968

9 Burglary

(1) A person is guilty of burglary if—

(a) he enters any building or part of a building as a trespasser and with intent to commit any such offence as is mentioned in subsection (2) below; or

(b) having entered into any building or part of a building as a trespasser he steals or attempts to steal anything in the building or that part of it or inflicts or attempts to inflict on any person therein any grievous bodily harm. [I] and [E]

(2) The offences referred to in subsection (1)(a) above are offences of stealing anything in the building or part of a building in question, of inflicting on any person therein any grievous bodily harm therein, and of doing unlawful damage to the building or anything therein.

(3) A person guilty of burglary shall on conviction on indictment be liable to imprisonment for a term not exceeding—

(a) where the offence was committed in respect of a building or part of a building which is a dwelling, fourteen years;

(b) in any other case, ten years.

(4) References in subsection (1) and (2) above to a building, and the reference in subsection (3) above to a building which is a dwelling, shall apply also to an inhabited vehicle or vessel, and shall apply to any such vehicle or vessel at times when the person having a habitation in it is not there as well as at times when he is.

10 Aggravated burglary

(1) A person is guilty of aggravated burglary if he commits any burglary and at the time has with him any firearm or imitation firearm, any weapon of offence, or any explosive; and for this purpose—

(a) 'firearm' includes an airgun or air pistol, and 'imitation firearm' means anything which has the appearance of being a firearm, whether capable of being discharged or not; and

(b) 'weapon of offence' means any article made or adapted for use for causing injury to or incapacitating a person, or intended by the person having it with him for such use; and

(c) 'explosive' means any article manufactured for the purpose of producing a practical effect by explosion, or intended by the person having it with him for that purpose. [I]

Firearms Act 1968

20 Trespassing with firearm

[See page 142]

Criminal Law Act 1977

6 Violence for securing entry

(1) Subject to the following provisions of this section, any person who, without lawful authority, uses or threatens violence for the purpose of securing entry into any premises for himself or for any other person is guilty of an offence, provided that—

(a) there is someone present on those premises at the time who is opposed to the entry which the violence is intended to secure; and

(b) the person using or threatening the violence knows that that is the case. [S]

(1A) Subsection (1) above does not apply to a person who is a displaced residential occupier or a protected intending occupier of the premises in question or who is acting on behalf of such an occupier; and if the accused adduces sufficient evidence that he was, or was acting on behalf of, such an occupier he shall be presumed to be, or to be acting on behalf of, such an occupier unless the contrary is proved by the prosecution.

(2) Subject to subsection (1A) above, the fact that a person has any interest in or right to possession or occupation of any premises shall not for the purposes of subsection (1) above constitute lawful authority for the use or threat of violence by him or anyone else for the purpose of securing his entry into those premises.

(4) It is immaterial for the purposes of this section—

(a) whether the violence in question is directed against the person or against the property; and

(b) whether the entry which the violence is intended to secure is for the purpose of acquiring possession of the premises in question or for any other purpose.

7 Adverse occupation of residential premises

(1) Subject to the following provisions of this section and to section 12A(9) below, any person who is on any premises as a trespasser after having entered as such is guilty of an offence if he fails to leave those premises on being required to do so by or on behalf of—

(a) a displaced residential occupier of the premises; or

(b) an individual who is a protected intending occupier of the premises. [S]

(2) In any proceedings for an offence under this section it shall be a defence for the accused to prove that he believed that the person requiring him to leave the premises was not a displaced residential occupier or protected intending occupier of the premises or a person acting on behalf of a displaced residential occupier or protected intending occupier.

(3) In any proceedings for an offence under this section it shall be a defence for the accused to prove—

(a) that the premises in question are or form part of premises used mainly for non-residential purposes; and

(b) that he was not on any part of the premises used wholly or mainly for residential purposes.

(4) Any reference in the preceding provisions of this section to any premises includes a reference to any access to them, whether or not any such access itself constitutes premises, within the meaning of this Part of this Act.

(7) Section 12 below contains provisions which apply for determining when any person is to be regarded for the purposes of this Part of this Act as a displaced residential occupier of any premises or of any access to any premises and section 12A below contains provisions which apply for determining when any person is to be regarded for the purposes of this Part of this Act as a protected intending occupier of any premises or of any access to any premises.

8 Trespassing with a weapon of offence

(1) A person who is on any premises as a trespasser, after having entered as such, is guilty of an offence if, without lawful authority or reasonable excuse, he has with him on the premises any weapon of offence. [S]

(2) In subsection (1) above 'weapon of offence' means any article made or adapted for use for causing injury to or incapacitating a person, or intended by the person having it with him for such use.

9 Trespassing on premises of foreign missions, etc.

(1) Subject to subsection (3) below, a person who enters or is on any premises to which this section applies as a trespasser is guilty of an offence. [S]

(2) This section applies to any premises which are or form part of—

- (a) the premises of a diplomatic mission within the meaning of the definition in Article 1(i) of the Vienna Convention on Diplomatic Relations signed in 1961 as that Article has effect in the United Kingdom by virtue of section 2 of and Schedule 1 to the Diplomatic Privileges Act 1964;
- (aa) the premises of a closed diplomatic mission;
- (b) consular premises within the meaning of the definition in paragraph 1(j) of Article 1 of the Vienna Convention on Consular Relations signed in 1963 as that Article has effect in the United Kingdom by virtue of section 1 of and Schedule 1 to the Consular Relations Act 1968;
- (bb) the premises of a closed consular post;
- (c) any other premises in respect of which any organisation or body is entitled to inviolability by or under any enactment; and
- (d) any premises which are the private residence of a diplomatic agent (within the meaning of Article 1(e) of the Convention mentioned in paragraph (a) above) or of any other person who is entitled to inviolability of residence by or under any enactment.

(3) In any proceedings for an offence under this section it shall be a defence for the accused to prove that he believed that the premises in question were not premises to which this section applies.

12 Supplementary provisions

(1) In this Part of this Act—

- (a) 'premises' means any building, any part of a building under separate occupation, any land ancillary to a building, the site comprising any building or buildings together with any land ancillary thereto, and (for the purposes only of sections 10 and 11 above) any other place; and
- (b) 'access' means, in relation to any premises, any part of any site or building within which those premises are situated which constitutes an ordinary means of access to those premises (whether or not that is its sole or primary use).

(2) References in this section to a building shall apply also to any structure other than a movable one, and to any movable structure, vehicle or vessel designed or adapted for use for residential purposes; and for the purposes of subsection (1) above—

- (a) part of a building is under separate occupation if anyone is in occupation or entitled to occupation of that part as distinct from the whole; and
- (b) land is ancillary to a building if it is adjacent to it and used (or intended for use) in connection with the occupation of that building or any part of it.

(3) Subject to subsection (4) below, any person who was occupying any premises as a residence immdiately before being excluded from occupation by anyone who entered those premises, or any access to those premises, as a trespasser is a displaced residential occupier of the premises for the purposes of this Part of this Act so long as he continues to be excluded from occupation of the premises by the original trespasser or by any subsequent trespasser.

(4) A person who was himself occupying the premises in question as a trespasser immediately before being excluded from occupation shall not by virtue of subsection above be a displaced residential occupier of the premises for the purposes of this Part of this Act.

(5) A person who by virtue of subsection (3) above is a displaced residential occupier of any premises shall be regarded for the purposes of this Part of this Act as a displaced residential occupier also of any access to those premises.

12A Protected intending occupiers: supplementary provisions

(1) For the purposes of this Part of this Act an individual is a protected intending occupier of any premises at any time if at that time he falls within subsections (2), (4) or (6) below.

(2) An individual is a protected occupier of any premises if—

- (a) he has in those premises a freehold interest or a leasehold interest with not less than two years still to run;
- (b) he requires the premises for his own occupation as a residence;
- (c) he is excluded from occupation of the premises by a person who entered them, or any access to them, as a trespasser; and
- (d) he or a person acting on his behalf holds a written statement—
  - (i) which specifies his interest in the premises;
  - (ii) which states that he requires the premises for occupation as a residence for himself; and
  - (iii) with respect to which the requirements in subsection (3) below are fulfilled.

(3) The requirements referred to in subsection (2)(d)(iii) above are—

- (a) that the statement is signed by the person whose interest is specified in it in the presence of a justice of the peace or commissioner for oaths; and
- (b) that the justice of the peace or commissioner for oaths has subscribed his name as a witness to the signature.

(4) An individual is also a protected intending occupier of any premises if—

- (a) he has a tenancy of those premises (other than a tenancy falling within subsection (2)(a) above or (6)(a) below) or a licence to occupy those premises granted by a person with a freehold interest or a leasehold interest with not less than two years still to run in the premises;
- (b) he requires the premises for his own occupation as a residence;
- (c) he is excluded from occupation of the premises by a person who entered them, or any access to them, as a trespasser; and
- (d) he or a person acting on his behalf holds a written statement—
  - (i) which states that he has been granted a tenancy of those premises or a licence to occupy those premises;
  - (ii) which specifies the interest in the premises of the person who granted that tenancy or licence to occupy ('the landlord');
  - (iii) which states that he requires the premises for occupation as a residence for himself; and
  - (iv) with respect to which the requirements in subsection (5) below are fulfilled.

(5) The requirements referred to in subsection (4)(d)(iv) above are—

- (a) that the statement is signed by the landlord and by the tenant or licensee in the presence of a justice of the peace or commissioner for oaths;
- (b) that the justice of the peace or commissioner for oaths has subscribed his name as a witness to the signatures.

(6) An individual is also a protected intending occupier of any premises if—

(a) he has a tenancy of those premises (other than a tenancy falling within subsection (2)(a) or (4)(a) above) or a licence to occupy those premises granted by an authority to which this subsection applies;

(b) he requires the premises for his own occupation as a residence;

(c) he is excluded from occupation of the premises by a person who entered the premises, or any access to them, as a trespasser; and

(d) there has been issued to him by or on behalf of the authority referred to in paragraph (a) above a certificate stating that—

(i) he has been granted a tenancy of those premises or a licence to occupy those premises as a residence by the authority; and

(ii) the authority which granted that tenancy or licence to occupy is one to which this subsection applies, being of a description specified in the certificate.

(7) Subsection (6) above applies to the following authorities—

(a) any body mentioned in section 14 of the Rent Act 1977 (landlord's interest belonging to local authority etc);

(b) the Housing Corporation; and . . .

(c) a registered social landlord within the meaning of the Housing Act 1985.

(8) A person is guilty of an offence if he makes a statement for the purposes of subsection (2) (d) or (4)(d) above which he knows to be false in a material particular or if he recklessly makes such a statement which is false in a material particular.

(9) In any proceedings for an offence under section 7 of this Act where the accused was requested to leave the premises by a person claiming to be or to act on behalf of a protected intending occupier of the premises—

(a) it shall be a defence for the accused to prove that, although asked to do so by the accused at the time the accused was requested to leave, that person failed at that time to produce to the accused such a statement as is referred to in subsection (2)(d) or (4)(d) above or such a certificate as is referred to in subsection (6)(d) above; and

(b) any document purporting to be a certificate under subsection (6)(d) above shall be received in evidence and, unless the contrary is proved, shall be deemed to have been issued by or on behalf of the authority stated in the certificate.

(11) A person who is protected intending occupier of any premises shall be regarded for the purposes of this Part of this Act as a protected intending occupier also of any access to those premises.

Night Poaching Act 1828

1 Persons taking or destroying game or rabbits by night, or entering any land for that purpose

. . . If any person shall . . . by night, unlawfully take or destroy any game or rabbits in any land, whether open or enclosed, or shall by night unlawfully enter or be in any land, whether open or enclosed, with any gun, net, engine, or other instrument, for the purpose of taking or destroying game, he shall be liable on summary conviction to a fine not exceeding level 3 on the standard scale. [S]

9 If persons to the number of three, being armed, enter any land for the purpose of taking or destroying game or rabbits, they shall be deemed guilty of a misdemeanour

. . . If any persons, to the number of three or more together, shall by night unlawfully enter or be on any land whether open or enclosed, for the purpose of taking or destroying game or rabbits, any of such persons being armed with any gun, crossbow, fire arms, bludgeon, or any other offensive weapon, each and every of such persons shall be guilty of a misdemeanour, . . . [S]

12 What time shall be considered night

Provided always...that for the purposes of this Act the night shall be considered and is hereby declared to commence at the expiration of the first hour of sunset, and to conclude at the beginning of the last hour before sunrise.

13 What shall be deemed game

...For the purposes of this Act the word 'game' shall be deemed to include hares, pheasants, partridges, grouse, heath or moor game, black game, and bustards.

Game Act 1831

30 Penalty on persons trespassing in the daytime upon lands in search of game, or woodcocks, etc.—Leave of occupier not to be a defence where game is reserved to landlord, etc.—Landlords and lords of manors,etc., to be deemed legal occupiers

... If any person whatsoever shall commit any trespass by entering or being in the daytime upon any land in search or pursuit of game, or woodcocks, snipes,...or conies, such person shall, on conviction thereof before a justice of the peace, forfeit and pay such sum of money, not exceeding level 3 on the standard scale, as to the justice shall seem meet,...; and...if any persons to the number of five or more together shall commit any trespass, by entering or being in the daytime upon any land in search or pursuit of game, woodcocks, snipes,...or conies, each of such persons shall, on conviction thereof before a justice of the peace, forfeit and pay such sum of money, not exceeding level 4 on the standard scale as to the said justice shall seem meet,...: Provided always, that any person charged with any such trespass shall be at liberty to prove, by way of defence, any matter which would have been a defence to an action at law for such trespass; save and except that the leave and licence of the occupier of the land so trespassed upon shall not be a sufficient defence in any case where the landlord, lessor, or other person shall have the right of killing the game upon such land, by virtue of any reservation or otherwise, as herein-before mentioned; but such landlord, lessor, or other person shall, for the purpose of prosecuting for each of the two offences herein last before mentioned, be deemed to be the legal occupier of such land, whenever the actual occupier thereof shall have given such leave or licence; and that the lord or steward of the crown of any manor, lordship, or royalty, or reputed manor, lordship, or royalty, shall be deemed to be the legal occupier of the land of the wastes or commons within such manor, lordship, or royalty, or reputed manor, lordship, or royalty. [S]

32 Penalty in case of five or more persons found armed in daytime in search of game, etc., and using violence, etc.

... Where any persons, to the number of five or more together, shall be found on any land,...in the daytime, in search or pursuit of game, or woodcocks, snipes,...or conies, any of such persons being then and there armed with a gun, and such persons or any of them shall then and there, by violence, intimidation, or menace, prevent or endeavour to prevent any person authorized as herein-before mentioned from approaching such persons so found, or any of them, for the purpose of requiring them or any of them to quit the land whereon they shall be so found, or to tell their or his christian name, surname, or place of abode respectively, as herein-before mentioned, every person so offending by such violence, intimidation, or menace as aforesaid, and every person then and there aiding or abetting such offender, shall, upon being convicted thereof before two justices of the peace, forfeit and pay for every such offence such penalty, not exceeding level 5 on the standard scale, as to the convicting justices shall seem meet,...; which said penalty shall be in addition to and independent of any other penalty to which any such person may be liable for any other offence against this Act. [S]

34 What to be deemed daytime

... For the purposes of this Act the daytime shall be deemed to commence at the beginning of the last hour before sunrise, and to conclude at the expiration of the first hour after sunset.

35 Provisions as to trespassers not to apply to certain persons

... Provided always, that the aforesaid provisions against trespassers and persons found on any land shall not extend to any lord or any steward of the crown of any manor, lordship, or royalty, or reputed manor, lordship or royalty, nor to any gamekeeper lawfully appointed by such lord or steward within the limits of such manor, lordship, or royalty, or reputed manor, lordship, or royalty.

Deer Act 1991

1 Poaching of deer

(1) Subject to subsection (3) below, if any person enters any land without the consent of the owner or occupier or other lawful authority in search or pursuit of any deer with the intention of taking, killing or injuring it, he shall be guilty of an offence. [S]

(2) Subject to subsection (3) below, if any person while on any land—

(a) intentionally takes, kills or injures, or attempts to take, kill or injure, any deer,

(b) searches for or pursues any deer with the intention of taking, killing or injuring it, or

(c) removes the carcase of any deer, without the consent of the owner or occupier of the land or other lawful authority, he shall be guilty of an offence. [S]

(3) A person shall not be guilty of an offence under subsection (1) or subsection (2) above by reason of anything done in the belief that—

(a) he would have the consent of the owner or occupier of the land if the owner or occupier knew of his doing it and the circumstances of it; or

(b) he has other lawful authority to do it.

Football (Offences) Act 1991

4 Going onto the playing area

[See page 294]

Criminal Justice and Public Order Act 1994

61 Power to remove trespassers on land

(1) If the senior police officer present at the scene reasonably believes that two or more persons are trespassing on land and are present there with the common purpose of residing there for any period, that reasonable steps have been taken by or on behalf of the occupier to ask them to leave and—

(a) that any of those persons has caused damage to the land or to property on the land or used threatening, abusive or insulting words or behaviour towards the occupier, a member of his family or an employee or agent of his, or

(b) that those persons have between them six or more vehicles on the land,

he may direct those persons, or any of them, to leave the land and to remove any vehicles or other property they have with them on the land.

(2) Where the persons in question are reasonably believed by the senior police officer to be persons who were not originally trespassers but have become trespassers on the land, the officer must reasonably believe that the other conditions specified in subsection (1) are satisfied after those persons became trespassers before he can exercise the power conferred by that subsection.

(3) A direction under subsection (1) above, if not communicated to the persons referred to in subsection (1) by the police officer giving the direction, may be communicated to them by any constable at the scene.

(4) If a person knowing that a direction under subsection (1) above has been given which applies to him—

(a) fails to leave the land as soon as reasonably practicable, or

(b) having left again enters the land as a trespasser within the period of three months beginning with the day on which the direction was given,

he commits an offence . . . [S]

(6) In proceedings for an offence under this section it is a defence for the accused to show—

(a) that he was not trespassing on the land, or

(b) that he had a reasonable excuse for failing to leave the land as soon as reasonably practicable or, as the case may be, for again entering the land as a trespasser.

(7) In its application in England and Wales to common land this section has effect as if in the preceding subsections of it—

(a) references to trespassing or trespassers were references to acts and persons doing acts which constitute either a trespass as against the occupier or an infringement of the commoners' rights; and

(b) references to 'the occupier' included the commoners or any of them or, in the case of common land to which the public has access, the local authority as well as any commoner.

(8) Subsection (7) above does not—

(a) require action by more than one occupier; or

(b) constitute persons trespassers as against any commoner or the local authority if they are permitted to be there by the other occupier.

(9) In this section—

'common land' means

(a) land registered as common land is a register of common land kept under Part I of the Commons Act 2006; and

(b) land to which Part I of that Act does not apply and which is subject to rights of common or defined in that Act;

'commoner' means a person with rights of common as so defined

'land' does not include—

(a) buildings other than—

(i) agricultural buildings within the meaning of, in England and Wales, paragraphs 3 to 8 of Schedule 5 to the Local Government Finance Act 1988 or

(ii) scheduled monuments within the meaning of the Ancient Monuments and Archaeological Areas Act 1979;

(b) land forming part of—

(i) a highway unless it falls within the classifications in section 54 of the Wildlife and Countryside Act 1981 (footpath, bridleway or byway open to all traffic or road used as a public path) or is a cycle track under the Highways Act 1980 or the Cycle Tracks Act 1984;

'the local authority', in relation to common land, means any local authority which has powers in relation to the land under section 45 of the Commons Act 2006;

'occupier' (and in subsection (8) 'the other occupier') means—

(a) in England and Wales, the person entitled to possession of the land by virtue of an estate or interest held by him;

'property' in relation to damage to property on land, means—

(a) in England and Wales, property within the meaning of section 10(1) of the Criminal Damage Act 1971;

and 'damage' includes the deposit of any substance capable of polluting the land;

'trespass' means, in the application of this section—

(a) In England and Wales, subject to the extensions effected by subsection (7) above, trespass as against the occupier of the land;

'trespassing' and 'trespasser' shall be construed accordingly;

'vehicle' includes—

(a) any vehicle, whether or not it is in a fit state for use on roads, and includes any chassis or body, with or without wheels, appearing to have formed part of such a vehicle, and any load carried by, and anything attached to, such a vehicle; and

(b) a caravan as defined in section 29(1) of the Caravan Sites and Control of Development Act 1960;

and a person may be regarded for the purposes of this section as having a purpose of residing in a place notwithstanding that he has a home elsewhere.

68 Offence of aggravated trespass

(1) A person commits the offence of aggravated trespass if he trespasses on land and, in relation to any lawful activity which persons are engaging in or are about to engage in on that or adjoining land, does there anything which is intended by him to have the effect—

(a) of intimidating those persons or any of them so as to deter them or any of them from engaging in that activity,

(b) of obstructing that activity, or

(c) of disrupting that activity. [S]

(2) Activity on any occasion on the part of a person or persons on land is 'lawful' for the purposes of this section if he or they may engage in the activity on the land on that occasion without committing an offence or trespassing on the land.

69 Powers to remove persons committing or participating in aggravated trespass

(1) If the senior police officer present at the scene reasonably believes—

(a) that a person is committing, has committed or intends to commit the offence of aggravated trespass on land; or

(b) that two or more persons are trespassing on land and are present there with the common purpose of intimidating persons so as to deter them from engaging in a lawful activity or of obstructing or disrupting a lawful activity,

he may direct that person or (as the case may be) those persons (or any of them) to leave the land.

(2) A direction under subsection (1) above, if not communicated to the persons referred to in subsection (1) by the police officer giving the direction, may be communicated to them by any constable at the scene.

(3) If a person knowing that a direction under subsection (1) above has been given which applies to him—

(a) fails to leave the land as soon as practicable, or

(b) having left again enters the land as a trespasser within the period of three months beginning with the day on which the direction was given,

he commits an offence . . . [S]

(4) In proceedings for an offence under subsection (3) it is a defence for the accused to show—

(a) that he was not trespassing on the land, or

(b) that he had a reasonable excuse for failing to leave the land as soon as practicable or, as the case may be, for again entering the land as a trespasser.

Merchant Shipping Act 1995

103 Stowaways

(1) If a person, without the consent of the master or of any other person authorised to give it, goes to sea or attempts to go to sea in a United Kingdom ship, he shall be liable on summary conviction to a fine not exceeding level 3 on the standard scale. [S]

104 Unauthorised presence on board ship

Where a United Kingdom ship or a ship registered in any other country is in a port in the United Kingdom and a person who is neither in Her Majesty's service nor authorised by law to do so—

(a) goes on board the ship without the consent of the master or of any other persons authorised to give it; or

(b) remains on board the ship after being requested to leave by the master, a constable, an officer authorised by the Secretary of State or an officer of customs and excise,

he shall be liable on summary conviction to a fine not exceeding level 5 on the standard scale. [S]

Education Act 1996

547 Nuisance or disturbance on school premises

(1) Any person who without lawful authority is present on premises to which this section applies and causes or permits nuisance or disturbance to the annoyance of persons who lawfully use those premises (whether or not any such persons are present at the time) is guilty of an offence. [S]

(2) This section applies to premises, including playgrounds, playing fields and other premises for outdoor recreation, of—

(a) any school maintained by a local education authority.

Sexual Offences Act 2003

63 Trespass with intent to commit a sexual offence

(1) A person commits an offence if—

(a) he is a trespasser on any premises,

(b) he intends to commit a relevant sexual offence on the premises, and

(c) he knows that, or is reckless as to whether, he is a trespasser.

(2) In this section—

'premises' includes a structure or part of a structure;

'relevant sexual offence' has the same meaning as in section 62;

'structure' includes a tent, vehicle or vessel or other temporary or movable structure. [E]

Serious Organised Crime and Police Act 2005

128 Offence of trespassing on designated site

(1) A person commits an offence if he enters, or is on, any protected site in England and Wales or Northern Ireland as a trespasser. [S]

(1A) In this section 'protected site' means—

(a) a nuclear site; or

(b) a designated site.

(1B) In this section 'nuclear site' means—

(a) so much of any premises in respect of which a nuclear site licence (within the meaning of the Nuclear Installations Act 1965) is for the time being in force as lies within the outer perimeter of the protection provided for those premises; and

(b) so much of any other premises of which premises falling within paragraph (a) form a part as lies within that outer perimeter.

(1C) For this purpose—

(a) the outer perimeter of the protection provided for any premises is the line of the outermost fences, walls or other obstacles provided or relied on for protecting those premises from intruders; and
(b) that line shall be determined on the assumption that every gate, door or other barrier across a way through a fence, wall or other obstacle is closed.

(2) A 'designated site' means a site—
(a) specified or described (in any way) in an order made by the Secretary of State, and
(b) designated for the purposes of this section by the order.

(3) The Secretary of State may only designate a site for the purposes of this section if—
(a) it is comprised in Crown land; or
(b) it is comprised in land belonging to Her Majesty in Her private capacity or to the immediate heir to the Throne in his private capacity; or
(c) it appears to the Secretary of State that it is appropriate to designate the site in the interests of national security.

(4) It is a defence for a person charged with an offence under this section to prove that he did not know, and had no reasonable cause to suspect, that the site in relation to which the offence is alleged to have been committed was a protected site.

(7) For the purposes of this section a person who is on any protected site as a trespasser does not cease to be a trespasser by virtue of being allowed time to leave the site.

(8) In this section—
(a) 'site' means the whole or part of any building or buildings, or any land, or both;
(b) 'Crown land' means land in which there is a Crown interest or a Duchy interest.

(9) For this purpose—

'Crown interest' means an interest belonging to Her Majesty in right of the Crown, and

'Duchy interest' means an interest belonging to Her Majesty in right of the Duchy of Lancaster or belonging to the Duchy of Cornwall.

Criminal Justice and immigration Act 2008

119 Offence of causing nuisance or disturbance on NHS premises

(1) A person commits an offence if—
(a) the person causes, without reasonable excuse and while on NHS premises, a nuisance or disturbance to an NHS staff member who is working there or is otherwise there in connection with work,
(b) the person refuses, without reasonable excuse, to leave the NHS premises when asked to do so by a constable or an NHS staff member, and
(c) the person is not on the NHS premises for the purpose of obtaining medical advice, treatment or care for himself or herself. [S]

(3) For the purposes of this section—
(a) a person ceases to be on NHS premises for the purpose of obtaining medical advice, treatment or care for himself or herself once the person has received the advice, treatment or care, and
(b) a person is not on NHS premises for the purpose of obtaining medical advice, treatment or care for himself or herself if the person has been refused the advice, treatment or care during the last 8 hours.

(b) Invasion of Privacy

Rehabilitation of Offenders Act 1974

9 Unauthorized disclosure of spent convictions

(1) In this section—

'official record' means a record kept for the purposes of its functions by any court, police force, Government department, local or other public authority in Great Britain, or a record kept, in Great Britain or elsewhere, for the purposes of any of Her Majesty's forces, being in either case a record containing information about persons convicted of offences; and

'specified information' means information imputing that a named or otherwise identifiable rehabilitated living person has committed or been charged with or prosecuted for or convicted of or sentenced for any offence which is the subject of a spent conviction.

(2) Subject to the provisions of any order made under subsection (5) below, any person who, in the course of his official duties, has or at any time has had custody of or access to any official record or the information contained therein, shall be guilty of an offence if, knowing or having reasonable cause to suspect that any specified information he has obtained in the course of those duties is specified information, he discloses it, otherwise than in the course of those duties, to another person. [S]

(3) in any proceedings for an offence under subsection (2) above it shall be a defence for the defendant (or, in Scotland, the accused person) to show that the disclosure was made—

- (a) to the rehabilitated person or to another person at the express request of the rehabilitated person; or
- (b) to a person whom he reasonably believed to be the rehabilitated person or to another person at the express request of a person whom he reasonably believed to be the rehabilitated person.

(4) Any person who obtains any specified information from any official record by means of any fraud, dishonesty or bribe shall be guilty of an offence.

Data Protection Act 1998

1 Basic interpretative provisions

(1) In this Act, unless the context otherwise requires—

'data' means information which—

- (a) is being processed by means of equipment operating automatically in response to instructions given for that purpose,
- (b) is recorded with the intention that it should be processed by means of such equipment,
- (c) is recorded as part of a relevant filing system or with the intention that it should form part of a relevant filing system, or
- (d) does not fall within paragraph (a), (b) or (c) but forms part of an accessible record as defined by section 68;

'data controller' means, subject to subsection (4), a person who (either alone or jointly or in common with other persons) determines the purposes for which and the manner in which any personal data are, or are to be, processed;

'data processor', in relation to personal data, means any person (other than an employee of the data controller) who processes the data on behalf of the data controller;

'data subject' means an individual who is the subject of personal data;

'personal data' means data which relate to a living individual who can be identified—

- (a) from those data, or

(b) from those data and other information which is in the possession of, or is likely to come into the possession of, the data controller,

and includes any expression of opinion about the individual and any indication of the intentions of the data controller or any other person in respect of the individual;

'processing', in relation to information or data, means obtaining, recording or holding the information or data or carrying out any operation or set of operations on the information or data, including—

(a) organisation, adaptation or alteration of the information or data,

(b) retrieval, consultation or use of the information or data,

(c) disclosure of the information or data by transmission, dissemination or otherwise making available, or

(d) alignment, combination, blocking, erasure or destruction of the information or data;

'relevant filing system' means any set of information relating to individuals to the extent that, although the information is not processed by means of equipment operating automatically in response to instructions given for that purpose, the set is structured, either by reference to individuals or by reference to criteria relating to individuals, in such a way that specific information relating to a particular individual is readily accessible.

(3) In determining for the purposes of this Act whether any information is recorded with the intention—

(a) that it should be processed by means of equipment operating automatically in response to instructions given for that purpose, or

(b) that it should form part of a relevant filing system,

it is immaterial that it is intended to be so processed or to form part of such a system only after being transferred to a country or territory outside the European Economic Area.

(4) Where personal data are processed only for purposes for which they are required by or under any enactment to be processed, the person on whom the obligation to process the data is imposed by or under that enactment is for the purposes of this Act the data controller.

55 Unlawful obtaining etc. of personal data

(1) A person must not knowingly or recklessly, without the consent of the data controller—

(a) obtain or disclose personal data or the information contained in personal data, or

(b) procure the disclosure to another person of the information contained in personal data.

(2) Subsection (1) does not apply to a person who shows—

(a) that the obtaining, disclosing or procuring—

(i) was necessary for the purpose of preventing or detecting crime, or

(ii) was required or authorised by or under any enactment, by any rule of law or by the order of a court,

(b) that he acted in the reasonable belief that he had in law the right to obtain or disclose the data or information or, as the case may be, to procure the disclosure of the information to the other person,

(c) that he acted in the reasonable belief that he would have had the consent of the data controller if the data controller had known of the obtaining, disclosing or procuring and the circumstances of it,

(ca) that he acted—

(i) for the special purposes,

(ii) with a view to the publication by any person of any journalistic, literary or artistic material, and

(iii) in the reasonable belief that in the particular circumstances the obtaining, disclosing or procuring was justified as being in the public interest, or

(d) that in the particular circumstances the obtaining, disclosing or procuring was justified as being in the public interest.

(3) A person who contravenes subsection (1) is guilty of an offence. [E]

(4) A person who sells personal data is guilty of an offence if he has obtained the data in contravention of subsection (1). [E]

(5) A person who offers to sell personal data is guilty of an offence if—

(a) he has obtained the data in contravention of subsection (1), or

(b) he subsequently obtains the data in contravention of that subsection. [E]

(6) For the purposes of subsection (5), an advertisement indicating that personal data are or may be for sale is an offer to sell the data.

(7) . . . for the purposes of subsections (4) to (6), 'personal data' includes information extracted from personal data.

56 Prohibition of requirement as to production of certain records

(1) A person must not, in connection with—

(a) the recruitment of another person as an employee,

(b) the continued employment of another person, or

(c) any contract for the provision of services to him by another person,

require that other person or a third party to supply him with a relevant record or to produce a relevant record to him.

(2) A person concerned with the provision (for payment or not) of goods, facilities or services to the public or a section of the public must not, as a condition of providing or offering to provide any goods, facilities or services to another person, require that other person or a third party to supply him with a relevant record or to produce a relevant record to him.

(3) Subsections (1) and (2) do not apply to a person who shows—

(a) that the imposition of the requirement was required or authorised by or under any enactment, by any rule of law or by the order of a court, or

(b) that in the particular circumstances the imposition of the requirement was justified as being in the public interest.

(4) Having regard to the provisions of Part V of the [1997 c. 50.] Police Act 1997 (certificates of criminal records etc.), the imposition of the requirement referred to in subsection (1) or (2) is not to be regarded as being justified as being in the public interest on the ground that it would assist in the prevention or detection of crime.

(5) A person who contravenes subsection (1) or (2) is guilty of an offence. [E]

(6) In this section 'a relevant record' means any record which—

(a) has been or is to be obtained by a data subject from any data controller specified in the first column of the Table below in the exercise of the right conferred by section 7, and

(b) contains information relating to any matter specified in relation to that data controller in the second column,

and includes a copy of such a record or a part of such a record.

Regulation of Investigatory Powers Act 2000

1 Unlawful interception

(1) It shall be an offence for a person intentionally and without lawful authority to intercept, at any place in the United Kingdom, any communication in the course of its transmission by means of—

(a) a public postal service; or

(b) a public telecommunication system. [E]

(2) It shall be an offence for a person—

(a) intentionally and without lawful authority, and

(b) otherwise than in circumstances in which his conduct is excluded by subsection (6) from criminal liability under this subsection,

to intercept, at any place in the United Kingdom, any communication in the course of its transmission by means of a private telecommunication system. [E]

. . .

(5) Conduct has lawful authority for the purposes of this section if, and only if—

(a) it is authorised by or under section 3 or 4;
(b) it takes place in accordance with a warrant under section 5 ('an interception warrant'); or
(c) it is in exercise, in relation to any stored communication, of any statutory power that is exercised (apart from this section) for the purpose of obtaining information or of taking possession of any document or other property;

and conduct (whether or not prohibited by this section) which has lawful authority for the purposes of this section by virtue of paragraph (a) or (b) shall also be taken to be lawful for all other purposes.

(6) The circumstances in which a person makes an interception of a communication in the course of its transmission by means of a private telecommunication system are such that his conduct is excluded from criminal liability under subsection (2) if—

(a) he is a person with a right to control the operation or the use of the system; or
(b) he has the express or implied consent of such a person to make the interception.

2 Meaning and location of 'interception', etc.

(1) In this Act—

'postal service' means any service which—

(a) consists in the following, or in any one or more of them, namely, the collection, sorting, conveyance, distribution and delivery (whether in the United Kingdom or elsewhere) of postal items; and
(b) is offered or provided as service the main purpose of which, or one of the main purposes of which, is to make available, or to facilitate, a means of transmission from place to place of postal items containing communications;

'private telecommunication system' means any telecommunication system which, without itself being a public telecommunication system, is a system in relation to which the following conditions are satisfied—

(a) it is attached. directly or indirectly and whether or not for the purposes of the communication in question, to a public telecommunication system; and
(b) there is apparatus comprised in the system which is both located in the United Kingdom and used (with or without other apparatus) for making the attachment to the public telecommunication system;

'public postal service' means any postal service which is offered or provided to, or to a substantial section of, the public in any one or more parts of the United Kingdom;

'public telecommunications service' means any telecommunications service which is offered or provided to, or to a substantial section of, the public in any one or more parts of the United Kingdom;

'public telecommunication system' means any such parts of a telecommunication system by means of which any public telecommunications service is provided as are located in the United Kingdom;

'telecommunications service' means any service that consists in the provision of access to, and of facilities for making use of, any telecommunication system (whether or not one provided by the person providing the service); and

'telecommunication system' means any system (including the apparatus comprised in it) which exists (whether wholly or partly in the United Kingdom or elsewhere) for the purpose of facilitating the transmission of communications by any means involving the use of electrical or electromagnetic energy.

(2) For the purposes of this Act, but subject to the following provisions of this section, a person intercepts a communication in the course of its transmission by means of a telecommunication system if, an only if, he—

(a) so modifies or interferes with the system, or its operation,
(b) so monitors transmissions made by means of the system, or
(c) so monitors transmissions made by wireless telegraphy to or from apparatus comprised in the system,

as to make some or all of the contents of the communication available, while being transmitted, to a person other than the sender or intended recipient of the communication.

(3) References in this Act to the interception of a communication do not include references to the interception of any communication broadcast for general reception.

(4) For the purposes of this Act the interception of a communication takes place in the United Kingdom if, and only if, the modification, interference or monitoring or, in the case of a postal item, the interception is effected by conduct within the United Kingdom and the communication is either—

(a) intercepted in the course of its transmission by means of a public postal service or public telecommunication system; or

(b) intercepted in the course of its transmission by means of a private telecommunication system in a case in which the sender or intended recipient of the communication is in the United Kingdom.

(5) References in this Act to the interception of a communication in the course of its transmission by means of a postal service or telecommunication system do not include references to—

(a) any conduct that takes place in relation only to so much of the communication as consists in any traffic data comprised in or attached to a communication (whether by the sender or otherwise) for the purposes of any postal service or telecommunication system by means of which it is being or may be transmitted; or

(b) any such conduct, in connection with conduct falling within paragraph (a), as gives a person who is neither the sender nor the intended recipient only so much access to a communication as is necessary for the purpose of identifying traffic data so comprised or attached.

(6) For the purposes of this section references to the modification of a telecommunication system include references to the attachment of any apparatus to, or other modification of or interference with—

(a) any part of the system; or

(b) any wireless telegraphy apparatus used for making transmissions to or from apparatus comprised in the system.

(7) For the purposes of this section the times while a communication is being transmitted by means of a telecommunication system shall be taken to include any time when the system by means of which the communication is being, or has been, transmitted is used for storing it in a manner that enables the intended recipient to collect it or otherwise to have access to it.

(8) For the purposes of this section the cases in which any contents of a communication are to be taken to be made available to a person while being transmitted shall include any case in which any of the contents of the communication, while being transmitted, are diverted or recorded so as to be available to a person subsequently.

(9) In this section 'traffic data', in relation to any communication, means—

(a) any data identifying, or purporting to identify, any person, apparatus or location to or from which the communication is or may be transmitted,

(b) any data identifying or selecting, or purporting to identify or select, apparatus through which, or by means of which, the communication is or may be transmitted,

(c) any data comprising signals for the actuation of apparatus used for the purposes of a telecommunication system for effecting (in whole or in part) the transmission of any communication, and

(d) any data identifying the data or other data as data comprised in or attached to a particular communication,

but that expression includes data identifying a computer file or computer program access to which is obtained, or which is run, by means of the communication to the extent only that the file or program is identified by reference to the apparatus in which it is stored.

(10) In this section—

(a) references, in relation to traffic data comprising signals for the actuation of apparatus, to a telecommunication system by means of which a communication is being or may be transmitted include references to any telecommunication system in which that apparatus is comprised; and

(b) references to traffic data being attached to a communication include references to the data and the communication being logically associated with each other;

and in this section 'data', in relation to a postal item, means anything written on the outside of the item.

(11) In this section 'postal item' means any letter, postcard or other such thing in writing as may be used by the sender for imparting information to the recipient, or any packet or parcel.

3 Lawful interception without an interception warrant

(1) Conduct by any person consisting in the interception of a communication is authorised by this section if the communication is one which, or which that person has reasonable grounds for believing, is both—

(a) a communication sent by a person who has consented to the interception; and
(b) a communication the intended recipient of which has so consented.

(2) Conduct by any person consisting in the interception of a communication is authorised by this section if—

(a) the communication is one sent by, or intended for, a person who has consented to the interception; and
(b) surveillance by means of that interception has been authorised under Part II.

(3) Conduct consisting in the interception of a communication is authorised by this section if—

(a) it is conduct by or on behalf of a person who provides a postal service or a telecommunications service; and
(b) it takes place for purposes connected with the provision or operation of that service or with the enforcement, in relation to that service, of any enactment relating to the use of postal services or telecommunications services.

(4) Conduct by any person consisting in the interception of a communication in the course of its transmission by means of wireless telegraphy is authorised by this section if it takes place—

(a) with the authority of a designated person under section 48 of the Wireless Telegraphy Act 2006 (interception and disclosure of wireless telegraphy messages); and
(b) for purposes connected with anything falling within subsection (5).

(5) Each of the following falls within this subsection—

(a) the grant of wireless telegraphy licences under the Wireless Telegraphy Act 2006;
(b) the prevention or detection of anything which constitutes interference with wireless telegraphy; and
(c) the enforcement of
 (i) any provision of Part 2 (other than Chapter 2 and sections 27 to 31) or Part 3 of that Act, or
 (ii) any enactment not falling within sub-paragraph (i),

that relates to such interference.

4 Power to provide for lawful interception

(1) Conduct by any person ('the interceptor') consisting in the interception of a communication in the course of its transmission by means of a telecommunication system is authorised by this section if—

(a) the interception is carried out for the purpose of obtaining information about the communications of a person who, or who the interceptor has reasonable grounds for believing, is in a country or territory outside the United Kingdom;
(b) the interception relates to the use of a telecommunications service provided to persons in that country or territory which is either—
 (i) a public telecommunications service; or
 (ii) a telecommunications service that would be a public telecommunications service if the persons to whom it is offered or provided were members of the public in a part of the United Kingdom;
(c) the person who provides that service (whether the interceptor or another person) is required by the law of that country or territory to carry out, secure or facilitate the interception in question;

(d) the situation is one in relation to which such further conditions as may be prescribed by regulations made by the Secretary of State are required to be satisfied before conduct may be treated as authorised by virtue of this subsection; and

(e) the conditions so prescribed are satisfied in relation to that situation.

19 Offence for unauthorised disclosures

(1) Where an interception warrant has been issued or renewed, it shall be the duty of every person falling within subsection (2) to keep secret all the matters mentioned in subsection (3).

(2) The persons falling within this subsection are—

(a) the persons specified in section 6(2);

(b) every person holding office under the Crown;

(c) every member of the staff of the Serious Organised Crime Agency;

(e) every person employed by or for the purposes of a police force;

(f) persons providing postal services or employed for the purposes of any business of providing such a service;

(g) persons providing public telecommunications services or employed for the purposes of any business of providing such a service;

(h) persons having control of the whole or any part of a telecommunication system located wholly or partly in the United Kingdom.

(3) Those matters are—

(a) the existence and contents of the warrant and of any section 8(4) certificate in relation to the warrant;

(b) the details of the issue of the warrant and of any renewal or modification of the warrant or of any such certificate;

(c) the existence and contents of any requirement to provide assistance with giving effect to the warrant;

(d) the steps taken in pursuance of the warrant or of any such requirement; and

(e) everything in the intercepted material, together with any related communications data.

(4) A person who makes a disclosure to another of anything that he is required to keep secret under this section shall be guilty of an offence.... [E]

(5) In proceedings against any person for an offence under this section in respect of any disclosure, it shall be a defence for that person to show that he could not reasonably have been expected, after first becoming aware of the matter disclosed, to take steps to prevent the disclosure.

(6) In proceedings against any person for an offence under this section in respect of any disclosure, it shall be a defence for that person to show that—

(a) the disclosure was made by or to a professional legal adviser in connection with the giving, by the adviser to any client of his, of advice about the effect of provisions of this Chapter; and

(b) the person to whom or, as the case may be, by whom it was made was the client or a representative of the client.

(7) In proceedings against any person for an offence under this section in respect of any disclosure, it shall be a defence for that person to show that the disclosure was made by a legal adviser—

(a) in contemplation of, or in connection with, any legal proceedings; and

(b) for the purposes of those proceedings.

(8) Neither subsection (6) nor subsection (7) applies in the case of a disclosure made with a view to furthering any criminal purpose.

(9) In proceedings against any person for an offence under this section in respect of any disclosure, it shall be a defence for that person to show that the disclosure was confined to a disclosure made to the Interception of Communications Commissioner or authorised—

(a) by that Commissioner;

(b) by the warrant or the person to whom the warrant is or was addressed;

(c) by the terms of the requirement to provide assistance; or

(d) by section 11(9).

Sexual Offences Act 2003

67 Voyeurism

(1) A person commits an offence if—

(a) for the purpose of obtaining sexual gratification, he observes another person doing a private act, and

(b) he knows that the other person does not consent to being observed for his sexual gratification.

(2) A person commits an offence if—

(a) he operates equipment with the intention of enabling another person to observe, for the purpose of obtaining sexual gratification, a third person (B) doing a private act, and

(b) he knows that B does not consent to his operating equipment with that intention.

(3) A person commits an offence if—

(a) he records another person (B) doing a private act,

(b) he does so with the intention that he or a third person will, for the purpose of obtaining sexual gratification, look at an image of B doing the act, and

(c) he knows that B does not consent to his recording the act with that intention.

(4) A person commits an offence if he installs equipment, or constructs or adapts a structure or part of a structure, with the intention of enabling himself or another person to commit an offence under subsection (1). [E]

68 Voyeurism: interpretation

(1) For the purposes of section 67, a person is doing a private act if the person is in a place which, in the circumstances, would reasonably be expected to provide privacy, and—

(a) the person's genitals, buttocks or breasts are exposed or covered only with underwear,

(b) the person is using a lavatory, or

(c) the person is doing a sexual act that is not of a kind ordinarily done in public.

(2) In section 67, 'structure' includes a tent, vehicle or vessel or other temporary or movable structure.

Wireless Telegraphy Act 2006

48 Interception and disclosure of messages

(1) A person commits an offence if, otherwise than under the authority of a designated person—

(a) he uses wireless telegraphy apparatus with intent to obtain information as to the contents, sender or addressee of a message (whether sent by means of wireless telegraphy or not) of which neither he nor a person on whose behalf he is acting is an intended recipient, or

(b) he discloses information as to the contents, sender or addressee of such a message. [S]

(2) A person commits an offence under this section consisting in the disclosure of information only if the information disclosed by him is information that would not have come to his knowledge but for the use of wireless telegraphy apparatus by him or by another person.

(3) A person does not commit an offence under this section consisting in the disclosure of information if he discloses the information in the course of legal proceedings or for the purpose of a report of legal proceedings.

(5) 'Designated person' means—

(a) the Secretary of State;

(b) the Commissioners for Her Majesty's Revenue and Customs; or

(c) any other person designated for the purposes of this section by regulations made by the Secretary of State.

Part X

Offensive Conduct

(a) Bigamy

Offences Against the Person Act 1861

57 Bigamy

Whosoever, being married, shall marry any other person during the life of the former husband or wife, whether the second marriage shall have taken place in England or Ireland or elsewhere, shall be guilty of felony, and being convicted thereof shall be liable to be kept in penal servitude for any term not exceeding seven years . . . : Provided, that nothing in this section contained shall extend to any second marriage contracted elsewhere than in England and Ireland by any other than a subject of Her Majesty, or to any person marrying a second time whose husband or wife shall have been continually absent from such person for the space of seven years then last past, and shall not have been known by such person to be living within that time, or shall extend to any person who, at the time of such second marriage, shall have been divorced from the bond of the first marriage, or to any person whose former marriage shall have been declared void by the sentence of any court of competent jurisdiction. [E]

Perjury Act 1911

3 False statements, etc., with reference to marriage

(1) If any person—

(a) for the purpose of procuring a marriage, or a certificate or licence for marriage, knowingly and wilfully makes a false oath, or makes or signs a false declaration, notice or certificate required under any Act of Parliament for the time being in force relating to marriage; or

(b) knowingly and wilfully makes, or knowingly and wilfully causes to be made, for the purpose of being inserted in any register of marriage, a false statement as to any particular required by law to be known and registered relating to any marriage; or

(c) forbids the issue of any certificate or licence for marriage by falsely representing himself to be a person whose consent to the marriage is required by law knowing such representation to be false, or

(d) with respect to a declaration made under section 16(1A) or 27B(2) of the Marriage Act 1949—

(i) enters a caveat under subsection (2) of the said section 16, or

(ii) makes a statement mentioned in subsection (4) of the said section 27B, which he knows to be false in a material particular, he shall be guilty of a misdemeanour, and, on conviction thereof on indictment shall be liable to penal servitude for a term not exceeding seven years. [I]

Forgery Act 1861

36 Destroying, injuring, forging, or falsifying registers of births, baptisms, marriages, deaths, or burials, or certified copies

Whosoever shall unlawfully destroy, deface, or injure, or cause or permit to be destroyed, defaced, or injured, any register of births, baptisms, marriages, deaths, or burials which now is or hereafter shall be by law authorised or required to be kept in England or Ireland, or any part of any such register, or any certified copy of any such register, or any part thereof, . . . or shall knowingly and unlawfully insert or cause or permit to be inserted in any such register, or in any certified copy thereof, any false entry of any matter relating to any birth, baptism, marriage, death, or burial, or shall knowingly and unlawfully give any false certificate relating to any birth, baptism, marriage, death, or burial, or shall certify any writing to be a copy or extract from any such register, knowing such writing, or the part of such register whereof such copy or extract shall be so given, to be false in any material particular . . . or shall offer, utter, dispose of, or put off any such register, entry, certified copy, certificate, . . . knowing the same to be false, . . . or shall offer, utter, dispose of, or put off any copy of any entry in any such register, knowing such entry to be false, . . . shall be guilty of felony, and being convicted thereof, shall be liable . . . to be kept in penal servitude for life . . . [I]

37 Making false entries in copies of registers of baptisms, marriages, or burials, directed to be sent to any registrar, or destroying or concealing copies of registers

Whosoever shall knowingly and wilfully insert or cause or permit to be inserted in any copy of any register directed or required by law to be transmitted to any registrar or other officer any false entry of any matter relating to any baptism, marriage, or burial . . . or shall knowingly and wilfully sign or verify any copy of any register so directed or required to be transmitted as aforesaid, which copy shall be false in any part thereof, knowing the same to be false, or shall unlawfully destroy, deface, or injure, or shall for any fraudulent purpose take from its place of deposit, or conceal, any such copy of any register, shall be guilty of felony, and being convicted thereof shall be liable . . . to be kept in penal servitude for life . . . [I]

(b) Surrogacy

Surrogacy Arrangements Act 1985

1 Meaning of 'surrogate mother', 'surrogacy arrangement' and other terms

(1) The following provisions shall have effect for the interpretation of this Act.

(2) 'Surrogate mother' means a woman who carries a child in pursuance of an arrangement—

(a) made before she began to carry the child, and

(b) made with a view to any child carried in pursuance of it being handed over to, and parental responsibility being met (so far as practicable) by, another person or other persons.

(3) An arrangement is a surrogacy arrangement if, were a woman to whom the arrangement relates to carry a child in pursuance of it, she would be a surrogate mother.

(4) In determining whether an arrangement is made with such a view as is mentioned in subsection (1) above regard may be had to the circumstances as a whole (and, in particular, where there is a promise or understanding that any payment will or may be made to the woman or for her

benefit in respect of the carrying of any child in pursuance of the arrangement, to that promise or understanding).

(5) An arrangement may be regarded as made with such a view though subject to conditions relating to the handing over of any child.

(6) A woman who carries a child is to be treated for the purposes of subsection (2)(a) above as beginning to carry it at the time of the insemination or of the placing in her of an embryo, of an egg in the process of fertilisation, or of sperm and eggs, as the case may be, that results in her carrying the child.

(7) 'Body of persons' means a body of persons corporate or unincorporate.

(8) 'Payment' means payment in money or money's worth.

(9) This Act applies to arrangements whether or not they are lawful.

2 Negotiating surrogacy arrangements on a commercial basis, etc.

(1) No person shall on a commercial basis do any of the following acts in the United Kingdom, that is—

- (a) initiate or take part in any negotiations with a view to the making of a surrogacy arrangement.
- (b) offer or agree to negotiate the making of a surrogacy arrangement, or
- (c) compile any information with a view to its use in making, or negotiating the making of, surrogacy arrangements;

and no person shall in the United Kingdom knowingly cause another to do any of those acts on a commercial basis.

(2) A person who contravenes subsection (1) above is guilty of an offence; but it is not a contravention of that subsection—

- (a) for a woman, with a view to becoming a surrogate mother herself, to do any act mentioned in that subsection or to cause such an act to be done, or
- (b) for any person, with a view to a surrogate mother carrying a child for him, to do such an act or to cause such an act to be done. [S]

(3) For the purpose of this section, a person does an act on a commercial basis (subject to subsection (4) below) if—

- (a) any payment is at any time received by himself or another in respect of it, or
- (b) he does it with a view to any payment being received by himself or another in respect of making, or negotiating or facilitating the making of, any surrogacy arrangement.

In this subsection 'payment' does not include payment to or for the benefit of a surrogate mother or prospective surrogate mother.

(4) In proceedings against a person for an offence under subsection (1) above, he is not to be treated as doing an act on a commercial basis by reason of any payment received by another in respect of the act if it is proved that—

- (a) in a case where the payment was received before he did the act, he did not do the act knowing or having reasonable cause to suspect that any payment had been received in respect of the act; and
- (b) in any other case, he did not do the act with a view to any payment being received in respect of it.

(5) Where—

- (a) a person acting on behalf of a body of persons takes any part in negotiating or facilitating the making of a surrogacy arrangement in the United Kingdom, and
- (b) negotiating or facilitating the making of surrogacy arrrangements is an activity of the body,

then, if the body at any time receives any payment made by or on behalf of—

- (i) a woman who carries a child in pursuance of the arrangement,
- (ii) the person or persons for whom she carries it, or
- (iii) any person connected with the woman or with that person or those persons,

the body is guilty of an offence. [S]

For the purposes of this subsection, a payment received by a person connected with a body is to be treated as received by the body.

(6) In proceeding against a body for an offence under subsection (5) above, it is a defence to prove that the payment concerned was not made in respect of the arrangement mentioned in paragraph (a) of the subsection

(7) A person who in the United Kingdom takes part in the management or control—

(a) of any body of persons, or

(b) of any of the activities of any body of persons, is guilty of an offence if the activity described in subsection (8) below is an activity of the body concerned.

(8) The activity referred to in subsection (7) above is negotiating or facilitating the making of surrogacy arrangements in the United Kingdom, being—

(a) arrangements the making of which is negotiated or facilitated on a commercial basis, or

(b) arrangements in the case of which payments are received (or treated for the purposes of subsection (5) above as received) by the body concerned in contravention of subsection (5) above.

(9) In proceedings against a person for an offence under subsection (7) above, it is a defence to prove that he neither knew nor had reasonable cause to suspect that the activity described in subsection (8) above was an activity of the body concerned; and for the purposes of such proceedings any arrangement falling within subsection (8)(b) above shall be disregarded if it is proved that the payment concerned was not made in respect of the arrangement.

3 Advertisement about surrogacy

(1) This section applies to any advertisement containing an indication (however expressed)—

(a) that any person is or may be willing to enter into a surrogacy arrangement or to negotiate or facilitate the making of a surrogacy arrangement, or

(b) that any person is looking for a woman willing to become a surrogate mother or for persons wanting a woman to carry a child as a surrogate mother.

(2) Where a newspaper or periodical containing an advertisement to which this section applies is published in the United Kingdom, any proprietor, editor or publisher of the newspaper or periodical is guilty of an offence. [S]

(3) Where an advertisement to which this section applies is conveyed by means of an electronic communication network so as to be seen or heard (or both) in the United Kingdom, any person who in the United Kingdom causes it to be so conveyed knowing it to contain such an indication as is mentioned in subsection (1) above is guilty of an offence. [S]

(4) A person who publishes or causes to be published in the United Kingdom an advertisement to which this section applies (not being an advertisement contained in a newspaper or periodical or conveyed by means of an electronic communication network) is guilty of an offence. [S]

(5) A person who distributes or causes to be distributed in the United Kingdom an advertisement to which this section applies (not being an advertisement contained in a newspaper or periodical published outside the United Kingdom or an advertisement conveyed by means of an electronic communication network) knowing it to contain such an indication as is mentioned in subsection (1) above is guilty of an offence. [S]

4 Offences

(3) Where an offence under this Act committed by a body corporate is proved to have been committed with the consent or connivance of, or to be attributable to any neglect on the part of, any director, manager, secretary or other similar officer of the body corporate or any person who was purporting to act in any such capacity, he as well as the body corporate is guilty of the offence and is liable to be proceeded against and punished accordingly.

(4) Where the affairs of a body corporate are managed by its members, subsection (3) above shall apply in relation to the acts and defaults of a member in connection with his functions of management as if he were a director of the body corporate.

(5) If any proceedings for an offence under section 2 of this Act, proof of things done or of words written, spoken or published (whether or not in the presence of any party to the proceedings) by any person taking part in the management or control of a body of persons or of any of the activities of the body, or by any person doing any of the acts mentioned in subsection (1)(a) to (c) of that section on behalf of the body, shall be admissible as evidence of the activities of the body.

(c) Medical Procedures

Human Fertilisation and Embryology Act 1990

1 Meaning of 'embryo', 'gamete' and associated expressions

(1) In this Act, except where otherwise stated—

(a) embryo means a live human embryo where fertilisation is complete, and

(b) references to an embryo include an egg in the process of fertilisation, and, for this purpose, fertilisation is not complete until the appearance of a two cell zygote.

(2) This Act, so far as it governs bringing about the creation of an embryo, applies only to bringing about the creation of an embryo outside the human body; and in this Act—

(a) references to embryos the creation of which was brought about in vitro (in their application to those where fertilisation is complete) are to those where fertilisation began outside the human body whether or not it was completed there, and

(b) references to embryos taken from a woman do not include embryos whose creation was brought about *in vitro*.

(3) This Act, so far as it governs the keeping or use of an embryo, applies only to keeping or using an embryo outside the human body.

(4) References in this Act to gametes, eggs or sperm, except where otherwise stated, are to live human gametes, eggs or sperm but references below in this Act to gametes or eggs do not include eggs in the process of fertilisation.

2 Other terms

(1) In this Act—...

'licence' means a licence under Schedule 2 to this Act and, in relation to a licence, 'the person responsible' has the meaning given by section 17 of this Act, and

'treatment services' means medical, surgical or obstetric services provided to the public or a section of the public for the purpose of assisting women to carry children.

(2) References in this Act to keeping, in relation to embryos or gametes, include keeping while preserved, whether preserved by cryopreservation or in any other way; and embryos or gametes so kept are referred to in this Act as 'stored' (and 'store' and 'storage' are to be interpreted accordingly).

(3) For the purposes of this Act, a woman is not to be treated as carrying a child until the embryo has become implanted.

3 Prohibitions in connection with embryos

(1) No person shall—

(a) bring about the creation of an embryo, or

(b) keep or use an embryo,

except in pursuance of a licence.

(2) No person shall place in a woman—

(a) a live embryo other than a human embryo, or

(b) any live gametes other than human gametes.

(3) A licence cannot authorise—

(a) keeping or using an embryo after the appearance of the primitive streak,

(b) placing an embryo in any animal,

(c) keeping or using an embryo in any circumstances in which regulations prohibit its keeping or use, or

(d) replacing a nucleus of a cell of an embryo with a nucleus taken from a cell of any person, embryo or subsequent development of an embryo.

(4) For the purposes of subsection (3)(a) above, the primitive streak is to be taken to have appeared in an embryo not later than the end of the period of 14 days beginning with the day when the gametes are mixed, not counting any time during which the embryo is stored.

3A Prohibition in connection with germ cells

(1) No person shall, for the purpose of providing fertility services for any woman, use female germ cells taken or derived from an embryo or a foetus or use embryos created by using such cells.

(2) In this section—

'female germ cells' means cells of the female germ line and includes such cells at any stage of maturity and accordingly includes eggs; and

'fertility services' means medical, surgical or obstetric services provided for the purpose of assisting women to carry children.

4 Prohibitions in connection with gametes

(1) No person shall—

(a) store any gametes, or

(b) in the course of providing treatment services for any woman, use the sperm of any man unless the services are being provided for the woman and the man together or use the eggs of any other woman, or

(c) mix gametes with the live gametes of any animal,

except in pursuance of a licence.

(2) A licence cannot authorise storing or using gametes in any circumstances in which regulations prohibit their storage or use.

(3) No person shall place sperm and eggs in a woman in any circumstances specified in regulations except in pursuance of a licence.

41 Offences

(1) A person who—

(a) contravenes section 3(2), 3A or 4(1)(c) of this Act, or

(b) does anything which, by virtue of section 3(3) of this Act, cannot be authorised by a licence,

is guilty of an offence . . . [I]

(2) A person who—

(a) contravenes section 3(1) of this Act, otherwise than by doing something which, by virtue of section 3(3) of this Act, cannot be authorised by a licence,

(b) keeps or uses any gametes in contravention of section 4(1)(a) or (b) of this Act,

(c) contravenes section 4(3) of this Act, or

(d) fails to comply with any directions given by virtue of section 24(7)(a) of this Act,

is guilty of an offence. [E]

Human Reproductive Cloning Act 2001

1 The offence

(1) A person who places in a woman a human embryo which has been created otherwise than by fertilisation is guilty of an offence. [I]

Human Tissue Act 2004

32 Prohibition of commercial dealings in human material for transplantation

(1) A person commits an offence if he—

(a) gives or receives a reward for the supply of, or for an offer to supply, any controlled material;

(b) seeks to find a person willing to supply any controlled material for reward;

(c) offers to supply any controlled material for reward;

(d) initiates or negotiates any arrangement involving the giving of a reward for the supply of, or for an offer to supply, any controlled material;

(e) takes part in the management or control of a body of persons corporate or unincorporate whose activities consist of or include the initiation or negotiation of such arrangements. [E]

(2) Without prejudice to subsection (1)(b) and (c), a person commits an offence if he causes to be published or distributed, or knowingly publishes or distributes, an advertisement—

(a) inviting persons to supply, or offering to supply, any controlled material for reward, or

(b) indicating that the advertiser is willing to initiate or negotiate any such arrangement as is mentioned in subsection (1)(d). [S]

(3) A person who engages in an activity to which subsection (1) or (2) applies does not commit an offence under that subsection if he is designated by the Authority as a person who may lawfully engage in the activity.

(6) For the purposes of subsections (1) and (2), payment in money or money's worth to the holder of a licence shall be treated as not being a reward where—

(a) it is in consideration for transporting, removing, preparing, preserving or storing controlled material, and

(b) its receipt by the holder of the licence is not expressly prohibited by the terms of the licence.

(7) References in subsections (1) and (2) to reward, in relation to the supply of any controlled material, do not include payment in money or money's worth for defraying or reimbursing—

(a) any expenses incurred in, or in connection with, transporting, removing, preparing, preserving or storing the material,

(b) any liability incurred in respect of—

(i) expenses incurred by a third party in, or in connection with, any of the activities mentioned in paragraph (a), or

(ii) a payment in relation to which subsection (6) has effect, or

(c) any expenses or loss of earnings incurred by the person from whose body the material comes so far as reasonably and directly attributable to his supplying the material from his body.

(8) For the purposes of this section, controlled material is any material which—

(a) consists of or includes human cells,

(b) is, or is intended to be removed, from a human body,

(c) is intended to be used for the purpose of transplantation, and

(d) is not of a kind excepted under subsection (9).

(9) The following kinds of material are excepted—

(a) gametes,

(b) embryos, and

(c) material which is the subject of property because of an application of human skill.

(10) Where the body of a deceased person is intended to be used to provide material which—

(a) consists of or includes human cells, and

(b) is not of a kind excepted under subsection (9),

for use for the purpose of transplantation, the body shall be treated as controlled material for the purposes of this section.

(11) In this section—

'advertisement' includes any form of advertising whether to the public generally, to any section of the public or individually to selected persons;

'reward' means any description of financial or other material advantage.

33 Restriction on transplants involving a live donor

(1) Subject to subsections (3) and (5), a person commits an offence if—

(a) he removes any transplantable material from the body of a living person intending that the material be used for the purpose of transplantation, and

(b) when he removes the material, he knows, or might reasonably be expected to know, that the person from whose body he removes the material is alive. [S]

(2) Subject to subsections (3) and (5), a person commits an offence if—

(a) he uses for the purpose of transplantation any transplantable material which has come from the body of a living person, and

(b) when he does so, he knows, or might reasonably be expected to know, that the transplantable material has come from the body of a living person. [S]

(3) The Secretary of State may by regulations provide that subsection (1) or (2) shall not apply in a case where—

(a) the Authority is satisfied—

(i) that no reward has been or is to be given in contravention of section 32, and

(ii) that such other conditions as are specified in the regulations are satisfied, and

(b) such other requirements as are specified in the regulations are complied with.

(4) Regulations under subsection (3) shall include provision for decisions of the Authority in relation to matters which fall to be decided by it under the regulations to be subject, in such circumstances as the regulations may provide, to reconsideration in accordance with such procedure as the regulations may provide.

(5) Where under subsection (3) an exception from subsection (1) or (2) is in force, a person does not commit an offence under that subsection if he reasonably believes that the exception applies.

(7) In this section—

'reward' has the same meaning as in section 32;

'transplantable material' means material of a description specified by regulations made by the Secretary of State.

49 Offences by bodies corporate

(1) Where an offence under this Act is committed by a body corporate and is proved to have been committed with the consent or connivance of or to be attributable to any neglect on the part of—

(a) any director, manager, secretary or other similar officer of the body corporate, or

(b) any person who was purporting to act in any such capacity,

he (as well as the body corporate) commits the offence and shall be liable to be proceeded against and punished accordingly.

(2) Where the affairs of a body corporate are managed by its members, subsection (1) applies in relation to the acts and defaults of a member in connection with his functions of management as if he were a director of the body corporate.

54 General interpretation

(2) In this Act—

(a) references to material from the body of a living person are to material from the body of a person alive at the point of separation, and

(b) references to material from the body of a deceased person are to material from the body of a person not alive at the point of separation.

(3) In this Act, references to transplantation are to transplantation to a human body and include transfusion.

(6) Subsections (1) and (4) of section 1 of the Human Fertilisation and Embryology Act 1990 (definitions of 'embryo' and 'gametes') have effect for the purposes of this Act as they have effect for the purposes of that Act (other than that section).

(7) For the purposes of this Act, material shall not be regarded as from a human body if it is created outside the human body.

(d) Sexual Acts

Sexual Offences Act 2003

64 Sex with an adult relative: penetration

(1) A person aged 16 or over (A) (subject to subsection (3A)) commits an offence if—

(a) he intentionally penetrates another person's vagina or anus with a part of his body or anything else, or penetrates another person's mouth with his penis,

(b) the penetration is sexual, and

(c) the other person (B) is aged 18 or over,

(d) A is related to B in a way mentioned in subsection (2), and

(e) A knows or could reasonably be expected to know that he is related to B in that way.

(2) The ways that A may be related to B are as parent, grandparent, child, grandchild, brother, sister, half-brother, half-sister, uncle, aunt, nephew or niece.

(3) In subsection (2)—

(za) 'parent' includes an adoptive parent;

(zb) 'child' includes an adopted person within the meaning of Chapter 4 of Part 1 of the Adoption and Children Act 2002;

(a) 'uncle' means the brother of a person's parent, and 'aunt' has a corresponding meaning;

(b) 'nephew' means the child of a person's brother or sister, and 'niece' has a corresponding meaning.

(3A) Where subsection (1) applies in a case where A is related to B as B's child by virtue of subsection (3)(zb), A does not commit an offence under this section unless A is 18 or over.

(4) Where in proceedings for an offence under this section it is proved that the defendant was related to the other person in any of those ways, it is to be taken that the defendant knew or could reasonably have been expected to know that he was related in that way unless sufficient evidence is adduced to raise an issue as to whether he knew or could reasonably have been expected to know that he was. [E]

(6) Nothing in—

(a) section 47 of the Adoption Act 1976 (which disapplies the status provisions in section 39 of that Act for the purposes of this section in relation to adoptions before 30 December 2005), or

(b) section 74 of the Adoption and Children Act 2002 (which disapplies the status provisions in section 67 of that Act for those purposes in relation to adoptions on or after that date),

is to be read as preventing the application of section 39 of the Adoption Act 1976 or section 67 of the Adoption and Children Act 2002 for the purposes of subsection (3)(za) and (zb) above.

65 Sex with an adult relative: consenting to penetration

(1) A person aged 16 or over (A) (subject to subsection (3A)) commits an offence if—

(a) another person (B) penetrates A's vagina or anus with a part of B's body or anything else, or penetrates A's mouth with B's penis,

(b) A consents to the penetration,

(c) the penetration is sexual,

(d) B is aged 18 or over,

(e) A is related to B in a way mentioned in subsection (2), and
(f) A knows or could reasonably be expected to know that he is related to B in that way.

(2) The ways that A may be related to B are as parent, grandparent, child, grandchild, brother, sister, half-brother, half-sister,uncle, aunt, nephew or niece.

(3) In subsection (2)—
(za) 'parent' includes an adoptive parent;
(zb) 'child' includes an adopted person within the meaning of Chapter 4 of Part 1 of the Adoption and Children Act 2002;
(a) 'uncle' means the brother of a person's parent, and 'aunt' has a corresponding meaning;
(b) 'nephew' means the child of a person's brother or sister, and 'niece' has a corresponding meaning.

(3A) Where subsection (1) applies in a case where A is related to B as B's child by virtue of subsection (3)(zb), A does not commit an offence under this section unless A is 18 or over.

(4) Where in proceedings for an offence under this section it is proved that the defendant was related to the other person in any of those ways, it is to be taken that the defendant knew or could reasonably have been expected to know that he was related in that way unless sufficient evidence is adduced to raise an issue as to whether he knew or could reasonably have been expected to know that he was. [E]

(6) Nothing in—
(a) section 47 of the Adoption Act 1976 (which disapplies the status provisions in section 39 of that Act for the purposes of this section in relation to adoptions before 30 December 2005), or
(b) section 74 of the Adoption and Children Act 2002 (which disapplies the status provisions in section 67 of that Act for those purposes in relation to adoptions on or after that date), is to be read as preventing the application of section 39 of the Adoption Act 1976 or section 67 of the Adoption and Children Act 2002 for the purposes of subsection (3)(za) and (zb) above.

69 Intercourse with an animal

(1) A person commits an offence if—
(a) he intentionally performs an act of penetration with his penis,
(b) what is penetrated is the vagina or anus of a living animal, and
(c) he knows that, or is reckless as to whether, that is what is penetrated.

(2) A person (A) commits an offence if—
(a) A intentionally causes, or allows, A's vagina or anus to be penetrated,
(b) the penetration is by the penis of a living animal, and
(c) A knows that, or is reckless as to whether, that is what A is being penetrated by. [E]

70 Sexual penetration of a corpse

(1) A person commits an offence if—
(a) he intentionally performs an act of penetration with a part of his body or anything else,
(b) what is penetrated is a part of the body of a dead person,
(c) he knows that, or is reckless as to whether, that is what is penetrated, and
(d) the penetration is sexual. [E]

71 Sexual activity in a public lavatory

(1) A person commits an offence if—
(a) he is in a lavatory to which the public or a section of the public has or is permitted to have access, whether on payment or otherwise,
(b) he intentionally engages in an activity, and,
(c) the activity is sexual.

(2) For the purposes of this section, an activity is sexual if a reasonable person would, in all the circumstances but regardless of any person's purpose, consider it to be sexual. [S]

74 'Consent'

[See page 47]

75 Evidential presumption about consent
[See page 47]

78 'Sexual'
[See page 48]

79 General interpretation
[See page 48]

(e) Prostitution

Sexual Offences Act 2003

47 Paying for sexual services of a child
[See page 75]

48 Causing or inciting child prostitution or pornography
[See page 75]

49 Controlling a child prostitute or a child involved in pornography
[See page 75]

50 Arranging or facilitating child prostitution or pornography
[See page 75]

51 Sections 48–50: interpretation
[See page 75]

52 Causing or inciting prostitution for gain
(1) A person commits an offence if—
- (a) he intentionally causes or incites another person to become a prostitute in any part of the world, and
- (b) he does so for or in the expectation of gain for himself or a third person. [E]

53 Controlling prostitution for gain
(1) A person commits an offence if—
- (a) he intentionally controls any of the activities of another person relating to that person's prostitution in any part of the world, and
- (b) he does so for or in the expectation of gain for himself or a third person. [E]

57 Trafficking into the UK for sexual exploitation
(1) A person commits an offence if, he intentionally arranges or facilitates the arrival or the entry into the United Kingdom of another person (B) and either—
- (a) he intends to do anything to or in respect of B, after B's arrival but in any part of the world, which if done will involve the commission of a relevant offence, or
- (b) he believes that another person is likely to do something to or in respect of B, after B's arrival but in any part of the world, which if done will involve the commission of a relevant offence. [E]

58 Trafficking within the UK for sexual exploitation
(1) A person (A) commits an offence if he intentionally arranges or facilitates travel within the United Kingdom by another person (B) and either—
- (a) he intends to do anything to or in respect of B, during or after the journey and in any part of the world, which if done will involve the commission of a relevant offence, or

(b) he believes that another person is likely to do something to or in respect of B, during or after the journey and in any part of the world, which if done will involve the commission of a relevant offence. [E]

59 Trafficking out of the UK for sexual exploitation

(1) A person (A) commits an offence if he intentionally arranges or facilitates the departure from the United Kingdom of another person (B) and either—

(a) he intends to do anything to or in respect of B, after B's departure but in any part of the world, which if done will involve the commission of a relevant offence, or

(b) he believes that another person is likely to do something to or in respect of B during or after of the journey and in any part of the world, which if done will involve the commission of a relevant offence. [E]

60 Sections 57 to 59: interpretation and jurisdiction

(1) In sections 57 to 59—

'relevant offence' means—

(a) an offence under this [Act],

(b) an offence under section 1(1)(a) of the Protection of Children Act 1978,

(e) anything done outside England and Wales and Northern Ireland which is not an offence within any of paragraphs (a) to (d) but would be if done in England and Wales or Northern Ireland;

(2) Sections 57 to 59 apply to anything done whether inside or outside the United Kingdom.

62 Committing an offence with intent to commit a sexual offence

[See page 46]

63 Trespass with intent to commit a sexual offence

[See page 230]

78 'Sexual'

[See page 48]

79 General interpretation

[See page 48]

Sexual Offences Act 1956

33 Keeping a brothel

It is an offence for a person to keep a brothel, or to manage, or act or assist in the management of, a brothel. [S]

33A Keeping a brothel used for prostitution

(1) It is an offence for a person to keep, or to manage, or act or assist in the management of, a brothel to which people resort for practices involving prostitution (whether or not also for other practices).

(2) In this section 'prostitution' has the meaning given by section 51(2) of the Sexual Offences Act 2003. [E]

34 Landlord letting premises for use as brothel

It is an offence for the lessor or landlord of any premises or his agent to let the whole or part of the premises with the knowledge that it is to be used, in whole or in part, as a brothel, or where the whole or part of the premises is used as a brothel, to be wilfully a party to that use continuing. [S]

35 Tenant permitting premises to be used as a brothel

(1) It is an offence for the tenant or occupier, or person in charge, of any premises knowingly to permit the whole or part of the premises to be used as a brothel. [S]

(2) Where the tenant or occupier of any premises is convicted (whether under this section or, for an offence committed before the commencement of this Act, under section thirteen of the Criminal Law Amendment Act, 1885) of knowingly permitting the whole or part of the premises to be used as a brothel, the First Schedule to this Act shall apply to enlarge the rights of the lessor or landlord with respect to the assignment or determination of the lease or other contract under which the premises are held by the person convicted.

(3) Where the tenant or occupier of any premises is so convicted, or was so convicted under the said section thirteen before the commencement of this Act, and either—

- (a) the lessor or landlord, after having the conviction brought to his notice, fails or failed to exercise his statutory rights in relation to the lease or contract under which the premises are or were held by the person convicted; or
- (b) the lessor or landlord, after exercising his statutory rights so as to determine that lease or contract, grants or granted a new lease or enters or entered into a new contract of tenancy of the premises to, with or for the benefit of the same person, without having all reasonable provisions to prevent the recurrence of the offence inserted in the new lease or contract;

then, if subsequently an offence under this section is committed in respect of the premises during the subsistence of the lease or contract referred to in paragraph (a) of this subsection or (where paragraph (b) applies) during the subsistence of the new lease or contract, the lessor or landlord shall be deemed to be a party to that offence unless he shows that he took all reasonable steps to prevent the recurrence of the offence.

36 Tenant permitting premises to be used for prostitution

It is an offence for the tenant or occupier of any premises knowingly to permit the whole or part of the premises to be used for the purposes of habitual prostitution (whether any prostitute involved is male or female). [S]

Sexual Offences Act 1967

6 Premises resorted to for homosexual practices

Premises shall be treated for purposes of section 33 to 35 of the Act of 1956 as a brothel if people resort to it for the purpose of lewd homosexual practices in circumstances in which resort thereto for lewd heterosexual practices would have led to its being treated as a brothel for the purposes of those sections.

Street Offences Act 1959

1 Loitering or soliciting for purposes of prostitution

(1) It shall be an offence for a common prostitute (whether male or female) to loiter or solicit in a street or public place for the purpose of prostitution. [S]

(4) For the purposes of this section 'street' includes any bridge, road, lane, footway, subway, square, court, alley or passage, whether a thoroughfare or not, which is for the time being open to the public; and the doorways and entrances of premises adjoining and open to a street, shall be treated as forming part of the street.

Sexual Offences Act 1985

1 Kerb-crawling

A person commits an offence if he solicits another person (or different persons) for the purpose of prostitution—

- (a) from a motor vehicle while it is in a street or public place; or
- (b) in a street or public place while in the immediate vicinity of a motor vehicle that he has just got out of or off, persistently or . . . in such manner or in such circumstances as to be likely

to cause annoyance to the person (or any of the persons) solicited, or nuisance to other persons in the neighbourhood. [S]

2 Persistent soliciting

(1) A person commits an offence if in a street or public place he persistently solicits another person (or different persons) for the purpose of prostitution. [S]

4 Interpretation

(1) Reference in this Act to a person soliciting another person for the purpose of prostitution are references to his soliciting that person for the purpose of obtaining that person's services as a prostitute.

(4) For the purposes of this Act 'street' includes any bridge, road, lane, footway, subway, square, court, alley or passage, whether a throughfare or not, which is for the time being open to the public; and the doorways and entrances of premises abutting on a street (as herein-before defined), and any ground adjoining and open to a street, shall be treated as forming part of the street.

Criminal Justice and Police Act 2001

46 Placing of advertisement relating to prostitution

(1) A person commits an offence if—

(a) he places on, or in the immediate vicinity of, a public telephone an advertisement relating to prostitution, and

(b) he does so with the intention that the advertisement should come to the attention of any other person or persons. [S]

(2) For the purposes of this section, an advertisement is an advertisement relating to prostitution if it—

(a) is for the services of a prostitute, whether male or female; or

(b) indicates that premises are premises at which such services are offered.

(3) In any proceedings for an offence under this section, any advertisement which a reasonable person would consider to be an advertisement relating to prostitution shall be presumed to be such an advertisement unless it is shown not to be.

(5) In this section—'public telephone' means—

(a) any telephone which is located in a public place and made available for use by the public, or a section of the public, and

(b) where such a telephone is located in or on, or attached to, a kiosk, booth, acoustic hood, shelter or other structure, that structure; and

'public place' means any place to which the public have or are permitted to have access, whether on payment or otherwise, other than—

(a) any place to which children under the age of 16 years are not permitted to have access, whether by law or otherwise, and

(b) any premises which are wholly or mainly used for residential purposes.

(f) Obscenity and Indecency

Obscene Publications Act 1959

1 Test of obscenity

(1) For the purpose of this Act an article shall be deemed to be obscene if its effect or (where the article comprises two or more distinct items) the effect of any one of its items is, if taken as a whole,

such as to tend to deprave and corrupt persons who are likely, having regard to all relevant circumstances, to read, see or hear the matter contained or embodied in it.

(2) In this Act 'article' means any description of article containing or embodying matter to be read or looked at or both, and sound record, and any film or other record of a picture or pictures.

(3) For the purposes of this Act a person publishes an article who—

(a) distributes, circulates, sells, lets on hire, gives, or lends it, or who offers it for sale or for letting on hire; or

(b) in the case of an article containing or embodying matter to be looked at or a record, shows, plays or projects it, or, where the matter is data stored electronically, transmits that data.

(4) For the purposes of this Act a person also publishes an article to the extent that any matter recorded on it is included by him in a programme included in a programme service.

(5) Where the inclusion of any matter in a programme so included would, if that matter were recorded matter, constitute the publication of an obscene article for the purposes of this Act by virtue of subsection (4) above, this Act shall have effect in relation to the inclusion of that matter in the programme as if it were recorded matter.

(6) In this section 'programme' and 'programme service' have the same meaning as in the Broadcasting Act 1990.

2 Prohibition of publication of obscene matter

(1) Subject as hereinafter provided, any person who, whether for gain or not publishes an obscene article or who has an obscene article for publication for gain (whether gain to himself or gain to another) shall be liable—

(a) on summary conviction to a fine not exceeding the prescribed sum or to imprisonment for a term not exceeding six months;

(b) on conviction on indictment to a fine or to imprisonment for a term not exceeding five years or both. [E]

(3) A prosecution for an offence against this section shall not be commenced more than two years after the commission of the offence.

(3A) Proceedings for an offence under this section shall not be instituted except by or with the consent of the Director of Public Prosecutions in any case where the article in question is a moving picture film of a width of not less than sixteen millimetres and the relevant publication or the only other publication which followed or could reasonably have been expected to follow from the relevant publication took place or (as the case may be) was to take place in the course of an exhibition of a film; and in this subsection 'the relevant publication' means—

(a) in the case of any proceedings under this section for publishing an obscene article, the publication in respect of which the defendant would be charged if the proceedings were brought; and

(b) in the case of any proceedings under this section for having an obscene article for publication for gain, the publication which, if the proceedings were brought, the defendant would be alleged to have had in contemplation.

(4) A person publishing an article shall not be proceeded against for an offence at common law consisting of the publication of any matter contained or embodied in the article where it is of the essence of the offence that the matter is obscene.

(4A) Without prejudice to subsection (4) above, a person shall not be proceeded against for an offence at common law—

(a) in respect of an exhibition of a film or anything said or done in the course of a film exhibition, where it is of the essence of the common law offence that the exhibition or, as the case may be, what was said or done was obscene, indecent, offensive, disgusting or injurious to morality; or

(b) in respect of an agreement to give an exhibition of a film or to cause anything to be said or done in the course of such an exhibition where the common law offence consists of conspiring to corrupt public morals or to do any act contrary to public morals or decency.

(5) A person shall not be convicted of an offence against this section if he proves that he had not examined the article in respect of which he is charged and had no reasonable cause to suspect that it was such that his publication of it would make him liable to be convicted of an offence against this section.

(6) In any proceedings against a person under this section the question whether an article is obscene shall be determined without regard to any publication by another person unless it could reasonably have been expected that the publication by the other person would follow from publication by the person charged.

(7) In this section 'exhibition of a film' has the meaning given in paragraph 15 of Schedule 2 to the Licensing Act 2003.

3 Powers of search and seizure

(1) If a justice of the peace is satisfied by information on oath that there is reasonable ground for suspecting that, in any premises, or on any stall or vehicle, being premises or a stall or vehicle specified in the information, obscene articles are, or are from time to time kept for publication for gain, the justice may issue a warrant under his hand empowering any constable to enter (if need be by force) and search the premises, or to search the stall or vehicle, and to seize and remove any articles found therein or thereon which the constable has reason to believe to be obscene articles and to be kept for publication for gain.

(2) A warrant under the foregoing subsection shall, if any obscene articles are seized under the warrant, also empower the seizure and removal of any documents found in the premises or, as the case may be, on the stall or vehicle which relate to a trade or business carried on at the premises or from the stall or vehicle.

(3) Subject to subsection (3A) of this section—

Any articles seized under subsection (1) of this section shall be brought before a justice of the peace acting in the local justice area in which the articles were seized, who may thereupon issue a summons to the occupier of the premises or, as the case may be, the user of the stall or vehicle to appear on a day specified in the summons before a magistrates' court acting in that local justice area to show cause why the articles or any of them should not be forfeited; and if the court is satisfied, as respects any of the articles, that at the time when they were seized they were obscene articles kept for publication for gain, the court shall order those articles to be forfeited:

Provided that if the person summoned does not appear, the court shall not make an order unless service of the summons is proved; Provided also that this subsection does not apply in relation to any article seized under subsection (1) of this section which is returned to the occupier of the premises or, as the case may be, to the user of the stall or vehicle in or on which it was found.

(3A) Without prejudice to the duty of a court to make an order for the forfeiture of an article where section 1(4) of the Obscene Publications Act 1964 applies (order made on conviction), in a case where by virtue of subsection (3A) of section 2 of this Act proceedings under the said section 2 for having an article for publication for gain could not be initiated except by or with the consent of the Director of Public Prosecutions; no order for the forfeiture of the article shall be made under this section unless the warrant under which the article was seized was issued on an information laid by or on behalf of the Director of Public Prosecutions.

(4) In addition to the person summoned, any other person being the owner, author or maker of any of the articles brought before the court, or any other person through whose hands they had passed before being seized, shall be entitled to appear before the court on the day specified in the summons to show cause why they should not be forfeited.

(7) For the purposes of this section the question whether an article is obscene shall be determined on the assumption that copies of it would be published in any manner likely having regard to the circumstances in which it was found, but in no other manner.

4 Defence of public good

(1) Subject to subsection (1A) of this section—

A person shall not be convicted of an offence against section two of this Act, and an order for forfeiture shall not be made under the foregoing section, if it is proved that publication of the article in question is justified as being for the public good on the ground that it is in the interests of science, literature, art or learning, or of other objects of general concern.

(1A) Subsection (1) of this section shall not apply where the article in question is a moving picture film or soundtrack, but—

(a) a person shall not be convicted of an offence against section 2 of this Act in relation to any such film or soundtrack, and

(b) an order for forfeiture of any such film or soundtrack shall not be made under section 3 of this Act,

if it is proved that publication of the film or soundtrack is justified as being for the public good on the grounds that it is in the interests of drama, opera, ballet or any other art, or of literature or learning.

(2) It is hereby declared that the opinion of experts as to the literary, artistic, scientific or other merits of an article may be admitted in any proceedings under this Act either to establish or to negative the said ground.

(3) In this section 'moving picture soundtrack' means any sound record designed for playing with a moving picture film, whether incorporated with the film or not.

Town Police Clauses Act 1847

28 Penalty on persons committing any of the offences herein named

Every person who in any street, to the obstruction, annoyance, or danger of the residents or passengers, commits any of the following offences, shall be liable to a penalty not exceeding level 3 on the standard scale for each offence of which he is convicted before the justice, (that is to say,)

... Every person who publicly offers for sale or distribution, or exhibits to public view any profane book, paper, print, drawing, printing or representation, or sings any profane or obscene song or ballad, or uses any profane or obscene language. [S]

Indecent Displays (Control) Act 1981

1 Indecent displays

(1) If any indecent matter is publicly displayed the person making the display and any person causing or permitting the display to be made shall be guilty of an offence. [E]

(2) Any matter which is displayed in or so as to be visible from any public place shall, for the purposes of this section, be deemed to be publicly displayed.

(3) In subsection (2) above, 'public place', in relation to the display of any matter, means any place to which the public have or are permitted to have access (whether on payment or otherwise) while that matter is displayed except—

(a) a place to which the public are permitted to have access only on payment which is or includes payment for that display; or

(b) a shop or any part of a shop to which the public can only gain access by passing beyond an adequate warning notice;

but the exclusions contained in paragraphs (a) and (b) above shall only apply where persons under the age of 18 years are not permitted to enter while the display in question is continuing.

(4) Nothing in this section applies in relation to any matter—

(a) included by any person in a television broadcasting service or other television programme service (within the meaning of Part I of the Broadcasting Act 1990); or

(b) included in the display of an art gallery or museum and visible only from within the gallery or museum; or

(c) displayed by or with the authority of, and visible only from within a building occupied by, the Crown or any local authority; or

(d) included in a performance of a play (within the meaning of paragraph 14(1) of Schedule 1 to the Licensing Act 2003); or

(e) included in an exhibition of a film within the meaning of paragraph 15 of Schedule 1 to the Licensing Act 2003—
 (i) given in a place which as regards that exhibition is required to be licensed under section 1 of that Act or by virtue only of section 5, 7 or 8 of that Act, is not required to be so licensed; or
 (ii) which is an exempted exhibition to which section 6 of that Act applies given by an exempted organisation as defined in subsection (6) of that section.

(5) In this section 'matter' includes anything capable of being displayed, except that it does not include an actual human body or any part thereof; and in determining for the purpose of this section whether any displayed matter is indecent—

(a) there shall be disregarded any part of that matter which is not exposed to view; and
(b) account may be taken of the effect of juxtaposing one thing with another.

(6) A warning notice shall not be adequate for the purposes of this section unless it complies with the following requirements—

(a) The warning notice must contain the following words, and no others—

'WARNING

Persons passing beyond this notice will find material on display which they may consider indecent. No admittance to persons under 18 years of age.'

(b) The word 'WARNING' must appear as a heading.
(c) No pictures or other matter shall appear on the notice.
(d) The notice must be so situated that no one could reasonably gain access to the shop or part of the shop in question without being aware of the notice and it must be easily legible by any person gaining such access.

Postal Services Act 2000

85 Prohibition on sending certain articles by post

(3) A person commits an offence if he sends by post a postal packet which encloses—

(a) any indecent or obscene print, painting, photograph, lithograph, engraving, cinematograph film or other record of a picture or pictures, book, card or written communication, or
(b) any other indecent or obscene article (whether or not of a similar kind to those mentioned in paragraph (a)). [E]

(4) A person commits an offence if he sends by post a postal packet which has on the packet, or on the cover of the packet, any words, marks or designs which are of an indecent or obscene character. [E]

Children and Young Persons (Harmful Publications) Act 1955

[See pages 81–82]

Unsolicited Goods and Services Act 1971

4 Unsolicited publications

(1) A person shall be guilty of an offence if he sends or causes to be sent to another person any book, magazine or leaflet (or advertising material for any such publication) which he knows or ought reasonably to know is unsolicited and which describes or illustrates human sexual techniques. [S]

6 Interpretation

(1) In this Act, unless the context or subject matter otherwise requires,—

'send' includes deliver and 'sender' shall be construed accordingly;

'unsolicited' means, in relation to goods sent to any person, that they are sent without any prior request made by him or on his behalf.

Theatres Act 1968

2 Prohibition of presentation of obscene performances of plays

(1) For the purposes of this section a performance of a play shall be deemed to be obscene if, taken as a whole, its effect was such as to tend to deprave and corrupt persons who were likely, having regard to all relevant circumstances, to attend it.

(2) Subject to sections 3 and 7 of this Act, if an obscene performance of a play is given, whether in public or private, any person who (whether for gain or not) presented or directed that performance shall be liable . . . [E]

(4) No person shall be proceeded against in respect of a performance of a play or anything said or done in the course of such a performance—

- (a) for an offence at common law where it is of the essence of the offence that the performance or, as the case may be, what was said or done was obscene, indecent, offensive, disgusting or injurious to morality; . . .

and no person shall be proceeded against for an offence at common law of conspiring to corrupt, or to do any act contrary to public morals or decency, in respect of an agreement to present or give a performance of a play, or to cause anything to be said or done in the course of such a performance.

3 Defence of public good

(1) A person shall not be convicted of an offence under section 2 of this Act if it is proved that the giving of the performance in question was justified as being for the public good on the ground that it was in the interests of drama, opera, ballet, or any other art, or of literature or learning.

(2) It is hereby declared that the opinion of experts as to the artistic, literary or other merits of a performance of a play may be admitted in any proceedings for an offence under section 2 of this Act either to establish or negative the said ground.

6 Provocation of breach of peace by means of public performance of a play

(1) Subject to section 7 of this Act, if there is given a public performance of a play involving the use of threatening, abusive or insulting words or behaviour, any person who (whether for gain or not) presented or directed that performance shall be guilty of an offence under this section if—

- (a) he did so with intent to provoke a breach of the peace; or
- (b) the performance, taken as a whole, was likely to occasion a breach of the peace. [S]

7 Exceptions for performances given in certain circumstances

(1) Nothing in sections 2 to 4 of this Act shall apply in relation to a performance of a play given on a domestic occasion in a private dwelling.

(2) Nothing in sections 2 to 6 of this Act shall apply in relation to a performance of a play given solely or primarily for one or more of the following purposes, that is to say—

- (a) rehearsal; or
- (b) to enable—
  - (i) a record or cinematograph film to be made from or by means of the performance; or
  - (ii) the performance to be broadcast; or
  - (iii) the performance to be included in a programme service (within the meaning of the Broadcasting Act 1990) other than a sound or television broadcasting service;

but in any proceedings for an offence under section 2, 5 or 6 of this Act alleged to have been committed in respect of a performance of a play or an offence at common law alleged to have been committed in

England and Wales by the publication of defamatory matter in the course of a performance of a play, if it is proved that the performance was attended by persons other than persons directly connected with the giving of the performance or the doing in relation thereto of any of the things mentioned in paragraph (b) above, the performance shall be taken not to have been given solely or primarily for one or more of the said purposes unless the contrary is shown.

18 Interpretation

(1) In this Act—

'Play' means—

(a) any dramatic piece, whether involving improvisation or not, which is given wholly or in part by one or more persons actually present and performing and in which the whole or a major proportion of what is done by the person or persons performing, whether by way of speech, singing or acting, involves the playing of a role; and

(b) any ballet given wholly or in part by one or more persons actually present and performing, whether or not it falls within paragraph (a) of this definition;

'premises' includes any place;

'public performance' includes any performance in a public place within the meaning of the Public Order Act 1936, any performance which is not open for the public but which is promoted for private gain; and any performance which the public or any section thereof are permitted to attend, whether on payment or otherwise;...

(2) For the purposes of this Act—

(a) a person shall not be treated as presenting a performance of a play by reason only of his taking part therein as a performer;

(b) a person taking part as a performer in a performance of a play directed by another person shall be treated as a person who directed the performance if without reasonable excuse he performs otherwise than in accordance with that person's direction; and

(c) a person shall be taken to have directed a performance of a play given under his direction notwithstanding that he was not present during the performance;

and a person shall not be treated as aiding or abetting the commission of an offence under section 2 or 6 of this Act in respect of a performance of a play by reason only of his taking part in that performance as a performer.

Video Recordings Act 1984

1 Interpretation of terms

(1) The provisions of this section shall have effect for the interpretation of terms used in this Act.

(2) 'Video work' means any series of visual images (with or without sound)—

(a) produced electronically by the use of information contained on any disc, magnetic tape or any other device capable of storing data electronically, and

(b) shown as a moving picture.

(3) 'Video recording' means any disc, magnetic tape or any other device capable of storing data electronically containing information by the use of which the whole or a part of a video work may be produced.

(4) 'Supply' means supply in any manner, whether or not for reward, and, therefore, includes supply by way of sale, letting on hire, exchange or loan; and references to a supply are to be interpreted accordingly.

2 Exempted works

(1) Subject to subsection (2) or (3) below, a video work is for the purposes of this Act an exempted work if, taken as a whole—

(a) it is designed to inform, educate or instruct;

(b) it is concerned with sport, religion or music; or

(c) it is a video game.

(2) A video work is not an exempted work for those purposes if, to any significant extent, it depicts—

(a) a human sexual activity or acts of force or restraint associated with such activity;

(b) mutilation or torture of, or other acts of gross violence towards, humans or animals;

(c) human genital organs or human urinary or excretory functions;

(d) techniques likely to be useful in the commission of offences;

or is likely to any significant extent to stimulate or encourage anything falling within paragraph (a) or, in the case of anything falling within paragraph (b), is likely to any extent to do so.

(3) A video work is not an exempted work for those purposes if, to any significant extent, it depicts criminal activity which is likely to any significant extent to stimulate or encourage the commission of offences.

3 Exempted supplies

(1) The provisions of this section apply to determine whether or not a supply of a video recording is an exempted supply for the purposes of this Act.

(2) The supply of a video recording by any person is an exempted supply if it is neither—

(a) a supply for reward, nor

(b) a supply in the course of furtherance of a business.

(3) Where on any premises facilities are provided in the course or furtherance of a business for supplying video recordings, the supply by any person of a video recording on those premises is to be treated for the purposes of subsection (2) above as a supply in the course or furtherance of a business.

(4) Where a person (in this subsection referred to as the 'original supplier') supplies a video recording to a person who, in the course of a business, makes video works or supplies video recordings, the supply is an exempted supply—

(a) if it is not made with a view to any further supply of that recording, or

(b) if it is so made, but is not made with a view to the eventual supply of that recording to the public or is made with a view to the eventual supply of that recording to the original supplier.

For the purposes of this subsection, any supply is a supply to the public unless it is—

(i) a supply to a person who, in the course of a business, makes video works or supplies video recordings,

(ii) an exempted supply by virtue of subsection (2) above or subsections (5) to (10) below, or

(iii) a supply outside the United Kingdom.

(5) Where a video work—

(a) is designed to provide a record of an event or occasion for those who took part in the event or occasion or are connected with those who did so,

(b) does not, to any significant extent, depict anything falling within paragraph (a), or of section 2(2) of this Act, and

(c) is not designed to any significant extent to stimulate or encourage anything falling within paragraph (a) of that subsection or, in the case of anything falling within paragraph (b) of that subsection, is not designed to any extent to do so,

the supply of a video recording containing only that work to a person who took part in the event or occasion or is connected with someone who did so is an exempted supply.

(6) The supply of a video recording for the purpose only of the exhibition of any video work contained in the recording in premises other than a dwelling-house—

(a) being premises mentioned in subsection (7) below, or

(b) being an exhibition which in England and Wales or Scotland would be a film exhibition to which section 6 of the Cinemas Act 1985 applies (film exhibition to which public not admitted or are admitted without payment)

is an exempted supply.

(7) The premises referred to in subsection (6) above are—

(za) premises in England and Wales which by virtue of an authorisation within the meaning of section 136 of the Licensing Act 2003, may be used for the exhibition of a film within the meaning of paragraph 15 of Schedule 1 to that Act.

(8) The supply of a video recording with a view only to its use for or in connection with—

(a) a programme service (within the meaning of the Broadcasting Act 1990) is an exempted supply.

(9) The supply of a video recording for the purpose only of submitting a video work contained in the recording for the issue of a classification certificate or otherwise only for purposes of arrangements made by the designated authority is an exempted supply.

(10) The supply of a video recording with a view only to its use—

(a) in training for or carrying on any medical or related occupation,

(b) for the purpose of—

(i) services provided in pursuance of the National Health Service Act 2006.

(c) in training persons employed in the course of services falling within paragraph (b) above, is an exempted supply.

(11) For the purposes of subsection (10) above, an occupation is a medical or related occupation if, to carry on the occupation, a person is required to be registered under the Health Professions Order 2001, the Nursing and Midwifery Order 2001, the Medical Act 1983, the Osteopaths Act 1993 or the Chiropractors Act 1994.

(12) The supply of a video recording otherwise than for reward, being a supply made for the purpose only of supplying it to a person who previously made an exempted supply of the recording, is also an exempted supply.

7 Classification certificates

(1) In this Act 'classification certificate' means a certificate—

(a) issued in respect of a video work in pursuance of arrangements made by the designated authority; and

(b) satisfying the requirements of subsection (2) below.

(2) Those requirements are that the certificate must contain the title assigned to the video work in accordance with section 4(1)(ia) of this Act and—

(a) a statement that the video work concerned is suitable for general viewing and unrestricted supply (with or without any advice as to the desirability of parental guidance with regard to the viewing of the work by young children or as to the particular suitability of the work for viewing by children or young children); or

(b) a statement that the video work concerned is suitable for viewing only by persons who have attained the age (not being more than eighteen years) specified in the certificate and that no video recording containing that work is to be supplied to any person who has not attained the age so specified; or

(c) the statement mentioned in paragraph (b) above together with a statement that no video recording containing that work is to be supplied other than in a licensed sex shop.

9 Supplying video recording of unclassified work

(1) A person who supplies or offers to supply a video recording containing a video work in respect of which no classification certificate has been issued is guilty of an offence unless—

(a) the supply is, or would if it took place be, an exempted supply, or

(b) the video work is an exempted work. [E]

(2) It is a defence to a charge of committing an offence under this section to prove that the accused believed on reasonable grounds—

(a) that the video work concerned or, if the video recording contained more than one work to which the charge relates, each of those works was either an exempted work or a work in respect of which a classification certificate had been issued, or

(b) that the supply was, or would if it took place be, an exempted supply by virtue of section 3(4) or (5) of this Act.

10 Possession of video recording of unclassified work for the purposes of supply

(1) Where a video recording contains a video work in respect of which no classification certificate has been issued, a person who has the recording in his possession for the purpose of supplying it is guilty of an offence unless—

(a) he has it in his possession for the purpose only of a supply which, if it took place, would be an exempted supply, or

(b) the video work is an exempted work. [E]

(2) It is a defence to a charge of committing an offence under this section to prove—

(a) that the accused believed on reasonable grounds that the video work concerned or, if the video recording contained more than one work to which the charge relates, each of those works was either an exempted work or a work in respect of which a classification certificate had been issued,

(b) that the accused had the video recording in his possession for the purpose only of a supply which he believed on reasonable grounds would, if it took place, be an exempted supply by virtue of section 3(4) or (5) of this Act, or

(c) that the accused did not intend to supply the video recording until a classification certificate had been issued in respect of the video work concerned.

11 Supplying video recording of classified work in breach of classification

(1) Where a classification certificate issued in respect of a video work states that no video recording containing that work is to be supplied to any person who has not attained the age specified in the certificate, a person who supplies or offers to supply a video recording containing that work to a person who has not attained the age so specified is guilty of an offence unless the supply is, or would if it took place be, an exempted supply. [S]

(2) It is a defence to a charge of committing an offence under this section to prove—

(a) that the accused neither knew nor had reasonable grounds to believe that the classification certificate contained the statement concerned,

(b) that the accused neither knew nor had reasonable grounds to believe that the person concerned had not attained that age, or

(c) that the accused believed on reasonable grounds that the supply was, or would if it took place be, an exempted supply by virtue of section 3(4) or (5) of this Act.

12 Certain video recordings only to be supplied in licensed sex shops

(1) Where a classification certificate issued in respect of a video work states that no video recording containing that work is to be supplied other than in a licensed sex shop, a person who at any place other than in a sex shop for which a licence is in force under the relevant enactment—

(a) supplies a video recording containing the work, or

(b) offers to do so, is guilty of an offence unless the supply is, or would if it took place be, an exempted supply. [S]

(2) It is a defence to a charge of committing an offence under subsection (1) above to prove—

(a) that the accused neither knew nor had reasonable grounds to believe that the classification certificate contained the statement concerned,

(b) that the accused believed on reasonable grounds that the place concerned was a sex shop for which a licence was in force under the relevant enactment, or

(c) that the accused believed on reasonable grounds that the supply was, or would if it took place be, an exempted supply by virtue of section 3(4) of this Act or subsection (6) below.

(3) Where a classification certificate issued in respect of a video work states that no video recording containing that work is to be supplied other than in a licensed sex shop, a person who has a video

recording containing the work in his possession for the purpose of supplying it at any place other than in such a sex shop is guilty of an offence, unless he has it in his possession for the purpose only of a supply which, if it took place, would be an exempted supply.

(4) It is a defence to a charge of committing an offence under subsection (3) above to prove—

(a) that the accused neither knew nor had reasonable grounds to believe that the classification certificate contained the statement concerned,

(b) that the accused believed on reasonable grounds that the place concerned was a sex shop for which a licence was in force under the relevant enactment, or

(c) that the accused had the video recording in his possession for the purpose only of a supply which he believed on reasonable grounds would, if it took place, be an exempted supply by virtue of section 3(4) of this Act or subsection (6) below.

(5) In this section 'relevant enactment' means Schedule 3 to the Local Government (Miscellaneous Provisions) Act 1982 . . . and 'sex shop' has the same meaning as in the relevant enactment.

(6) For the purposes of this section, where a classification certificate issued in respect of a video work states that no video recording containing that work is to be supplied other than in a licensed sex shop, the supply of a video recording containing that work—

(a) to a person who, in the course of a business, makes video works or supplies video recordings, and

(b) with a view to its eventual supply in sex shops, being sex shops for which licences are in force under the relevant enactment,

is an exempted supply.

14A General defence to offences under this Act

Without prejudice to any defence specified in the preceding provisions of this Act in relation to a particular offence, it is a defence to a charge of committing any offence under this Act to prove—

(a) that the commission of the offence was due to the act or default of a person other than the accused, and

(b) that the accused took all reasonable precautions and exercised all due diligence to avoid the commission of the offence by any person under his control.

16 Offences by bodies corporate

(1) Where an offence under this Act committed by a body corporate is proved to have been committed with the consent or connivance of, or to be attributable to any neglect on the part of, any director, manager, secretary or other similar officer of the body corporate, or any person who was purporting to act in any such capacity, he as well as the body corporate shall be guilty of the offence and shall be liable to be proceeded against and punished accordingly.

(2) Where the affairs of a body corporate are managed by its members, subsection (1) above shall apply in relation to the acts and defaults of a member in connection with his functions of management as if he were a director of the body corporate.

22 Other interpretation

(1) In this Act—

'business', except in section 3(4), includes any activity carried on by a club; and

'premises' includes any vehicle, vessel or stall.

(2) For the purposes of this Act, a video recording contains a video work if it contains information by the use of which the whole or a part of the work may be produced; but where a video work includes any extract from another video work, that extract is not to be regarded for the purposes of this subsection as a part of that other work.

(3) Where any alteration is made to a video work in respect of which a classification certificate has been issued, the classification certificate is not to be treated for the purposes of this Act as issued in respect of the altered work.

In this subsection, 'alteration' includes addition.

Criminal Justice and Immigration Act 2008

63 Possession of extreme pornographic images

(1) It is an offence for a person to be in possession of an extreme pornographic image. [E]

(2) An 'extreme pornographic image' is an image which is both—

(a) pornographic, and

(b) an extreme image.

(3) An image is 'pornographic' if it is of such a nature that it must reasonably be assumed to have been produced solely or principally for the purpose of sexual arousal.

(4) Where (as found in the person's possession) an image forms part of a series of images, the question whether the image is of such a nature as is mentioned in subsection (3) is to be determined by reference to—

(a) the image itself, and

(b) (if the series of images is such as to be capable of providing a context for the image) the context in which it occurs in the series of images.

(5) So, for example, where—

(a) an image forms an integral part of a narrative constituted by a series of images, and

(b) having regard to those images as a whole, they are not of such a nature that they must reasonably be assumed to have been produced solely or principally for the purpose of sexual arousal,

the image may, by virtue of being part of that narrative, be found not to be pornographic, even though it might have been found to be pornographic if taken by itself.

(6) An 'extreme image' is an image which—

(a) falls within subsection (7), and

(b) is grossly offensive, disgusting or otherwise of an obscene character.

(7) An image falls within this subsection if it portrays, in an explicit and realistic way, any of the following—

(a) an act which threatens a person's life,

(b) an act which results, or is likely to result, in serious injury to a person's anus, breasts or genitals,

(c) an act which involves sexual interference with a human corpse, or

(d) a person performing an act of intercourse or oral sex with an animal (whether dead or alive),

and a reasonable person looking at the image would think that any such person or animal was real.

(8) In this section 'image' means—

(a) a moving or still image (produced by any means); or

(b) data (stored by any means) which is capable of conversion into an image within paragraph (a).

(9) In this section references to a part of the body include references to a part surgically constructed (in particular through gender reassignment surgery).

64 Exclusion of classified films etc.

(1) Section 63 does not apply to excluded images.

(2) An 'excluded image' is an image which forms part of a series of images contained in a recording of the whole or part of a classified work.

(3) But such an image is not an 'excluded image' if—

(a) it is contained in a recording of an extract from a classified work, and

(b) it is of such a nature that it must reasonably be assumed to have been extracted (whether with or without other images) solely or principally for the purpose of sexual arousal.

(4) Where an extracted image is one of a series of images contained in the recording, the question whether the image is of such a nature as is mentioned in subsection (3)(b) is to be determined by reference to—

(a) the image itself, and

(b) (if the series of images is such as to be capable of providing a context for the image) the context in which it occurs in the series of images;

and section 63(5) applies in connection with determining that question as it applies in connection with determining whether an image is pornographic.

(5) In determining for the purposes of this section whether a recording is a recording of the whole or part of a classified work, any alteration attributable to—

(a) a defect caused for technical reasons or by inadvertence on the part of any person, or

(b) the inclusion in the recording of any extraneous material (such as advertisements),

is to be disregarded.

(7) In this section—

'classified work' means (subject to subsection (8)) a video work in respect of which a classification certificate has been issued by a designated authority (whether before or after the commencement of this section);

'classification certificate' and 'video work' have the same meanings as in the Video Recordings Act 1984;

'designated authority' means an authority which has been designated by the Secretary of State under section 4 of that Act;

'extract' includes an extract consisting of a single image;

'image' and 'pornographic' have the same meanings as in section 63;

'recording' means any disc, tape or other device capable of storing data electronically and from which images may be produced (by any means).

(8) Section 22(3) of the Video Recordings Act 1984 (effect of alterations) applies for the purposes of this section as it applies for the purposes of that Act.

65 Defences: general

(1) Where a person is charged with an offence under section 63, it is a defence for the person to prove any of the matters mentioned in subsection (2).

(2) The matters are—

(a) that the person had a legitimate reason for being in possession of the image concerned;

(b) that the person had not seen the image concerned and did not know, nor had any cause to suspect, it to be an extreme pornographic image;

(c) that the person—

(i) was sent the image concerned without any prior request having been made by or on behalf of the person, and

(ii) did not keep it for an unreasonable time.

(3) In this section 'extreme pornographic image' and 'image' have the same meanings as in section 63.

66 Defence: participation in consensual acts

(1) This section applies where—

(a) a person ('D') is charged with an offence under section 63, and

(b) the offence relates to an image that portrays an act or acts within paragraphs (a) to (c) (but none within paragraph (d)) of subsection (7) of that section.

(2) It is a defence for D to prove—

(a) that D directly participated in the act or any of the acts portrayed, and

(b) that the act or acts did not involve the infliction of any non-consensual harm on any person, and

(c) if the image portrays an act within section 63(7)(c), that what is portrayed as a human corpse was not in fact a corpse.

(3) For the purposes of this section harm inflicted on a person is 'non-consensual' harm if—

(a) the harm is of such a nature that the person cannot, in law, consent to it being inflicted on himself or herself; or

(b) where the person can, in law, consent to it being so inflicted, the person does not in fact consent to it being so inflicted.

(g) Intoxication: Alcohol and Other Drugs

Metropolitan Police Act 1839

44 Penalty on keepers of refreshment houses permitting drunkenness, disorderly conduct, etc., therein

...Every person who shall have or keep any house, shop, room, or place of public resort within the metropolitan police district, wherein provisions, liquors, or refreshments of any kind shall be sold or consumed, (whether the same shall be kept or retailed therein or procured elsewhere,) and who shall wilfully or knowingly permit drunkenness or other disorderly conduct in such house, shop, room, or place or knowingly permit or suffer prostitutes or persons of notoriously bad character to meet together and remain therein, shall for every such offence be liable to a penalty of not more than level 1 on the standard scale. [S]

Licensing Act 1872

12 Penalty on persons found drunk

Every person found drunk in any highway or other public place, whether a building or not, or on any licensed premises, shall be liable to a penalty not exceeding level 1 on the standard scale. [S]

Every person who is drunk while in charge on any highway or other public place of any carriage, horse, cattle, or steam engine, or who is drunk when in possession of any loaded firearms, shall be liable to a penalty not exceeding level 1 on the standard scale or in the discretion of the court to imprisonment...for any term not exceeding 51 weeks. [S]

Licensing Act 1902

8 Interpretation of 'public place'

[See page 61]

Criminal Justice Act 1967

91 Drunkenness in a public place

(1) Any person who in any public place is guilty, while drunk, of disorderly behaviour shall be liable on summary conviction to a fine not exceeding level 3 on the standard scale. [S]

(4) In this section 'public place' includes any highway and any other premises or place to which at the material time the public have or are permitted to have access, whether on payment or otherwise.

Licensing Act 2003

137 Exposing alcohol for unauthorised sale

(1) A person commits an offence if, on any premises, he exposes for sale by retail any alcohol in circumstances where the sale by retail of that alcohol on those premises would be an unauthorised licensable activity.

(2) For that purpose a licensable activity is unauthorised unless it is under and in accordance with an authorisation. [S]

138 Keeping alcohol on premises for unauthorised sale

(1) A person commits an offence if he has in his possession or under his control alcohol which he intends to sell by retail or supply in circumstances where that activity would be an unauthorised licensable activity.

(2) For that purpose a licensable activity is unauthorised unless it is under and in accordance with an authorisation.

(3) In subsection (1) the reference to the supply of alcohol is a reference to the supply of alcohol by or on behalf of a club to, or to the order of, a member of the club. [S]

139 Defence of due diligence

(1) In proceedings against a person for an offence to which subsection (2) applies, it is a defence that—

(a) his act was due to a mistake, or to reliance on information given to him, or to an act or omission by another person, or to some other cause beyond his control, and

(b) he took all reasonable precautions and exercised all due diligence to avoid committing the offence.

(2) This subsection applies to an offence under—

(a) section 136(1)(a) (carrying on unauthorised licensable activity),

(b) section 137 (exposing alcohol for unauthorised sale), or

(c) section 138 (keeping alcohol on premises for unauthorised sale).

140 Allowing disorderly conduct on licensed premises, etc.

(1) A person to whom subsection (2) applies commits an offence if he knowingly allows disorderly conduct on relevant premises.

(2) This subsection applies—

(a) to any person who works at the premises in a capacity, whether paid or unpaid, which authorises him to prevent the conduct,

(b) in the case of licensed premises, to—

(i) the holder of a premises licence in respect of the premises, and

(ii) the designated premises supervisor (if any) under such a licence,

(c) in the case of premises in respect of which a club premises certificate has effect, to any member or officer of the club which holds the certificate who at the time the conduct takes place is present on the premises in a capacity which enables him to prevent it, and

(d) in the case of premises which may be used for a permitted temporary activity by virtue of Part 5, to the premises user in relation to the temporary event notice in question. [S]

141 Sale of alcohol to a person who is drunk

(1) A person to whom subsection (2) applies commits an offence if, on relevant premises, he knowingly—

(a) sells or attempts to sell alcohol to a person who is drunk, or

(b) allows alcohol to be sold to such a person.

(2) This subsection applies—

(a) to any person who works at the premises in a capacity, whether paid or unpaid, which gives him authority to sell the alcohol concerned,

(b) in the case of licensed premises, to—

(i) the holder of a premises licence in respect of the premises, and

(ii) the designated premises supervisor (if any) under such a licence,

(c) in the case of premises in respect of which a club premises certificate has effect, to any member or officer of the club which holds the certificate who at the time the sale (or attempted sale) takes place is present on the premises in a capacity which enables him to prevent it, and

(d) in the case of premises which may be used for a permitted temporary activity by virtue of Part 5, to the premises user in relation to the temporary event notice in question.

(3) This section applies in relation to the supply of alcohol by or on behalf of a club to or to the order of a member of the club as it applies in relation to the sale of alcohol. [S]

142 Obtaining alcohol for a person who is drunk

(1) A person commits an offence if, on relevant premises, he knowingly obtains or attempts to obtain alcohol for consumption on those premises by a person who is drunk. [S]

143 Failure to leave licensed premises etc.

(1) A person who is drunk or disorderly commits an offence if, without reasonable excuse—

(a) he fails to leave relevant premises when requested to do so by a constable or by a person to whom subsection (2) applies, or

(b) he enters or attempts to enter relevant premises after a constable or a person to whom subsection (2) applies has requested him not to enter.

(2) This subsection applies—

(a) to any person who works at the premises in a capacity, whether paid or unpaid, which authorises him to make such a request,

(b) in the case of licensed premises, to—

(i) the holder of a premises licence in respect of the premises, or

(ii) the designated premises supervisor (if any) under such a licence,

(c) in the case of premises in respect of which a club premises certificate has effect, to any member or officer of the club which holds the certificate who is present on the premises in a capacity which enables him to make such a request, and

(d) in the case of premises which may be used for a permitted temporary activity by virtue of Part 5, to the premises user in relation to the temporary event notice in question. [S]

146 Sale of alcohol to children

(1) A person commits an offence if he sells alcohol to an individual aged under 18.

(2) A club commits an offence if alcohol is supplied by it or on its behalf—

(a) to, or to the order of, a member of the club who is aged under 18, or

(b) on the order of a member of the club, to an individual who is aged under 18.

(3) A person commits an offence if he supplies alcohol on behalf of a club—

(a) to, or to the order of, a member of the club who is aged under 18, or

(b) to the order of a member of the club, to an individual who is aged under 18.

(4) Where a person is charged with an offence under this section by reason of his own conduct it is a defence that—

(a) he believed that the individual was aged 18 or over, and

(b) either—

(i) he had taken all reasonable steps to establish the individual's age, or

(ii) nobody could reasonably have suspected from the individual's appearance that he was aged under 18.

(5) For the purposes of subsection (4), a person is treated as having taken all reasonable steps to establish an individual's age if—

(a) he asked the individual for evidence of his age, and

(b) the evidence would have convinced a reasonable person.

(6) Where a person ('the accused') is charged with an offence under this section by reason of the act or default of some other person it is a defence that the accused exercised all due diligence to avoid committing it. [S]

147 Allowing the sale of alcohol to children

(1) A person to whom subsection (2) applies commits an offence if he knowingly allows the sale of alcohol on relevant premises to an individual aged under 18.

(2) This subsection applies to a person who works at the premises in a capacity, whether paid or unpaid, which authorises him to prevent the sale.

(3) A person to whom subsection (4) applies commits an offence if he knowingly allows alcohol to be supplied on relevant premises by or on behalf of a club—

(a) to or to the order of a member of the club who is aged under 18, or

(b) to the order of a member of the club, to an individual who is aged under 18.

(4) This subsection applies to—

(a) a person who works on the premises in a capacity, whether paid or unpaid, which authorises him to prevent the supply, and

(b) any member or officer of the club who at the time of the supply is present on the relevant premises in a capacity which enables him to prevent it. [S]

147A Persistently selling alcohol to children

(1) A person is guilty of an offence if—

(a) on 3 or more different occasions within a period of 3 consecutive months alcohol is unlawfully sold on the same premises to an individual aged under 18;

(b) at the time of each sale the premises were either licensed premises or premises authorised to be used for a permitted temporary activity by virtue of Part 5; and

(c) that person was a responsible person in relation to the premises at each such time. [S]

(2) For the purposes of this section alcohol sold to an individual aged under 18 is unlawfully sold to him if—

(a) the person making the sale believed the individual to be aged under 18; or

(b) that person did not have reasonable grounds for believing the individual to be aged 18 or over.

(3) For the purposes of subsection (2) a person has reasonable grounds for believing an individual to be aged 18 or over only if—

(a) he asked the individual for evidence of his age and that individual produced evidence that would have convinced a reasonable person; or

(b) nobody could reasonably have suspected from the individual's appearance that he was aged under 18.

(4) A person is, in relation to premises and a time, a responsible person for the purposes of subsection (1) if, at that time, he is—

(a) the person or one of the persons holding a premises licence in respect of the premises; or

(b) the person or one of the persons who is the premises user in respect of a temporary event notice by reference to which the premises are authorised to be used for a permitted temporary activity by virtue of Part 5.

(5) The individual to whom the sales mentioned in subsection (1) are made may, but need not be, the same in each case.

(6) The same sale may not be counted in respect of different offences for the purpose—

(a) of enabling the same person to be convicted of more than one offence under this section; or

(b) of enabling the same person to be convicted of both an offence under this section and an offence under section 146 or 147.

(7) In determining whether an offence under this section has been committed, the following shall be admissible as evidence that there has been an unlawful sale of alcohol to an individual aged under 18 on any premises on any occasion—

(a) the conviction of a person for an offence under section 146 in respect of a sale to that individual on those premises on that occasion;

(b) the giving to a person of a caution (within the meaning of Part 5 of the Police Act 1997) in respect of such an offence; or

(c) the payment by a person of a fixed penalty under Part 1 of the Criminal Justice and Police Act 2001 in respect of such a sale.

148 Sale of liqueur confectionery to children under 16

(1) A person commits an offence if he—

(a) sells liqueur confectionery to an individual aged under 16, or

(b) he supplies such confectionery, on behalf of a club—

(i) to or to the order of a member of the club who is aged under 16, or

(ii) to the order of a member of the club, to an individual who is aged under 16.

(2) A club commits an offence if liqueur confectionery is supplied by it or on its behalf—

(a) to or to the order of a member of the club who is aged under 16, or

(b) to the order of a member of the club, to an individual who is aged under 16.

(3) Where a person is charged with an offence under this section by reason of his own conduct it is a defence that—

(a) he believed that the individual was aged 16 or over, and

(b) either—

(i) he had taken all reasonable steps to establish the individual's age, or

(ii) nobody could reasonably have suspected from the individual's appearance that he was aged under 16.

(4) For the purposes of subsection (3), a person is treated as having taken all reasonable steps to establish an individual's age if—

(a) he asked the individual for evidence of his age, and

(b) the evidence would have convinced a reasonable person.

(5) Where a person ('the accused') is charged with an offence under this section by reason of the act or default of some other person, it is a defence that the accused exercised all due diligence to avoid committing it.

(7) In this section 'liqueur confectionery' has the meaning given in section 191(2). [S]

149 Purchase of alcohol by or on behalf of children

(1) An individual aged under 18 commits an offence if—

(a) he buys or attempts to buy alcohol, or

(b) where he is a member of a club—

(i) alcohol is supplied to him or to his order by or on behalf of the club, as a result of some act or default of his, or

(ii) he attempts to have alcohol supplied to him or to his order by or on behalf of the club.

(2) But subsection (1) does not apply where the individual buys or attempts to buy the alcohol at the request of—

(a) a constable, or

(b) a weights and measures inspector,

who is acting in the course of his duty.

(3) A person commits an offence if—

(a) he buys or attempts to buy alcohol on behalf of an individual aged under 18, or

(b) where he is a member of a club, on behalf of an individual aged under 18 he—

(i) makes arrangements whereby alcohol is supplied to him or to his order by or on behalf of the club, or

(ii) attempts to make such arrangements.

(4) A person ('the relevant person') commits an offence if—

(a) he buys or attempts to buy alcohol for consumption on relevant premises by an individual aged under 18, or

(b) where he is a member of a club—

(i) by some act or default of his, alcohol is supplied to him, or to his order, by or on behalf of the club for consumption on relevant premises by an individual aged under 18, or

(ii) he attempts to have alcohol so supplied for such consumption.

(5) But subsection (4) does not apply where—

(a) the relevant person is aged 18 or over,

(b) the individual is aged 16 or 17,

(c) the alcohol is beer, wine or cider,

(d) its purchase or supply is for consumption at a table meal on relevant premises, and

(e) the individual is accompanied at the meal by an individual aged 18 or over.

(6) Where a person is charged with an offence under subsection (3) or (4) it is a defence that he had no reason to suspect that the individual was aged under 18. [S]

150 Consumption of alcohol by children

(1) An individual aged under 18 commits an offence if he knowingly consumes alcohol on relevant premises.

(2) A person to whom subsection (3) applies commits an offence if he knowingly allows the consumption of alcohol on relevant premises by an individual aged under 18.

(3) This subsection applies—

(a) to a person who works at the premises in a capacity, whether paid or unpaid, which authorises him to prevent the consumption, and

(b) where the alcohol was supplied by a club to or to the order of a member of the club, to any member or officer of the club who is present at the premises at the time of the consumption in a capacity which enables him to prevent it.

(4) Subsections (1) and (2) do not apply where—

(a) the individual is aged 16 or 17,

(b) the alcohol is beer, wine or cider,

(c) its consumption is at a table meal on relevant premises, and

(d) the individual is accompanied at the meal by an individual aged 18 or over. [S]

151 Delivering alcohol to children

(1) A person who works on relevant premises in any capacity, whether paid or unpaid, commits an offence if he knowingly delivers to an individual aged under 18—

(a) alcohol sold on the premises, or

(b) alcohol supplied on the premises by or on behalf of a club to or to the order of a member of the club.

(2) A person to whom subsection (3) applies commits an offence if he knowingly allows anybody else to deliver to an individual aged under 18 alcohol sold on relevant premises.

(3) This subsection applies to a person who works on the premises in a capacity, whether paid or unpaid, which authorises him to prevent the delivery of the alcohol.

(4) A person to whom subsection (5) applies commits an offence if he knowingly allows anybody else to deliver to an individual aged under 18 alcohol supplied on relevant premises by or on behalf of a club to or to the order of a member of the club.

(5) This subsection applies—

(a) to a person who works on the premises in a capacity, whether paid or unpaid, which authorises him to prevent the sale, and

(b) to any member or officer of the club who at the time of the supply in question is present on the premises in a capacity which enables him to prevent the supply.

(6) Subsections (1), (2) and (4) do not apply where—

(a) the alcohol is delivered at a place where the buyer or, as the case may be, person supplied lives or works, or

(b) the individual aged under 18 works on the relevant premises in a capacity, whether paid or unpaid, which involves the delivery of alcohol, or

(c) the alcohol is sold or supplied for consumption on the relevant premises. [S]

152 Sending a child to obtain alcohol

(1) A person commits an offence if he knowingly sends an individual aged under 18 to obtain—

(a) alcohol sold or to be sold on relevant premises for consumption off the premises, or

(b) alcohol supplied or to be supplied by or on behalf of a club to or to the order of a member of the club for such consumption.

(2) For the purposes of this section, it is immaterial whether the individual aged under 18 is sent to obtain the alcohol from the relevant premises or from other premises from which it is delivered in pursuance of the sale or supply.

(3) Subsection (1) does not apply where the individual aged under 18 works on the relevant premises in a capacity, whether paid or unpaid, which involves the delivery of alcohol.

(4) Subsection (1) also does not apply where the individual aged under 18 is sent by—

(a) a constable, or

(b) a weights and measures inspector,

who is acting in the course of his duty. [S]

153 Prohibition of unsupervised sales by children

(1) A responsible person commits an offence if on any relevant premises he knowingly allows an individual aged under 18 to make on the premises—

(a) any sale of alcohol, or

(b) any supply of alcohol by or on behalf of a club to or to the order of a member of the club,

unless the sale or supply has been specifically approved by that or another responsible person.

(2) But subsection (1) does not apply where—

(a) the alcohol is sold or supplied for consumption with a table meal,

(b) it is sold or supplied in premises which are being used for the service of table meals (or in a part of any premises which is being so used), and

(c) the premises are (or the part is) not used for the sale or supply of alcohol otherwise than to persons having table meals there and for consumption by such a person as an ancillary to his meal.

(4) In this section 'responsible person' means—

(a) in relation to licensed premises—

(i) the holder of the premises licence,

(ii) the designated premises supervisor, or

(iii) any individual aged 18 or over who is authorised for the purposes of this section by that holder or supervisor,

(b) in relation to premises in respect of which there is in force a club premises certificate, any member or officer of the club present on the premises in a capacity which enables him to prevent the supply in question, and

(c) in relation to premises which may be used for a permitted temporary activity by virtue of Part 5—

(i) the premises user, or

(ii) any individual aged 18 or over who is authorised for the purposes of this section by the premises user. [S]

159 Interpretation of this Part of this Act

In this Part—

'authorisation' has the meaning given in section 136(5);

'relevant premises' means—

(a) licensed premises, or

(b) premises in respect of which there is in force a club premises certificate, or

(c) premises which may be used for a permitted temporary activity by virtue of Part 5;

'table meal' means a meal eaten by a person seated at a table, or at a counter or other structure which serves the purpose of a table and is not used for the service of refreshments for consumption by persons not seated at a table or structure serving the purpose of a table . . .

187 Offences by bodies corporate etc.

(1) If an offence committed by a body corporate is shown—

(a) to have been committed with the consent or connivance of an officer, or
(b) to be attributable to any neglect on his part,

the officer as well as the body corporate is guilty of the offence and liable to be proceeded against and punished accordingly.

(2) If the affairs of a body corporate are managed by its members, subsection (1) applies in relation to the acts and defaults of a member in connection with his functions of management as if he were a director of the body.

(3) In subsection (1) 'officer', in relation to a body corporate, means—

(a) a director, member of the committee of management, chief executive, manager, secretary or other similar officer of the body, or a person purporting to act in any such capacity, and
(b) an individual who is a controller of the body.

(4) If an offence committed by a partnership is shown—

(a) to have been committed with the consent or connivance of a partner, or
(b) to be attributable to any neglect on his part,

the partner as well as the partnership is guilty of the offence and liable to be proceeded against and punished accordingly.

(5) In subsection (4) 'partner' includes a person purporting to act as a partner.

(6) If an offence committed by an unincorporated association (other than a partnership) is shown—

(a) to have been committed with the consent or connivance of an officer of the association or a member of its governing body, or
(b) to be attributable to any neglect on the part of such an officer or member,

that officer or member as well as the association is guilty of the offence and liable to be proceeded against and punished accordingly.

(8) In this section 'offence' means an offence under this Act.

191 Meaning of 'alcohol'

(1) In this Act, 'alcohol' means spirits, wine, beer, cider or any other fermented, distilled or spirituous liquor, but does not include—

(a) alcohol which is of a strength not exceeding 0.5% at the time of the sale or supply in question,
(b) perfume,
(c) flavouring essences recognised by the Commissioners of Customs and Excise as not being intended for consumption as or with dutiable alcoholic liquor,
(d) the aromatic flavouring essence commonly known as Angostura bitters,
(e) alcohol which is, or is included in, a medicinal product or a veterinary medicinal product,
(f) denatured alcohol,
(g) methyl alcohol,
(h) naphtha, or
(i) alcohol contained in liqueur confectionery.

(2) In this section—

'denatured alcohol' has the same meaning as in section 5 of the Finance Act 1995;

'dutiable alcoholic liquor' has the same meaning as in the Alcoholic Liquor Duties Act 1979;

'liqueur confectionery' means confectionery which—

(a) contains alcohol in a proportion not greater than 0.2 litres of alcohol (of a strength not exceeding 57%) per kilogram of the confectionery, and
(b) either consists of separate pieces weighing not more than 42g or is designed to be broken into such pieces for the purpose of consumption;

'medicinal product' has the same meaning as in section 130 of the Medicines Act 1968;

'strength' is to be construed in accordance with section 2 of the Alcoholic Liquor Duties Act 1979, and 'veterinary medicinal product' has the same meaning as in regulation 2 of the Veterinary Medicines Regulations 2006.

192 Meaning of 'sale by retail'

(1) For the purposes of this Act 'sale by retail', in relation to any alcohol, means a sale of alcohol to any person, other than a sale of alcohol that—

(a) is within subsection (2),

(b) is made from premises owned by the person making the sale, or occupied by him under a lease to which the provisions of Part 2 of the Landlord and Tenant Act 1954 (security of tenure) apply, and

(c) is made for consumption off the premises.

(2) A sale of alcohol is within this subsection if it is—

(a) to a trader for the purposes of his trade,

(b) to a club, which holds a club premises certificate, for the purposes of that club,

(c) to the holder of a personal licence for the purpose of making sales authorised by a premises licence,

(d) to the holder of a premises licence for the purpose of making sales authorised by that licence, or

(e) to the premises user in relation to a temporary event notice for the purpose of making sales authorised by that notice.

193 Other definitions

In this Act—

'beer' has the same meaning as in the Alcoholic Liquor Duties Act 1979;

'cider' has the same meaning as in that Act; . . .

'licensed premises' means premises in respect of which a premises licence has effect;

'licensing functions' is to be construed in accordance with section 4(1); . . .

'premises' means any place and includes a vehicle, vessel or moveable structure; . . .

'recognised club' means a club which satisfies conditions 1 to 3 of the general conditions in section 62;

. . . 'vehicle' means a vehicle intended or adapted for use on roads;

'vessel' includes a ship, boat, raft or other apparatus constructed or adapted for floating on water;

'wine' means—

(a) 'wine' within the meaning of the Alcoholic Liquor Duties Act 1979, and

(b) 'made-wine' within the meaning of that Act./

Sporting Events (Control of Alcohol etc.) Act 1985

1 Offences in connection with alcohol on coaches and trains

(1) This section applies to a vehicle which—

(a) is a public service vehicle or railway passenger vehicle, and

(b) is being used for the principal purpose of carrying passengers for the whole or part of a journey to or from a designated sporting event.

(2) A person who knowingly causes or permits alcohol to be carried on a vehicle to which this section applies is guilty of an offence—

(a) if the vehicle is a public service vehicle and he is the operator of the vehicle or the servant or agent of the operator, or

(b) if the vehicle is a hired vehicle and he is the person to whom it is hired or the servant or agent of that person. [S]

(3) A person who has alcohol in his possession while on a vehicle to which this section applies is guilty of an offence. [S]

(4) A person who is drunk on a vehicle to which this section applies is guilty of an offence. [S]

(5) In this section 'public service vehicle' and 'operator' have the same meaning as in the Public Passenger Vehicles Act 1981.

1A Alcohol on certain other vehicles

(1) This section applies to a motor vehicle which—

(a) is not a public service vehicle but is adapted to carry more than 8 passengers, and

(b) is being used for the principal purpose of carrying two or more passengers for the whole or part of a journey to or from a designated sporting event.

(2) A person who knowingly causes or permits alcohol to be carried on a motor vehicle to which this section applies is guilty of an offence—

(a) if he is its driver, or

(b) if he is not its driver but is its keeper, the servant or agent of its keeper, a person to whom it is made available (by hire, load or otherwise) by its keeper or the keeper's servant or agent, of the servant or agent of a person to whom it is so made available. [S]

(3) A person who has alcohol in his possession while on a motor vehicle to which this section applies is guilty of an offence. [S]

(4) A person who is drunk on a motor vehicle to which this section applies is guilty of an offence. [S]

(5) In this section—

'keeper', in relation to a vehicle, means the person having the duty to take out a licence for it under the Vehicle Excise and Registration Act 1994.

'motor vehicle' means a mechanically propelled vehicle intended or adapted for use on roads, and

'public service vehicle' has the same meaning as in the Public Passenger Vehicles Act 1981.

2 Offences in connection with alcohol, containers etc., at sports grounds

(1) A person who has alcohol or an article to which this section applies in his possession—

(a) at any time during the period of a designated sporting event when he is in any area of a designated sports ground from which the event may be directly viewed, or

(b) while entering or trying to enter a designated sports ground at any time during the period of a designated sporting event at that ground,

is guilty of an offence. [S]

(2) A person who is drunk in a designated sports ground at any time during the period of a designated sporting event at that ground or is drunk while entering or trying to enter such a ground at any time during the period of a designated sporting event at that ground is guilty of an offence. [S]

(3) This section applies to any article capable of causing injury to a person struck by it, being—

(a) a bottle, can or other portable container (including such an article when crushed or broken) which—

(i) is for holding any drink, and

(ii) is of a kind which, when empty, is normally discarded or returned to, or left to be recovered by, the supplier, or

(b) part of an article falling within paragraph (a) above; but does not apply to anything that is for holding any medicinal product (within the meaning of the Medicines Act 1968) or any veterinary medicinal product (within the meaning of the Veterinary Medicines Regulations 2006).

9 Interpretation

(1) The following provisions shall have effect for the interpretation of this Act.

(2) 'Designated sports ground' means any place—

(a) used (wholly or partly) for sporting events where accommodation is provided for spectators, and

(b) for the time being designated, or of a class designated, by order made by the Secretary of State;

and an order under this subsection may include provision for determining for the purposes of this Act the outer limit of any designated sports ground.

(3) 'Designated sporting event'—

(a) means a sporting event or proposed sporting event for the time being designated, or of a class designated, by order made by the Secretary of State, and

(b) includes a designated sporting event within the meaning of Part V of the Criminal Justice (Scotland) Act 1980;

and an order under this subsection may apply to events or proposed events outside Great Britain as well as those in England and Wales.

(4) The period of a designated sporting event is the period beginning two hours before the start of the event or (if earlier) two hours before the time at which it is advertised to start and ending one hour after the end of the event, but—

(a) where an event advertised to start at a particular time on a particular day is postponed to a later day, the period includes the period in the day on which it is advertised to take place beginning two hours before and ending one hour after that time, and

(b) where an event advertised to start at a particular time on a particular day does not take place, the period is the period referred to in paragraph (a) above.

(6) This Act does not apply to any sporting event or proposed sporting event—

(a) where all competitors are to take part otherwise than for reward, and

(b) to which all spectators are to be admitted free of charge.

Criminal Justice and Police Act 2001

12 Alcohol consumption in designated public places

(1) Subsection (2) applies if a constable reasonably believes that a person is, or has been, consuming alcohol in a designated public place or intends to consume alcohol in such a place.

(2) The constable may require the person concerned—

(a) not to consume in that place anything which is, or which the constable reasonably believes to be, alcohol;

(b) to surrender anything in his possession which is, or which the constable reasonably believes to be, alcohol or a container for alcohol.

(3) A constable may dispose of anything surrendered to him under subsection (2) in such manner as he considers appropriate.

(4) A person who fails without reasonable excuse to comply with a requirement imposed on him under subsection (2) commits an offence . . . [S]

(5) A constable who imposes a requirement on a person under subsection (2) shall inform the person concerned that failing without reasonable excuse to comply with the requirement is an offence.

13 Designated public places

(1) A place is, subject to section 14, a designated public place if it is—

(a) a public place in the area of a local authority; and

(b) identified in an order made by that authority under subsection (2).

(2) A local authority may for the purposes of subsection (1) by order identify any public place in their area if they are satisfied that—

(a) nuisance or annoyance to members of the public or a section of the public; or

(b) disorder;

has been associated with the consumption of alcohol in that place.

14 Places which are not designated public places

(1) A place is not a designated public place or a part of such a place if it is—

(a) premises in respect of which a premises licence has effect which authorises the premises to be used for the sale or supply of alcohol;

(aa) premises in respect of which a club premises certificate has effect which certifies that the premises may be used by the club for the sale or supply of alcohol;
(b) a place within the curtilage of premises within paragraph (a) or (aa);
(c) premises which by virtue of Part 5 of the Licensing Act 2003 may for the time being be used for the supply of alcohol or which, by virtue of that Part, could have been so used within the last 30 minutes;
(e) a place where facilities or activities relating to the sale or consumption of alcohol are for the time being permitted by virtue of a permission granted under section 115E of the Highways Act 1980 (highway related uses).

(1A) Subsection (1B) applies to premises falling within subsection (1)(a) if—
(a) the premises licence is held by a local authority in whose area the premises of part of the premises is situated; or
(b) the premises licence is held by another person but the premises are occupied by such an authority or are managed by or on behalf of such an authority.

(1B) Subsection (1) prevents premises to which this subsection applies from being, or being part of, a designated public place only—
(a) at times when it is being used for the sale or supply of alcohol; and
(b) at times falling within 30 minutes after the end of a period during which is has been so used.

(1C) In this section 'premises' licence and 'club premises certificate' have the same meaning as in the Licensing Act 2003.

16 Interpretation of sections 12 to 15

(1) In sections 12 to 15, unless the context otherwise requires—

['alcohol' has the same meaning as in the Licensing Act 2003;

'designated public place' has the meaning given by section 13(1);

'public place' means any place to which the public or any section of the public has access, on payment or otherwise, as of right or by virtue of express or implied permission; and

'supply of alcohol' has the meaning given by section 14 of the Licensing Act 2003.

(2) In sections 12 to 15 'local authority' means—
(a) in relation to England—
 (i) a unitary authority;
 (ii) a district council so far as they are not a unitary authority;
(b) in relation to Wales, a county council or a county borough council.

Misuse of Drugs Act 1971

2 Controlled drugs and their classification for purposes of this Act

(1) In this Act—
(a) the expression 'controlled drug' means any substance or product for the time being specified in Part I, II or III of Schedule 2 to this Act; and
(b) the expressions 'Class A drug', 'Class B drug', and 'Class C drug' mean any of the substances and products for the time being specified respectively in Part I, Part II and Part III of that Schedule;

and the provisions of Part IV of that Schedule shall have effect with respect to the meanings of expressions used in that Schedule.

3 Restriction of importation and exportation of controlled drugs

(1) Subject to subsection (2) below—
(a) the importation of a controlled drug; and
(b) the exportation of a controlled drug, are hereby prohibited.

(2) Subsection (1) above does not apply—

(a) to the importation or exportation of a controlled drug which is for the time being excepted from paragraph (a) or, as the case may be, paragraph (b) of subsection (1) above by regulations under section 7 of this Act; or

(b) to the importation or exportation of a controlled drug under and in accordance with the terms of a licence issued by the Secretary of State and in compliance with any conditions attached thereto.

4 Restriction of production and supply of controlled drugs

(1) Subject to any regulations under section 7 of this Act for the time being in force, it shall not be lawful for a person—

(a) to produce a controlled drug; or

(b) to supply or offer to supply a controlled drug to another.

(2) Subject to section 28 of this Act, it is an offence for a person—

(a) to produce a controlled drug in contravention of subsection (1) above; or

(b) to be concerned in the production of such a drug in contravention of that subsection by another. [E]

(3) Subject to section 28 of this Act, it is an offence for a person—

(a) to supply or offer to supply a controlled drug to another in contravention of subsection (1) above; or

(b) to be concerned in the supplying of such a drug to another in contravention of that subsection; or

(c) to be concerned in the making to another in contravention of that subsection of an offer to supply such a drug. [E]

4A Aggravation of offence of supply of controlled drug

(1) This section applies if—

(a) a court is considering the seriousness of an offence under section 4(3) of this Act, and

(b) at the time the offence was committed the offender had attained the age of 18.

(2) If either of the following conditions is met the court—

(a) must treat the fact that the condition is met as an aggravating factor (that is to say, a factor that increases the seriousness of the offence), and

(b) must state in open court that the offence is so aggravated.

(3) The first condition is that the offence was committed on or in the vicinity of school premises at a relevant time.

(4) The second condition is that in connection with the commission of the offence the offender used a courier who, at the time the offence was committed, was under the age of 18.

(5) In subsection (3), a relevant time is—

(a) any time when the school premises are in use by persons under the age of 18;

(b) one hour before the start and one hour after the end of any such time.

(6) For the purposes of subsection (4), a person uses a courier in connection with an offence under section 4(3) of this Act if he causes or permits another person (the courier)—

(a) to deliver a controlled drug to a third person, or

(b) to deliver a drug related consideration to himself or a third person.

(7) For the purposes of subsection (6), a drug related consideration is a consideration of any description which—

(a) is obtained in connection with the supply of a controlled drug, or

(b) is intended to be used in connection with obtaining a controlled drug.

(8) In this section—

'school premises' means land used for the purposes of a school excluding any land occupied solely as a dwelling by a person employed at the school; and

'school' has the same meaning—

(a) in England and Wales, as in section 4 of the Education Act 1996;

5 Restriction of possession of controlled drugs

(1) Subject to any regulations under section 7 of this Act for the time being in force, it shall not be lawful for a person to have a controlled drug in his possession.

(2) Subject to section 28 of this Act and to subsection (4) below, it is an offence for a person to have a controlled drug in his possession in contravention of subsection (1) above. [E]

(3) Subject to section 28 of this Act, it is an offence for a person to have a controlled drug in his possession, whether lawfully or not, with intent to supply it to another in contravention of section 4(1) of this Act. [E]

(4) In any proceedings for an offence under subsection (2) above in which it is proved that the accused had a controlled drug in his possession, it shall be a defence for him to prove—

- (a) that, knowing or suspecting it to be a controlled drug, he took possession of it for the purpose of preventing another from committing or continuing to commit an offence in connection with that drug and that as soon as possible after taking possession of it he took all such steps as were reasonably open to him to destroy the drug or to deliver it into the custody of a person lawfully entitled to take custody of it; or
- (b) that, knowing or suspecting it to be a controlled drug, he took possession of it for the purpose of delivering it into the custody of a person lawfully entitled to take custody of it and that as soon as possible after taking possession of it he took all such steps as were reasonably open to him to deliver it into the custody of such a person.

(4A) In any proceedings for an offence under subsection (3) above, if it is proved that the accused had an amount of a controlled drug in his possession which is not less than the prescribed amount, the court or jury must assume that he had the drug in his possession with the intent to supply it as mentioned in subsection (3).

(4B) Subsection (4A) above does not apply if evidence is adduced which is sufficient to raise an issue that the accused may not have had the drug in his possession with that intent.

(6) Nothing in subsection (4) above shall prejudice any defence which is open to a person charged with an offence under this section to raise apart from that subsection.

6 Restriction of cultivation of cannabis plants

(1) Subject to any regulations under section 7 of this Act for the time being in force, it shall not be lawful for a person to cultivate any plant of the genus Cannabis.

(2) Subject to section 28 of this Act, it is an offence to cultivate any such plant in contravention of subsection (1) above. [E]

7 Authorisation of activities otherwise unlawful under foregoing provisions

(1) The Secretary of State may by regulations—

- (a) except from section 3(1)(a) or (b), 4(1)(a) or (b) or 5(1) of this Act such controlled drugs as may be specified in the regulations; and
- (b) make such other provision as he thinks fit for the purpose of making it lawful for persons to do things which under any of the following provisions of this Act, that is to say sections 4(1), 5(1) and 6(1), it would otherwise be unlawful for them to do.

(2) Without prejudice to the generality of paragraph (b) of subsection (1) above, regulations under that subsection authorising the doing of any such thing as is mentioned in that paragraph may in particular provide for the doing of that thing to be lawful—

- (a) if it is done under and in accordance with the terms of a licence or other authority issued by the Secretary of State and in compliance with any conditions attached thereto; or
- (b) if it is done in compliance with such conditions as may be prescribed.

(3) Subject to subsection (4) below, the Secretary of State shall so exercise his power to make regulations under subsection (1) above as to secure—

- (a) that it is not unlawful under section 4(1) of this Act for a doctor, dentist, veterinary practitioner or veterinary surgeon, acting in his capacity as such, to prescribe, administer, manufacture, compound or supply a controlled drug, or for a pharmacist or a person lawfully conducting a retail pharmacy business, acting in either case in his capacity as such, to manufacture, compound or supply a controlled drug; and

(b) that it is not unlawful under section 5(1) of this Act for a doctor, dentist, veterinary practitioner, veterinary surgeon, pharmacist or person lawfully conducting a retail pharmacy business to have a controlled drug in his possession for the purpose of acting in his capacity as such.

(4) If in the case of any controlled drug the Secretary of State is of the opinion that it is in the public interest—

(a) for production, supply and possession of that drug to be either wholly unlawful or unlawful except for purposes of research or other special purposes; or

(b) for it to be unlawful for practitioners, pharmacists and persons lawfully conducting retail pharmacy business to do in relation to that drug any of the things mentioned in subsection (3) above except under a licence or other authority issued by the Secretary of State,

he may by order designate that drug as a drug to which this subsection applies; and while there is in force an order under this subsection designating a controlled drug as one to which this subsection applies subsection (3) above shall not apply as regards that drug.

(8) References in this section to a person's 'doing' things include references to his having things in his possession.

8 Occupiers, etc., of premises to be punishable for permitting certain activities to take place there

A person commits an offence if, being the occupier or concerned in the management of any premises, he knowingly permits or suffers any of the following activities to take place on those premises, that is to say—

(a) producing or attempting to produce a controlled drug in contravention of section 4 (1) of this Act;

(b) supplying or attempting to supply a controlled drug to another in contravention of section 4(1) of this Act, or offering to supply a controlled drug to another in contravention of section 4(1);

(c) preparing opium for smoking;

(d) smoking cannabis, cannabis resin or prepared opium.

9 Prohibition of certain activities, etc., relating to opium

Subject to section 28 of this Act, it is an offence for a person—

(a) to smoke or otherwise use prepared opium; or

(b) to frequent a place used for the purpose of opium smoking; or

(c) to have in his possession

(i) any pipes or other utensils made or adapted for use in connection with the smoking of opium, being pipes or utensils which have been used by him or with his knowledge and permission in that connection or which he intends to use or permit others to use in that connection; or

(ii) any utensils which have been used by him or with his knowledge and permission in connection with the preparation of opium for smoking. [E]

9A Prohibition of supply, etc., of articles for administering or preparing controlled drugs

(1) A person who supplies or offers to supply any article which may be used or adapted to be used (whether by itself or in combination with another article or other articles) in the administration by any person of a controlled drug to himself or another, believing that the article (or the article as adapted) is to be so used in circumstances where the administration is unlawful, is guilty of an offence. [S]

(2) It is not an offence under subsection (1) above to supply or offer to supply a hypodermic syringe, or any part of one.

(3) A person who supplies or offers to supply any article which may be used to prepare a controlled drug for administration by any person to himself or another believing that the article is to be so used in circumstances where the administration is unlawful is guilty of an offence. [S]

(4) For the purposes of this section, any administration of a controlled drug is unlawful except—

(a) the administration by any person of a controlled drug to another in circumstances where the administration of the drug is not unlawful under section 4(1) of this Act, or

(b) the administration by any person of a controlled drug to himself in circumstances where having the controlled drug in his possession is not unlawful under section 5(1) of this Act.

(5) In this section, references to administration by any person of a controlled drug to himself include a reference to his administering it to himself with the assistance of another.

19 Attempts, etc., to commit offences

It is an offence for a person to incite another to commit an offence under any other provision of this Act. [E] and [S]

20 Assisting in or inducing commission outside United Kingdom of offence punishable under a corresponding law

A person commits an offence if in the United Kingdom he assists in or induces the commission in any place outside the United Kingdom of an offence punishable under the provisions of a corresponding law in force in that place. [E]

28 Proof of lack of knowledge, etc., to be a defence in proceedings for certain offences

(1) This section applies to offences under any of the following provisions of this Act; that is to say section 4(2) and (3), section 5(2) and (3), section 6(2) and section 9.

(2) Subject to subsection (3) below, in any proceedings for an offence to which this section applies it shall be a defence for the accused to prove that he neither knew of nor suspected nor had reason to suspect the existence of some fact alleged by the prosecution which is necessary for the prosecution to prove if he is to be convicted of the offence charged.

(3) Where in any proceedings for an offence to which this section applies it is necessary, if the accused is to be convicted of the offence charged, for the prosecution to prove that some substance or product involved in the alleged offence was the controlled drug which the prosecution alleges it to have been, and it is proved that the substance or product in question was that controlled drug, the accused—

(a) shall not be acquitted of the offence charged by reason only of proving that he neither knew or suspected nor had reason to suspect that the substance or product in question was the particular controlled drug alleged; but

(b) shall be acquitted thereof—

(i) if he proves that he neither believed nor suspected nor had reason to suspect that the substance or product in question was a controlled drug; or

(ii) if he proves that he believed the substance or product in question to be a controlled drug, or a controlled drug of a description, such that, if it had in fact been that controlled drug or a controlled drug of that description, he would not at the material time have been committing any offence to which this section applies.

(4) Nothing in this section shall prejudice any defence which it is open to a person charged with an offence to which this section applies to raise apart from this section.

36 Meaning of 'corresponding law', and evidence of certain matters by certificate

(1) In this Act the expression 'corresponding law' means a law stated in a certificate purporting to be issued by or on behalf of the government of a country outside the United Kingdom to be a law providing for the control and regulation in that country of the production, supply, use, export and import of drugs and other substances in accordance with the provisions of the Single Convention on Narcotic Drugs signed at New York on 30th March 1961 or a law providing for the control and regulation in

that country of the production, supply, use, export and import of dangerous or otherwise harmful drugs in pursuance of any treaty, convention or other agreement or arrangement to which the government of that country and Her Majesty's Government in the United Kingdom are for the time being parties.

37 Interpretation

(1) In this Act, except in so far as the context otherwise requires, the following expressions have the meanings hereby assigned to them respectively, that is to say:—

'produce', where the reference is to producing a controlled drug, means producing it by manufacture, cultivation or any other method and 'production' has a corresponding meaning;

'supplying' includes distributing;

(2) References in this Act to misusing a drug are references to misusing it by taking it; and the reference in the foregoing provision to the taking of a drug is a reference to the taking of it by a human being by way of any form of self administration, whether or not involving assistance by another.

(3) For the purposes of this Act the things which a person has in his possession shall be taken to include any thing subject to his control which is in the custody of another.

Intoxicating Substances (Supply) Act 1985

1 Offence of supplying intoxicating substance to or for person under 18

(1) It is an offence for a person to supply or offer to supply a substance other than a controlled drug—

(a) to a person under the age of eighteen whom he knows, or has reasonable cause to believe, to be under that age; or

(b) to a person—

(i) who is acting on behalf of a person under that age; and

(ii) whom he knows, or has reasonable cause to believe, to be so acting, if he knows or has reasonable cause to believe that the substance is, or its fumes are, likely to be inhaled by the person under the age of eighteen for the purpose of causing intoxication. [S]

(2) In proceedings against any person for an offence under subsection (1) above it is a defence for him to show that at the time he made the supply or offer he was under the age of eighteen and was acting otherwise than in the course of furtherance of a business.

(4) In this section 'controlled drug' has the same meaning as in the Misuse of Drugs Act 1971.

(h) Noise

Criminal Justice and Public Order Act 1994

63 Raves

(1) This section applies to a gathering on land in the open air of 20 or more persons (whether or not trespassers) at which amplified music is played during the night (with or without intermissions) and is such as, by reason of its loudness and duration and the time at which it is played, is likely to cause serious distress to the inhabitants of the locality; and for this purpose—

(a) such a gathering continues during intermissions in the music and, where the gathering extends over several days, throughout the period during which amplified music is played at night (with or without intermissions); and

(b) 'music' includes sounds wholly or predominantly characterised by the emission of a succession of repetitive beats.

(1A) This section also applies to a gathering if—

(a) it is a gathering on land of 20 or more persons who are trespassing on the land; and

(b) it would be a gathering of a kind mentioned in subsection (1) above if it took place on land in the open air.

(2) If, as respects any land, a police officer of at least the rank of superintendent reasonably believes that—

(a) two or more persons are making preparations for the holding there of a gathering to which this section applies,

(b) ten or more persons are waiting for such a gathering to begin there, or

(c) ten or more persons are attending such a gathering which is in progress, he may give a direction that those persons and any other persons who come to prepare or wait for or to attend the gathering are to leave the land and remove any vehicles or other property which they have with them on the land.

(3) A direction under subsection (2) above, if not communicated to the persons referred to in subsection (2) by the police officer giving the direction, may be communicated to them by any constable at the scene.

(4) Persons shall be treated as having had a direction under subsection (2) above communicated to them if reasonable steps have been taken to bring it to their attention.

(5) A direction under subsection (2) above does not apply to an exempt person.

(6) If a person knowing that a direction has been given which applies to him—

(a) fails to leave the land as soon as reasonably practicable, or

(b) having left again enters the land within the period of 7 days beginning with the day on which the direction was given,

he commits an offence . . . [S]

(7) In proceedings for an offence under subsection 6 above it is a defence for the accused to show that he had a reasonable excuse for failing to leave the land as soon as reasonably practicable or, as the case may be, for again entering the land.

(7A) A person commits an offence if—

(a) he knows that a direction under subsection (2) above has been given which applies to him, and

(b) he makes preparations for or attends a gathering to which this section applies within the period of 24 hours starting when the direction was given.

(10) In this section—

'exempt person', in relation to land (or any gathering on land), means the occupier, any member of his family and any employee or agent of his and any person whose home is situated on the land;

'land in the open air' includes a place partly open to the air;

'occupier', 'trespasser' and 'vehicle' have the same meaning as in section 61.

(i) Fur Farming and Hunting with Dogs

Fur Farming (Prohibition) Act 2000

1 Offences relating to fur farming

(1) A person is guilty of an offence if he keeps animals solely or primarily—

(a) for slaughter (whether by himself or another) for the value of their fur, or

(b) for breeding progeny for such slaughter.

(2) A person is guilty of an offence if he knowingly causes or permits another to keep animals as mentioned in subsection (1). [S]

(3) The references in this section to keeping animals for slaughter or to breeding progeny for slaughter include keeping or (as the case may be) breeding them for sale for slaughter.

Hunting Act 2004

1 Hunting wild mammals with dogs

A person commits an offence if he hunts a wild mammal with a dog, unless his hunting is exempt. [S]

2 Exempt hunting

(1) Hunting is exempt if it is within a class specified in Schedule 1.

3 Hunting: assistance

(1) A person commits an offence if he knowingly permits land which belongs to him to be entered or used in the course of the commission of an offence under section 1.

(2) A person commits an offence if he knowingly permits a dog which belongs to him to be used in the course of the commission of an offence under section 1.

4 Hunting: defence

It is a defence for a person charged with an offence under section 1 in respect of hunting to show that he reasonably believed that the hunting was exempt.

5 Hare coursing

(1) A person commits an offence if he—

(a) participates in a hare coursing event,
(b) attends a hare coursing event,
(c) knowingly facilitates a hare coursing event, or
(d) permits land which belongs to him to be used for the purposes of a hare coursing event.

(2) Each of the following persons commits an offence if a dog participates in a hare coursing event—

(a) any person who enters the dog for the event,
(b) any person who permits the dog to be entered, and
(c) any person who controls or handles the dog in the course of or for the purposes of the event.

(3) A 'hare coursing event' is a competition in which dogs are, by the use of live hares, assessed as to skill in hunting hares.

10 Offence by body corporate

(1) This section applies where an offence under this Act is committed by a body corporate with the consent or connivance of an officer of the body.

(2) The officer, as well as the body, shall be guilty of the offence.

(3) In subsection (1) a reference to an officer of a body corporate includes a reference to—

(a) a director, manager or secretary,
(b) a person purporting to act as a director, manager or secretary, and
(c) if the affairs of the body are managed by its members, a member.

11 Interpretation

(1) In this Act 'wild mammal' includes, in particular—

(a) a wild mammal which has been bred or tamed for any purpose,
(b) a wild mammal which is in captivity or confinement,
(c) a wild mammal which has escaped or been released from captivity or confinement, and
(d) any mammal which is living wild.

(2) For the purposes of this Act a reference to a person hunting a wild mammal with a dog includes, in particular, any case where—

(a) a person engages or participates in the pursuit of a wild mammal, and

(b) one or more dogs are employed in that pursuit (whether or not by him and whether or not under his control or direction).

(3) For the purposes of this Act land belongs to a person if he—

(a) owns an interest in it,

(b) manages or controls it, or

(c) occupies it.

(4) For the purposes of this Act a dog belongs to a person if he—

(a) owns it,

(b) is in charge of it, or

(c) has control of it.

SCHEDULE 1 EXEMPT HUNTING

Stalking and flushing out

1. (1) Stalking a wild mammal, or flushing it out of cover, is exempt hunting if the conditions in this paragraph are satisfied.

(2) The first condition is that the stalking or flushing out is undertaken for the purpose of—

(a) preventing or reducing serious damage which the wild mammal would otherwise cause—

(i) to livestock,

(ii) to game birds or wild birds (within the meaning of section 27 of the Wildlife and Countryside Act 1981),

(iii) to food for livestock,

(iv) to crops (including vegetables and fruit),

(v) to growing timber,

(vi) to fisheries,

(vii) to other property, or

(viii) to the biological diversity of an area (within the meaning of the United Nations Environmental Programme Convention on Biological Diversity of 1992),

(b) obtaining meat to be used for human or animal consumption, or

(c) participation in a field trial.

(3) In sub-paragraph (2)(c) 'field trial' means a competition (other than a hare coursing event within the meaning of section 5) in which dogs—

(a) flush animals out of cover or retrieve animals that have been shot (or both), and

(b) are assessed as to their likely usefulness in connection with shooting.

(4) The second condition is that the stalking or flushing out takes place on land—

(a) which belongs to the person doing the stalking or flushing out, or

(b) which he has been given permission to use for the purpose by the occupier or, in the case of unoccupied land, by a person to whom it belongs.

(5) The third condition is that the stalking or flushing out does not involve the use of more than two dogs.

(6) The fourth condition is that the stalking or flushing out does not involve the use of a dog below ground otherwise than in accordance with paragraph 2 below.

(7) The fifth condition is that—

(a) reasonable steps are taken for the purpose of ensuring that as soon as possible after being found or flushed out the wild mammal is shot dead by a competent person, and

(b) in particular, each dog used in the stalking or flushing out is kept under sufficiently close control to ensure that it does not prevent or obstruct achievement of the objective in paragraph (a).

Use of dogs below ground to protect birds for shooting

2. (1) The use of a dog below ground in the course of stalking or flushing out is in accordance with this paragraph if the conditions in this paragraph are satisfied.

(2) The first condition is that the stalking or flushing out is undertaken for the purpose of preventing or reducing serious damage to game birds or wild birds (within the meaning of section 27 of the Wildlife and Countryside Act 1981 (c. 69)) which a person is keeping or preserving for the purpose of their being shot.

(3) The second condition is that the person doing the stalking or flushing out—

(a) has with him written evidence—

(i) that the land on which the stalking or flushing out takes place belongs to him, or

(ii) that he has been given permission to use that land for the purpose by the occupier or, in the case of unoccupied land, by a person to whom it belongs, and

(b) makes the evidence immediately available for inspection by a constable who asks to see it.

(4) The third condition is that the stalking or flushing out does not involve the use of more than one dog below ground at any one time.

(5) In so far as stalking or flushing out is undertaken with the use of a dog below ground in accordance with this paragraph, paragraph 1 shall have effect as if for the condition in paragraph 1 (7) there were substituted the condition that—

(a) reasonable steps are taken for the purpose of ensuring that as soon as possible after being found the wild mammal is flushed out from below ground,

(b) reasonable steps are taken for the purpose of ensuring that as soon as possible after being flushed out from below ground the wild mammal is shot dead by a competent person,

(c) in particular, the dog is brought under sufficiently close control to ensure that it does not prevent or obstruct achievement of the objective in paragraph (b),

(d) reasonable steps are taken for the purpose of preventing injury to the dog, and

(e) the manner in which the dog is used complies with any code of practice which is issued or approved for the purpose of this paragraph by the Secretary of State.

Rats

3. The hunting of rats is exempt if it takes place on land—

(a) which belongs to the hunter, or

(b) which he has been given permission to use for the purpose by the occupier or, in the case of unoccupied land, by a person to whom it belongs.

Rabbits

4. The hunting of rabbits is exempt if it takes place on land—

(a) which belongs to the hunter, or

(b) which he has been given permission to use for the purpose by the occupier or, in the case of unoccupied land, by a person to whom it belongs.

Retrieval of hares

5. The hunting of a hare which has been shot is exempt if it takes place on land—

(a) which belongs to the hunter, or

(b) which he has been given permission to use for the purpose of hunting hares by the occupier or, in the case of unoccupied land, by a person to whom it belongs.

Falconry

6. Flushing a wild mammal from cover is exempt hunting if undertaken—

(a) for the purpose of enabling a bird of prey to hunt the wild mammal, and

(b) on land which belongs to the hunter or which he has been given permission to use for the purpose by the occupier or, in the case of unoccupied land, by a person to whom it belongs.

Recapture of wild mammal

7. (1) The hunting of a wild mammal which has escaped or been released from captivity or confinement is exempt if the conditions in this paragraph are satisfied.

(2) The first condition is that the hunting takes place—

(a) on land which belongs to the hunter,
(b) on land which he has been given permission to use for the purpose by the occupier or, in the case of unoccupied land, by a person to whom it belongs, or
(c) with the authority of a constable.

(3) The second condition is that—
(a) reasonable steps are taken for the purpose of ensuring that as soon as possible after being found the wild mammal is recaptured or shot dead by a competent person, and
(b) in particular, each dog used in the hunt is kept under sufficiently close control to ensure that it does not prevent or obstruct achievement of the objective in paragraph (a).

(4) The third condition is that the wild mammal—
(a) was not released for the purpose of being hunted, and
(b) was not, for that purpose, permitted to escape.

Rescue of wild mammal

8. (1) The hunting of a wild mammal is exempt if the conditions in this paragraph are satisfied.

(2) The first condition is that the hunter reasonably believes that the wild mammal is or may be injured.

(3) The second condition is that the hunting is undertaken for the purpose of relieving the wild mammal's suffering.

(4) The third condition is that the hunting does not involve the use of more than two dogs.

(5) The fourth condition is that the hunting does not involve the use of a dog below ground.

(6) The fifth condition is that the hunting takes place—
(a) on land which belongs to the hunter,
(b) on land which he has been given permission to use for the purpose by the occupier or, in the case of unoccupied land, by a person to whom it belongs, or
(c) with the authority of a constable.

(7) The sixth condition is that—
(a) reasonable steps are taken for the purpose of ensuring that as soon as possible after the wild mammal is found appropriate action (if any) is taken to relieve its suffering, and
(b) in particular, each dog used in the hunt is kept under sufficiently close control to ensure that it does not prevent or obstruct achievement of the objective in paragraph (a).

(8) The seventh condition is that the wild mammal was not harmed for the purpose of enabling it to be hunted in reliance upon this paragraph.

Research and observation

9. (1) The hunting of a wild mammal is exempt if the conditions in this paragraph are satisfied.

(2) The first condition is that the hunting is undertaken for the purpose of or in connection with the observation or study of the wild mammal.

(3) The second condition is that the hunting does not involve the use of more than two dogs.

(4) The third condition is that the hunting does not involve the use of a dog below ground.

(5) The fourth condition is that the hunting takes place on land—
(a) which belongs to the hunter, or
(b) which he has been given permission to use for the purpose by the occupier or, in the case of unoccupied land, by a person to whom it belongs.

(6) The fifth condition is that each dog used in the hunt is kept under sufficiently close control to ensure that it does not injure the wild mammal.

Part XI

Disorder and Terrorism

(a) Disorder

Public Order Act 1986

PART 1

1 Riot

(1) Where 12 or more persons who are present together use or threaten unlawful violence for a common purpose and the conduct of them (taken together) is such as would cause a person of reasonable firmness present at the scene to fear for his personal safety, each of the persons using unlawful violence for the common purpose is guilty of riot. [I]

(2) It is immaterial whether or not the 12 or more use or threaten unlawful violence simultaneously.

(3) The common purpose may be inferred from conduct.

(4) No person of reasonable firmness need actually be, or be likely to be, present at the scene.

(5) Riot may be committed in private as well as in public places.

2 Violent disorder

(1) Where 3 or more persons who are present together use or threaten unlawful violence and the conduct of them (taken together) is such as would cause a person of reasonable firmness present at the scene to fear for his personal safety, each of the persons using or threatening unlawful violence is guilty of violent disorder. [E]

(2) It is immaterial whether or not the 3 or more use or threaten unlawful violence simultaneously.

(3) No person of reasonable firmness need actually be, or be likely to be, present at the scene.

(4) Violent disorder may be committed in private as well as in public places.

6 Mental element: miscellaneous

[See page 50]

8 Interpretation

[See page 50]

PART 3

17 Meaning of 'racial hatred'

In this Part 'racial hatred' means hatred against a group of persons defined by reference to colour, race, nationality (including citizenship) or ethnic or national origins.

18 Use of words or behaviour or display of written material

(1) A person who uses threatening, abusive or insulting words or behaviour, or displays any written material which is threatening, abusive or insulting, is guilty of an offence if—

(a) he intends thereby to stir up racial hatred, or

(b) having regard to all the circumstances racial hatred is likely to be stirred up thereby. [E]

(2) An offence under this section may be committed in a public or a private place, except that no offence is committed where the words or behaviour are used, or the written material is displayed, by a person inside a dwelling and are not heard or seen except by other persons in that or another dwelling.

(4) In proceedings for an offence under this section it is a defence for the accused to prove that he was inside a dwelling and had no reason to believe that the words or behaviour used, or the written material displayed, would be heard or seen by a person outside that or any other dwelling.

(5) A person who is not shown to have intended to stir up racial hatred is not guilty of an offence under this section if he did not intend his words or behaviour, or the written material, to be, and was not aware that it might be, threatening, abusive or insulting.

(6) This section does not apply to words or behaviour used, or written material displayed, solely for the purpose of being included in a programme included in a programme service.

19 Publishing or distributing written material

(1) A person who publishes or distributes written material which is threatening, abusive or insulting is guilty of an offence if—

(a) he intends thereby to stir up racial hatred, or

(b) having regard to all the circumstances racial hatred is likely to be stirred up thereby. [E]

(2) In proceedings for an offence under this section it is a defence for an accused who is not shown to have intended to stir up racial hatred to prove that he was not aware of the content of the material and did not suspect, and had no reason to suspect, that it was threatening, abusive or insulting.

(3) References in this Part to the publication or distribution of written material are to its publication or distribution to the public or a section of the public.

PART 3A

29A Meaning of 'religious hatred'

In this Part 'religious hatred' means hatred against a group of persons defined by reference to religious belief or lack of religious belief.

29AB Meaning of 'hatred on the grounds of sexual orientation'

In this Part 'hatred on the grounds of sexual orientation' means hatred against a group of persons defined by reference to sexual orientation (whether towards persons of the same sex, the opposite sex or both).

29B Use of words or behaviour or display of written material

(1) A person who uses threatening words or behaviour, or displays any written material which is threatening, is guilty of an offence if he intends thereby to stir up religious hatred or hatred on the grounds of sexual orientation. [E]

(2) An offence under this section may be committed in a public or a private place, except that no offence is committed where the words or behaviour are used, or the written material is displayed, by a person inside a dwelling and are not heard or seen except by other persons in that or another dwelling.

(4) In proceedings for an offence under this section it is a defence for the accused to prove that he was inside a dwelling and had no reason to believe that the words or behaviour used, or the written material displayed, would be heard or seen by a person outside that or any other dwelling.

(5) This section does not apply to words or behaviour used, or written material displayed, solely for the purpose of being included in a programme service.

29C Publishing or distributing written material

(1) A person who publishes or distributes written material which is threatening is guilty of an offence if he intends thereby to stir up religious hatred or hatred on the grounds of sexual orientation. [E]

(2) References in this Part to the publication or distribution of written material are to its publication or distribution to the public or a section of the public.

29D Public performance of play

(1) If a public performance of a play is given which involves the use of threatening words or behaviour, any person who presents or directs the performance is guilty of an offence if he intends thereby to stir up religious hatred or hatred on the grounds of sexual orientation. [E]

(2) This section does not apply to a performance given solely or primarily for one or more of the following purposes—

- (a) rehearsal,
- (b) making a recording of the performance, or
- (c) enabling the performance to be included in a programme service;

but if it is proved that the performance was attended by persons other than those directly connected with the giving of the performance or the doing in relation to it of the things mentioned in paragraph (b) or (c), the performance shall, unless the contrary is shown, be taken not to have been given solely or primarily for the purpose mentioned above.

(3) For the purposes of this section—

- (a) a person shall not be treated as presenting a performance of a play by reason only of his taking part in it as a performer,
- (b) a person taking part as a performer in a performance directed by another shall be treated as a person who directed the performance if without reasonable excuse he performs otherwise than in accordance with that person's direction, and
- (c) a person shall be taken to have directed a performance of a play given under his direction notwithstanding that he was not present during the performance;

and a person shall not be treated as aiding or abetting the commission of an offence under this section by reason only of his taking part in a performance as a performer.

(4) In this section 'play' and 'public performance' have the same meaning as in the Theatres Act 1968.

29E Distributing, showing or playing a recording

(1) A person who distributes, or shows or plays, a recording of visual images or sounds which are threatening is guilty of an offence if he intends thereby to stir up religious hatred or hatred on the grounds of sexual orientation. [E]

(2) In this Part 'recording' means any record from which visual images or sounds may, by any means, be reproduced; and references to the distribution, showing or playing of a recording are to its distribution, showing or playing to the public or a section of the public.

(3) This section does not apply to the showing or playing of a recording solely for the purpose of enabling the recording to be included in a programme service.

29F Broadcasting or including programme in programme service

(1) If a programme involving threatening visual images or sounds is included in a programme service, each of the persons mentioned in subsection (2) is guilty of an offence if he intends thereby to stir up religious hatred or hatred on the grounds of sexual orientation.

(2) The persons are—

- (a) the person providing the programme service,
- (b) any person by whom the programme is produced or directed, and
- (c) any person by whom offending words or behaviour are used.

29G Possession of inflammatory material

(1) A person who has in his possession written material which is threatening, or a recording of visual images or sounds which are threatening, with a view to—

(a) in the case of written material, its being displayed, published, distributed, or included in a programme service whether by himself or another, or

(b) in the case of a recording, its being distributed, shown, played, or included in a programme service, whether by himself or another,

is guilty of an offence if he intends thereby to stir up religious hatred or hatred on the grounds of sexual orientation. [E]

(2) For this purpose regard shall be had to such display, publication, distribution, showing, playing, or inclusion in a programme service as he has, or it may be reasonably be inferred that he has, in view.

29J Protection of freedom of expression

Nothing in this Part shall be read or given effect in a way which prohibits or restricts discussion, criticism or expressions of antipathy, dislike, ridicule, insult or abuse of particular religions or the beliefs or practices of their adherents, or of any other belief system or the beliefs or practices of its adherents, or proselytising or urging adherents of a different religion or belief system to cease practising their religion or belief system.

29JA Protection of freedom of expression (sexual orientation)

In this Part, for the avoidance of doubt, the discussion or criticism of sexual conduct or practices or the urging of persons to refrain from or modify such conduct or practices shall not be taken of itself to be threatening or intended to stir up hatred.

29K Savings for reports of parliamentary or judicial proceedings

(1) Nothing in this Part applies to a fair and accurate report of proceedings in Parliament, in the Scottish Parliament or in the National Assembly for Wales.

(2) Nothing in this Part applies to a fair and accurate report of proceedings publicly heard before a court or tribunal exercising judicial authority where the report is published contemporaneously with the proceedings or, if it is not reasonably practicable or would be unlawful to publish a report of them contemporaneously, as soon as publication is reasonably practicable and lawful.

29L Procedure and punishment

(1) No proceedings for an offence under this Part may be instituted except by or with the consent of the Attorney General.

(2) For the purposes of the rules against charging more than one offence in the same count or information, each of sections 29B to 29G creates one offence.

29M Offences by corporations

(1) Where a body corporate is guilty of an offence under this Part and it is shown that the offence was committed with the consent or connivance of a director, manager, secretary or other similar officer of the body, or a person purporting to act in any such capacity, he as well as the body corporate is guilty of the offence and liable to be proceeded against and punished accordingly.

(2) Where the affairs of a body corporate are managed by its members, subsection (1) applies in relation to the acts and defaults of a member in connection with his functions of management as it applies to a director.

29N Interpretation

In this Part—

'distribute', and related expressions, shall be construed in accordance with section 29C(2) (written material) and section 29E(2) (recordings);

'dwelling' means any structure or part of a structure occupied as a person's home or other living accommodation (whether the occupation is separate or shared with others) but does not include any part not so occupied, and for this purpose 'structure' includes a tent, caravan, vehicle, vessel or other temporary or movable structure;

'hatred on the grounds of sexual orientation' has the meaning given by section 29AB;

'programme' means any item which is included in a programme service; 'programme service' has the same meaning as in the Broadcasting Act 1990; 'publish', and related expressions, in relation to written material, shall be construed in accordance with section 29C(2);

'religious hatred' has the meaning given by section 29A;

'recording' has the meaning given by section 29E(2), and 'play' and 'show', and related expressions, in relation to a recording, shall be construed in accordance with that provision;

'written material' includes any sign or other visible representation.'

38 Contamination of or interference with goods with intention of causing public alarm or anxiety, etc.

(1) It is an offence for a person, with the intention—

(a) of causing public alarm or anxiety, or

(b) of causing injury to members of the public consuming or using the goods, or

(c) of causing economic loss to any person by reason of the goods being shunned by members of the public, or

(d) of causing economic loss to any person by reason of steps taken to avoid any such alarm or anxiety, injury or loss,

to contaminate or interfere with goods, or make it appear that goods have been contaminated or interfered with, or to place goods which have been contaminated or interfered with, or which appear to have been contaminated and interfered with, in a place where goods of that description are consumed, used, sold or otherwise supplied. [E]

(2) It is also an offence for a person, with any such intention as is mentioned in paragraph (a), (c) or (d) of subsection (1), to threaten that he or another will do, or claim that he or another has done, any of the acts mentioned in that subsection. [E]

(3) It is an offence for a person to be in possession of any of the following articles with a view to the commission of an offence under subsection (1)—

(a) materials to be used for contaminating or interfering with goods or making it appear that goods have been contaminated or interfered with, or

(b) goods which have been contaminated or interfered with, or which appear to have been contaminated or interfered with. [E]

(5) In this section 'goods' includes substances whether natural or manufactured and whether or not incorporated in or mixed with other goods.

(6) The reference in subsection (2) to a person claiming that certain acts have been committed does not include a person who in good faith reports or warns that such acts have been, or appear to have been, committed.

Crime and Disorder Act 1998

28 Meaning of 'racially or religiously aggravated'

(1) An offence is racially or religiously aggravated for the purposes of sections 29 to 32 below if—

(a) at the time of committing the offence, or immediately before or after doing so, the offender demonstrates towards the victim of the offence hostility based on the victim's membership (or presumed membership) of a racial or religious group; or

(b) the offence is motivated (wholly or partly) by hostility towards members of a racial group based on their membership of that group.

(2) In subsection (1)(a) above—

'membership', in relation to a racial or religious group, includes association with members of that group;

'presumed' means presumed by the offender.

(3) It is immaterial for the purposes of paragraph (a) or (b) of subsection (1) above whether or not the offender's hostility is also based, to any extent, on any other factor not mentioned in that paragraph.

(4) In this section 'racial group' means a group of persons defined by reference to race, colour, nationality (including citizenship) or ethnic or national origins.

(5) In this section 'religious group' means a group of persons defined by reference to religious belief or lack of religious belief.

29 Racially or religiously aggravated assaults

(1) A person is guilty of an offence under this section if he commits—

(a) an offence under section 20 of the Offences Against the Person Act 1861 (malicious wounding or grievous bodily harm);

(b) an offence under section 47 of that Act (actual bodily harm); or

(c) common assault,

which is racially or religiously aggravated for the purposes of this section. [E]

30 Racially or religiously aggravated criminal damage

(1) A person is guilty of an offence under this section if he commits an offence under section 1 (1) of the Criminal Damage Act 1971 (destroying or damaging property belonging to another) which is racially or religiously aggravated for the purposes of this section. [E]

(3) For the purposes of this section, section 28(1)(a) above shall have effect as if the person to whom the property belongs or is treated as belonging for the purposes of that Act were the victim of the offence.

31 Racially or religiously aggravated public order offences

(1) A person is guilty of an offence under this section if he commits—

(a) an offence under section 4 of the Public Order Act 1986 (fear or provocation of violence) [E];

(b) an offence under section 4A of that Act (intentional harassment, alarm or distress) [E] or

(c) an offence under section 5 of that Act (harassment, alarm or distress) [S],

which is racially or religiously aggravated for the purposes of this section.

(6) If, on the trial on indictment of a person charged with an offence falling within subsection (1) (a) or (b) above, the jury find him not guilty of the offence charged, they may find him guilty of the basic offence mentioned in that provision.

(7) For the purposes of subsection (1)(c) above, section 28(1)(a) above shall have effect as if the person likely to be caused harassment, alarm or distress were the victim of the offence.

32 Racially or religiously aggravated harassment, etc.

(1) A person is guilty of an offence under this section if he commits—

(a) an offence under section 2 of the Protection from Harassment Act 1997 (offence of harassment); or

(b) an offence under section 4 of that Act (putting people in fear of violence),

which is racially or religiously aggravated for the purposes of this section. [E]

(5) If, on the trial on indictment of a person charged with an offence falling within subsection (1)(a) above, the jury find him not guilty of the offence charged, they may find him guilty of the basic offence mentioned in that provision.

(6) If, on the trial on indictment of a person charged with an offence falling within subsection (1) (b) above, the jury find him not guilty of the offence charged, they may find him guilty of an offence falling within subsection (1)(a) above.

Football (Offences) Act 1991

1 Designated football matches

(1) In this Act a 'designated football match' means an association football match designated, or of a description designated, for the purposes of this Act by order of the Secretary of State.

Any such order shall be made by statutory instrument which shall be subject to annulment in pursuance of a resolution of either House of Parliament.

(2) References in this Act to things done at a designated football match include anything done at the ground—

(a) within the period beginning two hours before the start of the match or (if earlier) two hours before the time at which it is advertised to start and ending one hour after the end of the match; or

(b) where the match is advertised to start at a particular time on a particular day but does not take place on that day, within the period beginning two hours before and ending one hour after the advertised starting time.

2 Throwing of missiles

It is an offence for a person at a designated football match to throw anything at or towards—

(a) the playing area, or any area adjacent to the playing area to which spectators are not generally admitted, or

(b) any area in which spectators or other persons are or may be present, without lawful authority or lawful excuse (which shall be for him to prove). [S]

3 Indecent or racialist chanting

(1) It is an offence to engage or take part in chanting of an indecent or racialist nature at a designated football match. [S]

(2) For this purpose—

(a) 'chanting' means the repeated uttering of any words or sounds (whether alone or in concert with one or more others); and

(b) 'of a racialist nature' means consisting of or including matter which is threatening, abusive or insulting to a person by reason of his colour, race, nationality (including citizenship) or ethnic or national origins.

4 Going onto the playing area

It is an offence for a person at a designated football match to go onto the playing area, or any area adjacent to the playing area to which spectators are not generally admitted, without lawful authority or lawful excuse (which shall be for him to prove). [S]

(b) Terrorism

Explosive Substances Act 1883

2 Causing explosion likely to endanger life or property

A person who in the United Kingdom or (being a citizen of the United Kingdom and Colonies) in the Republic of Ireland unlawfully and maliciously causes by any explosive substance an explosion of a nature likely to endanger life or to cause serious injury to person or property shall, whether any injury to person or property has been actually caused or not, be guilty of an offence and on conviction on indictment shall be liable to imprisonment for life. [I]

3 Attempt to cause explosion, or making or keeping explosive with intent to endanger life or property

Any person who in the United Kingdom or a dependency or (being a citizen of the United Kingdom and Colonies) elsewhere unlawfully and maliciously—

(a) does any act with intent to cause, or conspires to cause, by an explosive substance an explosion of a nature likely to endanger life, or cause serious injury to property, whether in the United Kingdom or elsewhere, or

(b) makes or has in his possession or under his control an explosive substance with intent by means thereof to endanger life, or cause serious injury to property, whether in the United Kingdom or elsewhere, or to enable any other person so to do, shall, whether any explosion does not take place, and whether any injury to person or property has been actually caused or not, be guilty of an offence and on conviction on indictment shall be liable to imprisonment for life, and the explosive substance shall be forfeited. [I]

4 Making or possession of explosive under suspicious circumstances

(1) Any person who makes or knowingly has in his possession or under his control any explosive substance, under such circumstances as to give rise to a reasonable suspicion that he is not making it or does not have it in his possession or under his control for a lawful object, shall, unless he can show that he made it or had it in his possession or under his control for a lawful object, be guilty of felony, and, on conviction, shall be liable to penal servitude for a term not exceeding fourteen years, or to imprisonment for a term not exceeding two years with or without hard labour, and the explosive substance shall be forfeited. [I]

5 Punishment of accessories

Any person who within or (being a subject of Her Majesty) without Her Majesty's dominions by the supply of or solicitation for money, the providing of premises, the supply of materials, or in any manner whatsoever, procures, counsels, aids, abets, or is accessory to, the commission of any crime under this Act, shall be guilty of an offence, and shall be liable to be tried and punished for that crime, as if he had been guilty as a principal.

9 Definitions

(1) In this Act, unless the context otherwise requires—

The expression 'explosive substance' shall be deemed to include any materials for making any explosive substance; also any apparatus, machine, implement, or materials used, or intended to be used, or adapted for causing, or aiding in causing, any explosion in or with any explosive substance; also any part of any such apparatus, machine, or implement.

Taking of Hostages Act 1982

1 Hostage-taking

(1) A person, whatever his nationality, who, in the United Kingdom or elsewhere,—
- (a) detains any other person ('the hostage'), and
- (b) in order to compel a State, international governmental organisation or person to do or abstain from doing any act, threatens to kill, injure or continue to detain the hostage, commits an offence. [I]

Terrorism Act 2000

PART I INTRODUCTORY

1 Terrorism: interpretation

(1) In this Act 'terrorism' means the use or threat of action where—
- (a) the action falls within subsection (2),
- (b) the use or threat is designed to influence the government or an international governmental organisation or to intimidate the public or a section of the public, and
- (c) the use or threat is made for the purpose of advancing a political, religious or ideological cause.

(2) Action falls within this subsection if it—
- (a) involves serious violence against a person,
- (b) involves serious damage to property,

(c) endangers a person's life, other than that of the person committing the action,
(d) creates a serious risk to the health or safety of the public or a section of the public, or
(e) is designed seriously to interfere with or seriously to disrupt an electronic system.

(3) The use or threat of action falling within subsection (2) which involves the use of firearms or explosives is terrorism whether or not subsection (1)(b) is satisfied.

(4) In this section—
(a) 'action' includes action outside the United Kingdom,
(b) a reference to any person or to property is a reference to any person, or to property, wherever situated,
(c) a reference to the public includes a reference to the public of a country other than the United Kingdom, and
(d) 'the government' means the government of the United Kingdom, of a part of the United Kingdom or of a country other than the United Kingdom.

(5) In this Act a reference to action taken for the purposes of terrorism includes a reference to action taken for the benefit of a proscribed organisation.

PART II PROSCRIBED ORGANISATIONS

3 Proscription

(1) For the purposes of this Act an organisation is proscribed if—
(a) it is listed in Schedule 2, or
(b) it operates under the same name as an organisation listed in that Schedule.

11 Membership

(1) A person commits an offence if he belongs or professes to belong to a proscribed organisation. [I]

(2) It is a defence for a person charged with an offence under subsection (1) to prove—
(a) that the organisation was not proscribed on the last (or only) occasion on which he became a member or began to profess to be a member, and
(b) that he has not taken part in the activities of the organisation at any time while it was proscribed.

(4) In subsection (2) 'proscribed' means proscribed for the purposes of any of the following—
(a) this Act;
(b) the Northern Ireland (Emergency Provisions) Act 1996;
(c) the Northern Ireland (Emergency Provisions) Act 1991;
(d) the Prevention of Terrorism (Temporary Provisions) Act 1989;
(e) the Prevention of Terrorism (Temporary Provisions) Act 1984;
(f) the Northern Ireland (Emergency Provisions) Act 1978;
(g) the Prevention of Terrorism (Temporary Provisions) Act 1976;
(h) the Prevention of Terrorism (Temporary Provisions) Act 1974;
(i) the Northern Ireland (Emergency Provisions) Act 1973.

12 Support

(1) A person commits an offence if—
(a) he invites support for a proscribed organisation, and
(b) the support is not, or is not restricted to, the provision of money or other property (within the meaning of section 15). [I]

(2) A person commits an offence if he arranges, manages or assists in arranging or managing a meeting which he knows is—
(a) to support a proscribed organisation,
(b) to further the activities of a proscribed organisation, or
(c) to be addressed by a person who belongs or professes to belong to a proscribed organ-isation. [I]

(3) A person commits an offence if he addresses a meeting and the purpose of his address is to encourage support for a proscribed organisation or to further its activities. [I]

(4) Where a person is charged with an offence under subsection (2)(c) in respect of a private meeting it is a defence for him to prove that he had no reasonable cause to believe that the address mentioned in subsection (2)(c) would support a proscribed organisation or further its activities.

(5) In subsections (2) to (4)—

(a) 'meeting' means a meeting of three or more persons, whether or not the public are admitted, and

(b) a meeting is private if the public are not admitted.

13 Uniform

(1) A person in a public place commits an offence if he—

(a) wears an item of clothing, or

(b) wears, carries or displays an article,

in such a way or in such circumstances as to arouse reasonable suspicion that he is a member or supporter of a proscribed organisation. [E]

PART III TERRORIST PROPERTY

14 Terrorist property

(1) In this Act 'terrorist property' means—

(a) money or other property which is likely to be used for the purposes of terrorism (including any resources of a proscribed organisation),

(b) proceeds of the commission of acts of terrorism, and

(c) proceeds of acts carried out for the purposes of terrorism.

(2) In subsection (1)—

(a) a reference to proceeds of an act includes a reference to any property which wholly or partly, and directly or indirectly, represents the proceeds of the act (including payments or other rewards in connection with its commission), and

(b) the reference to an organisation's resources includes a reference to any money or other property which is applied or made available, or is to be applied or made available, for use by the organisation.

15 Fund-raising

(1) A person commits an offence if he—

(a) invites another to provide money or other property, and

(b) intends that it should be used, or has reasonable cause to suspect that it may be used, for the purposes of terrorism. [I]

(2) A person commits an offence if he—

(a) receives money or other property, and

(b) intends that it should be used, or has reasonable cause to suspect that it may be used, for the purposes of terrorism. [I]

(3) A person commits an offence if he—

(a) provides money or other property, and

(b) knows or has reasonable cause to suspect that it will or may be used for the purposes of terrorism. [I]

(4) In this section a reference to the provision of money or other property is a reference to its being given, lent or otherwise made available, whether or not for consideration.

16 Use and possession

(1) A person commits an offence if he uses money or other property for the purposes of terrorism.

(2) A person commits an offence if he—

(a) possesses money or other property, and
(b) intends that it should be used, or has reasonable cause to suspect that it may be used, for the purposes of terrorism. [I]

17 Funding arrangements

A person commits an offence if—

(a) he enters into or becomes concerned in an arrangement as a result of which money or other property is made available or is to be made available to another, and
(b) he knows or has reasonable cause to suspect that it will or may be used for the purposes of terrorism. [I]

18 Money laundering

(1) A person commits an offence if he enters into or becomes concerned in an arrangement which facilitates the retention or control by or on behalf of another person of terrorist property—

(a) by concealment,
(b) by removal from the jurisdiction,
(c) by transfer to nominees, or
(d) in any other way. [I]

(2) It is a defence for a person charged with an offence under subsection (1) to prove that he did not know and had no reasonable cause to suspect that the arrangement related to terrorist property.

19 Disclosure of information: duty

(1) This section applies where a person—

(a) believes or suspects that another person has committed an offence under any of sections 15 to 18, and
(b) bases his belief or suspicion on information which comes to his attention in the course of a trade, profession, business or employment.

(1A) But this section does not apply if the information came to the person in the course of a business in the regulated sector.

(2) The person commits an offence if he does not disclose to a constable as soon as is reasonably practicable—

(a) his belief or suspicion, and
(b) the information on which it is based. [E]

(3) It is a defence for a person charged with an offence under subsection (2) to prove that he had a reasonable excuse for not making the disclosure.

(4) Where—

(a) a person is in employment,
(b) his employer has established a procedure for the making of disclosures of the matters specified in subsection (2), and
(c) he is charged with an offence under that subsection, it is a defence for him to prove that he disclosed the matters specified in that subsection in accordance with the procedure.

(5) Subsection (2) does not require disclosure by a professional legal adviser of—

(a) information which he obtains in privileged circumstances, or
(b) a belief or suspicion based on information which he obtains in privileged circumstances

(6) For the purpose of subsection (5) information is obtained by an adviser in privileged circumstances if it comes to him, otherwise than with a view to furthering a criminal purpose—

(a) from a client or a client's representative, in connection with the provision of legal advice by the adviser to the client,
(b) from a person seeking legal advice from the adviser, or from the person's representative, or
(c) from any person, for the purpose of actual or contemplated legal proceedings.

(7) For the purposes of subsection (1)(a) a person shall be treated as having committed an offence under one of sections 15 to 18 if—

(a) he has taken an action or been in possession of a thing, and

(b) he would have committed an offence under one of those sections if he had been in the United Kingdom at the time when he took the action or was in possession of the thing.

(7A) The reference to a business in the regulated sector must be construed in accordance with Schedule 3A.

(7B) The reference to a constable includes a reference to a member of the staff of the Serious Organised Crime Agency authorised for the purposes of this section by the Director General of that Agency.

21 Cooperation with police

(1) A person does not commit an offence under any of sections 15 to 18 if he is acting with the express consent of a constable.

(2) Subject to subsections (3) and (4), a person does not commit an offence under any of sections 15 to 18 by involvement in a transaction or arrangement relating to money or other property if he discloses to a constable—

(a) his suspicion or belief that the money or other property is terrorist property, and

(b) the information on which his suspicion or belief is based.

(3) Subsection (2) applies only where a person makes a disclosure—

(a) after he becomes concerned in the transaction concerned,

(b) on his own initiative, and

(c) as soon as is reasonably practicable.

(4) Subsection (2) does not apply to a person if—

(a) a constable forbids him to continue his involvement in the transaction or arrangement to which the disclosure relates, and

(b) he continues his involvement.

(5) It is a defence for a person charged with an offence under any of sections 15(2) and (3) and 16 to 18 to prove that—

(a) he intended to make a disclosure of the kind mentioned in subsections (2) and (3), and

(b) there is reasonable excuse for his failure to do so.

(6) Where—

(a) a person is in employment, and

(b) his employer has established a procedure for the making of disclosures of the same kind as may be made to a constable under subsection (2),

this section shall have effect in relation to that person as if any reference to disclosure to a constable included a reference to disclosure in accordance with the procedure.

(7) A reference in this section to a transaction or arrangement relating to money or other property includes a reference to use or possession.

38B Information about acts of terrorism

(1) This section applies where a person has information which he knows or believes might be of material assistance—

(a) in preventing the commission by another person of an act of terrorism, or

(b) in securing the apprehension, prosecution or conviction of another person, in the United Kingdom, for an offence involving the commission, preparation or instigation of an act of terrorism.

(2) The person commits an offence if he does not disclose the information as soon as reasonably practicable in accordance with subsection (3). [E]

(3) Disclosure is in accordance with this subsection if it is made—

(a) in England and Wales, to a constable,

(b) in Scotland, to a constable, or

(c) in Northern Ireland, to a constable or a member of Her Majesty's forces.

(4) It is a defence for a person charged with an offence under subsection (2) to prove that he had a reasonable excuse for not making the disclosure.

(6) Proceedings for an offence under this section may be taken, and the offence may for the purposes of those proceedings be treated as having been committed, in any place where the person to be charged is or has at any time been since he first knew or believed that the information might be of material assistance as mentioned in subsection (1).

39 Disclosure of information, etc.

(1) Subsection (2) applies where a person knows or has reasonable cause to suspect that a constable is conducting or proposes to conduct a terrorist investigation.

(2) The person commits an offence if he—

(a) discloses to another anything which is likely to prejudice the investigation, or

(b) interferes with material which is likely to be relevant to the investigation. [E]

(3) Subsection (4) applies where a person knows or has reasonable cause to suspect that a disclosure has been or will be made under any of sections 19 to 21 or 38B.

(4) The person commits an offence if he—

(a) discloses to another anything which is likely to prejudice an investigation resulting from the disclosure under that section, or

(b) interferes with material which is likely to be relevant to an investigation resulting from the disclosure under that section. [E]

(5) It is a defence for a person charged with an offence under subsection (2) or (4) to prove—

(a) that he did not know and had no reasonable cause to suspect that the disclosure or interference was likely to affect a terrorist investigation, or

(b) that he had a reasonable excuse for the disclosure or interference.

(6) Subsections (2) and (4) do not apply to a disclosure which is made by a professional legal adviser—

(a) to his client or to his client's representative in connection with the provision of legal advice by the adviser to the client and not with a view to furthering a criminal purpose, or

(b) to any person for the purpose of actual or contemplated legal proceedings and not with a view to furthering a criminal purpose.

(8) For the purposes of this section—

(a) a reference to conducting a terrorist investigation includes a reference to taking part in the conduct of, or assisting, a terrorist investigation, and

(b) a person interferes with material if he falsifies it, conceals it, destroys it or disposes of it, or if he causes or permits another to do any of those things.

48 Authorisations

(1) An authorisation under this section authorises any constable in uniform to prohibit or restrict the parking of vehicles on a road specified in the authorisation.

(2) An authorisation may be given only if the person giving it considers it expedient for the prevention of acts of terrorism.

(3) An authorisation may be given—

(a) where the road specified is outside Northern Ireland and is wholly or partly within a police area other than one mentioned in paragraphs (b) or (c), by a police officer for the area who is of at least the rank of assistant chief constable;

(b) where the road specified is wholly or partly in the metropolitan police district, by a police officer for the district who is of at least the rank of commander of the metropolitan police;

(c) where the road specified is wholly or partly in the City of London, by a police officer for the City who is of at least the rank of commander in the City of London police force;

(d) where the road specified is in Northern Ireland, by a member of the Police Service of Northern Ireland who is of at least the rank of assistant chief constable.

(4) If an authorisation is given orally, the person giving it shall confirm it in writing as soon as is reasonably practicable.

49 Exercise of power

(1) The power conferred by an authorisation under section 48 shall be exercised by placing a traffic sign on the road concerned.

51 Offences

(1) A person commits an offence if he parks a vehicle in contravention of a prohibition or restriction imposed by virtue of section 48. [S]

(2) A person commits an offence if—

(a) he is the driver or other person in charge of a vehicle which has been permitted to remain at rest in contravention of any prohibition or restriction imposed by virtue of section 48, and

(b) he fails to move the vehicle when ordered to do so by a constable in uniform. [S]

(3) It is a defence for a person charged with an offence under this section to prove that he had a reasonable excuse for the act or omission in question.

(4) Possession of a current disabled person's badge shall not itself constitute a reasonable excuse for the purposes of subsection (3).

52 Interpretation

In sections 48 to 51—

'disabled person's badge' means a badge issued, or having effect as if issued, under any regulations for the time being in force under section 21 of the Chronically Sick and Disabled Persons Act 1970;

'driver' means, in relation to a vehicle which has been left on any road, the person who was driving it when it was left there;

'parking' means leaving a vehicle or permitting it to remain at rest;

'traffic sign' has the meaning given in section 142(1) of the Road Traffic Regulation Act 1984;

'vehicle' has the same meaning as in section 99(5) of the Road Traffic Regulation Act 1984

. . .

PART VI MISCELLANEOUS

54 Weapons training

(1) A person commits an offence if he provides instruction or training in the making or use of—

(a) firearms,

(aa) radioactive material or weapons designed or adapted for the discharge of any radioactive material,

(b) explosives, or

(c) chemical, biological or nuclear weapons. [E]

(2) A person commits an offence if he receives instruction or training in the making or use of—

(a) firearms,

(aa) radioative material or weapons designed or adapted for the discharge of any radioactive material.

(b) explosives, or

(c) chemical, biological or nuclear weapons. [E]

(3) A person commits an offence if he invites another to receive instruction or training and the receipt—

(a) would constitute an offence under subsection (2), or

(b) would constitute an offence under subsection (2) but for the fact that it is to take place outside the United Kingdom. [E]

(4) For the purpose of subsections (1) and (3)—

(a) a reference to the provision of instruction includes a reference to making it available either generally or to one or more specific persons, and

(b) an invitation to receive instruction or training may be either general or addressed to one or more specific persons.

(5) It is a defence for a person charged with an offence under this section in relation to instruction or training to prove that his action or involvement was wholly for a purpose other than assisting, preparing for or participating in terrorism.

55 Weapons training: interpretation

In section 54—

'biological weapon' means a biological agent or toxin (within the meaning of the Biological Weapons Act 1974) in a form capable of use for hostile purposes or anything to which section 1(1)(b) of that Act applies,

'chemical weapon' has the meaning given by section 1 of the Chemical Weapons Act 1996, and

'radioactive material' means radioactive material capable of endangering life or causing harm to human health.

56 Directing terrorist organisation

(1) A person commits an offence if he directs, at any level, the activities of an organisation which is concerned in the commission of acts of terrorism. [I]

57 Possession for terrorist purposes

(1) A person commits an offence if he possesses an article in circumstances which give rise to a reasonable suspicion that his possession is for a purpose connected with the commission, preparation or instigation of an act of terrorism. [E]

(2) It is a defence for a person charged with an offence under this section to prove that his possession of the article was not for a purpose connected with the commission, preparation or instigation of an act of terrorism.

(3) In proceedings for an offence under this section, if it is proved that an article—

- (a) was on any premises at the same time as the accused, or
- (b) was on premises of which the accused was the occupier or which he habitually used otherwise than as a member of the public,

the court may assume that the accused possessed the article, unless he proves that he did not know of its presence on the premises or that he had no control over it.

58 Collection of information

(1) A person commits an offence if—

- (a) he collects or makes a record of information of a kind likely to be useful to a person committing or preparing an act of terrorism, or
- (b) he possesses a document or record containing information of that kind. [E]

(2) In this section 'record' includes a photographic or electronic record.

(3) It is a defence for a person charged with an offence under this section to prove that he had a reasonable excuse for his action or possession.

59 Inciting terrorism overseas

(1) A person commits an offence if—

- (a) he incites another person to commit an act of terrorism wholly or partly outside the United Kingdom, and
- (b) the act would, if committed in England and Wales, constitute one of the offences listed in subsection (2).

(2) Those offences are—

- (a) murder,
- (b) an offence under section 18 of the Offences against the Person Act 1861 (wounding with intent),
- (c) an offence under section 23 or 24 of that Act (poison),
- (d) an offence under section 28 or 29 of that Act (explosions), and
- (e) an offence under section 1(2) of the Criminal Damage Act 1971 (endangering life by damaging property).

(3) A person guilty of an offence under this section shall be liable to any penalty to which he would be liable on conviction of the offence listed in subsection (2) which corresponds to the act which he incites.

(4) For the purposes of subsection (1) it is immaterial whether or not the person incited is in the United Kingdom at the time of the incitement.

(5) Nothing in this section imposes criminal liability on any person acting on behalf of, or holding office under, the Crown.

PART VIII GENERAL

118 Defences

(1) Subsection (2) applies where in accordance with a provision mentioned in subsection (5) it is a defence for a person charged with an offence to prove a particular matter.

(2) If the person adduces evidence which is sufficient to raise an issue with respect to the matter the court or jury shall assume that the defence is satisfied unless the prosecution proves beyond reasonable doubt that it is not.

(3) Subsection (4) applies where in accordance with a provision mentioned in subsection (5) a court—

(a) may make an assumption in relation to a person charged with an offence unless a particular matter is proved, or

(b) may accept a fact as sufficient evidence unless a particular matter is proved.

(4) If evidence is adduced which is sufficient to raise an issue with respect to the matter mentioned in subsection (3)(a) or (b) the court shall treat it as proved unless the prosecution disproves it beyond reasonable doubt.

(5) The provisions in respect of which subsections (2) and (4) apply are—

(a) sections 12(4), 39(5)(a), 54, 57, 58, 77 and 103 of this Act, . . .

121 Interpretation

In this Act—

'act' and 'action' include omission,

'article' includes substance and any other thing,

'British Transport Police Force' means the constables appointed under section 53 of the British Transport Commission 1949,

'customs officer' means an officer of Revenue and Customs,

'dwelling' means a building or part of a building used as a dwelling, and a vehicle which is habitually stationary and which is used as a dwelling,

'explosive' means—

(a) an article or substance manufactured for the purpose of producing a practical effect by explosion,

(b) materials for making an article or substance within paragraph (a),

(c) anything used or intended to be used for causing or assisting in causing an explosion, and

(d) a part of anything within paragraph (a) or (c),

'firearm' includes an air gun or air pistol,

'immigration officer' means a person appointed as an immigration officer under paragraph 1 of Schedule 2 to the Immigration Act 1971,

'the Islands' means the Channel Islands and the Isle of Man,

'organisation' includes any association or combination of persons,

'premises', except in section 63D, includes any place and in particular includes—

(a) a vehicle,

(b) an offshore installation within the meaning given in section 44 of the Petroleum Act 1998, and

(c) a tent or moveable structure,

'property' includes property wherever situated and whether real or personal, heritable or moveable, and things in action and other intangible or incorporeal property,

'public place' means a place to which members of the public have or are permitted to have access, whether or not for payment,

'road' has the same meaning as in the Road Traffic Act 1988 (in relation to England and Wales), . . . and includes part of a road, and

'vehicle', except in sections 48 to 52 and Schedule 7, includes an aircraft, hovercraft, train or vessel.

Anti-Terrorism, Crime and Security Act 2001

113 Use of noxious substances or things to cause harm and intimidate

(1) A person who takes any action which—

(a) involves the use of a noxious substance or other noxious thing;

(b) has or is likely to have an effect falling within subsection (2); and

(c) is designed to influence the government or an international governmental organisation or to intimidate the public or a section of the public,

is guilty of an offence. [E]

(2) Action has an effect falling within this subsection if it—

(a) causes serious violence against a person anywhere in the world;

(b) causes serious damage to real or personal property anywhere in the world;

(c) endangers human life or creates a serious risk to the health or safety of the public or a section of the public; or

(d) induces in members of the public the fear that the action is likely to endanger their lives or create a serious risk to their health or safety;

but any effect on the person taking the action is to be disregarded.

(3) A person who—

(a) makes a threat that he or another will take any action which constitutes an offence under subsection (1); and

(b) intends thereby to induce in a person anywhere in the world the fear that the threat is likely to be carried out,

is guilty of an offence. [E]

(5) In this section—

'the government' means the government of the United Kingdom, of a part of the United Kingdom or of a country other than the United Kingdom; and

'the public' includes the public of a country other than the United Kingdom.

114 Hoaxes involving noxious substances or things

(1) A person is guilty of an offence if he—

(a) places any substance or other thing in any place; or

(b) sends any substance or other thing from one place to another (by post, rail or any other means whatever);

with the intention of inducing in a person anywhere in the world a belief that it is likely to be (or contain) a noxious substance or other noxious thing and thereby endanger human life or create a serious risk to human health. [E]

(2) A person is guilty of an offence if he communicates any information which he knows or believes to be false with the intention of inducing in a person anywhere in the world a belief that a noxious substance or other noxious thing is likely to be present (whether at the time the information is communicated or later) in any place and thereby endanger human life or create a serious risk to human health. [E]

115 Sections 113 and 114: supplementary

(1) For the purposes of sections 113 and 114 'substance' includes any biological agent and any other natural or artificial substance (whatever its form, origin or method of production).

(2) For a person to be guilty of an offence under section 113(3) or 114 it is not necessary for him to have any particular person in mind as the person in whom he intends to induce the belief in question.

Terrorism Act 2006

1 Encouragement of terrorism

(1) This section applies to a statement that is likely to be understood by some or all of the members of the public to whom it is published as a direct or indirect encouragement or other inducement to them to the commission, preparation or instigation of acts of terrorism or Convention offences.

(2) A person commits an offence if—

(a) he publishes a statement to which this section applies or causes another to publish such a statement; and

(b) at the time he publishes it or causes it to be published, he—

(i) intends members of the public to be directly or indirectly encouraged or otherwise induced by the statement to commit, prepare or instigate acts of terrorism or Convention offences; or

(ii) is reckless as to whether members of the public will be directly or indirectly encouraged or otherwise induced by the statement to commit, prepare or instigate such acts or offences. [E]

(3) For the purposes of this section, the statements that are likely to be understood by members of the public as indirectly encouraging the commission or preparation of acts of terrorism or Convention offences include every statement which—

(a) glorifies the commission or preparation (whether in the past, in the future or generally) of such acts or offences; and

(b) is a statement from which those members of the public could reasonably be expected to infer that what is being glorified is being glorified as conduct that should be emulated by them in existing circumstances.

(4) For the purposes of this section the questions how a statement is likely to be understood and what members of the public could reasonably be expected to infer from it must be determined having regard both—

(a) to the contents of the statement as a whole; and

(b) to the circumstances and manner of its publication.

(5) It is irrelevant for the purposes of subsections (1) to (3)—

(a) whether anything mentioned in those subsections relates to the commission, preparation or instigation of one or more particular acts of terrorism or Convention offences, of acts of terrorism or Convention offences of a particular description or of acts of terrorism or Convention offences generally; and,

(b) whether any person is in fact encouraged or induced by the statement to commit, prepare or instigate any such act or offence.

(6) In proceedings for an offence under this section against a person in whose case it is not proved that he intended the statement directly or indirectly to encourage or otherwise induce the commission, preparation or instigation of acts of terrorism or Convention offences, it is a defence for him to show—

(a) that the statement neither expressed his views nor had his endorsement (whether by virtue of section 3 or otherwise); and

(b) that it was clear, in all the circumstances of the statement's publication, that it did not express his views and (apart from the possibility of his having been given and failed to comply with a notice under subsection (3) of that section) did not have his endorsement.

2 Dissemination of terrorist publications

(1) A person commits an offence if he engages in conduct falling within subsection (2) and, at the time he does so—

(a) he intends an effect of his conduct to be a direct or indirect encouragement or other inducement to the commission, preparation or instigation of acts of terrorism;

(b) he intends an effect of his conduct to be the provision of assistance in the commission or preparation of such acts; or

(c) he is reckless as to whether his conduct has an effect mentioned in paragraph (a) or (b). [E]

(2) For the purposes of this section a person engages in conduct falling within this subsection if he—

(a) distributes or circulates a terrorist publication;

(b) gives, sells or lends such a publication;

(c) offers such a publication for sale or loan;

(d) provides a service to others that enables them to obtain, read, listen to or look at such a publication, or to acquire it by means of a gift, sale or loan;

(e) transmits the contents of such a publication electronically; or

(f) has such a publication in his possession with a view to its becoming the subject of conduct falling within any of paragraphs (a) to (e).

(3) For the purposes of this section a publication is a terrorist publication, in relation to conduct falling within subsection (2), if matter contained in it is likely—

(a) to be understood, by some or all of the persons to whom it is or may become available as a consequence of that conduct, as a direct or indirect encouragement or other inducement to them to the commission, preparation or instigation of acts of terrorism; or

(b) to be useful in the commission or preparation of such acts and to be understood, by some or all of those persons, as contained in the publication, or made available to them, wholly or mainly for the purpose of being so useful to them.

(4) For the purposes of this section matter that is likely to be understood by a person as indirectly encouraging the commission or preparation of acts of terrorism includes any matter which—

(a) glorifies the commission or preparation (whether in the past, in the future or generally) of such acts; and

(b) is matter from which that person could reasonably be expected to infer that what is being glorified is being glorified as conduct that should be emulated by him in existing circumstances.

(5) For the purposes of this section the question whether a publication is a terrorist publication in relation to particular conduct must be determined—

(a) as at the time of that conduct; and

(b) having regard both to the contents of the publication as a whole and to the circumstances in which that conduct occurs.

(6) In subsection (1) references to the effect of a person's conduct in relation to a terrorist publication include references to an effect of the publication on one or more persons to whom it is or may become available as a consequence of that conduct.

(7) It is irrelevant for the purposes of this section whether anything mentioned in subsections (1) to (4) is in relation to the commission, preparation or instigation of one or more particular acts of terrorism, of acts of terrorism of a particular description or of acts of terrorism generally.

(8) For the purposes of this section it is also irrelevant, in relation to matter contained in any article whether any person—

(a) is in fact encouraged or induced by that matter to commit, prepare or instigate acts of terrorism; or

(b) in fact makes use of it in the commission or preparation of such acts.

(9) In proceedings for an offence under this section against a person in respect of conduct to which subsection (10) applies, it is a defence for him to show—

(a) that the matter by reference to which the publication in question was a terrorist publication neither expressed his views nor had his endorsement (whether by virtue of section 3 or otherwise); and

(b) that it was clear, in all the circumstances of the conduct, that that matter did not express his views and (apart from the possibility of his having been given and failed to comply with a notice under subsection (3) of that section) did not have his endorsement.

(10) This subsection applies to the conduct of a person to the extent that—

(a) the publication to which his conduct related contained matter by reference to which it was a terrorist publication by virtue of subsection (3)(a); and

(b) that person is not proved to have engaged in that conduct with the intention specified in subsection (1)(a).

(13) In this section—

'lend' includes let on hire, and 'loan' is to be construed accordingly;

'publication' means an article or record of any description that contains any of the following, or any combination of them—

(a) matter to be read;

(b) matter to be listened to;

(c) matter to be looked at or watched.

3 Application of ss. 1 and 2 to internet activity etc.

(1) This section applies for the purposes of sections 1 and 2 in relation to cases where—

(a) a statement is published or caused to be published in the course of, or in connection with, the provision or use of a service provided electronically; or

(b) conduct falling within section 2(2) was in the course of, or in connection with, the provision or use of such a service.

(2) The cases in which the statement, or the article or record to which the conduct relates, is to be regarded as having the endorsement of a person ('the relevant person') at any time include a case in which—

(a) a constable has given him a notice under subsection (3);

(b) that time falls more than 2 working days after the day on which the notice was given; and

(c) the relevant person has failed, without reasonable excuse, to comply with the notice.

(3) A notice under this subsection is a notice which—

(a) declares that, in the opinion of the constable giving it, the statement or the article or record is unlawfully terrorism-related;

(b) requires the relevant person to secure that the statement or the article or record, so far as it is so related, is not available to the public or is modified so as no longer to be so related;

(c) warns the relevant person that a failure to comply with the notice within 2 working days will result in the statement, or the article or record, being regarded as having his endorsement; and

(d) explains how, under subsection (4), he may become liable by virtue of the notice if the statement, or the article or record, becomes available to the public after he has complied with the notice.

(4) Where—

(a) a notice under subsection (3) has been given to the relevant person in respect of a statement, or an article or record, and he has complied with it, but

(b) he subsequently publishes or causes to be published a statement which is, or is for all practical purposes, the same or to the same effect as the statement to which the notice related, or to matter contained in the article or record to which it related, (a 'repeat statement');

the requirements of subsection (2)(a) to (c) shall be regarded as satisfied in the case of the repeat statement in relation to the times of its subsequent publication by the relevant person.

(5) In proceedings against a person for an offence under section 1 or 2 the requirements of subsection (2)(a) to (c) are not, in his case, to be regarded as satisfied in relation to any time by virtue of subsection (4) if he shows that he—

(a) has, before that time, taken every step he reasonably could to prevent a repeat statement from becoming available to the public and to ascertain whether it does; and

(b) was, at that time, a person to whom subsection (6) applied.

(6) This subsection applies to a person at any time when he—

(a) is not aware of the publication of the repeat statement; or

(b) having become aware of its publication, has taken every step that he reasonably could to secure that it either ceased to be available to the public or was modified as mentioned in subsection (3)(b).

(7) For the purposes of this section a statement or an article or record is unlawfully terrorism-related if it constitutes, or if matter contained in the article or record constitutes—

(a) something that is likely to be understood, by any one or more of the persons to whom it has or may become available, as a direct or indirect encouragement or other induce- ment to the commission, preparation or instigation of acts of terrorism or Convention offences; or

(b) information which—

(i) is likely to be useful to any one or more of those persons in the commission or preparation of such acts; and

(ii) is in a form or context in which it is likely to be understood by any one or more of those persons as being wholly or mainly for the purpose of being so useful.

(8) The reference in subsection (7) to something that is likely to be understood as an indirect encouragement to the commission or preparation of acts of terrorism or Convention offences includes anything which is likely to be understood as—

(a) the glorification of the commission or preparation (whether in the past, in the future or generally) of such acts or such offences; and

(b) a suggestion that what is being glorified is being glorified as conduct that should be emulated in existing circumstances.

(9) In this section 'working day' means any day other than—

(a) a Saturday or a Sunday;

(b) Christmas Day or Good Friday; or

(c) a day which is a bank holiday under the Banking and Financial Dealings Act 1971 in any part of the United Kingdom.

5 Preparation of terrorist acts

(1) A person commits an offence if, with the intention of—

(a) committing acts of terrorism, or

(b) assisting another to commit such acts,

he engages in any conduct in preparation for giving effect to his intention. [I]

(2) It is irrelevant for the purposes of subsection (1) whether the intention and preparations relate to one or more particular acts of terrorism, acts of terrorism of a particular description or acts of terrorism generally.

6 Training for terrorism

(1) A person commits an offence if—

(a) he provides instruction or training in any of the skills mentioned in subsection (3); and
(b) at the time he provides the instruction or training, he knows that a person receiving it intends to use the skills in which he is being instructed or trained—
(i) for or in connection with the commission or preparation of acts of terrorism or Convention offences; or
(ii) for assisting the commission or preparation by others of such acts or offences. [E]

(2) A person commits an offence if—
(a) he receives instruction or training in any of the skills mentioned in subsection (3); and
(b) at the time of the instruction or training, he intends to use the skills in which he is being instructed or trained—
(i) for or in connection with the commission or preparation of acts of terrorism or Convention offences; or
(ii) for assisting the commission or preparation by others of such acts or offences. [E]

(3) The skills are—
(a) the making, handling or use of a noxious substance, or of substances of a description of such substances;
(b) the use of any method or technique for doing anything else that is capable of being done for the purposes of terrorism, in connection with the commission or preparation of an act of terrorism or Convention offence or in connection with assisting the commission or preparation by another of such an act or offence; and
(c) the design or adaptation for the purposes of terrorism, or in connection with the commission or preparation of an act of terrorism or Convention offence, of any method or technique for doing anything.

(4) It is irrelevant for the purposes of subsections (1) and (2)—
(a) whether any instruction or training that is provided is provided to one or more particular persons or generally;
(b) whether the acts or offences in relation to which a person intends to use skills in which he is instructed or trained consist of one or more particular acts of terrorism or Convention offences, acts of terrorism or Convention offences of a particular description or acts of terrorism or Convention offences generally; and
(c) whether assistance that a person intends to provide to others is intended to be provided to one or more particular persons or to one or more persons whose identities are not yet known.

(7) In this section—
'noxious substance' means—
(a) a dangerous substance within the meaning of Part 7 of the Anti-terrorism, Crime and Security Act 2001 or
(b) any other substance which is hazardous or noxious or which may be or become hazardous or noxious only in certain circumstances;

'substance' includes any natural or artificial substance (whatever its origin or method of production and whether in solid or liquid form or in the form of a gas or vapour) and any mixture of substances.

8 Attendance at a place used for terrorist training

(1) A person commits an offence if—
(a) he attends at any place, whether in the United Kingdom or elsewhere;
(b) while he is at that place, instruction or training of the type mentioned in section 6(1) of this Act or section 54(1) of the Terrorism Act 2000 (weapons training) is provided there;
(c) that instruction or training is provided there wholly or partly for purposes connected with the commission or preparation of acts of terrorism or Convention offences; and
(d) the requirements of subsection (2) are satisfied in relation to that person. [E]

(2) The requirements of this subsection are satisfied in relation to a person if—

(a) he knows or believes that instruction or training is being provided there wholly or partly for purposes connected with the commission or preparation of acts of terrorism or Convention offences; or

(b) a person attending at that place throughout the period of that person's attendance could not reasonably have failed to understand that instruction or training was being provided there wholly or partly for such purposes.

(3) It is immaterial for the purposes of this section—

(a) whether the person concerned receives the instruction or training himself; and

(b) whether the instruction or training is provided for purposes connected with one or more particular acts of terrorism or Convention offences, acts of terrorism or Convention offences of a particular description or acts of terrorism or Convention offences generally.

(6) References in this section to instruction or training being provided include references to its being made available.

9 Making and possession of devices or materials

(1) A person commits an offence if—

(a) he makes or has in his possession a radioactive device, or

(b) he has in his possession radioactive material,

with the intention of using the device or material in the course of or in connection with the commission or preparation of an act of terrorism or for the purposes of terrorism, or of making it available to be so used. [I]

(2) It is irrelevant for the purposes of subsection (1) whether the act of terrorism to which an intention relates is a particular act of terrorism, an act of terrorism of a particular description or an act of terrorism generally.

(4) In this section—

'radioactive device' means—

(a) a nuclear weapon or other nuclear explosive device;

(b) a radioactive material dispersal device;

(c) a radiation-emitting device;

'radioactive material' means nuclear material or any other radioactive substance which—

(a) contains nuclides that undergo spontaneous disintegration in a process accompanied by the emission of one or more types of ionising radiation, such as alpha radiation, beta radiation, neutron particles or gamma rays; and

(b) is capable, owing to its radiological or fissile properties, of—

(i) causing serious bodily injury to a person;

(ii) causing serious damage to property;

(iii) endangering a person's life; or

(iv) creating a serious risk to the health or safety of the public.

(5) In subsection (4)—

'device' includes any of the following, whether or not fixed to land, namely, machinery, equipment, appliances, tanks, containers, pipes and conduits;

'nuclear material' has the same meaning as in the Nuclear Material (Offences) Act 1983 (see section 6 of that Act).

10 Misuse of devices or material and misuse and damage of facilities

(1) A person commits an offence if he uses—

(a) a radioactive device, or

(b) radioactive material,

in the course of or in connection with the commission of an act of terrorism or for the purposes of terrorism. [I]

(2) A person commits an offence if, in the course of or in connection with the commission of an act of terrorism or for the purposes of terrorism, he uses or damages a nuclear facility in a manner which—

(a) causes a release of radioactive material; or
(b) creates or increases a risk that such material will be released. [I]

(4) In this section—

'nuclear facility' means—

(a) a nuclear reactor, including a reactor installed in or on any transportation device for use as an energy source in order to propel it or for any other purpose; or
(b) a plant or conveyance being used for the production, storage, processing or transport of radioactive material;

'radioactive device' and 'radioactive material' have the same meanings as in section 9.

(5) In subsection (4)—

'nuclear reactor' has the same meaning as in the Nuclear Installations Act 1965 (c. 57) (see section 26 of that Act);

'transportation device' means any vehicle or any space object (within the meaning of the Outer Space Act 1986 (c. 38)).

11 Terrorist threats relating to devices, materials or facilities

(1) A person commits an offence if, in the course of or in connection with the commission of an act of terrorism or for the purposes of terrorism—

(a) he makes a demand—
  (i) for the supply to himself or to another of a radioactive device or of radioactive material;
  (ii) for a nuclear facility to be made available to himself or to another; or
  (iii) for access to such a facility to be given to himself or to another;
(b) he supports the demand with a threat that he or another will take action if the demand is not met; and
(c) the circumstances and manner of the threat are such that it is reasonable for the person to whom it is made to assume that there is real risk that the threat will be carried out if the demand is not met. [I]

(2) A person also commits an offence if—

(a) he makes a threat falling within subsection (3) in the course of or in connection with the commission of an act of terrorism or for the purposes of terrorism; and
(b) the circumstances and manner of the threat are such that it is reasonable for the person to whom it is made to assume that there is real risk that the threat will be carried out, or would be carried out if demands made in association with the threat are not met. [I]

(3) A threat falls within this subsection if it is—

(a) a threat to use radioactive material;
(b) a threat to use a radioactive device; or
(c) a threat to use or damage a nuclear facility in a manner that releases radioactive material or creates or increases a risk that such material will be released.

(5) In this section—

'nuclear facility' has the same meaning as in section 10; 'radioactive device' and 'radioactive material' have the same meanings as in section 9.

17 Commission of offences abroad

(1) If—

(a) a person does anything outside the United Kingdom, and
(b) his action, if done in a part of the United Kingdom, would constitute an offence falling within subsection (2),

he shall be guilty in that part of the United Kingdom of the offence.

(2) The offences falling within this subsection are—

(a) an offence under section 1 or 6 of this Act so far as it is committed in relation to any statement, instruction or training in relation to which that section has effect by reason of its relevance to the commission, preparation or instigation of one or more Convention offences;

(b) an offence under any of sections 8 to 11 of this Act;
(c) an offence under section 11(1) of the Terrorism Act 2000 (membership of proscribed organisations);
(d) an offence under section 54 of that Act (weapons training);
(e) conspiracy to commit an offence falling within this subsection;
(f) inciting a person to commit such an offence;
(g) attempting to commit such an offence;
(h) aiding, abetting, counselling or procuring the commission of such an offence.

(3) Subsection (1) applies irrespective of whether the person is a British citizen or, in the case of a company, a company incorporated in a part of the United Kingdom.

18 Liability of company directors etc.

(1) Where an offence under this Part is committed by a body corporate and is proved to have been committed with the consent or connivance of—

(a) a director, manager, secretary or other similar officer of the body corporate, or
(b) a person who was purporting to act in any such capacity,

he (as well as the body corporate) is guilty of that offence and shall be liable to be proceeded against and punished accordingly.

(3) In this section 'director', in relation to a body corporate whose affairs are managed by its members, means a member of the body corporate.

20 Interpretation of Part 1

(1) Expressions used in this Part and in the Terrorism Act 2000 have the same meanings in this Part as in that Act.

(2) In this Part—

'act of terrorism' includes anything constituting an action taken for the purposes of terrorism, within the meaning of the Terrorism Act 2000 (see section 1(5) of that Act);

'article' includes anything for storing data;

'Convention offence' means an offence listed in Schedule 1 or an equivalent offence under the law of a country or territory outside the United Kingdom;

'glorification' includes any form of praise or celebration, and cognate expressions are to be construed accordingly;

'public' is to be construed in accordance with subsection (3);

'publish' and cognate expressions are to be construed in accordance with subsection (4);

'record' means a record so far as not comprised in an article, including a temporary record created electronically and existing solely in the course of, and for the purposes of, the transmission of the whole or a part of its contents;

'statement' is to be construed in accordance with subsection (6).

(3) In this Part references to the public—

(a) are references to the public of any part of the United Kingdom or of a country or territory outside the United Kingdom, or any section of the public; and
(b) except in section 9(4), also include references to a meeting or other group of persons which is open to the public (whether unconditionally or on the making of a payment or the satisfaction of other conditions).

(4) In this Part references to a person's publishing a statement are references to—

(a) his publishing it in any manner to the public;
(b) his providing electronically any service by means of which the public have access to the statement; or
(c) his using a service provided to him electronically by another so as to enable or to facilitate access by the public to the statement;

but this subsection does not apply to the references to a publication in section 2.

(5) In this Part references to providing a service include references to making a facility available; and references to a service provided to a person are to be construed accordingly.

(6) In this Part references to a statement are references to a communication of any description, including a communication without words consisting of sounds or images or both.

(7) In this Part references to conduct that should be emulated in existing circumstances include references to conduct that is illustrative of a type of conduct that should be so emulated.

(8) In this Part references to what is contained in an article or record include references—

(a) to anything that is embodied or stored in or on it; and

(b) to anything that may be reproduced from it using apparatus designed or adapted for the purpose.

Part XII

Interference with Governmental or Public Services

Public Bodies Corrupt Practices Act 1889

1 Corruption in office a misdemeanour

(1) Every person who shall by himself or by or in conjunction with any other person, corruptly solicit or receive, or agree to receive, for himself, or for any other person, any gift, loan, fee, reward, or advantage whatever as an inducement to, or reward for, or otherwise on account of any member, officer, or servant of a public body as in this Act defined, doing or forbearing to do anything in respect of any matter or transaction whatsoever, actual or proposed, in which the said public body is concerned, shall be guilty of a misdemeanour. [E]

(2) Every person who shall by himself or by or in conjunction with any other person corruptly give, promise, or offer any gift, loan, fee, reward, or advantage whatsoever to any person, whether for the benefit of that person or of another person, as an inducement to or reward for or otherwise on account of any member, officer, or servant of any public body as in this Act defined, doing or forbearing to do anything in respect of any matter or transaction whatsoever, actual or proposed, in which such public body as aforesaid is concerned, shall be guilty of a misdemeanour. [E]

7 Interpretation

In this Act—

The expression 'public body' means any council of a county or county of a city or town, any council of a municipal borough, also any board, commissioners, select vestry, or other body which has power to act under and for the purposes of any Act relating to local government, or the public health, or to poor law or otherwise to administer money raised by rates in pursuance of any public general Act, and includes any body which exists in a country or territory outside the United Kingdom and is equivalent to any body described above.

The expression 'public office' means any office or employment of a person as a member, officer, or servant of such public body;

The expression 'person' includes a body of persons, corporate or unincorporate;

The expression 'advantage' includes any office or dignity, and any forbearance to demand any money or money's worth or valuable thing, and includes any aid, vote, consent, or influence, or pretended aid, vote, consent, or influence, and also includes any promise or procurement of or agreement or endeavour to procure, or the holding out of any expectation of any gift, loan, fee, reward, or advantage, as before defined.

Prevention of Corruption Act 1916

2 Presumption of corruption in certain cases

Where in any proceedings against a person for an offence under the Prevention of Corruption Act, 1906, or the Public Bodies Corrupt Practices Act, 1889, it is proved that any money, gift, or other consideration has been paid or given to or received by a person in the employment of His Majesty or any Government Department or a public body by or from a person, or agent of a person, holding or seeking to obtain a contract from His Majesty or any Government Department or public body, the money, gift, or consideration shall be deemed to have been paid or given and received corruptly as such inducement or reward as is mentioned in such Act unless the contrary is proved.

Anti-Terrorism, Crime and Security Act 2001

108 Bribery and corruption: foreign officers etc.

(1) For the purposes of any common law offence of bribery it is immaterial if the functions of the person who receives or is offered a reward have no connection with the United Kingdom and are carried out in a country or territory outside the United Kingdom.

109 Bribery and corruption committed outside the UK

(1) This section applies if—
- (a) a national of the United Kingdom or a body incorporated under the law of any part of the United Kingdom does anything in a country or territory outside the United Kingdom, and
- (b) the act would, if done in the United Kingdom, constitute a corruption offence (as defined below).

(2) In such a case—
- (a) the act constitutes the offence concerned, and
- (b) proceedings for the offence may be taken in the United Kingdom.

(3) These are corruption offences—
- (a) any common law offence of bribery;
- (b) the offences under section 1 of the Public Bodies Corrupt Practices Act 1889 (corruption in office);
- (c) the first two offences under section 1 of the Prevention of Corruption Act 1906 (bribes obtained by or given to agents).

(4) A national of the United Kingdom is an individual who is—
- (a) a British citizen, a British Overseas Territories citizen, a British National (Overseas) or a British Overseas citizen,
- (b) a person who under the British Nationality Act 1981 is a British subject, or
- (c) a British protected person within the meaning of that Act.

110 Presumption of corruption not to apply

Section 2 of the Prevention of Corruption Act 1916 (presumption of corruption in certain cases) is not to apply in relation to anything which would not be an offence apart from section 108 or section 109.

Official Secrets Act 1911

1 Penalties for spying

(1) If any person for any purpose prejudicial to the safety or interests of the State—
- (a) approaches, inspects, passes over or is in the neighbourhood of, or enters any prohibited place within the meaning of this Act; or
- (b) makes any sketch, plan, model, or note which is calculated to be or might be or is intended to be directly or indirectly useful to an enemy; or
- (c) obtains, collects, records, or publishes, or communicates to any other person any secret official code word or pass word, or any sketch, plan, model, article, or note, or other document or information which is directly or indirectly useful to an enemy; he shall be guilty of felony... [I]

(2) On a prosecution under this section, it shall not be necessary to show that the accused person was guilty of any particular act tending to show a purpose prejudicial to the safety or interests of the State, and, notwithstanding that no such act is proved against him, he may be convicted if, from the circumstances of the case, or his conduct, or his known character as proved, it appears that his purpose was a purpose prejudicial to the safety or interests of the State; and if any sketch, plan, model, article, note, document, or information relating to or used in any prohibited place within the meaning of this Act, or anything in such a place or any secret official code word or pass word, is made, obtained, collected, recorded, published, or communicated by any person other than a person acting under lawful authority, it shall be deemed to have been made, obtained, collected, recorded, published or communicated for a purpose prejudicial to the safety or interests of the State unless the contrary is proved.

3 Definition of prohibited place

For the purposes of this Act, the expression 'prohibited place' means—

(a) any work of defence, arsenal, naval or air force establishment or station, factory, dockyard, mine, minefield, camp, ship, or aircraft belonging to or occupied by or on behalf of His Majesty, or any telegraph, telephone, wireless or signal station, or office so belonging or occupied, and any place belonging to or occupied by or on behalf of His Majesty and used for the purpose of building, repairing, making or storing any munitions of war, or any sketches, plans, models or documents relating thereto, or for the purpose of getting any metals, oil or minerals of use in time of war;

(b) any place not belonging to His Majesty where any munitions of war, or any sketches, models, plans or documents relating thereto, are being made, repaired, gotten or stored under contract with, or with any person on behalf of, His Majesty, or otherwise on behalf of His Majesty; and

(c) any place belonging to or used for the purposes of His Majesty which is for the time being declared by order of a Secretary of State to be a prohibited place for the purposes of this section on the ground that information with respect thereto, or damage thereto, would be useful to an enemy; and

(d) any railway, road, way, or channel, or other means of communication by land or water (including any works or structures being part thereof or connected therewith), or any place used for gas, water, or electricity works or other works for purposes of a public character, or any place where any munitions of war, or any sketches, models, plans, or documents relating thereto, are being made, repaired, or stored otherwise than on behalf of His Majesty, which is for the time being declared by order of a Secretary of State to be a prohibited place for the purposes of this section, on the ground that information with respect thereto, or the destruction or obstruction thereof, or interference therewith, would be useful to an enemy.

7 Penalty for harbouring spies

If any person knowingly harbours any person whom he knows, or has reasonable grounds for supposing, to be a person who is about to commit or who has committed an offence under this Act, or knowingly permits to meet or assemble in any premises in his occupation or under his control any such persons, or if any person having harboured any such person, or permitted to meet or assemble in any premises in his occupation or under his control any such person, wilfully omits or refuses to disclose to a superintendent of police any information which it is in his power to give in relation to any such person he shall be guilty of a misdemeanour . . . [E]

Official Secrets Act 1920

1 Unauthorised use of uniforms; falsification of reports, personation, and false documents

(1) If any person for the purpose of gaining admission, or of assisting any other person to gain admission, to a prohibited place within the meaning of the Official Secrets Act 1911 (hereinafter

referred to as 'the principal Act'), or for any other purpose prejudicial to the safety or interests of the State within the meaning of the said Act—

(a) uses or wears, without lawful authority, any naval, military, air-force, police, or other official uniform, or any uniform so nearly resembling the same as to be calculated to deceive, or falsely represents himself to be a person who is or has been entitled to use or wear any such uniform; or

(b) orally, or in writing in any declaration or application, or in any document signed by him or on his behalf, knowingly makes or connives at the making of any false statement or any omission; or

(c) ... tampers with any passport or naval, military, air-force, police, or official pass, permit, certificate, licence, or other document of a similar character (hereinafter in this section referred to as an official document), ... or has in his possession any ... forged, altered, or irregular official document; or

(d) personates, or falsely represents himself to be a person holding, or in the employment of a person holding office under His Majesty, or to be or not to be a person to whom an official document or secret official code word or pass word has been duly issued or communicated, or with intent to obtain an official document, secret official code word or pass word, whether for himself or any other person, knowingly makes any false statement; or

(e) uses, or has in his possession or under his control, without the authority of the Government Department, or the authority concerned, any die, seal, or stamp of or belonging to, or used, made or provided by any Government Department, or by any diplomatic, naval, military, or air-force authority appointed by or acting under the authority of His Majesty, or any die, seal or stamp so nearly resembling any such die, seal or stamp as to be calculated to deceive, or counterfeits any such die, seal or stamp, or uses, or has in his possession, or under his control, any such counterfeited die, seal or stamp;

he shall be guilty of a misdemeanour.

(2) If any person—

(a) retains for any purpose prejudicial to the safety or interests of the State any official document, whether or not completed or issued for use, when he has no right to retain it, or when it is contrary to his duty to retain it, or fails to comply with any directions issued by any Government Department or any person authorised by such department with regard to the return or disposal thereof; or

(b) allows any other person to have possession of any official document issued for his use alone, or communicates any secret official code word or pass word so issued, or, without lawful authority or excuse, has in his possession any official document or secret official code word or pass word issued for the use of some person other than himself, or on obtaining possession of any official document by finding or otherwise, neglects or fails to restore it to the person or authority by whom or for whom or for whose use it was issued, or to a police constable; or

(c) without lawful authority or excuse, manufactures or sells, or has in his possession for sale any such die, seal or stamp as aforesaid;

he shall be guilty of a misdemeanour.

(3) In the case of any prosecution under this section involving the proof of a purpose prejudicial to the safety or interests of the State, subsection (2) of section one of the principal Act shall apply in like manner as it applies to prosecutions under that section.

2 Communications with foreign agents to be evidence of commission of certain offences

(1) In any proceedings against a person for an offence under section one of the principal Act, the fact that he has been in communication with, or attempted to communicate with, a foreign agent, whether within or without the United Kingdom, shall be evidence that he has for a purpose prejudicial to the safety or interests of the State, obtained or attempted to obtain information which is calculated to be or might be or intended to be directly or indirectly useful to an enemy.

(2) For the purpose of this section, but without prejudice to the generality of the foregoing provision—

(a) A person shall, unless he proves the contrary, be deemed to have been in communication with a foreign agent if—

(i) He has, either within or without the United Kingdom, visited the address of a foreign agent or consorted or associated with a foreign agent; or

(ii) Either, within or without the United Kingdom, the name or address of, or any other information regarding a foreign agent has been found in his possession, or has been supplied by him to any other person, or has been obtained by him from any other person;

(b) The expression 'foreign agent' includes a person who is or has been or is reasonably suspected of being or having been employed by a foreign power either directly or indirectly for the purpose of committing an act, either within or without the United Kingdom, prejudicial to the safety or interests of the State, or who has or is reasonably suspected of having, either within or without the United Kingdom, committed, or attempted to commit, such an act in the interests of a foreign power;

(c) Any address, whether within or without the United Kingdom, reasonably suspected of being an address used for the receipt of communications intended for a foreign agent, or any address at which a foreign agent resides, or to which he resorts for the purpose of giving or receiving communications, or at which he carries on any business, shall be deemed to be the address of a foreign agent, and communications addressed to such an address to be communications with a foreign agent.

3 Interfering with officers of the police or members of His Majesty's forces

No person in the vicinity of any prohibited place shall obstruct, knowingly mislead or otherwise interfere with or impede the chief officer or a superintendent or other officer of police, or any member of His Majesty's forces engaged on guard, sentry, patrol, or other similar duty in relation to the prohibited place, and, if any person acts in contravention of, or fails to comply with, this provision, he shall be guilty of a misdemeanour. [E]

7 Attempts, incitements, etc.

Any person who attempts to commit any offence under the principal Act or this Act, or solicits or incites or endeavours to persuade another person to commit an offence, or aids or abets and does any act preparatory to the commission of an offence under the principal Act or this Act, shall be guilty of a felony or a misdemeanour or a summary offence according as the offence in question is a felony, a misdemeanour or a summary offence, and on conviction shall be liable to the same punishment, and to be proceeded against in the same manner, as if he had committed the offence.

Official Secrets Act 1989

1 Security and intelligence

(1) A person who is or has been—

(a) a member of the security and intelligence services; or

(b) a person notified that he is subject to the provisions of this subsection, is guilty of an offence if without lawful authority he discloses any information, document or other article relating to security or intelligence which is or has been in his possession by virtue of his position as a member of any of those services or in the course of his work while the notification is or was in force. [E]

(2) The reference in subsection (1) above to disclosing information relating to security or intelligence includes a reference to making any statement which purports to be a disclosure of such information or is intended to be taken by those to whom it is addressed as being such a disclosure.

(3) A person who is or has been a Crown servant or government contractor is guilty of an offence if without lawful authority he makes a damaging disclosure of any information, document or other article relating to security or intelligence which is or has been in his possession by virtue of his position as such but otherwise than as mentioned in subsection (1) above.

(4) For the purposes of subsection (3) above a disclosure is damaging if—

(a) it causes damage to the work of, or of any part of, the security and intelligence services; or

(b) it is of information or a document or other article which is such that its unauthorised disclosure would be likely to cause such damage or which falls within a class or description of information, documents or articles the unauthorised disclosure of which would be likely to have that effect.

(5) It is a defence for a person charged with an offence under this section to prove that at the time of the alleged offence he did not know, and had no reasonable cause to believe, that the information, document or article in question related to security or intelligence or, in the case of an offence under subsection (2), that the disclosure would be damaging within the meaning of that subsection.

(6) Notification that a person is subject to subsection (1) above shall be effected by a notice in writing served on him by a Minister of the Crown; and such a notice may be served if, in the Minister's opinion, the work undertaken by the person in question is or includes work connected with the security and intelligence services and its nature is such that the interests of national security require that he should be subject to the provisions of that subsection.

(7) Subject to subsection (8) below, a notification for the purposes of subsection (1) above shall be in force for the period of five years beginning with the day on which it is served but may be renewed by further notices under subsection (6) above for periods of five years at a time.

(8) A notification for the purposes of subsection (1) above may at any time be revoked by a further notice in writing served by the Minister on the person concerned; and the Minister shall serve such a further notice as soon as, in his opinion, the work undertaken by that person ceases to be such as is mentioned in subsection (6) above.

(9) In this section 'security or intelligence' means the work of, or in support of, the security and intelligence services or any part of them, and references to information relating to security or intelligence include references to information held or transmitted by those services or by persons in support of, or of any part of, them.

2 Defence

(1) A person who is or has been a Crown servant or government contractor is guilty of an offence if without lawful authority he makes a damaging disclosure of any information, document or other article relating to defence which is or has been in his possession by virtue of his position as such.

(2) For the purposes of subsection (1) above a disclosure is damaging if—

(a) it damages the capability of, or of any part of, the armed forces of the Crown to carry out their tasks or leads to loss of life or injury to members of those forces or serious damage to the equipment or installations of those forces; or

(b) otherwise than as mentioned in paragraph (a) above, it endangers the interests of the United Kingdom abroad, seriously obstructs the promotion or protection by the United Kingdom of those interests or endangers the safety of British citizens abroad; or

(c) it is of information or of a document or article which is such that its unauthorised disclosure would be likely to have any of those effects.

(3) It is a defence for a person charged with an offence under this section to prove that at the time of the alleged offence he did not know, and had no reasonable cause to believe, that the information, document or article in question related to defence or that its disclosure would be damaging within the meaning of subsection (1) above.

(4) In this section 'defence' means—

(a) the size, shape, organisation, logistics, order of battle, deployment, operations, state of readiness and training of the armed forces of the Crown;

(b) the weapons, stores or other equipment of those forces and the invention, development, production and operation of such equipment and research relating to it;

(c) defence policy and strategy and military planning and intelligence;
(d) plans and measures for the maintenance of essential supplies and services that are or would be needed in time of war.

3 International relations

(1) A person who is or has been a Crown servant or government contractor is guilty of an offence if without lawful authority he makes a damaging disclosure of—

(a) any information, document or other article relating to international relations; or
(b) any confidential information, document or other article which was obtained from a State other than the United Kingdom or an international organisation,

being information or a document or article which is or has been in his possession by virtue of his position as a Crown servant or government contractor. [E]

(2) For the purposes of subsection (1) above a disclosure is damaging if—

(a) it endangers the interests of the United Kingdom abroad, seriously obstructs the promotion or protection by the United Kingdom of those interests or endangers the safety of British citizens abroad; or
(b) it is of information or of a document or article which is such that its unauthorised disclosure would be likely to have any of those effects.

(3) In the case of information or a document or article within subsection (1)(b) above—

(a) the fact that it is confidential, or
(b) its nature or contents,

may be sufficient to establish for the purposes of subsection (2)(b) above that the information, document or article is such that its unauthorised disclosure would be likely to have any of the effects there mentioned.

(4) It is a defence for a person charged with an offence under this section to prove that at the time of the alleged offence he did not know, and had no reasonable cause to believe, that the information, document or article in question was such as is mentioned in subsection (1) above or that its disclosure would be damaging within the meaning of that subsection.

(5) In this section 'international relations' means the relations between States, between international organisations or between one or more States and one or more such organisations and includes any matter relating to a State other than the United Kingdom or to an international organisation which is capable of affecting the relations of the United Kingdom with another State or with an international organisation.

(6) For the purposes of this section any information, document or article obtained from a State or organisation is confidential at any time while the terms on which it was obtained require it to be held in confidence or while the circumstances in which it was obtained make it reasonable for the State or organisation to expect that it would be so held.

4 Crime and special investigation powers

(1) A person who is or has been a Crown servant or government contractor is guilty of an offence if without lawful authority he discloses any information, document or other article to which this section applies and which is or has been in his possession by virtue of his position as such. [E]

(2) This section applies to any information, document or other article—

(a) the disclosure of which—
    (i) results in the commission of an offence; or
    (ii) facilitates an escape from legal custody or the doing of any other act prejudicial to the safekeeping of persons in legal custody; or
    (iii) impedes the prevention or detection of offences or the apprehension or prosecution of suspected offenders; or
(b) which is such that its unauthorised disclosure would be likely to have any of those effects.

(3) This section also applies to—

(a) any information obtained by reason of the interception of any communication in obedience to a warrant issued under section 2 of the Interception of Communications

Act 1985 or under the authority of an interception warrant under section 5 of the Reglation of Investigatory Powers Act 2000, any or under the authority of an interception warrant under section 5 of the Regulation of Investigatory Powers Act 2000, information relating to the obtaining of information by reason of any such interception and any document or other article which is or has been used or held for use in, or has been obtained by reason of, any such interception; and

(b) any information obtained by reason of action authorised by a warrant issued under section 3 of the Security Service Act 1989 or under section 5 of the Intelligence Services Act 1994 or by an authorisation given under section 7 of that Act, any information relating to the obtaining of information by reason of any such action and any document or other article which is or has been used or held for use in, or has been otained by reason of, any such action.

(4) It is a defence for a person charged with an offence under this section in respect of a disclosure falling within subsection (2)(a) above to prove that at the time of the alleged offence he did not know, and had no reasonable cause to believe, that the disclosure would have any of the effects there mentioned.

(5) It is a defence for a person charged with an offence under this section in respect of any other disclosure to prove that at the time of the alleged offence he did not know, and had no reasonable cause to believe, that the information, document or article in question was information or a document or article to which this section applies.

(6) In this section 'legal custody' includes detention in pursuance of any enactment or any instrument made under an enactment.

5 Information resulting from unauthorised disclosures or entrusted in confidence

(1) Subsection (2) below applies where—

(a) any information, document or other article protected against disclosure by the foregoing provisions of this Act has come into a person's possession as a result of having been—

(i) disclosed (whether to him or another) by a Crown servant or government contractor without lawful authority; or

(ii) entrusted to him by a Crown servant or government contractor on terms requiring it to be held in confidence or in circumstances in which the Crown servant or government contractor could reasonably expect that it would be so held; or

(iii) disclosed (whether to him or another) without lawful authority by a person to whom it was entrusted as mentioned in sub-paragraph (ii) above; and

(b) the disclosure without lawful authority of the information, document or article by the person into whose possession it has come is not an offence under any of those provisions.

(2) Subject to subsections (3) and (4) below, the person into whose possession the information, document or article has come is guilty of an offence if he discloses it without lawful authority knowing, or having reasonable cause to believe, that it is protected against disclosure by the foregoing provisions of this Act and that it has come into his possession as mentioned in subsection (1) above. [E]

(3) In the case of information or a document or article protected against disclosure by sections 1 to 3 above, a person does not commit an offence under subsection (2) above unless—

(a) the disclosure by him is damaging; and

(b) he makes it knowing, or having reasonable cause to believe, that it would be damaging;

and the question whether a disclosure is damaging shall be determined for the purposes of this subsection as it would be in relation to a disclosure of that information, document or article by a Crown servant in contravention of section 1(3), 2(1) or 3(1) above.

(4) A person does not commit an offence under subsection (2) above in respect of information or a document or other article which has come into his possession as a result of having been disclosed—

(a) as mentioned in subsection (1)(a)(i) above by a government contractor; or

(b) as mentioned in subsection (1)(a)(iii) above,

unless that disclosure was by a British citizen or took place in the United Kingdom, in any of the Channel Islands or in the Isle of Man or a colony.

(5) For the purposes of this section information or a document or article is protected against disclosure by the foregoing provisions of this Act if—

- (a) it relates to security or intelligence, defence or international relations within the meaning of section 1, 2 or 3 above or is such as is mentioned in section 3(1)(b) above; or
- (b) it is information or a document or article to which section 4 above applies; and information or a document or article is protected against disclosure by sections 1 to 3 above if it falls within paragraph (a) above.

(6) A person is guilty of an offence if without lawful authority he discloses any information, document or other article which he knows, or has reasonable cause to believe, to have come into his possession as a result of a contravention of section 1 of the Official Secrets Act 1911. [E]

6 Information entrusted in confidence to other States or international organisations

(1) This section applies where—

- (a) any information, document or other article which—
  - (i) relates to security or intelligence, defence or international relations; and
  - (ii) has been communicated in confidence by or on behalf of the United Kingdom to another State or to an international organisation,

has come into a person's possession as a result of having been disclosed (whether to him or another) without the authority of that State or organisation or, in the case of an organisation, of a member of it; and

- (b) the disclosure without lawful authority of the information, document or article by the person into whose possession it has come is not an offence under any of the foregoing provisions of this Act.

(2) Subject to subsection (2) below, the person into whose possession the information, document or article has come is guilty of an offence if he makes a damaging disclosure of it knowing, or having reasonable cause to believe, that it is such as is mentioned in subsection (1) above, that it has come into his possession as there mentioned and that its disclosure would be damaging. [E]

(3) A person does not commit an offence under subsection (2) above if the information, document or article is disclosed by him with lawful authority or has previously been made available to the public with the authority of the State or organisation concerned or, in the case of an organisation, of a member of it.

(4) For the purposes of this section 'security or intelligence', 'defence' and 'international relations' have the same meaning as in sections 1, 2 and 3 above and the question whether a disclosure is damaging shall be determined as it would be in relation to a disclosure of the information, document or article in question by a Crown servant in contravention of sections 1(3), 2 (1) and 3(1) above.

(5) For the purposes of this section information or a document or article is communicated in confidence if it is communicated on terms requiring it to be held in confidence or in circumstances in which the person communicating it could reasonably expect that it would be so held.

7 Authorised disclosures

(1) For the purposes of this Act a disclosure by—

- (a) a Crown servant; or
- (b) a person, not being a Crown servant or government contractor, in whose case a notification for the purposes of section 1(1) above is in force,

is made with lawful authority if, and only if, it is made in accordance with his official duty.

(2) For the purposes of this Act a disclosure by a government contractor is made with lawful authority if, and only if, it is made—

- (a) in accordance with an official authorisation; or
- (b) for the purposes of the functions by virtue of which he is a government contractor and without contravening an official restriction.

(3) For the purposes of this Act a disclosure made by any other person is made with lawful authority if, and only if, it is made—

(a) to a Crown servant for the purposes of his functions as such; or

(b) in accordance with an official authorisation.

(4) It is a defence for a person charged with an offence under any of the foregoing provisions of this Act to prove that at the time of the alleged offence he believed that he had lawful authority to make the disclosure in question and had no reasonable cause to believe otherwise.

(5) In this section 'official authorisation' and 'official restriction' mean, subject to subsection (6) below, an authorisation or restriction duly given or imposed by a Crown servant or government contractor or by or on behalf of a prescribed body or a body of a prescribed class.

(6) In relation to section 6 above 'official authorisation' includes an authorisation duly given by or on behalf of the State or organisation concerned or, in the case of an organisation, a member of it.

8 Safeguarding of information

(1) Where a Crown servant or government contractor, by virtue of his position as such, has in his possession or under his control any document or other article which it would be an offence under any of the foregoing provisions of this Act for him to disclose without lawful authority he is guilty of an offence if—

(a) being a Crown servant, he retains the document or article contrary to his official duty; or

(b) being a government contractor, he fails to comply with an official direction for the return or disposal of the document or article,

or if he fails to take such care to pevent the unauthorised disclosure of the document or article as a person in his position may reasonably be expected to take. [E]

(2) It is a defence for a Crown servant charged with an offence under subsection (1)(a) above to prove that at the time of the alleged offence he believed that he was acting in accordance with his official duty and had no reasonable cause to believe otherwise.

(3) In subsections (1) and (2) above references to a Crown servant include any person, not being a Crown servant or government contractor, in whose case a notification for the purposes of section 1(1) above is in force.

(4) Where a person has in his possession or under his control any document or other article which it would be an offence under section 5 above for him to disclose without lawful authority, he is guilty of an offence if—

(a) he fails to comply with an official direction for its return or disposal; or

(b) where he obtained it from a Crown servant or government contractor on terms requiring it to be held in confidence or in circumstances in which that servant or contractor could reasonably expect that it would be so held, he fails to take such care to prevent its unauthorised disclosure as a person in his position may reasonably be expected to take.

(5) Where a person has in his possession or under his control any document or other article which it would be an offence under section 6 above for him to disclose without lawful authority, he is guilty of an offence if he fails to comply with an official direction for its return or disposal.

(6) A person is guilty of an offence if he discloses any official information, document or other article which can be used for the purpose of obtaining access to any information, document or other article protected against disclosure by the foregoing provisions of this Act and the circumstances in which it is disclosed are such that it would be reasonable to expect that it might be used for that purpose without authority.

(7) For the purposes of subsection (6) above a person discloses information or a document or article which is official if—

(a) he has or has had it in his possession by virtue of his position as a Crown servant or government contractor; or

(b) he knows or has reasonable cause to believe that a Crown servant or government contractor has or has had it in his possession by virtue of his position as such.

(8) Subsection (5) of section 5 above applies for the purposes of subsection (6) above as it applies for the purposes of that section.

(9) In this section 'official direction' means a direction duly given by a Crown servant or government contractor or by or on behalf of a prescribed body or a body of a prescribed class.

12 'Crown servant' and 'government contractor'

(1) In this Act 'Crown servant' means—

(a) a Minister of the Crown; (ab)

(ab) The First Minister for Wales, a Welsh Minister appointed under section 48 of the Government of Wales Act 2006, the Counsel General to the Welsh Assembly Government or a Deputy Welsh Minister;

(c) any person employed in the civil service of the Crown, including Her Majesty's Diplomatic Service, Her Majesty's Overseas Civil Service, the civil service of Northern Ireland and the Northern Ireland Court Service;

(d) any member of the naval, military or air forces of the Crown, including any person employed by an association established for the purposes of Part XI the Reserve Forces Act 1996;

(e) any constable and any other person employed or appointed in or for the purposes of any police force (including the Police Service of Northern Ireland and the Police Service of Northern Ireland Reserve or of the Serious Organised Crime Agency;

(f) any person who is a member or employee of a prescribed body or a body of a prescribed class and either is prescribed for the purposes of this paragraph or belongs to a prescribed class of members or employees of any such body;

(g) any person who is the holder of a prescribed office or who is an employee of such a holder and either is prescribed for the purposes of this paragraph or belongs to a prescribed class of such employees.

(2) In this Act 'government contractor' means, subject to subsection (3) below, any person who is not a Crown servant but who provides, or is employed in the provision of, goods or services—

(a) for the purposes of any Minister or person mentioned in paragraph (a), (ab) or (b) of subsection (1) above, of any of the services, forces or bodies mentioned in that subsection or of the holder of any office prescribed under that subsection; or

(b) under an agreement or arrangement certified by the Secretary of State as being one to which the government of a State other than the United Kingdom or an international organisation is a party or which is subordinate to, or made for the purposes of implementing, any such agreement or arrangement.

(3) Where an employee or class of employees of any body, or of any holder of an office, is prescribed by an order made for the purposes of subsection (1) above—

(a) any employee of that body, or of the holder of that office, who is not prescribed or is not within the prescribed class; and

(b) any person who does not provide, or is not employed in the provision of, goods or services for the purposes of the performance of those functions of the body or the holder of the office in connection with which the employee or prescribed class of employees is engaged,

shall not be a government contractor for the purposes of this Act.

(4A) In this section the reference to a police force includes a reference to the Civil Nuclear Constabulary.

13 Other interpretation provisions

(1) In this Act—

'disclose' and 'disclosure', in relation to a document or other article, include parting with possession of it;

'international organisation' means, subject to subsections (2) and (3) below, an organisation of which only States are members and includes a reference to any organ of such an organisation;

'prescribed' means prescribed by an order made by the Secretary of State;

'State' includes the government of a State and any organ of its government and references to a State other than the United Kingdom include references to any territory outside the United Kingdom.

(2) In section 12(2)(b) above the reference to an international organisation includes a reference to any such organisation whether or not one of which only States are members and includes a commercial organisation.

(3) In determining for the purposes of subsection (1) above whether only States are members of an organisation, any member which is itself an organisation of which only States are members, or which is an organ of such an organisation, shall be treated as a State.

15 Acts done abroad

(1) Any act—

(a) done by a British citizen or Crown servant; or

(b) done by any person in any of the Channel Islands or the Isle of Man or any colony,

shall, if it would be an offence by that person under any provision of this Act other than section 8 (1), (4) or (5) when done by him in the United Kingdom, be an offence under that provision.

Incitement to Disaffection Act 1934

1 Penalty on persons endeavouring to seduce members of His Majesty's forces from their duty or allegiance

If any person maliciously and advisedly endeavours to seduce any member of His Majesty's forces from his duty or allegiance to His Majesty, he shall be guilty of an offence under this Act. [E]

2 Provisions for the prevention and detection of offences under this Act

(1) If any person, with intent to commit or to aid, abet, counsel, or procure the commission of an offence under section one of this Act, has in his possession or under his control any document of such a nature that the dissemination of copies thereof among members of His Majesty's forces would constitute such an offence, he shall be guilty of an offence under this Act. [S]

Emergency Workers (Obstruction) Act 2006

1 Obstructing or hindering certain emergency workers responding to emergency circumstances

(1) A person who without reasonable excuse obstructs or hinders another while that other person is, in a capacity mentioned in subsection (2) below, responding to emergency circumstances, commits an offence. [S]

(2) The capacity referred to in subsection (1) above is—

(a) that of a person employed by a fire and rescue authority in England and Wales;

(b) in relation to England and Wales, that of a person (other than a person falling within paragraph (a)) whose duties as an employee or as a servant of the Crown involve—

(i) extinguishing fires; or

(ii) protecting life and property in the event of a fire;

(c) that of a person employed by a relevant NHS body in the provision of ambulance services (including air ambulance services), or of a person providing such services pursuant to arrangements made by, or at the request of, a relevant NHS body;

(d) that of a person providing services for the transport of organs, blood, equipment or personnel pursuant to arrangements made by, or at the request of, a relevant NHS body;

(e) that of a member of Her Majesty's Coastguard;

(f) that of a member of the crew of a vessel operated by—

(i) the Royal National Lifeboat Institution, or

(ii) any other person or organisation operating a vessel for the purpose of providing a rescue service, or a person who musters the crew of such a vessel or attends to its launch or recovery.

(3) For the purposes of this section and section 2 of this Act, a person is responding to emergency circumstances if the person—

(a) is going anywhere for the purpose of dealing with emergency circumstances occurring there; or

(b) is dealing with emergency circumstances or preparing to do so.

(4) For the purposes of this Act, circumstances are 'emergency' circumstances if they are present or imminent and—

(a) are causing or are likely to cause—

(i) serious injury to or the serious illness (including mental illness) of a person;

(ii) serious harm to the environment (including the life and health of plants and animals);

(iii) serious harm to any building or other property; or

(iv) a worsening of any such injury, illness or harm; or

(b) are likely to cause the death of a person.

(5) In subsection (2) above 'relevant NHS body' means—

(a) in relation to England and Wales, an NHS foundation trust, National Health Service trust, Special Health Authority, Primary Care Trust or Local Health Board;

(b) in relation to Northern Ireland, a Health and Social Services trust or Health and Social Services Board.

2 Obstructing or hindering persons assisting emergency workers

(1) A person who without reasonable excuse obstructs or hinders another in the circumstances described in subsection (2) below commits an offence. [S]

(2) Those circumstances are where the person being obstructed or hindered is assisting another while that other person is, in a capacity mentioned in section 1(2) of this Act, responding to emergency circumstances.

3 Provisions supplementary to sections 1 and 2

(1) A person may be convicted of the offence under section 1 or 2 of this Act notwithstanding that it is—

(a) effected by means other than physical means; or

(b) effected by action directed only at any vehicle, vessel, apparatus, equipment or other thing or any animal used or to be used by a person referred to in that section.

(2) For the purposes of sections 1 and 2 of this Act, circumstances to which a person is responding are to be taken to be emergency circumstances if the person believes and has reasonable grounds for believing they are or may be emergency circumstances.

Fire and Rescue Services Act 2004

49 False alarms of fire

(1) A person commits an offence if he knowingly gives or causes to be given a false alarm of fire to a person acting on behalf of a fire and rescue authority. [S]

Postal Services Act 2000

88 Obstruction of business of universal service providers

(1) A person commits an offence if, without reasonable excuse, he—

(a) obstructs a person engaged in the business of a universal service provider in the execution of his duty in connection with the provision of a universal postal service, or

(b) obstructs, while in any universal postal service post office or related premises, the course of business of a universal service provider. [S]

(3) A person commits an offence if, without reasonable excuse, he fails to leave a universal postal service post office or related premises when required to do so by a person who—

(a) is engaged in the business of a universal service provider, and

(b) reasonably suspects him of committing an offence under subsection (1). [S]

(6) In this section 'related premises' means any premises belonging to a universal postal service post office or used together with any such post office.

Immigration Act 1971

24 Illegal entry and similar offences

(1) A person who is not a British citizen shall be guilty of an offence ... in any of the following cases:—

(a) if contrary to this Act he knowingly enters the United Kingdom in breach of a deportation order or without leave;

(b) if, having only a limited leave to enter or remain in the United Kingdom, he knowingly either—

(i) remains beyond the time limited by the leave; or

(ii) fails to observe a condition of the leave;

(c) if, having lawfully entered the United Kingdom without leave by virtue of section 8(1) above, he remains without leave beyond the time allowed by section 8(1);

(d) if, without reasonable excuse, he fails to comply with any requirement imposed on him under Schedule 2 to this Act to report to a medical officer of health or the chief administrative medical officer of a Health and Social Services Board, or to attend, or submit to a test or examination, as required by such an officer;

(e) if, without reasonable excuse, he fails to observe any restriction imposed on him under Schedule 2 or 3 to this Act as to residence, as to his employment or occupation or as to reporting to the police to an immigration officer or to the Secretary of State;

(f) if he disembarks in the United Kingdom from a ship or aircraft after being placed on board under Schedule 2 or 3 to this Act with a view to his removal from the United Kingdom;

(g) if he embarks in contravention of a restriction imposed by or under an Order in Council under section 3(7) of this Act. [S]

(1A) A person commits an offence under subsection (1)(b)(i) above on the day when he first knows that the time limited by his leave has expired and continues to commit it throughout any period during which he is in the United Kingdom thereafter; but a person shall not be prosecuted under that provision more than once in respect of the same limited leave.

(4) In proceedings for an offence against subsection (1)(a) above of entering the United Kingdom without leave,—

(a) any stamp purporting to have been imprinted on a passport or other travel document by an immigration officer on a particular date for the purpose of giving leave shall be presumed to have been duly so imprinted, unless the contrary is proved;

(b) proof that a person had leave to enter the United Kingdom shall lie on the defence if, but only if, he is shown to have entered within six months before the date when the proceedings were commenced.

24A Deception

(1) A person who is not a British citizen is guilty of an offence if, by means which include deception by him—

(a) he obtains or seeks to obtain leave to enter or remain in the United Kingdom; or

(b) he secures or seeks to secure the avoidance, postponement or revocation of enforcement action against him. [E]

(2) 'Enforcement action', in relation to a person, means—

(a) the giving of directions for his removal from the United Kingdom ('directions') under Schedule 2 to this Act or section 10 of the Immigration and Asylum Act 1999;

(b) the making of a deportation order against him under section 5 of this Act; or

(c) his removal from the United Kingdom in consequence of directions or a deportation order.

25 Assisting unlawful immigration to member State

(1) A person commits an offence if he—

(a) knowingly facilitates the commission of a breach of immigration law by an individual who is not a citizen of the European Union, or

(b) does anything which he has reasonable cause to believe may facilitate the commission of a breach of immigration law by an individual who is not a citizen of the European Union. [E]

(2) In subsection (1) 'immigration law' means a law which has effect in a member State and which controls, in respect of some or all persons who are not nationals of the State, entitlement to—

(a) enter the State,

(b) travel within the State, or

(c) be in the State.

(3) A document issued by the government of a member State certifying a matter of law in that State—

(a) shall be admissible in proceedings for an offence under this section, and

(b) shall be conclusive as to the matter certified.

(4) Subsection (1) applies to anything done—

(a) in the United Kingdom,

(b) outside the United Kingdom by an individual to whom subsection (5) applies, or

(c) outside the United Kingdom by a body incorporated under the law of a part of the United Kingdom.

(5) This subsection applies to—

(a) a British citizen,

(b) a British overseas territories citizen,

(c) a British National (Overseas),

(d) a British Overseas citizen,

(e) a person who is a British subject under the British Nationality Act 1981, and

(f) a British protected person within the meaning of that Act.

25A Helping asylum-seeker to enter United Kingdom

(1) A person commits an offence if—

(a) he knowingly and for gain facilitates the arrival in the United Kingdom of an individual, and

(b) he knows or has reasonable cause to believe that the individual is an asylum-seeker. [E]

(2) In this section 'asylum-seeker' means a person who intends to claim that to remove him from or require him to leave the United Kingdom would be contrary to the United Kingdom's obligations under—

(a) the Refugee Convention (within the meaning given by section 167(1) of the Immigration and Asylum Act 1999 (interpretation)), or

(b) the Human Rights Convention (within the meaning given by that section).

(3) Subsection (1) does not apply to anything done by a person acting on behalf of an organisation which aims to assist asylum-seekers.

(4) Subsections (4) to (6) of section 25 apply for the purpose of the offence in subsection (1) of this section as they apply for the purpose of the offence in subsection (1) of that section.

25B Assisting entry to united kingdom in breach of deportation order

(1) A person commits an offence if he—

(a) knowingly facilitates a breach of a deportation order in force against a citizen of the European Union, or

(b) does anything which he has reasonable cause to believe may facilitate a breach of a deportation order in force against a citizen of the European Union. [E]

(2) Subsections (4) to (6) of section 25 apply for the purpose of an offence under this section as they apply for the purpose of an offence under that section.

Immigration, Asylum and Nationality Act 2006

21 Employing unlawful immigrant

(1) A person commits an offence if he employs another ('the employee') knowing that the employee is an adult subject to immigration control and that—

(a) he has not been granted leave to enter or remain in the United Kingdom, or

(b) his leave to enter or remain in the United Kingdom—

(i) is invalid,

(ii) has ceased to have effect (whether by reason of curtailment, revocation, cancellation, passage of time or otherwise), or

(iii) is subject to a condition preventing him from accepting the employment. [E]

22 Offence: bodies corporate, etc.

(1) For the purposes of section 21(1) a body (whether corporate or not) shall be treated as knowing a fact about an employee if a person who has responsibility within the body for an aspect of the employment knows the fact.

(2) If an offence under section 21(1) is committed by a body corporate with the consent or connivance of an officer of the body, the officer, as well as the body, shall be treated as having committed the offence.

(3) In subsection (2) a reference to an officer of a body includes a reference to—

(a) a director, manager or secretary,

(b) a person purporting to act as a director, manager or secretary, and

(c) if the affairs of the body are managed by its members, a member.

(4) Where an offence under section 21(1) is committed by a partnership (whether or not a limited partnership) subsection (2) above shall have effect, but as if a reference to an officer of the body were a reference to—

(a) a partner, and

(b) a person purporting to act as a partner.

25 Interpretation

In sections 15 to 24—

(a) 'adult' means a person who has attained the age of 16,

(b) a reference to employment is to employment under a contract of service or apprenticeship, whether express or implied and whether oral or written,

(c) a person is subject to immigration control if under the Immigration Act 1971 he requires leave to enter or remain in the United Kingdom./

Customs and Excise Management Act 1979

50 Penalty for improper importation of goods

(1) Subsection (2) below applies to goods of the following descriptions, that is to say—

(a) goods chargeable with a duty which has not been paid; and

(b) goods the importation, landing or unloading of which is for the time being prohibited or restricted by or under any enactment.

(2) If any person with intent to defraud Her Majesty of any such duty or to evade any such prohibition or restriction as is mentioned in subsection (1) above—

(a) unships or lands in any port or unloads from any aircraft in the United Kingdom or from any vehicle in Northern Ireland any goods to which this subsection applies, or assists or is otherwise concerned in such unshipping, landing or unloading; or

(b) removes from their place of importation or from any approved wharf, examination station, transit shed or customs and excise station any goods to which this subsection applies or assists or is otherwise concerned in such removal,

he shall be guilty of an offence under this subsection and may be arrested. [E]

(3) If any person imports or is concerned in importing any goods contrary to any prohibition or restriction for the time being in force under or by virtue of any enactment with respect to those goods, whether or not the goods are unloaded, and does so with intent to evade the prohibition or restriction, he shall be guilty of an offence under this subsection and may be arrested. [E]

(7) In any case where a person would, apart from this subsection, be guilty of—

(a) an offence under this section in connection with the importation of goods contrary to a prohibition or restriction; and

(b) a corresponding offence under the enactment or other instrument imposing the prohibition or restriction, being an offence for which a fine or other penalty is expressly provided by that enactment or other instrument,

he shall not be guilty of the offence mentioned in paragraph (a) of this subsection.

170 Penalty for fraudulent evasion of duty, etc.

(1) Without prejudice to any other provision of the Customs and Excise Acts 1979, if any person—

(a) knowingly acquires possession of any of the following goods, that is to say—

(i) goods which have been unlawfully removed from a warehouse or Queen's warehouse;

(ii) goods which are chargeable with a duty which has not been paid;

(iii) goods with respect to the importation or exportation of which any prohibition or restriction is for the time being in force under or by virtue of any enactment; or

(b) is in any way knowingly concerned in carrying, removing, depositing, harbouring, keeping or concealing or in any manner dealing with any such goods, and does so with intent to defraud Her Majesty of any duty payable on the goods, or to evade any such prohibition or restriction with respect to the goods shall be guilty of an offence under this section and may be arrested. [E]

(2) Without prejudice to any other provision of the Customs and Excise Acts 1979, if any person is, in relation to any goods, in any way knowingly concerned in any fraudulent evasion or attempt at evasion—

(a) of any duty chargeable on the goods;

(b) of any prohibition or restriction for the time being in force with respect to the goods under or by virtue of any enactment; or

(c) of any provision of the Customs and Excise Acts 1979 applicable to the goods, he shall be guilty of an offence under this section and may be arrested. [E]

(5) In any case where a person would, apart from this subsection, be guilty of—

(a) an offence under this section in connection with a prohibition or restriction; and

(b) a corresponding offence under the enactment or other instrument imposing the prohibition or restriction, being an offence for which a fine or other penalty is expressly provided by that enactment or other instrument,

he shall not be guilty of the offence mentioned in paragraph (a) of this subsection.

(6) Where any person is guilty of an offence under this section, the goods in respect of which the offence was committed shall be liable to forfeiture.

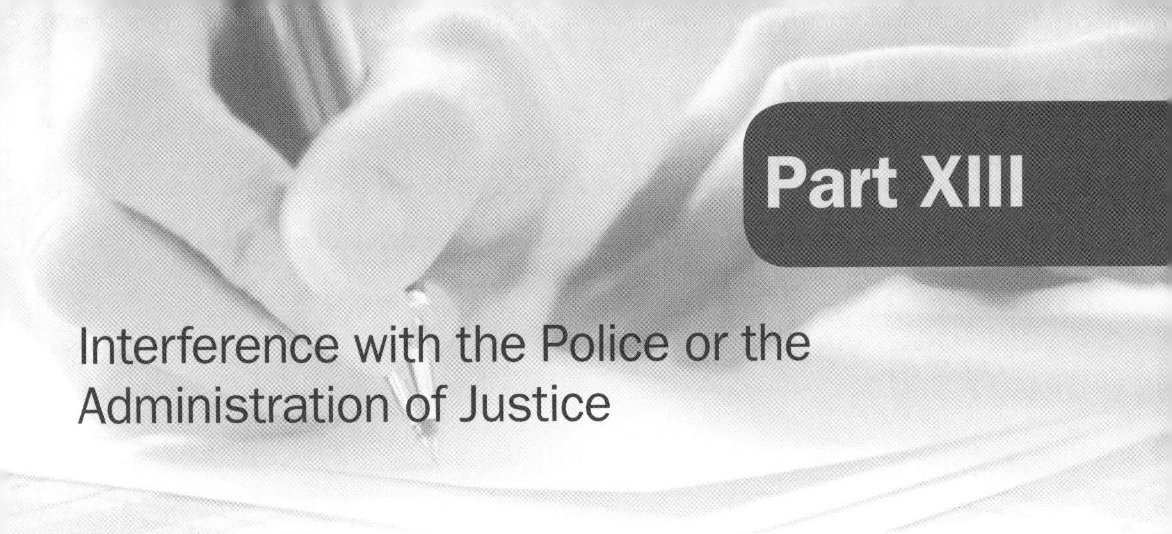

Part XIII

Interference with the Police or the Administration of Justice

Police Act 1996

89 Assaults on constables

(1) Any person who assaults a constable in the execution of his duty, or a person assisting a constable in the execution of his duty, shall be guilty of an offence . . . [S]

(2) Any person who resists or wilfully obstructs a constable in the execution of his duty, or a person assisting a constable in the execution of his duty shall be guilty of an offence . . . [S]

90 Impersonation, etc.

(1) Any person who with intent to deceive impersonates a member of a police force or special constable, or makes any statement or does any act calculated falsely to suggest that he is such a member or constable, shall be guilty of an offence . . . [S]

(2) Any person who, not being a constable, wears any article of police uniform in circumstances where it gives him an appearance so nearly resembling that of a member of a police force as to be calculated to deceive shall be guilty of an offence . . . [S]

(3) Any person who, not being a member of a police force or special constable, has in his possession any article of police uniform shall, unless he proves that he obtained possession of that article lawfully and has possession of it for a lawful purpose, be guilty of an offence . . . [S]

(4) In this section—

- (a) 'article of police uniform' means any article of uniform or any distinctive badge or mark or document of identification usually issued to members of police forces or special constables, or anything having the appearance of such an article, badge, mark or document;
- (ab) 'member of a police force' includes a member of the staff of the National Police Improvement Agency who is a constable, and
- (b) 'special constable' means a special constable appointed for a police area.

91 Causing disaffection

(1) Any person who causes, or attempts to cause, or does any act calculated to cause, disaffection amongst the members of any police force, or induces or attempts to induce, or does any act calculated to induce, any member of a police force to withhold his services, shall be guilty of an offence . . . [E]

(2) This section applies in the case of—

- (a) special constables appointed for a police area,
- (aa) members of the staff of the National Policing Improvement Agency who are constables,
- (b) members of the Civil Nuclear Constabulary, and
- (c) members of the British Transport Police Force,

as it applies in the case of members of a police of a police force.

Offences Against the Person Act 1861

18 Wounding or causing grievous bodily harm with intent to resist apprehension

[See page 40]

38 Assault with intent to resist arrest

[See page 45]

Perjury Act 1911

1 Perjury

(1) If any person lawfully sworn as a witness or as an interpreter in a judicial proceeding wilfully makes a statement material in that proceeding, which he knows to be false or does not believe to be true, he shall be guilty of perjury, and shall, on conviction thereof on indictment, be liable to imprisonment for a term not exceeding seven years, or to a fine or to both such imprisonment and fine. [I]

(2) The expression 'judicial proceeding' includes a proceeding before any court, tribunal, or person having by law power to hear, receive, and examine evidence on oath.

(3) Where a statement made for the purposes of a judicial proceeding is not made before the tribunal itself, but is made on oath before a person authorised by law to administer an oath to the person who makes the statement, and to record or authenticate the statement, it shall, for the purposes of this section, be treated as having been made in a judicial proceeding.

(4) A statement made by a person lawfully sworn in England for the purposes of a judical proceeding—

(a) in another part of Her Majesty's dominions; or

(b) in a British tribunal lawfully constituted in any place by sea or land outside Her Majesty's dominions; or

(c) in a tribunal of any foreign state,

shall, for the purposes of this section, be treated as a statement made in a judicial proceeding in England.

(5) Where for the purposes of a judicial proceeding in England, a person is lawfully sworn under the authority of an Act of Parliament—

(a) in any other part of Her Majesty's dominions; or

(b) before a British tribunal or a British officer in a foreign country, or within the jurisdiction of the Admiralty of England;

a statement made by such person so sworn as aforesaid (unless the Act of Parliament under which it was made otherwise specifically provides) shall be treated for the purposes of this section as having been made in the judicial proceeding in England for the purposes whereof it was made.

(6) The question whether a statement on which perjury is assigned was material is a question of law to be determined by the court of trial.

1A False unsworn statement under Evidence (Proceedings in other Jurisdictions) Act 1975

If any person in giving any testimony (either orally or in writing) otherwise than on oath, where required to do so by an order under section 2 of the Evidence (Proceedings in other Jurisdictions) Act 1975, makes a statement—

(a) which he knows to be false in a material particular, or

(b) which is false in a material particular and which he does not believe to be true,

he shall be guilty of an offence . . . [E]

2 False statements on oath made otherwise than in a judicial proceeding

If any person—

(1) being required or authorised by law to make any statement or oath for any purpose, and being lawfully sworn (otherwise than in a judicial proceeding) wilfully makes a statement which is material for that purpose and which he knows to be false or does not believe to be true; or

(2) wilfully uses any false affidavit for the purposes of the Bills of Sale Act, 1878, as amended by any subsequent enactment, he shall be guilty of a misdemeanour, . . . [E]

4 False statements, etc., as to births or deaths

(1) If any person—

(a) wilfully makes any false answer to any question put to him by any registrar of births or deaths relating to the particulars required to be registered concerning any birth or death, or, wilfully gives to any such registrar any false information concerning any birth or death or the cause of any death; or

(b) wilfully makes any false certificate or declaration under or for the purposes of any Act relating to the registration of births or deaths, or, knowing any such certificate or declaration to be false, uses the same as true or gives or sends the same as true to any person; or

(c) wilfully makes, gives or uses any false statement or declaration as to a child born alive as having been still-born, or as to the body of a deceased person or a still-born child in any coffin, or falsely pretends that any child born alive was still-born; or

(d) makes any false statement with intent to have the same inserted in any register of births or deaths,

he shall be guilty of a misdemeanour . . . [E]

5 False statutory declarations and other false statements without oath

If any person knowingly and wilfully makes (otherwise than on oath) a statement false in a material particular, and the statement is made—

(a) in a statutory declaration; or

(b) in an abstract, account, balance sheet, book, certificate, declaration, entry, estimate, inventory, notice, report, return, or other document which he is authorised or required to make, attest, or verify, by any public general Act of Parliament for the time being in force; or

(c) in any oral declaration or oral answer which he is required to make by, under, or in pursuance of any public general Act of Parliament for the time being in force, he shall be guilty of a misdemeanour . . . [E]

6 False declarations, etc., to obtain registration, etc., for carrying on a vocation

If any person—

(a) procures or attempts to procure himself to be registered on any register or roll kept under or in pursuance of any public general Act of Parliament for the time being in force of persons qualified by law to practise any vocation or calling; or

(b) procures or attempts to procure a certificate of the registration of any person on any such register or roll as aforesaid,

by wilfully making or producing or causing to be made or produced either verbally or in writing, any declaration, certificate, or representation which he knows to be false or fraudulent, he shall be guilty of misdemeanour . . . [E]

7 Aiders, abettors, suborners, etc.

(1) Every person who aids, abets, counsels, procures, or suborns another person to commit an offence against this Act shall be liable to be proceeded against, indicted, tried and punished as if he were a principal offender.

(2) Every person who incites another person to commit an offence against this Act shall be guilty of a misdemeanour, . . . [E]

15 Interpretation, etc.

(1) For the purposes of this Act, the forms and ceremonies used in administering an oath are immaterial, if the court or person before whom the oath is taken has power to administer an oath for the purpose of verifying the statement in question, and if the oath has been administered in a form and with ceremonies which the person taking the oath has accepted without objection, or has declared to be binding on him.

(a) In this Act—

The expression 'oath' includes 'affirmation' and 'declaration', and the expression 'swear' includes 'affirm' and 'declare'; and

The expression 'statutory declaration' means a declaration made by virtue of the Statutory Declarations Act, 1835, or of any Act, Order in Council, rule or regulation applying or extending the provisions thereof.

Criminal Justice Act 1967

89 False written statements tendered in evidence

(1) If any person in a written statement tendered in evidence in criminal proceedings by virtue of section 9 of this Act wilfully makes a statement material in those proceedings which he knows to be false or does not believe to be true, he shall be liable on conviction on indictment to imprisonment for a term not exceeding two years or a fine or both. [I]

(2) The Perjury Act 1911 shall have effect as if this section were contained in that Act.

Contempt of Court Act 1981

1 The strict liability rule

In this Act 'the strict liability rule' means the rule of law whereby conduct may be treated as a contempt of court as tending to interfere with the course of justice in particular legal proceedings regardless of intent to do so.

2 Limitation of scope of strict liability

(1) The strict liability rule applies only in relation to publications, and for this purpose 'publication' includes any speech, writing, programme included in a programme service or other communication in whatever form, which is addressed to the public at large or any section of the public.

(2) The strict liability rule applies only to a publication which creates a substantial risk that the course of justice in the proceedings in question will be seriously impeded or prejudiced.

(3) The strict liability rule applies to a publication only if the proceedings in question are active within the meaning of this section at the time of the publication.

(5) In this section 'programme service' has the same meaning as in the Broadcasting Act 1990.

3 Defence of innocent publication or distribution

(1) A person is not guilty of contempt of court under the strict liability rule as the publisher of any matter to which that rule applies if at the time of publication (having taken all reasonable care) he does not know and has no reason to suspect that relevant proceedings are active.

(2) A person is not guilty of contempt of court under the strict liability rule as the distributor of a publication containing any such matter if at the time of distribution (having taken all reasonable care) he does not know that it contains such matter and has no reason to suspect that it is likely to do so.

(3) The burden of proof of any fact tending to establish a defence afforded by this section to any person lies upon that person.

4 Contemporary reports of proceedings

(1) Subject to this section a person is not guilty of contempt of court under the strict liability rule in respect of a fair and accurate report of legal proceedings held in public, published contemporaneously and in good faith.

(2) In any such proceedings the court may, where it appears to be necessary for avoiding a substantial risk of prejudice to the administration of justice in those proceedings, or in any other proceedings pending or imminent, order that the publication of any report of the proceedings, or any part of the proceedings, be postponed for such period as the court thinks necessary for that purpose.

(2A) Where in proceedings for any offence which is an administration of justice offence for the purposes of section 54 of the Criminal Procedure and Investigations Act 1996 (acquittal tainted by an administration of justice offence) it appears to the court that there is a possibility that (by virtue of that section) proceedings may be taken against a person for an offence of which he has been acquitted, subsection (2) of this section shall apply as if those proceedings were pending or imminent.

(3) For the purposes of subsection (1) of this section a report of proceedings shall be treated as published contemporaneously—

- (a) in the case of a report of which publication is postponed pursuant to an order under subsection (2) of this section, if published as soon as practicable after that order expires;
- (b) in the case of a report of allocation or sending proceedings of which publication is permitted by virtue only of subsection (6) of section 52A of the Crime and Disorder Act 1998 ('The 1998 Act') if published as soon as practicable after publication is so permitted;
- (c) in the case of a report of an application of which publication is permitted by virtue only of sub-paragraph (5) or (7) of paragraph 3 of Schedule 3 to the 1998 Act, if published as soon as practicable after publication is so permitted.

5 Discussion of public affairs

A publication made as or as part of a discussion in good faith of public affairs or other matters of general public interest is not to be treated as a contempt of court under the strict liability rule if the risk of impediment or prejudice to particular legal proceedings is merely incidental to the discussion.

6 Savings

Nothing in the foregoing provisions of this Act—

- (a) prejudices any defence available at common law to a charge of contempt of court under the strict liability rule;
- (b) implies that any publication is punishable as contempt of court under that rule which would not be so punishable apart from those provisions;
- (c) restricts liability for contempt of court in respect of conduct intended to impede or prejudice the administration of justice.

8 Confidentiality of jury's deliberations

(1) Subject to subsection (2) below, it is a contempt of court to obtain, disclose or solicit any particulars of statements made, opinions expressed, arguments advanced or votes cast by members of a jury in the course of their deliberations in any legal proceedings.

(2) This section does not apply to any disclosure of any particulars—

- (a) in the proceedings in question for the purpose of enabling the jury to arrive at their verdict, or in connection with the delivery of that verdict, or
- (b) in evidence in any subsequent proceedings for an offence alleged to have been committed in relation to the jury in the first mentioned proceedings, or to the publication of any particulars so disclosed.

9 Use of tape recorders

(1) Subject to subsection (4) below, it is a contempt of court—

- (a) to use in court, or bring into court for use, any tape recorder or other instrument for recording sound, except with the leave of the court;

(b) to publish a recording of legal proceedings made by means of any such instrument, or any recording derived directly or indirectly from it, by playing it in the hearing of the public or any section of the public, or to dispose of it or any recording so derived, with a view to such publication;

(c) to use any such recording in contravention of any conditions of leave granted under paragraph (a).

(2) Leave under paragraph (a) of subsection (1) may be granted or refused at the discretion of the court, and if granted may be granted subject to such conditions as the court thinks proper with respect to the use of any recording made pursuant to the leave; and where leave has been granted the court may at the like discretion withdraw or amend it either generally or in relation to any particular part of the proceedings.

(4) This section does not apply to the making or use of sound recordings for purposes of official transcripts of proceedings.

Criminal Justice and Public Order Act 1994

51 Intimidation, etc., of witnesses, jurors and others

(1) A person commits an offence if—

(a) he does an act which intimidates, and is intended to intimidate, another person ('the victim'),

(b) he does the act knowing or believing that the victim is assisting in the investigation of an offence or is a witness or potential witness or a juror or potential juror in proceedings for an offence, and

(c) he does it intending thereby to cause the investigation or the course of justice to be obstructed, perverted or interfered with. [E]

(2) A person commits an offence if—

(a) he does an act which harms, and is intended to harm, another person or, intending to cause another person to fear harm, he threatens to do an act which would harm that other person,

(b) he does or threatens to do the act knowing or believing that the person harmed or threatened to be harmed ('the victim'), or some other person, has assisted in an investigation into an offence or has given evidence or particular evidence in proceedings for an offence, or has acted as a juror or concurred in a particular verdict in proceedings for an offence, and

(c) he does or threatens to do it because of that knowledge or belief. [E]

(3) For the purposes of subsections (1) and (2) it is immaterial that the act is or would be done, or that the threat is made—

(a) otherwise than in the presence of the victim, or

(b) to a person other than the victim.

(4) The harm that may be done or threatened may be financial as well as physical (whether to the person or a person's property) and similarly as respects an intimidatory act which consists of threats.

(5) The intention required by subsection (1)(c) and the motive required by subsection (2)(c) above need not be the only or the predominating intention or motive with which the act is done or, in the case of subsection (2), threatened.

(7) If, in proceedings against a person for an offence under subsection (1) above, it is proved that he did an act falling within paragraph (a) with the knowledge or belief required by paragraph (b), he shall be presumed, unless the contrary is proved, to have done the act with the intention required by paragraph (c) of that subsection.

(8) If, in proceedings against a person for an offence under subsection (2) above, it is proved that within the relevant period—

(a) he did an act which harmed, and was intended to harm, another person, or

(b) intending to cause another person fear of harm, he threatened to do an act which would harm that other person. and that he did the act, or (as the case may be) threatened to do the act, with the knowledge or belief required by paragraph (b), he shall be presumed, unless the contrary is proved, to have done the act or (as the case may be) threatened to do the act with the motive required by paragraph (c) of that subsection.

(9) In this section—

'investigation into an offence' means such an investigation by the police or other person charged with the duty of investigating offences or charging offenders;

'offence' includes an alleged or suspected offence;

'potential', in relation to a juror, means a person who has been summoned for jury service at the court at which proceedings for the offence are pending; and

'the relevant period'—

(a) in relation to a witness or juror in any proceedings for an offence, means the period beginning with the institution of the proceedings and ending with the first anniversary of the conclusion of the trial or, if there is an appeal or reference under section 9 or 11 of the Criminal Appeal Act 1995, of the conclusion of the appeal;

(b) in relation to a person who has, or is believed by the accused to have assisted in an investigation into an offence, but was not also a witness in proceedings for an offence, means the period of one year beginning with any act of his, or any act believed by the accused to be an act of his, assisting in the investigation; and

(c) in relation to a person who both has, or is believed by the accused to have, assisted in the investigation into an offence and was a witness in proceedings for the offence, means the period beginning with any act of his, or any act believed by the accused to be an act of his, assisting in the investigation and ending with the anniversary mentioned in paragraph (a) above;

'public prosecutor', 'requisition' and 'written charge' have the same meaning as in section 29 of the Criminal Justice Act 2003;

(10) For the purposes of the definition of the relevant period in subsection (9) above—

(a) proceedings for an offence are instituted at the earliest of the following times—

(i) when a justice of the peace issues a summons or warrant under section 1 of the Magistrates' Courts Act 1980 in respect of the offence;

(ia) when a public prosecutor issues a written charge and requisition in respect of the offence;

(ii) when a person is charged with the offence after being taken into custody without a warrant;

(iii) when a bill of indictment is preferred by virtue of section 2(2)(b) of the Administration of Justice (Miscellaneous Provisions) Act 1933;

(b) proceedings at a trial of an offence are concluded with the occurrence of any of the following, the discontinuance of the prosecution, the discharge of the jury without a finding, otherwise than in circumtances where the proceedings are continued without a jury, the acquittal of the accused or the sentencing of or other dealing with the accused for the offence of which he was convicted; and

(c) proceedings on an appeal are concluded on the determination of the appeal or the abandonment of the appeal.

(11) This section is in addition to, and not in derogation of, any offence subsisting at common law.

Criminal Justice and Police Act 2001

39 Intimidation of witnesses

(1) A person commits an offence if—

(a) he does an act which intimidates, and is intended to intimidate, another person ('the victim');
(b) he does the act—
(i) knowing or believing that the victim is or may be a witness in any relevant proceedings; and
(ii) intending, by his act, to cause the course of justice to be obstructed, perverted or interfered with; and
(c) the act is done after the commencement of those proceedings. [E]

(2) For the purposes of subsection (1) it is immaterial—
(a) whether or not the act that is done is done in the presence of the victim;
(b) whether that act is done to the victim himself or to another person; and
(c) whether or not the intention to cause the course of justice to be obstructed, perverted or interfered with is the predominating intention of the person doing the act in question.

(3) If, in proceedings against a person for an offence under this section, it is proved—
(a) that he did any act that intimidated, and was intended to intimidate, another person, and
(b) that he did that act knowing or believing that that other person was or might be a witness in any relevant proceedings that had already commenced,

he shall be presumed, unless the contrary is shown, to have done the act with the intention of causing the course of justice to be obstructed, perverted or interfered with.

(5) References in this section to a witness, in relation to any proceedings, include references to a person who provides, or is able to provide, any information or any document or other thing which might be used as evidence in those proceedings or which (whether or not admissible as evidence in those proceedings)—
(a) might tend to confirm evidence which will be or might be admitted in those proceedings;
(b) might be referred to in evidence given in those proceedings by another witness; or
(c) might be used as the basis for any cross examination in the course of those proceedings.

(6) References in this section to doing an act include references to issuing any threat (whether against a person or his finances or property or otherwise), or making any other statement.

(7) This section is in addition to, and not in derogation of, any offence subsisting at common law.

40 Harming witnesses etc.

(1) A person commits an offence if, in circumstances falling within subsection (2)—
(a) he does an act which harms, and is intended to harm, another person; or
(b) intending to cause another person to fear harm, he threatens to do an act which would harm that other person. [E]

(2) The circumstances fall within this subsection if—
(a) the person doing or threatening to do the act does so knowing or believing that some person (whether or not the person harmed or threatened or the person against whom harm is threatened) has been a witness in relevant proceedings; and
(b) he does or threatens to do that act because of that knowledge or belief.

(3) If, in proceedings against a person for an offence under this section, it is proved that, within the relevant period—
(a) he did an act which harmed, and was intended to harm, another person, or
(b) intending to cause another person to fear harm, he threatened to do an act which would harm that other person,

and that he did the act, or (as the case may be) threatened to do the act, with the knowledge or belief required by paragraph (a) of subsection (2), he shall be presumed, unless the contrary is shown, to have done the act, or (as the case may be) threatened to do the act, because of that knowledge or belief.

(4) For the purposes of this section it is immaterial—

(a) whether or not the act that is done or threatened, or the threat that is made, is or would be done or is made in the presence of the person who is or would be harmed or of the person who is threatened;
(b) whether or not the motive mentioned in subsection (2)(b) is the predominating motive for the act or threat; and
(c) whether the harm that is done or threatened is physical or financial or is harm to a person or to his property.

(6) In this section 'the relevant period', in relation to an act done, or threat made, with the knowledge or belief that a person has been a witness in any relevant proceedings, means the period that begins with the commencement of those proceedings and ends one year after they are finally concluded.

(7) References in this section to a witness, in relation to any proceedings, include references to a person who has provided any information or any document or other thing which was or might have been used as evidence in those proceedings or which (whether or not it was admissible as evidence in those proceedings)—
(a) tended to confirm or might have tended to confirm any evidence which was or could have been given in those proceedings;
(b) was or might have been referred to in evidence given in those proceedings by another witness; or
(c) was or might have been used as the basis for any cross examination in the course of those proceedings.

(8) This section is in addition to, and not in derogation of, any offence subsisting at common law.

41 Relevant proceedings

(1) A reference in section 39 or 40 to relevant proceedings is a reference to any proceedings in or before the Court of Appeal, the High Court, the Crown Court or any county court or magistrates' court which—
(a) are not proceedings for an offence; and
(b) were commenced after the coming into force of that section.

(2) For the purposes of any reference in section 39 or 40 or this section to the commencement of any proceedings relevant proceedings are commenced (subject to subsection (5)) at the earliest time at which one of the following occurs—
(a) an information is laid or application, claim form, complaint, petition, summons or other process made or issued for the purpose of commencing the proceedings;
(b) any other step is taken by means of which the subject matter of the proceedings is brought for the first time (whether as part of the proceedings or in anticipation of them) before the court.

(3) For the purposes of any reference in section 39 or 40 to the time when any proceedings are finally concluded, relevant proceedings are finally concluded (subject to subsection (4))—
(a) if proceedings for an appeal against, or an application for a review of, those proceedings or of any decision taken in those proceedings are brought or is made, at the time when proceedings on that appeal or application are finally concluded;
(b) if the proceedings are withdrawn or discontinued, at the time when they are withdrawn or discontinued; and
(c) in any other case, when the court in or before which the proceedings are brought finally disposes of all the matters arising in those proceedings.

(4) Relevant proceedings shall not be taken to be finally concluded by virtue of subsection (3)(a) where—
(a) the matters to which the appeal or application relate are such that the proceedings in respect of which it is brought or made continue or resume after the making of any determination on that appeal or application; or

(b) a determination made on that appeal or application requires those proceedings to continue or to be resumed.

(5) Where, after having appeared to be finally concluded, any relevant proceedings continue by reason of—

(a) the giving of permission to bring an appeal after a fixed time for appealing has expired,

(b) the lifting of any stay in the proceedings,

(c) the setting aside, without an appeal, of any judgment or order, or

(d) the revival of any discontinued proceedings,

sections 39 and 40 and this section shall have effect as if the proceedings had concluded when they appeared to, but as if the giving of permission, the lifting of the stay, the setting aside of the judgment or order or, as the case may be, the revival of the discontinued proceedings were the commencement of new relevant proceedings.

Criminal Law Act 1967

4 Penalties for assisting offenders

(1) Where a person has committed a relevant offence, any other person who, knowing or believing him to be guilty of the offence or of some other relevant offence, does without lawful authority or reasonable excuse any act with intent to impede his apprehension or prosecution shall be guilty of an offence. [I] and [E]

(1A) In this section and section 5 below, 'relevant offence' means—

(a) an offence for which the sentence is fixed by law,

(b) an offence for which a person of 18 years or over (not previously convicted) may be sentenced to imprisonment for a term of five years (or might be so sentenced but for the restrictions imposed by section 33 of the Magistrates' Courts Act 1980).

(2) If on the trial of an indictment for a relevant offence the jury are satisfied that the offence charged (or some other offence of which the accused might on that charge be found guilty) was committed, but find the accused not guilty of it, they may find him guilty of any offence under subsection (1) above of which they are satisfied that he is guilty in relation to the offence charged (or that other offence).

(3) A person committing an offence under subsection (1) above with intent to impede another person's apprehension or prosecution shall on conviction on indictment be liable to imprisonment according to the gravity of the other person's offence, as follows:—

(a) if that offence is one for which the sentence is fixed by law, he shall be liable to imprisonment for not more than ten years; [I]

(b) if it is one for which a person (not previously convicted) may be sentenced to imprisonment for a term of fourteen years, he shall be liable to imprisonment for not more than seven years; [I]

(c) if it is not one included above but is one for which a person (not previously convicted) may be sentenced to imprisonment for a term of ten years, he shall be liable to imprisonment for not more than five years; [E]

(d) in any other case, he shall be liable to imprisonment for not more than three years. [E]

5 Penalties for concealing offences or giving false information

(1) Where a person has committed a relevant offence, any other person who, knowing or believing that the offence or some other relevant offence has been committed, and that he has information which might be of material assistance in securing the prosecution or conviction of an offender for it, accepts or agrees to accept for not disclosing that information any consideration other than the making good of loss or injury caused by the offence, or the making of reasonable compensation for that loss or injury, shall be liable on conviction on indictment to imprisonment for not more than two years. [I] and [E]

(2) Where a person causes any wasteful employment of the police by knowingly making to any person a false report tending to show that an offence has been committed, or to give rise to apprehension for the safety of any persons or property, or tending to show that he has information material to any police inquiry, he shall be liable on summary conviction to imprisonment for not more than six months or to a fine of not more than level 4 on the standard scale or to both. [S]

(5) The compounding of an offence other than treason shall not be an offence otherwise than under this section.

Prison Act 1952

39 Assisting prisoner to escape

(1) A person who—

(a) assists a prisoner in escaping or attempting to escape from a prison, or

(b) intending to facilitate the escape of a prisoner—

(i) brings, throws or otherwise conveys anything into a prison,

(ii) causes another person to bring, throw or otherwise convey anything into a prison, or

(iii) gives anything to a prisoner or leaves anything in any place (whether inside or outside a prison),

is guilty of an offence. [I]

40A Sections 40B and 40C: classification of articles

(1) This section defines the categories of articles which are referred to in sections 40B and 40C.

(2) A List A article is any article or substance in the following list ('List A')—

(a) a controlled drug (as defined for the purposes of the Misuse of Drugs Act 1971);

(b) an explosive;

(c) any firearm or ammunition (as defined in section 57 of the Firearms Act 1968);

(d) any other offensive weapon (as defined in section 1(9) of the Police and Criminal Evidence Act 1984).

(3) A List B article is any article or substance in the following list ('List B')—

(a) alcohol (as defined for the purposes of the Licensing Act 2003);

(b) a mobile telephone;

(c) a camera;

(d) a sound-recording device.

(4) In List B—

'camera' includes any device by means of which a photograph (as defined in section 40E) can be produced;

'sound-recording device' includes any device by means of which a sound-recording (as defined in section 40E) can be made.

(5) The reference in paragraph (b), (c) or (d) of List B to a device of any description includes a reference to—

(a) a component part of a device of that description; or

(b) an article designed or adapted for use with a device of that description (including any disk, film or other separate article on which images, sounds or information may be recorded).

(6) A List C article is any article or substance prescribed for the purposes of this subsection by prison rules.

40B Conveyance etc. of List A articles into or out of prison

(1) A person who, without authorisation—

(a) brings, throws or otherwise conveys a List A article into or out of a prison,

(b) causes another person to bring, throw or otherwise convey a List A article into or out of a prison,

(c) leaves a List A article in any place (whether inside or outside a prison) intending it to come into the possession of a prisoner, or

(d) knowing a person to be a prisoner, gives a List A article to him,

is guilty of an offence. [I]

(2) In this section 'authorisation' means authorisation given for the purposes of this section—

(a) in relation to all prisons or prisons of a specified description, by prison rules or by the Secretary of State; or

(b) in relation to a particular prison, by the Secretary of State or by the governor or director of the prison.

In paragraph (a) 'specified' means specified in the authorisation.

(3) Authorisation may be given to specified persons or persons of a specified description—

(a) in relation to specified articles or articles of a specified description;

(b) in relation to specified acts or acts of a specified description; or

(c) on such other terms as may be specified.

In this subsection 'specified' means specified in the authorisation.

(4) Authorisation given by the Secretary of State otherwise than in writing shall be recorded in writing as soon as is reasonably practicable after being given.

(5) Authorisation given by the governor or director of a prison shall—

(a) be given in writing; and

(b) specify the purpose for which it is given.

40C Conveyance etc. of List B or C articles into or out of prison

(1) A person who, without authorisation—

(a) brings, throws or otherwise conveys a List B article into or out of a prison,

(b) causes another person to bring, throw or otherwise convey a List B article into or out of a prison,

(c) leaves a List B article in any place (whether inside or outside a prison) intending it to come into the possession of a prisoner, or

(d) knowing a person to be a prisoner, gives a List B article to him,

is guilty of an offence. [E]

(2) A person who, without authorisation—

(a) brings, throws or otherwise conveys a List C article into a prison intending it to come into the possession of a prisoner,

(b) causes another person to bring, throw or otherwise convey a List C article into a prison intending it to come into the possession of a prisoner,

(c) brings, throws or otherwise conveys a List C article out of a prison on behalf of a prisoner,

(d) causes another person to bring, throw or otherwise convey a List C article out of a prison on behalf of a prisoner,

(e) leaves a List C article in any place (whether inside or outside a prison) intending it to come into the possession of a prisoner, or

(f) while inside a prison, gives a List C article to a prisoner,

is guilty of an offence. [S]

(3) A person who attempts to commit an offence under subsection (2) is guilty of that offence.

(4) In proceedings for an offence under this section it is a defence for the accused to show that—

(a) he reasonably believed that he had authorisation to do the act in respect of which the proceedings are brought, or

(b) in all the circumstances there was an overriding public interest which justified the doing of that act.

(7) In this section 'authorisation' means authorisation given for the purposes of this section; and subsections (1) to (3) of section 40E apply in relation to authorisations so given as they apply to authorisations given for the purposes of section 40D.

40D Other offences relating to prison security

(1) A person who, without authorisation—

(a) takes a photograph, or makes a sound-recording, inside a prison, or
(b) transmits, or causes to be transmitted, any image or any sound from inside a prison by electronic communications for simultaneous reception outside the prison,

is guilty of an offence. [E]

(2) It is immaterial for the purposes of subsection (1)(a) where the recording medium is located.

(3) A person who, without authorisation—

(a) brings or otherwise conveys a restricted document out of a prison or causes such a document to be brought or conveyed out of a prison, or
(b) transmits, or causes to be transmitted, a restricted document (or any information derived from a restricted document) from inside a prison by means of electronic communications,

is guilty of an offence. [E]

(4) In proceedings for an offence under this section it is a defence for the accused to show that—

(a) he reasonably believed that he had authorisation to do the act in respect of which the proceedings are brought, or
(b) in all the circumstances there was an overriding public interest which justified the doing of that act.

40E Section 40D: meaning of 'authorisation' and other interpretation

(1) In section 40D (and the following provisions of this section) "authorisation" means authorisation given for the purposes of that section—

(a) in relation to all prisons or prisons of a specified description, by prison rules or by the Secretary of State;
(b) in relation to a particular prison—
  (i) by the Secretary of State;
  (ii) by the governor or director of the prison;
  (iii) by a person working at the prison who is authorised by the governor or director to grant authorisation on his behalf.

(2) Authorisation may be given—

(a) to persons generally or to specified persons or persons of a specified description; and
(b) on such terms as may be specified.

In this subsection 'specified' means specified in the authorisation.

(3) Authorisation given by or on behalf of the governor or director of a prison must be in writing.

(4) In section 40D 'restricted document' means the whole (or any part of)—

(a) a photograph taken inside the prison;
(b) a sound-recording made inside the prison;
(c) a personal record (or a document containing information derived from a personal record);
(d) any other document which contains—
  (i) information relating to an identified or identifiable relevant individual, if the disclosure of that information would or might prejudicially affect the interests of that individual; or
  (ii) information relating to any matter connected with the prison or its operation, if the disclosure of that information would or might prejudicially affect the security or operation of the prison.

(5) In subsection (4)—

'personal record' means any record which is required by prison rules to be prepared and maintained in relation to any prisoner (and it is immaterial whether or not the individual concerned is still a prisoner at the time of any alleged offence);

'relevant individual' means an individual who is or has at any time been—

(a) a prisoner or a person working at the prison; or
(b) a member of such a person's family or household.

(6) In section 40D and this section—

'document' means anything in which information is recorded (by whatever means);

'electronic communications' has the same meaning as in the Electronic Communications Act 2000;

'photograph' means a recording on any medium on which an image is produced or from which an image (including a moving image) may by any means be produced; and

'sound-recording' means a recording of sounds on any medium from which the sounds may by any means be reproduced.

40F Offences under sections 40B, 40C or 40D: extension of Crown immunity

(1) An individual who—

(a) works at a prison;

(b) does not do that work as a servant or agent of the Crown; and

(c) has been designated by the Secretary of State for the purposes of this section,

shall be treated for the purpose of the application of sections 40B, 40C or 40D as if he were doing that work as a servant or agent of the Crown.

(2) A designation for the purposes of this section may be given—

(a) in relation to persons specified in the designation or persons of a description so specified; and

(b) in relation to all work falling within subsection (1)(a) or only in relation to such activities as the designation may provide.

Prison Security Act 1992

1 Offence of prison mutiny

(1) Any prisoner who takes part in a prison mutiny shall be guilty of an offence and liable, on conviction on indictment, to imprisonment for a term not exceeding ten years or to a fine or to both. [I]

(2) For the purposes of this section there is a prison mutiny where two or more prisoners, while on the premises of any prison, engage in conduct which is intended to further a common purpose of overthrowing lawful authority in that prison.

(3) For the purposes of this section the intentions and common purpose of prisoners may be inferred from the form and circumstances of their conduct and it shall be immaterial that conduct falling within subsection (2) above takes a different form in the case of different prisoners.

(4) Where there is a prison mutiny, a prisoner who has or is given a reasonable opportunity of submitting to lawful authority and fails, without reasonable excuse, to do so shall be regarded for the purposes of this section as taking part in the mutiny.

(6) In this section—

'conduct' includes acts and omissions;

'prison' means any prison, or young offender institution which is under the general superintendence of, or is provided by, the Secretary of State under the Prison Act 1952, including a contracted out prison within the meaning of Part IV of the Criminal Justice Act 1991;

'prisoner' means any person for the time being in a prison as a result of any requirement imposed by a court or otherwise that he be detained in legal custody.

Public Order Act 1936

1 Prohibition of uniforms in connection with political objects

(1) Subject as hereinafter provided, any person who in any public place or at any public meeting wears uniform signifying his association with any political organisation or with the promotion of any political object shall be guilty of an offence:

Provided that, if the chief officer of police is satisfied that the wearing of any such uniform as aforesaid on any ceremonial, anniversary, or other special occasion will not be likely to involve risk of public disorder, he may, with the consent of a Secretary of State, by order permit the wearing of such uniform on that occasion either absolutely or subject to such conditions as may be specified in the order. [S]

2 Prohibition of quasi-military organisations

(1) If the members or adherents of any association of persons, whether incorporated or not, are—

(a) organised or trained or equipped for the purpose of enabling them to be employed in usurping the functions of the police or of the armed forces of the Crown; or

(b) organised and trained or organised and equipped either for the purpose of enabling them to be employed for the use or display of physical force in promoting any political object, or in such manner as to arouse reasonable apprehension that they are organised and either trained or equipped for that purpose;

then any person who takes part in the control or management of the association, or in so organising or training as aforesaid any members or adherents thereof, shall be guilty of an offence under this section:

Provided that in any proceedings against a person charged with the offence of taking part in the control or management of such an association as aforesaid it shall be a defence to that charge to prove that he neither consented to nor connived at the organisation, training, or equipment of members or adherents of the association in contravention of the provisions of this section. [E]

Bail Act 1976

6 Offence of absconding by person released on bail

(1) If a person who has been released on bail in criminal proceedings fails without reasonable cause to surrender to custody he shall be guilty of an offence. [S]

(2) If a person who—

(a) has been released on bail in criminal proceedings, and

(b) having reasonable cause therefor, has failed to surrender to custody, fails to surrender to custody at the appointed place as soon after the appointed time as is reasonably practicable he shall be guilty of an offence.

(3) It shall be for the accused to prove that he had reasonable cause for his failure to surrender to custody.

(4) A failure to give to a person granted bail in criminal proceedings a copy of the record of the decision shall not constitute a reasonable cause for that person's failure to surrender to custody.

9 Offence of agreeing to indemnify sureties in criminal proceedings

(1) If a person agrees with another to indemnify that other against any liability which that other may incur as a surety to secure the surrender to custody of a person accused or convicted of or under arrest for an offence, he and that other person shall be guilty of an offence. [E]

(2) An offence under subsection (1) above is committed whether the agreement is made before or after the person to be indemnified becomes a surety and whether or not he becomes a surety and whether the agreement contemplates compensation in money or in money's worth.

Part XIV

Preliminary Offences

Criminal Attempts Act 1981

1 Attempting to commit an offence

(1) If, with intent to commit an offence to which this section applies, a person does an act which is more than merely preparatory to the commission of the offence, he is guilty of attempting to commit the offence. [I] [E]

(1A) Subject to section 8 of the Computer Misuse Act 1990 (relevance of external law), if this subsection applies to an act, what the person doing it had in view shall be treated as an offence to which this section applies.

(1B) Subsection (1A) above applies to an act if—

(a) it is done in England and Wales; and

(b) it would fall within subsection (1) above as more than merely preparatory to the commission of an offence under section 3 of the Computer Misuse Act 1990 but for the fact that the offence, if completed, would not be an offence triable in England and Wales.

(2) A person may be guilty of attempting to commit an offence to which this section applies even though the facts are such that the commission of the offence is impossible.

(3) In any case where—

(a) apart from this subsection a person's intention would not be regarded as having amounted to an intent to commit an offence: but

(b) if the facts of the case had been as he believed them to be, his intention would be so regarded, then, for the purposes of subsection (1) above, he shall be regarded as having had an intent to commit that offence.

(4) This section applies to any offence which, if it were completed, would be triable in England and Wales as an indictable offence, other than—

(a) conspiracy (at common law or under section 1 of the Criminal Law Act 1977 or any other enactment);

(b) aiding, abetting, counselling, procuring or suborning the commission of an offence;

(c) offences under section 4 (1) (assisting offenders) or 5 (1) (accepting or agreeing to accept consideration for not disclosing information about an arrestable offence) of the Criminal Law Act 1967.

1A Extended jurisdiction in relation to certain attempts

(1) If this section applies to an act, what the person doing the act had in view shall be treated as an offence to which section 1(1) above applies.

(2) This section applies to an act if—

(a) it is done in England and Wales, and

(b) it would fall within section 1(1) above as more than merely preparatory to the commission of a Group A offence but for the fact that that offence, if completed, would not be an offence triable in England and Wales.

(3) In this section 'Group A offence' has the same meaning as in Part 1 of the Criminal Justice Act 1993.

(4) Subsection (1) above is subject to the provisions of section 6 of the Act of 1993 (relevance of external law).

(5) Where a person does any act to which this section applies, the offence which he commits shall for all purposes be treated as the offence of attempting to commit the relevant Group A offence.

4 Trial and penalties

(1) A person guilty by virtue of section 1 above of attempting to commit an offence shall—

(a) if the offence attempted is murder or any other offence the sentence for which is fixed by law, be liable on conviction on indictment to imprisonment for life; and

(b) if the offence attempted is indictable but does not fall within paragraph (a) above, be liable on conviction on indictment to any penalty to which he would have been liable on conviction on indictment of that offence; and

(c) if the offence attempted is triable either way, be liable on summary conviction to any penalty to which he would have been liable on summary conviction of that offence.

(3) Where, in proceedings against a person for an offence under section 1 above, there is evidence sufficient in law to support a finding that he did an act falling within subsection (1) of that section, the question whether or not his act fell within that subsection is a question of fact.

6 Effect on common law

(1) The offence of attempt at common law and any offence at common law of procuring materials for crime are hereby abolished for all purposes not relating to acts done before the commencement of this Act.

(2) Except as regards offences committed before the commencement of this Act, references in any enactment passed before this Act which fall to be construed as references to the offence of attempt at common law shall be construed as references to the offence under section 1 above.

9 Interference with vehicles

(1) A person is guilty of the offence of vehicle interference if he interferes with a motor vehicle or trailer or with anything carried in or on a motor vehicle or trailer with the intention that any offence specified in subsection (2) below shall be committed by himself or some other person. [S]

(2) The offences mentioned in subsection (1) above are—

(a) theft of the motor vehicle or trailer or part of it;

(b) theft of anything carried in or on the motor vehicle or trailer; and

(c) an offence under section 12(1) of the Theft Act 1968 (taking and driving away without consent);

and, if it is shown that a person accused of an offence under this section intended that one of those offences should be committed, it is immaterial that it cannot be shown which it was.

(5) In this section 'motor vehicle' and 'trailer' have the meanings assigned to them by section 185(1) of the Road Traffic Act 1988.

Serious Crime Act 2007

PART 2 ENCOURAGING OR ASSISTING CRIME

44 Intentionally encouraging or assisting an offence

(1) A person commits an offence if—

(a) he does an act capable of encouraging or assisting the commission of an offence; and

(b) he intends to encourage or assist its commission. [I] [E]

(2) But he is not to be taken to have intended to encourage or assist the commission of an offence merely because such encouragement or assistance was a foreseeable consequence of his act.

45 Encouraging or assisting an offence believing it will be committed

A person commits an offence if—

(a) he does an act capable of encouraging or assisting the commission of an offence; and

(b) he believes—

(i) that the offence will be committed; and

(ii) hat his act will encourage or assist its commission. [I] [E]

46 Encouraging or assisting offences believing one or more will be committed

(1) A person commits an offence if—

(a) he does an act capable of encouraging or assisting the commission of one or more of a number of offences; and

(b) he believes—

(i) that one or more of those offences will be committed (but has no belief as to which); and

(ii) that his act will encourage or assist the commission of one or more of them. [I]

(2) It is immaterial for the purposes of subsection (1)(b)(ii) whether the person has any belief as to which offence will be encouraged or assisted.

(3) If a person is charged with an offence under subsection (1)—

(a) the indictment must specify the offences alleged to be the 'number of offences' mentioned in paragraph (a) of that subsection; but

(b) nothing in paragraph (a) requires all the offences potentially comprised in that number to be specified.

(4) In relation to an offence under this section, reference in this Part to the offences specified in the indictment is to the offences specified by virtue of subsection (3)(a).

47 Proving an offence under this Part

(1) Sections 44, 45 and 46 are to be read in accordance with this section.

(2) If it is alleged under section 44(1)(b) that a person (D) intended to encourage or assist the commission of an offence, it is sufficient to prove that he intended to encourage or assist the doing of an act which would amount to the commission of that offence.

(3) If it is alleged under section 45(b) that a person (D) believed that an offence would be committed and that his act would encourage or assist its commission, it is sufficient to prove that he believed—

(a) that an act would be done which would amount to the commission of that offence; and

(b) that his act would encourage or assist the doing of that act.

(4) If it is alleged under section 46(1)(b) that a person (D) believed that one or more of a number of offences would be committed and that his act would encourage or assist the commission of one or more of them, it is sufficient to prove that he believed—

(a) that one or more of a number of acts would be done which would amount to the commission of one or more of those offences; and

(b) that his act would encourage or assist the doing of one or more of those acts.

(5) In proving for the purposes of this section whether an act is one which, if done, would amount to the commission of an offence—

(a) if the offence is one requiring proof of fault, it must be proved that—

(i) D believed that, were the act to be done, it would be done with that fault;

(ii) D was reckless as to whether or not it would be done with that fault; or

(iii) D's state of mind was such that, were he to do it, it would be done with that fault; and

(b) if the offence is one requiring proof of particular circumstances or consequences (or both), it must be proved that—

(i) D believed that, were the act to be done, it would be done in those circumstances or with those consequences; or

(ii) D was reckless as to whether or not it would be done in those circumstances or with those consequences.

(6) For the purposes of subsection (5)(a)(iii), D is to be assumed to be able to do the act in question.

(7) In the case of an offence under section 44—

(a) subsection (5)(b)(i) is to be read as if the reference to 'D believed' were a reference to 'D intended or believed'; but

(b) D is not to be taken to have intended that an act would be done in particular circumstances or with particular consequences merely because its being done in those circumstances or with those consequences was a foreseeable consequence of his act of encouragement or assistance.

(8) Reference in this section to the doing of an act includes reference to—

(a) a failure to act;

(b) the continuation of an act that has already begun;

(c) an attempt to do an act (except an act amounting to the commission of the offence of attempting to commit another offence).

(9) In the remaining provisions of this Part (unless otherwise provided) a reference to the anticipated offence is—

(a) in relation to an offence under section 44, a reference to the offence mentioned in subsection (2); and

(b) in relation to an offence under section 45, a reference to the offence mentioned in subsection (3).

48 Proving an offence under section 46

(1) This section makes further provision about the application of section 47 to an offence under section 46.

(2) It is sufficient to prove the matters mentioned in section 47(5) by reference to one offence only.

(3) The offence or offences by reference to which those matters are proved must be one of the offences specified in the indictment.

(4) Subsection (3) does not affect any enactment or rule of law under which a person charged with one offence may be convicted of another and is subject to section 57.

49 Supplemental provisions

(1) A person may commit an offence under this Part whether or not any offence capable of being encouraged or assisted by his act is committed.

(2) If a person's act is capable of encouraging or assisting the commission of a number of offences—

(a) section 44 applies separately in relation to each offence that he intends to encourage or assist to be committed; and

(b) section 45 applies separately in relation to each offence that he believes will be encouraged or assisted to be committed.

(3) A person may, in relation to the same act, commit an offence under more than one provision of this Part.

(4) In reckoning whether—

(a) for the purposes of section 45, an act is capable of encouraging or assisting the commission of an offence; or

(b) for the purposes of section 46, an act is capable of encouraging or assisting the commission of one or more of a number of offences;

offences under this Part and listed offences are to be disregarded.

(5) 'Listed offence' means—

(a) in England and Wales, an offence listed in Part 1, 2 or 3 of Schedule 3; and
(b) in Northern Ireland, an offence listed in Part 1, 4 or 5 of that Schedule.

(7) For the purposes of sections 45(b)(i) and 46(1)(b)(i) it is sufficient for the person concerned to believe that the offence (or one or more of the offences) will be committed if certain conditions are met.

50 Defence of acting reasonably

(1) A person is not guilty of an offence under this Part if he proves—
(a) that he knew certain circumstances existed; and
(b) that it was reasonable for him to act as he did in those circumstances.

(2) A person is not guilty of an offence under this Part if he proves—
(a) that he believed certain circumstances to exist;
(b) that his belief was reasonable; and
(c) that it was reasonable for him to act as he did in the circumstances as he believed them to be.

(3) Factors to be considered in determining whether it was reasonable for a person to act as he did include—
(a) the seriousness of the anticipated offence (or, in the case of an offence under section 46, the offences specified in the indictment);
(b) any purpose for which he claims to have been acting;
(c) any authority by which he claims to have been acting.

51 Protective offences: victims not liable

(1) In the case of protective offences, a person does not commit an offence under this Part by reference to such an offence if—
(a) he falls within the protected category; and
(b) he is the person in respect of whom the protective offence was committed or would have been if it had been committed.

(2) 'Protective offence' means an offence that exists (wholly or in part) for the protection of a particular category of persons ("the protected category").

52 Jurisdiction over offences of assisting or encouraging an offence

(1) If a person (D) knows or believes that what he anticipates might take place wholly or partly in England or Wales, he may be guilty of an offence under section 44, 45 or 46 no matter where he was at any relevant time.

(2) If it is not proved that D knows or believes that what he anticipates might take place wholly or partly in England or Wales, he is not guilty of an offence under section 44, 45 or 46 unless paragraph 1, 2 or 3 of Schedule 4 applies.

(3) A reference in this section (and in any of those paragraphs) to what D anticipates is to be read as follows—
(a) in relation to an offence under section 44 or 45, it refers to the act which would amount to the commission of the anticipated offence;
(b) in relation to an offence under section 46, it refers to an act which would amount to the commission of any of the offences specified in the indictment.

55 Mode of trial

(1) An offence under section 44 or 45 is triable in the same way as the anticipated offence.

56 Persons who may be perpetrators or encouragers etc.

(1) In proceedings for an offence under this Part ('the inchoate offence') the defendant may be convicted if—
(a) it is proved that he must have committed the inchoate offence or the anticipated offence; but

(b) it is not proved which of those offences he committed.

(2) For the purposes of this section, a person is not to be treated as having committed the anticipated offence merely because he aided, abetted, counselled or procured its commission.

(3) In relation to an offence under section 46, a reference in this section to the anticipated offence is to be read as a reference to an offence specified in the indictment.

57 Alternative verdicts and guilty pleas

(1) If in proceedings on indictment for an offence under section 44 or 45 a person is not found guilty of that offence by reference to the specified offence, he may be found guilty of that offence by reference to an alternative offence.

(2) If in proceedings for an offence under section 46 a person is not found guilty of that offence by reference to any specified offence, he may be found guilty of that offence by reference to one or more alternative offences.

(3) If in proceedings for an offence under section 46 a person is found guilty of the offence by reference to one or more specified offences, he may also be found guilty of it by reference to one or more other alternative offences.

(4) For the purposes of this section, an offence is an alternative offence if—

(a) it is an offence of which, on a trial on indictment for the specified offence, an accused may be found guilty; or

(b) it is an indictable offence, or one to which section 40 of the Criminal Justice Act 1988 applies (power to include count for common assault etc. in indictment), and the condition in subsection (5) is satisfied.

(5) The condition is that the allegations in the indictment charging the person with the offence under this Part amount to or include (expressly or by implication) an allegation of that offence by reference to it.

(6) Subsection (4)(b) does not apply if the specified offence, or any of the specified offences, is murder or treason.

(7) In the application of subsection (5) to proceedings for an offence under section 44, the allegations in the indictment are to be taken to include an allegation of that offence by reference to the offence of attempting to commit the specified offence.

(8) Section 49(4) applies to an offence which is an alternative offence in relation to a specified offence as it applies to that specified offence.

(9) In this section—

(a) in relation to a person charged with an offence under section 44 or 45, 'the specified offence' means the offence specified in the indictment as the one alleged to be the anticipated offence;

(b) in relation to a person charged with an offence under section 46, 'specified offence' means an offence specified in the indictment (within the meaning of subsection (4) of that section), and related expressions are to be read accordingly.

(10) A person arraigned on an indictment for an offence under this Part may plead guilty to an offence of which he could be found guilty under this section on that indictment.

(11) This section applies to an indictment containing more than one count as if each count were a separate indictment.

(12) This section is without prejudice to—

(a) section 6(1)(b) and (3) of the Criminal Law Act 1967;

59 Abolition of common law replaced by this Part

The common law offence of inciting the commission of another offence is abolished.

Interpretation: Part 2

64 Encouraging or assisting the commission of an offence

A reference in this Part to encouraging or assisting the commission of an offence is to be read in accordance with section 47.

65 Being capable of encouraging or assisting

(1) A reference in this Part to a person's doing an act that is capable of encouraging the commission of an offence includes a reference to his doing so by threatening another person or otherwise putting pressure on another person to commit the offence.

(2) A reference in this Part to a person's doing an act that is capable of encouraging or assisting the commission of an offence includes a reference to his doing so by—

(a) taking steps to reduce the possibility of criminal proceedings being brought in respect of that offence;

(b) failing to take reasonable steps to discharge a duty.

(3) But a person is not to be regarded as doing an act that is capable of encouraging or assisting the commission of an offence merely because he fails to respond to a constable's request for assistance in preventing a breach of the peace.

66 Indirectly encouraging or assisting

If a person (D1) arranges for a person (D2) to do an act that is capable of encouraging or assisting the commission of an offence, and D2 does the act, D1 is also to be treated for the purposes of this Part as having done it.

67 Course of conduct

A reference in this Part to an act includes a reference to a course of conduct, and a reference to doing an act is to be read accordingly.

Criminal Law Act 1977

1 The offence of conspiracy

(1) Subject to the following provisions of this Part of this Act, if a person agrees with any other person or persons that a course of conduct shall be pursued which, if the agreement is carried out in accordance with their intentions, either—

(a) will necessarily amount to or involve the commission of any offence or offences by one or more parties to the agreement, or

(b) would do so but for the existence of facts which render the commission of the offence or any offences impossible,

he is guilty of conspiracy to commit the offence or offences in question. [I] [E]

(2) Where liability for any offence may be incurred without knowledge on the part of the person committing it of any particular fact or circumstance necessary for the commission of the offence, a person shall nevertheless not be guilty of conspiracy to commit that offence by virtue of subsection (1) above unless he and at least one other party to the agreement intend or know that that fact or circumstance shall or will exist at the time when the conduct constituting the offence is to take place.

(4) In this Part of this Act 'offence' means an offence triable in England and Wales.

1A Conspiracy to commit offences outside the United Kingdom

(1) Where each of the following conditions is satisfied in the case of an agreement, this Part of this Act has effect in relation to the agreement as it has effect in relation to an agreement falling within section 1(1) above.

(2) The first condition is that the pursuit of the agreed course of conduct would at some stage involve—

(a) an act by one or more of the parties, or

(b) the happening of some other event, intended to take place in a country or territory outside the United Kingdom.

(3) The second condition is that that act or other event constitutes an offence under the law in force in that country or territory.

(4) The third condition is that the agreement would fall within section 1(1) above as an agreement relating to the commission of an offence but for the fact that the offence would not be an offence triable in England and Wales if committed in accordance with the parties' intentions.

(5) The fourth condition is that—

(a) a party to the agreement, or a party's agent, did anything in England and Wales in relation to the agreement before its formation, or

(b) a party to the agreement became a party in England and Wales (by joining it either in person or through an agent), or

(c) a party to the agreement, or a party's agent, did or omitted anything in England and Wales in pursuance of the agreement.

(6) In the application of this Part of this Act to an agreement in the case of which each of the above conditions is satisfied, a reference to an offence is to be read as a reference to what would be the offence in question but for the fact that it is not an offence triable in England and Wales.

(7) Conduct punishable under the law in force in any country or territory is an offence under that law for the purposes of this section, however it is described in that law.

(8) Subject to subsection (9) below, the second condition is to be taken to be satisfied unless, not later than rules of court may provide, the defence serve on the prosecution a notice—

(a) stating that, on the facts as alleged with respect to the agreed course of conduct, the condition is not in their opinion satisfied.

(b) showing their grounds for that opinion, and

(c) requiring the prosecution to show that it is satisfied.

(9) The court may permit the defence to require the prosecution to show that the second condition is satisfied without the prior service of a notice under subsection (8) above.

(10) In the Crown Court the question whether the second condition is satisfied shall be decided by the judge alone, and shall be treated as a question of law for the purposes of—

(a) section 9(3) of the Criminal Justice Act 1987 (preparatory hearing in fraud cases), and

(b) section 31(3) of the Criminal Procedure and Investigations Act 1996 (preparatory hearing in other cases).

(11) Any act done by means of a message (however communicated) is to be treated for the purposes of the fourth condition as done in England and Wales if the message is sent or received in England and Wales.

(12) In any proceedings in respect of an offence triable by virtue of this section, it is immaterial to guilt whether or not the accused was a British citizen at the time of any act or other event proof of which is required for conviction of the offence.

(13) References in any enactment, instrument or document (except those in this Part of this Act) to an offence of conspiracy to commit an offence include an offence triable in England and Wales as such a conspiracy by virtue of this section (without prejudice to subsection (6))

(14) Nothing in this section—

(a) applies to an agreement entered into before the day on which the Criminal Justice (Terrorism and Conspiracy) Act 1998 was passed, or

(b) imposes criminal liability on any person acting on behalf of, or holding office under, the Crown.

2 Exemptions from liability for conspiracy

(1) A person shall not by virtue of section 1 above be guilty of conspiracy to commit any offence if he is an intended victim of that offence.

(2) A person shall not by virtue of section 1 above be guilty of conspiracy to commit any offence or offences if the only other person or persons with whom he agrees are (both initially and at all times during the currency of the agreement) persons of any one or more of the following descriptions, that is to say—

(a) his spouse or civil partner;

(b) a person under the age of criminal responsibility; and

(c) an intended victim of that offence or of each of those offences.

(3) A person is under the age of criminal responsibility for the purposes of subsection (2)(b) above so long as it is conclusively presumed, by virtue of section 50 of the Children and Young Persons Act 1933, that he cannot be guilty of any offence.

3 Penalties for conspiracy

(1) A person guilty by virtue of section 1 above of conspiracy to commit any offence or offences shall be liable on conviction on indictment—

(a) in a case falling within subsection (2) or (3) below, to imprisonment for a term related in accordance with that subsection to the gravity of the offence or offences in question (referred to below in this section as the relevant offence or offences); and

(b) in any other case, to a fine.

Paragraph (b) above shall not be taken as prejudicing the application of section 30(1) of the Powers of Criminal Courts Act 1973 (general power of court to fine offender convicted on indictment) in a case falling within subsection (2) or (3) below.

(2) Where the relevant offence or any of the relevant offences is an offence of any of the following descriptions, that is to say—

(a) murder, or any other offence the sentence for which is fixed by law;

(b) an offence for which a sentence extending to imprisonment for life is provided; or

(c) an indictable offence punishable with imprisonment for which no maximum term of imprisonment is provided,

the person convicted shall be liable to imprisonment for life.

(3) Where in a case other than one to which subsection (2) above applies the relevant offence or any of the relevant offences is punishable with imprisonment, the person convicted shall be liable to imprisonment for a term not exceeding the maximum term provided for that offence or (where more than one such offence is in question) for any one of those offences (taking the longer or the longest term as the limit for the purposes of this section where the terms provided differ).

In the case of an offence triable either way the references above in this subsection to the maximum term provided for that offence are references to the maximum term so provided on conviction on indictment.

4 Restrictions on the institution of proceedings for conspiracy

(1) Subject to subsection (2) below proceedings under section 1 above for conspiracy to commit any offence shall not be instituted against any person except by or with the consent of the Director of Public Prosecutions if the offence or (as the case may be) each of the offences in question is a summary offence.

(2) In relation to the institution of proceedings under section 1 above for conspiracy to commit—

(a) an offence which is subject to a prohibition by or under any enactment on the institution of proceedings otherwise than by, or on behalf or with the consent of, the Attorney-General, or

(b) two or more offences of which at least one is subject to such a prohibition, subsection (1) above shall have effect with the substitution of a reference to the Attorney-General for the reference to the Director of Public Prosecutions.

(3) Any prohibition by or under any enactment on the institution of proceedings for any offence which is not a summary offence otherwise than by, or on behalf or with the consent of, the Director of Public Prosecutions or any other person shall apply also in relation to proceedings under section 1 above for conspiracy to commit that offence.

(4) Where—

(a) an offence has been committed in pursuance of any agreement; and

(b) proceedings may not be instituted for that offence because any time limit applicable to the institution of any such proceedings has expired, proceedings under section 1 above for conspiracy to commit that offence shall not be instituted against any person on the basis of that agreement.

(5) Subject to subsection (6) below, no proceedings for an offence triable by virtue of section 1A above may be instituted except by or with the consent of the Attorney-General.

(6) The Secretary of State may by order provide that subsection (5) above shall not apply, or shall not apply to any case of a description specified in the order.

5 Abolitions, savings, transitional provisions, consequential amendment and repeals

(1) Subject to the following provisions of this section, the offence of conspiracy at common law is hereby abolished.

(2) Subsection (1) above shall not affect the offence of conspiracy at common law so far as relates to conspiracy to defraud.

(3) Subsection (1) above shall not affect the offence of conspiracy at common law if and in so far as it may be committed by entering into an agreement to engage in conduct which—

(a) tends to corrupt public morals or outrages public decency; but

(b) would not amount to or involve the commission of an offence if carried out by a single person otherwise than in pursuance of an agreement.

(6) The rules laid down by sections 1 and 2 above shall apply for determining whether a person is guilty of an offence of conspiracy under any enactment other than section 1 above, but conduct which is an offence under any such other enactment shall not also be an offence under section 1 above.

(8) The fact that the person or persons who, so far as appears from the indictment on which any person has been convicted of conspiracy, were the only other parties to the agreement on which his conviction was based have been acquitted of conspiracy by reference to that agreement (whether after being tried with the person convicted or separately) shall not be a ground for quashing his conviction unless under all the circumstances of the case his conviction is inconsistent with the acquittal of the other person or persons in question.

(9) Any rule of law or practice inconsistent with the provisions of subsection (8) above is hereby abolished.

8 Trespassing with a weapon of offence

[See page 223]

Trade Union and Labour Relations (Consolidation) Act 1992

242 Restriction of offence of conspiracy

(1) Where in pursuance of any such agreement as is mentioned in section 1(1) of the Criminal Law Act 1977 (which provides for the offence of conspiracy) the acts in question in relation to an offence are to be done in contemplation or furtherance of a trade dispute, the offence shall be disregarded for the purposes of that subsection if it is a summary offence which is not punishable with imprisonment.

244 Meaning of 'trade dispute'

(1) In this Part a 'trade dispute' means a dispute between workers and their employer which relates wholly or mainly to one or more of the following—

(a) terms and conditions of employment, or the physical conditions in which any workers are required to work;

(b) engagement or non-engagement, or termination or suspension of employment or the duties of employment, of one or more workers;

(c) allocation of work or the duties of employment between workers or groups of workers;

(d) matters of discipline;

(e) a worker's membership or non-membership of a trade union;

(f) facilities for officials of trade unions; and

(g) machinery for negotiation or consultation, and other procedures, relating to any of the above matters, including the recognition by employers or employers' associations of the right of a trade union to represent workers in such negotiations of the right of a trade union to represent workers in such negotiation or consultation or in the carrying out of such procedures.

(2) A dispute between a Minister of the Crown and any workers shall, notwithstanding that he is not the employer of those workers, be treated as a dispute between those workers and their employer if the dispute relates to matters which—

(a) have been referred for consideration by a joint body on which, by virtue of provision made by or under any enactment, he is represented, or

(b) cannot be settled without him exercising a power conferred on him by or under an enactment.

(3) There is a trade dispute even though it relates to matters occurring outside the United Kingdom, so long as the person or persons whose actions in the United Kingdom are said to be in contemplation or furtherance of a trade dispute relating to matters occurring outside the United Kingdom are likely to be affected in respect of one or more of the matters specified in subsection (1) by the outcome of the dispute.

(4) An act, threat or demand done or made by one person or organisation against another which, if resisted, would have led to a trade dispute with that other, shall be treated as being done or made in contemplation of a trade dispute with that other, notwithstanding that because that other submits to the act or threat or accedes to the demand no dispute arises.

(5) In this section—

'employment' includes any relationship whereby one person personally does work or performs services for another; and

'worker', in relation to a dispute with an employer, means—

(a) a worker employed by that employer; or

(b) a person who has ceased to be so employed if his employment was terminated in connection with the dispute or if the termination of his employment was one of the circumstances giving rise to the dispute.

Criminal Justice Act 1987

12 Charges of conspiracy to defraud

(1) If—

(a) a person agrees with any other person or persons that a course of conduct shall be pursued; and

(b) that course of conduct will necessarily amount to or involve the commission of any offence or offences by one or more of the parties to the agreement if the agreement is carried out in accordance with their intentions,

the fact that it will do so shall not preclude a charge of conspiracy to defraud being brought against any of them in respect of the agreement. [I]

Criminal Justice Act 1993

5 Extended jurisdiction over conspiracies to defraud

[See page 16]

6 Relevance of external law

[See page 17]

Vagrancy Act 1824

4 Persons committing certain offences shall be deemed rogues and vagabonds and may be imprisoned for three months

. . . Every person committing any of the offences herein-before mentioned, after having been convicted as an idle and disorderly person; . . . every person wandering abroad and lodging in any barn or outhouse, or in any deserted or unoccupied building, or in the open air, or under a tent, or in any cart or waggon, . . . and not giving a good account of himself or herself; . . . ; every person wandering abroad, and endeavouring by the exposure of wound or deformities to obtain or gather alms; every person going about as a gatherer or collector of alms, or endeavouring to procure charitable contributions of any nature or kind, under any false or fraudulent pretence; . . . ; every person being found in or upon any dwelling house, warehouse, coach-house, stable, or outhouse, or in any inclosed yard, garden, or area, for any unlawful purpose; . . . ; and every person apprehended as an idle and disorderly person, and violently resisting any constable, or other peace officer so apprehending him or her, and being subsequently convicted of the offence for which he or she shall have been so apprehended; shall be deemed a rogue and vagabond, within the true intent and meaning of this Act; and, subject to section 70 of the Criminal Justice Act 1982, it shall be lawful for any justice of the peace to commit such offender (being thereof convicted before him by the confession of such offender, or by the evidence on oath of one or more credible witness or witnesses,) to the house of correction . . . for any time not exceeding three calender months; . . . [S]

Offences Against the Person Act 1861

4 Soliciting to commit murder

Whosoever shall solicit, encourage, persuade, or endeavour to persuade, or shall propose to any person, to murder any other person, whether he be a subject of Her Majesty or not, and whether he be within the Queen's dominions or not, shall be guilty of a misdemeanour, and being convicted thereof shall be liable to imprisonment for life. [I]

18 Wounding with intent to cause grievous bodily harm or to resist apprehension

[See page 40]

21 Attempting to choke, etc., in order to commit or assist in the committing of any indictable offence

[See page 40]

22 Using chloroform, etc., to commit or assist in the committing of any indictable offence

[See page 40]

29 Causing gunpowder to explode, or sending to any person an explosive substance, or throwing corrosive fluid on a person, with intent to grievous bodily harm

[See page 41]

30 Placing gunpowder near a building etc., with intent to do bodily injury to any person

[See page 41]

64 Making or having anything with intent to commit an offence in this Act
[See page 42]

Explosive Substances Act 1883

2 Causing explosion likely to endanger life or property
[See page 294]

3 Attempt to cause explosion, or making or keeping explosive with intent to endanger life or property
[See page 294]

4 Making or possession of explosive under suspicious circumstances
[See page 295]

5 Punishment of accessories
[See page 295]

9 Definitions
[See page 295]

Prevention of Crime Act 1953

1 Prohibition of the carrying of offensive weapons without lawful authority or reasonable excuse

(1) Any person who without lawful authority or reasonable excuse, the proof whereof shall lie on him, has with him in any public place any offensive weapon shall be guilty of an offence. [E]

(2) Where any person is convicted of an offence under subsection (1) of this section the court may make an order for the forfeiture or disposal of any weapon in respect of which the offence was committed.

(4) In this section 'public place' includes any highway and any other premises or place to which at the material time the public have or are permitted to have access, whether on payment or otherwise; and 'offensive weapon' means any article made or adapted for use for causing injury to the person, or intended by the person having it with him for such use by him or by some other person.

Restriction of Offensive Weapons Act 1959

1 Penalties for offences in connection with dangerous weapons

(1) Any person who manufactures, sells or hires or offers for sale or hire or exposes or has in his possession for the purpose of sale or hire, or lends or gives to any other person—

(a) any knife which has a blade which opens automatically by hand pressure applied to a button, spring or other device in or attached to the handle of the knife, sometimes known as a 'flick knife' or 'flick gun'; or

(b) any knife which has a blade which is released from the handle or sheath thereof by the force of gravity or the application of centrifugal force and which, when released, is locked into place by means of a button, spring, lever, or other device, sometimes known as a 'gravity knife';

shall be guilty of an offence. [S]

(2) The importation of any such knife as is described in the foregoing subsection is hereby prohibited.

Firearms Act 1968

16 Possession of firearm with intent to injure

[See page 141]

17 Use of firearm to resist arrest

[See page 141]

18 Carrying firearm with criminal intent

[See page 141]

Criminal Justice Act 1988

139 Having article with blade or point in public place

(1) Subject to subsections (4) and (5) below, any person who has an article to which this section applies with him in a public place shall be guilty of an offence. [E]

(2) Subject to subsection (3) below, this section applies to any article which has a blade or is sharply pointed except a folding pocketknife.

(3) This section applies to a folding pocketknife if the cutting edge of its blade exceeds 3 inches.

(4) It shall be a defence for a person charged with an offence under this section to prove that he had good reason or lawful authority for having the article with him in a public place.

(5) Without prejudice to the generality of subsection (4) above, it shall be a defence for a person charged with an offence under this section to prove that he had the article with him—

(a) for use at work;
(b) for religious reasons; or
(c) as part of any national costume.

(7) In this section 'public place' includes any place to which at the material time the public have or are permitted access, whether on payment or otherwise.

139A Offence of having article with blade or point (or offensive weapon) on school premises

(1) Any person who has an article to which section 139 of this Act applies with him on school premises shall be guilty of an offence. [E]

(2) Any person who has an offensive weapon within the meaning of section 1 of the Prevention of Crime Act 1953 with him on school premises shall be guilty of an offence. [E]

(3) It shall be a defence for a person charged with an offence under subsection (1) or (2) above to prove that he had good reason or lawful authority for having the article or weapon with him on the premises in question.

(4) Without prejudice to the generality of subsection (3) above, it shall be a defence for a person charged with an offence under subsection (1) or (2) above to prove that he had the article or weapon in question with him—

(a) for use at work,
(b) for educational purposes,
(c) for religious reasons, or
(d) as part of any national costume.

(6) In this section and section 139B, 'school premises' means land used for the purposes of a school excluding any land occupied solely as a dwelling by a person employed at the school; and 'school' has the meaning given by section 4 of the Education Act 1996.

141 Offensive weapons

(1) Any person who manufactures, sells or hires or offers for sale or hire, exposes or has in his possession for the purpose of sale or hire, or lends or gives to any other person, a weapon to which this section applies shall be guilty of an offence . . . [S]

(2) The Secretary of State may by order made by statutory instrument direct that this section shall apply to any description of weapon specified in the order except—

(a) any weapon subject to the Firearms Act 1968; and

(b) crossbows.

(4) The importation of a weapon to which this section applies is hereby prohibited.

(5) It shall be a defence for any person charged in respect of any conduct of his relating to a weapon to which this section applies—

(a) with an offence under subsection (1) above; or

(b) with an offence under section 50(2) or (3) of the Customs and Excise Management Act 1979 (improper importation),

to show that his conduct was only for the purposes of functions carried out on behalf of the Crown or of a visiting force.

(8) It shall be a defence for any person charged in respect of any conduct of his relating to a weapon to which this section applies—

(a) with an offence under subsection (1) above; or

(b) with an offence under section 50(2) or (3) of the Customs and Excise Management Act 1979,

to show that the conduct in question was only for the purposes of making the weapon available to a museum or gallery to which this subsection applies.

(9) If a person acting on behalf of a museum or gallery to which subsection (8) above applies is charged with hiring or lending a weapon to which this section applies, it shall be a defence for him to show that he had reasonable grounds for believing that the person to whom he lent or hired it would use it only for cultural, artistic or educational purposes.

(10) Subsection (8) above applies to a museum or gallery only if it does not distribute profits.

(11A) It shall be a defence for a person charged in respect of conduct of his relating to a weapon to which this section applies—

(a) with an offence under subsection (1) above, or

(b) with an offence under section 50(2) or (3) of the Customs and Excise Management Act 1979,

to show that his conduct was for the purpose only of making the weapon in question available for one or more of the purposes specified in subsection (11B).

(11B) Those purposes are—

(a) the purposes of theatrical performances and of rehearsals for such performances;

(b) the production of films (within the meaning of Part 1 of the Copyright, Designs and Patents Act 1988—see section 5B of that Act);

(c) the production of television programmes (within the meaning of the Communications Act 2003–see section 405(1) of that Act).

(11C) For the purposes of this section a person shall be taken to have shown a matter specified in subsection (5), (8), (9) or (11A) if—

(a) sufficient evidence of that matter is adduced to raise an issue with respect to it; and

(b) the contrary is not proved beyond a reasonable doubt.

141A Sale of knives and certain articles with blade or point to persons under eighteen

(1) Subject to subsection (3A) below any person who sells to a person under the age of eighteen years an article to which this section applies shall be guilty of an offence. [S]

(2) Subject to subsection (3) below, this section applies to—

(a) any knife, knife blade or razor blade,

(b) any axe,

(ba) any sword, and

(c) any other article which has a blade or which is sharply pointed and which is made or adapted for use for causing injury to the person.

(3) This section does not apply to any article described in—

(a) section 1 of the Restriction of Offensive Weapons Act 1959,

(b) an order made under section 141(2) of this Act, or

(c) an order made by the Secretary of State under this section.

(3A) It is not an offence under subsection (i) to sell or knife to a person if—

(a) the person is aged 16 or over and

(b) the knife or blade is designed for domestic use.

(4) It shall be a defence for a person charged with an offence under subsection (1) above to prove that he took all reasonable precautions and exercised all due diligence to avoid the commission of the offence.

Knives Act 1997

1 Unlawful marketing of knives

(1) A person is guilty of an offence if he markets a knife in a way which—

(a) indicates, or suggests, that it is suitable for combat; or

(b) is otherwise likely to stimulate or encourage violent behaviour involving the use of the knife as a weapon. [E]

(2) 'Suitable for combat' and 'violent behaviour' are defined in section 10.

(3) For the purposes of this Act, an indication or suggestion that a knife is suitable for combat may, in particular, be given or made by a name or description—

(a) applied to the knife;

(b) on the knife or on any packaging in which it is contained; or

(c) included in any advertisement which, expressly or by implication, relates to the knife.

(4) For the purposes of this Act, a person markets a knife if—

(a) he sells or hires it;

(b) he offers, or exposes, it for sale or hire; or

(c) he has it in his possession for the purpose of sale or hire.

2 Publications

(1) A person is guilty of an offence if he publishes any written, pictorial or other material in connection with the marketing of any knife and that material—

(a) indicates, or suggests, that the knife is suitable for combat; or

(b) is otherwise likely to stimulate or encourage violent behaviour involving the use of the knife as a weapon. [E]

3 Exempt trades

(1) It is a defence for a person charged with an offence under section 1 to prove that—

(a) the knife was marketed—

(i) for use by the armed forces of any country;

(ii) as an antique or curio; or

(iii) as falling within such other category (if any) as may be prescribed;

(b) it was reasonable for the knife to be marketed in that way; and

(c) there were no reasonable grounds for suspecting that a person into whose possession the knife might come in consequence of the way in which it was marketed would use it for an unlawful purpose.

(2) It is a defence for a person charged with an offence under section 2 to prove that—

(a) the material was published in connection with marketing a knife—

(i) for use by the armed forces of any country;
(ii) as an antique or curio; or
(iii) as falling within such other category (if any) as may be prescribed.

4 Other defences

(1) It is a defence for a person charged with an offence under section 1 to prove that he did not know or suspect, and had no reasonable grounds for suspecting, that the way in which the knife was marketed—

(a) amounted to an indication or suggestion that the knife was suitable for combat; or
(b) was likely to stimulate or encourage violent behaviour involving the use of the knife as a weapon.

(2) It is a defence for a person charged with an offence under section 2 to prove that he did not know or suspect, and had no reasonable grounds for suspecting, that the material—

(a) amounted to an indication or suggestion that the knife was suitable for combat; or
(b) was likely to stimulate or encourage violent behaviour involving the use of the knife as a weapon.

(3) It is a defence for a person charged with an offence under section 1 or 2 to prove that he took all reasonable precautions and exercised all due diligence to avoid committing the offence.

9 Offences by bodies corporate

(1) If an offence under this Act committed by a body corporate is proved—

(a) to have been committed with the consent or connivance of an officer, or
(b) to be attributable to any neglect on his part,

he as well as the body corporate is guilty of be offence and liable to be proceeded against and punished accordingly.

(2) In subsection (1) 'officer', in relation to a body corporate, means a director, manager, secretary or other similar officer of the body, or a person purporting to act in any such capacity.

(3) If the affairs of a body corporate are managed by its members, subsection (1) applies in relation to the acts and defaults of a member in connection with his functions of management as if he were a director of the body corporate.

10 Interpretation

In this Act—

'the court' means—

(a) in relation to England and Wales or Northern Ireland, the Crown Court or a magistrate's court;

'knife' means an instrument which has a blade or is sharply pointed;

'marketing' and related expressions are to be read with section 1(4);

'publication' includes a publication in electronic form and, in the case of a publication which is, or may be, produced from electronic data, any medium on which the data are stored;

'suitable for combat' means suitable for use as a weapon for inflicting injury on a person or causing a person to fear injury:

'violent behaviour' means an unlawful act inflicting injury on a person or causing a person to fear injury.

Fraud Act 2006

6 Possession etc. of articles for use in frauds

[See page 192]

7 Making or supplying articles for use in frauds

[See page 192]

Violent Crime Reduction Act 2006

28 Using someone to mind a weapon

(1) A person is guilty of an offence if—

(a) he uses another to look after, hide or transport a dangerous weapon for him; and

(b) he does so under arrangements or in circumstances that facilitate, or are intended to facilitate, the weapon's being available to him for an unlawful purpose. [I]

(2) For the purposes of this section the cases in which a dangerous weapon is to be regarded as available to a person for an unlawful purpose include any case where-

(a) the weapon is available for him to take possession of it at a time and place; and

(b) his possession of the weapon at that time and place would constitute, or be likely to involve or to lead to, the commission by him of an offence.

(3) In this section 'dangerous weapon' means—

(a) a firearm other than an air weapon or a component part of, or accessory to, an air weapon; or

(b) a weapon to which section 141 or 141A of the Criminal Justice Act 1988 applies (specified offensive weapons, knives and bladed weapons).

32 Sales of air weapons by way of trade or business to be face to face

(1) This section applies where a person sells an air weapon by way of trade or business to an individual in Great Britain who is not registered as a firearms dealer.

(2) A person is guilty of an offence if, for the purposes of the sale, he transfers possession of the air weapon to the buyer otherwise than at a time when both—

(a) the buyer, and

(b) either the seller or a representative of his,

are present in person. [E]

(3) The reference in subsection (2) to a representative of the seller is a reference to—

(a) a person who is employed by the seller in his business as a registered firearms dealer;

(b) a registered firearms dealer who has been authorised by the seller to act on his behalf in relation to the sale; or

(c) a person who is employed by a person falling within paragraph (b) in his business as a registered firearms dealer.

36 Manufacture, import and sale of realistic imitation firearms

(1) A person is guilty of an offence if—

(a) he manufactures a realistic imitation firearm;

(b) he modifies an imitation firearm so that it becomes a realistic imitation firearm;

(c) he sells a realistic imitation firearm; or

(d) he brings a realistic imitation firearm into Great Britain or causes one to be brought into Great Britain. [S]

(2) Subsection (1) has effect subject to the defences in section 37.

(11) In this section 'realistic imitation firearm' has the meaning given by section 38.

37 Specific defences applying to the offence under s. 36

(1) It shall be a defence for a person charged with an offence under section 36 in respect of any conduct to show that the conduct was for the purpose only of making the imitation firearm in question available for one or more of the purposes specified in subsection (2).

(2) Those purposes are—

(a) the purposes of a museum or gallery;

(b) the purposes of theatrical performances and of rehearsals for such performances;

(c) the production of films (within the meaning of Part 1 of the Copyright, Designs and Patents Act 1988—see section 5B of that Act);

(d) the production of television programmes (within the meaning of the Communications Act 2003—see section 405(1) of that Act);

(e) the organisation and holding of historical re-enactments organised and held by persons specified or described for the purposes of this section by regulations made by the Secretary of State;

(f) the purposes of functions that a person has in his capacity as a person in the service of Her Majesty.

(3) It shall also be a defence for a person charged with an offence under section 36 in respect of conduct falling within subsection (1)(d) of that section to show that the conduct—

(a) was in the course of carrying on any trade or business; and

(b) was for the purpose of making the imitation firearm in question available to be modified in a way which would result in its ceasing to be a realistic imitation firearm.

(4) For the purposes of this section a person shall be taken to have shown a matter specified in subsection (1) or (3) if—

(a) sufficient evidence of that matter is adduced to raise an issue with respect to it; and

(b) the contrary is not proved beyond a reasonable doubt.

(7) In this section—

'historical re-enactment' means any presentation or other event held for the purpose of re- enacting an event from the past or of illustrating conduct from a particular time or period in the past;

'museum or gallery' includes any institution which—

(a) has as its purpose, or one of its purposes, the preservation, display and interpretation of material of historical, artistic or scientific interest; and

(b) gives the public access to it.

38 Meaning of 'realistic imitation firearm'

(1) In sections 36 and 37 'realistic imitation firearm' means an imitation firearm which—

(a) has an appearance that is so realistic as to make it indistinguishable, for all practical purposes, from a real firearm; and

(b) is neither a de-activated firearm nor itself an antique.

(2) For the purposes of this section, an imitation firearm is not (except by virtue of subsection (3)(b)) to be regarded as distinguishable from a real firearm for any practical purpose if it could be so distinguished only—

(a) by an expert;

(b) on a close examination; or

(c) as a result of an attempt to load or to fire it.

(3) In determining for the purposes of this section whether an imitation firearm is distinguishable from a real firearm—

(a) the matters that must be taken into account include any differences between the size, shape and principal colour of the imitation firearm and the size, shape and colour in which the real firearm is manufactured; and

(b) the imitation is to be regarded as distinguishable if its size, shape or principal colour is unrealistic for a real firearm.

(7) In this section—

'colour' is to be construed in accordance with subsection (9);

'de-activated firearm' means an imitation firearm that consists in something which—

(a) was a firearm; but

(b) has been so rendered incapable of discharging a shot, bullet or other missile as no longer to be a firearm;

'real firearm' means—

(a) a firearm of an actual make or model of modern firearm (whether existing or discontinued); or

(b) something falling within a description which could be used for identifying, by reference to their appearance, the firearms falling within a category of actual modern firearms which, even though they include firearms of different makes or models (whether existing or discontinued) or both, all have the same or a similar appearance.

(8) In subsection (7) 'modern firearm' means any firearm other than one the appearance of which would tend to identify it as having a design and mechanism of a sort first dating from before the year 1870.

(9) References in this section, in relation to an imitation firearm or a real firearm, to its colour include references to its being made of transparent material.

Official Secrets Act 1920

7 Attempts, incitements, etc.

[See page 318]

Incitement to Disaffection Act 1934

2 Provisions for the prevention and detection of offences

[See page 325]

Theft Act 1968

9 Burglary

[See page 221]

10 Aggravated burglary

[See page 221]

17 False accounting

[See page 177]

20(1) Suppression, etc., of documents

[See page 178]

21 Blackmail

[See page 178]

25 Going equipped for stealing, etc.

[See page 180]

Criminal Damage Act 1971

3 Possessing anything with intent to destroy or damage property

[See page 168]

Forgery and Counterfeiting Act 1981

5 Offences relating to money orders, share certificates, passports, etc.

[See page 185]

16 Offences involving the custody or control of counterfeit notes and coins
[See page 188]

17 Offences involving the making or custody or control of counterfeiting materials and implements
[See page 188]

Computer Misuse Act 1990

2 Unauthorised access with intent to commit or facilitate commission of further offences
[See page 170]

Social Security Administration Act 1992

111A Dishonest representations for obtaining benefit etc.

(1) If a person dishonestly—

(a) makes a false statement or representation; or

(b) produces or furnishes, or causes or allows to be produced or furnished, any document or information which is false in a material particular;

with a view to obtaining any benefit or other payment or advantage under the relevant social security legislation (whether for himself or for some other person), he shall be guilty of an offence. [E]

(1A) A person shall be guilty of an offence if—

(a) there has been a change of circumstances affecting any entitlement of his to any benefit or other payment or advantage under any provision of the relevant social security legislation;

(b) the change is not a change that is excluded by regulations from the changes that are required to be notified;

(c) he knows that the change affects an entitlement of his to such a benefit or other payment or advantage; and

(d) he dishonestly fails to give a prompt notification of that change in the prescribed manner to the prescribed person. [E]

(1B) A person shall be guilty of an offence if—

(a) there has been a change of circumstances affecting any entitlement of another person to any benefit or other payment or advantage under any provision of the relevant social security legislation;

(b) the change is not a change that is excluded by regulations from the changes that are required to be notified;

(c) he knows that the change affects an entitlement of that other person to such a benefit or other payment or advantage; and

(d) he dishonestly causes or allows that other person to fail to give a prompt notification of that change in the prescribed manner to the prescribed person. [E]

(1C) This subsection applies where—

(a) there has been a change of circumstances affecting any entitlement of a person ('the claimant') to any benefit or other payment or advantage under any provision of the relevant social security legislation;

(b) the benefit, payment or advantage is one in respect of which there is another person ('the recipient') who for the time being has a right to receive payments to which the claimant has, or (but for the arrangements under which they are payable to the recipient) would have, an entitlement; and

(c) the change is not a change that is excluded by regulations from the changes that are required to be notified.

(1D) In a case where subsection (1C) above applies, the recipient is guilty of an offence if—

(a) he knows that the change affects an entitlement of the claimant to a benefit or other payment or advantage under a provision of the relevant social security legislation;

(b) the entitlement is one in respect of which he has a right to receive payments to which the claimant has, or (but for the arrangements under which they are payable to the recipient) would have, an entitlement; and

(c) he dishonestly fails to give a prompt notification of that change in the prescribed manner to the prescribed person. [E]

(1E) In a case where that subsection applies, a person other than the recipient is guilty of an offence if—

(a) he knows that the change affects an entitlement of the claimant to a benefit or other payment or advantage under a provision of the relevant social security legislation;

(b) the entitlement is one in respect of which the recipient has a right to receive payments to which the claimant has, or (but for the arrangements under which they are payable to the recipient) would have, an entitlement; and

(c) he dishonestly causes or allows the recipient to fail to give a prompt notification of that change in the prescribed manner to the prescribed person. [E]

(1F) In any case where subsection (1C) above applies but the right of the recipient is confined to a right, by reason of his being a person to whom the claimant is required to make payments in respect of a dwelling, to receive payments of housing benefit—

(a) a person shall not be guilty of an offence under subsection (1D) or (1E) above unless the change is one relating to one or both of the following—

(i) the claimant's occupation of that dwelling

(ii) the claimant's liability to make payments in respect of that dwelling; but

(b) subsections (1D)(a) and (1E)(a) above shall each have effect as if after 'knows' there were inserted 'or could reasonably be expected to know'.

(1G) For the purposes of subsections (1A) to (1E) above a notification of a change is prompt if, and only if, it is given as soon as reasonably practicable after the change occurs.

112 Making false statements for the purpose of obtaining benefit

(1) If a person for the purpose of obtaining any benefit or other payment under the relevant social security legislation whether for himself or some other person, or for any purpose connected with that legislation—

(a) makes a statement or representation which he knows to be false; or

(b) produces or furnishes or knowingly causes or knowingly allows to be produced or furnished any document or information which he knows to be false in any material particular;

he shall be guilty of a summary offence. [S]

(1A) A person shall be guilty of an offence if—

(a) there has been a change of circumstances affecting any entitlement of his to any benefit or other payment or advantage under any provision of the relevant social security legislation;

(b) the change is not a change that is excluded by regulations from the changes that are required to be notified;

(c) he knows that the change affects an entitlement of his to such a benefit or other payment or advantage; and

(d) he fails to give a prompt notification of that change in the prescribed manner to the prescribed person. [E]

(1B) A person is guilty of an offence under this section if—

(a) there has been a change of circumstances affecting any entitlement of another person to any benefit or other payment or advantage under any provision of the relevant social security legislation;

(b) the change is not a change that is excluded by regulations from the changes that are required to be notified;

(c) he knows that the change affects an entitlement of that other person to such a benefit or other payment or advantage; and

(d) he causes or allows that other person to fail to give a prompt notification of that change in the prescribed manner to the prescribed person. [E]

(1C) In a case where subsection (1C) of section 111A above applies, the recipient is guilty of an offence if—

(a) he knows that the change affects an entitlement of the claimant to a benefit or other payment or advantage under a provision of the relevant social security legislation;

(b) the entitlement is one in respect of which he has a right to receive payments to which the claimant has, or (but for the arrangements under which they are payable to the recipient) would have, an entitlement; and

(c) he fails to give a prompt notification of that change in the prescribed manner to the prescribed person. [E]

(1D) In a case where that subsection applies, a person other than the recipient is guilty of an offence if—

(a) he knows that the change affects an entitlement of the claimant to a benefit or other payment or advantage under a provision of the relevant social security legislation;

(b) the entitlement is one in respect of which the recipient has a right to receive payments to which the claimant has, or (but for the arrangements under which they are payable to the recipient) would have, an entitlement; and

(c) he causes or allows the recipient to fail to give a prompt notification of that change in the prescribed manner to the prescribed person. [E]

(1E) Subsection (1f) of section 111A above applies in relation to subsections (1C) and (1D) above as it applies in relation to subsections (1D) and (1E) of that section.

(1F) For the purposes of subsections (1A) to (1D) above a notification of a change is prompt if, and only if, it is given as soon as reasonably practicable after the change occurs.

Terrorism Act 2000

11 Membership
[See page 296]

12 Support
[See page 296]

15 Fund-raising
[See page 297]

16 Use and possession
[See page 297]

17 Funding arrangements
[See page 298]

54 Weapons training
[See page 301]

57 Possession for terrorist purposes
[See page 302]

58 Collection of information
[See page 302]

Communications Act 2003

126 Possession or supply of apparatus for dishonestly obtaining communications services
[See page 183]

Sexual Offences Act 2003

61 Administering a substance with intention of enabling sexual activity
[See page 46]

62 Committing an offence with intent to commit a sexual offence
[See page 46]

63 Trespass with intent to commit a sexual offence
[See page 230]

Anti-social Behaviour Act 2003

54 Sale of aerosol paint to children
[See page 167]

Identity Cards Act 2006

25 Possession of false identity documents etc.

(1) It is an offence for a person with the requisite intention to have in his possession or under his control—

(a) an identity document that is false and that he knows or believes to be false;

(b) an identity document that was improperly obtained and that he knows or believes to have been improperly obtained; or

(c) an identity document that relates to someone else. [I]

(2) The requisite intention for the purposes of subsection (1) is—

(a) the intention of using the document for establishing registrable facts about himself; or

(b) the intention of allowing or inducing another to use it for establishing, ascertaining or verifying registrable facts about himself or about any other person (with the exception, in the case of a document within paragraph (c) of that subsection, of the individual to whom it relates).

(3) It is an offence for a person with the requisite intention to make, or to have in his possession or under his control—

(a) any apparatus which, to his knowledge, is or has been specially designed or adapted for the making of false identity documents; or

(b) any article or material which, to his knowledge, is or has been specially designed or adapted to be used in the making of false identity documents. [I]

(4) The requisite intention for the purposes of subsection (3) is the intention—

(a) that he or another will make a false identity document; and

(b) that the document will be used by somebody for establishing, ascertaining or verifying registrable facts about a person.

(5) It is an offence for a person to have in his possession or under his control, without reasonable excuse—

(a) an identity document that is false;
(b) an identity document that was improperly obtained;
(c) an identity document that relates to someone else; or
(d) any apparatus, article or material which, to his knowledge, is or has been specially designed or adapted for the making of false identity documents or to be used in the making of such documents. [E]

(8) For the purposes of this section—

(a) an identity document is false only if it is false within the meaning of Part 1 of the Forgery and Counterfeiting Act 1981 (see section 9(1) of that Act); and
(b) an identity document was improperly obtained if false information was provided, in or in connection with the application for its issue or an application for its modification, to the person who issued it or (as the case may be) to a person entitled to modify it;

and references to the making of a false identity document include references to the modification of an identity document so that it becomes false.

(10) In this section 'identity document' has the meaning given by section 26.

26 Identity documents for the purposes of s. 25

(1) In section 25 'identity document' means any document that is, or purports to be—

(a) an ID card;
(b) a designated document;
(c) an immigration document;
(d) a United Kingdom passport (within the meaning of the Immigration Act 1971);
(e) a passport issued by or on behalf of the authorities of a country or territory outside the United Kingdom or by or on behalf of an international organisation;
(f) a document that can be used (in some or all circumstances) instead of a passport;
(g) a UK driving licence; or
(h) a driving licence issued by or on behalf of the authorities of a country or territory outside the United Kingdom.

(2) In subsection (1) 'immigration document' means—

(a) a document used for confirming the right of a person under the Community Treaties in respect of entry or residence in the United Kingdom;
(b) a document which is given in exercise of immigration functions and records information about leave granted to a person to enter or to remain in the United Kingdom; or
(c) a registration card (within the meaning of section 26A of the Immigration Act 1971);

and in paragraph (b) 'immigration functions' means functions under the Immigration Acts (within the meaning of the Asylum and Immigration (Treatment of Claimants, etc.) Act 2004).

(3) In that subsection 'UK driving licence' means—

(a) a licence to drive a motor vehicle granted under Part 3 of the Road Traffic Act 1988; or
(b) a licence to drive a motor vehicle granted under Part 2 of the Road Traffic (Northern Ireland) Order 1981.

27 Unauthorised disclosure of information

(1) A person is guilty of an offence if, without lawful authority—

(a) he provides any person with information that he is required to keep confidential; or
(b) he otherwise makes a disclosure of any such information. [I]

(2) For the purposes of this section a person is required to keep information confidential if it is information that is or has become available to him by reason of his holding an office or employment the duties of which relate, in whole or in part, to—

(a) the establishment or maintenance of the Register;
(b) the issue, manufacture, modification, cancellation or surrender of ID cards; or
(c) the carrying out of the Commissioner's functions.

(3) For the purposes of this section information is provided or otherwise disclosed with lawful authority if, and only if the provision or other disclosure of the information—

(a) is authorised by or under this Act or another enactment;

(b) is in pursuance of an order or direction of a court or of a tribunal established by or under any enactment;

(c) is in pursuance of a Community obligation; or

(d) is for the purposes of the performance of the duties of an office or employment of the sort mentioned in subsection (2).

(4) It is a defence for a person charged with an offence under this section to show that, at the time of the alleged offence, he believed, on reasonable grounds, that he had lawful authority to provide the information or to make the other disclosure in question.

28 Providing false information

(1) A person is guilty of an offence if, in circumstances falling within subsection (2), he provides false information to any person—

(a) for the purpose of securing the making or modification of an entry in the Register;

(b) in confirming (with or without changes) the contents of an entry in the Register; or

(c) for the purpose of obtaining for himself or another the issue or modification of an ID card. [E]

(2) Those circumstances are that, at the time of the provision of the information he—

(a) knows or believes the information to be false; or

(b) is reckless as to whether or not it is false.

29 Tampering with the Register etc.

(1) A person is guilty of an offence under this section if—

(a) he engages in any conduct that causes an unauthorised modification of information recorded in the Register; and

(b) at the time when he engages in the conduct, he has the requisite intent. [E]

(2) For the purposes of this section a person has the requisite intent if he—

(a) intends to cause a modification of information recorded in the Register; or

(b) is reckless as to whether or not his conduct will cause such a modification.

(3) For the purposes of this section the cases in which conduct causes a modification of information recorded in the Register include—

(a) where it contributes to a modification of such information; and

(b) where it makes it more difficult or impossible for such information to be retrieved in a legible form from a computer on which it is stored by the Secretary of State, or contributes to making that more difficult or impossible.

(4) It is immaterial for the purposes of this section—

(a) whether the conduct constituting the offence, or any of it, took place in the United Kingdom; or

(b) in the case of conduct outside the United Kingdom, whether it is conduct of a British citizen.

(5) For the purposes of this section a modification is unauthorised, in relation to the person whose conduct causes it, if—

(a) he is not himself entitled to determine if the modification may be made; and

(b) he does not have a consent to the modification from a person who is so entitled.

(6) In proceedings against a person for an offence under this section in respect of conduct causing a modification of information recorded in the Register it is to be a defence for that person to show that, at the time of the conduct, he believed, on reasonable grounds—

(a) that he was a person entitled to determine if that modification might be made; or

(b) that consent to the modification had been given by a person so entitled.

(9) In this section—

'conduct' includes acts and omissions; and

'modification' includes a temporary modification.

Part XV

Disposal of Proceeds of Crimes

Theft Act 1968

22 Handling stolen goods
[See page 178]

23 Advertising rewards for return of goods stolen or lost
[See page 179]

24 Scope of offences relating to stolen goods
[See page 179]

27 Evidence and procedure on charge of theft or handling stolen goods
[See page 180]

Salmon Act 1986

32 Handling salmon in suspicious circumstance
[See page 181]

Proceeds of Crime Act 2002

PART 7 MONEY LAUNDERING

327 Concealing etc.

(1) A person commits an offence if he—

(a) conceals criminal property;

(b) disguises criminal property;

(c) converts criminal property;

(d) transfers criminal property;

(e) removes criminal property from England and Wales or from Scotland or from Northern Ireland. [E]

(2) But a person does not commit such an offence if—

(a) he makes an authorised disclosure under section 338 and (if the disclosure is made before he does the act mentioned in subsection (1)) he has the appropriate consent;

(b) he intended to make such a disclosure but had a reasonable excuse for not doing so;

(c) the act he does is done in carrying out a function he has relating to the enforcement of any provision of this Act or of any other enactment relating to criminal conduct or benefit from criminal conduct.

(2A) Nor does a person commit an offence under subsection (1) if—

(a) he knows, or believes on reasonable grounds, that the relevant criminal conduct occurred in a particular country or territory outside the United Kingdom, and

(b) the relevant criminal conduct—

(i) was not, at the time it occurred, unlawful under the criminal law then applying in that country or territory, and

(ii) is not of a description prescribed by an order made by the Secretary of State.

(2B) In subsection (2A) 'the relevant criminal conduct' is the criminal conduct by reference to which the property concerned is criminal property.

(2C) A deposit-taking body that does an act mentioned in paragraph (c) or (d) of subsection (1) does not commit an offence under that subsection if—

(a) it does the act in operating an account maintained with it, and

(b) the value of the criminal property concerned is less than the threshold amount determined under section 339A for the act.

(3) Concealing or disguising criminal property includes concealing or disguising its nature, source, location, disposition, movement or ownership or any rights with respect to it.

328 Arrangements

(1) A person commits an offence if he enters into or becomes concerned in an arrangement which he knows or suspects facilitates (by whatever means) the acquisition, retention, use or control of criminal property by or on behalf of another person. [E]

(2) But a person does not commit such an offence if—

(a) he makes an authorised disclosure under section 338 and (if the disclosure is made before he does the act mentioned in subsection (1)) he has the appropriate consent;

(b) he intended to make such a disclosure but had a reasonable excuse for not doing so;

(c) the act he does is done in carrying out a function he has relating to the enforcement of any provision of this Act or of any other enactment relating to criminal conduct or benefit from criminal conduct.

(3) Nor does a person commit an offence under subsection (1) if—

(a) he knows, or believes on reasonable grounds, that the relevant criminal conduct occurred in a particular country or territory outside the United Kingdom, and

(b) the relevant criminal conduct—

(i) was not, at the time it occurred, unlawful under the criminal law then applying in that country or territory, and

(ii) is not of a description prescribed by an order made by the Secretary of State.

(4) In subsection (3) 'the relevant criminal conduct' is the criminal conduct by reference to which the property concerned is criminal property.

(5) A deposit-taking body that does an act mentioned in subsection (1) does not commit an offence under that subsection if—

(a) it does the act in operating an account maintained with it, and

(b) the arrangement facilitates the acquisition, retention, use or control of criminal property of a value that is less than the threshold amount determined under section 339A for the act.

329 Acquisition, use and possession

(1) A person commits an offence if he—

(a) acquires criminal property;

(b) uses criminal property;

(c) has possession of criminal property. [E]

(2) But a person does not commit such an offence if—

(a) he makes an authorised disclosure under section 338 and (if the disclosure is made before he does the act mentioned in subsection (1)) he has the appropriate consent;
(b) he intended to make such a disclosure but had a reasonable excuse for not doing so;
(c) he acquired or used or had possession of the property for adequate consideration;
(d) the act he does is done in carrying out a function he has relating to the enforcement of any provision of this Act or of any other enactment relating to criminal conduct or benefit from criminal conduct.

(2A) Nor does a person commit an offence under subsection (1) if—
(a) he knows, or believes on reasonable grounds, that the relevant criminal conduct occurred in a particular country or territory outside the United Kingdom, and
(b) the relevant criminal conduct—
(i) was not, at the time it occurred, unlawful under the criminal law then applying in that country or territory, and
(ii) is not of a description prescribed by an order made by the Secretary of State.

(2B) In subsection (2A) 'the relevant criminal conduct' is the criminal conduct by reference to which the property concerned is criminal property.

(2C) A deposit-taking body that does an act mentioned in subsection (1) does not commit an offence under that subsection if—
(a) it does the act in operating an account maintained with it, and
(b) the value of the criminal property concerned is less than the threshold amount determined under section 339A for the act.

(3) For the purposes of this section—
(a) a person acquires property for inadequate consideration if the value of the consideration is significantly less than the value of the property;
(b) a person uses or has possession of property for inadequate consideration if the value of the consideration is significantly less than the value of the use or possession;
(c) the provision by a person of goods or services which he knows or suspects may help another to carry out criminal conduct is not consideration.

330 Failure to disclose: regulated sector

(1) A person commits an offence if the conditions in subsections (2) to (4) are satisfied. [E]

(2) The first condition is that he—
(a) knows or suspects, or
(b) has reasonable grounds for knowing or suspecting,
that another person is engaged in money laundering.

(3) The second condition is that the information or other matter—
(a) on which his knowledge or suspicion is based, or
(b) which gives reasonable grounds for such knowledge or suspicion,
came to him in the course of a business in the regulated sector.

(3A) The third condition is—
(a) that he can identify the other person mentioned in subsection (2) or the whereabouts of any of the laundered property, or
(b) that he believes, or it is reasonable to expect him to believe, that the information or other matter mentioned in subsection (3) will or may assist in identifying that other person or the whereabouts of any of the laundered property.

(4) The fourth condition is that he does not make the required disclosure to—
(a) a nominated officer, or
(b) a person authorised for the purposes of this Part by the Director General of the Serious Organised Crime Agency,
as soon as is practicable after the information or other matter mentioned in subsection (3) comes to him.

(5) The required disclosure is a disclosure of—
(a) the identity of the other person mentioned in subsection (2), if he knows it,

(b) the whereabouts of the laundered property, so far as he knows it, and
(c) the information or other matter mentioned in subsection (3).

(5A) The laundered property is the property forming the subject-matter of the money laundering that he knows or suspects, or has reasonable grounds for knowing or suspecting, that other person to be engaged in.

(6) But he does not commit an offence under this section if—
(a) he has a reasonable excuse for not making the required disclosure,
(b) he is a professional legal adviser or other relevant professional adviser and—
(i) if he knows either of the things mentioned in subsection (5)(a) and (b), he knows the thing because of information or other matter that came to him in privileged circumstances, or
(ii) the information or other matter mentioned in subsection (3) came to him in privileged circumstances, or
(c) subsection (7) or (7B) applies to him.

(7) This subsection applies to a person if—
(a) he does not know or suspect that another person is engaged in money laundering, and
(b) he has not been provided by his employer with such training as is specified by the Secretary of State by order for the purposes of this section.

(7A) Nor does a person commit an offence under this section if—
(a) he knows, or believes on reasonable grounds, that the money laundering is occurring in a particular country or territory outside the United Kingdom, and
(b) the money laundering—
(i) is not unlawful under the criminal law applying in that country or territory, and
(ii) is not of a description prescribed in an order made by the Secretary of State.

(7B) This subsection applies to a person if—
(a) he is employed by, or is in partnership with, a professional legal adviser or a relevant professional adviser to provide the adviser with assistance or support,
(b) the information or other matter mentioned in subsection (3) comes to the person in connection with the provision of such assistance or support, and
(c) the information or other matter came to the adviser in privileged circumstances.

(8) In deciding whether a person committed an offence under this section the court must consider whether he followed any relevant guidance which was at the time concerned—
(a) issued by a supervisory authority or any other appropriate body,
(b) approved by the Treasury, and
(c) published in a manner it approved as appropriate in its opinion to bring the guidance to the attention of persons likely to be affected by it.

(9) A disclosure to a nominated officer is a disclosure which—
(a) is made to a person nominated by the alleged offender's employer to receive disclosures under this section, and
(b) is made in the course of the alleged offender's employment.

(9A) But a disclosure which satisfies paragraphs (a) and (b) of subsection (9) is not to be taken as a disclosure to a nominated officer if the person making the disclosure—
(a) is a professional legal adviser or other relevant professional adviser,
(b) makes it for the purpose of obtaining advice about making a disclosure under this section, and
(c) does not intend it to be a disclosure under this section.

(10) Information or other matter comes to a professional legal adviser or other relevant professional advisor in privileged circumstances if it is communicated or given to him—
(a) by (or by a representative of) a client of his in connection with the giving by the adviser of legal advice to the client,
(b) by (or by a representative of) a person seeking legal advice from the adviser, or
(c) by a person in connection with legal proceedings or contemplated legal proceedings.

(11) But subsection (10) does not apply to information or other matter which is communicated or given with the intention of furthering a criminal purpose.

(12) Schedule 9 has effect for the purpose of determining what is—

(a) a business in the regulated sector;

(b) a supervisory authority.

(13) An appropriate body is any body which regulates or is representative of any trade, profession, business or employment carried on by the alleged offender.

(14) A relevant professional adviser is an accountant, auditor or tax adviser who is a member of a professional body which is established for accountants, auditors or tax advisers (as the case may be) and which makes provision for—

(a) testing the competence of those seeking admission to membership of such a body as a condition for such admission; and

(b) imposing and maintaining professional and ethical standards for its members, as well as imposing sanctions for non-compliance with those standards.

331 Failure to disclose: nominated officers in the regulated sector

(1) A person nominated to receive disclosures under section 330 commits an offence if the conditions in subsections (2) to (4) are satisfied. [E]

(2) The first condition is that he—

(a) knows or suspects, or

(b) has reasonable grounds for knowing or suspecting,

that another person is engaged in money laundering.

(3) The second condition is that the information or other matter—

(a) on which his knowledge or suspicion is based, or

(b) which gives reasonable grounds for such knowledge or suspicion,

came to him in consequence of a disclosure made under section 330.

(3A) The third condition is—

(a) that he knows the identity of the other person mentioned in subsection (2), or the whereabouts of any of the laundered property, in consequence of a disclosure made under section 330,

(b) that that other person, or the whereabouts of any of the laundered property, can be identified from the information or other matter mentioned in subsection (3), or

(c) that he believes, or it is reasonable to expect him to believe, that the information or other matter will or may assist in identifying that other person or the whereabouts of any of the laundered property.

(4) The fourth condition is that he does not make the required disclosure to a person authorised for the purposes of this Part by the Director General of the Serious Organised Crime Agency as soon as is practicable after the information or other matter mentioned in subsection (3) comes to him.

(5) The required disclosure is a disclosure of—

(a) the identity of the other person mentioned in subsection (2), if disclosed to him under section 330,

(b) the whereabouts of the laundered property, so far as disclosed to him under section 330, and

(c) the information or other matter mentioned in subsection (3).

(5A) The laundered property is the property forming the subject-matter of the money laundering that he knows or suspects, or has reasonable grounds for knowing or suspecting, that other person to be engaged in.

(6) But he does not commit an offence under this section if he has a reasonable excuse for not making the required disclosure.

(6A) Nor does a person commit an offence under this section if—

(a) he knows, or believes on reasonable grounds, that the money laundering is occurring in a particular country or territory outside the United Kingdom, and
(b) the money laundering—
(i) is not unlawful under the criminal law applying in that country or territory, and
(ii) is not of a description prescribed in an order made by the Secretary of State.

(7) In deciding whether a person committed an offence under this section the court must consider whether he followed any relevant guidance which was at the time concerned—
(a) issued by a supervisory authority or any other appropriate body,
(b) approved by the Treasury, and
(c) published in a manner it approved as appropriate in its opinion to bring the guidance to the attention of persons likely to be affected by it.

(8) Schedule 9 has effect for the purpose of determining what is a supervisory authority.

(9) An appropriate body is a body which regulates or is representative of a trade, profession, business or employment.

332 Failure to disclose: other nominated officers

(1) A person nominated to receive disclosures under section 337 or 338 commits an offence if the conditions in subsections (2) to (4) are satisfied. [E]

(2) The first condition is that he knows or suspects that another person is engaged in money laundering.

(3) The second condition is that the information or other matter on which his knowledge or suspicion is based came to him in consequence of a disclosure made under the applicable section.

(3A) The third condition is—
(a) that he knows the identity of the other person mentioned in subsection (2), or the whereabouts of any of the laundered property, in consequence of a disclosure made under section 330,
(b) that that other person, or the whereabouts of any of the laundered property, can be identified from the information or other matter mentioned in subsection (3), or
(c) that he believes, or it is reasonable to expect him to believe, that the information or other matter will or may assist in identifying that other person or the whereabouts of any of the laundered property.

(4) The fourth condition is that he does not make the required disclosure to a person authorised for the purposes of this Part by the Director General of the Serious Organised Crime Agency as soon as is practicable after the information or other matter mentioned in subsection (3) comes to him.

(5) The required disclosure is a disclosure of—
(a) the identity of the other person mentioned in subsection (2), if disclosed to him under section,
(b) the whereabouts of the laundered property, so far as disclosed to him under the applicable section, and
(c) the information or other matter mentioned in subsection (3).

(5A) The laundered property is the property forming the subject-matter of the money laundering that he knows or suspects, or has reasonable grounds for knowing or suspecting, that other person to be engaged in.

(5B) The applicable section is section 337 or, as the case may be, section 338.

(6) But he does not commit an offence under this section if he has a reasonable excuse for not making the required disclosure.

(7) Nor does a person commit an offence under this section if—
(a) he knows, or believes on reasonable grounds, that the money laundering is occurring in a particular country or territory outside the United Kingdom, and
(b) the money laundering—
(i) is not unlawful under the criminal law applying in that country or territory, and
(ii) is not of a description prescribed in an order made by the Secretary of State.

333 Tipping off

(1) A person commits an offence if—

(a) he knows or suspects that a disclosure falling within section 337 or 338 has been made, and

(b) he makes a disclosure which is likely to prejudice any investigation which might be conducted following the disclosure referred to in paragraph (a). [E]

(2) But a person does not commit an offence under subsection (1) if—

(a) he did not know or suspect that the disclosure was likely to be prejudicial as mentioned in subsection (1);

(b) the disclosure is made in carrying out a function he has relating to the enforcement of any provision of this Act or of any other enactment relating to criminal conduct or benefit from criminal conduct;

(c) he is a professional legal adviser and the disclosure falls within subsection (3).

(3) A disclosure falls within this subsection if it is a disclosure—

(a) to (or to a representative of) a client of the professional legal adviser in connection with the giving by the adviser of legal advice to the client, or

(b) to any person in connection with legal proceedings or contemplated legal proceedings.

(4) But a disclosure does not fall within subsection (3) if it is made with the intention of furthering a criminal purpose.

335 Appropriate consent

(1) The apropriate consent is—

(a) the consent of a nominated officer to do a prohibited act if an authorised disclosure is made to the nominated officer;

(b) the consent of a constable to do a prohibited act if an authorised disclosure is made to a constable;

(c) the consent of a customs officer to do a prohibited act if an authorised disclosure is made to a customs officer.

(2) A person must be treated as having the appropriate consent if—

(a) he makes an authorised disclosure to a constable or a customs officer, and

(b) the condition in subsection (3) or the condition in subsection (4) is satisfied.

(3) The condition is that before the end of the notice period he does not receive notice from a constable or customs officer that consent to the doing of the act is refused.

(4) The condition is that—

(a) before the end of the notice period he receives notice from a constable or customs officer that consent to the doing of the act is refused, and

(b) the moratorium period has expired.

(5) The notice period is the period of seven working days starting with the first working day after the person makes the disclosure.

(6) The moratorium period is the period of 31 days starting with the day on which the person receives notice that consent to the doing of the act is refused.

(7) A working day is a day other than a Saturday, a Sunday, Christmas Day, Good Friday or a day which is a bank holiday under the Banking and Financial Dealings Act 1971 in the part of the United Kingdom in which the person is when he makes the disclosure.

(8) References to a prohibited act are to an act mentioned in section 327(1), 328(1) or 329(1) (as the case may be).

(9) A nominated officer is a person nominated to receive disclosures under section 338.

(10) Subsections (1) to (4) apply for the purposes of this Part.

336 Nominated officer: consent

(1) A nominated officer must not give the appropriate consent to the doing of a prohibited act unless the condition in subsection (2), the condition in subsection (3) or the condition in subsection (4) is satisfied.

(2) The condition is that—

(a) he makes a disclosure that property is criminal property to a person authorised for the purposes of this Part by the Director General of the Serious Organised Crime Agency, and

(b) such a person gives consent to the doing of the act.

(3) The condition is that—

(a) he makes a disclosure that property is criminal property to a person authorised for the purposes of this Part by the Director General of the Serious Organised Crime Agency, and

(b) before the end of the notice period he does not receive notice from such a person that consent to the doing of the act is refused.

(4) The condition is that—

(a) he makes a disclosure that property is criminal property to a person authorised for the purposes of this Part by the Director General of the Serious Organised Crime Agency,

(b) before the end of the notice period he receives notice from such a person that consent to the doing of the act is refused, and

(c) the moratorium period has expired.

(5) A person who is a nominated officer commits an offence if—

(a) he gives consent to a prohibited act in circumstances where none of the conditions in subsections (2), (3) and (4) is satisfied, and

(b) he knows or suspects that the act is a prohibited act. [E]

(7) The notice period is the period of seven working days starting with the first working day after the nominated officer makes the disclosure.

(8) The moratorium period is the period of 31 days starting with the day on which the nominated officer is given notice that consent to the doing of the act is refused.

(9) A working day is a day other than a Saturday, a Sunday, Christmas Day, Good Friday or a day which is a bank holiday under the Banking and Financial Dealings Act 1971 in the part of the United Kingdom in which the nominated officer is when he gives the appropriate consent.

(10) References to a prohibited act are to an act mentioned in section 327(1), 328(1) or 329(1) (as the case may be).

(11) A nominated officer is a person nominated to receive disclosures under section 338.

337 Protected disclosures

(1) A disclosure which satisfies the following three conditions is not to be taken to breach any restriction on the disclosure of information (however imposed).

(2) The first condition is that the information or other matter disclosed came to the person making the disclosure (the discloser) in the course of his trade, profession, business or employment.

(3) The second condition is that the information or other matter—

(a) causes the discloser to know or suspect, or

(b) gives him reasonable grounds for knowing or suspecting, that another person is engaged in money laundering.

(4) The third condition is that the disclosure is made to a constable, a customs officer or a nominated officer as soon as is practicable after the information or other matter comes to the discloser.

(4A) Where a disclosure consists of a disclosure protected under subsection (1) and a disclosure of either or both of—

(a) the identity of the other person mentioned in subsection (3), and

(b) the whereabouts of property forming the subject-matter of the money laundering that the discloser knows or suspects, or has reasonable grounds for knowing or suspecting, that other person to be engaged in,

the disclosure of the thing mentioned in paragraph (a) or (b) (as well as the disclosure protected under subsection (1)) is not to be taken to breach any restriction on the disclosure of information (however imposed).

(5) A disclosure to a nominated officer is a disclosure which—

(a) is made to a person nominated by the discloser's employer to receive disclosures under section 330 or this section, and
(b) is made in the course of the discloser's employment.

338 Authorised disclosures

(1) For the purposes of this Part a disclosure is authorised if—
(a) it is a disclosure to a constable, a customs officer or a nominated officer by the alleged offender that property is criminal property, and
(b) the first, second or third condition set out below is satisfied.

(2) The first condition is that the disclosure is made before the alleged offender does the prohibited act.

(2A) The second condition is that—
(a) the disclosure is made while the alleged offender is doing the prohibited act,
(b) he began to do the act at a time when, because he did not then know or suspect that the property constituted or represented a person's benefit from criminal conduct, the act was not a prohibited act, and
(c) the disclosure is made on his own initiative and as soon as is practicable after he first knows or suspects that the property constitutes or represents a person's benefit from criminal conduct.

(3) The third condition is that—
(a) the disclosure is made after the alleged offender does the prohibited act,
(b) there is a good reason for his failure to make the disclosure before he did the act, and
(c) the disclosure is made on his own initiative and as soon as it is practicable for him to make it.

(4) An authorised disclosure is not to be taken to breach any restriction on the disclosure of information (however imposed).

(5) A disclosure to a nominated officer is a disclosure which—
(a) is made to a person nominated by the alleged offender's employer to receive authorised disclosures, and
(b) is made in the course of the alleged offender's employment.

(6) References to the prohibited act are to an act mentioned in section 327(1), 328(1) or 329(1) (as the case may be).

339A Threshold amounts

(1) This section applies for the purposes of sections 327(2C), 328(5) and 329(2C).

(2) The threshold amount for acts done by a deposit-taking body in operating an account is £250 unless a higher amount is specified under the following provisions of this section (in which event it is that higher amount).

(3) An officer of Revenue and Customs, or a constable, may specify the threshold amount for acts done by a deposit-taking body in operating an account—
(a) when he gives consent, or gives notice refusing consent, to the deposit-taking body's doing of an act mentioned in section 327(1), 328(1) or 329(1) in opening, or operating, the account or a related account, or
(b) on a request from the deposit-taking body.

(4) Where the threshold amount for acts done in operating an account is specified under subsection (3) or this subsection, an officer of Revenue and Customs, or a constable, may vary the amount (whether on a request from the deposit-taking body or otherwise) by specifying a different amount.

(5) Different threshold amounts may be specified under subsections (3) and (4) for different acts done in operating the same account.

(6) The amount specified under subsection (3) or (4) as the threshold amount for acts done in operating an account must, when specified, not be less than the amount specified in subsection (2).

(7) The Secretary of State may by order vary the amount for the time being specified in subsection (2).

(8) For the purposes of this section, an account is related to another if each is maintained with the same deposit-taking body and there is a person who, in relation to each account, is the person or one of the persons entitled to instruct the body as respects the operation of the account.

340 Interpretation

(1) This section applies for the purposes of this Part.

(2) Criminal conduct is conduct which—

(a) constitutes an offence in any part of the United Kingdom, or

(b) would constitute an offence in any part of the United Kingdom if it occurred there.

(3) Property is criminal property if—

(a) it constitutes a person's benefit from criminal conduct or it represents such a benefit (in whole or part and whether directly or indirectly), and

(b) the alleged offender knows or suspects that it constitutes or represents such a benefit.

(4) It is immaterial—

(a) who carried out the conduct;

(b) who benefited from it;

(c) whether the conduct occurred before or after the passing of this Act.

(5) A person benefits from conduct if he obtains property as a result of or in connection with the conduct.

(6) If a person obtains a pecuniary advantage as a result of or in connection with conduct, he is to be taken to obtain as a result of or in connection with the conduct a sum of money equal to the value of the pecuniary advantage.

(7) References to property or a pecuniary advantage obtained in connection with conduct include references to property or a pecuniary advantage obtained in both that connection and some other.

(8) If a person benefits from conduct his benefit is the property obtained as a result of or in connection with the conduct.

(9) Property is all property wherever situated and includes—

(a) money;

(b) all forms of property, real or personal, heritable or moveable;

(c) things in action and other intangible or incorporeal property.

(10) The following rules apply in relation to property—

(a) property is obtained by a person if he obtains an interest in it;

(b) references to an interest, in relation to land in England and Wales or Northern Ireland, are to any legal estate or equitable interest or power;

(c) references to an interest, in relation to land in Scotland, are to any estate, interest, servitude or other heritable right in or over land, including a heritable security;

(d) references to an interest, in relation to property other than land, include references to a right (including a right to possession).

(11) Money laundering is an act which—

(a) constitutes an offence under section 327, 328 or 329,

(b) constitutes an attempt, conspiracy or incitement to commit an offence specified in paragraph (a),

(c) constitutes aiding, abetting, counselling or procuring the commission of an offence specified in paragraph (a), or

(d) would constitute an offence specified in paragraph (a), (b) or (c) if done in the United Kingdom.

(12) For the purposes of a disclosure to a nominated officer—

(a) references to a person's employer include any body, association or organisation (including a voluntary organisation) in connection with whose activities the person exercises a function (whether or not for gain or reward), and

(b) references to employment must be construed accordingly.

(13) References to a constable include references to a person authorised for the purposes of this Part by the Director General of the Serious Organised Crime Agency.

(14) 'Deposit-taking body' means—

(a) a business which engages in the activity of accepting deposits, or

(b) the National Savings Bank.

Dealing in Cultural Objects (Offences) Act 2003

1 Offence of dealing in tainted cultural objects

(1) A person is guilty of an offence if he dishonestly deals in a cultural object that is tainted, knowing or believing that the object is tainted.

(2) It is immaterial whether he knows or believes that the object is a cultural object. [E]

2 Meaning of 'tainted cultural object'

(1) 'Cultural object' means an object of historical, architectural or archaeological interest.

(2) A cultural object is tainted if, after the commencement of this Act—

(a) a person removes the object in a case falling within subsection (4) or he excavates the object, and

(b) the removal or excavation constitutes an offence.

(3) It is immaterial whether—

(a) the removal or excavation was done in the United Kingdom or elsewhere,

(b) the offence is committed under the law of a part of the United Kingdom or under the law of any other country or territory.

(4) An object is removed in a case falling within this subsection if—

(a) it is removed from a building or structure of historical, architectural or archaeological interest where the object has at any time formed part of the building or structure, or

(b) it is removed from a monument of such interest.

(5) 'Monument' means—

(a) any work, cave or excavation,

(b) any site comprising the remains of any building or structure or of any work, cave or excavation,

(c) any site comprising, or comprising the remains of, any vehicle, vessel, aircraft or other movable structure, or part of any such thing.

(6) 'Remains' includes any trace or sign of the previous existence of the thing in question.

(7) It is immaterial whether—

(a) a building, structure or work is above or below the surface of the land,

(b) a site is above or below water.

(8) This section has effect for the purposes of section 1.

3 Meaning of 'deals in'

(1) A person deals in an object if (and only if) he—

(a) acquires, disposes of, imports or exports it,

(b) agrees with another to do an act mentioned in paragraph (a), or

(c) makes arrangements under which another person does such an act or under which another person agrees with a third person to do such an act.

(2) 'Acquires' means buys, hires, borrows or accepts.

(3) 'Disposes of' means sells, lets on hire, lends or gives.

(4) In relation to agreeing or arranging to do an act, it is immaterial whether the act is agreed or arranged to take place in the United Kingdom or elsewhere.

(5) This section has effect for the purposes of section 1.

5 Offences by bodies corporate

(1) If an offence under section 1 committed by a body corporate is proved—

(a) to have been committed with the consent or connivance of an officer, or

(b) to be attributable to any neglect on his part,

he (as well as the body corporate) is guilty of the offence and liable to be proceeded against and punished accordingly.

(2) 'Officer', in relation to a body corporate, means—

(a) a director, manager, secretary or other similar officer of the body,

(b) a person purporting to act in any such capacity.

(3) If the affairs of a body corporate are managed by its members, subsection (1) applies in relation to the acts and defaults of a member in connection with his functions of management as if he were a director of the body.

Appendix 1

Code for Crown Prosecutors—2004

[issued pursuant to Prosecution of Offences Act 1985, s. 10]

1 Introduction

1.1 The decision to prosecute an individual is a serious step. Fair and effective prosecution is essential to the maintenance of law and order. Even in a small case a prosecution has serious implications for all involved–victims, witnesses and defendants. The Crown Prosecution Service applies the Code for Crown Prosecutors so that it can make fair and consistent decisions about prosecutions.

1.2 The Code helps the Crown Prosecution Service to play its part in making sure that justice is done. It contains information that is important to police officers and others who work in the criminal justice system and to the general public. Police officers should take account of the Code when they are deciding whether to charge a person with an offence.

1.3 The Code is also designed to make sure that everyone knows the principles that the Crown Prosecution Service applies when carrying out its work. By applying the same principles, everyone involved in the system is helping to treat victims fairly and to prosecute fairly but effectively.

2 General principles

2.1 Each case is unique and must be considered on its own facts and merits. However, there are general principles that apply to the way in which Crown Prosecutors must approach every case.

2.2 Crown Prosecutors must be fair, independent and objective. They must not let any personal views about ethnic or national origin, sex, religious beliefs, political views or the sexual orientation of the suspect, victim or witness influence their decisions. They must not be affected by improper or undue pressure from any source.

2.3 It is the duty of Crown Prosecutors to make sure that the right person is prosecuted for the right offence. In doing so, Crown Prosecutors must always act in the interests of justice and not solely for the purpose of obtaining a conviction.

2.4 Crown Prosecutors should provide guidance and advice to investigators throughout the investigative and prosecuting process. This may include lines of inquiry, evidential requirements and assistance in any pre-charge procedures. Crown Prosecutors will be proactive in identifying and, where possible, rectifying evidential deficiencies and in bringing to an early conclusion those cases that cannot be strengthened by further investigation.

2.5 It is the duty of Crown Prosecutors to review, advise on and prosecute cases, ensuring that the law is properly applied, that all relevant evidence is put before the court and that obligations of disclosure are complied with, in accordance with the principles set out in this Code.

2.6 The CPS is a public authority for the purposes of the Human Rights Act 1998. Crown Prosecutors must apply the principles of the European Convention on Human Rights in accordance with the Act.

3 The decision to prosecute

3.1 In most cases, Crown Prosecutors are responsible for deciding whether a person should be charged with a criminal offence, and if so, what that offence should be. Crown Prosecutors make these decisions in accordance with this Code and the Director's Guidance on Charging. In those cases where the police determine the charge, which are usually more minor and routine cases, they apply the same provisions.

3.2 Crown Prosecutors make charging decisions in accordance with the Full Code Test (see section 5 below), other than in those limited circumstances where the Threshold Test applies (see section 6 below).

3.3 The Threshold Test applies where the case is one in which it is proposed to keep the suspect in custody after charge, but the evidence required to apply the Full Code Test is not yet available.

3.4 Where a Crown Prosecutor makes a charging decision in accordance with the Threshold Test, the case must be reviewed in accordance with the Full Code Test as soon as reasonably practicable, taking into account the progress of the investigation.

4 Review

4.1 Each case the Crown Prosecution Service receives from the police is reviewed to make sure that it is right to proceed with a prosecution. Unless the Threshold Test applies, the Crown Prosecution Service will only start or continue with a prosecution when the case has passed both stages of the Full Code Test.

4.2 Review is a continuing process and Crown Prosecutors must take account of any change in circumstances. Wherever possible, they should talk to the police first if they are thinking about changing the charges or stopping the case. Crown Prosecutors should also tell the police if they believe that some additional evidence may strengthen the case. This gives the police the chance to provide more information that may affect the decision.

4.3 The Crown Prosecution Service and the police work closely together, but the final responsibility for the decision whether or not a charge or a case should go ahead rests with the Crown Prosecution Service.

5 The Full Code Test

5.1 The Full Code Test has two stages. The first stage is consideration of the evidence. If the case does not pass the evidential stage it must not go ahead no matter how important or serious it may be. If the case does pass the evidential stage, Crown Prosecutors must proceed to the second stage and decide if a prosecution is needed in the public interest. The evidential and public interest stages are explained below.

The evidential stage

5.2 Crown Prosecutors must be satisfied that there is enough evidence to provide a 'realistic prospect of conviction' against each defendant on each charge. They must consider what the defence case may be, and how that is likely to affect the prosecution case.

5.3 A realistic prospect of conviction is an objective test. It means that a jury or bench of magistrates, or judge hearing a case alone properly directed in accordance with the law, is more likely than not to convict the defendant of the charge alleged. This is a separate test from the one that the criminal courts themselves must apply. A court should only convict if satisfied so that it is sure of a defendant's guilt.

5.4 When deciding whether there is enough evidence to prosecute, Crown Prosecutors must consider whether the evidence can be used and is reliable. There will be many cases in which the evidence does not give any cause for concern. But there will also be cases in which the evidence may not be as strong as it first appears. Crown Prosecutors must ask themselves the following questions:

Can the evidence be used in court?

(a) Is it likely that the evidence will be excluded by the court? There are certain legal rules which might mean that evidence which seems relevant cannot be given at a trial. For example, is it likely that the evidence will be excluded because of the way in which it was gathered? If so, is there enough other evidence for a realistic prospect of conviction?

Is the evidence reliable?

(b) Is there evidence which might support or detract from the reliability of a confession? Is the reliability affected by factors such as the defendant's age, intelligence or level of understanding?
(c) What explanation has the defendant given? Is a court likely to find it credible in the light of the evidence as a whole? Does it support an innocent explanation?
(d) If the identity of the defendant is likely to be questioned, is the evidence about this strong enough?
(e) Is the witness's background likely to weaken the prosecution case? For example, does the witness have any motive that may affect his or her attitude to the case, or a relevant previous conviction?
(f) Are there concerns over the accuracy or credibility of a witness? Are these concerns based on evidence or simply information with nothing to support it? Is there further evidence which the police should be asked to seek out which may support or detract from the account of the witness?

5.5 Crown Prosecutors should not ignore evidence because they are not sure that it can be used or is reliable. But they should look closely at it when deciding if there is a realistic prospect of conviction.

The Public Interest Stage

5.6 In 1951, Lord Shawcross, who was Attorney General, made the classic statement on public interest, which has been supported by Attorneys General ever since: 'It has never been the rule in this country—I hope it never will be—that suspected criminal offences must automatically be the subject of prosecution'. (House of Commons Debates, volume 483, column 681, 29 January 1951.)

5.7 The public interest must be considered in each case where there is enough evidence to provide a realistic prospect of conviction. Although there may be public interest factors against prosecution in a particular case, often the prosecution should go ahead and those factors should be put to the court for consideration when sentence is being passed. A prosecution will usually take place unless there are public interest factors tending against prosecution which clearly outweigh those tending in favour, or it appears more appropriate in all the circumstances of the case to divert the person from prosecution (see section 8 below).

5.8 Crown Prosecutors must balance factors for and against prosecution carefully and fairly. Public interest factors that can affect the decision to prosecute usually depend on the seriousness of the offence or the circumstances of the suspect. Some factors may increase the need to prosecute but others may suggest that another course of action would be better.

The following lists of some common public interest factors, both for and against prosecution, are not exhaustive. The factors that apply will depend on the facts in each case.

Some common public interest factors in favour of prosecution

5.9 The more serious the offence, the more likely it is that a prosecution will be needed in the public interest. A prosecution is likely to be needed if:

(a) a conviction is likely to result in a significant sentence;
(b) a conviction is likely to result in a confiscation or any other order;
(c) a weapon was used or violence was threatened during the commission of the offence;
(d) the offence was committed against a person serving the public (for example, a police or prison officer, or a nurse);
(e) the defendant was in a position of authority or trust;
(f) the evidence shows that the defendant was a ringleader or an organiser of the offence;
(g) there is evidence that the offence was premeditated;
(h) there is evidence that the offence was carried out by a group;

(i) the victim of the offence was vulnerable, has been put in considerable fear, or suffered personal attack, damage or disturbance;
(j) the offence was committed in the presence of, or in close proximity to, a child;
(k) the offence was motivated by any form of discrimination against the victim's ethnic or national origin, disability, sex, religious beliefs, political views or sexual orientation, or the suspect demonstrated hostility towards the victim based on any of those characteristics;
(l) there is a marked difference between the actual or mental ages of the defendant and the victim, or if there is any element of corruption;
(m) the defendant's previous convictions or cautions are relevant to the present offence;
(n) the defendant is alleged to have committed the offence whilst under an order of the court;
(o) there are grounds for believing that the offence is likely to be continued or repeated, for example, by a history of recurring conduct;
(p) the offence, although not serious in itself, is widespread in the area where it was committed; or
(q) a prosecution would have a significant positive impact on maintaining community confidence.

Some common public interest factors against prosecution

5.10 A prosecution is less likely to be needed if:
(a) the court is likely to impose a nominal penalty;
(b) the defendant has already been made the subject of a sentence and any further conviction would be unlikely to result in the imposition of an additional sentence or order, unless the nature of the particular offence requires a prosecution or the defendant withdraws consent to have an offence taken into consideration during sentencing;
(c) the offence was committed as a result of a genuine mistake or misunderstanding (these factors must be balanced against the seriousness of the offence);
(d) the loss or harm can be described as minor and was the result of a single incident, particularly if it was caused by a misjudgement;
(e) there has been a long delay between the offence taking place and the date of the trial, unless:
- the offence is serious;
- the delay has been caused in part by the defendant;
- the offence has only recently come to light; or
- the complexity of the offence has meant that there has been a long investigation;

(f) a prosecution is likely to have a bad effect on the victim's physical or mental health, always bearing in mind the seriousness of the offence;
(g) the defendant is elderly or is, or was at the time of the offence, suffering from significant mental or physical ill health, unless the offence is serious or there is a real possibility that it may be repeated. The Crown Prosecution Service, where necessary, applies Home Office guidelines about how to deal with mentally disordered offenders. Crown Prosecutors must balance the desirability of diverting a defendant who is suffering from significant mental or physical ill health with the need to safeguard the general public;
(h) the defendant has put right the loss or harm that was caused (but defendants must not avoid prosecution solely because they pay compensation); or
(i) details may be made public that could harm sources of information, international relations or national security.

5.11 Deciding on the public interest is not simply a matter of adding up the number of factors on each side. Crown Prosecutors must decide how important each factor is in the circumstances of each case and go on to make an overall assessment.

The relationship between the victim and the public interest

5.12 The Crown Prosecution Service does not act for victims or the families of victims in the same way as solicitors act for their clients. Crown Prosecutors act on behalf of the public and not just in the interests of any particular individual. However, when considering the public interest test Crown Prosecutors should always take into account the consequences for the victim of the decision whether or not to prosecute, and any views expressed by the victim or the victim's family.

5.13 It is important that a victim is told about a decision which makes a significant difference to the case in which they are involved. Crown Prosecutors should ensure that they follow any agreed procedures.

6 The Threshold Test

6.1 The Threshold Test requires Crown Prosecutors to decide whether there is at least a reasonable suspicion that the suspect has committed an offence, and if there is, whether it is in the public interest to charge that suspect.

6.2 The Threshold Test is applied to those cases in which it would not be appropriate to release a suspect on bail after charge, but the evidence to apply the Full Code Test is not yet available.

6.3 There are statutory limits that restrict the time a suspect may remain in police custody before a decision has to be made whether to charge or release the suspect. There will be cases where the suspect in custody presents a substantial bail risk if released, but much of the evidence may not be available at the time the charging decision has to be made. Crown Prosecutors will apply the Threshold Test to such cases for a limited period.

6.4 The evidential decision in each case will require consideration of a number of factors including:

- the evidence available at the time;
- the likelihood and nature of further evidence being obtained;
- the reasonableness for believing that evidence will become available;
- the time it will take to gather that evidence and the steps being taken to do so;
- the impact the expected evidence will have on the case;
- the charges that the evidence will support.

6.5 The public interest means the same as under the Full Code Test, but will be based on the information available at the time of charge which will often be limited.

6.6 A decision to charge and withhold bail must be kept under review. The evidence gathered must be regularly assessed to ensure the charge is still appropriate and that continued objection to bail is justified. The Full Code Test must be applied as soon as reasonably practicable.

7 Selection of Charges

7.1 Crown Prosecutors should select charges which:

(a) reflect the seriousness and extent of the offending;

(b) give the court adequate sentencing powers and impose appropriate post-conviction orders; and

(c) enable the case to be presented in a clear and simple way.

This means that Crown Prosecutors may not always choose or continue with the most serious charge where there is a choice.

7.2 Crown Prosecutors should never go ahead with more charges than are necessary just to encourage a defendant to plead guilty to a few. In the same way, they should never go ahead with a more serious charge just to encourage a defendant to plead guilty to a less serious one.

7.3 Crown Prosecutors should not change the charge simply because of the decision made by the court or the defendant about where the case will be heard.

8 Diversion from Prosecution

Adults

8.1 When deciding whether a case should be prosecuted in the courts, Crown Prosecutors should consider the alternatives to prosecution. Where appropriate, the availability of suitable rehabilitative, reparative or restorative justice processes can be considered.

8.2 Alternatives to prosecution for adult suspects include a simple caution and a conditional caution.

Simple caution

8.3 A simple caution should only be given if the public interest justifies it and in accordance with Home Office guidelines. Where it is felt that such a caution is appropriate, Crown Prosecutors must inform the police so they can caution the suspect. If the caution is not administered, because the suspect refuses to accept it, a Crown Prosecutor may review the case again.

Conditional caution

8.4 A conditional caution may be appropriate where a Crown Prosecutor considers that while the public interest justifies a prosecution, the interests of the suspect, victim and community may be better served by the suspect complying with suitable conditions aimed at rehabilitation or reparation. These may include restorative processes.

8.5 Crown Prosecutors must be satisfied that there is sufficient evidence for a realistic prospect of conviction and that the public interest would justify a prosecution should the offer of a conditional caution be refused or the offender fail to comply with the agreed conditions of the caution.

8.6 In reaching their decision, Crown Prosecutors should follow the Conditional Cautions Code of Practice and any guidance on conditional cautioning issued or approved by the Director of Public Prosecutions.

8.7 Where Crown Prosecutors consider a conditional caution to be appropriate, they must inform the police, or other authority responsible for administering the conditional caution, as well as providing an indication of the appropriate conditions so that the conditional caution can be administered.

Youths

8.8 Crown Prosecutors must consider the interests of a youth when deciding whether it is in the public interest to prosecute. However Crown Prosecutors should not avoid prosecuting simply because of the defendant's age. The seriousness of the offence or the youth's past behaviour is very important.

8.9 Cases involving youths are usually only referred to the Crown Prosecution Service for prosecution if the youth has already received a reprimand and final warning, unless the offence is so serious that neither of these were appropriate or the youth does not admit committing the offence. Reprimands and final warnings are intended to prevent re-offending and the fact that a further offence has occurred indicates that attempts to divert the youth from the court system have not been effective. So the public interest will usually require a prosecution in such cases, unless there are clear public interest factors against prosecution.

9 Mode of trial

9.1 The Crown Prosecution Service applies the current guidelines for magistrates who have to decide whether cases should be tried in the Crown Court when the offence gives the option and the defendant does not indicate a guilty plea. Crown Prosecutors should recommend Crown Court trial when they are satisfied that the guidelines require them to do so.

9.2 Speed must never be the only reason for asking for a case to stay in the magistrates' courts. But Crown Prosecutors should consider the effect of any likely delay if they send a case to the Crown Court, and any possible stress on victims and witnesses if the case is delayed.

10 Accepting guilty pleas

10.1 Defendants may want to plead guilty to some, but not all, of the charges. Alternatively, they may want to plead guilty to a different, possibly less serious, charge because they are admitting only part of the crime. Crown Prosecutors should only accept the defendant's plea if they think the court is able to pass a sentence that matches the seriousness of the offending, particularly where there are aggravating features. Crown Prosecutors must never accept a guilty plea just because it is convenient.

10.2 In considering whether the pleas offered are acceptable, Crown Prosecutors should ensure that the interests of the victim and, where possible, any views expressed by the victim or victim's family, are taken into account when deciding whether it is in the public interest to accept the plea. However, the decision rests with the Crown Prosecutor.

10.3 It must be made clear to the court on what basis any plea is advanced and accepted. In cases where a defendant pleads guilty to the charges but on the basis of facts that are different from the prosecution case, and where this may significantly affect sentence, the court should be invited to hear evidence to determine what happened, and then sentence on that basis.

10.4 Where a defendant has previously indicated that he or she will ask the court to take an offence into consideration when sentencing, but then declines to admit that offence at court, Crown Prosecutors will consider whether a prosecution is required for that offence. Crown Prosecutors should explain to the defence advocate and the court that the prosecution of that offence may be subject to further review.

10.5 Particular care must be taken when considering pleas which would enable the defendant to avoid the imposition of a mandatory minimum sentence. When pleas are offered, Crown Prosecutors must bear in mind the fact that ancillary orders can be made with some offences but not with others.

11 Prosecutors' role in sentencing

11.1 Crown Prosecutors should draw the court's attention to:

- any aggravating or mitigating factors disclosed by the prosecution case;
- any victim personal statement;
- where appropriate, evidence of the impact of the offending on a community;
- any statutory provisions or sentencing guidelines which may assist;
- any relevant statutory provisions relating to ancillary orders (such as anti-social behaviour orders).

11.2 The Crown Prosecutor should challenge any assertion made by the defence in mitigation that is inaccurate, misleading or derogatory. If the defence persist in the assertion, and it appears relevant to the sentence, the court should be invited to hear evidence to determine the facts and sentence accordingly.

12 Re-starting a prosecution

12.1 People should be able to rely on decisions taken by the Crown Prosecution Service. Normally, if the Crown Prosecution Service tells a suspect or defendant that there will not be a prosecution, or that the prosecution has been stopped, that is the end of the matter and the case will not start again. But occasionally there are special reasons why the Crown Prosecution Service will re-start the prosecution, particularly if the case is serious.

12.2 These reasons include:

(a) rare cases where a new look at the original decision shows that it was clearly wrong and should not be allowed to stand;

(b) cases which are stopped so that more evidence which is likely to become available in the fairly near future can be collected and prepared. In these cases, the Crown Prosecutor will tell the defendant that the prosecution may well start again; and

(c) cases which are stopped because of a lack of evidence but where more significant evidence is discovered later.

12.3 There may also be exceptional case in which, following an acquittal of a serious offence, the Crown Prosecutor may, with the written consent of the Director of Public Prosecutions, apply to the Court of Appeal for an order quashing the acquittal and requiring the defendant to be retried, in accordance with Part 10 of the Criminal Justice Act 2003.

Appendix 2

'Legislating the Criminal Code'

Participating in Crime [Draft] Bill 2007

(Law Commission Report No. 305)

PART 1

Chapter 1: Liability for offences committed or acts done by others

1 Assisting or encouraging an offence

(1) Where a person (P) has committed an offence, another person (D) is also guilty of the offence if—

(a) D did an act with the intention that one or more of a number of other acts would be done by another person,

(b) P's criminal act was one of those acts,

(c) D's behaviour assisted or encouraged P to do his criminal act, and

(d) subsection (2) or (3) is satisfied.

(2) This subsection is satisfied if D believed that a person doing the act would commit the offence.

(3) This subsection is satisfied if D's state of mind was such that had he done the act he would have committed the offence.

2 Participating in a joint criminal venture

(1) This section applies where two or more persons participate in a joint criminal venture.

(2) If one of the (P) commits an offence, another participant (D) is also guilty of the offence if P's criminal act falls within the scope of the venture.

(3) The existence or scope of a joint criminal venture may be interred from the conduct of the participants (whether or not there is an express agreement).

(4) D does not escape liability under this section for an offence committed by P at a time when D is a participant in the venture merely because D is at the time—

(a) absent,

(b) against the venture's being carried out, or

(c) indifferent as to whether it is carried out.

3 Liability not restricted by special characteristics required of offender

D may be guilty under this Chapter of an offence even though—

(a) the offence is one that may be committed only by a person who meets a particular description, and

(b) D does not meet that description.

4 Using an innocent agent

(1) If a person (D) uses an innocent agent (P) to commit an offence, D is guilty of that offence.

(2) P is an innocent agent in relation to an offence if—

(a) he does a criminal act, and

(b) he does not commit the offence itself for one of the following reasons—

(i) he is under the age of 10,

(ii) he has a defence of insanity, or

(iii) he acts without the fault required for conviction,

and there is no other reason why he does not commit it.

(3) D uses P to commit an offence if—

(a) D intends to cause a person (whether or not P) to do a criminal act in relation to the offence,

(b) D causes P to do the criminal act, and

(c) subsection (4) or (5) is satisfied.

(4) If a particular state of mind requires to be proved for conviction of the offence that D uses P to commit, D's state of mind must be such that, were he to do the act that he intends to cause to be done, he would do it with the state of mind required for conviction of the offence.

(5) If the offence which D uses P to commit is a no-fault offence, D must know or believe that, were a person to do the act that D intends to cause to be done, that person would do it—

(a) in the circumstances (if any), and

(b) with the consequences (if any),

proof of which is required for conviction of the offence.

Chapter 2: Causing a no-fault offence

5 Offence of causing a no-fault offence

(1) A person commits an offence if he causes another person to commit a no-fault offence, and—

(a) it is his intention that a person should commit the offence, or

(b) he knows or believes that his behaviour will cause a person to commit it.

(2) 'No-fault offence' means an offence that does not require proof of fault.

PART 2: LIMITATIONS ON LIABILITY IMPOSED BY PART 1

6 Protective offences: victims not liable

(1) D is not liable under Chapter 1 of Part 1 for a protective offence if—

(a) he falls within the protected category, and

(b) he is the person in respect of whom it was committed.

(2) D does not commit an offence under section 5 if—

(a) the no-fault offence is a protective offence,

(b) he falls within the protected category, and

(c) he is the person in respect of whom it was committed.

'Protective offence' means an offence that exists (wholly or in part) for the protection of a particular category of persons ('the protected category').

7 Defence of acting to prevent commission of offence etc.

(1) In proceedings for an offence to which this section applies, a person is not guilty of the offence if he proves on the balance of probabilities that—

(a) he acted for the purpose of—

(i) preventing the commission of that offence or another offence, or

(ii) preventing, or limiting, the occurrence of harm, and

(b) it was reasonable for him to act as he did.

(2) This section applies to an offence of which a person is alleged to be guilty as a result of section 1 or 2.

PART 3: INTERPRETATION

8 Encouraging and assisting

(1) A reference in this Act to encouraging a person to do an act includes a reference to threatening or otherwise putting pressure on him to do it.

(2) A reference in this Act to encouraging or assisting a person to do an act includes a reference to—

(a) taking steps to reduce the possibility of criminal proceedings being brought in respect of the act's being done,

(b) failing to take reasonable steps to discharge a duty.

(3) But a person is not to be regarded as encouraging or assisting another person to do an act merely because he fails to respond to a constable's request for assistance in preventing a breach of the peace.

9 Indirectly encouraging or assisting

If a person (D1) arranged for a person (D2) to do something that will encourage or assist another person to do an act, and D2 does any such thing, D1 is also to be treated for the purposes of this Act as having done it.

10 Committing an offence

(1) For the purposes of sections 1 and 2 and of Part 2 (so far as it relates to those sections), a reference to a person (P) who commits an offence is to a person who—

(a) acts with the fault required for conviction of the offence,

(b) is of or over the age of 10, and

(c) does not have a defence of insanity.

(2) For those purposes, it is immaterial whether P has any other defence.

11 Acts, criminal acts and no-fault offences

(1) A reference in this Act to an act includes a reference to a course of conduct and a reference to the doing of an act is to be read accordingly.

(2) A reference in this Act to a criminal act is, in relation to an offence, a reference to an act (or a failure to act) that falls within the definition of the act (or failure to act) that must be proved in order for a person to be convicted of the offence.

(3) A reference in this Act to the doing of a criminal act includes a reference to—

(a) the continuation of an act that has already begun,

(b) an attempt to do an act (except in relation to an offence of attempting to commit another offence).

(4) A reference in this Act to a no-fault offence is to read in accordance with section 5(2).

Participating in Crime (Jurisdiction, Procedure and Consequential Provisions) [Draft] Bill 2007

(Law Commission Report No. 305)

1 Meaning and application of 'the codifying Act'

(1) In this Act 'the codifying Act' means the Participating in Crime Act 2006.

(2) Any expression used in this Act in connection with a provision of the codifying Act has the same meaning as it has in that provision.

2 Liability under sections 1 and 2 of the codifying Act

(1) If P's offence is committed in England or Wales, D may be guilty under section 1 or 2 of the codifying Act of the same offence no matter where he was at any relevant time.

(2) If P's offence is committed outside England and Wales, D is not guilty under either of those sections of the same offence unless paragraph 1 or 2 of Schedule 1 applies.

3 Liability under section 4 of the codifying Act

(1) If the offence that P would have committed ('the principal offence') would have been committed in England or Wales, D may be guilty under section 4 of the codifying Act of that offence no matter where he was at any relevant time.

(2) If the principal offence would have been committed outside England and Wales, D is not guilty under that section of that offence unless paragraph 3 or 4 of Schedule 1 applies.

4 Offences under section 5 of the codifying Act

A person does not commit an offence under section 5 of the codifying Act unless—

(a) P commits the no-fault offence in England or Wales; and

(b) any relevant behaviour of D's takes place wholly or partly in England or Wales.

5 Persons who may be perpetrators or encouragers etc.

(1) A person may be convicted of an offence if, although it is not proved whether—

(a) he is guilty of the offence on the basis that he committed it and has no defence, or

(b) he is guilty under section 1 or 2 of the codifying Act of the offence,

it is proved that he must be one or the other.

(2) For the purposes of subsection (1)(a), a person who used an innocent agent to commit an offence is guilty of that offence on the basis that he committed it.

8 Abolition of common law replaced by the codifying Act

The following (which are replaced by provisions of the codifying Act) are abolished—

(a) the rules of the common law relating to the circumstances in which a person is liable for an offence because he has aided, abetted, counselled or procured its commission; and

(b) the rules of the common law relating to the circumstances in which a person commits an offence through an innocent agent.

Criminal Law [Draft] Bill 1993

(Law Commission Report No. 218)

PART II GENERAL DEFENCES AND OTHER PROVISIONS

24 Application of this Part

The provisions of this Part apply in relation to all offences under the law of England and Wales, . . .

Duress

25 Duress by threats

(1) No act of a person constitutes an offence if the act is done under duress by threats.

(2) A person does an act under duress by threats if he does it because he knows or believes—

(a) that a threat has been made to cause death or serious injury to himself or another if the act is not done, and

(b) that the threat will be carried out immediately if he does not do the act or, if not immediately, before he or that other can obtain effective official protection, and

(c) that there is no other way of preventing the threat being carried out, and the threat is one which in all the circumstances (including any of his personal characteristics that affect its gravity) he cannot reasonably be expected to resist.

It is for the defendant to show that the reason for his act was such knowledge or belief as is mentioned in paragraphs (a) to (c).

(3) This section applies in relation to omissions as it applies in relation to acts.

(4) This section does not apply to a person who knowingly and without reasonable excuse exposed himself to the risk of the threat made or believed to have been made.

If the question arises whether a person knowingly and without reasonable excuse exposed himself to such a risk, it is for him to show that he did not.

26 Duress of circumstances

(1) No act of a person constitutes an offence if the act is done under duress of circumstances.

(2) A person does an act under duress of circumstances if—

(a) he does it because he knows or believes that it is immediately necessary to avoid death or serious injury to himself or another, and

(b) the danger that he knows or believes to exist is such that in all the circumstances (including any of his personal characteristics that affect its gravity) he cannot reasonably be expected to act otherwise.

It is for the defendant to show that the reason for his act was such knowledge or belief as is mentioned in paragraph (a).

(3) This section applies in relation to omissions as it applies in relation to acts.

(4) This section does not apply to a person who knowingly and without reasonable excuse exposed himself to the danger known or believed to exist.

If the question arises whether a person knowingly and without reasonable excuse exposed himself to that danger, it is for him to show that he did not.

(5) This section does not apply to—

(a) an act done in the knowledge or belief that a threat has been made to cause death or serious injury to himself or another (see section 25), or

(b) the use of force within the meaning of section 27 or 28, or an act immediately preparatory to the use of force, for the purposes mentioned in section 27(1) or 28(1).

Self-defence, prevention of crime, etc.

27 Justifiable use of force: protection of person or property, prevention of crime, etc.

(1) The use of force by a person for any of the following purposes, if only such as is reasonable in the circumstances as he believes them to be, does not constitute an offence—

(a) to protect himself or another from injury, assault or detention caused by a criminal act;

(b) to protect himself or (with the authority of that other) another from trespass to the person;

(c) to protect his property from appropriation, destruction or damage caused by a criminal act or from trespass or infringement;

(d) to protect property belonging to another from appropriation, destruction or damage caused by a criminal act or (with the authority of the other) from trespass or infringement; or

(e) to prevent crime or a breach of the peace.

(2) The expressions 'use of force' and 'property' in subsection (1) are defined and extended by sections 29 and 30 respectively.

(3) For the purposes of this section an act involves a 'crime' or is 'criminal' although the person committing it, if charged with an offence in respect of it, would be acquitted on the ground that—

(a) he was under ten years of age, or
(b) he acted under duress, whether by threats or of circumstances, or
(c) his act was involuntary, or
(d) he was in a state of intoxication, or
(e) he was insane, so as not to be responsible, according to law, for the act.

(4) The references in subsection (1) to protecting a person or property from anything include protecting him or it from its continuing; and the reference to preventing crime or a breach of the peace shall be similarly construed.

(5) For the purposes of this section the question whether the act against which force is used is of a kind mentioned in any of paragraphs (a) to (e) of subsection (1) shall be determined according to the circumstances as the person using the force ('D') believes them to be.

In the following provisions of this section references to unlawful or lawful acts are to acts which are or are not of such a kind.

(6) Where an act is lawful by reason only of a belief or suspicion which is mistaken, the defence provided by this section applies as in the case of an unlawful act, unless—
(a) D knows or believes that the force is used against a constable or a person assisting a constable, and
(b) the constable is acting in the execution of his duty,

in which case the defence applies only if D believes the force to be immediately necessary to prevent injury to himself or another.

(7) The defence provided by this section does not apply to a person who causes conduct or a state of affairs with a view to using force to resist or terminate it.

But the defence may apply although the occasion for the use of force arises only because he does something he may lawfully do, knowing that such an occasion may arise.

28 Justifiable use of force: effecting or assisting arrest

(1) The use of force by a person in effecting or assisting in a lawful arrest, if only such as is reasonable in the circumstances as he believes them to be, does not constitute an offence.

(2) The expression 'use of force' in subsection (1) is defined and extended by section 29.

(3) For the purposes of this section the question whether the arrest is lawful shall be determined according to the circumstances as the person using the force believed them to be.

29 Meaning of 'use of force' and related provisions

(1) For the purposes of sections 27 and 28—
(a) a person uses force in relation to another person or property not only where he applies force to, but also where he causes an impact on, the body of that person or that property;
(b) a person shall be treated as using force in relation to another person if—
(i) he threatens him with its use, or
(ii) he detains him without actually using it; and
(c) a person shall be treated as using force in relation to property if he threatens a person with its use in relation to property.

(2) Those sections apply in relation to acts immediately preparatory to the use of force as they apply in relation to acts in which force is used.

(3) A threat of force may be reasonable although the actual use of force would not be.

(4) The fact that a person had an opportunity to retreat before using force shall be taken into account, in conjunction with other relevant evidence, in determining whether the use of force was reasonable.

30 Meaning of 'property' and related provisions

(1) For the purposes of section 27(1)(c) and (d) (justifiable use of force: protection of property) the expression 'property' means property of a tangible nature, whether real or personal, or any right, interest or privilege in or over any such property, whether created by grant, licence or otherwise.

The expression also includes—

(a) money,
(b) wild creatures which have been tamed or are ordinarily kept in captivity, and
(c) any other wild creatures or their carcasses if, but only if, they have been reduced into possession which has not been lost or abandoned or are in the course of being reduced into possession,

but not mushrooms growing wild on any land or flowers, fruit or foliage of a plant growing wild on any land.

For this purpose 'mushroom' includes any fungus and 'plant' includes any shrub or tree.

(2) Property shall be treated for the purposes of section 27(1)(c) and (d) as belonging to any person—

(a) having the custody or control of it,
(b) having in it any proprietary right or interest (not being an equitable interest arising only from an agreement to transfer or grant an interest), or
(c) having a charge on it;

and where a property is subject to a trust, the persons to whom it belongs shall be treated as including any person having a right to enforce the trust.

Property of a corporation sole shall be treated as belonging to the corporation notwithstanding a vacancy in the corporation.

34 Interpretation of Part II

In this Part—

'fault', in relation to an offence, means an element of the offence consisting of either or both of the following—

(a) a state of mind with which a person acts, or
(b) a failure to comply with a standard of conduct, and references to a person being at fault shall be construed accordingly; and

'injury' means—

(a) physical injury, including pain, unconsciousness, or any other impairment of a person's physical condition, or
(b) impairment of a person's mental health.

Offences Against the Person [Draft] Bill 1998

(Home Office, Violence—Reforming the Offences Against the Person Act 1861 (February 1998))

Injury and assault

1 Intentional serious injury

(1) A person is guilty of an offence if he intentionally causes serious injury to another.

(2) A person is guilty of an offence if he omits to do an act which he has a duty to do at common law, the omission results in serious injury to another, and he intends the omission to have that result.

(3) An offence under this section is committed notwithstanding that the injury occurs outside England and Wales if the act causing injury is done in England and Wales or the omission resulting in injury is made there.

(4) A person guilty of an offence under this section is liable on conviction on indictment to imprisonment for life.

2 Reckless serious injury

(1) A person is guilty of an offence if he recklessly causes serious injury to another.

(2) An offence under this section is committed notwithstanding that the injury occurs outside England and Wales if the act causing injury is done in England and Wales.

(3) A person guilty of an offence under this section is liable—

(a) on conviction on indictment, to imprisonment for a term not exceeding 7 years;
(b) on summary conviction, to imprisonment for a term not exceeding 6 months or a fine not exceeding the statutory maximum or both.

3 Intentional or reckless injury

(1) A person is guilty of an offence if he intentionally or recklessly causes injury to another.

(2) An offence under this section is committed notwithstanding that the injury occurs outside England and Wales if the act causing injury is done in England and Wales.

(3) A person guilty of an offence under this section is liable—
(a) on conviction on indictment, to imprisonment for a term not exceeding 5 years;
(b) on summary conviction, to imprisonment for a term not exceeding 6 months or a fine not exceeding the statutory maximum or both.

4 Assault

(1) A person is guilty of an offence if—
(a) he intentionally or recklessly applies force to or causes an impact on the body of another, or
(b) he intentionally or recklessly causes the other to believe that any such force or impact is imminent.

(2) No such offence is committed if the force or impact, not being intended or likely to cause injury, is in the circumstances such as is generally acceptable in the ordinary conduct of daily life and the defendant does not know or believe that it is in fact unacceptable to the other person.

(3) A person guilty of an offence under this section is liable on summary conviction to imprisonment for a term not exceeding 6 months or a fine not exceeding level 5 on the standard scale or both.

5 Assault on a constable

(1) A person is guilty of an offence if he assaults—
(a) a constable acting in the execution of his duty, or
(b) a person assisting a constable acting in the execution of his duty.

(2) For the purposes of this section a person assaults if he commits the offence under section 4.

(3) A reference in this section to a constable acting in the execution of his duty includes a reference to a constable who is a member of a police force maintained in Scotland or Northern Ireland when he is executing a warrant, or otherwise acting in England or Wales, by virtue of an enactment conferring powers on him in England and Wales.

(4) For the purposes of subsection (3) each of the following is a police force—
(a) a police force within the meaning given by section 50 of the Police (Scotland) Act 1967;
(b) the Royal Ulster Constabulary and the Royal Ulster Constabulary Reserve.

(5) A person guilty of an offence under this section is liable on summary conviction to imprisonment for a term not exceeding 6 months or a fine not exceeding level 5 on the standard scale or both.

6 Causing serious injury to resist arrest etc.

(1) A person is guilty of an offence if he causes serious injury to another intending to resist, prevent or terminate the lawful arrest or detention of himself or a third person.

(2) The question whether the defendant believes the arrest or detention is lawful must be determined according to the circumstances as he believes them to be.

(3) A person guilty of an offence under this section is liable on conviction on indictment to imprisonment for life.

7 Assault to resist arrest etc.

(1) A person is guilty of an offence if he assaults another intending to resist, prevent or terminate the lawful arrest or detention of himself or a third person.

(2) The question whether the defendant believes the arrest or detention is lawful must be determined according to the circumstances as he believes them to be.

(3) For the purposes of this section a person assaults if he commits the offence under section 4.

(4) A person guilty of an offence under this section is liable—

(a) on conviction on indictment, to imprisonment for a term not exceeding 2 years;
(b) on summary conviction, to imprisonment for a term not exceeding 6 months or a fine not exceeding the statutory maximum or both.

Dangerous substances

8 Dangerous substances: intending or risking serious injury

(1) A person is guilty of an offence if he acts as mentioned in subsection (2) and—
(a) he intends to cause serious injury, or
(b) he is reckless whether serious injury is caused.

(2) A person acts as mentioned in this subsection if he—
(a) causes an explosive substance to explode,
(b) places a dangerous substance in any place,
(c) delivers or sends a dangerous substance to a person,
(d) throws a dangerous substance at or near a person, or
(e) applies a dangerous substance to a person.

(3) For the purposes of subsection (2) a dangerous substance is an explosive substance of any other dangerous substance.

(4) In this section 'explosive substance' has the same meaning as in the Explosive Substances Act 1883.

(5) A person guilty of an offence under this section is liable on conviction on indictment to imprisonment for life.

9 Dangerous substances: intending or risking injury

(1) A person is guilty of an offence if he acts as mentioned in section 8(2) and—
(a) he intends to cause injury, or
(b) he is reckless whether injury is caused.

(2) A person guilty of an offence under this section is liable on conviction on indictment to imprisonment for a term not exceeding 14 years.

Other offences

10 Threats to kill or cause serious injury

(1) A person is guilty of an offence if he makes to another a threat to cause the death of, or serious injury to, that other or a third person, intending that other to believe that it will be carried out.

(2) A person guilty of an offence under this section is liable—
(a) on conviction on indictment, to imprisonment for a term not exceeding 10 years;
(b) on summary conviction, to imprisonment for a term not exceeding 6 months or a fine not exceeding the statutory maximum or both.

11 Administering a substance capable of causing injury

(1) A person is guilty of an offence if—
(a) he administers a substance to another or causes it to be taken by him and (in either case) he does so intentionally or recklessly,
(b) he knows the substance is capable of causing injury to the other, and
(c) it is unreasonable to adminster the substance or cause it to be taken having regard to the circumstances as he knows or believes them to be.

(2) A person guilty of an offence under this section is liable—
(a) on conviction on indictment, to imprisonment for a term not exceeding 5 years;
(b) on summary conviction, to imprisonment for a term not exceeding 6 months or a fine not exceeding the statutory maximum or both.

12 Torture

(1) A person is guilty of an offence if he intentionally inflicts severe pain or suffering on another and he does the act—
(a) in the performance or purported performance of his official duties as a public official, or

(b) at the instigation or with the consent or acquiescence of a public official who is performing or purporting to perform his official duties.

(2) A person is guilty of an offence if—

(a) he omits to do an act which he has a duty to do at common law.

(b) he makes the omission as mentioned in subsection (1)(a) or (b).

(c) the omission results in the infliction of severe pain or suffering on another, and

(d) he intends the omission to have that result.

(3) The following are immaterial—

(a) the nationality of the persons concerned;

(b) whether anything occurs in the United Kingdom or elsewhere;

(c) whether the pain or suffering is physical or mental.

(4) References in this section to an official include references to a person acting in an official capacity.

(5) Proceedings for an offence under this section may be instituted only by or with the consent of the Attorney General.

(6) A person guilty of an offence under this section is liable on conviction on indictment to imprisonment for life.

13 Causing danger on railways

(1) A person is guilty of an offence if he intentionally or recklessly causes danger to a person who is on a railway or is being carried on a railway.

(2) A person is guilty of an offence if he omits to do an act which he has a duty to do at common law, the omission results in danger to a person who is on a railway or is being carried on a railway, and he intends the omission to have that result or is reckless whether it will have that result.

(3) A person guilty of an offence under this section is liable—

(a) on conviction on indictment, to imprisonment for a term not exceeding 2 years;

(b) on summary conviction, to imprisonment for a term not exceeding 6 months or a fine not exceeding the statutory maximum or both.

Meaning of fault terms and of injury

14 Meaning of fault terms

(1) A person acts intentionally with respect to a result if—

(a) it is his purpose to cause it, or

(b) although it is not his purpose to cause it he knows that it would occur in the ordinary course of events if he were to succeed in his purpose of causing some other result.

(2) A person acts recklessly with respect to a result if he is aware of a risk that it will occur and it is unreasonable to take that risk having regard to the circumstances as he knows or belies them to bc.

(3) A person intends an omission to have a result if—

(a) it is his purpose that the result will occur, or

(b) although it is not his purpose that the result will occur, he knows that it would occur in the ordinary course of events if he were to succeed in his purpose that some other result will occur.

(4) A person is reckless whether an omission will have a result if he is aware of a risk that the result will occur and it is unreasonable to take that risk having regard to the circumstances as he knows or believes them to be.

(5) Related expressions must be construed accordingly.

(6) This section has effect for the purposes of this Act.

15 Meaning of injury

(1) In this Act 'injury' means—

(a) physical injury, or

(b) mental injury.

(2) Physical injury does not include anything caused by disease but (subject to that) it includes pain, unconsciousness and any other impairment of a person's physical condition.

(3) Mental injury does not include anything caused by disease but (subject to that) it includes any impairment of a person's mental health.

(4) In its application to section 1 this section applies without the exceptions relating to things caused by disease.

Matters affecting liability

16 Supervening fault

(1) Where it is an offence under this Act to be at fault in causing a result by an act and a person lacks the fault required when he does an act that may cause or does cause the result, he nevertheless commits the offence if—

(a) being aware that he has done the act and that the result may occur or (as the case may be) has occurred and may continue, and

(b) with the fault required,

he falls to take reasonable steps to prevent the result occurring or continuing and it does occur or continue.

(2) Where it is an offence under this Act to be at fault in causing a result by an omission and a person lacks the fault required when he makes an omission that may cause or does cause the result, he nevertheless commits the offence if—

(a) being aware that he has made the omission and that the result may occur or (as the case may be) has occurred and may continue, and

(b) with the fault required, he fails to take reasonable steps to prevent the result occurring or continuing and it does occur or continue.

(3) For the purposes of this section fault is intention or recklessness, and references to a person being at fault must be construed accordingly.

(4) Common law rules relating to matters provided for in this section do not apply to offences under this Act.

17 Transferred fault

(1) This section applies in determining whether a person is guilty of an offence under this Act.

(2) A person's intention, or awareness of a risk, that his act will cause a result in relation to a person capable of being the victim of the offence must be treated as an intention or (as the case may be) awareness of a risk that his act will cause that result in relation to any other person affected by his act.

(3) A person's intention, or awareness of a risk, that his omission will have a result in relation to a person capable of being the victim of the offence must be treated as an intention or (as the case may be) awareness of a risk that his omission will have that result in relation to any other person affected as a result of his omission.

(4) Common law rules relating to matters provided for in this section do not apply to offences under this Act.

18 General defences etc.

(1) The provisions of this Act have effect subject to any enactment or rule of law providing—

(a) a defence, or

(b) lawful authority, justification or excuse for an act or omission.

(2) In the application of subsection (1) to section 12 'lawful authority, justification or excuse' means—

(a) in relation to pain or suffering inflicted in the United Kingdom, lawful authority, justification or excuse under the law of the part of the United Kingdom where it was inflicted;

(b) in relation to pain or suffering inflicted outside the United Kingdom by (or as a result of an omission by) a United Kingdom official acting under the law of the United Kingdom or any part of the United Kingdom, lawful authority, justification or excuse under that law;

(c) in any other case, lawful authority, justification or excuse under the law of the place where the pain or suffering was inflicted.

(3) The reference in this section to an official includes a reference to a person acting in an official capacity.

19 Effect of voluntary intoxication

(1) For the purposes of this Act a person who was voluntarily intoxicated at any material time must be treated—

(a) as having been aware of any risk of which he would have been aware had he not been intoxicated, and

(b) as having known or believed in any circumstances which he would have known or believed in had he not been intoxicated.

(2) Whether a person is voluntarily intoxicated for this purpose must be determined in accordance with the following provisions.

(3) A person is voluntarily intoxicated if—

(a) he takes an intoxicant otherwise than properly for a medicinal purpose,

(b) he is aware that it is or may be an intoxicant, and

(c) he takes it in such a quantity as impairs his awareness or understanding.

(4) An intoxicant, although taken for a medicinal purpose, is not properly so taken if—

(a) the intoxicant is not taken on medical advice, and the taker is aware that the taking may result in his doing an act or making an omission capable of constituting an offence of the kind in question, or

(b) the intoxicant is taken on medical advice, but the taker fails then or afterwards to comply with any forming condition forming part of the advice and he is aware that the failure may result in his doing an act or making an omission capable of constituting an offence of the kind in question.

(5) Intoxication must be presumed to have been voluntary unless there is adduced such evidence as might lead the court or jury to conclude that there is a reasonable possibility that the intoxication was involuntary.

(6) An intoxicant is any alcohol, drug or other thing which, when taken into the body, may impair the awareness or understanding of the person taking it.

(7) A person must be treated as taking an intoxicant if he permits it to be administered to him.

20 Attempts

(1) This section applies for the purpose of deciding whether a person is guilty under section 1 of the Criminal Attempts Act 1981 of attempting to commit an offence under this Act.

(2) For that purpose a person acts with intent with respect to a result if—

(a) it is his purpose to cause it, or

(b) although it is not his purpose to cause it, he knows that it would occur in the ordinary course of events if he were to succeed in his purpose of causing some other result.

Charges and verdicts

21 Charging more than one offence

For the purposes of the rules against charging more than one offence in the same count or information, each of sections 1 to 13 creates one offence.

22 Alternative verdicts

(1) For the purposes of the application of section 6(3) of the Criminal Law Act 1967 (alternative verdicts) to the trial of a person on indictment for any offence under this Act, an allegation in the indictment of intention includes an allegation of recklessness.

(2) If on the trial on indictment of a person charged with an offence under section 1, 2, 3, 6 or 7 the jury find him not guilty of the offence charged, they may (without prejudice to section 6(3) of the Criminal Law Act 1967) find him guilty of an offence under section 4.

(3) If on the summary trial of a person charged with an offence under section 2 the magistrates' court find him not guilty of that offence, they may find him guilty of an offence under section 3 or 4.

(4) If on the summary trial of a person charged with an offence under section 3, 5 or 7 the magistrates' court find him not guilty of that offence, they may find him guilty of an offence under section 4.

(5) If—

(a) on the summary trial of a person charged with an offence under section 2 the magistrates' court convict him of that offence and make no decision whether he is guilty of an offence under section 3 or 4, and

(b) he appeals to the Crown Court against the conviction, the Crown Court may reverse the conviction and find him guilty of an offence under section 3 or 4.

(6) If—

(a) on the summary trial of a person charged with an offence under section 3, 5 or 7 the magistrates' court convict him of that offence and make no decision whether he is guilty of an offence under section 4, and

(b) he appeals to the Crown Court against the conviction, the Crown Court may reverse the conviction and find him guilty of an offence under section 4.

Amendments etc.

23 Abolition of certain common law offences

The following common law offences are abolished—

(a) common assault;

(b) battery;

(c) mayhem.

Appendix 3

Assisted Dying for the Terminally Ill Bill [H.L.] 2005

1 Authorisation of assisted dying

Subject to the provisions of this Act, it shall be lawful for—

(a) a physician to assist a patient who is a qualifying patient to die—

(i) by prescribing such medication, and

(ii) in the case of a patient for whom it is impossible or inappropriate orally to ingest that medication, by prescribing and providing such means of self-administration of that medication,

as will enable the patient to end his own life, and

(b) a person who is a member of a health care team to work in conjunction with a physician to whom paragraph (a) of this section applies.

2 Qualifying conditions

(1) Before the assisting physician can assist a patient to die the conditions specified in subsections (2) and (3) must be satisfied, the patient must have made a declaration in accordance with section 4 and the requirements of section 5(3) must have been complied with.

(2) The first condition is that the attending physician shall have—

(a) been informed by the patient in a written request signed by the patient that the patient wishes to be assisted to die;

(b) examined the patient and the patient's medical records and satisfied himself that the patient does not lack capacity;

(c) determined that the patient has a terminal illness;

(d) concluded that the patient is suffering unbearably as a result of that terminal illness;

(e) informed the patient of—

(i) his medical diagnosis;

(ii) his prognosis;

(iii) the process of being assisted to die; and

(iv) the alternatives to assisted dying, including, but not limited to, palliative care, care in a hospice and the control of pain;

(f) ensured that a specialist in palliative care, who shall be a physician or a nurse, has attended the patient to inform the patient of the benefits of the various forms of palliative care,

(g) recommended to the patient that the patient notifies his next of kin of his request for assistance to die,

(h) if the patient persists with his request to be assisted to die, satisfied himself that the request is made voluntarily and that the patient has made an informed decision; and

(i) referred the patient to a consulting physician.

(3) The second condition is that the consulting physician shall have—

(a) been informed by the patient that the patient wishes to be assisted to die;

(b) examined the patient and the patient's medical records and satisfied himself that the patient does not lack capacity;

(c) confirmed the diagnosis and prognosis made by the attending physician;
(d) concluded that the patient is suffering unbearably as a result of the terminal illness;
(e) informed the patient of the alternatives to assisted dying including, but not limited to, palliative care, care in a hospice and the control of pain;
(f) if the patient still persists with his request to be assisted to die, satisfied himself that the request is made voluntarily and that the patient has made an informed decision; and
(g) advised the patient that prior to being assisted to die the patient will be required to complete a declaration which the patient can revoke.

(4) For the purposes of this Act, a person lacks capacity in relation to being assisted to die if at the material time he is unable to make a decision for himself in relation to that matter because of an impairment of, or a disturbance in the functioning of, the mind or brain resulting from any disability or disorder of the mind or brain.

3 Determination of lack of capacity

(1) If, in the opinion of either the attending or the consulting physician, a patient who wishes to make a declaration may lack capacity, the attending physician shall refer the patient to a consultant psychiatrist, or a psychologist, who shall be independent of the attending and consulting physicians, for an opinion as to the patient's capacity.

(2) No assistance to end the patient's life may be given unless the consultant psychiatrist or the psychologist has determined that the patient does not lack capacity.

4 Declaration

(1) When the qualifying conditions have been met, a patient who wishes to be assisted to die must make a declaration of his wish to die in the form prescribed by regulations made by the Secretary of State.

(2) The declaration must be witnessed by two individuals one of whom shall be either a solicitor who holds a current practising certificate or a public notary.

(3) The solicitor or public notary may only witness the declaration if—
(a) the patient is personally known to, or has proved his identity to, him;
(b) it appears to him that the patient is of sound mind and has made the declaration voluntarily; and
(c) he is satisfied that the patient understands the effect of the declaration.

(4) The patient and witnesses shall sign and witness the declaration respectively at the same time and each in the presence of the others.

(5) Neither the attending or consulting physician, nor a member of the health care team, a consultant psychiatrist or a psychologist consulted under section 3, nor a relative or partner (by blood, marriage or adoption) of the patient who wishes to be assisted to die, may witness the declaration.

(6) No person who owns, operates or is employed at a health care establishment where the patient is a resident or is receiving medical treatment may witness the declaration.

5 Duties of assisting physician

(1) The assisting physician shall be either the attending physician or the consulting physician.

(2) The assisting physician shall not take any action to assist the patient to die until after the expiration of a period of 14 days from the date on which the patient informed the attending physician under section 2(2)(a) that the patient wished to be assisted to die.

(3) Before taking any step to assist the patient to die the existing physician shall have—
(a) informed the patient of his right to revoke the declaration, and
(b) asked the patient to confirm that the declaration has not been revoked, and received such confirmation.

6 Revocation of declaration

(1) A patient may revoke his declaration orally or in any other manner and irrespective of his physical or mental state.

(2) In the event of a declaration being revoked, the assisting physician, or if there is no assisting physician, the attending physician, shall ensure that a note recording its revocation is made on the patient's file.

7 Conscientious objection

(1) No person shall be under any duty to participate in any diagnosis, treatment or other action authorised by this Act, apart from subsection (6), to which he has a conscientious objection.

(2) No hospice, hospital, nursing home, clinic or other health care establishment shall be under any obligation to permit an assisted death on its premises.

(3) No person shall be under any duty to raise the option of assisted dying with a patient, to refer a patient to any other source for obtaining information or advice pertaining to assistance to die, or to refer a patient to any other person for assistance to die under the provisions of this Act.

(4) If an attending physician whose patient makes a request to be assisted to die in accordance with this Act has a conscientious objection as provided in subsection (1), the patient shall be free to consult another physician who does not have a conscientious objection and who, for the purposes of this Act, shall then be the patient's attending physician.

(5) If a consulting physician to whom a patient has been referred in accordance with section 2(2)(i) has a conscientious objection as provided in subsection (1), the patient shall be free to consult another consulting physician who does not have a conscientious objection and who, for the purposes of this Act, shall then be the patient's consulting physician.

(6) Where a patient has consulted a physician under subsection (4) or (5) the physician who has a conscientious objection shall immediately, on receipt of a request to do so, transfer the patient's medical records to the new physician.

8 Protection for health care professionals and other persons

(1) A physician who assists a qualifying patient to die, or attempts to do so, in accordance with the requirements of this Act, shall not, by so doing, be guilty of an offence.

(2) A member of a health care team who works in conjunction with a physician who assists a qualifying patient to die, or attempts to do so, in accordance with the requirements of this Act, or in reliance on information supplied to him that the requirements of this Act in relation to the patient had been fully complied with, shall not by so doing be guilty of an offence.

(3) A person who is present when—

(a) a qualifying patient dies, having received assistance to die, or

(b) an attempt is made to assist a qualifying patient to die,

shall not be guilty of an offence provided that he is present in reliance on information provided to him that the requirements of this Act in relation to the patient have been complied with.

(4) A physician to whom subsection (1) of this section applies or a member of a health care team to whom subsection (2) of this section applies, shall be deemed not to be in breach of any professional oath or affirmation.

(5) No physician, psychiatrist, psychologist or member of a health care team may take any part in assisting a qualifying patient to die, or in giving an opinion in respect of such a patient, nor may any person act as a witness, if he has grounds for believing that he will benefit financially or in any other way, except for his proper professional fees or salary, as a result of the death of that patient.

9 Offences

(1) A person commits an offence if he wilfully falsifies or forges a declaration made or purporting to be made under section 4 with the intent or effect of causing the patient's death. [I]

(2) A person guilty of an offence under subsection (1) shall be liable, on conviction on indictment, to imprisonment for life.

(3) A person commits an offence if he makes a statement as a witness to a declaration made, or purporting to be made, under section 4 that he knows to be false. [I]

(4) A person commits an offence if he wilfully conceals or destroys a declaration. [I]

(5) A physician, psychiatrist, psychologist, or member of a health care team who takes any part in assisting a qualifying patient to die, or who gives an opinion in respect of such a patient, and who has grounds for believing that he will benefit financially or in any other way, except for his proper professional fees or salary, as the result of the death of that patient, contrary to section 8(5) commits an offence. [I]

(7) No provision of this Act shall be taken to affect a person's liability on conviction to criminal penalties for conduct which is inconsistent with the provisions of this Act.

11 Requirements as to documentation in medical records and reporting requirements

(1) The assisting physician shall ensure that the following are documented and filed in the patient's medical records—

(a) all evidence, data and records which demonstrate that the qualifying conditions have been met;

(b) any written request by the patient for assistance to end his life;

(c) the declaration; and

(d) a note by the assisting physician stating that he was satisfied, at the date and time of his having assisted the patient to die, that all requirements under this Act had been met and indicating the steps taken to end the patient's life including the description and quantity of the medication and any means of self-administration prescribed or provided.

(2) The assisting physician shall send a copy of each of the documents referred to in subsection (1) of this section to the monitoring commission for the region concerned within seven days of the qualifying patient having been assisted to die or of an attempt so to assist having been made.

12 Monitoring commission

(1) The Secretary of State shall by order establish such number of monitoring commissions covering regions forming parts of England and Wales as he may determine, to review the operation of this Act and to hold and monitor records maintained pursuant to this Act.

(2) A monitoring commission shall consist of three members appointed by the Secretary of State, of whom—

(a) one shall be a registered medical practitioner;

(b) one shall be a solicitor or barrister; and

(c) one shall be a lay person having first hand experience in caring for a person with a terminal illness.

(3) If, in relation to documents sent to a monitoring commission in accordance with section 11(2), two of its members consider that the qualifying conditions have not been met, the declaration had not been validly made or had been revoked, or that the requirements of this Act had not been complied with, the monitoring commission shall refer the matter to the district coroner.

(4) A monitoring commission to which documents have been sent in accordance with section 11(2) shall confirm to the assisting physician concerned whether all the requirements of this Act have been complied with as soon as reasonably possible after the date of receiving such notification of the patient having been assisted to die or of an attempt so to assist having been made.

13 Interpretation

(1) In this Act—

'assisting physician' means the physician who assists the patient to die;

'attending physician' means the physician who has primary responsibility for the care of the patient and the treatment of the patient's illness;

'consulting physician' means a consultant physician who is qualified by specialty to make a professional diagnosis and prognosis regarding the patient's illness and who is independent of the attending physician;

'declaration' means a witnessed declaration in writing made under section 4 by the patient;

'health care team' means a person or persons assisting the attending physician or the consulting physician;

'informed decision' means a decision by a patient to request assistance to die, which is based on an appreciation of the relevant facts and after having been fully informed in accordance with section 2 of—

(a) his medical diagnosis;
(b) his prognosis;
(c) the process of being assisted to die; and
(d) the alternatives to being assisted to die, including, but not limited to, palliative care, care in a hospice and the control of pain;

'monitoring commission' means a commission set up by the Secretary of State to monitor the workings of this Act in a region forming a part of England and Wales;

'nurse' means a nurse practitioner who is registered with the Nursing and Midwifery Council;

'patient' means a person who is under the care of a physician;

'physician' means a medical practitioner who is fully registered with the General Medical Council;

'psychiatrist' means a physician who is a specialist in psychiatry;

'psychologist' means a person who is registered with the British Psychological Society as a chartered clinical psychologist;

'qualifying conditions' means the conditions set out in section 2(2) to (4);

'qualifying patient' means a patient who—

(a) has reached the age of majority, and
(b) after having been registered for primary health care in England and Wales for a period of at least twelve months has made a declaration that is for the time being in force;

and in respect of whom—

(i) all the qualifying conditions have been met, and
(ii) the requirements of section 5(3) have been complied with;

'signed' in relation to the signature of a patient on a document means executed—

(a) by the patient writing his own signature, or
(b) where the patient cannot write legibly either through illiteracy or physical infirmity, by the patient leaving his mark, or
(c) where the patient through physical infirmity cannot either sign or make his mark, by a third party signing for the patient at his direction and so indicating on the document after the signature and adding his own full name and address;

'terminal illness' means an illness which in the opinion of both the attending and the consulting physician—

(a) is inevitably progressive,
(b) cannot be reversed by treatment (although treatment may be successful in relieving symptoms temporarily), and
(c) will be likely to result in the patient's death within six months;

'unbearable suffering' means suffering whether by reason of pain, distress or otherwise which the patient finds so severe as to be unacceptable; and

'witness' means a person who signs a declaration by way of attestation.

(2) Grammatical variations of words and expressions to which definitions are assigned in this section shall be construed in accordance with the definitions.

15 Amendment of the Suicide Act 1961

Section 2 of the Suicide Act 1961 is amended by inserting after subsection (3)—

'(3A) Subsection (1) does not apply where a person assists another person to die, or where a person helps another person to assist a third person to die, or where a person is present when another person ends his own life or attempts to do so, in accordance with sections 1 and 8 of the Assisted Dying for the Terminally Ill Act 2005.'

Index